Jossey-Bass Teacher

Jossey-Bass Teacher provides educators with practical knowledge and tools to create a positive and lifelong impact on student learning. We offer classroom-tested and research-based teaching resources for a variety of grade levels and subject areas. Whether you are an aspiring, new, or veteran teacher, we want to help you make every teaching day your best.

From ready-to-use classroom activities to the latest teaching framework, our value-packed books provide insightful, practical, and comprehensive materials on the topics that matter most to K–12 teachers. We hope to become your trusted source for the best ideas from the most experienced and respected experts in the field.

THE SOURCEBOOK FOR TEACHING SCIENCE

Strategies, Activities, and Instructional Resources

GRADES 6–12

NORMAN HERR

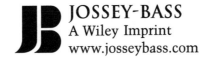
JOSSEY-BASS
A Wiley Imprint
www.josseybass.com

Published by Jossey-Bass
A Wiley Imprint
989 Market Street, San Francisco, CA 94103-1741—www.josseybass.com

Jossey-Bass books and products are available through most bookstores. To contact Jossey-Bass directly call our Customer Care Department within the U.S. at 800-956-7739, outside the U.S. at 317-572-3986, or fax 317-572-4002.

Jossey-Bass also publishes its books in a variety of electronic formats. Some content that appears in print may not be available in electronic books.

Library of Congress Cataloging-in-Publication Data

Herr, Norman.
    The sourcebook for teaching science, grades 6–12 : strategies, activities, and instructional resources / Norman Herr. — 1st ed.
        p. cm.
    Includes bibliographical references and index.
    ISBN 978-0-7879-7298-1 (pbk.)
        1. Science—Study and teaching (Middle school)   2. Science—Study and teaching (Secondary)   I. Title.
    LB1585.H473 2008
    507.1'2—dc22

                                                                                                2008000873

Printed in the United States of America
FIRST EDITION
PB Printing 10 9 8 7 6 5

About This Book

The Sourcebook for Teaching Science, Grades 6–12: Strategies, Activities, and Instructional Resources provides new and experienced teachers a wealth of teaching strategies, resources, lessons, activities, and ideas to enhance the teaching and learning of physics, chemistry, biology, and the earth and space sciences. Resources are based on learning theory and are designed to stimulate student interest and involvement. As students engage in the activities in this book, they develop higher-order reasoning skills and a deeper understanding of scientific concepts and their relevance to their everyday life.

The Sourcebook for Teaching Science, Grades 6–12 is designed to complement any secondary school science curriculum. Science teachers will find ready-to-use demonstrations, experiments, illustrations, games, puzzles, analogies, lessons, activities, and strategies, as well as explanations of how to adapt these for English Language Learners and diverse student populations. All topics are accompanied by extensive background material, providing teachers with the scientific, organizational, and pedagogical principles necessary for successful classroom implementation.

The Sourcebook for Teaching Science, Grades 6–12 complements *Hands-On Physics Activities with Real-Life Applications* and *Hands-On Chemistry Activities with Real-Life Applications,* authored by Norman Herr and James Cunningham, and published by Jossey-Bass, John Wiley & Sons, Inc. The activities in all three of these resources address the National Science Education Standards and state science content standards.

Technological resources for teaching and learning science are incorporated throughout this book, and teachers who desire additional resources will find them on the free companion Web site, *sciencesourcebook.com.* The directory structure of the Web site mirrors the table of contents, giving teachers immediate access to numerous interactive resources and downloadable files.

Norman Herr, Ph.D.
California State University, Northridge

About the Author

Norman Herr, Ph.D., is a professor of science and computer education at California State University, Northridge. He earned his doctorate from the University of California, Los Angeles, and has worked as a scientist, high school science teacher, college science instructor, science education consultant, and director of graduate programs in science education. Herr has published research in the field of science education and is the coauthor of *Hands-On Physics Activities with Real-Life Applications* and *Hands-On Chemistry Activities with Real-Life Applications.*

To my wife, Roberta,
our children Christiana, Stephen, and John,
and
to my father, Herbert Herr,
and the loving memory of my mother, Elizabeth Herr.

Acknowledgments

I am grateful to Kate Bradford, senior editor; Constance Santisteban, senior editorial assistant; Susan Geraghty, production editor; and Bev Miller, copyeditor; of Jossey-Bass, John Wiley & Sons, for their professional assistance and guidance. I am indebted to the biology, chemistry, physics, and geoscience credential students and the science education graduate students at California State University, Northridge, who have implemented and reviewed the activities, and to my wife, Roberta, who has proofed the text. I am deeply grateful to my family for their support and encouragement. I created the diagrams in this book using Macromedia Freehand.

Contents

About the Author   vii

Acknowledgments   xi

PART ONE   **Developing Scientific Literacy**   1

1   Building a Scientific Vocabulary   3

    For the Teacher   3

    1.1   Biology Vocabulary   4

    1.2   Chemistry Vocabulary   15

    1.3   Physics Vocabulary   24

    1.4   Earth and Space Science Vocabulary   28

    Answers to Chapter Activities   33

2   Developing Science Reading Skills   35

    For the Teacher   35

    2.1   Science Reading Comprehension: Cloze   38

    2.2   Science Reading Comprehension: Jigsaw   39

    2.3   Science Vocabulary in Spanish and English   39

    2.4   Scientific Terminology: Linking Languages   41

    Answers to Chapter Activities   42

3   Developing Science Writing Skills   45

    For the Teacher   45

    3.1   Science Note Taking   46

    3.2   Science Journaling   47

    3.3   Science Essay Questions   49

3.4	Types of Science Writing	51
3.5	Science Writing Style	53
	Answers to Chapter Activities	57

4 Science, Technology, and Society ... 58

For the Teacher ... 58

4.1	Science and Society	59
4.2	Science and Other Subjects	61
4.3	Careers in Science	67
4.4	Science and Technological Innovation	70
	Answers to Chapter Activities	74

PART TWO   Developing Scientific Reasoning ... 77

5 Employing Scientific Methods ... 79

For the Teacher ... 79

5.1	Discrepant Events: Establishing a "Need to Know"	80
5.2	Developing Scientifically Oriented Questions	83
5.3	Observation Versus Inference	86
5.4	Brainstorming and Hypothesizing	87
5.5	Experimental Design	90
5.6	Independent Variables	92
5.7	Writing Clear Procedures	94
5.8	Using History to Teach Scientific Methods	95
5.9	Indirect Evidence: "Black Box" Experiments	99
5.10	Evaluating Hypotheses	101
	Answers to Chapter Activities	102

6 Developing Scientific Reasoning Skills ... 106

For the Teacher ... 106

| 6.1 | Levels of Reasoning | 108 |
| 6.2 | Inductive Reasoning | 111 |

6.3   Deductive Reasoning   116

6.4   Lateral Thinking   121

Answers to Chapter Activities   122

7   Thinking Critically and Resolving Misconceptions   **125**

For the Teacher   125

7.1   Critical Thinking   126

7.2   Evaluating Claims   129

7.3   Using a Decision-Making Matrix   131

7.4   Misconceptions in Physics   132

7.5   Misconceptions in Chemistry   135

7.6   Misconceptions in Biology   137

7.7   Misconceptions in Earth and Space Science   139

Answers to Chapter Activities   142

PART THREE   **Developing Scientific Understanding**   **149**

8   Organizing Science Information and Concepts   **151**

For the Teacher   151

8.1   Advance Organizers   153

8.2   Orders of Magnitude: The Universe in
       Powers of Ten   154

8.3   Organizational Hierarchy in Biology   157

8.4   Organization of the Chemistry Curriculum   161

8.5   Organization of the Physics Curriculum   161

8.6   Earth Systems Interactions   162

Answers to Chapter Activities   165

9   Graphic Organizers for Science   **168**

For the Teacher   168

9.1   Conceptual Grids   169

9.2   Venn Diagrams   172

9.3   Flowcharts   **174**

9.4   Mind Maps   **176**

9.5   Concept Maps   **178**

        Answers to Chapter Activities   **182**

10   Learning Science Concepts with Analogies   **184**

        For the Teacher   **184**

10.1   Extended Science Analogies   **187**

10.2   Analogies for Learning Physics   **195**

10.3   Analogies for Learning Chemistry   **197**

10.4   Analogies for Learning Biology   **198**

10.5   Analogies for Learning Earth and Space Science   **199**

        Answers to Chapter Activities   **200**

11   Tools for Improving Memory in Science   **203**

        For the Teacher   **203**

11.1   The Primacy and Recency Effect   **211**

11.2   Expanding Short-Term Memory by Chunking   **211**

11.3   Science Acronyms and Abbreviations   **215**

11.4   Acrostics for Memorizing Lists   **216**

        Answers to Chapter Activities   **219**

12   Structure and Function in Science   **225**

        For the Teacher   **225**

12.1   Form and Function in Machines   **226**

12.2   Structure and Function in Anatomy
        and Physiology   **229**

12.3   Structure and Function in Plants   **233**

12.4   Structure and Function at a Molecular Level   **235**

12.5   Model Building   **238**

        Answers to Chapter Activities   **239**

13   Games for Learning Science   243

For the Teacher   243

13.1   Science Jeopardy   244

13.2   Science Taboo   247

13.3   Science Bingo   248

13.4   Science Pictionary   248

13.5   Science Bowl   250

13.6   Science Baseball   252

13.7   What in the World?   252

13.8   Twenty Questions   255

13.9   Logic Games   256

PART FOUR   **Developing Scientific Problem-Solving Skills**   259

14   Science Word Problems   261

For the Teacher   261

14.1   Translating Common Words into Mathematical Symbols   263

14.2   Translating Natural Language into Algebraic Expressions   264

14.3   Translating Algebraic Expressions into Natural Language   266

Answers to Chapter Activities   268

15   Geometric Principles in Science   270

For the Teacher   270

15.1   Developing Measurement Scales   271

15.2   Indirect Measurement in Science   273

15.3   Ratios for Solving Problems in Science   275

15.4   Surface Area to Volume Ratios   277

15.5   Surface Area to Volume Ratios in Living Systems   279

15.6   The Inverse Square Law in the Physical Sciences   283

15.7   Scientific Applications of Conic Sections   287

Answers to Chapter Activities   290

16 Diagramming and Visualizing Problems in Science   293

For the Teacher   293

16.1   Vector Diagrams   295

16.2   Interpreting Scientific Diagrams   298

16.3   Pictorial Riddles   301

16.4   Analyzing Photographs   304

16.5   Digital Movies and Animations   310

16.6   Extrapolation   316

16.7   Interactive Scientific Simulations   318

Answers to Chapter Activities   319

17 Dimensional Analysis   322

For the Teacher   322

17.1   Unit Measures   326

17.2   Fundamental Quantities   329

17.3   SI and Non-SI Units   332

17.4   CGS and MKS Units   334

17.5   Discovering Physical Laws Using
        Fundamental Units   335

17.6   Simplifying Calculations with the
        Line Method   337

17.7   Solving Problems with Dimensional Analysis   339

Answers to Chapter Activities   346

18 Stoichiometry: Interactions of Matter   351

For the Teacher   351

18.1   Predicting Oxidation States and Ions   354

18.2   Predicting Polyatomic Ions, Reactants,
        and Products   360

18.3   Techniques for Balancing Equations   363

Answers to Chapter Activities   366

PART FIVE		**Developing Scientific Research Skills**	**371**
19		Scientific Databases	**373**
		For the Teacher	373
	19.1	Databases in Chemistry	374
	19.2	Databases in Biology	378
	19.3	Databases in Health	382
	19.4	Databases in Earth and Space Science	385
	19.5	Databases in Physics	387
		Answers to Chapter Activities	389
20		Spreadsheets, Graphs, and Scientific Data Analysis	**392**
		For the Teacher	392
	20.1	Calculations and Computer Modeling	394
	20.2	Relating Graphs to Real-World Experiences	398
	20.3	Graphing Stories	400
	20.4	Scatter and Line Graphs	402
	20.5	Column and Bar Graphs	406
	20.6	Pie and Area Graphs	410
	20.7	High-Low, Combination, and Log Plots	413
	20.8	Statistics	418
		Answers to Chapter Activities	420
21		Mapping and Visualizing Scientific Data	**426**
		For the Teacher	426
	21.1	Map Construction	427
	21.2	Topographic Maps	428
	21.3	Mapping Data Electronically	434
	21.4	Weather Maps	438
	21.5	Environmental Maps	444

21.6   Astronomy Maps   446

21.7   Interpreting Aerial and Satellite Photographs   452

Answers to Chapter Activities   454

22   Science Inquiry and Research   458

For the Teacher   458

22.1   Inquiry   459

22.2   Sensors and Probeware   461

22.3   Problem-Based Learning   465

22.4   Forums and Debates   466

22.5   Rotating Laboratories   468

22.6   Citing Research   470

Answers to Chapter Activities   471

23   Science Projects and Fairs   473

For the Teacher   473

23.1   Writing Research Questions   474

23.2   Developing a Research Proposal   486

23.3   Conducting Research   487

23.4   Sharing Your Findings   488

Answers to Chapter Activities   490

PART SIX   Resources for Teaching Science   491

24   Science Curriculum and Instruction   493

24.1   The Nature of Science   493

24.2   Theories and Perspectives in Science Education   496

24.3   Developments in Science Curriculum and Instruction 498

24.4   The Science Curriculum   502

24.5   Advanced Placement and International Baccalaureate
        Curricula   504

24.6   Teaching Science Inquiry   506

24.7   Teaching Science to English Language Learners   508

24.8   Teaching Science with Humor   **511**

24.9   Professional Development in Science Education   **513**

24.10   Science Field Trips and Guest Speakers   **515**

25   Planning and Managing Science Instruction   **517**

25.1   Establishing Science Learning Objectives   **517**

25.2   Developing a Science Lesson Plan   **517**

25.3   Developing a Science Semester Plan   **519**

25.4   Getting to Know Your Students   **519**

25.5   Managing the Classroom Effectively   **522**

25.6   Assessing Student Performance   **525**

25.7   Evaluating Teaching Performance   **528**

26   The Science Laboratory   **529**

26.1   Equipping the Science Laboratory   **529**

26.2   Writing Successful Grant Proposals   **533**

26.3   Common and Inexpensive Sources of Chemicals   **534**

26.4   Preparing Solutions   **538**

26.5   Laboratory Safety   **540**

26.6   Safety Equipment Checklist   **540**

26.7   Chemical Hazards and Storage   **542**

26.8   Disposal of Chemicals   **546**

26.9   Accidents   **547**

27   Science Reference Information   **549**

27.1   Writing Style Guidelines   **549**

27.2   Units, Constants, and Conversions   **551**

27.3   Chemical Properties   **554**

27.4   Graph Paper, Protractors, and Rulers   **559**

Notes   **567**

Index   **577**

Part One

Developing Scientific Literacy

Chapter One

Building a Scientific Vocabulary

For the Teacher 3

1.1 Biology Vocabulary 4

1.2 Chemistry Vocabulary 15

1.3 Physics Vocabulary 24

1.4 Earth and Space Science Vocabulary 28

Answers to Chapter Activities 33

For the Teacher

During the fourteenth century, sailors and traders on the Mediterranean Sea learned a variety of Italian, Turkish, French, Spanish, Greek, and Arabic phrases so they could communicate with one another. Eventually an international language of trade developed, known as *lingua franca,* borrowing words and sounds from each people. The term *lingua franca* has come to mean any language used by a group of people whose first languages are different. Today scientists from around the world communicate in English, and English has therefore become the lingua franca of science. The English lexicon (the entire stock of words belonging to the language) is much greater than any other due in part to the scientific words that are added daily. The English scientific vocabulary is increasingly rich and complex, allowing scientists and others to express themselves more precisely than ever before. Unfortunately the growing vocabulary of scientific English makes it increasingly difficult for students to master, particularly for those who learn it as a

second language. This chapter presents resources and activities to make this task easier.

Scientists give names to new discoveries, concepts, theories, and inventions using classical Latin and Greek roots, prefixes, and suffixes. Since these languages are no longer spoken (they were replaced by modern Italian and Greek), the meanings of words never change. For example, the ancient Greeks used the word *therme* to describe heat, and today we use the root *therm* to mean "heat" in a variety of English words, such as *homeotherm, thermometer, thermistor, ectotherm, poikilotherm, thermophilic, thermoregulation, thermochemistry, endothermic, exothermic, thermite, thermodynamics, thermoelectric, thermocouple, thermonuclear, thermal, isotherm,* and *thermocline.* A simple science root word can provide clues to numerous other words, greatly reducing the amount of memorization necessary to master this new vocabulary and making it easier for people speaking different first languages to understand.

A knowledge of Greek and Latin root words can greatly enhance student understanding of scientific terms and provide a better understanding of English and other European languages. Approximately 50 percent of all words in English have Latin roots, many of them shared by Spanish, French, Portuguese, and Italian words. Learning scientific root words thereby helps us understand the vocabulary of a variety of languages, particularly English. The activities in this chapter focus on scientific terms, but the roots are used in other words as well. For example, the prefix *anti-* means "against" or "opposite" as in the following scientific terms: *antiseptic, antibiotic, antigen, antibody, antibacterial, antioxidant, anticodon, antacid, antinodes, antimatter, antiquark, antiparticle, anticline,* and *anticyclone*. This same prefix is used in many nonscientific terms as well, such as *anticlimactic, antifreeze, antiperspirant, antidepressant,* and *antiterrorism*. Thus, an understanding of the roots introduced in this chapter helps us all master both scientific and nonscientific terms and become more proficient in the use of language.

I suggest that teachers provide their students with copies of the relevant root word lists that follow in this chapter to keep in the back of their notebooks alongside the glossaries that they develop. Each time a new term is introduced in class, students should analyze its prefixes, suffixes, and roots and add the entry to their personal glossaries as described in the activities that follow.

1.1 Biology Vocabulary

Biology has a larger vocabulary than any other branch of science, but fortunately nearly all biological terms contain roots, prefixes, and suffixes with predictable meanings, many of which appear in Table 1.1. Knowing these roots greatly simplifies the acquisition of new terms, and the following activities will help in memorizing and understanding these roots.

Table 1.1 Roots, Prefixes, and Suffixes in Biology

a, an	**not, without:** asymptomatic, aphasia, anemia, aseptic, amorphous, asexual, anhydrous, anaerobic A patient is asymptomatic if he or she does **not** have symptoms.
ab	**away from:** abductor, absent, aberrant, abstain, abnormal, abscission, abscissic acid An abductor is a muscle that moves a limb **away** from the body.
acu	**sharp:** acute, acupuncture, accurate, acumen Acute pains are **sharp** pains.
ad	**toward:** adductor, addiction, adhesion, additive, adhere Adductor muscles brings limbs **toward** the body.
ag, act	**do, move, cause:** agent, reaction, reagent, agitate, action Disease agents **cause** diseases.
-al	**relating to, at:** nocturnal, diurnal, arboreal, terrestrial, biological Nocturnal animals are active **at** night.
alb	**white:** albino, albacore, albedo, albumin, linea alba Albinos appear **white** due to an absence of pigmentation.
ambul	**to walk:** ambulatory, amble, ambulance, somnambulist Ambulatory patients can **walk.**
amph	**double, both:** amphibian, amphoteric, amphibious, Amphipoda Amphibians live **both** on land and in the water.
amyl	**starch:** amylase, amylose, amylopectin, amyloplast Amylase is an enzyme that converts **starch** to simple sugars.

an	**upward, apart:** anaphase, anode, analysis, anabolism During anaphase, chromosomes are pulled **apart.**
andr, anth	**male, man:** androgen, anthropology, anther, antheridia, anthropomorphic Androgens are **male** hormones.
ann, enni	**circle, year:** perennial, annelid, annular rings, annual, biennial Perennial plants stay alive through all seasons of the **year.**
ante	**before, front:** antenna, anterior, antedate, antebrachium The antennae are located on the **front** of the organism.
anti	**against, opposite:** antiseptic, antibiotic, antigen, antibody, antibacterial, antioxidant, anticodon Antibodies protect **against** antigens.
arbor	**tree:** arboreal, arboretum, arborvitae, arborist Arboreal species live in **trees.**
-arium	**place:** aquarium, terrarium, planetarium, vivarium Aquariums are **places** for aquatic organisms.
arth	**joint:** arthritis, arthropod, arthroscope, arthrogram, Arthropoda Arthritis is an inflammation of the **joints.**
aud	**sound:** auditory meatus, audible, audiologist, audiogram, audience **Sound** waves travel through the auditory meatus to the eardrum.
auto	**self:** autotrophic, autoimmune, autocatalytic, autonomic nervous system, automatic, autonomous Autotrophic organisms are considered **self**-feeders because they produce their own food.
av, avi	**bird:** Aves, aviary, aviation, avian flu, aviculture Aves is the class of animals composed of **birds.**
bio	**life:** biology, biochemistry, biometrics, biome, biosphere, antibiotic Biology is the study of **living** systems.
blast	**germ, embryo:** blastula, blastocoel, blastocyst, cytoblast, erythroblast The blastula is an early stage of **embryonic** development.
bol	**clod:** bolus, anabolism, catabolism, metabolism A bolus is a **clod** of food in the digestive tract.
brachi	**arm:** biceps brachii, brachial artery, brachial plexus, triceps brachii The biceps brachii is a two-headed muscle of the **arm.**
calor	**heat:** calorie, caloric, calorimeter, kilocalorie A calorie is a unit of **heat** energy.
cap, cep	**head:** triceps, cephalopod decapitate, capital, cap, captain The triceps is a muscle with three **heads.**
cardi	**heart:** pericardium, tachycardia, cardiac arrest, bradycardia, electrocardiogram The pericardium is the sac around the **heart.**
carp	**wrist:** carpal bones, carpus, metacarpal, carpal tunnel syndrome The **wrist** is made up of carpal bones.
cep, cept	**take:** receptor, intercept, forceps, except, accept Receptors **take** and transmit information on the environment.
cephal	**head, brain:** electroencephalogram, Cephalopoda, hydrocephaly, cephalothorax, encephalitis An electroencephalogram is a record of **brain** wave activity.

(Continued)

Table 1.1 *(Continued)*

chlor	**green:** chlorophyll, chloroplast, chlorine, chlorella, chlorosis Chlorophyll is the **green** pigment in plant cells.
chond	**cartilage, granular:** mitochondria, chondroblast, chondrocyte, chondrichthyes Mitochondria appear as **granular** objects in the cell.
chord	**a chord, string:** Chordata, Hemichordata, notochord, chordae tendineae Chordata is the phylum of animals with dorsal nerve **chords.**
chrom	**color:** chromosome, chromatic, monochrome, chromatophore, chromatography Chromosomes appear as **colorful** bodies when stained appropriately.
cide, cis	**to kill, to cut:** pesticide, herbicide, fungicide, incision, excision, germicide Pesticides are used to **kill** agricultural pests.
cili	**a small hair:** ciliary muscle, cilia, Ciliophora, aciliate Ciliary muscles are **small hair**like muscles in the eye.
circ	**ring, around:** circulatory system, circa, circulation, circumflex artery The circulatory system conducts blood **around** the body.
co, com	**together:** community, commensalism, conjugal, communicate, conjugation A community is a group of organisms that live **together** in the same environment.
coel	**hollow:** coelenterate, coelenteron, blastocoel, pseudocoelomate, Coelenterata Coelenterates have **hollow** bodies.
cogn	**know, think:** prognosis, diagnosis, recognize, cognitive Physicians make prognoses about what they **think** will happen to a patient.
corp	**body:** corpus callosum, corpse, corpulent, corpus luteum, blood corpuscle, pacinian corpuscle The corpus callosum is the **body** that unites the two cerebral hemispheres.
crani	**skull:** craniotomy, cranium, cranial nerve, epicranium, cranial artery Craniotomy surgery involves opening the **skull.**
crypt	**hidden:** cryptic, encrypted, cryptic coloration, cryptozoa, cryptogrammic Cryptically colored animals are easily **hidden** in the environment.
cyan	**dark blue:** anthocyanin, hemocyanin, cyan, cyanosis, cyanide Anthocyanin is the **dark blue** pigment found in blue and purple flowers.
cyst	**bladder, sac:** cyst, sporocyst, blastocyst, cystic fibrosis, nematocyst, oocyst A cyst is a membranous **sac** in the body.
cyt	**cell:** cytology, erythrocyte, chondrocyte, cytokinin, phagocyte, cytoplasm Erythrocytes are red blood **cells.**
de	**without:** denature, decomposition, dehydrate, deciduous, defibrillate, deforestation, DNA Denatured proteins are **without** the structure necessary to function.
dem	**people:** demography, epidemic, pandemic, epidemiology An epidemic is a widespread disease among **people.**
dendr	**tree, bush:** dendrites, dendritic, dendrology, rhododendron, dendrochronology Dendrites are **tree**-shaped extensions on a neuron.
dent, dont	**tooth:** dentin, dentist, dentifrice, orthodontist, periodontal, dentate Dentin is the hard part of the **tooth** beneath the enamel.
derm	**skin:** dermatology, epidermis, hypodermic, ectoderm, endoderm Dermatology is the study of the **skin.**
dis, dys	**away, not:** dystrophy, disease, dysfunction, distemper, disinfect, dyslexia, dislocation Muscular dystrophy results in a wasting **away** of muscles.

dors	**back:** latissimus dorsi, dorsal fin, dorsal lip, dorsiflexor, dorsiflexion The latissimus dorsi is a large, lateral muscle of the **back.**
dura	**hard, lasting:** dura matter, durable, duration, endure The dura matter is a **hard,** tough membrane protecting the brain.
e, ex, ef	**out, without, from:** exocytosis, efferent, exchange, exoskeleton, exogenous During exocytosis, contents of vacuoles go **out** of a cell.
echino	**spiny:** echinoderm, Echinodermata, echinate, echinoid Echinoderms have **spiny** skin.
eco	**house, environment:** ecology, ecosystem, ecophysiology, ecocline Ecologists study the interaction of organisms with their **environments.**
ecto	**outside, external:** ectoparasite, ectoderm, ectoplasm, ectopic, ectothermal A flea is an ectoparasite because it lives **outside** its host.
ectomy	**cut out:** appendectomy, tonsillectomy, lumpectomy, hysterectomy, mastectomy During appendectomy surgery, the physician **cuts out** the patient's appendix.
endo, en	**within:** endoskeleton, endosperm, endocrine, endometrium, endothermic, endemic, endoparasite Vertebrates have endoskeletons, which support their bodies from **within.**
epi	**upon:** epidermis, epithelial, epicotyl, epicondyle, epiglottis, epiphyte The epidermis is the top layer of the skin and rests **upon** the dermis.
eryth	**reddish:** erythrocyte, erythroblastosis fetalis, erythropoiesis, erythroblast Erythrocytes, or red blood cells, have a **reddish** color due to their iron content.
eu	**good, true:** eukaryote, eugenics, eubacteria, euphoria Eukaryotes are organisms with **true** nuclei.
ex, exo	**outside of:** exoskeleton, exocrine, exotic, extraterrestrial, extinct Crustaceans, like crabs and lobsters, have exoskeletons on the **outside** of their bodies.
fer	**to carry, bear:** conifer, porifera, transfer, infer, refer Conifers, such as pines and firs, are cone-**bearing** trees.
flex, flect	**bend:** flexor, flex, reflex, flexible, inflexibility, circumflex, dorsiflex Flexor muscles, such as the biceps, **bend** limbs at the joints.
foramen	**hole, perforation:** foramen magnum, Foraminifera, optic foramen The foramen magnum is the largest **hole** in the cranium.
form	**form, shape:** fusiform, coliform, form, uniform, conform, formal Fusiform cells are spindle **shaped,** while coliform bacteria are rod **shaped.**
gam	**marriage, sex cell:** gametes, monogamy, gametogenesis, gametocyte, gametophyte Gametes are the **sex cells** that combine in fertilization to yield a zygote.
gastr	**stomach:** gastritis, gastric, gastronomic, gastropod, gastrointestinal system Gastritis is the inflammation of the **stomach.**
gen	**origin:** genetics, gene, generate, antigen, pathogen Genetics gives us an understanding of the **origin** of phenotypic traits.
germ	**sprout:** germination, germ, germ cell, germ layer, germicide During germination, the seed **sprouts,** and the plant grows.
gest	**carry, bear:** gestation, congest, digest, indigestion Gestation is the period during which a mother **carries** the developing offspring.
gloss, glot	**tongue:** glossopharyngeal nerve, glossary, polyglot, epiglottis The glossopharyngeal nerve innervates the **tongue** and pharynx.

(Continued)

Table 1.1 *(Continued)*

glu, glo	**lump, bond:** glomerulus, glue, agglutinate, conglomerate Glomeruli contain **lumps** of vessels.
glyc	**sugar:** hypoglycemia, glycogen, glycolysis, glycolipid, glycerin, glycerides The blood **sugar** of people with hypoglycemia is too low.
gnath	**jaw:** Agnatha, gnathostomata, gnaw, orthognathous, gnathic Members of Agnatha, such as the lamprey, have no **jaws.**
gram	**writing, picture:** electrocardiogram, radiogram, thermogram, mammogram, electroencephalogram An electrocardiogram gives a **picture** of the electrical activity of the heart.
gyn	**woman:** gynecologist, gynecology, gynarchy, monogynous, epigynous Gynecologists specialize in medical issues specific to **women.**
hal	**breathe:** inhalation, exhalation, inhale, exhale, halitosis, inhalant Inhalation is the process of **breathing** air in, and exhalation is the process of **breathing** out.
hem	**blood:** hematology, hemorrhage, hemoglobin, hemophilia, hematocrit, heme, hemocyte Hematology is the study of the physiology of the **blood.**
hemi	**half:** hemiplegia, hemisphere, Hemichordata, hemicellulose, hemiparasite Hemiplegia is paralysis of the right or left **half** of the body.
hepat	**liver:** hepatitis, hepatic artery, hepatocyte, hepatoma Hepatitis is a disease characterized by an inflammation of the **liver.**
herb	**plants:** herbivore, herbaceous, herbs, herbarium Herbivores feed on **plants.**
hetero	**other, different:** heterotroph, heterogeneous, heterosexual, heterozygous Heterotrophs get their energy from **other** organisms.
histo	**tissue:** histology, histochemical, histogenic, histologist Histology is the study of **tissues.**
hom	**same, alike:** homologous, homeostasis, homogeneous, homogenize, homeostatic, homeotherm Homologous chromosomes have the **same** structural features and patterns of genes.
hyper	**over, above:** hypertensive, hypersensitive, hyperventilate, hyperextension, hyperglycemia Hypertensive patients exhibit **above**-normal blood pressure.
hypo	**below, beneath:** hypodermic, hypotension, hypoglycemia, hypoallergenic, hypothermia, hypoxia Hypodermic needles are used to inject medicine **beneath** the skin.
ichth	**fish:** Chondrichthyes, ichthyology, Osteichthyes, ichthyosaurus, ichthyologist The Chondricthyes are bony **fish.**
-ile	**quality, state:** juvenile hormones, mobile, contractile, fertile, flexible Juvenile hormones maintain the larval **state.**
im, in	**not:** independent variable, immiscible, immobile, innocuous, invalid, insane The independent variable does **not** depend on dependent variables.
immun	**safe:** immunization, immunology, immunoglobulin, immunosupressor, immunity Immunizations are administered to keep patients **safe** from diseases.
inter	**between:** intercostals, internal, interface, intercellular, interbreed, interneurons, interact, interbreed Intercostal muscles are found **between** the ribs.
intra	**within, into:** intracellular, intracranial, intravenous, intravascular, intramuscular Intravenous injections go directly **into** veins.

-ion	**process:** respiration, reproduction, decomposition, abscission, addiction Respiration, reproduction, and decomposition are important biological **processes.**
-ist	**one who studies:** biologist, biochemist, ecologist, geneticist, radiologist, cardiologist A biologist is **one who studies** living systems.
-itis	**inflammation:** tendonitis, hepatitis, appendicitis, bursitis, arthritis Bursitis is **inflammation** of the bursa in the knee, elbow, or shoulder.
junct	**join:** conjunctive tissue, nondisjunction, conjunctiva, disjunction, gap junction Conjunctive tissue **joins** tissues together.
juven	**young:** juvenile diabetes, juvenile, rejuvenate, juvenile hormones Juvenile diabetes is expressed when one is **young.**
kilo	**thousand:** kilocalorie, kilogram, kilojoule, kilometer, kilobase A kilocalorie is one **thousand** calories.
kine	**motion:** kinesiology, kinetochore, cytokinesis, kinesthetic, kinetic energy Kinesiology is the study of human **motion.**
lact	**milk:** lactase, lactic acid, lactose, lactate, lactobacillus, lactoglobulin Lactase is an enzyme that breaks down **milk** sugar (lactose).
lip	**fat:** lipoprotein, lipid, lipase, liposuction, lipoid, liposphere Lipoproteins are proteins that combine with **fat** in the blood.
loc	**place, position:** dislocate, locale, allocate, locomotion, location Dislocated limbs are not in the correct **position.**
lys	**loose, break:** lysosome, plasmolysis, lyse, paralysis, analysis Lysosomes are organelles that contain enzymes that **break** down materials.
macro	**large:** macromolecule, macronutrient, macroscopic, macromere, macrophage, macrostructure Macromolecules are **large** molecules, such as proteins and nucleic acids.
mal	**bad, badly:** malignant, malformation, malady, malodorous, malaise, malaria, malfunction Malignant tumors are **bad** because they are metastatic and invasive.
mamm	**breast:** mammary gland, mammal, mammogram, Mammalia Mammary glands, or **breasts,** are found in mammals and provide milk to the young.
man	**hand:** manipulate, manual, manage, manufacture, maneuver We can manipulate tools with our **hands.**
medi	**middle, between:** mediastinum, medial, medial artery, gluteus medius, mediate, median nerve The mediastinum is the membrane **between** the lungs.
medic	**physician:** medical doctor, medicine, medic, medicate, medicinal Medical doctors are **physicians.**
mes	**middle, between:** mesoderm, mesencephalon, mesoglea, mesophyll, mesoplankton, mesenteron Mesoderm is located **between** the endoderm and ectoderm.
meta	**change, between:** metamorphosis, metabolism, metathorax, metacognition, metacarpal, metastasis Metamorphosis is the **change** in insects or amphibians from an immature form to an adult form.
meter	**measure:** metric system, thermometer, millimeter, multimeter, calorimeter, sphygmomanometer The metric system is a standardized system of **measurement.**
micro	**small:** microvilli, microscope, micrometer, microbiology, microbe, microclimate, microtubule Microvilli are **small,** finger-like projections that increase cell surface area.

(Continued)

Table 1.1 *(Continued)*

migra	**wander:** migratory, migrate, emigrate, immigrate, immigrant Migratory mammals **wander** from one habitat to another.
mis	**bad, wrong:** misidentify, miscarriage, misnomer, mistake, misalign, misdiagnose, mislabel Misidentification of symptoms can lead to a **wrong** diagnosis.
moll	**soft:** mollusk, Mollusca, emolliate, emollient, mollify Mollusks, such as snails and slugs, have **soft** bodies.
mono	**single:** monocot, monotremes, monocotyledon, monecious, monogamy Monocots, such as grasses and palms, have only a **single** cotyledon.
morph	**form:** morphogen, metamorphosis, morphology, isomorphic, morphogenesis Morphogens are chemicals that stimulate a change in **form** or shape.
mort	**mortal, death:** postmortem, mortality, mortal, mortician, mortuary Postmortem exams are used to determine the cause of **death.**
mut	**change:** mutagen, mutant, mutability, mutate, mutation Mutagens cause **changes** in genetic composition.
myo	**muscle:** myocardium, myofibril, myositis, myoglobin, myology, myopathic The myocardium is the **muscular** tissue of the heart.
nas, nos	**nose:** nasal, nostril, nasopharynx, nasal cavity, nasal concha The nasal bone provides structure for the **nose.**
nat	**born, birth:** innate, natal, native, prenatal, postnatal, nature, natural Innate reflexes, such as grasping or rooting reflexes, are present at **birth.**
neo	**new, recent:** neoplasm, neotropics, neophyte, neonate, neonatology, neolith Neoplasms are **new,** abnormal growths associated with cancer.
nephr	**kidney:** nephritis, epinephrine, nephrectomy, nephron, nephridia Nephritis is an inflammation of the kidney.
neur	**nerve:** neuritis, neuropathology, neurologist, neural, neurula, neuron, neuroma, neurosis, neurobiology Neuritis is an inflammation of peripheral **nerves.**
nom	**name, order:** taxonomy, binomial nomenclature, autonomic, autonomy Taxonomy is the branch of science concerned with classification and **naming.**
nuc	**center:** nucleus, nuclear, nucleic acid, nucleotide, enucleate, nucleolus The nucleus is the control **center** of the cell.
ocu	**eye:** ocular lens, binocular, ocular nerve, interocular The ocular lens of a microscope is the one closest to the **eye.**
-oid	**resemble, like:** amoeboid, haploid, diploid, steroid, deltoid, thyroid, thylakoid, trapezoid Organisms that **resemble** amoebas are said to be amoeboid.
olfact	**to smell:** olfactory nerve, olfactory, olfaction, olfactory cell The olfactory nerve is involved in the sense of **smell.**
ology	**study of:** biology, physiology, pathology, pharmacology, ecology, embryology, zoology, ecology Biology is the **study of** living systems.
oo	**egg:** oocyte, oogonium, oocyst, oogenesis, oospore An oocyte is an **egg** cell.
oper	**work:** operon, operate, cooperate, operator, operation, operant conditioning An operon controls the **work** of genes responsible for protein synthesis.

ortho	**straight, correct:** Orthoptera, orthodontist, orthopedic, orthoptics, orthotic Orthoptera, including grasshoppers and crickets, have **straight** wings.
-osis	**process, condition:** metamorphosis, neurosis, thrombosis, mitosis, halitosis Metamorphosis is the **process** of changing shape.
oss, osteo	**bone:** osteoblast, osteocyte, ossify, osteology, osteoporosis, osteoclast Osteoblasts secrete the matrix for **bone** formation.
oto	**ear:** otolith, otology, otoscope, otopathology, ototoxic, otologist Otoliths in the inner **ear** are used in the detection of gravity.
ov	**egg:** ovum, oviduct, ovary, ovulate, ova, ovulation, oviparous The ovum, or **egg,** passes through the oviduct during ovulation.
para	**alongside:** parasympathetic, paramedic, paraphrase, parallel, parapodia, parasite The parasympathetic nervous system works **alongside** the sympathetic nervous system.
pariet	**wall:** parietal lobe, parietal bone, parietal cell, parietal The parietal bones comprise the side **walls** of the skull.
pater, pat	**father:** sympatry, paternal, paternity, allopatry, patriarch, sympatric Sympatric species are from the same "**father**land."
path	**disease:** pathology, pathologist, allelopathy, sympathetic nervous system, allopathy Pathologists study the causes and effects of **diseases.**
ped, pod	**foot:** arthropod, cephalopod, gastropod, millipede, centipede, podiatry, bipedal, tripod, orthopedics Arthropods, such as insects, spiders, and crustaceans, have jointed **feet.**
phag	**eat:** phagocytosis, macrophage, bacteriophage, esophagus, phagocyte Phagocytosis occurs when amoeboid protozoa **eat** bacteria and other material.
phob	**fear:** arachnophobia, hydrophobic, phobia, claustrophobia, acrophobia, aquaphobia Arachnophobia is an irrational **fear** of spiders.
photo	**light:** photoperiodism, photosynthesis, photomicrograph, photon, photoreceptor Photoperiodism is the response of plants to seasonal changes in the amount of day**light.**
phyll	**leaf:** phylloquinone, mesophyll, chlorophyll, xanthophyll, phyllopod Phylloquione is one of the K vitamins found in **leafy** green vegetables.
phys	**body, nature:** physiology, biophysics, physical medicine, physician, physique Physiology is the study of the **body.**
phyt	**plant:** epiphyte, phytochemistry, phytoplankton, sporophyte, gametophyte, phytonutrient, phytotoxin Epiphytes, such as orchids, are nonparasitic plants that live on other **plants.**
pneum	**lung:** pneumococcus, pneumatic, pneumonia, pneumocystis, pneumothorax Pneumococcus is a spherical-shaped bacterium found in some **lung** infections.
pole, polar	**end of axis:** vegetal pole, animal pole, polar bear, polarize, depolarize The vegetal pole is at the **end of one axis** of an embryo.
poly	**many:** polysaccharide, polyploid, polymerize, polymerase, polydactyl, polymer Polymerization is the binding together of **many** subunits.
pop	**people, inhabitants:** population, populous, populace, depopulate, populate, repopulate A population is a group of interbreeding organisms that **inhabit** the same region.
port	**carry:** transport, portable, export, import, report Electron transport chains **carry** electrons across membranes during phosphorylation.

(Continued)

Table 1.1 *(Continued)*

post	**after:** postpartum, posterior, posthumous, posterity, postnasal, postsurgery The postpartum period is the period **after** birth.
pre	**before:** prefix, prefrontal, precede, preborn, predict, presynaptic Prefixes appear **before** root words and modify meanings.
prim	**first:** primary succession, primitive, primal, primary consumer, primordial Primary succession occurs **first** following retreating glaciers or volcanic eruptions.
pseudo	**not true, false:** pseudopodia, pseudocoel, Pseudotsuga, pseudoscience Pseudopodia are **not true** feet, but they have footlike characteristics.
psych	**mind:** neuropsychiatry, psychology, psychiatry, psychobiology, psychosis Neuropsychiatry is concerned with the organic aspects of disorders of the **mind.**
pter	**wing:** Orthoptera, Archaeopteryx, Pterodactyl The Pterodactyl had "**winged** fingers."
pulmo	**lung:** pulmonary, cardiopulmonary system, pulmonary cavity, pulmonary artery The pulmonary cavity contains the **lungs.**
re	**back, again:** retract, reforest, repopulate, regrow, return, react Reforestation is necessary to bring **back** forests following logging and erosion.
rhiz	**root:** rhizome, rhizoid, rhizobium, mycorrhizae Rhizomes are **root**like underground stems.
sacchar	**sugar:** monosaccharide, disaccharide, polysaccharide, Saccharomyces Monosaccharides, such as glucose and fructose, are **sugars.**
saur	**lizard:** dinosaur, brontosaurus, ichthyosaurus, stegosaurus, tyrannosaurus Dinosaurs had some **lizard**-like characteristics.
sci	**know:** science, conscious, unconscious, scientific Science is one way of **knowing** things.
scop	**see, monitor:** arthroscope, stethoscope, microscope, endoscope, bronchoscope Physicians use arthroscopes to **see** inside joints.
script	**to write:** transcription, prescription, reverse transcriptase, description, superscript, subscript Transcription is the process in which DNA code is **written** as RNA code.
sect	**cut:** section, dissect, transect, intersect, vivisection, bisect A longitudinal section requires a **cut** from the top to bottom of a structure.
sed, sess	**seated, fixed:** sedentary, sessile, residue, sedate, sedative Kelp are sessile because holdfasts keep them **fixed** to the rocks on the ocean floor.
semi	**half:** semitendinosus, semipermeable, semilunar valve, semimembranosus, semicircular canal The semitendinosus muscle is **half** muscle and **half** tendon.
sens	**feel:** sensory, sense, sensation, sensitive, sensor, sensorimotor Without sensory neurons, you would not be able to **feel** anything.
serv	**save:** conservationist, preserve, conserve, reservation, conservation, preservation Conservationists work to **save** resources for the future.
sperm	**seed:** angiosperm, sperm, gymnosperm, endosperm, spermatozoa In angiosperms (flowering plants), **seeds** are found within fruits.
sphere	**ball, sphere:** biosphere, cerebral hemisphere, troposphere, hydrosphere, atmosphere The biosphere is the **spherical** zone around the Earth in which life exists.

spir	**breathe:** spiracles, inspire, respiration, perspiration, respirometer Insects **breathe** through pores known as spiracles.
stom	**mouth, pore:** stomata, stoma, stomach, protostome, deuterostome Stomata are tiny **pores** that regulate the flow of gases in and out of leaves.
sub	**under, below:** subclavian, subalpine, subarctic, subcortical, subcutaneous, subgenus, subspecies The subclavian artery is located **below** the clavicle.
super	**above, over:** superior vena cava, superior, superior oblique muscle, superior rectus muscle The superior vena cava is located **above** the heart.
syn	**together, with:** synapse, photosynthesis, synchronize, syndrome, chemosynthesis The synapse is where two neurons come **together.**
tact, tag	**touch:** contagious, tactile, contact, intact, geotactic Many contagious diseases spread by **touch.**
taxis	**movement response:** phototactic, geotaxis, phototaxis, chemotaxis, barotaxis Phototactic bacteria **move in response** to light.
tele, telo	**far, end:** telophase, telomere, telodendrion, telescope During telophase, the chromosomes are **far** apart.
ten, tin	**hold:** tendon, extension, retention, abstention, contents, tension, tentacle Tendons **hold** muscles to bones.
therm	**heat:** homeotherm, thermometer, thermistor, ectotherm, poikilotherm, thermophilic, thermoregulation Homeotherms regulate internal **heat** to maintain constant body temperature.
tom	**cut:** microtome, atom, appendectomy, tonsillectomy, dichotomy, anatomy, tomography Microtomes are used to **cut** extremely thin tissue sections for examination under a microscope.
tox	**poison:** toxemia, toxic, intoxicate, antitoxin, cytotoxic, detoxification Toxemia is blood **poisoning** by toxins from a local bacterial infection.
trans	**across:** neurotransmitter, transfusion, tranferase, translation, transcription, transect, transpiration Neurotransmitters carry signals **across** synapses.
trop	**turning, change:** tropomysosin, geotropism, phototropism, troposphere, troponin, tropics Tropomyosin is a muscle protein that **changes** direction, causing muscles to contract.
trich	**hair:** trichome, trichocyst, Trichoptera, trichotomy Trichomes are small **hairs** in the epidermis of plants.
troph	**nutrition, food:** autotroph, atrophy, hypertrophy, heterotroph, trophic layers, chemotroph Autotrophs produce their own **food** through photosynthesis or chemosynthesis.
ultra	**beyond:** ultrasound, ultracentrifuge, ultrafiltrate, ultraviolet, ultrastructure Ultrasound is a frequency **beyond** the range of human hearing.
ur	**urine:** urea, urologist, urinary, ureter, urethra, urinalysis Urea is a nitrogenous waste product found in **urine.**
vas	**vessel:** cardiovascular, vascular bundle, vascularity, vasoconstrictor, vasodilator, vas deferens The cardiovascular system is the system of the heart and blood **vessels.**
ven	**vein:** venule, vena cava, venous, intravenous, vein Venules are tiny **veins** that collect blood from capillaries.

(Continued)

Table 1.1 *(Continued)*

vid, vis	**see:** visible, video, evident, evidence, revise, vision We **see** visible light, while other organisms see ultraviolet or infrared light.
viv, vita	**alive, life:** vitamin, vital, revitalize, survive, revive, vivisection Vitamins are essential for normal **life** functions.
vor	**eat:** herbivorous, voracious, carnivorous, omnivorous, devour Herbivorous animals **eat** plant material.
zoo, zoa	**animal:** zoo, zoology, protozoan, spermatozoa, zooplankton Zoology is the study of the anatomy, physiology, classification, and behavior of **animals.**

ACTIVITY 1.1.1 *Understanding Biology Root Words*

Table 1.1 lists the most common roots, prefixes, and suffixes in biology. Following each definition in the table is a series of biological terms that share this root. For example, *cyt-* means cell. *Cytology* is therefore the study of cells, *erythrocytes* are red blood cells, *chondrocytes* are cartilage cells, *cytokinin* is a plant hormone that stimulates cell division, *phagocytes* are cells that engulf particles, and *cytoplasm* is the liquid of the cell. By knowing the meanings of a few roots, one can determine the meanings of many terms. Construct a sentence for each biology vocabulary word provided by your teacher. These may come from readings, lectures, or Table 1.1. Show the relationship between these biology words and their roots by **highlighting** root word meanings as illustrated in the sentences of Table 1.1.

ACTIVITY 1.1.2 *Developing a Biology Glossary*

Construct a three-column chart with the headings used in Table 1.2. Each time you encounter an unfamiliar term in class or in your reading, enter its meaning and roots as shown in the examples. Add to this table for the duration of the class,

Table 1.2 Biology Glossary

Term	Meaning	Roots (Meanings)
Biology	The study of living systems	Bio- (life); -ology (study of)
Autotrophic	An organism that makes its own food	Auto- (self); -troph (food)
Cytoplasm	The liquid of the cell	Cyto- (cell); -plasm (liquid)
↓ New words	↓	↓

Table 1.3 Deciphering Biology Terms: Classification

		Term		Definitions and Examples
↓	1	Annelida	a	Class of animals with large head and "foot": *octopus, squid*
	2	Arthropoda	b	Class of *birds, seagulls, eagles, pigeons*
	3	Aves	c	Class of the cartilaginous fish: *sharks, rays*
	4	Cephalopoda	d	Order of insects with straight wings: *wasps, grasshoppers*
	5	Chondricthyes	e	Phylum of organisms with cordlike backbone: *humans*
	6	Chordata	f	Phylum with jointed feet: *insects, spiders, crustaceans*
	7	Ciliphora	g	Phylum with soft bodies: *snails, slugs*
	8	Echinodermata	h	Phylum with spiny skin: *sea stars, urchins*
	9	Mollusca	i	Phylum with circular, segmented bodies: *earthworms*
	10	Orthoptera	j	Protozoans propelled by hairlike structures: *paramecia*

referring to the list of biology roots (Table 1.1) whenever necessary.

ACTIVITY 1.1.3 *Deciphering Biology Terms: Taxonomy and Classification*

Once you know basic root words for a science, you can determine the meanings of new terms. Table 1.3 has a list of animal classifications, many of which you may find unfamiliar or even unpronounceable. Analyze the roots using Table 1.1, and match each phylum, class, or order to a likely definition (the first term is done as an example). Do not consult a dictionary or glossary; rather, draw conclusions based on your analysis of the root words.

1.2 Chemistry Vocabulary

The periodic table of elements is a central feature of introductory chemistry classes. Many students memorize the names of the elements but do not realize that these names are descriptive. For example, *helium* derives its name from the Greek word *helios*, meaning "sun," because the first evidence of its existence was obtained by analyzing the spectrum of sunlight. The word *hydrogen* comes from the Greek words *hydro*, meaning "water" (as in *hydroelectric* and *hydrolysis*) and *gen*, meaning "beginning" (as in *Genesis*, *gene*, and *genetics*). Thus, the word *hydrogen* means "water former," an appropriate name for a substance that forms water when it combusts. Examine Table 1.4, and note that every element has a meaningful name.

ACTIVITY 1.2.1 *Understanding Chemistry Root Words*

Table 1.5 lists the most common roots, prefixes, and suffixes used in chemistry. Following each definition is a series of chemical terms that share this root. For example, *ferr-* means "iron." *Ferromagnetism* is the type of magnetism displayed by iron, *ferrous* refers to materials containing iron (II), *ferric* refers to materials containing iron (III), *ferrite* is a form of pure iron occurring in

Table 1.4 Meaning of Element Names

Element	Symbol	Number	Date Discovered	Meaning of Name
Actinium	Ac	89	1900	Greek: *aktis*, ray
Aluminum	Al	13	1825	Latin: *alumen*, substance with astringent taste
Americium	Am	95	1944	English: *America*
Antimony	Sb	51	1400s	Greek: *antimonos*, opposite to solitude
Argon	Ar	18	1894	Greek: *argos*, inactive
Arsenic	As	33	1200s	Greek: *arsenikon*, valiant
Astatine	At	85	1940	Greek: *astatos*, unstable
Barium	Ba	56	1808	Greek: *barys*, heavy
Berkelium	Bk	97	1949	English: University of California, *Berkeley*
Beryllium	Be	4	1797	Greek: *beryllos*, a mineral
Bismuth	Bi	83	1400s	German: *bisemutum*, white mass
Boron	B	5	1808	Arabic: *bawraq*, white, borax
Bromine	Br	35	1826	Greek: *bromos*, a stench
Cadmium	Cd	48	1817	Latin: *cadmia*, calamine, a zinc ore
Calcium	Ca	20	1808	Latin: *calcis*, lime
Californium	Cf	98	1950	English: State and University of *California*
Carbon	C	6	prehistoric	Latin: *carbo*, coal
Cerium	Ce	58	1804	English: The asteroid *Ceres*, discovered 1803
Cesium	Cs	55	1860	Latin: *caesius*, sky blue
Chlorine	Cl	17	1808	Greek: *chloros*, grass green

(Continued)

Table 1.4 *(Continued)*

Element	Symbol	Number	Date Discovered	Meaning of Name
Chromium	Cr	24	1797	Greek: *chroma*, color
Cobalt	Co	27	1735	Greek: *kobolos*, a goblin
Copper	Cu	29	prehistoric	Latin: *cuprum*, copper
Curium	Cm	96	1944	French: Marie and Pierre *Curie*
Dysprosium	Dy	66	1886	Greek: *dysprositos*, hard to get at
Einsteinium	Es	99	1952	German: *Albert Einstein*
Erbium	Er	68	1843	Swedish: *Ytterby*, town where discovered
Europium	Eu	63	1900	English: *Europe*
Fermium	Fm	100	1953	Italian: Enrico *Fermi*
Fluorine	F	9	1886	Latin: *fluere*, to flow
Francium	Fr	87	1939	French: *France*
Gadolinium	Gd	64	1886	Finnish: Johan *Gadolin*, Finnish chemist
Gallium	Ga	31	1875	Latin: *Gaul*, or France
Germanium	Ge	32	1886	German: *Germany*
Gold	Au	79	prehistoric	Anglo-Saxon: for gold; *aurum*, gold
Hafnium	Hf	72	1922	Latin: *Hafnia*, the city of Copenhagen, Denmark
Helium	He	2	1895	Greek: *helios*, the Sun
Holmium	Ho	67	1879	Latin: *Holmia*, the city Stockholm, Sweden
Hydrogen	H	1	1766	Greek *hydro genes*, water former
Indium	In	49	1863	Latin: *indicum*, produces an indigo-blue spectrum
Iodine	I	53	1811	Greek: *iodes*, produces a violet-like *spectrum line*
Iridium	Ir	77	1804	Latin: *iridis*, rainbow
Iron	Fe	26	prehistoric	Anglo Saxon: *iren*, symbol from Latin *ferrum*
Krypton	Kr	36	1898	Greek: *kryptos*, hidden
Lanthanum	La	57	1839	Greek: *lanthanien*, to be concealed
Lawrencium	Lw	103	1961	English: Ernest *Lawrence*, inventor of cyclotron
Lead	Pb	82	prehistoric	Anglo Saxon: *lead*; symbol from Latin: *plumbum*
Lithium	Li	3	1817	Greek: *lithos*, stone
Lutetium	Lu	71	1905	Latin: *Lutetia*, ancient name of Paris
Magnesium	Mg	12	1774	Latin: *magnes*, magnet
Mendelevium	Md	101	1955	Russian: Dmitri *Mendeleev*, devised periodic table
Mercury	Hg	80	prehistoric	Latin: *Mercury*, messenger; symbol *Hydrarygus*
Molybdenum	Mo	42	1782	Greek: *molybdos*, lead
Neodymium	Nd	60	1885	Greek: *neos*, new, and *didymos*, twin
Neon	Ne	10	1898	Greek: *neos*, new
Neptunium	Np	93	1940	English: planet *Neptune*
Nickel	Ni	28	1750	German: *kupfernickel*, false copper
Niobium	Nb	41	1801	Greek: *Niobe*, mythological daughter of Tantalus
Nitrogen	N	7	1772	Latin: *nitro*, native soda, and *gen*, born
Nobelium	No	102	1957	Swedish: Alfred *Nobel*, discoverer of dynamite
Osmium	Os	76	1804	Greek: *osme*, odor of volatile tetroxide

Element	Symbol	Number	Date Discovered	Meaning of Name
Oxygen	O	8	1774	Greek: *oxys*, sharp, and *gen*, born
Palladium	Pd	46	1803	English: planetoid *Pallas*, discovered 1801
Phosphorus	P	15	1669	Greek: *phosphoros*, light bringer
Platinum	Pt	78	1735	Spanish: *plata*, silver
Plutonium	Pu	94	1940	English: *Pluto*, the planet
Polonium	Po	84	1898	Polish: *Poland*, country of codiscoverer Marie Curie
Potassium	K	19	1807	English: *potash*; symbol Latin *kalium*
Praseodymium	Pr	59	1885	Greek: *Praseos*, leek green, and *didymos*, a twin
Promethium	Pm	61	1947	Greek: *Prometheus*, fire bringer
Protactinium	Pa	91	1917	Greek: *protos*, first
Radium	Ra	88	1898	Latin: *radius*, ray
Radon	Rn	86	1900	Latin: from *radium*, to radiate energy
Rhenium	Re	75	1924	Latin: *Rhenus*, Rhine province of Germany
Rhodium	Rh	45	1804	Greek: *rhodon*, a rose
Rubidium	Rb	37	1860	Latin: *rubidus*, red
Ruthenium	Ru	44	1845	Latin: *Ruthenia*, Russia
Samarium	Sm	62	1879	Russian: *Samarski*, a Russian engineer
Scandium	Sc	21	1879	Scandinavian: *Scandinavia*
Selenium	Se	34	1817	Greek: *selene*, moon
Silicon	Si	14	1823	Latin: *silex*, flint
Silver	Ag	47	prehistoric	Anglo-Saxon: *siolful*; symbol Latin: *argentum*
Sodium	Na	11	1807	Latin: *sodanum* for headache remedy; Na: *natrium*
Strontium	Sr	38	1808	Scottish: town of *Strontian*, Scotland
Sulfur	S	16	prehistoric	Latin: *sulphur*, sulfur
Tantalum	Ta	73	1802	Greek: *Tantalus* of Greek mythology
Technetium	Tc	43	1937	Greek: *technetos*, artificial
Tellurium	Te	52	1782	Latin: *tellus*, the Earth
Terbium	Tb	65	1843	Swedish: *Ytterby*, town in Sweden
Thallium	Tl	81	1862	Greek: *thallos*, a young shoot
Thorium	Th	90	1819	Scandinavian: *Thor* from Scandinavian mythology
Thulium	Tm	69	1879	Latin: *Thule*, northerly part of the habitable world
Tin	Sn	50	prehistoric	Latin: Etruscan god *Tinia*; symbol Latin: *stannum*
Titanium	Ti	22	1791	Greek: mythology, *Titans*, first sons of the Earth
Tungsten	W	74	1783	Swedish: *tung sten*, heavy stone, W: German:
Uranium	U	92	1789	English: Planet *Uranus*
Vanadium	V	23	1830	Scandinavian: goddess *Vanadis* of mythology
Xenon	Xe	54	1898	Greek: *xenos*, strange
Ytterbium	Yb	70	1905	Scandinavian: Ytterby, a town in Sweden
Yttrium	Y	39	1843	Scandinavian: Ytterby, a town in Sweden
Zinc	Zn	30	prehistoric	German: *Zink*, akin to *Zinn*, tin
Zirconium	Zr	40	1824	named for the mineral *zircon*

low-carbon steel, and a *ferroalloy* is an alloy of iron with one or more metals. When you know the meanings of a few roots, you can determine the meanings of many terms. Construct a sentence for each chemistry vocabulary word that your teacher has selected from Table 1.5. Illustrate the relationship between these words and their roots by **highlighting** root word meanings, as illustrated in the sentences of Table 1.5.

ACTIVITY 1.2.2 *Developing a Chemistry Glossary*

Construct a three-column chart with the headings used in Table 1.6. Each time you encounter an unfamiliar term in class or in your reading, enter its meaning and roots as shown. Contribute to this table for the duration of the class, referring to Table 1.5 whenever there is an unfamiliar root, prefix, or suffix.

ACTIVITY 1.2.3 *Eciphering Chemistry Terms*

Once you know the basic roots, you can determine the meanings of new chemistry terms. Table 1.7 contains a list of random chemistry words, many of which may be unfamiliar to you. Analyze the roots using Table 1.5, matching each term to a likely definition (the first term is done as an example). Do not consult a dictionary or glossary; rather, draw conclusions based on your analysis of the words.

Table 1.5 Roots, Prefixes, and Suffixes in Chemistry

a, an	**not, without:** amorphous, anhydrous, anaerobic, atypical Amorphous carbon does **not** display crystalline structure.
acid, acri	**sour, sharp:** acid, acidity, acrid, acidify, acidophilus Acids, such as those in lemons and other citrus fruits, produce a **sour** taste.
ag, act	**move, proceed:** reagent, action, reaction, agent, activity Chemical reagents are necessary for a reaction to **proceed.**
al, allo	**other, different:** allotrope, alloy, alter, allosteric, alias, alien Graphite, charcoal, and diamond are allotropes (**different** forms) of carbon.
alpha	**first:** alpha particle, alpha helix, alpha ray, alpha position, alpha test Alpha radiation was the **first** radiation characterized by Ernest Rutherford.
amin	**amine:** amine, amino acid, vitamin, acetaminophen, deaminate, ammonia At the center of amino acids are **amine** groups.
amph	**double, both:** amphoteric, amphibolite, amphibole Amphoteric species can act as **both** acids and bases.
an	**apart:** analytical, analysis, anode, anabolism, anabolic Analytical chemists break compounds **apart** to determine chemical structure.
-ane	**single covalent bond:** methane, alkane, ethane, propane, butane, pentane, hexane, octane Methane, ethane, propane, and butane have only **single** bonds.
-ate	**negatively charged ion:** carbonate, phosphate, sulfate, hydrate, bromate, chlorate, iodate Carbonate, phosphate, and sulfate are **negatively charged ions.**
anti	**against, opposite, inhibit:** antioxidant, antifreeze, antacid, antinodes, antimatter Antioxidants, such as vitamins C and E, **inhibit** oxidation.
aqu	**water:** aqueous, aqua regia, aquamarine, aquatic In aqueous solutions, the solute is dissolved in **water.**
baro	**pressure:** barometer, bar, barometry, barometric pressure, hyperbaric chamber Barometers are used to measure air **pressure.**
beta	**second:** beta particle, beta decay, beta ray, betatron Beta radiation was the **second** type of radiation that Ernest Rutherford characterized.

bi	**two:** bivalent, binary compounds, bicarbonate, bimetallic Bivalent (divalent) elements have a valence of **two.**
bio	**life, living:** biochemistry, bioassay, biocatalyst, biodegradable Biochemistry is the chemistry of **living** systems.
calor	**heat:** calorimeter, calorie, caloric, kilocalorie, calorimetry Calorimeters measure **heat** released or absorbed in reactions.
carb	**coal, carbon:** carbohydrate, carbonic acid, bicarbonate, carbon dioxide, carbide, carboxylic acid Carbohydrates are **carbon**-based molecules, including sugars, starch, and cellulose.
cat	**down, negative:** cathode, catalyst, catabolism, catastrophe Cathodes are **negatively** charged electrodes.
cau, caus	**burn, heat:** caustic, cauldron, cauterize, caustic soda Caustic substances, such as sodium hydroxide, can **burn** organic tissues.
chem	**chemical:** chemisorption, chemistry, biochemistry, chemoautotroph, chemoreceptor, chemist In chemisorption, the adsorbed substance is held by **chemical** bonds.
chrom	**color:** chromium, chromosphere, chromatography, monochrome, dicrhomate Chromium compounds are very **colorful.**
co, com	**with, together:** conjugate, composition, coefficient, colligative, compress, conduction, convection Conjugate acids and bases exist **with** each other, differing only by the presence of a proton.
cry	**cold:** crystal, cryogenic, crystalline, liquid crystal, crystallize, cryoprecipitate Crystals form when supersaturated solutions are **cooled.**
de	**down, lack, from:** denature, decomposition, dehydrate, decant, deformation Denatured proteins **lack** the critical three-dimensional structure required to function.
dens	**thick:** density, dense, condense, condenser, densimeter Density is a measure of "**thickness**" (amount of mass per unit volume).
di	**double:** disaccharide, dipeptide, dichloride, dioxide, dibromide, disulfide, dichroic Disaccharides are formed by the bonding of **two** monosaccharides.
dis, dif	**separate, apart:** dissociation, discontinuity, disperse, dispersion, differentiate Salts dissociate when component ions **separate** in solution.
duc, -t	**led, pulled:** ductile, product, conduct, induce, deduce, deduction Metals are ductile and can be **pulled** to produce wires.
e, ex, ef	**out, without, from:** emit, evaporation, explosion, exothermic, effervescence, effect, effuse Thermochemists measure the amount of heat emitted **from** reactions.
electr	**electricity:** electrolyte, electricity, electrode, electromotive force, dielectric, electron **Electricity** flows in solutions containing electrolytes.
elem	**basic:** elements, elemental, elementary particle Elements cannot be broken down into more **basic** substances by normal chemical means.
en	**in, into:** endothermic, endergonic, energy, enthalpy Endothermic reactions take heat energy **in** from the environment.
-ene	**double covalent bond:** benzene, alkene, ethene, propene, butene, pentene, polypropylene, toluene Benzene forms a six-carbon ring with three **double covalent bonds.**

(Continued)

Table 1.5 *(Continued)*

equ	**equal:** equilibrium, equate, equation, equal, equidistant Equilibrium is a dynamic condition in which two opposing reactions occur at **equal** rates.
erg	**work:** energy, erg, bond energy, energetics Energy is the capacity to perform **work.**
ex, exo	**out, outside:** exothermic, extrinsic, exterior, extrapolate, external Exothermic reactions release heat to the **outside** environment.
ferr, ferro	**iron:** ferromagnetism, ferrous, ferric, ferricyanide, ferrite, ferroalloy Ferromagnetic materials, such as **iron,** are strongly attracted to magnets.
fiss	**cleft, split:** nuclear fission, fissionable, fission bomb Nuclei **split** during nuclear fission.
fix	**fix, fasten:** fixation, fixture, affix, prefix, suffix, fix During carbon fixation, atmospheric carbon is **fixed** into molecules of glucose.
flu	**flow:** fluids, reflux, fluctuate, influx, flux, flux density Liquids and gases are classified as fluids because they **flow.**
fract	**break, broken:** fractional distillation, fraction, refract, fractionate During fractional distillation, mixtures are **broken** down and separated by different boiling points.
glyc	**sweet, sugar:** glycolysis, glycogen, glycolipid, glyceride, glycol During glycolysis, glucose **sugar** is broken down, and pyruvic acid and energy are released.
graph	**writing, printing:** graphite, chromatography, crystallography, thermography, photography Graphite is a planar form of carbon that makes gray marks when **writing** with pencils.
halo	**salt:** halogens, halocline, halite, halogenate Halogens (group VII) often combine with metals to form **salts.**
here, hes	**stick to:** cohesive, cohesion, cohere, adhere, adhesion, adhesive, coherent Cohesive substances **stick to** each other, and adhesive substances **stick to** other substances.
hybrid	**combination:** hybrid orbital, hybridize, sp3 hybridization, hybrid bond, hyperon Hybrid orbitals are produced by the **combination** of two or more orbitals of the same atom.
hydr	**water:** hydrazine, hydrolysis, dehydrate, hydrogen, rehydrate, dehydration synthesis Although very different chemically, hydrazine resembles **water** in that both are colorless liquids.
hyper	**over, above:** (hy)perchloric acid, hypertonic solution, (hy)perchlorate, hyperbaric, hyperacidic The oxidation state of chlorine in perchloric acid is **above** the oxidation state in chloric acid.
hypo	**under, beneath:** hypochlorous acid, hypotonic, hypothesis The oxidation state of chlorine in hypochlorous acid is **lower** than in chlorous acid.
-ic	**higher valence:** sulfuric, hydrochloric, phosphoric, nitric, bromic, ferric Sulfur in sulfuric acid has a **higher valence** than in sulfurous acid.
-ide	**derived from:** bromide, chloride, fluoride, iodide, oxide, dioxide, monoxide, sulfide, hydride Bromides **are derived from** bromine.
ign	**fire:** ignite, lignite, ignition, ignitable, igneous Sulfur can be ignited with a hot **flame.**
-ile	**describing:** ductile, volatile, tensile, percentile, mobile Volatility **describes** a substance's vapor pressure.

-ion	**process:** fusion, fission, dilution, solution, adhesion Fusion is the **process** of combining (fusing) nuclei to form a heavier nucleus.
iso	**equal, same:** isomers, isotonic, isometric, isotope, isosceles Isomers are compounds that have the **same** molecular formula but different structures.
-ist	**one who studies:** chemist, biochemist, organic chemist, geomorphologist, metallurgist A chemist is **one who studies** chemistry.
-ite	**negatively charged ion:** nitrite, chlorite, bromite, flourite, sulfite Nitrite is a **negatively charged ion.**
kilo	**thousand:** kilogram, kilocalorie, kilojoule, kilopascal, kiloton, kilowatt A kilogram is one **thousand** grams.
liqu	**fluid, liquid:** deliquescence, liquefy, liquid, liquefaction Deliquescence is the tendency to become **liquid.**
lys, lyz	**loosening, breaking:** electrolysis, hydrolysis, catalysis, hydrolyze, acidolysis Electrolysis is the **breaking** apart of a substance by an electric current.
malle	**hammer:** malleable, mallet, malleability Malleability is the ability to bend when hit by a **hammer.**
mer	**a part:** dimer, polymer, polymerization, monomer, dimerize Dimers, such as O_2 or C_{12}, are made of two identical **parts.**
meter	**measure:** meter, voltmeter, thermometer, metric system, calorimeter, colorimeter, eudiometer Thermometers are used to **measure** the intensity of heat energy.
mill	**one thousand:** milliliter, milligram, millibar, milliamp, millimole A milliliter is **one-thousandth** of a liter.
misc, mix	**mix:** miscible, immiscible, mix, mixer, mixture Oil and water are immiscible, unable to **mix** to form a homogeneous mixture.
mon	**single:** monomer, monosodium glutamate, monoglyceride, monobasic, monochromatic, monoxide Monomers are **single** molecular units that can join to form polymers.
morph	**form, shape:** amorphous sulfur, dimorphic, geomorphology Amorphous sulfur does not have a consistent **shape.**
neg	**no:** negligible, negate, negative, negligence, negate A negligible measurement error will have **no** effect.
neutr	**neither:** neutral, neutron, neutralize, neutrality Neutrons are **neither** positive nor negative.
nitro	**nitrogen:** nitrogen dioxide, nitroglycerin, nitride, nitric, nitrogen, nitrile, nitrite, nitrosyl, nitrous Nitrogen dioxide is composed of one **nitrogen** and two oxygen atoms
non	**not:** nonpolar, nonferrous, nonabrasive, nonenzymatic Nonpolar substances, such as butane, do **not** demonstrate polarity.
oct	**eight:** octet rule, octane, octanol, octyl, octagonal The octet rule describes the tendency of atoms to establish a full set of **eight** valence electrons.
-on	**unit:** electron, proton, lepton, baryon, fermion, photon, boson The electron is the smallest **unit** of electricity.
-ous	**lower valence:** sulfurous, nitrous, bromous, ferrous Iron in ferrous oxide has a **lower valence** than in ferric oxide.

(Continued)

Table 1.5 *(Continued)*

oxid, oxy	**oxygen:** oxidizer, oxide, dioxide, oxidize, oxidation, oxidize Oxidizers resemble **oxygen,** removing electrons from other substances.
pent	**five:** pentahydrate, pentane, pentose, pentoxide, pentachloride Copper sulfate pentahydrate binds **five** water molecules per copper sulfate unit.
phil	**love:** hydrophilic, nucleophilic, acidophilic, basophilic Hydrophilic substances are "water **loving**" and dissolve rapidly in water.
photo	**light:** photochemical smog, photon, photolysis, photocatalysis, photochemistry Photochemical smog contains pollutants that are synthesized in the presence of sun**light.**
polar	**end of axis:** polar covalent, polar, dipole, polarimeter, nonpolar In polar molecules, the **ends of the axes** carry partial charges.
poly	**many:** polyester, polymer, polysaccharide, polyacrylic, polyvinyl chloride, polyacrylamide Polyester is a polymer made by bonding **many** ester groups.
pre	**before:** precursor, precaution, predict, preheat, precede Precursors are substances that arise **before** products form.
pyr	**fire, heat:** pyrolysis, pyrotechnics, pyrite, pyroclastic, pyrometer Pyroloysis is decomposition by **heat** at high temperatures.
quant	**amount:** quantum, quantity, quantify, quantitative A quantum is a discrete **amount** of energy.
radi, ray	**ray, radius:** radioactive, radius, ray, radiant, gamma ray Radioactive materials emit **rays** of electromagnetic energy.
re	**back, again:** reflux, reabsorb, reaction, reactant, reactive, rehydrate, remove, reduction, reheat During reflux, vapor condenses, returns, and is vaporized **again.**
sacchar	**sugar:** monosaccharide, disaccharide, polysaccharide, Saccharomyces Monosaccharides, such as glucose and fructose, are **sugars.**
sat	**full, maximum:** saturate, satisfy, polyunsaturated, supersaturated, unsaturated Saturated solutions contain the **maximum** amount of solute that can be held in solution.
semi	**half, partial:** semiconductor, semipermeable, semisolid, semicrystalline Semiconductors are **partially** conductive.
sol	**dissolve:** solubility, solution, dissolve, soluble, solvent Solubility is a measure of a substance's potential to **dissolve** in a specific solvent.
spec	**look:** spectator ions, specimen, specific, spectrum, specifications Spectator ions "**look** on" but are not involved in reactions.
sub	**under, below:** subscript, subatomic, submerge, subtract, subscale, sublimation, sublimate, substrate Subscripts are numbers or letters placed **below** a term, such as the "2" in H_2O.
super	**above, beyond:** supersaturate, superheat, supercool, superscript, superfluid, supernatant, superoxide A solution is supersaturated when its concentration is increased **beyond** the saturation point.
therm	**heat:** thermochemistry, thermometer, therm, endothermic, exothermic, thermite Thermochemistry studies changes in **heat** energy accompanying chemical and physical changes.
thesis	**statement, arranging:** hypothesis, synthesis, thesis, photosynthesis, chemosynthesis A hypothesis is a testable **statement** and proposed explanation.

trans	**across, through:** trans–fatty acid, transition elements, transaminase, trans-, transfer, transmutation
	In trans–fatty acids, carbons are situated **across** from each other at the double bonds.
un	**not:** unsaturated, unbonded, untested, unheated, undissociated, unstable, unfavorable
	Unsaturated bonds have **not** been saturated with hydrogen.
vac	**empty:** vacuum, vacate, evacuate, vacant, vacuous
	A vacuum is an **empty** place, void of matter.
val	**strength, worth:** equivalence point, equivalent, validate, validity, evaluate, value
	At the equivalence point, the **strength** of the base is equal to the strength of the acid.
-yne	**triple covalent bond:** alkyne, ethyne, butyne, propyne
	Alkynes have one or more **triple covalent bonds.**

Table 1.6 Chemistry Glossary

Term	Meaning	Roots (Meanings)
Exothermic	Reaction that releases heat	Exo (out), therm (heat)
Photocatalysis	Light stimulated breakdown	Photo (light), cat (down), lys (break)
Carlorimeter	Measures heat of reaction	Calor (heat), meter (measure)
↓new words	↓	↓

Table 1.7 Deciphering Chemistry Terms

		Term		Definitions
↓	1	*aqua regia*	a	A binary carbon compound
	2	*barometer*	b	A device that records air pressure
	3	*carbide*	c	A mixture used for dissolving platinum and gold
	4	*conduction*	d	An instrument that measures the absorbed dose of radiation
	5	*cryogen*	e	Atoms with same atomic number but different mass
	6	*deliquesce*	f	Capable of having its nucleus split
	7	*dosimeter*	g	Carbohydrates made of many joined monosaccharides
	8	*effluent*	h	Having or exhibiting many colors or wavelengths
	9	*electrophoresis*	i	Iron-containing plant proteins that act as electron carriers
	10	*ferredoxin*	j	Large enough to be examined by the unaided eye
	11	*fissionable*	k	Liquid waste from industrial processes
	12	*hypoxia*	l	Low levels of oxygen in the blood
	13	*isotope*	m	Measurement of temperature
	14	*macroscopic*	n	Process of adding a phosphate group into a molecule
	15	*microradiography*	o	Refrigerants used to obtain very low temperatures
	16	*phosphorylation*	p	Study of the relationships between heat and other energy
	17	*polychromatic*	q	The migration of molecules in an electric field
	18	*polysaccharide*	r	Transmission through a medium or passage
	19	*thermodynamics*	s	To become liquid by absorbing moisture from the air
	20	*thermometry*	t	X-ray photography showing minute internal structure

1.3 Physics Vocabulary

ACTIVITY 1.3.1 *Understanding Physics Root Words*

Table 1.8 lists the most common roots, prefixes, and suffixes used in physics. Following each definition is a series of physics terms that share this root. For example, *vect-* means "to carry, convey, or move." Velocity

vectors are arrows that indicate the magnitude and direction of motion, and are used to show how objects move. *Convection* is the movement of heat as a gas warms and rises, and *advection* is the horizontal movement of heat within an ocean or atmospheric current. When you know the meanings of a few roots, you can determine the meanings of many terms. Construct a sentence for each physics vocabulary

Table 1.8 Roots, Prefixes, and Suffixes in Physics

acceler	**faster:** accelerate, accelerometer, angular acceleration, centripetal acceleration To accelerate is to go progressively **faster.**
aero	**air:** aerodynamics, aeronautics, aerosol, aeroballistics Aerodynamics studies the properties of moving air and the forces it exerts.
alter	**other:** alternating current, alternator, alternate interior angle, alterable An alternating current switches from one polarity to the **other.**
anti	**against, opposite:** antiquark, antimatter, antiparticle, antilogarithm The antiquark is an **opposite,** or antiparticle, of the quark.
astr, aster	**star:** astronomy, asteroid, astrophysics, astronaut, astronomical Astronomy is the study of the **stars.**
avi	**bird, flight:** avionics, aviation, circumnavigation Avionics are the electronics that control **flight** in airplanes.
calor	**heat:** calorie, caloric, calorimeter, kilocalorie A calorie is the amount of **heat** to raise 1 gram of water by 1 degree Celsius.
capac	**amount:** capacitor, capacity, capacitance A capacitor stores an **amount** of charge.
centr	**center:** centripetal, concentric, centrifugal, eccentric Centripetal acceleration is always toward the **center.**
circ	**ring, around:** circuit, circumference, integrated circuit, short circuit An electrical circuit is a closed **ring** or path.
co, com	**together:** condensation, compression, conduction, convection, collinear Molecules come **together** during condensation.
cosm	**universe:** cosmology, cosmos, cosmonaut, cosmic rays Cosmology is the study of the **universe.**
counter	**against, opposite:** counterforce, counterflow, counterbalance, countercurrent A counterforce **opposes** another force.
cur, curs	**run, flow:** current, recur, occur, cursor, precursor Current is the **flow** of electricity or fluid.
de	**down, without:** depolarize, decelerate, detach, declination, deduce A depolarized surface is **without** charge.
dec	**tenth:** decibel, decimal, decimeter, decade A decibel has the sound intensity of one-**tenth** of a bel.
di, dia	**across:** diameter, dielectric, diagnoal, diagram, diamagnetic The diameter is the distance **across** an object.

duc, -t	**to lead, carry:** transducer, conduct, deduct, induce, induce, deduce A transducer **carries** energy from one system to another.
dyn	**power, force:** dyne, dynamometer, dynamic, dynamite, dynamo, aerodynamics, hydrodynamics A dyne is a unit of **force.**
electr	**electricity:** electrode, electricity, electromotive force, electronics, dielectric, electron, electroscope An electrode is a conductor through which **electricity** enters or leaves an object.
empir	**experience:** empirical, empiricist, unempirical An empirical study is based on **experience** and observation.
erg	**work:** energy, erg, kinetic energy, potential energy, energetics Energy is the capacity to do **work.**
fin	**end, finish, boundary:** finite, final, finish, confine, infinite, define, definite A finite object has **boundaries.**
flect, flex	**to bend:** reflection, flexible, deflect, reflect Reflected rays **bend** away from the reflecting surface.
flu	**flow:** flux, fluids, fluctuate, influx, reflux, magnetic flux Flux is the **flow** of radiant or magnetic energy.
fract	**break, broken:** refraction, diffraction, fraction, fracture, refractive Refracted rays appear **broken.**
fus	**melt, join:** fusion, fuse, fusion bomb, nuclear fusion, fusible, heat of fusion During nuclear fusion, nuclei **join** together.
grav	**heavy, weighty:** gravity, gravitational, microgravity, graviton The greater the gravity, the **heavier** an object is.
gyr	**circle, rotation:** gyroscope, gyration, gyrostabilizer, gyrocompass Gyroscopes are stablized by **rotational** inertia.
infra	**beneath, lower:** infrared, infrastructure, near-infrared, infrasonic Infrared light has **lower** energy than red light.
inter	**between:** interference, interferometry, Internet, intersect, interpolate Interference patterns form due to the interaction **between** waves.
-ion	**process:** fusion, revolution, extension, compression, fission Nuclear fusion is the **process** in which two hydrogen atoms fuse into one helium atom.
-ist	**one who studies:** physicist, astrophysicist, empiricist, cosmologist A physicist is **one who studies** physics.
ject	**to throw:** trajectory, reject, eject, project, projectile The path of a **thrown** object is its trajectory.
kilo	**thousand:** kilopascal, kilogram, kilometer, kilojoule, kilohertz, kilovolt, kiloton, kilowatt A kilopascal has one **thousand** times the pressure of a pascal.
kine	**motion:** kinetic energy, kinetics, hydrokinetics, kinetic friction Kinetic energy is the energy of **motion.**
lu, lum	**light:** luminescence, translucent, luster, luminosity, luminous, lux, lumen Luminescence is the emission of **light** from an unheated object.

(Continued)

Table 1.8 *(Continued)*

mega	**great, million:** megahertz, megabyte, megawatt, megavolt, megaton, megajoule A megahertz wave oscillates at 1 **million** times the frequency of a 1 hertz wave.
meter	**measure:** ammeter, meter, barometer, thermometer, metric system, interferometer An ammeter **measures** electric current in amps.
micro	**small, one-millionth:** microwave, micrometer, microgram, micron, microfarad, microprocessor Microwaves are **smaller** (shorter wavelength) than normal radio waves.
milli	**thousandth:** millisecond, millivolt, millirem, milliamp, milliwatt A millisecond is one-**thousandth** of a second.
min	**small:** minor, minuscule, minute, minimum, minority Minor forces are **smaller** than major forces.
mit, miss	**to send:** transmit, emit, emission, transmission, missile Transmitting antennas **send** radio signals.
mot, mov	**move:** locomotion, electromotive force (emf), motion, motility, movement Electromotive force is the difference in potential that **moves** electrons and creates a current.
multi	**many:** multiply, multiplex, multistage, multitude, multiple star Multiplexing allows the simultaneous transmission of **many** messages through one medium.
nano	**billionth:** nanosecond, nanotechnology, nanogram, nanoscale A nanogram is one-**billionth** of a gram.
numer	**number:** numeral, numeration, enumerate, innumerable, numerator, numerous To enumerate is to determine the **number** of something.
-on	**unit:** photon, elecrtron, proton, lepton, baryon, fermion, boson Photons are the smallest **units** of light.
pel, puls	**drive, push:** propulsion, expel, repel, pulse, impulse, pulsate, repulsion, propel Rockets must have propulsion to **push** forward.
pend, pens	**hang, weigh:** pendulum, suspend, pending, suspension, pendant A pendulum is a swinging, **hanging weight.**
photo	**light:** photon, photoelectric effect, photoemission, photoluminescence A photon is a particle of **light** with zero rest mass.
phys	**body/nature:** physics, physical science, Newtonian physics, particle physics, geophysics, astrophysics Physics is the study of the **nature** of matter and energy.
polar	**end of axis:** polar, dipole, polarization, polarized, polarity, polar coordinates, monopole Polar molecules have positive and negative **ends.**
pot	**power:** electrical potential, potential energy, potentiometer, potential difference, action potential Potential energy is the **power** to perform work.
prim	**first:** primary coil, primary colors, primary pigments, prime A magnetic field forms **first** in the primary coil before a current is induced in the secondary coil.
pro	**before, positive:** proton, progress, projectile, propel Protons carry a **positive** charge.
radi, ray	**ray, radius:** radioactive, radius, ray, radiant, radiate, irradiate, X-ray, radiator, radiation **Rays** of radiation emanate from radioactive sources.

re	**back, again:** reflect, reactance, rebound, react, reflection, refraction, resonance
	Reflected light bounces **back** toward the source.
rect	**straight:** rectifier, rectify, direct current, erect, directrix
	A rectifier changes, or "**straightens**," an AC current into a DC current.
scop	**see, watch:** spectroscope, telescope, oscilloscope, microscopic, galvanoscope
	Spectroscopes allow physicists to **see** and analyze the spectrum of light.
sign	**sign, mark:** signal, signature, design, significant, designate
	Radio signals are used to **mark** a satellite's position.
sim	**same, like:** simulation, similar, assimilate, simulate, simultaneous
	Good physics simulations behave **like** the phenomena they model.
son	**sound:** ultrasonic, sonic, sonar, resonate, unison, ultrasound, resonance
	Ultrasonic waves have a frequency higher than **sound** waves.
stat	**stay, position:** stationary, static electricity, statics, station, thermostat, rheostat
	Thermostats ensure that temperatures remain in the **same** range.
sub	**under, below:** subscript, subsonic, submerge, subscript, subtend, subtract, subzero
	Subscripts are placed **below** the line (e.g., v1, v2).
super	**above, over:** superposition, superpose, superimpose, superheat, superior, supersonic
	Superposition is the addition of one wave **over** another to determine the final pattern.
therm	**heat:** thermodynamics, therm, thermoelectric, thermocouple, thermonuclear, thermistor
	Thermodynamics is the science of **heat** energy.
tort, tors	**twist:** torque, torsion, distort, contort, torque converter, torsion balance
	Torque can be described as a **twisting** force.
tract	**to draw or drag:** abstract, attract, traction, extract, retract, subtract, contract, extract, protractor
	Abstract ideas may be **drawn** from careful observations.
trans	**across:** transmitter, transducer, transformer, transceiver, transistor, translucent, transmission
	Radio transmitters send messages **across** long distances.
ultra	**beyond:** ultraviolet, ultrasound, ultrahigh frequency (UHF), ultrahigh vacuum
	Ultraviolet radiation has a frequency **beyond** violet radiation.
uni	**one, same:** uniform, unit, unify, universal, universe
	Uniform techniques are employed to keep controls the **same.**
vect	**to carry:** vector, convection, convect, advection, vector product
	Heat and smoke are **carried** away from a fire by convection.

word provided by your teacher. These may come from readings, lectures, or Table 1.8. Illustrate the relationship between these words and their roots by **highlighting** root word meanings as illustrated in the sentences in Table 1.8.

unfamiliar term in class or in your reading, enter its meaning and roots as shown. Contribute to this table for the duration of the class, referring to Table 1.8 whenever you encounter an unfamiliar root, prefix, or suffix.

ACTIVITY 1.3.2 *Developing a Physics Glossary*
Construct a three-column chart with the headings used in Table 1.9. Each time you encounter an

ACTIVITY 1.3.3 *Deciphering Physics Terms*
Once you know basic roots, you can determine the meanings of new physics terms. Table 1.10

Table 1.9 Physics Glossary

Term	Meaning	Roots (Meanings)
Fusion	Joining of nuclei	Fus (melt, join), -ion (process)
Infrasonic	Below audible frequency	Infra (below), son (sound)
Astrophysics	Study of the nature of stars	Astro (star), phys (nature)
↓new words	↓	↓

Table 1.10 Deciphering Physics Terms

		Term		Definitions
↓	1	thermodynamics	a	Producing electricity from a difference of temperatures
	2	electrodynamics	b	Flow in the opposite direction
	3	dynamometer	c	Instrument that measures the power output of an engine
	4	aerodynamics	d	Interaction of electric currents and fields
	5	thermoelectric	e	The production of electricity using energy from light
	6	electromotive	f	Produces an electric current
	7	countercurrent	g	Light resulting from absorption of electromagnetic radiation
	8	photoluminescence	h	Study of the relation of heat, energy, and power
	9	photoelectric	i	The loss of electrons when light strikes a surface
	10	photoemission	j	The properties of moving air and the forces it exerts

contains a list of physics words, many of which may be unfamiliar to you. Analyze the roots (using Table 1.8), and match each term to a likely definition (the first term is done as an example). Do not consult a dictionary or glossary; rather, draw conclusions based on your analysis of the roots.

1.4 Earth and Space Science Vocabulary

ACTIVITY 1.4.1 *Understanding Earth and Space Science Root Words*

Table 1.11 lists the most common roots, prefixes, and suffixes in the earth and space sciences. Following each definition is a series of earth and space science terms that share this root. For example, *iso-* means "same." An *isosceles* triangle has equal sides, an *isobar* is a line on a map that connects points having the same atmospheric pressure, an *isotherm* is a line connecting all points of the same temperature, an *isocline* connects all points with the same slope, and *isotopes* are forms of the same element. By knowing the meanings of a few roots, you can determine the meanings of many terms. Construct a sentence for each earth or space science vocabulary word your teacher uses. These may come from readings, lectures, or Table 1.11. Illustrate the relationship between these words and their roots by **highlighting** root word meanings as illustrated in the sentences in Table 1.11.

ACTIVITY 1.4.2 *Developing an Earth and Space Science Glossary*

Construct a three-column chart with the headings used in Table 1.12. Each time you encounter an unfamiliar term in class or in your reading, enter its meaning and roots as shown in Table 1.11. Add to this table for the duration of the course, referring to Table 1.11 whenever there is an unfamiliar root.

Table 1.11 Roots, Prefixes, and Suffixes in Earth and Space Science

-al	**relating to:** geological, alluvial, astronomical, terrestrial, altitudinal The U.S. Geological Survey examines issues **related to** the topography and resources of the Earth.
alt	**high:** altocumulus, altitude, altimeter, altiplano, altostratus Altocumulus are **high** cumulus cloud formations.
anti	**against, opposite:** anticline, anticyclone, antilogarithm, antitrades An anticline is characterized by slopes angled **opposite** directions down from the crest.
aqu	**water:** aquifer, aqueous, aquarium, aquatic, aqueduct, aquaculture An **aquifer** is a body of permeable rock that contains water.
baro	**pressure:** barometer, bar, barometry, barometric pressure, hyperbaric chamber Barometers are used to measure air **pressure.**
bi	**two:** binary star, bimetallic, bifurcate, bimetallic, bicarbonate Binary stars occur in **twos.**
benth	**bottom of the sea:** benthos, benthic, zoobenthos The benthos refers to the environment or the flora and fauna on the **bottom** of the sea.
calci	**lime:** calcium oxide, calcified, calcium, calcite, decalcified, calcium carbonate **Lime** is composed of calcium oxide, obtained by heating limestone.
calor	**heat:** calorimeter, calorie, caloric, kilocalorie, calorimetry Calorimeters are used to measure the **heat** energy in oil-bearing rocks.
carb	**coal, carbon:** carbon dioxide, carbonic acid, bicarbonate, carboniferous, calcium carbonate Carbon dioxide and carbonic acid are **carbon**-based chemicals.
cent	**hundred, hundredth:** centigrade, centimeter, centigram, percent There are one **hundred** degrees between freezing and boiling on the centigrade scale.
chrom	**color:** chromium, chromosphere, chromatography, monochrome, dicrhomate Chromium compounds are very **colorful.**
chron	**time:** geochronologist, geochronology, chronology, chronic, chronicle, chronometer, synchronize Geochronologists try to determine the **time** rocks were formed.
circ	**ring, around:** circumference, circumlunar, circulate, circumpolar, circumsolar The equatorial circumference of the Earth is the distance **around** the Earth at the equator.
clin	**slope:** clinometer, incline, decline, halocline, anticline, syncline, thermocline A clinometer measures the **slope.**
clud, clus	**to close:** occluded front, exclude, exclusive, conclude, cluster, star cluster An occluded front occurs when a cold front **closes** in on a warm front.
co, com	**with, together:** cogeneration, conglomerate, condense, compress, confluence Cogeneration plants produce electricity and heat **together.**
cosm	**universe, world:** cosmic dust, cosmos, cosmology, cosmonaut, cosmic rays, cosmography Cosmic dust is composed of small particles distributed throughout the **universe.**
crust	**shell:** crust, encrusted, crustose, crustal The Earth's crust is the hard rocky **shell** above the mantle.
cycl	**circle, cycle:** cyclone, cyclical, cycle, rock cycle, anticyclone, cyclotron, nitrogen cycle Cyclones are strong wind systems flowing in **circles** around low-pressure zones.

(Continued)

Table 1.11 *(Continued)*

de	**down, without, from:** declination, decomposition, deduce, deform, degenerate, deoxygenate Declination is measured in degrees **from** the celestial equator.
deci	**tenth:** decibel, decimeter, decimal, deciliter A decibel has one-**tenth** the sound intensity of a bel.
dia	**through, across:** diameter, diagonal, diaphragm, diagram Diameter is the measure **across** a circle or other shape.
e, ec, ex	**out, without, from:** eclipse, eccentric, ecliptic, elongation, exothermic, effluent The Earth is **without** direct light from the Sun during total solar eclipses.
epi	**upon, above:** epicenter, epibenthos, epilimnion, epicycle The epicenter is directly **above** the focus of an earthquake.
equi	**equal:** equinox, equidistant, equilateral, equilibrium, equation, equator The length of day and night are **equal** at the equinoxes.
flu, fluc	**flowing:** confluence, fluid, flue, fluctuate, effluvium, magnetic flux The confluence of two rivers is the point where they **flow** together as one.
geo	**Earth:** geothermal, geology, geode, geocentric, geomorphology, geography, geotropism Geothermal energy comes from the **Earth.**
glaci	**ice:** glacier, glaciation, glacial, glaciology, glacial polish, glaze Glaciers are large, slowly moving rivers of **ice.**
grad	**step, go:** retrograde, prograde, grade, gradual, graduate, graduated, gradient Planets periodically exhibit retrograde motion and appear to **go** backward.
graph	**writing, drawing:** geography, graphite, oceanography, photography, cartography, topography Geographers represent landforms using maps and other **drawings.**
halo	**salt:** halite, halogens, halocline, halophyte Halite is rock **salt.**
helio	**Sun:** aphelion, perihelion, heliograph, heliocentric, heliostat, heliosphere, heliopause The aphelion is the point in orbit when a planet or comet is farthest from the **Sun.**
hydr, hygr	**water:** hydroelectric, hydraulics, hydrate, hydrology, hydrothermal, hydropower, hygrometer Hydroelectric power plants produce electricity from the energy in falling **water.**
-ic	**relating to:** benthic, pelagic, atmospheric, acidic, basic The term *pelagic* **relates to** the open sea.
ign	**fire:** ignite, igneous, ignition, igneous fusion, metaigneous Igneous rocks are "born of **fire**" in volcanoes or the depth of the Earth.
im, in	**not:** independent variable, inversion, immobile, immiscible, inversion layer Independent variables do **not** depend on dependent variables.
-ion	**process:** erosion, conservation, pollution, decomposition, evolution, liquefaction Erosion is a **process** in which soil and rock are worn away.
iso	**equal:** isobar, isotherm, isocline, isostasy, isotope Isobars are lines on meteorological maps that connect points of **equal** pressure.
-ist	**one who studies:** meteorologist, geologist, geophysicist, environmentalist, conservationist Meteorologists **study** the atmosphere and weather.
-ite	**ore, rock, crystal:** bauxite, bentonite, chalcopyrite, dolomite, granite, rhyolite, graphite Bauxite is an aluminum **ore.**
kilo	**thousand:** kilopascal, kilogram, kilometer, kilovolt, kiloton, kilowatt, kilowatt-hour A kilopascal is one **thousand** pascals of pressure.

liqu	**fluid, liquid:** liquefaction, liquefy, liquid, liquid crystal During earthquakes, some soils undergo liquefaction and are more **fluid** than normal.
lith	**rock:** lithosphere, batholith, neolithic, Paleolithic, lithify The lithosphere is the **rocky** crust and outer portion of the mantle.
lu, lum	**light:** luminous, translucent, luster, luminescence, luminosity Stars are luminous, producing **light** during nuclear reactions.
magn	**great:** order of magnitude, magnify, magnitude, magnification Each order of magnitude is ten times **greater** than the previous one.
mar	**sea:** Mare Tranquilis, marine, mariner, marsh, maritime, mare Mare Tranquilis, the "**Sea** of Tranquility," is a large, dark, basalt plain on the Moon.
medi	**half, middle:** medial moraine, Mediterranean, medium, median Medial moraines form in the **middle** between two adjacent glaciers.
meso	**middle, between:** mesosphere, mesocyclone, meson, Mesozoic, Mesoamerica The mesosphere is **between** the stratosphere and thermosphere.
meta	**between, change:** metamorphic, metastable, metamorphism, metathesis Metamorphic rock has undergone **change** as a result of heat, pressure, and time.
meter	**measure:** anemometer, barometer, thermometer, altimeter, diameter, hygrometer Anemometers are used to **measure** wind speed.
nimb	**rain:** nimbus, cumulonimbus, nimbostratus Nimbus clouds usually produce **rain.**
nov	**new:** nova, supernova, innovation, novice, Nova Scotia, novel, novice Novas are stars that display a **new,** rapid increase in brilliance.
nox, noc	**night:** nocturnal, vernal equinox, autumnal equinox, noctilucent clouds At the vernal and autumnal equinoxes, day and **night** are of equal length.
-oid	**like, form:** metalloid, colloid, asteroid, meteoroid, crystalloid Metalloids are **like** metals in many ways.
-ology	**study of:** seismology, meteorology, petrology, climatology, mineralogy, geology, meteorology Seismology is the **study of** earthquakes and related phenomena.
orb	**circle:** orbital velocity, orbit, orbiter, orb Satellites must travel at orbital velocity to continue **circling** the Earth.
ortho	**straight, correct:** orthoclase, orthogonal, orthoquartzite, orthoslice Orthoclase crystals are common in granite and exhibit **straight** planes of cleavage.
-ous, -us	**characterized by:** aqueous, nebulous, igneous, carboniferous, nimbus, cumulus Aqueous solutions are **characterized by** water, the "universal solvent."
paleo	**ancient:** paleontology, Paleozoic, paleobotany, paleomagnetism Paleobotany is the study of **ancient,** fossilized plants.
pel, puls	**push, pulse:** pulsar, pulsate, impulse, propel, repel Pulsars are thought to be rapidly rotating neutron stars that emit **pulses** of radio waves.
pelag	**the sea:** pelagic, bathypelagic, abbysalpelagic Fish living in the open **sea** are known as pelagic fish.
peri	**around:** perimeter, periscope, perigee, perihelion The perimeter of an island is the length **around** its shores.

(Continued)

Table 1.11 *(Continued)*

petr	**rock:** petrified, petrification, petrology, petrochemical, petrography, petroleum Petrified wood was once organic but now is **rock.**
phys	**nature:** physicist, physics, physiography, physical geography, physical science, geophysics Physicists study the **nature** of energy and matter.
plan	**flat:** altiplano, planar, plains, floodplain, coplanar The high, **flat** tableland of South America is known as the altiplano.
pole, polar	**end of axis:** Polaris, circumpolar, North and South Poles, polar cap, polar projection, aurora Polaris Polaris, the pole star, is in line with the Earth's **axis.**
pos	**put, laid:** deposit, expose, position, composite, opposite Alluvial deposits have been **laid** down over time.
quad	**four:** quadrat, quadrangle, quadrilateral, quadrillion, quadruple A quadrat is a **four**-sided parcel of land used in field studies.
re	**back, again:** nonrenewable, renewable, report, retain, research, reaction Once depleted, nonrenewable resources cannot be tapped **again.**
retro	**back, again:** retrograde, retrorocket, retrofit, retrogression During retrograde, planets appear to move **backward.**
rupt	**break:** eruption, erupt, rupture, interrupt, abrupt, disrupt During eruptions, magma **breaks** through the Earth's crust.
sal	**salt:** desalination, salinity, saline, salt, salinization Desalination removes **salt** from water.
sed, sid	**sit, settle:** sediment, subside, residue, sedimentary, residual Sediments form when particulates **settle** out of a mixture.
solar	**sun:** solar wind, solar cell, solar flare, solar system, solarize Solar wind is a flow of charged particles from the **Sun.**
sphere	**ball, sphere:** lithosphere, stratosphere, exosphere, asthenosphere, thermosphere, atmosphere The lithosphere is the outermost **spherical** layer of the Earth.
struct	**build:** infrastructure, structure, construct, instruct, obstruct, destruction Infrastructure must be **built** before superstructures are erected.
sub	**under, below:** subsoil, subduct, submerge, subduction zone, subscript, subarctic, substrata, substrate Subsoil lies immediately **below** surface soil.
super	**above, over:** superstratum, supernova, superheat, supercool, supersaturate, superscript The superstratum lies **above** other layers.
syn	**together, with:** syncline, geosynchronous, synthesis, geosyncline Water flowing down the opposite slopes of a syncline will come **together.**
terr	**Earth:** subterranean, terrain, territory, terrestrial, extraterrestrial, terrace, terrarium Subterranean structures are located below the surface of the **Earth.**
therm	**heat:** thermal, thermometer, geothermal, isotherm, thermocline Thermals are upward currents of **heated** air.
trans	**across, through:** translucent, transoceanic, transit, transmit, transect, transparent Light goes **through** translucent objects.

trib	**give:** tributary, contribute, attribute, distribute Tributaries **give** their water to other rivers.
typ	**type:** prototype, type, typical, typology, typify Prototypes are the first of their **type.**
ultra	**beyond:** ultraviolet, ultrasound, ultrahigh frequency (UHF), ultramafic Ultraviolet radiation has a frequency **beyond** that of violet radiation.
umb	**shadow:** umbra, penumbra, umbrella The umbra is the darkest **shadow** in an eclipse.
vert, vers	**turn:** diversion dam, divert, invert, reverse, convert Diversion dams **turn** the course of rivers or streams.
volcan	**fire, volcano:** volcanologist, volcano, vulcanize, volcanology, volcanism Volcanologists study **volcanoes.**

Table 1.12 Earth and Space Science Glossary

Term	Meaning	Roots (Meanings)
Barometer	Measures air pressure	Bar (pressure), meter (measure)
Translucent	Allows light through	Trans (through), luc (light)
Heliocentric	Sun centered	Helio (sun), centr (centered)
↓new words	↓	↓

Table 1.13 Deciphering Terms from Earth and Space Science

		Term		Definitions
↓	1	anticline	a	Instrument that measures the moisture or humidity of air
	2	anticyclone	b	Instrument that measures slope angle
	3	antitrades	c	Process in which organic materials are transformed to rock
	4	clinometer	d	Process of becoming liquid or behaving like a liquid
	5	hydrology	e	Steady winds that blow opposite the trade winds
	6	hygrometer	f	Stratified rock sloping in opposite directions from a crest
	7	liquefaction	g	Study of the appearance and classification of rocks
	8	petrifaction	h	Study of the Earth's water
	9	petrography	i	Study of the origin, structure, and composition of rocks
	10	petrology	j	Winds that move opposite storm winds

ACTIVITY 1.4.3 *Deciphering Earth and Space Science Terms*

Once you know basic root words, you can determine the meanings of many new terms. Table 1.13 contains a list of earth and space science words, many of which may be unfamiliar to you. Analyze the roots using Table 1.11. and match each term to a likely definition (the first term is done as an example). Do not consult a dictionary or glossary; rather, draw conclusions based on your analysis of the root words.

Answers to Chapter Activities

1.1.1 Students develop sentences using the format illustrated in Table 1.3. The teacher is encouraged to select current terms from readings, laboratories, lectures, and discussions.

1.1.2 Students maintain a glossary for the course according to the format shown in Table 1.1.

1.1.3 1(i), 2(f), 3(b), 4(a), 5(c), 6(e), 7(j), 8(h), 9(g), 10(d).

1.2.1 Students develop sentences using the format illustrated in Table 1.7. The teacher is encouraged to select current terms from readings, laboratories, lectures, and discussions.

1.2.2   Students maintain a glossary for the course according to the format shown in Table 1.5.

1.2.3   1(c), 2(b), 3(a), 4(r), 5(o), 6(s), 7(d), 8(k), 9(q), 10(i), 11(f), 12(l), 13(e), 14(j), 15(t), 16(n), 17(h), 18(g), 19(p), 20(m).

1.3.1   Students develop sentences using the format illustrated in Table 1.10. The teacher is encouraged to select current terms from readings, laboratories, lectures, and discussions.

1.3.2   Students maintain a glossary for the course according to the format shown in Table 1.8.

1.3.3   1(h), 2(d), 3(c), 4(j), 5(a), 6(f), 7(b), 8(g), 9(e), 10(i).

1.4.1   Students develop sentences using the format illustrated in Table 1.13. The teacher is encouraged to select current terms from readings, laboratories, lectures, and discussions.

1.4.2   Students maintain a glossary for the course according to the format shown in Table 1.11.

1.4.3   1(f), 2(j), 3(e), 4(b), 5(h), 6(a), 7(d), 8(c), 9(g), 10(i).

Chapter Two

Developing Science Reading Skills

For the Teacher 35

2.1 Science Reading Comprehension: Cloze 38

2.2 Science Reading Comprehension: Jigsaw 39

2.3 Science Vocabulary in Spanish and English 39

2.4 Scientific Terminology: Linking Languages 41

Answers to Chapter Activities 42

For the Teacher

The Importance of Science Literacy

Educators, scientists, engineers, economists, entrepreneurs, and politicians have expressed the need for a scientifically literate population. According to the American Association for the Advancement of Science, a scientifically literate person is

> one who is aware that science, mathematics, and technology are interdependent human enterprises with strengths and limitations; understands key concepts and principles of science; is familiar with the natural world and recognizes both its diversity and unity; and uses scientific knowledge and scientific ways of thinking for individual and social purposes.[1]

The National Academy of Science states:

> Scientific literacy means that a person can ask, find, or determine answers to questions derived from curiosity about everyday experiences. It means that a person has the ability to describe, explain, and predict natural phenomena. Scientific literacy entails being able to read with understanding articles about science in the popular press and to engage in social conversation about the validity of the conclusions. Scientific literacy implies that a person can identify scientific issues underlying national and local decisions and express positions that are scientifically and technologically informed. A literate citizen should be able to evaluate the quality of scientific information on the basis of its source and the methods used to generate it. Scientific literacy also implies the capacity to pose and evaluate arguments based on evidence and to apply conclusions from such arguments appropriately.[2]

Finally the Programme for International Student Assessment defines scientific literacy:

> As the capacity to use scientific knowledge, to identify questions and to draw evidence-based conclusions in order to understand and help

make decisions about the natural world and the changes made to it through human activity.[3]

A scientifically literate person is able to read and write about scientific topics. The person who speaks English has a distinct advantage in this regard, since more scientific research is published in English than any other language. English-language literacy strategies promote scientific literacy by providing the tools necessary to read scientific material. In this chapter, we introduce strategies that are useful for English learners as well as native speakers.

Developing Strategic Readers

Many students believe that they are good readers, when in fact they are simply good decoders.

Decoding is the transformation of an encoded message into a usable form; reading requires comprehension. Therefore, if students have poor comprehension, they are poor readers even if they can decode fluently. Fortunately, there are techniques to help poor readers become good readers. Table 2.1 contrasts the habits of poor readers with strategic readers. It is important for teachers to recognize these characteristics so they can diagnose reading problems and help students improve.

Techniques for Improving Reading

This book introduces a variety of strategies for improving science literacy by improving science

Table 2.1 Characteristics of Poor and Strategic Readers

		Poor readers . . .	Strategic readers . . .
Before reading	Focus	Do not eliminate distractions	Establish an environment free of distractions
	Background	Start reading without thinking about content	Review background information before reading
	Structure	Do not review the structure established by the author	Review structure, author notes, headings, and formatted terms
	Goals	Do not have specific goals for what they hope to accomplish	Set specific goals before they start reading
While reading	Notes	Do not take notes	List the key points and summarize major ideas
	Vocabulary	Ignore words they do not understand	Use roots, semantic, and syntactic clues to determine meanings
	Re-reading	Continue "reading" even if they do not understand key points	Re-read confusing sections
	Synthesis	Do not relate new information with prior knowledge	Integrate new material with prior understanding
	Reflection	Do not reflect on what they have read	Generate questions from the reading
	Highlights	Highlight and underline too much or not at all	Highlight or underline only key points
	Assessment	Do not assess understanding, or only at the end of the passage	Assess understanding by outlining and solving problems
After reading	Evaluation	Do not have any goals to evaluate	Determine if they have reached their goals
	Paraphrase	Memorize material verbatim or not at all.	Express key points in their own words
	Discussion	Do not "self-talk" or discuss the material with others	Conduct "self-talk" and discuss concepts with others
	Review	Do not review the material they have read	Integrate new information with prior knowledge

reading comprehension. Many of these strategies are found in other chapters. Following is a summary of these techniques (the number in parentheses is the section number where the full discussion may be found):

Cornell notes (3.1): Cornell notes are commonly used in lectures, but can also be helpful for understanding and remembering the structure and content of written material. Students must take notes (brief phrases, words, and diagrams) and identify cues (key words or questions) from the reading. They then cover their notes and use the cues to quiz themselves and see what they have remembered. Eventually they summarize the key points.

Advanced organizers (8.1): Students preread the science text to understand its structure and the scope of its content. By consciously analyzing and recording the author's outline and advance organizers, they are better prepared to understand the text when they read it.

Mind (semantic) maps (9.4): Mind mapping is a brainstorming technique in which a radial "map" is developed showing the relationship of a central idea to supporting facts and concepts. Mind maps can be used to review and discuss the central theme of a chapter.

Concept maps (9.5): Students can develop a concept map for the theme of a chapter or section. This technique requires a good understanding of the material and can be used as a postreading activity to develop comprehension.

KWL (8.0): Students discuss what they **K**now and what they **W**ant to know prior to reading and what they have **L**earned after reading a passage. This approach is used to develop reading goals so students can read with a purpose.

SQ3R (8.0): SQ3R is the acronym for a technique known as **S**urvey, **Q**uestion, **R**ead, **R**ecite, **R**eview. SQ3R is a structured approach that focuses on comprehension.

Root words (1.1–1.4): Students learn how to construct and decipher scientific words by understanding the meanings of roots, prefixes, and suffixes common to biology, chemistry, physics, and the earth and space sciences.

Cloze (2.1): Cloze activities (providing closure to passages with missing words) are used to assess the readability of a passage. The higher the cloze scores for a given population, the more readable the passage is. In this chapter, we introduce cloze as a technique for developing and assessing reading comprehension.

Jigsaw (2.2): Jigsaw is a technique whereby students develop reading skills by consulting with others, preparing notes, and teaching their peers.

Cognates (2.3–4): Cognates are words in different languages that have the same linguistic roots. Once students recognize the similarities between English and their native language, they will be better prepared to figure out the meanings of unfamiliar words.

Choosing Textbooks for English Learners

Students learn English and science fastest if their science textbooks are well structured, match the curriculum, and include well-documented charts, diagrams, and pictures. Teachers should review the following features before adopting a science textbook for English learners:

Organization: Is the text clearly organized with appropriate chapters, headings, and subheadings?

Guide questions: Does the text have questions that guide the reading?

Terms and principles: Are key terms and principles highlighted using special formatting?

Diagrams: Is the text illustrated with clear, informational diagrams? Are these diagrams annotated and labeled?

Illustrations: Are key ideas illustrated with informative diagrams, charts, or pictures?

Sentence structure: Are sentences clear, concise, and instructive?

Summaries: Does the text include section summaries and key points to remember?

Glossary: Does the text include a comprehensive glossary showing the relationship between roots and science terms?

2.1 Science Reading Comprehension: Cloze

Look at Figures 2.1A, 2.1B, and 2.1C, and record the shapes you see. Most people see a square in Figure 2.1A, a circle in Figure 2.1B, and a triangle in Figure 2.1C, but if you look again, you will note that none of these shapes is actually found in the diagram. Your mind sees clues and provides "closure" to the partial patterns it detects. Similarly, your mind provides closure if you don't decode every word when you are reading.

Reading specialists believe that your ability to provide closure is a measure of reading comprehension and have developed the cloze activity to assess and develop this skill. A passage of two hundred to three hundred words in length is selected. The first and last sentences are kept intact, and every fifth word of the remaining text is replaced

by a blank. The blanks are of equal length so as not to give the reader clues other than the context. Students work individually or in groups to infer or predict words that provide meaning. Readers use syntax, context, and prior knowledge to predict the hidden words.

ACTIVITY 2.1.1 *Develop a Science Cloze Worksheet*

Create a science cloze worksheet for another student by doing the following:

1. Select a 200- to 300-word passage from your science textbook, science magazine, or related resource.
2. Transcribe the first sentence intact.
3. Transcribe all but the last sentence, replacing every fifth word with a blank of equal length, as illustrated in Exhibit 2.1.
4. Transcribe the last sentence intact.
5. Make a list of the missing words on a separate sheet of paper.

ACTIVITY 2.1.2 *Complete a Science Cloze Activity*

Exchange papers with a fellow student, and fill in the worksheet you received with words that make

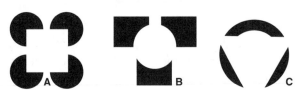

Figure 2.1 What Shapes Do You See?

Exhibit 2.1 *Sample Science Cloze Worksheet*

All known physical interactions of matter occur through four fundamental forces: gravitation, electromagnetism, strong nuclear force, and weak nuclear force. The most pervasive force _____ gravitation, in that every _____ of matter attracts every _____ particle. Without gravity you _____ have no weight, objects _____ float in midair, the _____ would slowly disintegrate, and _____ solar system and galaxy _____ fly apart! Electromagnetic forces _____ between those particles that _____ electric charge and/or a _____ moment. Electromagnetic forces are _____ for electricity, magnetism, and _____. In addition, they control _____ way atoms interact, and _____ the bases for all _____ reactions, both in living _____ nonliving systems. Muscle _____, the explosions in an _____ engine, and the adhesion _____ glues are but a _____ of the many expressions _____ electromagnetic forces. The nuclear _____ are crucial for the _____ of matter as we _____ it. Strong nuclear forces _____ neutrons and protons together _____ nuclei while the weak _____ forces are involved in _____ nuclear decay processes. Without _____ forces, atoms, the building _____ of matter, could not _____! We will investigate force and Newton's laws, which describe the effects and interactions of force.

sense. Alternatively, you may receive prepared cloze activities from your teacher. Exhibit 2.1 is a sample worksheet. What percentage of the terms did you guess correctly? What percentage were synonyms for the missing words?

2.2 Science Reading Comprehension: Jigsaw

A proverb says: "Tell me, and I'll forget. Show me, and I may remember. Involve me, and I'll understand." One of the most effective ways to be involved in the learning process is to share your understanding with another. In the process of explaining to others, you develop a deeper and more comprehensive understanding. In this activity, students study a science passage and explain it to their peers.

Each student is assigned to a home group (groups 1–4, Figure 2.2A) and an expert group (groups A–D, Figure 2.2B). The text from a chapter or other reading is divided into as many sections as there are expert groups. Students go to their "expert group" to study their portion of the chapter. In the example (Figure 2.2), the chapter on fundamental forces is divided such that group A studies gravity, group B studies electromagnetism, group C studies strong nuclear force, and group D studies weak nuclear force. In expert groups, students read the pertinent portion of the chapter and prepare to teach by developing a summary, list of key terms, diagrams, and questions. They consult with each other, share explanations, and prepare to teach.

The "experts" return to their home groups and teach their peers using the materials prepared in the expert group. In the example (Figure 2.2) the A's teach about gravity, the B's electromagnetism, the C's strong nuclear force, and the D's weak nuclear force. The content will vary depending on the material the teacher selects.

ACTIVITY 2.2.1 *Peer Teaching with the Jigsaw Technique*
Divide into expert groups as directed by the teacher. Dialogue with the other experts and prepare a summary, list of key terms, set of diagrams, and questions for the passage designated that the teacher has designated. Return to your home group, and teach your colleagues using the material you have prepared.

2.3 Science Vocabulary in Spanish and English

Spanish (Español) is one of the most influential languages in the world, particularly in the Western Hemisphere, where it is the dominant language in Central and South America. Spanish is also prevalent in the United States, where it is the first language of many immigrants. Spanish is a Latin-based language and shares much in common with other Romance languages, such as Italian, French, and

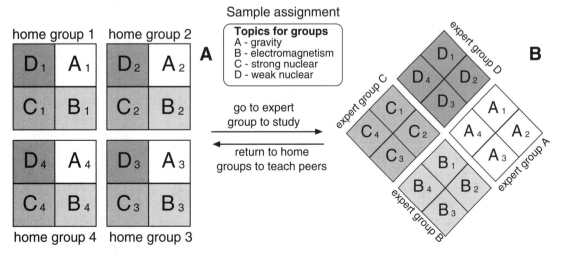

Figure 2.2 Jigsaw Strategy

Portuguese. It also shares much in common with English, particularly in science, where many words in both languages are based on Latin roots. As a result, an English-speaking scientist with no formal training in Spanish can recognize many scientific words in Spanish, and a Spanish-speaking scientist with no formal training in English can recognize many scientific words in English. Words that have similar linguistic roots are known as *cognates*. A list of a few English/Spanish science cognates appears in Table 2.2.

ACTIVITY 2.3.1 *Translating Science Terms for Native Spanish Speakers*
Complete Table 2.3. Try to determine the Spanish equivalent of each science term without referring to an English/Spanish dictionary. Not all scientific terms are cognates. Which of the terms in the table are?

ACTIVITY 2.3.2 *Translating Science Terms for Native English Speakers*
Complete Table 2.4. Try to determine the English equivalent of each Spanish science term without

Table 2.2 English/Spanish Science Cognates

English	Spanish	English	Spanish
anatomy	anatomía	inertia	inercia
asteroid	asteroide	lung	pulmón
atmosphere	atmósfera	meteorology	meteorología
bacterium	bacteria	mitochondrion	mitocondrio
biome	bioma	motion	movimiento
combustion	combustión	optics	óptica
condensation	condensación	oxidation	oxidación
desert	desierto	physiology	fisiología
electricity	electricidad	protein	proteína
electron	electrón	science	ciencia
energy	energía	solar system	sistema solar
flower	flor	telescope	telescopio
friction	fricción	torque	momento de torsión
gravity	gravitación	tsunami	tsunami
hibernation	hibernación	universe	universo
igneous	ígneo	voltage	voltaje

Table 2.3 English/Spanish Cognates

English → Spanish

English	Spanish
artery	_____
atherosclerosis	_____
atom	_____
biochemistry	_____
cancer	_____
comet	_____
dehydration	_____
earthquake	_____
electromagnetism	_____
element	_____
evaporation	_____
forest	_____
galaxy	_____
heart	_____
hurricane	_____

Table 2.4 Spanish/English Cognates

English ← Spanish

English	Spanish
_____	inercia
_____	magnetismo
_____	microscopio
_____	molécula
_____	Sistema nervioso
_____	Órbita
_____	oxígeno
_____	polinización
_____	radiación
_____	esqueleto
_____	taxonomía
_____	termodinámica
_____	transistor
_____	tuberculosis
_____	volcán

referring to a Spanish/English dictionary. Not all scientific terms are cognates. Which of the terms in the table are?

2.4 Scientific Terminology: Linking Languages

Many languages employ the same root words for scientific terms. Table 2.5 shows the similarity of some common scientific terms among five major Western European languages. Pronounce each term as best you can, and note that words in different languages sound similar even if they have different spellings.

There are also many similarities between English scientific words and scientific words in languages not native to Western Europe. These similarities arise when both languages rely on Latin and Greek roots to coin new terms or when English words are imported, as shown by the widespread adoption of the word *ecology* (Table 2.6).

ACTIVITY 2.4.1 *Matching Scientific Terms from 20 Common Languages*
Table 2.7 lists a variety of scientific terms. Match these terms with the correct non-English science terms from the word bank. When you have completed the table, you will have matched English science terms with corresponding terms from the 20 common languages listed.

ACTIVITY 2.4.2 *Matching Scientific Terms from 20 Uncommon Languages*
Table 2.8 lists a variety of scientific terms. Match these terms with the correct non-English science

Table 2.5 Comparison of Scientific Terms in Five European Languages

English	Italian	Spanish	French	German
chemistry	chimica	química	chimie	Chemie
biology	biologia	Biología	biologie	Biologie
physics	fisica	física	physique	Physik
geology	geologia	geología	géologie	Geologie
astronomy	astronomia	Astronomía	astronomie	Astronomie
meteorology	meteorologia	meteorología	météorologie	Meteologishe
photosynthesis	fotosintesi	fotosíntesis	photosynthèse	Photosynthese
metamorphosis	metamorfosi	metamorfosis	métamorphosse	Metamorphose
cell	cellula	célula	cellule	Zelle
organism	organismo	organismo	organisme	Organismus
ecology	ecologia	ecología	écologie	Ökologie

Table 2.6 Comparison of a Scientific Term in 36 Languages

Afrikaans	ekologie	French	écologie	Polish	ekologia
Albanian	ekologji	German	Ökologie	Portuguese	ecologia
Basque	ekologia	Greek	οικολογία	Romanian	ecologie
Bulgarian	екология	Hungarian	ökológia	Russian	экология
Chinese	生态学	Indonesian	ekologi	Serbian	екологија
Croatian	ekologija	Italian	ecologia	Slovak	ekológia
Czech	ekologie	Japanese	エコロジー	Spanish	ecología
Danish	økologi	Korean	생태학	Swedish	ekologi
Dutch	ecologie	Kurdish	êkolojî	Turkish	ekoloji
English	ecology	Latvian	ekoloģija	Ukrainian	екологія
Estonian	ökoloogia	Norwegian	økologi	Yiddish	ekologye
Finnish	ekologia	Persian	بوم زیست		

Table 2.7 Matching Scientific Terms from 20 Common Languages

1	bacterium	Czech		11	tsunami	Japanese	
2	magnetism	Danish		12	voltage	Polish	
3	thermodynamics	Dutch		13	combustion	Portuguese	
4	comet	Finnish		14	hydrology	Romanian	
5	sedimentary	French		15	atmosphere	Russian	
6	nervous system	German		16	pollination	Spanish	
7	tectonics	Greek		17	carbohydrate	Swedish	
8	periodic table	Hungarian		18	energy	Turkish	
9	cancer	Indonesian		19	microscope	Ukrainian	
10	hibernation	Italian		20	oxygen; O	Vietnamese	

Word bank				
baktérie	*ibernazione*	*magnetisme*	*polinización*	*Τεκτονικη*
combustão	*kanker*	*Nervensystem*	*sédimentaire*	*атмосфера*
enerji	*kolhyrdrater*	*Ôxy*	*thermodynamiek*	*мікроскоп*
hidrologie	*komeetta*	*periódusos rendszer*	*woltaż*	津波

Table 2.8 Matching Scientific Terms from 20 Uncommon Languages

1	heart	Flemish		11	molecule	Lithuanian	
2	hurricane	Afrikaans		12	anatomy	Paduan	
3	physiology	Albanian		13	optics	Romagnolo	
4	gravity	Basque		14	orbit	Serbian	
5	taxonomy	Bulgarian		15	universe	Sicilian	
6	tuberculosis	Croatian		16	dehydration	Slovak	
7	solar system	Esperanto		17	volcano	Swahili	
8	inertia	Furlan		18	friction	Valencian	
9	igneous	Galician		19	science	Venetian	
10	artery	Latvian		20	biochemistry	Welsh	

Word bank				
artêrija	friccio	inerzie	orkaan	universu
biocemeg	grabitazio	molêkulė	siensa	volkeni
dehydratácia	hart	'natomìa	sunsistemo	орбита
fiziologji	ígneo	òptich	tuberkuloza	таксономия

terms from the word bank. When you have completed the table, you will have matched English science terms with corresponding terms from the 20 uncommon languages listed.

Answers to Chapter Activities

2.1.1 Students develop a cloze activity similar to Exhibit 2.1.

2.1.2 Answers to the missing words of the sample cloze are in bold: "All known physical interactions of matter occur through four fundamental forces: gravitation, electromagnetism, strong nuclear force, and weak nuclear force. The most pervasive force **is** gravitation, in that every **particle** of matter attracts every **other** particle. Without gravity you **would** have no weight, objects **would** float in mid-air, the **Earth** would slowly disintegrate, and **our** solar system and galaxy **would** fly apart! Electromagnetic forces **exist** between those particles that **have** electric charge and/or a **magnetic** moment. Electromagnetic forces are **responsible** for electricity, magnetism, and **light**. In addition, they control **the** way atoms interact, and **are** the bases for all **chemical** reactions, both in living **and** nonliving systems. Muscle **action**, the explosions in an **automobile** engine, and the adhesion **of** glues are but a **few** of

Table 2.9 Answers to Activity 2.3.1

English	Spanish
artery	arteria
atherosclerosis	aterosclerosis
atom	átomo
biochemistry	bioquímica
cancer	cáncer
comet	cometa
dehydration	deshidratación
earthquake	terremoto
electromagnetism	electromagnetismo
element	elemento
evaporation	evaporación
forest	floresta
galaxy	galaxia
heart	corazón
hurricane	huracán

Table 2.10 Answers to Activity 2.3.2

English	Spanish
inertia	inercia
magnetism	magnetismo
microscope	microscopio
molecule	molécula
nervous system	sistema nervioso
orbit	órbita
oxygen; O	oxígeno
pollination	polinización
Radiation	radiación
skeleton	esqueleto
taxonomy	taxonomía
thermodynamics	termodinámica
transistor	transistor
tuberculosis	tuberculosis
volcano	volcán

Table 2.11 Science Terms in 20 Common Langauges

1	bacterium	Czech	baktérie	11	tsunami	Japanese	津波
2	magnetism	Danish	magnetisme	12	voltage	Polish	woltaż
3	thermodynamics	Dutch	thermodynamiek	13	combustion	Portuguese	combustão
4	comet	Finnish	komeetta	14	hydrology	Romanian	hidrologie
5	sedimentary	French	sédimentaire	15	atmosphere	Russian	атмосфера
6	nervous system	German	Nervensystem	16	pollination	Spanish	polinización
7	tectonics	Greek	Τεκτονική	17	carbohydrate	Swedish	kolhyrdrater
8	periodic table	Hungarian	periódusos ren.	18	energy	Turkish	enerji
9	cancer	Indonesian	kanker	19	microscope	Ukrainian	мікроскоп
10	hibernation	Italian	ibernazione	20	oxygen; O	Vietnamese	Ôxy

Table 2.12 Science Terms in 20 Uncommon Languages

1	heart	Flemish	hart	11	molecule	Lithuanian	molékulé
2	hurricane	Afrikaans	orkaan	12	anatomy	Paduan	'natomìa
3	physiology	Albanian	fiziologji	13	optics	Romagnolo	òptich
4	gravity	Basque	grabitazio	14	orbit	Serbian	орбита
5	taxonomy	Bulgarian	таксономия	15	universe	Sicilian	universu
6	tuberculosis	Croatian	tuberkuloza	16	dehydration	Slovak	dehydratácia
7	solar system	Esperanto	sunsistemo	17	volcano	Swahili	volkeni
8	inertia	Furlan	inerzie	18	friction	Valencian	friccio
9	igneous	Galician	ígneo	19	science	Venetian	siensa
10	artery	Latvian	artêrija	20	biochemistry	Welsh	biocemeg

the many expressions **of** electromagnetic forces. The nuclear **forces** are crucial for the **existence** of matter as we **know** it. Strong nuclear forces **hold** neutrons and protons together **in** nuclei, while the weak **nuclear** forces are involved in **many** nuclear decay processes. Without **nuclear** forces, atoms, the building **blocks** of matter, could not **exist**! We will investigate force and Newton's laws that describe the effects and interactions of force."

2.2.1   Students use their summary, list of key terms, and set of diagrams as they explain their material. They use their questions to assess for understanding and reteach sections that are not understood by their home team.

2.3.1   See Table 2.9. The italicized words are cognates.

2.3.2   See Table 2.10. The italicized words are cognates.

2.4.1   See Table 2.11.

2.4.2   See Table 2.12.

Chapter Three

Developing Science Writing Skills

For the Teacher 45

3.1 Science Note Taking 46

3.2 Science Journaling 47

3.3 Science Essay Questions 49

3.4 Types of Science Writing 51

3.5 Science Writing Style 53

Answers to Chapter Activities 57

For the Teacher

Writing is foundational to science. Scientists share their hypotheses, findings, and criticisms through writing. Upon completion of their research, they write manuscripts describing their hypotheses, methods, materials, results, and conclusions. These manuscripts are examined by other scientists, who write reviews to determine if the research is worthy of publication. This process of *peer review* is central to the scientific endeavor.

In 1989, two chemists, Stanley Pons and Martin Fleischman, broke this convention when they made a startling announcement of their achievement of "cold fusion" to the media without first committing their work to writing and submitting it for peer review.[1] These scientists claimed to have achieved nuclear fusion (the process that releases energy in the Sun and other stars) at room temperature, an achievement that offered the promise of a limitless supply of energy for the world. While Pons and Fleischman were enjoying worldwide attention, their colleagues were expressing outrage that media announcements had been made prior to peer review of the work. Since the work had never been submitted for peer review or published in a reputable journal, other scientists were unable to assess its validity. For years, other chemists continued to work on the problem but were unable to replicate the results. Pons and Fleischman were widely discredited in the scientific community not because of their experiments, but because they had announced their findings to the media without first committing them to writing and submitting them for peer review. The cold fusion scandal underscores the importance of writing to the scientific endeavor.

Writing is an essential element of many professions and is fundamental to business and communication. Ernest Boyer, one of the most influential spokesmen of higher education, said that "perhaps more than any other form of communication, writing holds us responsible for our words and ultimately makes us more thoughtful human beings."[2]

Unfortunately a large percentage of students never gain this benefit because they do not write very often or very much. No one becomes a professional athlete without extensive practice, and no one becomes an excellent writer without extensive practice. Just as coaches schedule workouts for their athletes, teachers should schedule writing opportunities for their students. The activities in this chapter are "workouts" designed to help students become better writers of science.

Scientific writing offers special challenges for English learners. English learners may simultaneously be learning to use conversational English in their language acquisition courses, write creative essays in English, review opinion papers in government, write slang in instant messages, and draft lab reports in science. Learning to write in many forms is challenging for native speakers and can be overwhelming for English learners, particularly if they are unfamiliar with such forms of writing in their native languages. It is therefore important that teachers model scientific writing and provide examples to their students, showing how it differs from other literary forms. Scientific writing is precise, economical, and formal, and it is helpful to read good examples of scientific writing aloud to illustrate these principles to your students. Encourage all of your students to read their own writing aloud, since hearing the text is one of best ways to see if it flows and makes sense. It may also be helpful for students to use the speech synthesis feature of their computer to listen to their written work.

3.1 Science Note Taking

Lectures are a hallmark of secondary and higher education. Unlike video recordings, lectures are live performances, requiring mental and physical participation on the part of students. Many students think that the primary use of note taking is to capture the teacher's ideas so they can be studied after class. Although this is a value of note taking, it is minor in comparison with the potential learning that can take place during active engagement in thoughtful, reflective note taking. True note taking requires discernment, filtering, and processing and is quite different from dictation. The verbatim copying of notes from a screen or board or the verbatim copying of a teacher's spoken words reduces the time and energy for understanding and integrating the information presented.

Many students think that it is unnecessary to take notes if they can understand what their instructor is saying. This misconception arises when students view note taking as a form of dictation rather than an integral portion of the learning process. When students take notes correctly, they are actively engaged in the lecture and remember concepts and ideas better, even if they never review the notes. The very process of distilling the thoughts of the lecturer is helpful in comprehending and remembering the material. Here are some rules for effective note taking.

Rules for Effective Note Taking

Review: Review previous notes before the lecture begins. This provides context and allows you to connect new ideas and information with previously learned material.

Think! Notes should include your thoughts as you process the lecture. You must be actively engaged, thinking about the content while you are taking notes.

Key concepts: As you listen to and see information presented in lecture, identify and record key concepts, and skip less meaningful details and information. Filter what the teacher says, and take notes on ideas that will prompt your memory.

Notes, not dictation: Do not write in full sentences as this requires too much time and may cause you to miss important points. Substitute phrases for sentences and words for phrases whenever possible.

Use your own words: Whenever possible, put ideas in your own words rather than quoting the teacher. This requires comprehension and will help you remember material longer.

Format: Use an informal but uniform format. Underline main concepts and indent subconcepts. Leave space for later additions.

Organization: Number your pages, and keep the notes in order. Using a bound notebook helps maintain the pages in sequential order.

Rework: Rework your notes shortly after completing them. Add points, diagrams, and other reminders, but do not rewrite them as this detracts from time that is better spent in other activities.

Review: Review your notes shortly after completing them and prior to the next lecture or assessment.

One of the most popular and effective note-taking methods is the Cornell notes system. This system was developed at Cornell University to help students learn more effectively from lectures and readings, and it is now widely used in secondary schools as well. To begin, divide a piece of paper into three sections as illustrated in Figure 3.1. The largest section is devoted to notes; the side column is reserved for cues, key words, and concepts; and the bottom row is allocated for a summary.

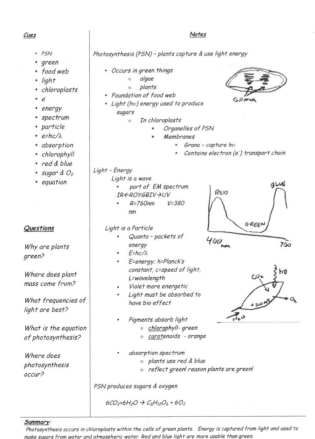

ACTIVITY 3.1.1 *Note Taking with the Cornell Notes System: Lecture*

Take Cornell notes of your class lecture or discussion for a day, week, or other period defined by your instructor. Follow these guidelines when using Cornell notes:

Notes: Write your raw notes in the "notes" column using brief phrases, words, and diagrams.

Cues: Shortly after class, write a list of key words and questions in the "cue" column.

Recite: Cover the notes, and using the cue words to trigger your memory, try to deliver the key points of the lecture to yourself or another student.

Summary: Summarize the key points in the summary section.

ACTIVITY 3.1.2 *Note Taking with the Cornell Notes System: Reading*

Cornell notes are useful for organizing the concepts in a section or chapter of a book or magazine. Following the directions listed for Activity 3.1.1, write Cornell notes for a chapter or other portion of your text.

3.2 Science Journaling

Publilius Syrus, a first century B.C. author, wrote, "Practice is the best of all instructors." Syrus knew that only those who practice can become excellent writers. More recently it has been said that the secret of becoming a writer is to write, write, and keep on writing. Athletes do not become good at their sport with an occasional game, but through regular practice and competition. Similarly, people do not become good writers by writing occasional brief notes, but only through regular informal and formal writing. Unfortunately many students never develop good writing skills because they fail to write enough. Many get so bogged down with the mechanics of writing (style, spelling, punctuation, form, and syntax) that they never get enough writing practice to improve. A popular technique to give students ample writing practice is known as *journaling*.

Journaling is a widely used technique in which individuals keep a daily written record of their

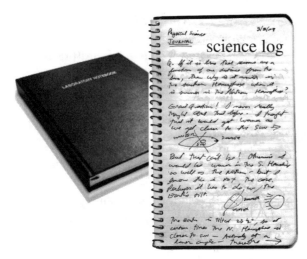

Figure 3.2 Notebook for Science Journaling

thoughts and activities. Writing gives them the opportunity to clarify their thoughts, opinions, and plans. In the science classroom, journaling can be used to provide students with writing practice while they reflect on relevant topics. Students record their thoughts in a bound notebook and share their writings periodically with their teacher. The process of translating an idea into writing helps students process and clarify ideas. The idea eventually takes shape for a learner when he or she must discuss a concept in writing.

Journals are typically evaluated on the basis of the quality and quantity of thoughts expressed, not on the quality of the syntax, spelling, and form. Journals should be kept in a bound notebook (Figure 3.2) with the date written at the top of each page. It is important to have regular entries, so assignments should be kept short and distinctly different from traditional worksheets or homework. Following is a list of journaling topics for the science classroom:

• *Current events (seeing the connection between science, technology, and society).* Summarize an article about a relevant scientific discovery. The summary should contain the title, date, author, and source, and a one-paragraph summary of the article written in your own words. There are numerous sources of current events in science, including the science sections of many newspapers. These can generally

be accessed online (*sciencesourcebook.com* or search "New York Times science").

• *Observations (building observational skills).* Record as many observations as possible about an object or process selected by the teacher. Be certain to record only observations, and not inferences that you have made (see section 5.3). Suitable observations include teacher demonstrations or experiments, samples of items from the natural world (rocks, fossils, plants, insects), chemical reactions (for example, Faraday's burning candle activity in section 5.2.1), photographs (plant communities, machines, animals), and video clips (athletic feats, natural processes, technological innovations). Observations can include color, shape, odor, texture, structure, composition, organization, movement, direction, location, temperature, magnetism, and pressure.

• *Longitudinal studies (recording observations over time).* Scientific observations and experiments often take place over numerous days (these are called *longitudinal studies*) and require careful note taking. Record your observations and measurements of a long-term process on a regular basis of such things as bacterial growth on an agar plate, the germination of a seed, the growth response of a plant with respect to gravity or light, the decomposition of plant material in a plastic bottle decomposition chamber, or the growth of crystals in an evaporating dish.

• *Prior knowledge (reflecting on what you already know).* Write down everything you know about a particular topic before it is introduced in class. For example, if the topic is electricity, write down all know about electricity: how it is produced, what it is used for, how it is delivered to your home, how it is stored, how it is purchased, who produces it, and so forth. This can be done for virtually any topic in science.

• *Misconceptions (using critical reasoning).* There are many common misconceptions in science that may serve as prompts for journal entries. For example, many people think that the reason temperatures are higher in the summer is that the Earth is closer to the Sun at this time. To explore this misconception, a journal prompt could ask, "If it is true that seasons are a function of our distance from the Sun, then why is it winter in the Southern Hemisphere when it is summer in the Northern Hemisphere? Provide a reasonable explanation for seasonality." Students will gain experience writing as they wrestle with such misconceptions. See sections 7.4 to 7.7 for a series of misconceptions that may be used as journal prompts.

ACTIVITY 3.2.1 *Journaling in Science*

Maintain a bound journal (Figure 3.2) for your science class. Record entries for all prompts (current events, observations, longitudinal studies, prior knowledge, misconceptions, and so forth) provided by your teacher. For each journal entry, include the date, the prompt, and your answer or response to the prompt.

3.3 Science Essay Questions

Educators use essays to assess analytical skills, written expression, and content mastery. Essays are a common element of standardized assessments such as the Scholastic Aptitude and Advanced Placement tests. Unfortunately many students do poorly on such assessments because they do not accurately analyze the essay questions before starting to write. Consequently they may write lengthy essays that are interesting, but off-topic, so they receive little or no credit for their efforts.

In my own experience as a consultant for national testing agencies, I have noted common problems that arise when students do not adequately analyze essay questions. These problems are illustrated in response to two past Advanced Placement Biology Exam questions:

Sample Question

Discuss the processes of exchange of O_2 and CO_2 that occur at the alveoli and muscle cells of mammals. Include in your answer a description of the transport of these gases in the blood.

Problems

Hasty assumptions: A large percentage of students wrote lengthy essays on the respiratory system and included diagrams of the trachea, bronchi, bronchioles, lungs, and diaphragm. They immediately saw the formulas for oxygen and carbon dioxide and assumed the question dealt with the respiratory system. Being familiar with the mechanics of respiration, they proceeded to write lengthy off-topic essays. Not only did such students receive no points for their efforts, but this diversion took away valuable writing time.

Incomplete responses: Many students wrote good essays about one component of the question but forgot to address the other components. For example, some focused entirely on oxygen, alveoli, or processes of exchange and failed to discuss carbon dioxide, muscle cells, or transport in the blood. Their incomplete responses cost them points on the test.

Sample Question

Discuss the processes of cleavage, gastrulation, and neurulation in the frog embryo. Tell what each process accomplishes. Describe an experiment that illustrates the importance of induction in development.

Problems

Inability to generalize: Many students wrote comments such as, "We only studied chicken embryology, so I know nothing about frogs!" Such students panicked when they saw "frog embryo," not realizing that vertebrates have similar embryological development and that the question could have been answered adequately using knowledge from the embryology of other vertebrates such as the chicken.

Poor time allocation: "Primacy" and "recency" effects cause us to remember the beginning and ends of questions more than the material in the middle. In this instance, some students spent the majority of their time focusing on the induction experiment (the most recent item in the question), even though it was only a fourth of the question and points.

Disorganized responses: Many students never organized their thoughts before writing, and as a result, their answers were rambling and incoherent. This and the other problems can be avoided by developing a framework or conceptual grid as shown in the next section.

Preparing a Response

If you do not check your map before driving to a new location, you will probably waste a lot of time and gasoline and may never arrive at your destination. Similarly, if you do not analyze the "road map" inherent in an essay question before you start to write, you will likely waste a lot of time and energy and may never meet the requirements. To ensure an accurate "road map" when writing essay, do the following before writing:

• Read the question twice.
• Highlight and categorize key terms.
• Develop a grid (Exhibit 3.1) or outline of the question.
• Write notes of items to discuss in each section.

These steps are illustrated in the following examples. In question 1, we have put boxes around the two major topics of exchange and transport, double underlined the two gases in question, and underlined the regions where we must discuss exchange and transport. This can be expressed as a matrix or table, as shown in Exhibit 3.1. The table

indicates that a complete response to the question should address six specific issues, indicated by the six boxes in the table.

For question 2 we have boxed the major issues (processes, accomplishments, and experimentation) and underlined the categories to which these apply (cleavage, gastrulation, neurulation, and the importance of induction), then charted the question as shown in Exhibit 3.2. Once the specifics have been filled in, one can proceed to write the essay.

ACTIVITY 3.3.1 *Preparing an Outline or Grid for an Essay Question*

Highlight the key terms in the following essay questions and create grids or frameworks similar to those shown in Exhibit 3.1. It is not necessary to have an understanding of the topics because the questions provide sufficient information to develop an outline or grid. You do not need to fill in the cells with notes unless you have recently studied these topics.

1. Discuss how the rate of photosynthesis varies in C3, C4, and CAM plants with respect to temperature, wavelength, and light intensity.
2. Compare the inner planets with the outer planets with respect to composition, size, and orbital velocity.

Exhibit 3.1 *Grid for Answering an Essay Question*

(1) Discuss the processes of exchange *of* O_2 *and* CO_2 *that occur at the* alveoli *and* muscle *cells of mammals. Include in your answer a description of the* transport *of these gases in the* blood.

	Exchange	
	O_2	CO_2
alveoli		
muscle cells		

	Transport	
blood		

Exhibit 3.2 *Grid and Notes for Answering an Essay Question*

(2) Discuss the ⎡processes⎤ *of* <u>cleavage</u>, <u>gastrulation</u>, *and* <u>neurulation</u> *in the frog embryo; tell what each process* ⎡accomplishes⎤ *. Describe an* ⎡experiment⎤ *that* <u>illustrates the importance of induction in development.</u>

	Cleavage	Gastrulation	Neurulation
process	Rapid mitosis No cell growth Grey crescent	Cell migration Involution Invagination	Folds form Neural folds fuse
accomplishment	Forms blastula Unequal distribution	3 tissue layers Gut	Neural tube Neurula

	Induction experiment
description	Dorsal lip experiment
illustration	Cells influence development of neighbors Induces differentiation Influences gene expression

3. Compare and contrast the nutritional requirements and means of acquiring nutrition of angiosperms (flowering plants) and vertebrates.
4. Explain how energy transfer occurs and how ATP is involved in cellular movement, fermentation, chemiosmosis, and active transport.

ACTIVITY 3.3.2 *Completing an Outline or Grid for an essay question*

Develop an outline or grid for essay questions provided by your teacher. Fill in the cells from your knowledge of the topic as illustrated in Exhibit 3.2.

3.4 Types of Science Writing

There are many types of literary genre, including poetry, novels, history, ballads, plays, and short stories, each with its own rules and nuances. Similarly, there are a variety of scientific genres, including lab report, open essay, directed essay, library research review, and scientific journal report, each with its own distinctive rules and nuances. This section includes activities for writing a variety of scientific genre.

All work that is not your own should be cited. The MLA (Modern Language Association), ACS (American Chemical Society), Chicago (University of Chicago), APA (American Psychological Society), and CBE (Council of Biology Editors) style manuals are commonly used, and you should check with your teacher regarding the preferred format at your school. Table 3.1 illustrates sample citations based on the *APA Style Manual*.

ACTIVITY 3.4.1 *Writing a Science Lab Report*

The laboratory report derives its structure from the scientific method and is similar in structure to research papers found in scientific journals. The lab report is used to document laboratory work done in class. Write your laboratory reports using the following structure:

Problem: Statement of the question or problem to be researched
Background: Description of what is already known

Table 3.1 Citing References Using APA Style

Citations as They Appear in the Bibliography or Reference Section	Citations as They Appear in the Text
Books	
Herr, N., & Cunningham, J. (1999). *Hands-on chemistry activities with real-life applications.* West Nyack, NY: Center for Applied Research in Education.	(Herr & Cunningham, 1999)
Journals	
Herr, N. (1993). The relationship between Advanced Placement and honors science courses. *School Science and Mathematics, 93*(4), 183–187.	(Herr, 1993)
Chapters in a book	
Herr, N. (1992). *Using an electronic database to solve practical problems in nutrition.* In E. Murdock & P. Desberg (Eds.), *Computers in the curriculum: Exercises for integrating technology into instruction* (pp. 133–154). Long Beach, CA: California State University Press.	(Herr, 1992)
Web sites	
Herr, N. (2007). *Science education.* Retrieved January 3, 2007, from California State University, Science Education Web site: http://www.csun.edu/science.	(Herr, 2006)

Source: American Psychological Association. (2005). *Concise Rules of APA Style.* Washington, DC: American Psychological Association.

Hypothesis: Tentative explanation based on background knowledge

Experiment: Discussion of the methods and materials used

Results: Data, expressed in tables, charts, and graphs

Conclusion: Explanation of how the data support or refute the hypothesis

ACTIVITY 3.4.2 *Writing an Open Essay*

Students are often required to write essays on a scientific topic of their choice. In such situations, it is recommended that students adopt the classic essay structure: introduction, body, and conclusion. Write your open essays using the following structure:

Introduction: The introduction is the first paragraph of an essay and presents a clear statement of the intent of the essay and a brief summary of what will follow in the body.

Body: The body presents concrete evidence to support the ideas expressed in the introduction. It is supported by specific examples and references to findings in the literature or laboratory. Each paragraph has a topic statement, summarizing the key points addressed.

Conclusion: The conclusion summarizes and interprets the essay.

ACTIVITY 3.4.3 *Writing a Directed Essay*

Directed essays have specific prompts that dictate the structure of the essay. Students should develop a conceptual outline or grid (see section 3.3) that reflects the issues that must be addressed and write the essay accordingly.

Write your directed essays using the following guidelines:

Response to prompt: Examine the essay prompt and identify each major question and all subquestions (see section 3.3). The essay should answer these in a logical manner, which is generally the sequence in which they were asked. Directed essays require specific material, and it is therefore generally not necessary to provide an introduction and conclusion, but ask your teacher for clarification.

ACTIVITY 3.4.4 *Writing a Library Research Paper*

A library research paper summarizes the findings of other researchers. It does not include new information, although it may be assembled in a novel or concise manner. It is often given as a special assignment or extra-credit project.

Write your library research papers using the following structure:

Introduction: The introduction is one or more paragraphs that include a clear statement of the research topic and any specific questions addressed.

Body: The body elaborates on the issues discussed in the introduction. All references are according to the style you are using.

Summary: The summary reviews major findings and raises questions for future research.

References: Many science journals use the name-year system for citing references (Table 3.1).

ACTIVITY 3.4.5 *Writing a Scientific Journal Paper*

Scientific research published in journals usually has the following format, which you should follow in writing your scientific journal papers:

Title: The title concisely describes the contents of the paper.

Authors and affiliations: The primary investigator's name is first, followed by the names of the other researchers. Each author's name is followed by his or her institution.

Abstract: The abstract summarizes the paper in 300 words or less. It includes a brief statement of the question, experimental design and methods, major findings including key quantitative results or trends, and a brief summary of the researcher's interpretations and conclusions.

Introduction: The introduction establishes the context of the research by discussing primary research (with citations); summarizing current understanding of the issues; stating the purposes of the research in the form of a hypothesis, question, or problem to be investigated; and explaining the rationale for the research.

Methods: The methods section explains how the research was conducted, including details on subjects (plants, animals, rocks), study site (global positioning system coordinates, slope, aspect), and experimental or sampling design (controls, treatments, independent variable, dependent variables, replications, and procedures for collecting data).

Results: The results section presents the data in an orderly and logical sequence, using tables, charts, figures, and graphs as appropriate. Summaries, highlights, and negative results are included.

Discussion: The discussion interprets the hypothesis or problem statement in the light of the data and shows how the study has helped move our understanding forward.

References: All references are cited using one of the accepted formats (see above).

3.5 Science Writing Style

Each type of literary genre has its own style conventions. For example, the repetition of a line may be appropriate in the lyrics of a poem or song but inappropriate when writing a book on English grammar. Science has its own writing style conventions that differ from those in other disciplines, but many students don't understand these conventions because they learned to write in English classes, not in science classes. The following are characteristics of scientific writing.

Scientific Writing Is Logical

- Start each paragraph with a topic sentence. Subsequent sentences in each paragraph should relate to the topic sentence. Do not use unlinked ideas in the same paragraph.

- Do not change the direction of an argument more than once in a paragraph. For example, do not use the word *however* more than once per paragraph.
- Organize your writing into appropriate sections and subsections.
- Explain abbreviations and acronyms in parentheses the first time they are used—for example, NASA (National Aeronautics and Space Administration) or BMI (body mass index).
- Focus your thoughts by writing the summary first. Make certain that the body of text is consistent with the summary.
- Format your document to show its logical structure:
  - Put headings in **BOLD UPPER CASE**.
  - Put subheadings in **Bold Title Case**.
  - Use *italics* for emphasis and **bold** for strong emphasis.

Scientific Writing Is Economical

Scientists write economically. They avoid redundancy and use as few words as necessary to communicate. The following list has examples of phrases that may be expressed more economically by deleting unnecessary or redundant words as shown.

~~a total of~~ *n* samples	four ~~different~~ groups
~~absolutely~~ essential	in ~~close~~ proximity
~~also~~ included	~~in order~~ to
except ~~for~~	~~period of~~ time
for ~~the purpose of~~	summarize ~~briefly~~
found ~~previously~~	the reason is ~~because~~

Scientific Writing Is Precise

Scientists write with precision, choosing words that communicate as accurately as possible. Scientists avoid unwarranted generalizations by using specific terminology. Examine Table 3.2. Although the terms in the left column may be accurate, they are not precise. By contrast, the terms in the right column are precise and therefore more appropriate in most scientific writing.

Table 3.2 General Versus Precise Descriptions

General	More Specific	Precise
tree	pine	*Pinus ponderosa*
patients	cancer patients	lung cancer patients
star	red giant	*Betelgeuse*
slope	steep slope	slope of 48 degrees
sedimentary	sandstone	quartzose sandstone
most	more than half	58.2%
chemical	organic chemical	ethanol
force	nuclear force	strong nuclear force
fast	supersonic	mach 1.5
fluid	water	seawater

Scientific Writing Is Standardized

Scientific writing is standardized. There is a standard way of representing units (*mks*), unit symbols, unit names, and numbers. Standardization makes it easy to compare information from a variety of sources. The standards accepted by most scientists follow.

Standard Units   Le Systéme International des Unités (SI) is an internationally recognized system of measurement adopted in 1960 by the General Conference of Weights and Measures. Scientists are encouraged to express all measurements in SI units so colleagues around the world can interpret them readily. There are seven fundamental units from which all other units can be derived:

Quantity	Unit	Symbol
distance	meter	m
mass	kilogram	kg
time	second	s
temperature	kelvin	K
amount	mole	mol
charge	coulomb	C
luminous intensity	candela	cd

The far-right column in Table 3.3 shows how *mks* units are expressed in terms of these seven units.

Table 3.3 Fundamental (in Bold) and Derived Units Frequently Used in Science

	Symbol	SI Measurement Units	Symbol	Unit Dimensions
Distance	d	meter	m	m
Mass	m	kilogram	kg	kg
Time	t	second	s	s
Charge[a]	Q	coulomb	C	C
Temperature	T	kelvin	K	K
Amount	n	mole	mol	mol
Luminous intensity	I	candela	cd	cd
Acceleration	a	meter per second squared	m/s^2	m/s^2
Area	A	square meter	m^2	m^2
Capacitance	C	farad	F	$C^2{\cdot}s^2/kg{\cdot}m^2$
Concentration	$[C]$	molar	M	mol/dm^3
Density	D	kilogram per cubic meter	kg/m^3	kg/m^3
Electric current	I	ampere	A	C/s
Electric field intensity	E	newton per coulomb	N/C	$kg{\cdot}m/C{\cdot}s^2$
Electric resistance	R	ohm	Ω	$kg{\cdot}m^2/C^2{\cdot}s$
Emf	ξ	volt	V	$kg{\cdot}m^2/C{\cdot}s^2$
Energy	E	joule	J	$kg{\cdot}m^2/s^2$
Force	F	newton	N	$kg{\cdot}m/s^2$
Frequency	f	hertz	Hz	s^{-1}
Heat	Q	joule	J	$kg{\cdot}m^2/s^2$
Illumination	E	lux (lumen per square meter)	lx	cd/m^2
Inductance	L	henry	H	$kg{\cdot}m^2/C^2$
Magnetic flux	ϕ	weber	Wb	$kg{\cdot}m^2/C{\cdot}s$
Potential difference	V	volt	V	$kg{\cdot}m^2/C{\cdot}s^2$
Power	P	watt	W	$kg{\cdot}m^2/s^3$
Pressure	p	pascal (newton per square meter)	Pa	$kg/m{\cdot}s^2$
Velocity	v	meter per second	m/s	m/s
Volume	V	cubic meter	m^3	m^3
Work	W	joule	J	$kg{\cdot}m^2/s^2$

Note: [a] The official SI quantity is electrical current, and the base unit is the ampere. Electrical current is the amount of electrical charge (measured in coulombs) per unit of time.

Standardized Number Formatting

- For numbers less than 1, a zero precedes the decimal point: 0.0453, *not* .0453.
- A tilde (~) is used to indicate "approximately equal": ~57 kg.
- A space is placed between numbers and units: 82 m, *not* 82m.
- The number of significant figures includes all of the certain digits plus the first uncertain digit.
- Numbers beginning sentences should be spelled out. Rewrite sentences so that large numbers are not at the beginning of sentences.

Standardized Unit Names
When written in full, units begin with a lowercase letter:

Correct: kelvin, farad, newton, joule, hertz, degree

Incorrect: Kelvin, Farad, Newton, Joule, Hertz, Degree

Standardized Unit Symbols The first letter in a unit symbol is uppercase when the unit name is derived from a person's name. The following list shows units that are named after scientists. Note that the unit name is not capitalized, but the unit symbol is.

ampere	A	André Ampère discovered basic principles of electrodynamics.
coulomb	C	Charles Coulomb discovered the law of force between charged bodies.
farad	F	Michael Faraday pioneered research in electricity and magnetism.
henry	H	Joseph Henry discovered electromagnetic induction and self-induction.
hertz	Hz	Heinrich Hertz discovered radio waves.
joule	J	James Joule pioneered research in thermodynamics.
kelvin	K	William Thomson (Lord Kelvin) developed the absolute temperature scale.
newton	N	Isaac Newton pioneered work in forces, calculus, optics, and gravitation.
ohm	Ω	Georg Ohm discovered the relationship between current, voltage, and resistance.
pascal	Pa	Blaise Pascal discovered basic principles of hydrostatics.
tesla	T	Nikola Tesla developed the AC motor and high-voltage transformers.
volt	V	Allesandro Volta invented the first battery.
watt	W	James Watt developed the steam engine as a practical power source.
weber	Wb	Wilhelm Weber performed early research in electricity and magnetism.

The following units are not named after people, and therefore their symbols are not capitalized: meter, m; kilogram, kg; second, s; mole, mol; candle, cd; lux, lx; degree, °.

Unit Prefixes The symbols for all prefixes representing factors less than 1 million are never capitalized (y, z, a, f, p, n, k, m, c, d, da, h, k). The symbols representing factors equal to or greater than 1 million are always capitalized (M, G, T, P, X, Z, Y).

Prefix	Symbol	Multiplier
yotta-	Y	10^{24}
zetta-	Z	10^{21}
exa-	X	10^{18}
peta-	P	10^{15}
tera-	T	10^{12}
giga-	G	10^{9}
mega-	M	10^{6}
kilo-	k	10^{3}
hecto-	h	10^{2}
deca-	da	10^{1}
deci-	d	10^{-1}
centi-	c	10^{-2}
milli-	m	10^{-3}
micro-	μ	10^{-6}
nano-	n	10^{-9}
pico-	p	10^{-12}
femto-	f	10^{-15}
atto-	a	10^{-18}
zepto-	z	10^{-21}
yocto-	y	10^{-24}

Compound Units A centered dot is used to indicate that a unit is the product of two or more units (N·m, *not* Nm). The following are examples of common compound units: volt = $kg \cdot m^2 / A \cdot s^3$, newton = $kg \cdot m / s^2$, watt = $kg \cdot m^2 / s^3$, and joule = $kg \cdot m^2 / s^2$.

Quantity Symbols Versus Unit Symbols By convention, quantity symbols are italicized, and unit symbols are not. Quantity symbols represent a physical quantity such as time, mass, and length; unit symbols represent specific measures of those quantities, such as seconds, kilograms, and meters.

Quantity Symbols	Unit Symbols
time, t	seconds, s
mass, m	kilograms, kg
length, l	meter, m
heat, Q	joule, J

ACTIVITY 3.5.1 *Principles of Style*

Review the principles of style for scientific writing, and identify the best expression from each pair:

1	it is suggested that a relationship may exist	a relationship may exist
2	because	based on the fact that
3	the reason is because	because
4	very strong storm	category 4 hurricane
5	low pressure	950 mb
6	83% of all those tested	many
7	the same	one and the same
8	0.0567	.0567
9	temperature of 273 K	temperature of 273 k
10	length (l) and mass (m) . . .	length (*l*) and mass (*m*) . . .
11	length of 5 m and mass of 10 kg	length of 5 *m* and mass of 10 *kg*
12	how many newtons of force?	how many Newtons of force?
13	current of 25 a (amperes)	current of 25 A (amperes)
14	pressure of 1000 Pa (pascals)	pressure of 1000 pa (Pascals)
15	$15 \ kg \cdot m/s^2$	$15 \ Kgm/s^2$
16	1 calorie of energy	4.1868 joules of energy
17	1 pascal of pressure	10 bayre of pressure
18	1 kilometer	0.621 miles
19	32 Fahrenheit	273 Kelvin
20	44.7 meters/second	100 miles per hour

Answers to Chapter Activities

3.1.1 Students will develop Cornell notes such as shown in Figure 3.1.

3.1.2 Students will develop Cornell notes such as shown in Figure 3.1.

3.2.1 Students will maintain a science journal as specified. It is suggested that teachers periodically collect these notebooks and assess them on the basis of the quality and quantity of thoughts expressed, not on the quality of the syntax, spelling, and form.

3.3.1 Students will develop grids such as illustrated in Exhibit 3.1.

3.3.2 Students will develop grids and add notes as illustrated in Exhibit 3.2.

3.4.1–3.4.5 Students will write lab reports, open essays, directed essays, library research papers, and scientific journal papers according to the principles and structures discussed in section 3.4.

3.5.1 (1) a relationship may exist, (2) because, (3) because, (4) category 4 hurricane, (5) 950 mb, (6) 83% of all those tested, (7) the same, (8) 0.0567, (9) temperature of 273 K, (10) length (*l*) and mass (*m*) . . . , (11) length of 5 m and mass of 10 kg, (12) how many newtons of force? (13) current of 25 A (amperes), (14) pressure of 1000 Pa (pascals), (15) $15 \ kg \cdot m/s^2$, (16) 4.1868 joules of energy, (17) 1 pascal of pressure, (18) 1 kilometer, (19) 273 Kelvin, (20) 44.7 meters/second.

Chapter Four

Science, Technology, and Society

For the Teacher 58

4.1 Science and Society 59

4.2 Science and Other Subjects 61

4.3 Careers in Science 67

4.4 Science and Technological Innovation 70

Answers to Chapter Activities 74

For the Teacher

Many students become interested in science when they see its significance to society and relevance to their lives. Kinematics, bonding, DNA, and seismology are esoteric topics until one understands how they are used in the design of safer automobiles, better pharmaceuticals, frost-resistant varieties of crops, and new oil wells. The activities in this chapter will help students understand the significance of scientific research to the development of technology and the relevance of scientific and technological developments to their everyday lives. Understanding the relationship of science, technology, and society is foundational to scientific literacy.

Significance of Science

Activity 4.1.1 focuses on the significance of chemistry to society by discussing chemical products that have altered agriculture, food, health, medicine, transportation, electronics, technology,

the household, and the environment. This activity can be adapted to discuss the significance of physics, biology, and the earth and space sciences. For example, the class can discuss the significance of biological discoveries to agriculture (plant breeding, bioengineered crops, hormone treatments, cloning), food (nutritional requirements, metabolic disorders, pasteurization, diets for those with diabetes), and other areas. Teachers should consider dividing the class into study groups and assigning each a specific connection to investigate. The groups can then share their information with other students through class presentations or electronically through a news group, Web site, or related medium.

Relevance of Science

Activity 4.1.2 focuses on the relevance of physics to other fields of study by giving specific examples of how physics principles provide a richer understanding of music, botany, health, geology, biology, chemistry, geology, astronomy, literature, sports, shop, home economics, history, government, math, drama, business, foreign languages, and computers. This activity can be adapted to show the relevance of other sciences as well. For example, it can be shown that an understanding of earth science leads to a better understanding of health (asbestosis, earthquake preparedness, pollen count), business (mineral exploration, mining, seismic retrofitting), and other fields.

Science Careers and Guest Speakers

The section on science-related careers will help students see the importance of science to the economy. Students are encouraged to write research reports on careers of their choice but should realize that some of the job titles listed are very specific, and it may be necessary to generalize their research to gain sufficient information. We encourage teachers to invite guest speakers to their classes to discuss science-related careers. Teachers can gather information about potential parent guest speakers through voluntary student surveys, letters to parents, Web site notices, or personal conversations with parents at open house and back-to-school night. In addition, many science- and technology-related businesses provide guest speakers or offer company tours.

When inviting guest speakers to your class, provide them clear expectations regarding the topics you wish them to discuss and the time frame they will have with your students. Encourage them to bring handouts and Internet addresses for further information.

The Influence of Science on Technology and Medicine

Activity 4.4.2 focuses on the influence of science on technology and medicine. I have provided a list of some of the most significant inventions and inventors of the past four hundred years. Students research the significance of these inventions to society and investigate the scientific principles that made them possible. After researching inventions of the past, students focus on current discoveries

and inventions to learn that science is a growing and developing field that will ultimately yield many new innovations and inventions for them and generations to follow.

4.1 Science and Society

ACTIVITY 4.1.1 *The Significance of Chemistry to Society*

Many people have an inaccurate understanding of chemistry and chemists. Chemists rarely appear in the movies or other media, and when shown, they often are portrayed as unkempt, isolated, asocial individuals or as "mad scientists" bent on destruction. Similarly, many people view all chemicals as hazardous, not realizing that their very bodies, the clothing they wear, and the houses they live in are made of chemicals.

Chemistry is the study of matter, and chemists study the properties and uses of matter. Chemists often develop new substances that have practical significance to society, yet they rarely get media attention for their discoveries or developments. Many of these products have life-saving potential, such as sodium azide, which powers automobile air bags; epinephrine, which prevents anaphylactic shock in those allergic to bee stings; and tempered glass, which eliminates the threat of glass cuts in automobile accidents. Many chemical products are less glamorous yet support our way of life. For example, chemists have been involved in the development and study of virtually everything in your classroom. The paint on the wall, the linoleum or concrete on the floor, the gas in the fluorescent lights, the ink in your pens, and the dyes in your clothing are but a few of the many things in your room that were developed by chemists. Chemistry is a basic science and is foundational to an understanding of other sciences, such as biology (biochemistry, molecular genetics), physiology (nutrition, metabolism) geology (geochemistry), and physics (nuclear physics).

In the activities that follow you will investigate the significance of chemistry to the world around you by considering the products that are made possible because of the work of chemists.

• *Chemistry and agriculture.* Agriculture is the most basic profession; without it we would starve, yet the percentage of farmers in the labor force has declined steadily for many years. In 1900, about 41 percent of the United States labor force worked on farms, but by 2000, less than 2 percent did (Figure 4.1). This monumental shift in the labor force resulted from increasing agricultural efficiency due largely to advances in agricultural chemistry. Research and describe one or more types of agricultural chemicals that influence the way we raise crops and animals (see Figure 4.2;

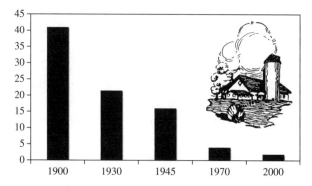

Figure 4.1 U.S. Agricultural Workforce, in Percentage

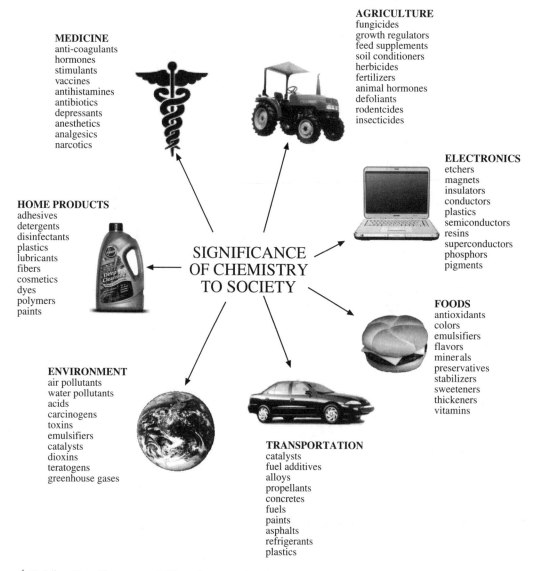

MEDICINE
anti-coagulants
hormones
stimulants
vaccines
antihistamines
antibiotics
depressants
anesthetics
analgesics
narcotics

AGRICULTURE
fungicides
growth regulators
feed supplements
soil conditioners
herbicides
fertilizers
animal hormones
defoliants
rodentcides
insecticides

ELECTRONICS
etchers
magnets
insulators
conductors
plastics
semiconductors
resins
superconductors
phosphors
pigments

HOME PRODUCTS
adhesives
detergents
disinfectants
plastics
lubricants
fibers
cosmetics
dyes
polymers
paints

SIGNIFICANCE OF CHEMISTRY TO SOCIETY

FOODS
antioxidants
colors
emulsifiers
flavors
minerals
preservatives
stabilizers
sweeteners
thickeners
vitamins

ENVIRONMENT
air pollutants
water pollutants
acids
carcinogens
toxins
emulsifiers
catalysts
dioxins
teratogens
greenhouse gases

TRANSPORTATION
catalysts
fuel additives
alloys
propellants
concretes
fuels
paints
asphalts
refrigerants
plastics

Figure 4.2 The Significance of Chemistry to Society

fertilizers, soil conditioners, plant growth regulators, animal hormones, feed supplements, insecticides, rodentcides, herbicides, fungicides). Describe the role these chemicals play in modern agriculture, and give three or more specific examples.

• *Chemistry and foods.* Research one or more types of food chemicals (see Figure 4.2, additives, preservatives, artificial flavors, artificial colors, stabilizers, emulsifiers, vitamins, thickeners, minerals, antioxidants). Describe the role these chemicals play, and provide three or more specific examples.

• *Chemistry and medicine.* Figure 4.3 shows that life expectancy in the United States has increased dramatically since 1900. Much of this increase is due to advances in chemistry that have yielded products that directly or indirectly influence health. Research and describe three or more chemical products that have benefited public health and medicine (see Figure 4.2; antibiotics, vaccines, medical plastics, artificial blood plasma, artificial hormones, depressants, stimulants, narcotics, analgesics, antihistamines, anticoagulants, and others).

• *Chemistry and transportation.* How has chemistry influenced transportation (see Figure 4.2)? Research and describe three or more specific chemicals or processes that chemists have developed that improve our means of transportation. For example, identify specific fuels, fuel additives, or vehicular materials that allow us to move faster or more efficiently on land and water or in the air and space.

• *Chemistry and household products.* It is impossible to escape chemistry, even at home!

Look around your house, and identify and research three or more chemicals that have application in household products. For general classifications of household chemicals, refer to Figure 4.2.

• *Chemistry and electronics.* Computers, electronics, and related technologies are made possible because of a variety of chemicals with very specific properties. Identify and research three or more chemicals that are essential to computers or other high-tech applications (see Figure 4.2), and explain how the specific properties of these chemicals have facilitated the technology revolution.

• *Chemistry and the environment.* Many industrial and household chemicals have adverse effects on the environment, and chemists are employed to find ways of reducing these problems (see Figure 4.2). Research and describe three or more environmental problems that have a chemical basis or chemical solutions or both chemical bases and solutions. For example, you may research the chemistry of air and water pollution, the greenhouse effect, environmental toxins, and the ways chemists address these and other chemically related environmental problems.

ACTIVITY 4.1.2 *The Significance of Physics to Society*

Adapt Activity 4.1.1 for physics. Show the significance of physics to each of these seven areas (agriculture, foods, medicine, transportation, household products, electronics, and environment) or other areas (energy, defense, engineering, manufacturing, and communications) by giving specific examples of products or processes that have been made available by an understanding of physics.

4.2 Science and Other Subjects

Relevance of Physics to Other Fields of Study

Physics is the most basic science because it is concerned with the nature and properties of matter and energy. Physics studies mechanics, heat, light, radiation, sound, electricity, magnetism,

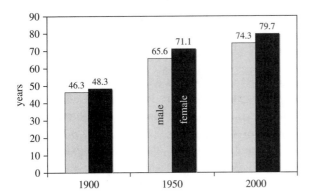

Figure 4.3 U.S. Life Expectancy at Birth, 1900, 1950, and 2000

and the nature of matter, and it is essential for an understanding of other sciences, such as chemistry, biology, physiology, geology, meteorology, astronomy, health, and environmental science. Physics also helps us understand seemingly unrelated fields, such as music, art, literature, political science, history, sports, and home economics, as the following examples illustrate.

Relevance of Physics to Music *Sound waves: Music* is an artistic expression in the form of organized vibrations. Vibrating strings in *string instruments* and columns of air in *wind instruments* generate sound by vibrating at fundamental frequencies or multiples of these frequencies known as *harmonics.* An *octave* is a harmonic that is double or half the frequency of a given note. Sound travels as longitudinal, compression waves, the frequency of which determines the *pitch,* and the amplitude of which determines the *volume.*

Law of strings: The first law of strings states that the frequency at which a string vibrates is inversely proportional to its length: $f/f' = l'/l$; where f = original frequency, f' = new frequency, l = original length, and l' = new length. Thus, the musician can play a *higher note* on a *guitar, banjo, violin,* or other stringed instrument by shortening the length of the string. To facilitate this, these instruments are equipped with narrow lateral ridges underneath the strings known as *frets.* The musician presses the wire against these frets to shorten the length of the string that is plucked. A second law of strings states *that the frequency of a string is directly proportional to the square root of its tension:* $f/f' = \sqrt{T}/\sqrt{T'}$, where T represents tension. Thus, if the tension on a string is quadrupled, the frequency of the string is doubled ($f' = f\sqrt{T'})/\sqrt{T}$). All string instruments are *tuned* by adjusting the tension of the *strings.*

Relevance of Physics to Art *Frequency, wavelength, color:* Red, green, and blue are the fundamental colors of light, and by mixing them in different ratios, you can obtain any desired color. *Stage lights, televisions,* and *monitors* mix red, green, and blue to get the desired colors by addition of

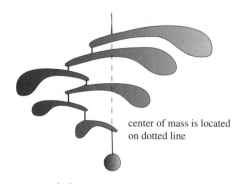

center of mass is located on dotted line

Figure 4.4 Center of Mass in a Mobile

lights. This is known as additive mixing. The mixing of red, green, and blue light produces white light. By contrast, cyan, yellow, and magenta are the three fundamental pigments that can be combined in different ratios to produce a wide variety of colors of *paint, dye,* or *ink. Pigments* reflect light, and therefore the more pigments that are present, the less light is reflected. When pigments are mixed, colors are subtracted, The mixing of cyan, yellow, and magenta pigments produces a black pigment that reflects no light. Artists who understand the properties of light and pigments can achieve the desired effects for their artwork.

Center of mass: The center of mass is a point representing the mean position of the matter in a body or system. Many works of art rely on the principle that an object will return to stable equilibrium as long as its center of mass passes within the base of support or below the pivot point. Ancient sculptors used this principle to ensure stability of *sculptures,* and more recent art, such as Alexander Calder's *kinetic sculptures* or *mobiles* (Figure 4.4), are dramatic illustrations of this principle.

Relevance of Physics to Literature *Physics terms:* Physics terms are frequently used in literature to explain events in everyday life. For example, authors may use terms such as *quantum leap, free fall, light-years, black holes, leverage, force, power, inertia, energy, work, resonance,* and phrases such as "on the same wavelength," "magnetic attraction," and "gaining momentum" to explain by analogy to physics concepts.

Physics authors: Great physics literature has had a profound influence on science and literature. Nicholas Copernicus (*On the Revolutions of the Heavenly Spheres,* 1543), Johannes Kepler (*A New Astronomy,* 1609), and Isaac Newton (*Principia—Mathematical Principles of Natural Philosophy,* 1687) are a few of the physics authors who popularized scientific writing as an acceptable literary form. More recently, books on exotic theories in physics, such as Stephen Hawking's best-selling *A Brief History of Time* (2002), have provided themes for movies, fictional literature, and pop culture.

Relevance of Physics to Political Science

Bosons/atomic structure: The Higgs boson is a hypothetical massive scalar *elementary particle.* To test for the existence of this particle and to further studies in the *basic nature of matter,* Congress approved the development of the *superconducting super collider* (SSC), a multibillion-dollar facility. Various congressmen argued to have it in their district because of the prestige and jobs it would create, and eventually construction was started on an 87 km circumference underground collider in Texas. Debate again erupted in Congress, and in 1993 the project was canceled when it was decided the government did not have the funds to build the collider and the International Space Station simultaneously, leaving a $2 billion hole in Texas.

Nuclear X-ray laser: A nuclear *X-ray laser* was designed at Lawrence Livermore laboratories in California, and President Ronald Reagan was told of its potential for destroying enemy missiles. In his famous Star Wars speech, Reagan said, "I call upon the scientific community who gave us nuclear weapons to turn their great talents to the cause of mankind and world peace: to give us the means of rendering these nuclear weapons impotent and obsolete." Reagan initiated the Strategic Defense Initiative (SDI), a multibillion-dollar program, to develop this technology. There was much criticism of the program, and it failed to achieve its goals before being abandoned by the Clinton administration. The George W. Bush administration revived the program and the national missile defense, and in 2005 a test missile was intercepted using the physics principles discovered and the technology developed in the program.

Relevance of Physics to History

Special relativity and nuclear fission: In 1905 Albert Einstein published his theory *of special relativity,* suggesting that a small amount of mass could be converted into a huge amount of energy ($E = mc^2$). Further discoveries by physicists Ernst Rutherford, James Chadwick, Enrico Fermi, and Leo Szilárd produced additional information about the nature of matter and the potential to develop a nuclear bomb. Albert Einstein warned President Roosevelt that the Nazis might develop a nuclear weapon, and the president decided to initiate the *Manhattan Project,* which resulted in the design, production, and detonation of three *atomic bombs* in 1945. The bombs hastened the end of World War II and opened the nuclear arms race of the cold war between the Soviet Union and the United States.

Levers and torque: The principle of leverage has been applied for thousands of years in the *building of civilizations.* The ancient Egyptians used levers to upright obelisks weighing in excess of 100 tons. In the third century B.C., Archimedes wrote, "Give me the place to stand, and I shall move the earth," illustrating his understanding that levers can be used to multiply force (when the effort is farther from the fulcrum than the load). Alternatively, levers magnify speed if the effort is inside the fulcrum. First-class levers (the effort and load are on opposite sides of the fulcrum) are found in *oars* (used to move ancient galleys and modern rowboats), *trebuchets* (medieval siege engines), and many tools such as *wrenches* and *pliers.* Second-class levers (the effort is beyond the load on same side of fulcrum) are found in *wheelbarrows* and *nutcrackers,* and third-class levers (the effort is before the load on the same side of the fulcrum) are found in *hoes, scythes, brooms,* and *catapults* to amplify speed. Imagine how different the world would be if these tools had not been developed.

Relevance of Physics to Sports

Inertia: Inertia is a property of matter by which it continues in its existing state of rest or uniform motion in a straight line unless that state is changed by an external force. Newton's first law describes inertia: an object at rest tends to stay at rest, and an object in motion tends to stay in motion with the same speed and in the same direction, unless acted on by an outside force. This principle is important in contact sports such as football and boxing. *Football coaches* recruit heavier players to serve as *linemen*, knowing that their greater mass will mean greater inertia and make it more difficult for the opposing team to penetrate the line. *Boxers* compete only against others in their *weight class* (bantamweight, featherweight, lightweight, middleweight, and heavy weight) because unequal weights would create uneven matches due to differences in inertia. Rotational inertia is useful in sports such as bicycling and ice skating. *Bicyclists* maintain their upright position due to the rotational inertia of the wheels, and *ice skaters* adjust the rate of their spin by changing the moment of inertia as they move their arms or legs.

Impulse and momentum: Momentum (p) is the product of mass and velocity ($p = mv$). Impulse (I) is the product of force and time ($I = F\delta t$, for constant force) and changes momentum $F\delta t = mv$. *Baseball* players want to increase the time of contact with the *bat* (δt) to increase the velocity (v) imparted to the ball. When *catching* a ball, baseball players recoil to increase the time (δt) of the impulse, and thereby decrease the force (F) necessary to stop the ball. *Football running backs* who have large mass (m) and are fast (v) will have greater momentum and be more difficult to stop.

Relevance of Physics to Home Economics

Convection, conduction, radiation: Thermodynamics studies the movement of energy and the effect of energy on movement. It helps us understand how conventional ovens, convection ovens, and microwave ovens work. *Conventional ovens* transfer heat to food by radiation (radiant energy from the flame or heating element reaches the food), convection (warm air in the oven moves past the food, transferring energy to it), or conduction (metal racks or pans conduct heat to the food).

Convection ovens are more effective because they have fans that move air past the food. *Microwave ovens* send microwave radiation (2450 MHz) through food. Water, sugar, and fat molecules absorb energy through dielectric heating as they vibrate in the alternating electric field induced by the oven.

Thermal conductivity: Thermal conductivity is an intensive property of matter that describes the tendency to conduct heat. Copper has a thermal conductivity of 386 $W \cdot m^{-1} \cdot K^{-1}$ while iron has a conductivity of only 80 $W \cdot m^{-1} \cdot K^{-1}$. To increase the transfer of heat to food, manufacturers coat the bottoms of *pots* and *pans* with copper. To increase the speed of cooking turkeys or other large items, cooks use aluminum *cooking pins* that conduct heat into the food.

ACTIVITY 4.2.1 *The Relationship of Physics to Other Subjects*

Figure 4.5 shows a variety of classes commonly taught in secondary schools. Unfortunately, we often see these classes as distinct entities with no overlap or relationship to one another. Although the curricular emphasis of each class may be unique, the concepts are not. Information from one class is often helpful for another. For example, the grammatical rules students learn in English class help

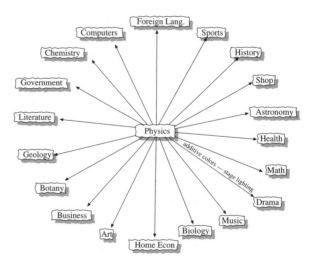

Figure 4.5 Diagram for Giving Examples of How Physics Principles Are Used in Other Classes

them understand the rules in other languages, and an understanding of American government helps in understanding the events of American history. Most students, however, see little connection between physics and other classes because these connections were not made explicit in readings or lectures.

The following list sets out a physics principle, and then an example of a phenomenon it explains. Read each description, and identify a class other than physics for which this information is useful. Write the summary relationship on the appropriate connecting lines in Figure 4.5 (the first is given as an example). Your completed diagram will illustrate how physics principles are used in all of these classes.

1.   *Additive colors → stage lighting.* A color gel, or filter, is a translucent or transparent colored material used in theaters to produce colored lighting. By illuminating red, green, and blue (the fundamental colors of light) gels in different proportions, lighting experts use the principle of color addition to achieve the desired color and mood.

2.   *Wave interference → tuning.* Beats are periodic fluctuations in the intensity of a sound when two sound waves of slightly different frequencies interfere. A musician can tune a stringed instrument by using a tuning fork of known frequency and changing the tension on a string of the same note until no beats are heard.

3.   *Bernoulli's principle → curve ball.* Pitchers put a spin on baseballs to cause them to curve. The air carried along by the stitching on the side of a spinning baseball travels faster relative to the surrounding air than does the air on the other side where the surface motion is opposite the movement of the ball. According to Bernoulli's principle, faster-moving fluids experience lower pressure, causing the baseball to veer to the side where the surface motion is in the same direction as the ball's forward movement.

4.   *Buoyancy → swim bladder.* Gas-filled sacs located on the dorsal side of fish are known as gas or swim bladders and are used to control buoyancy. When gases are introduced into the bladder, fish become slightly larger, displace more water, and become more buoyant according to

Archimedes' principle. When gases are absorbed from the bladder into the bloodstream, fish displace less water, becomes less buoyant, and sink.

5.   *Circuits → microprocessors.* Microprocessors are digital electronic components with miniaturized transistors on a single semiconductor integrated circuit and often serve as the central processing unit for computers and related devices. Microprocessors rely on numerous miniature circuits to perform logic functions.

6.   *Coulomb's law → ionic bonding.* Coulomb's law states that the magnitude of the electrostatic force between two point charges is directly proportional to the magnitudes of each charge and inversely proportional to the square of the distance between them. Electrostatic bonds form between two ions when the distances between them are small.

7.   *Physics terms → cognates. Cognates* are words in different languages that have the same linguistic roots. Most English physics terms have cognates in other languages. For example, the English word *thermodynamics* has the following cognates: *termodinámica* (Spanish), *thermodinamique* (French), *Thermodynamik* (German), and *termodinamica* (Italian).

8.   *Evaporative cooling → refrigeration.* Energy is required to evaporate liquids. Heat is removed from the body to evaporate sweat, causing body temperature to drop. Refrigerators and freezers use this same principle. Compressors on the outside of the refrigerator liquefy ammonia or other refrigerant, releasing heat to the room. The refrigerant is pumped to tubes inside the unit, where it evaporates, removing heat from the surrounding air, and causing the temperature to drop.

9.   *Sound intensity → inverse square law.* The surface area of a sphere is $4\pi r^2$, where r represents the radius. Assuming sound expands spherically from a point source, such as an omnidirectional speaker, its intensity (power per unit area) falls off as the inverse square of the radius from the source ($I = P/4\pi r^2$) as the same amount of power is distributed over an ever-expanding spherical surface.

10.   *Heat engine → industrial revolution.* A heat engine converts heat energy to mechanical work by using the temperature gradient between

a warmer "source" and a cooler "sink," according to the laws of thermodynamics. The development of the first practical steam engine by James Watt spurred the industrial revolution.

11. *Photons → photosynthesis.* Photons are quanta of light that can be perceived as waves or particles, depending on how they are measured. Photons are captured by antenna complexes in chlorophyll within the chloroplasts of plant cells, and their energy is ultimately used to produce sugars and oxygen. Virtually all life is dependent on the products of photosynthesis.

12. *Physics literature → realism.* Romanticism, a popular literary movement in late eighteenth-century Europe, emphasized strong emotion and imagination. Publication of an increasing number of scientific works in the middle of the nineteenth century ushered in a new literary movement known as realism, which deemphasized emotion and imagination and focused on reality as defined by the methods of science.

13. *Ram pressure → meteors.* Ram pressure is the pressure exerted on supersonic bodies traveling through a fluid such as air. Meteors may travel in excess of 15 km per second, causing violent compression of air in front of them. Compressional heating, combined with frictional forces on the meteor, causes the meteor to become extremely hot and glow, making it appear as a "shooting star."

14. *Physics research → appropriations.* The large electron positron collider in Switzerland is a circular tube 3.8 m (12 ft 6 in.) in diameter and 27 km (17 mi) in circumference and has been used to study the smallest particles of matter by accelerating electrons and positrons that collided with each other. The establishment of such an expensive research facility was accomplished only because of political and economic support from 20 European countries. Such political and economic cooperation was also necessary to establish the International Space Station (ISS), a joint project of NASA (United States), the Russian Federal Space Agency, the European Space Agency, the Japan Aerospace Exploration agency, the Canadian Space Agency, and the Brazilian Space Agency.

15. *Subtractive pigments → paint mixing.* The three primary colors of light our eyes see are red, green, and blue. Pigments absorb some wavelengths of light and reflect others. Artists use cyan, magenta, and yellow (the same three colors in a color printer) dyes to create the myriad of colors we see in a painting. Cyan dyes absorb red light and reflect blue and green, which our brains perceive as cyan. Magenta dyes absorb green light and reflect red and blue, which our brains perceive as magenta. Yellow dyes absorb blue light and reflect red and green light, which our brains perceive as yellow. Thus, if you mix cyan and magenta dyes, red and green light will be absorbed so that the surface reflects only blue. Similarly, if cyan and yellow are mixed, red and blue are absorbed so that only green is reflected. Finally, if yellow and magenta are mixed, blue and green are absorbed so that only red is reflected. If cyan, magenta, and yellow are mixed, then red, green and blue are absorbed, and the surface appears black. Mixing of pigments results in the subtraction (absorption) of more wavelengths of light and is used to create a myriad of colors. Artists have used this principle for centuries to create the variety of colors exhibited in such works as Leonardo da Vinci's *Mona Lisa*, Vincent van Gogh's *Starry Night*, and Paul Cézanne's *Still Life*.

16. *Technological applications → venture capital.* As physicists study the nature of matter and energy, they often discover principles that have potential applications in technology. It was noted that carbon dust adheres electrostatically to paper that has been illuminated. When an image is projected on the page, carbon toner particles are attracted to the electrostatic latent image, creating a visible image. Although this technique was developed by Chester Carlton in 1938, it wasn't until a great deal of venture capital was poured into research and development that the photocopier became a consumer product. In 1959 the Xerox Company introduced the first one-piece plain paper photocopier, and in the decades that followed, many patient investors became millionaires off the money had they invested as the company expanded and stock prices soared. Venture capital is sometimes necessary to make useful products from the discoveries physicists make.

17. *Torque → wrenches.* Torque causes rotation and is defined as $F \times r$, where F is the force and

r is the radius (torque arm) between the pivot and applied force. Torque is directly proportional to the length of the torque arm. Thus, a mechanic can develop twice the torque on a nut simply by using a wrench that is twice as long.

18. *Radiation → cancer.* Electromagnetic radiation can have a physiological effect only if it is absorbed. Radio waves stream through the body continuously but have no physiological effect because they are not absorbed. Infrared and visible light are absorbed by the skin and warm the body but do not have sufficient energy to cause tissue damage. Ultraviolet light, however, is strongly absorbed by the skin and has sufficient energy to ionize molecules and cause genetic errors. It is responsible for various forms of skin cancer. Higher-energy radiation, such as X-rays and gamma rays, although absorbed less by tissues, can cause mutations and cancer or can be focused to kill malignant tissues in the process of radiation therapy.

19. *Wave reflection → oil exploration.* New oil deposits are found using geophysical techniques such as the reflection of shock waves. Explosives are detonated in the ground or water, and scientists watch for reflections using seismometers or hydrophones. Oil deposits reflect shock waves differently than they do surrounding rock, allowing scientists to predict potential oil reserves.

ACTIVITY 4.2.2 *Relationship of Chemistry to Other Subjects*

Create a diagram like Figure 4.5, but put chemistry in the center box. Then write connections between chemistry and other subjects on the connecting lines. You may select principles of chemistry that help you understand other subjects, or principles from other subjects related to chemistry. Label each line with a connecting idea as illustrated in Figure 4.5. For example, to connect chemistry and computers, you could discuss the chemical processes for growing the semiconductor crystals that are used in the integrated circuits of computers. On the connecting line between chemistry and computers, write "semiconductor crystals (chemistry)—integrated circuits (computers)."

ACTIVITY 4.2.3 *The Relationship of Biology to Other Subjects*

Create a diagram like Figure 4.5, but put biology in the center box. Write connections between biology and the other subjects on the connecting lines. You may select principles of biology that help you understand other subjects, or principles from other subjects related to biology. Label each line with a connecting idea as illustrated in Figure 4.5. For example, to connect biology and geology, you could discuss the processes in which the plant materials in swamp ecosystems are gradually compacted, chemically altered, and metamorphosed by heat and pressure to form coal. On the connecting between biology and geology write "swamp ecosystems (biology)—coal (geology)."

ACTIVITY 4.2 *The Relationship of Earth and Space Science to Other Subjects*

Create a diagram like Figure 4.5, but put earth and space science in the center box. Label each line with a connecting idea as illustrated in Figure 4.5. For example, to connect astronomy and government, you could discuss the role NASA (National Aeronautics and Space Administration) plays in the study of the planets. On the connecting line between earth and space science and government write "planetary science (earth and space science)—NASA space exploration (government)."

4.3 Careers in Science

Most high school graduates or college freshmen have only a vague idea of what they want to pursue as a career. They may register in college as a biology, chemistry, physics, geology, or astronomy major, but have no idea what they will do when they earn their degree. You are therefore strongly encouraged to take a career and interest survey before graduating from high school. Such surveys and related information are available from the school counselor or online through free or commercial services (for example, *sciencesourcebook.com*, or search using "career interest survey"). After responding to a series of questions regarding your interests and aptitudes, the surveys identify professions for which you might be well suited. Although such tests are helpful in providing ideas, you should also talk to professionals in the field to gain more insights. Ask your school counselor for more information regarding interest surveys, colleges, and career contacts.

ACTIVITY 4.3.1 *Science Careers*

Write a report on a science-related career of your choice, including the components listed below. Much information can be obtained from the U.S. Bureau of Labor Statistics' online *Occupational Outlook Handbook*[1] or official sites of organizations representing specific professions (*sciencesourcebook.com*, www.bls.gov/oco; or search "Occupational Outlook Handbook"). You can find colleges that excel in preparing students for specific careers by visiting the College Board Web site (collegeboard.com).

ACTIVITY 4.3.2 *Careers in Biology*

Select one or more of the biology-related careers listed in Table 4.1, and write a paper that includes the information specified in Exhibit 4.1.

If possible, interview a professional in this field, and incorporate his or her responses in your report.

ACTIVITY 4.3.3 *Careers in Chemistry*

Select one or more of the chemistry-related careers listed in Table 4.2, and write a paper that includes the information listed in Exhibit 4.1. If possible, interview an individual who works in your chosen field and include this person's ideas in your report.

ACTIVITY 4.3.4 *Careers in Physics*

Select one or more of the physics-related careers listed in Table 4.3, and write a paper that includes the information listed in Exhibit 4.1. If possible, interview an individual who works in your chosen field and use this person's information in your report.

ACTIVITY 4.3.5 *Careers in Earth and Space Science*

Select one or more of the earth science-related careers listed in Table 4.4, and write a paper that includes the information listed in Exhibit 4.1.

Exhibit 4.1 *Components of a Career Report*

Job description

- What is the job title?
- What are typical job responsibilities?
- What aspects of the job interest you most?
- What are the working conditions?

Training and education

- What classes should one take in high school?
- What science and math classes are necessary in college?
- What major and what college degrees are necessary?
- What colleges offer good preparation?

Potential earning

- What is the salary range?
- What benefits (health insurance, retirement, and others) can one expect?
- Include a job announcement from the Internet.

Job prospects

- What is the employment outlook for the coming five to ten years?
- Is this an expanding, static, or shrinking field?
- Who are the potential employers?

Table 4.1 Careers Requiring a Background in Biology

Agricultural engineer	Cytologist	Herpetologist	Park ranger
Agricultural entomologist	Dental hygienist	Horticulturalist	Pathologist
Agricultural genetic engineer	Dentist	Ichthyologist	Pediatrician
	Dermatologist	Immunologist	Pharmaceutical researcher
Agricultural inspector	Developmental biologist	Industrial hygienist	
Agrochemist	Dietician	Intensive care nurse	Pharmacist
Agronomist	Embryologist	Laboratory technician	Pharmacologist
Allergist	Emergency medical technician	Limnologist	Phycologist
Anatomist	Endocrinologist	Lobbyist	Physical therapist
Anesthesiologist	Enologist	Mammalogist	Physician
Animal breeder	Entomologist	Marine biologist	Physician's assistant
Animal trainer	Environmental attorney	Medical technologist	Physiological ecologist
Aquatic botanist	Environmental engineer	Microbiologist	
Aquatic ecologist	Environmental health officer	Microscopist	Physiologist
Arboretum manager		Molecular biologist	Phytochemist
Arborist	Environmental impact analyst	Molecular geneticist	Plant breeder
Audiologist		Mycologist	Plant ecologist
Bacteriologist	Environmental toxicologist	Natural resource manager	Plastic surgeon
Biochemist			Podiatrist
Biogeographer	Environmentalist	Naturalist	Pomologist
Biological engineer	Epidemiologist	Nematologist	Population biologist
Biological illustrator	Estuarine ecologist	Neonatologist	Population geneticist
Biology professor	Ethologist	Nephrologist	Psychiatrist
Biology teacher	Exercise physiologist	Neurobiologist	Pulmonary physician
Biomathematician	Family medicine physician	Neurologist	Radiologist
Biomedical engineer		Neurosurgeon	Range conservationist
Biophysicist	Farmer	Nurse	Rangeland manager
Biostatistician	Fish and wildlife specialist	Nurse practitioner	Reconstructive surgeon
Botanist		Nutritionist	
Cardiologist	Fishery biologist	Obstetrician/gynecologist	Research assistant
Cardiothoracic surgeon	Floriculturist		Restoration ecologist
	Food and drug inspector	Occupational therapist	Rheumatologist
Cardiovascular pathologist	Food scientist	Oncologist	Silviculturalist
	Forensics scientist	Ophthalmologist	Surgeon
Cell biologist	Forest ecologist	Oral surgeon	Surgical technologist
Chiropractor	Forester	Ornithologist	Systems ecologist
Clinical laboratory technician	Genetic counselor	Orthodontist	Taxonomist
	Genetic engineer	Orthopedic surgeon	Technical writer
Clinical nutritionist	Geneticist	Orthotics technician	Toxicologist
Clinical pharmacologist	Gerontologist	Osteologist	Urologist
Community health nurse	Gynecologist	Osteopathic physician	Veterinarian
	Hand surgeon		Veterinary assistant
Conservation biologist	Head and neck surgeon	Otolaryngologist	Virologist
Coroner		Paleontologist	Viticulturist
Crime lab analyst	Health educator	Paramedic	Wildlife biologist
Crime scene investigator	Hematologist	Parasitologist	Wildlife conservation
Crop scientist		Park naturalist	Zoo director
			Zoologist

Table 4.2 Careers Requiring a Background in Chemistry

Agrochemist	Educational coordinator	Pharmaceutical attorney
Analytical chemist	Environmental attorney	Pharmacist
Anesthesiologist	Environmental engineer	Physical chemist
Aquatic chemist	Environmental health officer	Pharmaceutical chemist
Assayer	Environmental impact analyst	Physical chemist
Atmospheric chemist	Environmental toxicologist	Pollution control chemist
Biochemist	Food and drug inspector	Polymer chemist
Chemical analyst	Food chemist	Production chemist
Chemical distributor	Forensic chemist	Pharmaceutical
Chemical engineer	Geochemist	representative
Chemical lab technician	Hazardous waste specialist	Pharmaceutical researcher
Chemical safety officer	Industrial chemist	Quality control
Chemical sales representative	Inorganic chemist	Quality control chemist
Chemistry professor	Laboratory technician	Quality control technician
Chemistry teacher	Lobbyist	Recycling plant manager
Clinical chemist	Materials scientist	Research assistant
Crime lab analyst	Metallurgist	Research chemist
Crime scene investigator	Organic chemist	Spectroscopist
Crystallographer	Patent attorney	Technical writer

Table 4.3 Careers Requiring a Background in Physics

Acoustics engineer	Computer engineer	Nuclear physicist
Aeronautical engineer	Cosmologist	Optical physicist
Agricultural engineer	Crime lab analyst	Particle physicist
Astronaut	Crime scene investigator	Patent attorney
Astronomer	Electrical engineer	Physics professor
Astrophysicist	Engineering geologist	Physics teacher
Atmospheric physicist	Environmental engineer	Plasma physicist
Atomic physicist	Geophysicist	Radiological engineer
Ballistics expert	High-energy physicist	Radiologist
Biomedical physicist	Laboratory technician	Research assistant
Biophysicist	Lobbyist	Solid state physicist
Chemical engineer	Mechanical engineer	Structural engineer
Civil engineer	Medical physicist	Technical writer

If possible, interview someone who works in this profession, and incorporate information you gain from the interview in your report.

4.4 Science and Technological Innovation

Consider the following quotes by reputable scientists, inventors, and technologists of the latter part of the nineteenth century:

"The abdomen, the chest, and the brain will forever be shut from the intrusion of the wise and humane surgeon." Sir John Eric Ericksen, British surgeon, appointed Surgeon-Extraordinary to Queen Victoria, 1873. Today such surgeries are common, and there are abdominal, thoracic, and brain surgery specialties.

"This 'telephone' has too many shortcomings to be seriously considered as a means of communication. The device is inherently of no value to us." Western Union internal memo,

Table 4.4 Careers Requiring a Background in Earth and Space Science

Astronomer	Geochemist	Meteorologist	Seismologist
Astrophysicist	Geodynamicist	Mineralogist	Soil conservationist
Atmospheric chemist	Geologist	Natural resource	Soil scientist
Atmospheric physicist	Geomorphologist	manager	Stratigrapher
Cartographer	Geophysicist	Oceanographer	Technical writer
Climatologist	Geoscience professor	Paleoclimatologist	Volcanologist
Cosmologist	Geoscience teacher	Petroleum geologist	Waste management
Economic geologist	GIS specialist	Petrologist	specialist
Engineering geologist	Glaciologist	Physical oceanographer	Water conservation
Environmental attorney	Hazardous waste	Planetary geologist	officer
Environmental engineer	manager	Prospector	Water quality
Environmental geologist	Hydrologist	Rangeland manager	analyst
Environmental impact	Interpretive naturalist	Research assistant	Water resources
analyst	Lobbyist	Restoration ecologist	specialist
Environmentalist	Marine geologist	Sedimentologist	Watershed manager

1876. Today wireless phone communication is common throughout the world.

"I have always consistently opposed high-tension and alternating systems of electric lighting (AC current) . . . not only on account of danger, but because of their general unreliability and unsuitability for any general system of distribution."[2] Thomas Edison, 1889. Today power lines deliver alternating current to virtually every household and business in the United States.

People have become accustomed to change and expect rapid developments in science and technology, but as these quotations show, this has not always been so. Each day brings new discoveries or innovations in science, technology, and medicine, many of which may eventually influence our life or culture significantly. Scientists provide the basic research to discover new principles, and engineers apply these concepts to produce new products that change the way we live and work.

ACTIVITY 4.4.1 *Science and the Development of Technology*

Table 4.5 lists many of the most significant inventions and inventors of the past four centuries. Each of these inventions has played a significant role in

society, and each is dependent on the scientific and technological discoveries of others who went before. For example, Hans Lippershey is credited with designing the first practical telescope, but his work was preceded by ancient Greeks and Romans who first developed convex glass lenses for starting fires, and by Pliny and Seneca who described the magnifying effect of a glass globe filled with water. Lippershey used the collective knowledge of spectacle makers and lens crafters when assembling his first telescope. Galileo was one of the first to use Lippershey's design, and from it he developed an improved telescope that led to the discovery of four of Jupiter's moons, the phases of Venus, the transit of Mercury, and evidence verifying the Copernican heliocentric model of the solar system. Thus, Lippershey's telescope, which was based on principles discovered by ancient Greeks and Romans, contributed to the development of modern astronomy and science.

Select one or more of the inventions from Table 4.5. Describe (1) the invention, (2) the underlying scientific principles that preceded its development, and (3) the impact of the invention on science, technology, and society. (Look for information online at *sciencesourcebook.com* or wikipedia.com, or search by inventor and invention). See Exhibit 4.2 for a sample report.

Table 4.5 Major Inventions and Inventors, 1600–2000

1608: Telescope: Hans Lippershey	1862: Revolving machine gun: Richard J. Gatling
1610: Microscope: Galileo Galilei	1862: Pasteurization: Louis Pasteur, Claude Bernard
1620: Slide rule: William Oughtred	1865: Compression ice machine: Thaddeus Lowe
1642: Adding machine: Blaise Pascal	1866: Dynamite: Alfred Nobel
1643: Barometer: Evangelista Torricelli	1868: Air brake: George Westinghouse
1645: Vacuum pump: Otto von Guericke	1868: Oleomargarine: Mege Mouries
1657: Pendulum clock: Christiaan Huygens	1869: Vacuum cleaner: I. W. McGaffers
1698: Steam engine: Thomas Savery	1870: Stock ticker: Thomas Alva Edison
1714: Mercury thermometer: Daniel Fahrenheit	1871: Compressed air rock drill: Simon Ingersoll
1752: Lightning rod: Benjamin Franklin	1875: Dynamo: William A. Anthony
1762: Iron smelting process: Jared Eliot	1876: Telephone: Alexander Graham Bell
1767: Carbonated water: Joseph Priestley	1876: Gasoline carburetor: Daimler
1769: Steam engine: James Watt	1877: Induction motor: Nikola Tesla
1783: Parachute: Jean Pierre Blanchard	1877: Phonograph: Thomas Alva Edison
1783: Hot air balloon: Montgolfier brothers	1877: Electric welding: Elihu Thomson
1784: Bifocals: Benjamin Franklin	1878: Cathode ray tube: William Crookes
1793: Cotton gin: Eli Whitney	1879: Automobile engine: Karl Benz
1798: Vaccination: Edward Jenner	1880: Roll film: George Eastman
1800: Electric battery: Alessandro Volta	1880: Seismograph: John Milne
1801: Jacquard loom: Joseph Jacquard	1881: Electric welding machine: Elihu Thomson
1805: Refrigerator: Oliver Evans	1881: Metal detector: Alexander Graham Bell
1807: Steamboat: Robert Fulton	1882: Electric fan: Schuyler Wheeler
1816: Miner's safety lamp: Humphry Davy	1883: Two-phase (AC) induction motor: Nikola Tesla
1816: Stethoscope: René Laennec	1884: Punched card accounting: Herman Hollerith
1821: Electric motor: Michael Faraday	1885: Automobile, differential gear: Karl Benz
1823: Electromagnet: William Sturgeon	1885: Motorcycle: Gottlieb Daimler
1826: Internal combustion engine: Samuel Morey	1885: AC transformer: William Stanley
1827: Insulated wire: Joseph Henry	1886: Gasoline engine: Gottlieb Daimler
1827: Screw propeller: Josef Ressel	1887: Automobile, gasoline: Gottlieb Daimler
1827: Friction match: John Walker	1888: Kodak hand camera: George Eastman
1831: Multiple coil magnet: Joseph Henry	1892: Color photography: Frederic E. Ives
1831: Magnetic acoustic telegraph: Joseph Henry	1893: Wireless communication: Nikola Tesla
1831: Electrical generator: Michael Faraday	1895: Diesel engine: Rudolf Diesel
1835: Morse code: Samuel Morse	1895: Radio signals: Guglielmo Marconi
1835: Electromechanical relay: Joseph Henry	1896: Steam turbine: Charles Curtis
1836: Sewing machine: Josef Madersberger	1897: Automobile, magneto: Robert Bosch
1837: Photography: Louis Daguerre	1899: Magnetic tape recorder: Valdemar Poulsen
1837: Steel plow: John Deere	1900: Rigid dirigible: Ferdinand von Zeppelin
1838: Electric telegraph: Charles Wheatstone	1901: Mercury vapor lamp: Peter C. Hewitt
1839: Vulcanization of rubber: Charles Goodyear	1902: Rayon cellulose ester: Arthur D. Little
1842: Anesthesia: Crawford Long	1903: Electrocardiograph (EKG): Willem Einthoven
1844: Telegraph: Samuel Morse	1903: Powered airplane: Wilbur and Orville Wright
1845: Portland cement: William Aspdin	1905: Radio tube diode: John Fleming
1852: Airship: Henri Giffard	1907: Radio amplifier: Lee DeForest
1852: Elevator: Elisha Otis	1907: Electric vacuum cleaner: James Spangler
1852: Gyroscope: Léon Foucault	1909: Bakelite (first plastic): Leo Baekeland
1853: Glider: Sir George Cayley	1911: Air conditioner: Willis Carrier
1855: Bunsen burner: Robert Bunsen	1911: Cellophane: Jacques Brandenburger
1855: Bessemer process: Henry Bessemer	1911: Hydroplane: Glenn Curtiss

1913: Gyroscope stabilizer: Elmer A. Sperry

1913: Geiger counter: Hans Geiger

1913: Radio receiver tuning: Ernst Alexanderson

1913: Stainless steel: Harry Brearley

1914: Liquid fuel rocket: Robert Goddard

1915: Tungsten filament: Irving Langmuir

1915: Radio tube oscillator: Lee DeForest

1917: Sonar echolocation: Paul Langevin

1922: Radar: Robert Watson-Watt

1923: Sound film: Lee DeForest

1923: Television: Philo Farnsworth

1923: Wind tunnel: Max Munk

1923: Xenon flash lamp: Harold Edgerton

1925: Ultra-centrifuge: Theodor Svedberg

1928: Antibiotics: Alexander Fleming

1929: Electroencephalograph (EEG): Hans Berger

1930: Neoprene: Wallace Carothers

1930: Nylon: Wallace Carothers

1932: Polaroid glass: Edwin Land

1935: Microwave radar: Robert Watson-Watt

1937: Jet engine: Frank Whittle, Hans von Ohain

1938: Fiberglass: Russell Slayter, John Thomas

1938: Computer: Konrad Zuse, John Atanasoff

1939: FM radio: Edwin Armstrong

1939: Helicopter: Igor Sikorsky

1943: Aqua-lung: Jacques-Yves Cousteau

1945: Atomic bomb: Manhattan Project

1946: Microwave oven: Percy Spencer

1947: Transistor: William Shockley, Walter Brattain, and John Bardeen

1952: Fusion bomb: Edward Teller and Stanislaw Ulam

1955: Nuclear reactor: Enrico Fermi, Leó Szilárd

1957: EEG topography: Walter Grey

1958: Integrated circuit: Jack Kilby, Robert Noyce

1960: Laser: Theodore Maiman

1962: Light-emitting diode: Nick Holonyak

1968: Videoconferencing: AT&T

1971: MRI: Raymond V. Damadian

1972: Computed tomography: Godfrey Hounsfield

1973: Ethernet: Bob Metcalfe and David Boggs

1985: Polymerase chain reaction: Kary Mullis

1985: DNA fingerprinting: Alec Jeffreys

1989: World Wide Web protocol: Tim Berners-Lee

1993: Global positioning system: U.S. Department of Defense

1995: DVD: various companies

1996: Cloning of sheep: Ian Wilmut and others

Exhibit 4.2 *Sample Report on the Steel Plow*

(1) *Invention*: John Deere produced the first commercial steel plow in 1837.

(2) *Scientific principles*: An alloy is a mixture of two or more elements, at least one of which is a metal. Alloys may have different properties from their component elements. Metallurgists worked for centuries perfecting steel, an alloy of iron and carbon (0.02%–1.7% by weight) that is substantially harder than iron. John Deere selected steel for his plows because it was hard to break up the tough sod of the American Great Plains.

(3) *Impact of invention*: The steel plow made it possible to cultivate grasslands and led to the rapid growth and settlement of the Great Plains, as well as the demise of native prairie ecosystems. The steel plow paved the way for a variety of steel-based agricultural machines (seeders, planters, combines, harvesters) that increased efficiency while reducing the need for farmers, thereby increasing productivity while accelerating migration to the cities.

ACTIVITY 4.4.2 *Current Developments in Science, Technology, and Medicine*

Each day ushers in new discoveries and developments in science, technology, and medicine. Many electronic newspapers and magazines provide sections devoted entirely to these fields (look online at *sciencesourcebook.com* or search "technology news"). Maintain a weekly log or journal of recent discoveries, inventions, or studies related to your course. Your entries can be in one of the forms described below, as directed by your instructor.

Ways of Summarizing Science and Technology Articles

1. *Summary:* Summarize the article by recording the topic, title, main idea, supporting facts, name of source, date of source, and reference or URL.
2. *Reporter:* Answer reporter questions: Who? What? Where? When? Why? How? What are the implications?
3. *Compare and contrast:* Compare and contrast the story as presented by two different sources.
4. *Perspectives:* Rewrite the article from a different viewpoint. The facts should remain the same, but the article should represent a different perspective.
5. *Diagram or cartoon:* Create a diagram or cartoon to summarize the article.
6. *Vocabulary:* List key vocabulary words and definitions.
7. *Future research:* What new questions does this research, discovery, or study raise?
8. *Nature of science:* After reading an article, describe how science is an ongoing process that changes in response to new information and discoveries. Use examples from the article.

Answers to Chapter Activities

4.1.1 The following lists provide examples of the application of chemistry to agriculture, food, medicine, transportation, household products, electronics and the environment. Vary the length and number of questions to address the specific needs of your class. Alternatively, you may wish to discuss the significance of chemistry to society by leading a discussion in which you provide select examples from the list below. Students should understand that chemistry has a significant impact on many aspects of society and the world around them.

Applications of Chemistry to Agriculture

Strychnine is an *avicide* used to **control birds** that might destroy crops.

Warfarin is a *rodentcide* used to **control rodents** that might destroy crops.

2,4-dichlorophenoxyacetic acid (2,4-D) is an *herbicide* used to **kill weeds** that compete with crops.

1,1,1-trichloro-2,2-bis(ρ-chlorophenyl)ethane (DDT) was the first widely used *insecticide* used to **control insects** that might destroy crops.

Quinone inhibitors are *fungicides* used to **control fungi** that destroy crops.

Nitrogen, phosphorous, and *potassium (NPK)* **fertilizers** are used to increase crop yield.

Humic acid is a complex mixture of organic acids used to **increase the availability of plant nutrients** and increase water penetration in the soil.

Calcium sulfate, known as *gypsum,* can be used to **reduce soil acidity** and is also useful for lightening the structure of heavy clays.

Sulfur is added to agricultural soils to **increase soil acidity.**

Ethylene is a plant hormone used to **ripen fruit** when it is ready for delivery.

Indole acetic acid (IAA) is a plant hormone used to **prevent fruit from dropping** prematurely.

Growth hormone (GH) and other animal hormones are used to **stimulate growth in livestock.**

Applications of Chemistry to Food

Saccharin, aspartame, sucralose, neotame, and *acesulfame-K* are **artificial sweeteners** added to foods to increase sweetness without increasing caloric value.

Isoamyl acetate, cinnamic aldehyde, ethyl propionate, d-limonine, ethyl-(E,Z)-2,4-decadienoate, allyle hexanoate, and *methyl salicylate* are **artificial flavors** that simulate banana, cinnamon, fruity, orange, pear, pineapple, and wintergreen, respectively.

Olestra, a **fat substitute,** is an indigestible molecule that has the flavor of fat but no caloric value.

Sodium nitrate, sodium nitrite, sulfur dioxide, sodium bisulfate, potassium bisulfate, and *disodium EDTA* are **food preservatives** that prevent microbial growth on foods.

Chlorella, cochineal, annatto, and *FD&C dyes* are **food dyes** added to color foods.

Phospholipid lecithin is used as an **emulsifier** to stabilize food emulsions in products such as mayonnaise.

Monosodium glutamate is added in cooking as a **flavor enhancer.**

Applications of Chemistry to Health and Medicine

Retionol, thiamine, riboflavin, niacin, ascorbic acid, and *folic acid* are **vitamins** added to foods to protect or improve health.

Activated charcoal (carbon) is used in water filters to **purify water.**

Fluoride ions are added to municipal water supply to **reduce tooth decay.**

Ozone and *chlorine* are added to municipal water systems to **kill waterborne bacteria.**

Tetrasodium EDTA is added to soaps to **kill bacteria on the skin.**

Insulin is administered to **fight diabetes** and prolong life.

Beta-blockers, alpha-blockers, and *vasodilators* are used to **reduce blood pressure** in patients with hypertension.

Hydrogen peroxide is used to **sterilize** wounds.

Isopropyl alcohol is rubbing alcohol and is used to **clean the skin.**

Penicillins, sulfonamides, and *tetracyclines* are **antibiotics** used to combat bacterial infections.

Interferons are **antiviral drugs** used to combat viral infections.

Paclitaxel (Taxol) is an **anticancer drug** used in chemotherapy.

Benzoyl peroxide is used to **combat acne.**

Acetylsalicylic acid (aspirin) and *acetaminophen* are used to **reduce pain** and headaches.

Lithium salts are **mood stabilizers** used to treat bipolar disorder.

Stannous fluoride is added to **toothpastes** to prevent tooth decay.

Cuprates and other superconducting materials are used in the construction of **MRI** (magnetic resonance imaging) machines used to diagnose medical problems.

Silver chloride and *silver bromide* are photosensitive chemicals used to make **X-ray film.**

Applications of Chemistry to Transportation

Gasoline is a mixture of C_7H_{16} to $C_{11}H_{24}$ hydrocarbons used to **power automobiles.**

Kerosene is a mixture of $C_{12}H_{26}$ to $C_{15}H_{32}$ hydrocarbons used as **fuel in jet airplanes.**

Diesel fuel is a mixture of $C_{16}H_{34}$ to $C_{18}H_{38}$ hydrocarbons used to **power diesel trucks and busses.**

Liquid oxygen and hydrogen (O_2, H_2) are burned in liquid rocket motors to **power the space shuttle** into orbit.

Methane (CH_4), a gas produced in landfills, is compressed as liquefied natural gas (LNG) and used to **power environmentally friendly "green" vehicles.**

Ethanol (C_2H_5OH) is made from fermentation of plant products. It is a renewable resource and potentially a valuable **automotive fuel.**

Nitromethane (CH_3NO_2) is used to **fuel dragsters** and funny cars.

Hydrogen and oxygen (O_2, H_2) are used in **fuel cells** to power a growing number of vehicles.

Lithium ion batteries and other batteries are used in gasoline/electric **hybrid cars.**

MTBE (methyl tertiary-butyl ether) is one of many **fuel additives** used to raise the oxygen content of gasoline and improve performance.

Uranium-235 is used to **power nuclear submarines** by a process of nuclear fission.

Crystalline silicon and *gallium arsenide* are used in photovoltaic cells in the **solar panels of spacecraft** and other vehicles.

Asphalt is primarily *bitumen,* a thick organic liquid left by fractional distillation of oil, and is used to surface many **roads and highways.**

Concrete is a combination of calcium, silicon, aluminum, iron, and other minor ingredients and is used to make many **roads, freeways, and bridges.**

Steel is a metal alloy of *iron* and *carbon* and is used in **railroad tracks** and **bridges.**

Tar is a viscous liquid made from the destructive distillation of *coal* and is used to cover dirt **roads** and **landing fields** (tarmacs).

Fiberglass is material made from extremely fine fibers of *glass* and reinforced with an *epoxy resin.* It is used to make the hulls of many **sailboats** and **motorboats,** as well as some **car bodies.**

Aluminum alloys are used to make **engine blocks** lighter than if made of *steel.*

Sulfur, carbon, and *silicon* are used to vulcanize rubber to make **bicycle tires** more durable.

Carbon fiber, aluminum alloy, and *titanium* are used to construct lightweight **bicycle frames.**

Styrene butadiene rubber is used to make automobile **tires.**

Applications of Chemistry to Household Products

Nylon, rayon, and *polyester* are synthetic fibers used extensively in **clothing.**

Polyurethane is a versatile group of polymers used for **foam** in couches, **varnish** on wood, and the tops of **desks** and **tables** and elastic **sport clothing.**

Polytetrafluoroethylene (Teflon) is used in low-friction applications such as **nonstick pans, ball bearings,** and **gears.**

Polypropylene is a synthetic polymer used in **plastic bottles** and **carpet.**

Polyethylene is used to make **plastic bags, wire insulation,** and **squeeze bottles.**

Polystyrene is used in **disposable cups** and **utensils.**

Polyvinylchloride is used for clear food **wrap, floor coverings, synthetic leather,** and garden **water pipes.**

Polyacrylonitrile is a synthetic fiber used in knit **shirts, sweaters, blankets,** and **carpets.**

Polyvinyl acetate is used in **adhesives** and household **paints.**

Paradichlorobenzene is used for **mothballs** to protect clothing from insect damage.

Sodium hypochlorite is the active ingredient in **bleach.**

Fatty acid salts are used as **soaps** and **detergents.**

Iron oxide is used to give red coloration to **lipstick.**

Ammonium hydroxide (ammonia) is used in many floor and window **cleaning solutions.**

Sodium hydroxide is used to **unclog drains.**

Calcium sulfate dihydrate (gypsum) is a main component in **drywall, plaster, cement, and paints.**

Applications of Chemistry to Electronics and Technology

Silicon, germanium, and *gallium arsenide* are semiconductors used in **microprocessors.**

Haloalkanes (halons) are used in **fire extinguishers** to protect electronic equipment.

Iron oxide particles are used to record data magnetically on **disk drives** and **magnetic tape.**

Epoxy resins are used to make the **circuit boards** on which electronic circuits are printed.

Aluminum and *copper* are used in **power lines** and **electrical wiring.**

Gold is used for **fine wires** and **connectors** in electric circuits.

Tungsten is used in **light bulb** filaments.

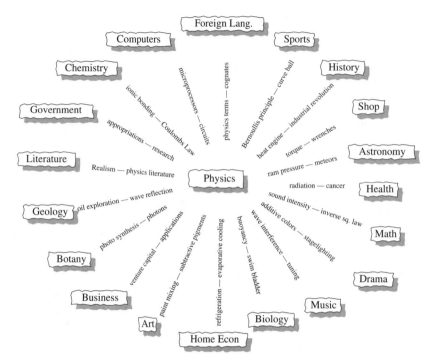

Figure 4.6 Connections Between Physics and Other Subjects

Mercury vapor and *sodium vapor* are used for efficient, long-life **lamps.**

Iodine and *bromine* gases are used in **halogen lamps** to allow filaments to burn brighter.

Teflon and other materials are used to **insulate wires** in electronic equipment.

Carbon is used for toner in **photocopiers** and **laser printers.**

Reinforced carbon carbon (RCC) and *silicon-based tiles* are used on the space shuttle to **shield from intense heating** on atmospheric reentry.

Applications of Chemistry to the Environment

Hydrocarbons and *nitrogen oxides* from automotive exhaust react in sunlight to form a secondary pollutant known as *ozone* (O_3) that can **harm lung function.**

Platinum, rhodium, and *palladium* are used in **catalytic converters** to reduce the emission of *carbon monoxide, volatile organics,* and *nitrogen oxides.*

Dioxins, such as TCDD, are by-products of industrial production and are **toxic** *chlorinated organic compounds* that bioaccumulate in humans and wildlife.

Carbon dioxide, methane, and *nitrous oxide* are products of industrial societies that contribute to the **greenhouse effect** and **global warming.**

CFCs (chlorinated fluorocarbons) are industrial pollutants known to **destroy the stratospheric** ozone that protects the Earth from damaging ultraviolet rays.

Sulfur dioxide and other industrial waste gases combine with *water* in the atmosphere to form **acid rain,** which may harm terrestrial and aquatic plants.

Calcium carbonate is used in **scrubbers** to remove *sulfur dioxide* pollutants from industrial smokestacks and minimize the emissions that contribute to acid rain.

Heavy metals such as *mercury, lead,* and *cadmium,* are produced in various industrial products and can cause **serious illness** in humans and animals.

Polynuclear aromatic hydrocarbons in **oil spills** endanger marine wildlife.

Emulsifiers are used to **clean up oil spills.**

Polyethylene, Styrofoam, and other packaging materials contribute to **nonbiodegradable trash.**

GMO free starch, vegetable oil, and other renewable resources are used in the production of **biodegradable packaging materials.**

Asbestos, a group of hydrous magnesium silicates used in fireproofing, insulation, and brakes, has been found to **cause cancer.**

4.1.2   Student answers will vary. You may wish to adapt this activity for biology or earth and space science, or both.

4.2.1   See Figure 4.6.

4.2.2–4.2.4   Student diagrams will vary but should resemble Figure 4.6 in format, but with different subjects in the center.

4.3.1–4.3.4   Students will write reports using the format specified in Table 4.1. Encourage them to interview professionals and visit the associated occupation and college Web sites.

4.4.1   Student responses will resemble the example in Activity 4.4.1.

4.4.2   Student responses will vary.

Part Two

Developing Scientific Reasoning

Chapter Five

Employing Scientific Methods

For the Teacher 79

5.1   Discrepant Events: Establishing a
      "Need to Know" 80

5.2   Developing Scientifically Oriented Questions 83

5.3   Observation Versus Inference 86

5.4   Brainstorming and Hypothesizing 87

5.5   Experimental Design 90

5.6   Independent Variables 92

5.7   Writing Clear Procedures 94

5.8   Using History to Teach Scientific Methods 95

5.9   Indirect Evidence: "Black Box" Experiments 99

5.10 Evaluating Hypotheses 101

Answers to Chapter Activities 102

For the Teacher

Merriam-Webster's Dictionary defines *science* in terms of the *scientific method,* stating that it is the "knowledge or a system of knowledge . . . obtained and tested through scientific method."[1] An early form of the scientific method was proposed in 1620 by the English philosopher Francis Bacon in his work *Novum Organum* (New Instrument), in which he emphasized the importance of asking questions, making observations, generating possible explanations, and evaluating these explanations in the light of additional observations. Today most science textbooks define the scientific method as a technique in which the researcher defines a problem, makes observations, generates a hypothesis, designs an experiment to test this hypothesis, and uses data from this experiment to draw conclusions concerning the validity of the hypothesis so he or she can answer the research question. The scientific method is often presented in outline form:

Research question: Define the question to be answered.

Observations: Make observations related to this question.

Hypothesis: Offer a possible explanation.

Experiment: Design an experiment to test the validity of this hypothesis.

Conclusions: Evaluate the hypothesis in the light of experimental data, and offer an answer to the research question.

Although many science textbooks imply that there is but one scientific method (generally in this form), the Nobel Prize–winning physicist Percy Bridgman states, "There are as many scientific methods as there are individual scientists." Bridgman says that the scientist "is not consciously following any prescribed course of action, but feels complete freedom to utilize any method or device whatever, which in the particular situation before him seems likely to yield the correct answer. In his attack on his specific problem he suffers no inhibitions of precedent or authority, but is completely free to adopt any course that his ingenuity is capable of suggesting to him."[2]

Bridgman's comments are a good reminder that science is a creative endeavor and that scientists are not restricted to a cookbook methodology in their pursuit of knowledge. Nonetheless, the scientific method, as commonly presented, is a good tool for learning how to answer problems, and like any other tool, it is best understood through use.

In this chapter, students will employ the scientific method in a variety of ways to answer real problems. They will also use scientific vocabulary, including the following key terms:

Key Terminology Related to the Scientific Method

Variable: A variable is something that is capable of changing or varying.

Independent variable: An independent variable is independent of others. A change in the dependent variable does not cause a change in the independent variable. In most graphs it is plotted on the *x*-axis.

Dependent variable: A dependent variable depends on the independent variable. A change in the independent variable may cause a change in the dependent variable.

Quantitative variable: A quantitative variable has numerical values (height, age, temperature, velocity, distance). Quantitative data are displayed in scatter plots or histograms.

Categorical (qualitative) variables: A categorical variable includes data grouped on a given property, such as genus, chemical family, or population. Categorical data are best displayed in bar graphs or pie charts.

Control: A control is a subject or object in an experiment that is not involved in the procedures affecting the rest of the experiment, thus acting as a standard against which experimental results can be compared.

Constants: These are factors that are held constant during an experiment. To determine the effect of an independent variable on a dependent variable, all other potential factors must be held constant.

5.1 Discrepant Events: Establishing a "Need to Know"

Early bacteriologists and microbiologists determined to identify microbes involved in disease. Such a task was challenging for early workers, and samples were often contaminated by fungi and other microorganisms. In 1928, a researcher by the name of Alexander Fleming was studying a group of bacteria (*staphylococci*) when he noticed a slight discrepancy in their growth pattern. Bacteria that would normally cover the growth medium were not found near spots of fungal contamination. These observations were not consistent with Fleming's prior experiences, and he immediately set out to determine the cause for this discrepancy. After much research, Fleming isolated a substance from the mold that inhibits the growth of bacteria and named it *penicillin.* Ten years later, English researchers Ernst Chain and Howard Florey demonstrated the therapeutic effects of penicillin in the treatment of bacterial infections. Penicillin became the first widespread antibiotic and has since saved many lives.

One man's interest in a slight discrepancy (the lack of bacteria surrounding fungal contamination) led to many subsequent discoveries, and ultimately the introduction of antibiotics. Students, like researchers, tend to pay more attention if something does not behave the way they expect it to. Such discrepant events engender curiosity and stimulate a *need to know*. Those who have a need to know are likely to investigate in more depth.

Educators employ discrepant events in an effort to capture student interest and provide parameters in which students will naturally develop a need to know. In this section, we introduce a few discrepant events and many more may be found in *Hands-On Physics with Real-Life Applications* and *Hands-On Chemistry with Real-Life Applications.*[3]

ACTIVITY 5.1.1 *A Reversible, Spontaneous Color Change: Teacher Demonstration*

Materials: methylene blue, potassium hydroxide, flasks, dextrose.

We are not accustomed to seeing liquids spontaneously change color, much less revert back to their original color when shaken. In this demonstration, the teacher fills a flask with a liquid that turns blue when shaken (Figure 5.1A), but reverts to clear when allowed to stand (Figure 5.1B). This discrepant event can be used to introduce the importance of observation in the scientific method.

The teacher should put on protective eyewear and a lab coat. Add the following to an Erlenmeyer flask: 200 mL of 0.5 *M* potassium hydroxide (5.7 grams KOH in 200 mL water; allow to cool before

adding other substances), 7 grams of dextrose (glucose), and a few drops of methylene blue indicator solution (or approximately 0.5 g of methylene blue powder). In a basic solution, methylene blue is reduced to its colorless state:

$$\underset{\text{(blue)}}{\overset{oxidized}{\text{methylene blue}}} \xrightarrow{\text{reducing environment}} \underset{\text{(colorless)}}{\overset{reduced}{\text{methylene blue}}}$$

Methylene blue may be subsequently oxidized by shaking the flask vigorously. Atmospheric oxygen dissolves into solution, oxidizing methylene blue to the blue state.

$$\underset{\text{(colorless)}}{\overset{reduced}{\text{methylene blue}}} \xrightarrow{\text{oxidizing environment}} \underset{\text{(blue)}}{\overset{oxidized}{\text{methylene blue}}}$$

After shaking, allow the flask to stand undisturbed until it returns to clear. This process can be repeated numerous times.

When students observe this phenomenon, they will start to ask questions concerning how it works. The teacher can use this discrepant event to whet student curiosity about science or launch an exploration of the underlying principles of oxidation and reduction.

ACTIVITY 5.1.2 *The Collapsing Can: Teacher Demonstration*

Materials: 12 oz soda can, water, hot plate, beaker tongs, safety goggles, lab coat.

This is a teacher demonstration only. Put on goggles and a laboratory coat.

Obtain a large beaker or bucket, and fill it with water. Pour water into an empty, opened, aluminum soft drink can to a depth of approximately 1 cm, and place the can on a hot plate until the water boils (Figure 5.2A). *Do not allow the can to boil dry!* After the water has boiled (watch for steam) for approximately 1 minute, use tongs to remove the can from the heat source and place it in an upright position with the base in water (Figure 5.2B). Students will notice no changes in the can. Repeat the process, but this time invert the can and submerge the opening in the water, as illustrated in (Figure 5.2C). This time the can will immediately collapse. Ask your students to draw a diagram of the experimental setup and indicate

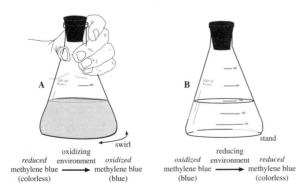

Figure 5.1 Spontaneous Color Change

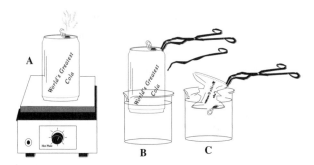

Figure 5.2 The Collapsing Soda Can

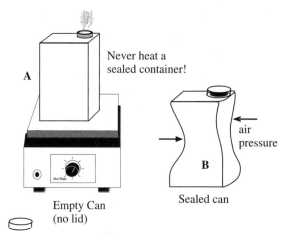

Figure 5.3 The Collapsing Can

where the pressure must be highest and where it must be lowest to produce the observed results.

When 1 mL of water boils (vaporizes), it changes into approximately 1000 mL of steam. As the water in the soft drink can boils, it displaces air originally in the can. When the can is sealed and cooled, steam condenses to liquid water but now occupies only approximately 1/1000 the volume it occupied as steam. In other words, for every 1 mL of steam that condenses inside the sealed can, approximately 999 mL of vacuum are left behind. The air pressure outside the can remains the same while the pressure inside drops, creating a pressure differential that collapses the can.

Air pressure can also be illustrated in a very dramatic manner by using a resealable metal can such as those used to package paint thinner and other solvents. *The instructor should make certain the can is completely clean and dry prior to the demonstration or else dangerous fumes may enter the atmosphere when the can is heated.*

Seal the can, and ask a student to crush it with his or her hands. It will be very difficult for the student to do much more than dent the sealed can because the air inside resists compression. Remove the lid and cover the threads with plumber's Teflon tape. Add water to a depth of 1 cm and heat unsealed until the water boils (Figure 5.3A). **Never heat a sealed container!** Using potholders, remove the can from the heat, and seal with the lid (Figure 5.3B). **Do not reseal the can while it is being heated, or an explosion may occur.**

As the can is allowed to cool on a bench top, it will gradually collapse as the water vapor condenses and the internal pressure drops to a fraction of the external atmospheric pressure. Cooling the outside of the can with water or a damp cloth will accelerate this process. Students can calculate the force on the can by calculating the surface area (A) and then solving the equation $F = PA$, where P (atmospheric pressure) is approximately 101,325 N/m^2.

Under normal circumstances, empty cans do not spontaneously collapse, so when students observe them imploding in this activity, their curiosity is immediately aroused. You can use this discrepant event as an introduction to the importance of observation to scientific method or to introduce students to air pressure and the gas laws.

ACTIVITY 5.1.3 *Retinal Fatigue: What You Perceive Is Not Always Real!: Teacher Demonstration*

Materials: overhead transparency; yellow, green, and black overhead pens; overhead projector.

When you are photographed with a camera equipped with an electronic flash (strobe), you may have noticed a dark afterimage of the strobe long after the flash of light disappeared. The flash is so intense that it fatigues photoreceptive cells in your retina (see Figure 5.4) so they are temporarily unresponsive to light. As a result, a black image of the flash appears in your vision. Your retinas may also fatigue after staring at colored objects for long periods of time. However, when you look toward a white surface, you will not see a black afterimage but rather one that is the complementary color of

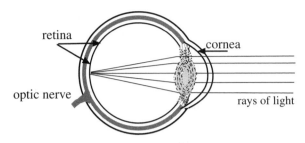

Figure 5.4 Light Focuses on the Retina

the object you were staring at. For example, if you stare intensely for 1 minute at a red dot and then turn your eyes toward a sheet of white paper, you will see a cyan (the complementary color of red) afterimage of the dot. Light reflected from white paper normally stimulates the red, green, and blue cones (photoreceptive cells) of the retina, but if you have first fatigued the red cones by staring at a red object, these cells temporarily will not respond to red light. As a result, only the green and blue cones in that region of the retina are stimulated, causing the image to appear cyan (the combination of green and blue light), the complementary color of red!

For this activity, color an American flag on an overhead transparency using the colors indicated in Figure 5.5, or project the flag image from the companion Web site of this sourcebook (*sciencesourcebook.com*). Instruct your students to cover one eye, and stare intensely at the middle of the flag with the other. After 1 minute, remove the transparency, and instruct students to keep

their eyes focused on the same point on the white screen. They should soon see the American flag, correctly colored in red, white, and blue!

Instruct your students to draw a solid red circle on a white sheet of paper using a marker or paintbrush. They should cover one eye, place the circle in bright light, and stare at it. At the end of 1 minute, instruct them to quickly refocus on a well-lit sheet of white paper and ask them to identify the color of the afterimage (it will be cyan). Repeat this process with green and blue dots, and discuss the results. Students should identify magenta as the complementary color of green and yellow as the complementary color of blue.

Under normal circumstances, we don't see colors where none exist, so when students observe colors when they stare at a sheet of white paper, their curiosity is immediately aroused. You can use this discrepant event as an introduction to the importance of observation in the scientific method or to introduce students to vision and retinal physiology.

5.2 Developing Scientifically Oriented Questions

Michael Faraday (1791–1867) was a British scientist who invented the first electric motor and dynamo, demonstrated the relationship between electricity and chemical bonding, and discovered the effect of magnetism on light. Faraday was not only a brilliant scientist but also a well-known educator who brought science to the public through lectures he delivered each Christmas season at the Royal Society in London.[4] Faraday's Christmas Lectures were popular because he illustrated concepts with numerous hands-on activities and experiments.

Faraday knew the importance of observation in science and began his most famous lecture series by asking his audience to record as many observations as possible about a burning candle. Even today science teachers use Faraday's activity to encourage the development of observation skills. Douglas Osheroff, the 1997 Nobel Prize

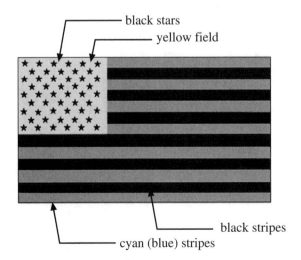

Figure 5.5 Flag in Complementary Colors

winner in physics (for discovery of the superfluid phases of ³H), reflected on the importance of this activity in his own intellectual development: "I remember quite well one class assignment: to record our own observations of a burning candle. I knew pretty well how a candle worked, and simply wrote down an explanation of how radiant heat from the flame melted the wax, which was then drawn up into the wick by capillary action, etc. Mr. Hock (the teacher) read my explanation, and then came to me and pointed out that what I had written could not possibly have been drawn from my own observations."[5] Osheroff had not made observations as requested but had relied on his prior knowledge to explain what he was seeing. Hock's comments helped Osheroff distinguish observation from inference, and this distinction ultimately helped him in his career as a scientist.

Table 5.1 Observations to Make About a Burning Candle

Flame
initial speed of burning
speed of burning once the wax starts to melt
height of flame in the open air
colors of flame
colors of flame light reflected off white paper
quality of light generated by flame
color distribution within flame
shape of flame
response of flame to air movement
response of flame to water
changes in flame height when beaker is lowered
changes in flame color when beaker is lowered
direction flame burns when candle is tilted
duration of smoke when candle is extinguished
time candle burns under large beaker
time candle burns under medium beaker
time candle burns under small beaker
shape of flame when water is placed in well

Condensate
appearance of condensate in beaker
conditions under which condensate forms
location where condensate forms
rate at which condensate forms
rate at which condensate disappears if flame is removed

Deposits
color of deposits on beaker
location where deposits form
rate deposits form on beaker
conditions under which deposits form
texture of deposits

Smoke
color of smoke
quantity of smoke
distribution of smoke

change in smoke production with funnel
distance from which candle can be relit
color bromthymol blue turns in the smoke

Candle (Paraffin)
color of candle
texture of candle
shape of candle
rate candle is consumed
appearance of wax when candle is burning
color of tip of wick when burning
rate candle is consumed if wax in well is drained
rate candle is consumed if wax is not drained
width of tracks left by flowing wax

Wick
position of wick of unlit candle
color of wick of unlit candle
structure of wick of unlit candle
ability of wick to burn if placed in water
ability of wick to burn if placed in lamp fluid
color of base of wick when burning
color of stalk of wick when burning
flow patterns of liquid wax
rate wick burns when not in wax
rate wick burns when in candle
apparent dryness or wetness of base of wick

Odors
odors produced by unlit candle
odors produced by burning candle
odors released by extinguished candle

Sound
sound produced by burning candle
sound of candle when water is placed in well

Heat
heat distribution around flame (top, sides, base)
side of hand that feels heat when near flame

ACTIVITY 5.2.1 *Observations of a Candle*

Materials: small candle, matches, tongs, beaker, funnel, clay or putty, bromthymol blue or phenol red indicator, test tube clamp, safety glasses, dull butter knife, lamp oil (optional).

The purpose of this activity is to record as many observations of a candle as possible. Refer to Table 5.1 for ideas on the types of observations that may be made. Record your observations in a laboratory notebook or worksheet.

Firmly plant a candle in a small clump of clay. Using beaker tongs, suspend a clean, cool beaker over the unlit candle, as illustrated in (Figure 5.6A), and record your observations. Repeat the procedure with a funnel on which there are drops of the pH indicator methylene blue or phenol red (Figure 5.6B). Does the indicator change color?

Put on safety goggles, and light the candle. Record all observations (Figure 5.6C). Using beaker tongs, suspend a cooled beaker over the flame, as shown in Figure 5.6D. What observations can you make about the inside of the beaker? Repeat the procedure with a funnel in which there are drops of bromthymol blue (Figure 5.6E).

Place a dry, clean beaker over the flame (Figure 5.6F), and make observations as the flame is extinguished. Repeat the procedure with different sizes of glass beakers. Is there any correlation between the size of the glass beaker and the time it takes to extinguish the flame? Remove the beaker, and relight the candle by placing a match in the smoke near the wick (Figure 5.6G). Is it possible to relight the candle simply by moving the flame into the smoke?

Using a dull knife, cut the wick free from the candle, and place one end of the wick in a dish of water. Light the other end of the wick (Figure 5.6H). What do you observe? Dry the wick off, place it in a dish of lamp oil, and relight it. What do you observe?

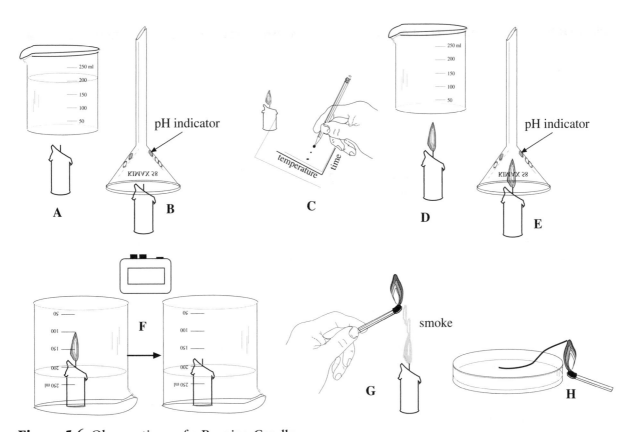

Figure 5.6 Observations of a Burning Candle

ACTIVITY 5.2.2 *Developing Questions About the Candle*

In his introduction to the classic candle activity, Michael Faraday wrote, "We come here to be philosophers; and I hope you will always remember that whenever results happen, especially if it be new, you should say, 'What is the cause? Why does it occur?' and you in the course of time will find out the answer."

Write down as many questions as you can based on the observations you made in Activity 5.2.1. For example: What is wax? What is the wick? Why is the wax soft? Why does the wick turn black? Why does the wax melt? Why does the smoke ignite? What is the substance that appears on the glass above the flame? Why does the indicator turn color when placed over the candle? Do all candles burn the same?

5.3 Observation Versus Inference

Science is based largely on observations and inferences. An *observation* is a record resulting from the study of an event or object, whereas an *inference* is a conclusion drawn from evidence or reasoning based on observations. Unfortunately many people cannot distinguish observations from inferences and use the concepts interchangeably. The following activities are designed to help students understand the differences between observations and inferences and help them use each appropriately.

ACTIVITY 5.3.1 *Observations Versus Inferences of a "Plant"—Teacher Demonstration*

Place a realistic-looking silk plant with flowers in a pot containing soil (Figure 5.7A). Place the plant in the front of the class, and ask your students to record all of their observations of the plant on a sheet of paper. After a few minutes, ask students to read their observations, and list them on the board or an overhead transparency. Do not allow any of your students to discuss the "observations" that appear on the list. Because many students do not understand the difference between observation and

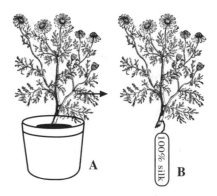

Figure 5.7 Observations Versus Inferences of a "Plant"

inference, the list will probably include inferences such as flower scent, root structure, photosynthesis, and respiration, in addition to true observations, such as leaf color, leaf shape, and flower color. Once the list is complete, pull the plant out of the pot and pass it around the room (Figure 5.7B). It will now be evident that many of the "observations" were merely incorrect inferences made because the students assumed that the plant was real. Draw another column on the list, and ask students to identify which of the "observations" should be categorized as inferences.

ACTIVITY 5.3.2 *Observations Versus Inferences of "Raisidia"—Teacher Demonstration*

"Raisidia" is a humorous activity designed to help students differentiate observations from inferences. Before class begins, place raisins in a cup of tapwater for at least 20 minutes. During this time, the raisins hydrate, and their densities decrease. Without allowing students to see the raisins, drain off the water, and place them in a tall, clean, clear drinking glass, and fill the glass with a clear carbonated drink such as lemon-lime soda or club soda. After the fizzing has subsided and the raisins begin to bob up and down, present the cup to the students and ask them to make as many observations as possible (Figure 5.8).

Do not allow the students to approach the container. You may wish to tell them a tall tale about how you collected these "creatures" (*raisidia*) in a nearby bog or gutter. When asked

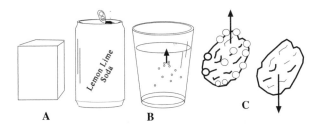

Figure 5.8 Observations Versus Inferences of "Raisidia"

to make observations, many will describe how the creatures swim to the surface and dive back, or how they congregate on the bottom before swimming to the top. Record all of the students' observations of the "raisidia" on the board. After your students complete all of their observations, you may wish to astound them by drinking the contents of the glass. Students will be shocked until you pull out the raisin box and tell them that the "creatures" are actually raisins. Draw another column on the list and have the students identify which of the "observations" should be categorized as inferences.

The English scientist William Henry (1774–1836) observed that the concentration of gas in a solution increases in a linear fashion as the pressure of the gas above the solution increases:

$$C_{gas} = kP_{gas}$$

where C_{gas} = molar concentration of the gas in the solution, k = Henry's law constant for that gas at a particular temperature, and P_{gas} = partial pressure of the gas above the solution.

Carbonated soft drinks are packaged under pressure, forcing a large amount of carbon dioxide to dissolve in solution. When a can of carbonated soft drink is opened, the external pressure is reduced to atmospheric pressure, and the carbon dioxide comes out of solution as bubbles (the fizz). Bubbles of carbon dioxide form on the surface of the submerged raisins, and the raisins are soon buoyed to the surface where the bubbles break, causing the raisins to sink (Figure 5.8).

This activity illustrates Archimedes' principle, which states that an object is buoyed up by a force

equivalent to the weight of the fluid displaced. The bubbles on the raisins displace sufficient soft drink so that the buoyant force on the raisins exceeds the force of gravity, and they rise to the surface. When the bubbles break, the raisins displace less fluid and experience a buoyant force that is less than that of their own weight, causing them to sink once again to the bottom. The raisins will continue to bob up and down until the soda becomes flat (no more carbon dioxide escapes from solution).

5.4 Brainstorming and Hypothesizing

Brainstorming is a group problem-solving technique that involves the spontaneous contribution of ideas from all members of the group. Scientists often hold brainstorming sessions to generate possible solutions to difficult problems, particularly in the hypothesis generation phase of the scientific method. Often the comments of one team member stimulate the thought processes of another, creating a chain reaction of ideas. The following guidelines should be used in a brainstorming session:

- Do not discuss or evaluate ideas until the brainstorming session is complete.
- Focus on quantity, not quality. You want to get many ideas for discussion.
- Build on the ideas of others, combining or modifying ideas already presented.

In the first activity, students engage in a classic brainstorming session that has been used as a team-building activity in many schools and organizations. Teams are told to imagine that they are part of a lunar exploration mission and that their craft has experienced mechanical difficulties, leaving them stranded some distance from the lunar research station. They are asked to develop consensus regarding the relative value of various items that may be taken with them from the wreckage on their trek to the research station.

The activity presented here is a variation of the original exercise, modified to encourage brainstorming, consensus building, and evaluative reasoning. Before proceeding with the activity, you may wish to show images and videos of the Moon's surface (online at *sciencesourcebook.com*, or search "lunar photos") to familiarize students with the lunar environment.

ACTIVITY 5.4.1 *Lost on the Moon: Brainstorming and Consensus Building*

Divide students into teams of three to five members, and read the following paragraphs aloud to the class:

> You are members of a scientific team bound for a permanent research station on the surface of the moon. Unfortunately, your lunar craft malfunctions, forcing an emergency landing in Mare Crisium, approximately 300 km from the research station at Mare Serenitatis. Both you and the research station are on the lighted surface of the moon. During the landing process, much of the equipment aboard has been damaged, and since your survival depends on reaching the research station, only the most critical items must be chosen for the trek.
>
> These 15 items have been left intact following the emergency landing [project the list so everyone can see it]. As a group, you must reach consensus regarding the relative importance of these items in your mission to reach help at the research station.
>
> Here is the list of 15 items:

box of matches	two 100 kg tanks of oxygen	stellar map
10 kg dehydrated food	traditional signal flares	first aid kit
50 m of nylon rope	solar-powered FM radio	10 L water
portable heating unit	two 45 caliber pistols	case of dehydrated milk
life raft	magnetic compass	parachute silk

Now provide these instructions:

1. *Brainstorming:* Write down as many ideas as possible regarding the potential use of the 15 items for your trek to the research station. At this time, do not discuss or evaluate the merit of these ideas.

2. *Analysis:* Review the maps, photos, movies, and data on the moon available on the Web site. Record the similarities and differences between the Earth and the Moon with respect to gravity, atmosphere, lighting, radiation, magnetic field, visibility, surface, and so forth.

3. *Evaluation and consensus building:* Discuss the merits of the ideas presented during the brainstorming session, and develop a consensus within your group regarding the relative value of each of the items. Place a 1 by the item you value most and a 15 by the item you value least, recording the rationale for your ranking.

4. *Discussion and defense of position:* Compare your ranking with those of other groups. If there are differences, discuss them, presenting reasoned arguments for your ranking.

ACTIVITY 5.4.2 *The Mysterious Bottle: Generating a Hypothesis—Teacher Demonstration*

Materials: surgical tubing, pliers, burner, ring stand, nail, beakers, food coloring, utility knife, black electrician's tape, foil.

A *discrepant or counterintuitive event* is a demonstration or activity that produces unexpected results, causing the observer to ask questions. You can use discrepant events to create an environment in which your students, rather than you, are asking the questions. The "mysterious bottle" is a discrepant event that can be used as a brainstorming activity in which students build on each other's ideas to surmise the contents of a covered container that exhibits some very unusual properties. They then evaluate each other's hypotheses in the light of their observations.

The preparation for this activity should be done in a location where none of the students will see how the device is assembled. Obtain a 2 L plastic soda bottle. Put on protective eyewear. Using insulated pliers, hold the tip of a large nail

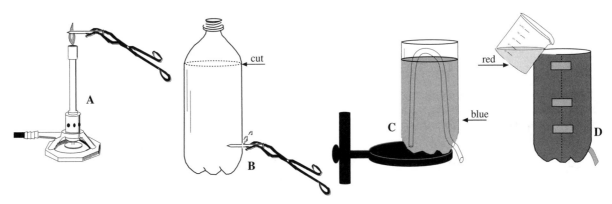

Figure 5.9 Setup for the Mysterious Bottle Activity

in the flame of a laboratory burner (Figure 5.9A), and then use the heated nail to melt a hole in the side (near the base, Figure 5.9B) of the 2 L bottle. Slowly move the nail around in a circle until the diameter of the hole is just slightly smaller than the diameter of flexible latex surgical tubing. Using a sharp utility knife or scissors, cut off the top of the bottle as shown in Figure 5.9. Pinch the end of the tubing so it will fit through the hole, and then pull the tubing until it is positioned as shown in Figure 5.9C. Test the seal by adding water to the container. Leakage may occur if you use Tygon or other stiff plastic tubing, or if the hole is too large.

Empty the bottle, and place it on a ring stand equipped as illustrated in Figure 5.9C. Place a few drops of blue food coloring in the base of the container, and add water until the level is just below the base of the arch in the tubing. Hide the contents of the container from view by wrapping the bottle in aluminum foil and taping the tube that protrudes with black electrician's tape (Figure 5.9D).

Place a few drops of red food coloring in a small beaker, and add water. Place the full assembly in view of the class. Pour water from the beaker into the bottle until water starts to flow out of the exit tube and into a 2 L collection flask, beaker, or cylinder. Ask students to record their observations, for example, the amount and color of fluid added and the amount and color of fluid that exits.

Students will be surprised to see much more water leave the bottle than entered it. Ask students to use these observations when generating ideas regarding the possible contents of the container.

Provide students with overhead transparencies and pens, and instruct them to draw diagrams of what they think may be in bottle. Ask for volunteers to explain their hypotheses using the overhead projector. Encourage the participation of all students, and allow them to build on the ideas of others.

After the final presentation, discuss each idea to see if it explains all of the observed phenomenon (e.g., increase in amount of fluid, change in color). Keeping the bottle covered, pour an equal quantity of red water as before into the container. The students will note that nothing comes out of the container. Ask them to evaluate their hypotheses to see if they can explain these new data. The class should be able to rule out many of the hypotheses on the basis of the observations that they have made. After completing this process, ask students to vote on the hypothesis that they believe best explains the observations. Commend students for their contributions and critiques, and discuss how scientists use similar processes to generate a variety of hypotheses before focusing in on one to be tested.

Although the primary purpose of this activity is to engage students in brainstorming and hypothesis generation, students will undoubtedly want to

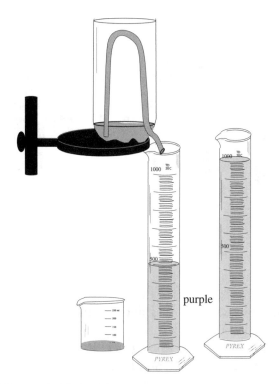

Figure 5.10 Siphon

see the contents of the bottle to determine if their hypotheses were correct. Remove the aluminum foil, and show the simple siphon (Figure 5.10). The action of the siphon is dependent on differences in gravitational attraction on the fluid in the two arms of the siphon. There is greater pull on the side of the tube with a higher vertical column of water (in this case, the tube exiting the bottle) than there is on the shorter branch (the section inside the bottle). Water exhibits significant cohesive forces that prevent the column of water from breaking. As water starts to flow out the exit tube, water is pulled in through the inlet. The column of water "falls" toward the lowest point in much the way that a short section of rope placed over a railing falls to the side on which more of the rope hangs.

For a siphon to function, there must be a difference in pressure at the two ends of the tubing. In the siphon in this activity, the atmospheric pressure is approximately the same at both ends

of the tube, but the liquid pressure is different. Liquid pressure can be calculated by multiplying the density of the fluid ($\rho = 1$ g/cm³ for water) by the acceleration due to gravity ($g = 9.8$ m/s²) by the height differential (h). Thus, a 20 cm column in the intake arm exerts a pressure of approximately 2 kPa (2000 N/m²) while a 30 cm column of water in the exit tube exerts (not to scale shown in diagram) a pressure of approximately 3 kPa (3000 N/m²).

$$\begin{array}{l} \textit{Fluid} \\ \textit{pressure in} \\ \textit{intake tube} \end{array} = \rho g h = (1g/cm^3)\left(\frac{9.8m}{s^2}\right)(0.2m) \approx 2\,kPa$$

$$\begin{array}{l} \textit{Fluid} \\ \textit{pressure in} \\ \textit{exit tube} \end{array} = \rho g h = (1g/cm^3)\left(\frac{9.8m}{s^2}\right)(0.3m) \approx 3\,kPa$$

Thus, pressure in the intake arm is 99 kPa (101 kPa of air pressure -2 kPa of water pressure) while pressure in the lower (exit) arm is only 98 kPa (101 kPa of air pressure -3 kPa of water pressure). Since the net pressure in the intake arm is greater than in the exit arm, water flows toward the exit. The greater the difference in height, the greater the pressure differential, and the greater the rate of flow.

This activity provides a great model for "black-box" research. Researchers are often unable to see the thing that they are studying and must rely on observations of inputs and outputs. In this activity, the addition of water is an input, and the water exiting is an output. Scientists draw inferences based on inputs and outputs, especially when they cannot see the inner workings.

5.5 Experimental Design

Assume that you sit on the council of a major city, and the fire commissioner comes to request more funding to hire additional firefighters. In the course of the presentation, the commissioner presents the data as shown in Figure 5.11A.

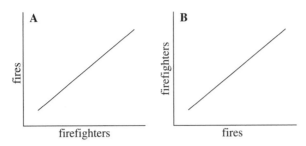

Figure 5.11 Relationship of Fires and Firefighters

On the basis of these data, would you vote to hire more firefighters? I hope not! The graph suggests that the numbers of fires in your city are proportional to the number of firefighters. Note that the number of firefighters is plotted on the *x*-axis, while the number of fires is plotted on the *y*-axis. By convention, we plot the independent variable (the variable that we change independently of the other) on the *x*-axis, while plotting the dependent variable (the variable that changes in response to the independent variable) on the *y*-axis. The data in Figure 5.11A suggest that if you hire more firefighters (the independent variable), your city will experience more fires (dependent variable). As a city council member, you would probably not be reelected if your constituency learned that you voted in favor of the fire commissioner's request on the basis of these data! If, however, the commissioner presented the data as shown in Figure 5.11B, your vote would not provoke concern. These data suggest that as the number of fires (the independent variable on the *x*-axis) has grown, the city has hired more firefighters (the dependent variable on the *y*-axis).

As you can see, much confusion can be generated by not following the standard convention for plotting data. By convention, the independent variable should be plotted on the *x*-axis (horizontal axis) and the dependent variable on the *y*-axis (vertical axis):

• *Independent variable:* Mathematicians traditionally refer to the *horizontal axis* of a graph as the *x-axis* or the *abscissa*; scientists refer to it as the *independent variable.* An independent variable is one that is unaffected by changes in the dependent variable. For example, when the influence of temperature on photosynthesis is examined, temperature is the independent variable because it does not depend on photosynthetic rate. A change in the photosynthetic rate does not affect the temperature of the air! Experimenters often manipulate independent variables and look for changes in dependent variables in order to understand basic relationships.

• *Dependent variable:* Mathematicians refer to the *vertical axis* of the graph as the *y-axis* or *ordinate,* and scientists refer to it as the *dependent variable.* The dependent variable is dependent on changes in the independent variable. For example, photosynthesis is dependent on temperature. A change in air temperature will result in a change in photosynthetic production.

• *Constants:* To conduct an experiment, it is necessary to keep factors other than the independent variable constant. For example, if a food scientist is studying the relationship between the concentration of preservative and the growth rate of bread mold, it is important that the temperature, humidity, light, and other factors be the same for all bread used in the study. If these are not kept constant, it is impossible to determine the effect of the variable that you are intending to test.

• *Controls:* Experiments also require a control, that is, a specimen that is not subjected to the procedures affecting the rest of the experiment, thus acting as the standard against which the results are compared.

ACTIVITY 5.5.1 *Interpreting Graphs*
Figures 5.12A to 5.12H show the data from a variety of experiments and studies. For each graph, (1) identify the independent variable, (2) identify the dependent variable, (3) list factors that must be held constant, (4) describe an experiment that would produce such data, and (5) give a simple interpretation of the data.

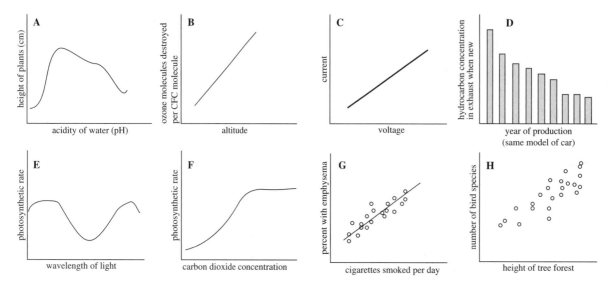

Figure 5.12 Graphs of Experimental Data

5.6 Independent Variables

In 1976, the United States celebrated its two-hundredth anniversary, and many people flocked to Philadelphia to celebrate and commemorate the signing of the Declaration of Independence. Shortly after the celebrations, 180 people who had attended the American Legion Convention in Philadelphia contracted pneumonia-like symptoms, and 34 eventually died from related complications.

"Legionnaires' disease," as it was called, prompted a massive medical investigation. Researchers knew that all who had suffered from Legionnaires' disease had attended the American Legion convention, but beyond that, they did not have much information. Was the disease caused by an environmental toxin, a virus, bacteria, or other pathogen? Was it transmitted by food, water, air, or direct contact? To find the cause, medical researchers isolated and studied single variables and then studied these in conjunction with others. After much methodical research, scientists were successful in identifying the disease agent (the bacteria *Legionella pneumophila*) and the environmental parameters (mists containing the bacteria) that set the stage for this deadly outbreak.

As with Legionnaires' disease, most other real-life problems are complex and contain many variables, each of which may influence the outcome individually or in conjunction with other variables. In Activity 5.6.1, you will be confronted with a complex situation in which many things happen simultaneously, and you must use a methodical approach of isolating variables to determine the causes of the phenomena you see.

ACTIVITY 5.6.1 *Isolating Variables in a Complex Chemical Reaction*
Materials: resealable sandwich bags, plastic spoons, plastic beral pipettes, anhydrous calcium chloride, sodium bicarbonate, phenol red solution (0.01 gram solid phenol red/liter of solution), beakers

Put on a laboratory coat and protective eyewear. Place 5 g (approximately 1 teaspoon) of sodium bicarbonate ($NaHCO_3$) in one corner of a plastic bag with a zipper lock and an equal amount of anhydrous calcium chloride in another. Be careful not to mix the powders. Place a plastic beral pipette filled with phenol red solution (made by dissolving 0.1 g of phenol red powder in 100 mL of water) in the bag with the tip positioned so no solution leaks into the powder. Seal the bag, and mix all the components as rapidly as possible. Once the contents are thoroughly mixed, set the bag on a table, and record any changes (such as color, temperature, and appearance) you observe in Table 5.2.

Table 5.2 Observations of Mixing Components

Phenol Red	Sodium Bicarbonate	Calcium Chloride	Color	Temperature ↑ *Indicates Rise* ↓ *Indicates Loss*	Appearance *(e.g., Gases, Precipitates)*
✓	✓	✓			
✓	✓				
✓		✓			
	✓	✓			

Although a variety of changes occur when the phenol red, sodium bicarbonate, and calcium chloride are mixed, it is not possible to determine the specific causes of each change because there are too many variables. For example, is the observed color change due to the mixing of phenol red solution with sodium bicarbonate, the mixing of phenol red solution with calcium chloride, the mixing of sodium bicarbonate and calcium chloride, or the mixing of all three items? To answer such questions, it is necessary to change one variable at a time while controlling, or keeping constant, the rest. For example, rather than mixing all three substances together at once, try mixing small quantities of pairs of chemicals independently in small beakers and then mixing the resulting mixtures with the remaining substance.

Mix phenol red and sodium bicarbonate, and report your observations in Table 5.2. Mix phenol red and calcium chloride in a separate bag, and record your observations. Finally, mix sodium bicarbonate and calcium chloride without any phenol red, and again record your observations.

Repeat the original process, but starting with a mixture of two substances as shown in Table 5.3. Record your observations in the appropriate columns, and then add the final substance to each mixture as specified in the table. Answer the following questions.

1. Which combination is necessary for the formation of a precipitate?
2. Which combination(s) is(are) exothermic (the temperature rises)?
3. Which combination(s) is(are) endothermic (the temperature drops)?
4. Is a precipitate formed as a result of mixing two powders, a powder and phenol red, or the two solutions?

Table 5.3 Observations of Mixing a Mixture with a Single Component

Sodium Bicarbonate, Phenol Red	Calcium Chloride, Phenol Red	Calcium Chloride, Sodium Bicarbonate	Calcium Chloride	Sodium Bicarbonate	Phenol Red	Color	Temperature ↑ *Indicates Rise* ↓ *Indicates Loss*	Appearance *(e.g., Gases, Precipitates)*
✓			✓					
	✓			✓				
		✓			✓			

5. Is gas formed as a result of mixing the two powders, a powder and phenol red, or the two solutions? Explain your answer.

5.7 Writing Clear Procedures

In September 1999, the Mars Global Surveyor, a $125 million NASA spacecraft, disappeared as it was about to enter orbit around the red planet. When an investigation was performed, it was learned that Lockheed Martin Corporation, the company that built the spacecraft, had programmed it using pounds of thrust, a customary or English system of measuring force, while the navigators at Jet Propulsion Laboratory were assuming it was programmed in newtons, a metric unit of measuring thrust. This major loss highlighted the need of scientists and engineers to communicate in clear and unambiguous terms. The following activities help students learn the difference between ambiguous and unambiguous procedures and observations.

ACTIVITY 5.7.1 *Assembling a Peanut Butter and Jelly Sandwich*

Tell your students to write instructions for the construction of a peanut butter and jelly sandwich. Collect their papers, and select a few for illustration. Read their instructions, and follow them in a manner consistent with the writing, not necessarily with the intent of the author. For example:

Student instruction: Place a dinner plate on a flat table surface.
Your response: Place the plate upside down on the table.

Student instruction: Take two pieces of bread from the loaf.
Your response: Grab two pieces of bread through the wall of the bag.

Student instruction: Put peanut butter on the bread.
Your response: Place the unopened container of peanut butter on the slice of bread.

Student instruction: Spread the peanut butter on the bread with the knife.
Your response: Hold the blade and spread the peanut butter with the handle.

Student instruction: Spread jelly on the other slice of bread.
Your response: Spread jelly on the crust of the other slice.

Student instruction: Place the two pieces of bread together.
Your response: Place the two pieces together, but with the peanut butter and jelly on the outsides.

Use this humorous activity to illustrate the importance of writing instructions or recording observations in a precise and unambiguous manner. You may wish to share the following set of more precise procedures with your students:

1. Place a plate on a table with the concave side facing up.
2. Gently hold a loaf of bread on the table with your nondominant hand.
3. Using your dominant hand, twist the tie-wire counterclockwise until it is completely unwound.
4. Using your dominant hand, remove the tie, and place it on the table.
5. Using your dominant hand, remove the second and third slices of bread from the sack through the opening.
6. Lay both pieces of bread flat on the plate.
7. Grasp the jar of peanut butter with your nondominant hand.
8. Place the palm of your nondominant hand on the side of an unopened jar.
9. Grasp the lid of the jar with your dominant hand, and twist the cap in a counterclockwise direction until the jar opens, and set the cap down on the table.
10. Release your dominant hand, and use it to grasp the handle of the knife and dip the blade into the peanut butter, scooping out approximately 2 tablespoons of peanut butter.

11. Spread the peanut butter that is now on the knife blade as evenly as possible onto the upper surface of one slice of bread.
12. Repeat steps 7 to 11, substituting jelly for peanut butter and applying jelly to the exposed face of the second slice of bread.
13. Place the faces of the bread together with the peanut butter and jelly sides in the middle.

ACTIVITY 5.7.2 *Writing Unambiguous Procedures*

Pierre Fermat (1601–1665) was one of the most famous number theorists who ever lived, but unfortunately he was not a great communicator and published only one mathematical paper in his entire life. One of Fermat's most famous unpublished works is known as Fermat's Last Theorem. It states that

$$x^n + y^n = z^n$$

has no nonzero integer solutions for *x, y,* and *z* when $n > 2$. Fermat wrote, "I have discovered a truly remarkable proof which this margin is too small to contain." But he never documented his proof, and for centuries mathematicians have been seeking to rediscover it. Scientists, like mathematicians, need to document their work and share it with others. They need to clearly explain their observations, experimental procedures, and findings.

In this activity you will repeat the process in the preceding activity, although you will be writing instructions for one of the following: (1) putting on a jacket, (2) shuffling a deck of cards, or (3) drawing a map to your home. Your directions should be unambiguous so that they can be followed without any assumptions.

5.8 Using History to Teach Scientific Methods

Isaac Newton, one of the most influential physicists of all time, said: "If I have seen farther than other men, it is because I have stood upon the shoulders of giants." Newton, like all other scientists, did not make his discoveries in a vacuum but relied heavily on the methodologies, data, and conclusions of others who had gone before him.

Although educators often do a good job introducing their students to the conclusions of scientists, most do not take time to introduce the methodologies and thought processes that lead to these conclusions. Unfortunately this may lead students to believe that science is merely a set of conclusions rather than a vital endeavor of discovery.

An apprentice electrician learns the trade not by merely analyzing wiring diagrams or finished circuits but by watching and imitating the procedures practiced by a master electrician. In a similar manner, a surgical intern learns surgery not by looking at the results of a successful surgery but by accompanying an experienced surgeon through diagnostic and surgical procedures. To learn science, students need to observe not only the conclusions of scientific research but also the processes that lead to these conclusions. In the activities that follow, students are led through historical accounts of major discoveries and must learn to ask and answer appropriate questions the way the original scientists did.

ACTIVITY 5.8.1 *Tracking Down the Cause of Beriberi Disease*

I suggest that the teacher read the narrations and questions and ask for student responses. The questions are designed to reflect those raised by the original researchers.

Narration 1: The Republic of Indonesia encompasses the world's largest archipelago, a chain of islands on the equator north of Australia, stretching one-eighth of the earth's circumference. Indonesia is the fifth most populated country in the world and was the largest Dutch colony before it gained its independence in 1949. In 1602 (eighteen years before the *Mayflower* sailed to America), Dutch merchants formed the Dutch East Indies Company to protect a lucrative trade that they had established with the people of those islands. The Dutch who came to live or trade in the Indonesian archipelago soon learned of numerous diseases never seen in their native Holland. One of the most famous diseases was beriberi, an often fatal condition marked by extreme weakness. The Dutch wanted to find the cause of this dreaded disease so they might also be able to find a cure.

By the mid-nineteenth century, French scientist Louis Pasteur had demonstrated that fermentation (the production of alcohol in aging plant material) and putrefaction (the rotting of food) were caused by microscopic organisms in the air. The work of Pasteur and others led to the establishment of germ theory, which suggests that many diseases are caused by microorganisms. The Dutch East Indies Company was aware of Pasteur's work and commissioned a team of scientists to go to the archipelago to identify the germ causing beriberi. Assume that you were one of the researchers on this team as you address the following questions.

Question: What is the research question that must be answered?

Note to teacher: Research begins with a research question or problem. Just as a golfer needs to see the flag of the next hole before teeing off, a researcher needs to develop a research question before initiating research. In projects like this, students often raise questions that are too specific. For example, their first question might be, "Is beriberi caused by mosquito bites?" or "Is it transmitted through the water?" Guide your students to ask more general questions so they can gather sufficient data to proceed.

Possible Student Responses
- What is the germ that causes beriberi?
- What is the cause of beriberi?

Narration 2: In the late 1800s, the Dutch research team arrived in Java, the most heavily populated island of the Indonesian archipelago. Before the team could find the germ responsible for beriberi, it was first necessary to collect more data and make more observations.

Question: What additional observations would you need to make if you were a member of this research team?

Possible Student Responses
- What are the symptoms of beriberi?
- What are the characteristics of those who have beriberi and the characteristics of those who do not have beriberi?

- Where is beriberi most common?
- Is beriberi correlated with any environmental conditions such as water supply, sanitation, light, or something else?

Narration 3: The Dutch researchers noticed that beriberi is accompanied by muscle weakness, weight loss, nervous disorders, and ultimately paralysis and death. They found that beriberi was common on Java, the heavily populated island that was the seat of the colonial government. They looked for correlations between beriberi and various environmental factors (sanitation, water quality, air quality, light intensity, and others) but found none.

Question: The research team was commissioned to find the germ that caused beriberi. What would you do try to find the germ?

Note to teacher: Students should see the need for a control in both observation and experimentation. For example, it is not sufficient to look at the body fluids of sick people alone, because there is no basis of comparison and no way of concluding if something is abnormal unless you first establish what "normal" is.

Possible Student Responses
- Compare the body fluids and tissues of healthy people with those who have beriberi.
- Examine under a microscope the saliva, blood, and urine of diseased patients.

Narration 4: Using microscopes, the research team observed the blood, urine, and saliva of diseased individuals but found no germs. Finally, after nine months, they left their youngest member, Christiaan Eijkman, in charge of the tiny research station and went home to Holland. Eijkman continued his research for 10 years.

Question: If you were Christiaan Eijkman, what would your next step be?

Note to teacher: Students often think that if an experiment does not go as planned, it is a failure. Thomas Edison, perhaps the world's greatest inventor, had numerous "failed experiments" in his efforts to invent a light bulb, but said, "I have not failed. I just found 10,000 ways that won't work."

Edison did not view negative results with distain and said, "I am not discouraged, because every wrong attempt discarded is another step forward."

Possible Student Responses

- Collect more data. Make more observations.
- Determine if there are other organisms that demonstrate beriberi characteristics.

Narration 5: Eijkman continued to collect more data on the characteristics of beriberi and those who had it. While working at the research station, Eijkman noticed that some of the chickens living at the research station contracted beriberi-like symptoms. Many of the chickens were sick for several months, and some died, while others recovered. Eijkman tried to correlate the onset of the sickness with environmental variables and noticed that the chickens got sick only after a shipment of their red rice failed to arrive, and they were fed higher-grade polished white rice instead. (In nature, rice is covered by a red or brown husk. Polishing removes the husk and allows rice to be stored much longer with a lesser risk of spoilage.) When the superintendent of the research station noticed that they were being fed polished white rice, he reordered a shipment of unhusked red rice to reduce his costs. Eijkman noticed that the health of the chickens recovered after they were fed the unhusked rice. Most people would have shrugged off this observation, but Eijkman recognized its significance. As Thomas Edison said, "The eye sees a great many things, but the average brain records very few of them." Eijkman did not have an "average brain."

Question: What could cause the chickens to recover when fed the brown rice?

Possible Student Responses

- There may have been a germ in the white rice that was causing the sickness, and this germ was not present in the red rice.
- Perhaps beriberi is not caused by a germ but by a lack of something that exists in unhusked rice.

Narration 6: Eijkman was not certain that the symptoms exhibited by the sick chickens were due

to beriberi but decided to investigate further. He noticed that chickens at the research station survived almost entirely on a diet of rice and determined to see if there might be a link between diet and the disease. Eijkman examined health reports from Indonesian prisons and noticed that beriberi was reported in 34 of 63 prisons where polished rice was served, but was rarely reported among 27 other prisons where red, unhusked rice was served. The prisoners, like the chickens at his research station, survived on a diet consisting almost entirely of rice.

Question: What can you hypothesize about the possible cause of beriberi?

Possible Student Responses

- There is a poison in rice that is countered by an antidote in the husk.
- Beriberi is not caused by a germ or a poison, but rather by the lack of some substance found in unhusked rice.

Narration 7: Eijkman hypothesized that beriberi was not caused by germs but rather by toxins in the polished rice that were checked by antidote substances in the unhusked rice. He designed an experiment to find the toxin.

Question: How would you design an experiment to find a toxin in the white rice?

Note to the teacher: Students should mention two treatments: one with the presumed toxin, and one without it (*control*). Emphasize the need for controls when designing an experiment. Without a control, it is impossible to interpret the results. Emphasize that it is necessary to change only one variable at time. If two or three potential toxins are tested at a time, it will be unclear which one has caused the problem.

Possible Student Response

- Separate the components of rice, and feed each to a different group of chickens.

Narration 8: In his experiment, Eijkman separated healthy chickens into three groups and fed one group only whole grain rice, a second group only rice with the husk removed, and a

Table 5.4 Results of Christiaan Eijkman's Experiment

Group	Diet	Result
Group 1	Unhusked whole grain rice	Remained healthy
Group 2	Rough rice: rice with husk removed	Remained healthy
Group 3	Polished rice with husk and silver skin (pericarpium) removed	Demonstrated beriberi-like symptoms

third group only rice from which both the outer husk and the inner silver skin membrane were removed. Table 5.4 shows the results of his study.

Question: What can you conclude from Eijkman's data?

Possible Student Response

- Beriberi is not caused by a germ or toxin but by the absence of something found in the silver skin.

Narration 9: Eijkman's research indicated that there is a vital substance in the pericarpium (silver skin) of rice that prevents the onset of beriberi. Later this substance became known as a "vital-amine," or vitamin. Although the specific chemical was not yet identified, the concept of vitamins was introduced for the first time. The inspector-general of public health in the Dutch East Indies ordered that all prisoners receive unhusked rice, and within a very short time beriberi disappeared from the prison system. It was later shown that this same vital substance could be found in barley, prompting the Japanese navy to include barley with polished rice in the food given to sailors, thereby eliminating beriberi from their navy.

Eijkman originally set out to find the germ responsible for beriberi but instead discovered that the disease was caused by the absence of a "vital substance" (vitamin). In 1929, Christiaan Eijkman was awarded the Nobel Prize in physiology and medicine for the discovery of vitamins, a group

of organic substances essential in small quantities for animal nutrition and metabolism. Years later, Casimir Funk, a Polish emigrant to the United States, identified Eijkman's vital material as thiamine, or vitamin B_1.

Eijkman's research can be used to help us understand other historical occurrences as well. As early as the fifth century B.C., Hippocrates described a condition now known as scurvy, characterized by bleeding gums, hemorrhaging, and death. Scurvy became a dreaded disease among all who embarked on long voyages. On one of Christopher Columbus's voyages, some Portuguese sailors developed scurvy and requested to be dropped off on one of the newly discovered islands so they could die on land rather than at sea. On a later voyage, Columbus returned to the island and found the men alive and healthy, and named the island Curaçao, meaning "cure." In the middle of the eighteenth century, the Scottish physician James Lind noted that sailors given a diet rich in citrus fruit rapidly recovered from the dreaded scourge. In response to Lind's work, the British navy soon required crews to carry citrus such as lime on all voyages, and the British sailors thus acquired the nickname *limeys*.

Question: Is there any relationship between these cures for scurvy and the cure that Eijkman found for beriberi?

Possible Student Response

- Yes. Scurvy, like beriberi, is due to a vitamin deficiency (lack of vitamin C). Prior to refrigeration, sailors survived on diets consisting of fish, salted meats, and hardtack, but no vitamin-rich fruits or vegetables. Columbus's abandoned crew members were able to eat vitamin-rich fruits on Curaçao, prompting their recovery from scurvy. In a similar manner, James Lind's patients recovered because of the vitamin C in their citrus-rich diets.

ACTIVITY 5.8.2 *The Scientific Method Seen in Other Discoveries*

A review of Activity 5.7.1 shows that Christiaan Eijkman did not follow the steps of the scientific method in rigid order, but rather used scientific methods as they were appropriate. Although each path to discovery is unique, just as each scientist is unique, methods of science are found in each discovery. Select one of the discoveries below, and research how the discovery was made. Identify the (1) research question, (2) key observations, (3) hypotheses, (4) experiment, and (5) conclusions that were made.

Insulin—Frederick Banting

Pulsars—Jocelyn Bell

Nylon—Wallace Carothers

Electron, isotopes—J. J. Thompson

Other galaxies—Edwin Hubble

Polio vaccine—Jonas Salk

DNA—James Watson and Francis Crick

Electromagnetism—Hans Christiaan Orsted

5.9 Indirect Evidence: "Black Box" Experiments

In science texts you will find diagrams showing the cross-section of the Earth (Figure 5.13A), electron orbital clouds (Figure 5.13B), and the position of our solar system within in the Milky Way Galaxy (Figure 5.13C). Most of us accept such diagrams without asking how we know what the core of the earth looks like because no one has ever been there, or how we can diagram the structure of an atom if it is too small to be seen, or how we can determine our position in the Milky Way if it is impossible to

move outside of it to get a view. These are but of few of the many instances in which scientists must draw conclusions on the basis of indirect evidence. Experiments in which the researcher can neither see nor measure the object of interest are referred to as "black box" experiments. In such instances, researchers must make inferences from inputs, outputs, and other indirect evidence.

ACTIVITY 5.9.1 *Determining the Contents of a "Black Box"*

Materials: shoe boxes, duct tape, adhesive (panel adhesive, hot glue, etc.), 2" 3 2" board and saw or children's blocks, marble

Teacher preparation: Ask students to bring shoeboxes to class. Using a wood saw, cut 2 in. lengths from a 2" × 2" board (available at most hardware or home improvement stores). Using paneling adhesive, hot glue, or similar adhesive, position the blocks in the base of each box according to the plans shown in Figure 5.14A. Place one marble or ball bearing in each box, and seal the box with duct tape. Mark the design pattern on the lid using a code so students will not know the design but you will be able to check without opening the box. Alternatively, students can prepare these boxes by gluing children's building blocks or other similar objects to the floors of the boxes. Distribute one box to each lab group.

Student participation: Determine the internal structure of your box by evidence (sound or vibrations, for example) produced by the moving marble. You may use any technique you wish

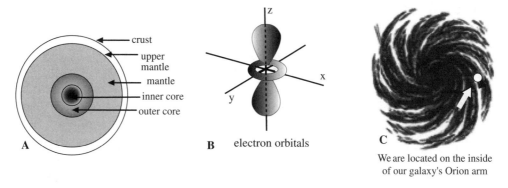

Figure 5.13 Common Drawings of Things That Have Never Been Seen

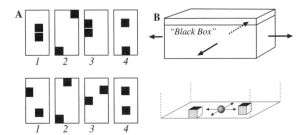

Figure 5.14 Black Box Experiment

as long as it does not damage the box or break the seal (Figure 5.14B). Draw a diagram indicating where you believe the blocks are located. Compare your diagram with the correct one as recorded by your teacher. Were you able to determine the positions of the hidden blocks? If so, you did so on the basis of indirect evidence because you never opened the box.

ACTIVITY 5.9.2 *Determining the Structure of the Atom with Indirect Evidence*

Materials: Pegboard, dowels, marbles, graph paper, and rulers.

In 1897, the English physicist Joseph John Thomson confirmed the existence of the electron, a fundamental particle of matter with a negative charge. Thomson believed that an atom was a uniform sphere of positive matter in which negative electrons were embedded, somewhat like raisins in a bowl of pudding (Figure 5.15A). In his model, the positive and negative charges were evenly distributed in space. Consequently a particle with positive charge traveling through the space occupied by the negative and positive charges would be traveling through a "neutral zone" because the

effects of the positive and negative charges would cancel and the particle would experience no unbalanced force to move it one way or another. In other words, a positive particle would move straight through the "plum pudding" model, experiencing no deflection.

In the early part of the twentieth century, English physicist Ernest Rutherford investigated the structure of the atom by shooting alpha particles (positively charged helium ions; helium nuclei) through very thin foils of gold and other metals. Most of the incoming alpha particles passed through the foil either undeflected or with only a slight deflection, as would be predicted by the Thomson model. However, there were some startling occurrences in which the alpha particles were deflected at large angles and, at times, straight back in the direction from which they had come (Figure 5.15B). Rutherford explained these results by proposing that the atom is mostly empty space (which explains why most of the alpha particles pass through undeflected) with positive charges concentrated in a dense central core (which explains why positively charged alpha particles are occasionally deflected or reflected).

Rutherford never saw an atom but inferred its structure by observing the interaction of alpha particles with atoms. Rutherford's classic black box experiments revolutionized our understanding of the atom. The following black box experiment imitates Rutherford's original experiment. Students are asked to determine the position of pegs ("nuclei") in a hidden pegboard by studying their interaction with marbles ("alpha particles").

Students should work in pairs for this activity. Obtain three pegs and a pegboard that has at least 2 holes on a side (minimum of 25 holes per board, approximately 3 cm apart). Wooden pegs may be made by cutting and sanding dowels that have a diameter similar to the holes in the pegboard. The pegs should be long enough that marbles can freely move under the apparatus when set up as shown in Figure 5.16A. While one student looks away, the other places three pegs randomly in pegboard holes and turns the board over, placing it so that the pegs are lying on a flat surface and the board is parallel to the desk surface. A sheet

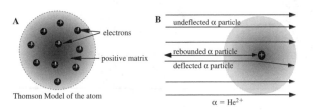

Figure 5.15 (A) Thomson Model of an Atom. (B) Rutherford Experiment.

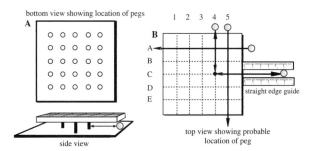

Figure 5.16 Determining the Structure of the Atom

of graph paper should be placed on the board to hide the holes. Without looking under the board to see the position of the pegs, the second student should now roll marbles under the pegboard at selected intervals and record on the graph paper the original path of the marble and any resulting deflections. To ensure that marbles travel straight, they should be launched between two straight edges (Figure 5.16B). This activity should be repeated for at least two adjacent sides of the pegboard. If the ball is deflected, it indicates that there is a peg in that row or column. Analyze the results to identify the positions of the pegs. Repeat the procedure until you can accurately determine and record the positions of all three pegs.

5.10 Evaluating Hypotheses

Perhaps the most prodigious inventor of all time was Thomas Alva Edison, holder of 1093 patents and inventor of the first reliable electric light bulb (Figure 5.17), movie camera, and sound recording device (phonograph). Although the public remembers Edison for his numerous inventions that revolutionized the way we live and work, scientists remember him primarily for the development of the first industrial research laboratory.

Edison assembled a wide array of chemists, physicists, inventors, machinists, botanists, materials experts, and other professionals from around the world to work at his laboratories in Menlo Park and East Orange, New Jersey. In Edison's laboratories, everyone had to be a team player. Edison

Figure 5.17 Thomas Edison

and his research associates set research agendas, determined job descriptions, worked together toward common goals, and in a short time introduced the world to a dazzling array of useful inventions. Today Edison's model is used worldwide as engineers and scientists work together with common objectives. The power of scientific teamwork was profoundly illustrated when NASA's (National Aeronautics and Space Administration) team of engineers and scientists landed men on the Moon, and when a nationwide team of biologists announced the sequencing of the human genome. The activity that follows illustrates the value of teamwork and the need to reevaluate hypotheses in light of new data.

ACTIVITY 5.19.1 *Tangrams and Team-work*
Teacher preparation: This activity must be prepared in advance by the teacher. Download the tangram sheet from the sourcebook Web site *(sciencesourcebook.com)* or make your own using the scale diagram in Figure 5.18, making certain each piece is labeled appropriately. Cut the shapes as shown and make a set of five envelopes for each team as follows: (a) I,E,H; (b) A,A,A,C; (c) A,J; (d) D,F; (e) B,C,F,G. Indicate the contents of each envelope by writing the components on

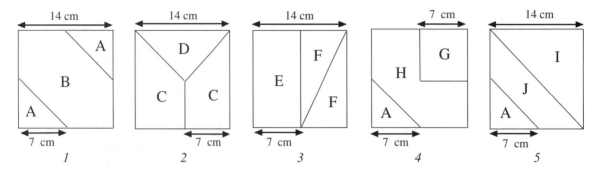

Figure 5.18 Tangrams

the outside. Separate students into teams of five, and read the following instructions.

- Each team member gets one of the envelopes.
- Each team must assemble five separate squares from the pieces provided.
- Each team member must construct a square. You cannot work on others' squares.
- You may not talk or make gestures.
- You cannot take any pieces from another student; you can only give pieces.

Then ask these questions:

1. What does this teach about scientific teamwork?
2. What does this teach about the scientific method?

Note to teacher: Although a variety of squares can be made from the pieces of paper provided, not all are part of the final five-square solution. Therefore, if one student constructs a square that is not part of the solution and is unwilling to break his or her square and distribute the pieces to team mates, the team can never construct all five squares. Participants must keep their attention on the group goal of constructing all five squares and be willing to give up their own work to achieve the final team goal.

This exercise is an excellent tool in teaching teamwork, a necessary element in any modern research laboratory. Students must look at the needs of the group, not just their own needs, if their team is to be successful in achieving the final goal. They must pay careful attention to the needs

of others and be willing to disassemble their own squares to provide pieces needed by others.

This exercise is also an excellent way to introduce the need to maintain flexibility when developing hypotheses. Although a hypothesis may appear to explain experimental results, it may have to be replaced by a different hypothesis that is more consistent with the data. Students who are unwilling to disassemble their own "hypotheses" (in this case, the squares they have made) will be unable to reach a final conclusion.

Answers to Chapter Activities

5.1.1–5.1.3 The activities in this section are designed to develop a need to know. Although this is difficult to quantify, the teacher will know when it has occurred by student attitudes and the questions they raise

5.2.1 This activity has been used throughout the years to encourage students to make careful and comprehensive observations. By observing both the unlit and the burning candle, students can see the influence of the flame. Table 5.1 is a partial list of the types of observations that can be made. You may wish to award points on the quantity of observations, detracting points for statements that are not observations (inferences, inaccurate observations, irrelevant comments.)

5.2.2 Students should generate a wide variety of questions. The following information may help you prepare for such questions. The cotton wicks of some new candles are dipped in paraffin, while others are not. If there is no paraffin in the wick, it will burn rather rapidly until the heat from the flame starts to melt the paraffin below it. The wick is a string, and liquid paraffin is drawn up it and into the flame by capillary action. The light and heat produced by the combustion of the wick are insignificant compared to the light and heat produced by the combustion of the paraffin. A thin candle will burn much more rapidly than a thick candle because it runs out of fuel more quickly. Similarly, a candle will burn down much more rapidly if the melted paraffin is allowed to drain out of the reservoir away from the wick.

Paraffin has a rather low melting point (53°C) and becomes a liquid as the flame approaches. Liquid paraffin flows into the well created by the flame and then moves up the wick by capillary action. As the liquid paraffin approaches the flame, it vaporizes. The flash point of paraffin is 198°C. When it reaches this temperature it combusts:

$$2C_{30}H_{62} + 91O_2(g) \rightarrow 60CO_2(g) + 62H_2O(g)$$

Oxygen and paraffin are consumed, and carbon dioxide and water vapor are produced. The condensate that students observe forming on the sides of a cooled beaker placed over the candle is from the water formed during combustion. The carbon dioxide will dissolve into the bromthymol blue droplets placed on the funnel. Dissolved carbon dioxide reacts with water to form carbonic acid (H_2CO_3):

$$CO_2 + H_2O \rightarrow H_2CO_3$$

Bromthymol blue turns greenish as the pH drops due to the formation of carbonic acid. The combustion requires oxygen, and thus the flame will be extinguished if all of the oxygen is consumed. The length of time that a candle will burn when placed under a beaker is directly proportional to the volume of the air trapped in the beaker. Thus, students should notice that the flame burns twice as long when placed under a 1000 mL beaker as when placed under a 500 mL beaker.

Another common product of combustion is soot, a black powdery form of carbon that rises up in fine particles within the flames and smoke. Soot collects on glassware that is held immediately above the flame. Soot production is more rapid when there is less oxygen, and therefore students will notice the rate of soot deposition increases rapidly as oxygen is depleted when a beaker is lowered partially over the flame. Soot and unburned hydrocarbons are released in the smoke of the flame, making it possible to relight a candle by igniting the smoke. It is generally possible to relight a smoking candle from a distance of about 1 cm.

5.3.1   Observations may include only those things that are actually observed, such as color, shape, and height. Students should not make inferences, such as growth, root structure, or type of "plant."

5.3.2   Observations may include only those things that are actually observed, such as color, appearance, shape, and movement. Students should not make inferences such as the nature of the raisidia, the composition of the liquid, or the composition of the bubbles.

5.4.1   It is likely that each group will derive a different ranking, and these differences can provide an interesting platform for discussion. During the discussion phase,

make certain that each team provides a rationale for its rankings. Often different rankings are a result of different assumptions. Encourage students to state their assumptions and discuss the logic of their responses given these assumptions. Table 5.5 lists potential benefits of the items listed.

5.4.2   Students will explain their drawings using the overhead projector.

5.5.1   Graphing and experimental design:

(a)   (1) pH of water. (2) height of plants. (3) type of plant, age of seeds, temperature, light, soil, etc. (4) Seeds of the same plant were grown in containers that were given water of different pH. (5) The growth of this species is a function of the pH of the water it receives. When pH is too low or too high, growth is little, but when the pH is in an intermediate zone, growth is significant.

(b)   (1) altitude. (2) molecules of ozone destroyed per CFC molecule. (3) source of air, ozone concentration, temperature, light intensity, etc. (4) A series of chambers is established with atmospheric conditions of differing altitudes. An equal amount of chlorofluorocarbon (CFC) is introduced into each, and the level of ozone is measured after a given time. (5) CFCs are stable molecules that served as coolants in air-conditioning units and propellants in aerosol cans. Although CFCs do not interact with ozone at lower elevations, they cause significant degradation at higher elevations. Since ozone protects us by filtering ultraviolet light, such research has led many countries to ban various uses of CFCs.

(c)   (1) voltage. (2) current. (3) resistance, circuit design, etc. (4) The current in a circuit is measured as you increase the voltage. (5) An increase in voltage causes an increase in current. Physicists know this relationship as Ohm's law, $V = IR$.

(d)   (1) year car was manufactured. (2) the concentration of hydrocarbons in the exhaust. (3) make and model of car, manner in which exhaust is measured, etc. (4) The exhaust of new cars is analyzed as the cars roll off the production lines. The average hydrocarbon exhaust data for each production year are plotted. (5) Each year the automobile manufacturer in this study produces cars with lower hydrocarbon emissions.

(e)   (1) wavelength of light. (2) rate of photosynthesis. (3) temperature, type of plant, way in which photosynthesis is measured, etc. (4) Plants are grown in a growth chamber with all conditions being similar except the wavelength of light to which they are exposed. (5) Plants grow fastest in relatively short and long wavelength light, and slower in mid-wavelength light.

(f)   (1) carbon dioxide concentration. (2) rate of photosynthesis. (3) type of light, temperature, humidity, soil moisture, etc. (4) Plants are grown in controlled chambers of differing carbon dioxide concentration. (5) At low and mid-carbon dioxide concentrations, an increase in the carbon dioxide concentration results in an increased rate of photosynthesis, but at high carbon dioxide concentrations, the rate changes little.

Table 5.5 Possible Uses of Items While on the Surface of the Moon

Two 100 kg tanks of oxygen	Oxygen is necessary for respiration. Humans can survive only about 5 minutes without oxygen.
10 L of water	Water is necessary for all biological processes. Without water, humans can survive only about 5 to 9 days.
Stellar map	A stellar map can be used to orient oneself for the journey to the research station.
10 kg dehydrated food	Food is required for energy for the long trek, but some students will note that it will be impossible to eat food unless it can be delivered to the mouth without breaking the seal of the astronaut's suit. Some students may rank this item low, supposing that there will be no way to prepare it outside the pressurized environment of the space capsule.
Solar-powered FM two-way radio	The FM radio can be used to transmit a distress signal to the research station. FM radios, however, transmit only by line of sight, which will be more difficult to obtain on the moon given the greater curvature of the moon's surface. The lack of an atmosphere should not hamper FM transmission because FM signals do not reflect off the ionosphere (which does not exist on the moon) as do AM signals.
50 m of nylon rope	Rope may be useful for climbing or tying things together.
First aid kit	The first aid kit will be of value only if it is designed to be used with space suits. Conventional first aid kits will be useless since astronauts will not be able to open their suits to apply any first aid.
Parachute silk	Due to the lack of atmosphere, the solar radiation on the lighted side of the moon is very intense, and the silk can provide a good shelter from the solar rays.
Life raft	Life rafts often contain compressed carbon dioxide, which may have use as a propellant. The raft can be used to carry other items.
Traditional signal flares	Signal flares can be used to make distress signals. Flares produce their own oxygen and may therefore work in the atmosphere-free environment of the moon.
Two 0.45 caliber pistols	Some students will argue that these can be used for self-propulsion, but they would be of very limited value. Oxygen is released from the chemicals in the gunpowder, allowing the pistols to work on the surface of the moon.
Case of dehydrated milk	This could provide some nutrition if there is a way to mix it and ingest it in the absence of atmospheric pressure.
Portable heating unit	Most portable heating units emit infrared radiation, but unfortunately most of this heat would probably reflect off the surfaces of the space suits and therefore have little effect on keeping the astronauts warm.
Magnetic compass	There are no magnetic poles on the moon, so a magnetic compass would be useless.
Box of matches	Matches require oxygen to burn, and therefore would be useless in the oxygen-free environment of the moon.

(g) (1) number of cigarettes smoked per day. (2) percentage of population with emphysema. (3) This is a study rather than an experiment. Since it is unethical to perform such experiments on humans, one can collect human data only by examining statistics from the population. To minimize the influence of other factors, one could study only individuals from the same gender, occupation, and age. (4) Conduct a survey in which you ask people how many cigarettes they smoke per day on average and whether they have emphysema. (5) Emphysema is a lung disorder in which there is a loss in the oxygen-absorbing air sacs known as alveoli. The data suggest that smoking causes emphysema.

(h) (1) height of the forest tree canopy. (2) number of bird species identified. (3) type of forest, location, climate, technique for counting species. (4) Identify the number of bird species found within given plot of land. Measure the average height of the forest canopy. Repeat these measurements for other regions within the forest. (5) As a forest matures and the canopy gets higher, it supports a greater diversity of bird species.

5.6.1 Phenol red solution is primarily water, and both calcium chloride and sodium bicarbonate dissolve within it. The dissolution of calcium chloride is an exothermic process and produces heat (temperature rises):

$$CaCl_2 + H_2O \rightarrow Ca^{+2}(aq) + 2Cr(aq) + heat$$

The dissolution of sodium bicarbonate, however, is an endothermic process and consumes heat (temperature falls):

$$NaHCO_3 + H_2O + heat \rightarrow Na^+(aq) + HCO_3^-(aq)$$

The observed temperature changes are due primarily to the interaction of these two reactions. The calcium ions then react with the bicarbonate ions to produce a white precipitate (calcium carbonate), water, and carbon dioxide gas. Carbon dioxide is the gas that causes the plastic bag to expand. Calcium carbonate is the precipitate that settles in the bottom of the bag.

$$Ca^{2+}(aq) + 2HCO_3^-(aq) \rightarrow CaCO_3(s) + H_2O(l) + CO_2(g)$$

The carbon dioxide produced in this reaction reacts with water to form carbonic acid (H_2CO_3), which turns phenol red from red to yellow.

$$CO_2 + H_2O \rightarrow H_2CO_3$$

As a result of their research, students should be able to isolate the variables responsible for different phenomenon and answer the questions:

(1) Calcium ions and bicarbonate ions react to produce calcium bicarbonate, a white precipitate.
(2) The dissolution of calcium chloride in water is exothermic.
(3) The dissolution of sodium bicarbonate in water is endothermic.
(4) The precipitate (calcium carbonate) is formed by mixing two solutions (sodium bicarbonate and calcium chloride solutions).
(5) Carbon dioxide is produced only when the two solutions are mixed.

5.7.1 After two or three tries, students should be able to write unambiguous instructions for assembling a peanut butter and jelly sandwich.

5.7.2 Students should be able to write unambiguous procedures for each of the activities.

5.8.1 This is an interactive discussion. No written response is required.

5.8.2 Students will write a history of one of these great discoveries, clearly identifying the (1) research question, (2) key observations, (3) hypotheses, (4) experiment, and (5) conclusions that were made.

5.9.1 After they make their observations, students should draw diagrams of the contents, including the positions and relative sizes of each object in the box, and then copy these diagrams to transparencies so they can be projected and discussed by the class. Students should explain the various techniques used in the developing their hypotheses. Some students may determine the center of gravity by balancing the box on their finger and then making inferences about the distribution of masses within. Other students may tilt the box gently back and forth and listen for when the marbles hit obstructions. Still others may shake, rotate, or slide the box to gather information. Following the discussion, you may wish to open the boxes to show students their internal design.

5.9.2 Students should correctly locate the position of the pegs ("nuclei") on the graph paper by noting the rows and columns in which marbles ("alpha particles") are deflected or reflected.

5.10.1 (1) This activity shows that researchers must work together to solve problems. When an individual is unwilling to share his or her information with others, the team goal cannot be achieved. Individuals should look at the needs of the team, and not just at their own needs. (2) The scientific method is not linear. Often the researcher has to redesign experiments or reevaluate hypotheses in the light of new data. Researchers must be flexible and willing to reassess their ideas in the light of empirical data.

Chapter Six

Developing Scientific Reasoning Skills

For the Teacher 106

6.1 Levels of Reasoning 108

6.2 Inductive Reasoning 111

6.3 Deductive Reasoning 116

6.4 Lateral Thinking 121

Answers to Chapter Activities 122

For the Teacher

Although the goal of education is to develop thinkers and lifelong learners, few classroom activities encourage students to monitor or improve their own thinking and learning processes. *Metacognition,* or thinking about and regulating one's own thought processes, is a skill that differentiates expert from novice learners.[1] Expert learners employ effective learning techniques, monitor their own learning, and develop and adapt strategies to become more effective learners. The activities in this chapter require students to think about their own thinking, with the goal of developing better metacognitive skills and becoming more effective learners.

Novice learners rarely evaluate their comprehension, examine the quality of their work, or make adjustments in their learning strategies. They are generally satisfied with superficial explanations and do not strive to make connections or understand the relevance of material learned. By contrast, expert learners think about their thinking, know when they don't understand something,

reflect on the quality of their work, make revisions in learning strategies as they proceed, search for deeper explanations, and strive to understand how concepts are interrelated.

Metacognition involves the *development, implementation,* and *evaluation* of a learning plan. During *development,* learners establish goals (what needs to be learned and to what depth), determine relevant prior knowledge and skills, define task requirements (time, schedule, evaluation criteria), and select resources (books, peers, authorities, electronic references) that will assist them in reaching their goals. During *implementation,* learners apply strategies (e.g., mnemonics, induction, deduction, concept mapping, outlining, dimensional analysis, elaboration, pacing), *evaluate* the effectiveness of these strategies (using formative assessments including self-questioning, checklists, outlines, and notes), and modify their plans as necessary. As individuals become more skilled with metacognitive strategies, they gain confidence and become independent learners, determining and pursuing their own intellectual needs.

This chapter focuses on the identification and development of essential reasoning skills, and much of the rest of this book deals with specific strategies. Teachers should implement learning activities that develop these skills and instruments that assess them. As students learn to identify and develop their reasoning skills, they become more effective and independent learners and better able to use the strategies introduced throughout this book.

Inductive reasoning (drawing conclusions from the natural world through observation and experimentation) is a process of making generalizations from specific information. By contrast, *deductive reasoning* (deriving testable predictions about specific cases from established principles) is a process of making specific conclusions by the application of general principles. Scientists and others employ both in their work and everyday lives.

In an effort to categorize reasoning and learning skills, a committee of psychologists and educators, directed by Benjamin Bloom, developed a taxonomy of affective, psychomotor, and cognitive skills.[2] The taxonomy of cognitive objectives (*knowledge, comprehension, application, analysis, synthesis, evaluation*) became widely used by educators and curriculum developers (Figure 6.1A). Recently, experts have proposed modifications (Figure 6.1B), but although I see merit in the revised classification, the activities in this book use the original format because of its familiarity and widespread acceptance in literature and practice.[3] Although designed as a hierarchy, the elements are not strictly hierarchical in practice, so the position within the hierarchy should not be overemphasized. Bloom's taxonomy gives us the opportunity to examine our teaching emphasis, and it is noted

that most secondary instruction focuses on basic knowledge and comprehension and gives minimal attention to the development of higher-order reasoning skills. Fortunately, the sciences provide an environment that is conducive to the development of these skills, and many teachers capitalize on this to help develop critical thinkers.

Expert learners use metacognitive strategies to monitor and improve their learning, employ inductive and deductive logic to make discoveries, and exhibit knowledge, comprehension, application, analysis, synthesis, and evaluation as they study and work. In addition, they demonstrate critical thinking, creativity, fluency, flexibility, originality, lateral thinking, transferability, and elaboration.

Critical thinking is the process of analyzing and evaluating information on the basis of evidence and logic. Critical thinkers evaluate statements, opinions, and hypotheses by collecting, analyzing, and evaluating data, issues, and arguments from different sources and perspectives. Critical thinking is the theme of Chapter Seven and is used to identify misconceptions in science.

Creativity may involve insight, inventiveness, imagination, innovation, originality, initiative, and resourcefulness to develop new hypotheses, products, or ways of thinking. It is difficult to teach creativity, but teachers can provide activities that help develop the requisite skills of *fluency* (the ability to generate many ideas), *flexibility* (the ability to see things from different perspectives), and *elaboration* (the ability to build on existing ideas. Fluent individuals generally consider many options and "think outside the box." Brainstorming activities, such as those introduced in Chapter Five, are helpful for accomplishing this. Flexible thinkers can analyze problems and issues from a variety of perspectives.

This chapter provides *lateral thinking* exercises, designed to help students approach problems from a variety of perspectives. Finally, much emphasis is given in this book (and in the companion books *Hands-On Physics Activities with Applications* and *Hands-On Chemistry Activities with Real-Life Applications*) to *transferability*—the aptitude for applying ideas across a wide variety of contexts.[4]

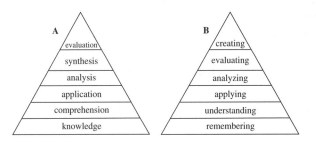

Figure 6.1 (A) Bloom's Taxonomy, 1956. (B) Revised Taxonomy, 2001

6.1 Levels of Reasoning

Any discussion of thought processes requires first agreeing on terms and interpretations. Perhaps the most widely used classification of human thought is one known as Bloom's taxonomy. Benjamin Bloom and his team of researchers wrote extensively on the subject, particularly on six basic levels of cognitive outcomes they identified: knowledge, comprehension, application, analysis, synthesis, and evaluation. Bloom's taxonomy is hierarchical, with knowledge, comprehension, and application as fundamental levels, and analysis, synthesis, and evaluation as advanced levels. When educators refer to higher-level reasoning, they are generally referring to analysis, synthesis, and evaluation.

According to Bloom's team, *knowledge* (remembering previously learned material) represents the most basic learning outcome, and *comprehension* (the ability to gain meaning) represents the basic level of understanding. *Application* (the ability to use learned material) is a more advanced skill because it requires both knowledge and comprehension. *Analysis* (the examination of structure and relationships) is the most basic of the higher-order skills and is required for *synthesis* (the ability to assemble ideas to create new patterns, ideas, or structures). *Evaluation* (assessing merit) is the highest level because it relies on elements of knowledge, comprehension, application, analysis, and synthesis. Table 6.1 summarizes the key concepts in Bloom's taxonomy (Figure 6.1).

Table 6.2 lists verbs commonly associated with each of the levels of reasoning. This table is helpful when constructing questions to target different skills, but students should realize that words alone do not ensure a given skill.

The following questions from a physics test on motion represent all six levels of Bloom's taxonomy. A rationale is provided for each classification, but alternative classifications are possible depending on the prior knowledge of the students. For example, the comprehension question could be considered a knowledge question if students had memorized a textbook explanation. After reviewing the physics questions on motion below, classify the chemistry, biology, and earth science questions. The questions are written so each set has representatives from all six levels of Bloom's taxonomy. Note that it is not necessary to understand the content of these questions in order to identify the level of reasoning they represent.

Knowledge: Write the formula that describes the motion of a falling object near the Earth's surface. *Rationale:* This requires recalling the memorized formula.

Comprehension: Explain why objects fall more slowly on the Moon than on Earth.

Table 6.1 Bloom's Taxonomy of Cognitive Skills

Knowledge: Remembering and recalling specifics (terminology, facts, figures), ways and means (trends, classification, criteria, methodology), and abstractions (principles, generalizations, theories)

Comprehension: Demonstrating understanding by translation (words to numbers, one language to another), interpretation (explaining, summarizing), and extrapolation (making inferences, predicting consequences)

Application: Using facts, techniques, rules, methods, concepts, principles, theories, and laws to solve or resolve problems or issues

Analysis: Examining and breaking information into components to identify facts and hypotheses, distinguish relevant from irrelevant, and understand relationships, structure, and organizational principles

Synthesis: Creating new hypotheses, plans, patterns, solutions, structures, communications, or abstract relationships

Evaluation: Judging the validity and usefulness of hypotheses, theories, statements, reports, solutions, or relationships using criteria, evidence, and logic

Table 6.2 Verbs Commonly Associated with Levels of Reasoning

Knowledge	Comprehension	Application	Analysis	Synthesis	Evaluation
cite	associate	apply	analyze	adapt	appraise
copy	classify	calculate	arrange	assemble	argue
define	convert	chart	categorize	collaborate	assess
describe	describe	choose	classify	compose	conclude
duplicate	differentiate	compute	compare	construct	convince
identify	discuss	construct	contrast	create	criticize
label	distinguish	demonstrate	correlate	design	decide
list	estimate	determine	detect	develop	deduce
match	explain	develop	diagram	devise	defend
memorize	express	discover	differentiate	formulate	determine
name	extend	employ	dissect	generalize	infer
order	group	examine	distinguish	generate	interpret
quote	identify	illustrate	divide	hypothesize	judge
recall	indicate	interview	examine	imagine	justify
recognize	order	modify	experiment	integrate	persuade
record	paraphrase	operate	group	invent	prioritize
recount	predict	practice	identify	modify	rate
repeat	report	prepare	inspect	plan	rank
show	restate	produce	interpret	predict	recommend
specify	retell	relate	inventory	produce	relate
state	review	report	investigate	propose	revise
when	select	show	order	reconstruct	score
what	summarize	sketch	outline	reorganize	support
where	translate	solve	survey	revise	value
who	understand	transfer	test	speculate	validate

Rationale: This requires understanding the difference between the masses of the Moon and Earth and how this affects acceleration.

Application: A baseball falls from a height of 30 m. Ignoring air resistance, calculate the time the ball hits the ground. *Rationale:* This requires applying a kinematics equation to derive the answer to this problem.

Analysis: A bullet is fired from a rifle aimed at the horizon, and at the same time an identical bullet is dropped from the same height as the muzzle of the gun. Ignoring air resistance, compare and contrast the trajectory of both bullets and the time required to hit the ground. *Rationale:* This requires examining the similarities and differences of the trajectories, and distinguishing relevant from irrelevant information to answer the question.

Synthesis: Bowling balls, basketballs, baseballs, golf balls, and Ping-Pong balls fall at the same rate in a vacuum. Develop a hypothesis that predicts the order they will hit the ground if dropped from a height of 1000 m in air. Explain your reasoning. *Rationale:* This question requires generating and substantiating a hypothesis based on established principles, prior knowledge, and experience.

Evaluation: Legend has it that Galileo investigated the motion of falling bodies by dropping cannon balls from the leaning tower of Pisa. In reality, his studies of motion were conducted by rolling objects down inclined planes. Discuss the advantages this method may have held for Galileo. *Rationale:* This requires judging the merits of Galileo's approach using criteria and logic.

ACTIVITY 6.1.1 *Determining Levels of Reasoning Required by Biology Questions*
Classify the biology questions below with the levels of Bloom's taxonomy that they best represent. *Reminder:* It is not necessary to understand the content of these questions in order to identify the level of reasoning they represent.

1. Explain why pea plants served as a good subject for Mendel's work, knowing that peas produce many offspring and have visible traits that exist in only two forms.
2. Design an experiment that is likely to determine the genotype of tall pea plants with colored seeds.
3. Predict the ratio of offspring resulting from the cross of a heterozygous tall plant (Tt) with a homozygous short plant (tt).
4. Mendel did much of his genetics work using pea plants, but in recent years, geneticists turned to yeast (*Saccharomyces cerevisiae*), fruit flies (*Drosophila melanogaster*), and bacteria (*Escherichia coli*) for much of their work. Explain the benefits these organisms provide for modern genetics studies.
5. Examine the following data and determine the likely genotypes of the parent plants. F1 cross yielded:

   27 tall plants with colored seeds, terminal flowers, and yellow pods
   9 tall plants with white seeds, terminal flowers, and yellow pods

   10 short plants with colored seeds, terminal flowers, and yellow pods
   3 short plants with white seeds, terminal flowers, and yellow pods

T-tall	C-colored seeds	A-axial flowers	G-green pods
t-short	c-white	a-terminal flowers	g-yellow pods

6. Define phenotype, genotype, allele, and gene.

ACTIVITY 6.1.2 *Determining Levels of Reasoning Required by Chemistry Questions*
Classify the chemistry questions below with the levels of Bloom's taxonomy that they best represent. *Reminder:* It is not necessary to understand the content of these questions in order to identify the level of reasoning they represent.

1. Which two elements have properties similar to those of calcium: (a) beryllium and barium, (b) potassium and bromine, (c) chromium and molybdenum, (d) sodium and strontium?
2. Examine Table 6.3, and determine which properties are periodic: (1) element, (2) atomic mass, (3) melting point, (4) ionization energy, (5) atomic radius. Explain your answer.
3. Plot atomic radius as a function of atomic number using data in Table 6.3. Predict the shape of an electron affinity versus atomic number graph.

Table 6.3 Which Properties Are Periodic?

1 X	2 (amu)	3 (K)	4 (kJ/mol)	5 (Å)	1 X	2 (amu)	3 (K)	4 (kJ/mol)	5 (Å)
H	1	14	1312	0.32	Na	23	371	496	1.90
He	4	1	2372	0.50	Mg	24	923	738	1.60
Li	7	454	520	1.55	Al	27	934	578	1.43
Be	9	1560	899	1.12	Si	28	1685	786	1.32
B	11	2450	801	0.98	P	31	317	1012	1.28
C	12	3920	1086	0.91	S	32	388	1000	1.27
N	14	63	1402	0.92	Cl	35	172	1251	0.99
O	16	54	1314	0.73	Ar	40	84	1521	0.98
F	19	54	1681	0.72	K	39	337	419	2.35
Ne	20	25	2081	0.71	Ca	40	1123	590	1.97

4. It is said that atomic radius can be used to predict ionization energy. Defend this statement using evidence from Table 6.3.

5. Which of the following is a correct definition of electronegativity?

   a. Energy required to remove an electron from a gaseous atom

   b. The arrangement of electrons around the nucleus of an atom in its ground state

   c. Tendency to repel protons

   d. Tendency to attract electrons from another element

6. Which is the correct electron configuration for vanadium?

   a. $1s^2 2s^2 2p^1$

   b. $1s^2 2s^2 2p^6 3s^2$

   c. $1s^2 2s^2 2p^6 3s^2 3p^6 3d^3 4s^2$

   d. $1s^2 2s^2 2p^6 3s^2 3p^5$

ACTIVITY 6.1.3 *Determining Levels of Reasoning Required by Earth Science Questions*

Classify the earth science questions below with the levels of Bloom's taxonomy that they best represent. *Reminder:* It is not necessary to understand the content of these questions in order to identify the level of reasoning they represent.

1. Explain why the air pressure in Death Valley (280 feet below sea level) is greater than on top of Mount Whitney (14,495 feet above sea level).

2. Design a barometer using only the following items: plastic soda bottle, balloon, straw, and tape. Illustrate your design with an annotated diagram.

3. Define standard atmospheric temperature and pressure (STP).

4. Assess the benefits and shortcomings of barometric and global positioning system altimeters for use in private aircraft.

5. A mercury barometer reads 760 mm (1 atmosphere). What minimum height would the barometer need to be to measure this pressure if it were made using water, knowing that the density of mercury is 13.56 times that of water?

6. A noodle dish cooked at sea level is fine, while the same dish cooked for the same length of time at 10,000 feet is crunchy. Analyze the differences between the two cooking environments, and offer an explanation for the difference.

ACTIVITY 6.1.4 *Writing Questions That Test Each Educational Objective*

Good scientists know how to ask good questions. Good questions develop the mind and lead to other good questions. Write six questions for a theme you are currently studying, one for each level of reasoning. Write one knowledge question, one comprehension question, one application question, one analysis question, one synthesis question, and one evaluation question. Identify the level of reasoning required to answer each.

6.2 Inductive Reasoning

Science may be defined as the development and organization of knowledge of the physical universe through observation, experiment, and reason, and the body of knowledge gained from such activities. The word *science* comes from the Latin *scientia,* meaning knowledge, because science is a way of knowing about the physical world. One of the primary ways scientists discover new knowledge is through *inductive reasoning:* the logic of developing generalizations, hypotheses, and theories from specific observations and experiments. The premises or observations support the conclusion or generalization but do not ensure it. The following examples of inductive reasoning illustrate how it is used to develop reasonable, although not certain, conclusions.

Physicists have repeatedly measured the acceleration due to gravity at sea level to be 9.8 m/s^2, and this value is now an accepted constant, even though it has not been tested everywhere that is at sea level on the Earth's surface. As with all other conclusions derived by induction, it is possible that this generalization is flawed. It is possible, although extremely unlikely, that newer measurements will show different values at places not yet measured.

Scientists have noted that (1) ice in Greenland is melting faster than it is forming, (2) glaciers in Alaska are retreating, (3) the Northwest Passage is navigable for the first time in history, and (4) Antarctic ice is receding. Based on these and other observations, scientists infer that global temperature is rising. Although these observations support the conclusion, they do not ensure it. Other explanations, though unlikely, could explain the observed phenomenon. For example, it is possible that the ice fields are shrinking not because of increasing temperatures but because of decreasing ones. If temperatures are cooler, there is less oceanic evaporation, there are fewer clouds, and there is less snowfall over the ice fields. Although it is highly unlikely, the retreat of ice fields may be due not to increased melting but due to decreased snowfall to replenish that which has been lost to melting. As seen in both of the examples, the premises or observations used in inductive reasoning support the conclusion or generalization but do not ensure it.

ACTIVITY 6.2.1 *Deriving the Pendulum Equation by Inductive Reasoning (Physics)*

Newton's second law of motion (*F 5 ma*) and the ideal gas law (*PV 5 nRT*) were derived by generalizing from empirical data. In this activity, you will develop part of an equation for the period (the time of one cycle) of a pendulum as a function of mass and length. You can develop your own pendulum with lengths and masses of your choosing, or use the data from Table 6.4. Plot the period of the pendulum on the *y*-axis and the length on the *x*-axis. The period of a pendulum is the time required for the pendulum to return to its original position. To determine the period, measure 10 cycles and take the average.

On a second graph, plot the period of the pendulum on the *y*-axis and the mass on the *x*-axis. Compare the graphs with those in Figure 6.2. If the graph is a horizontal line, such as *y = 4*, then there is no relationship between the two variables and the factor (the variable plotted on the *x*-axis) is not in the equation. If it resembles the *square* ($y = x^2$), *direct* ($y = x$), or *square root* ($y = x^{1/2}$)

Table 6.4 Pendulum Data

L (m)	T (s)	m (kg)	T (s)
1	2.01	1	4.51
2	2.84	2	4.49
3	3.48	3	4.48
4	4.01	4	4.49
5	4.49	5	4.52
6	4.92	6	4.49
7	5.31	7	4.49
8	5.68	8	4.51
9	6.02	9	4.49
10	6.35	10	4.49

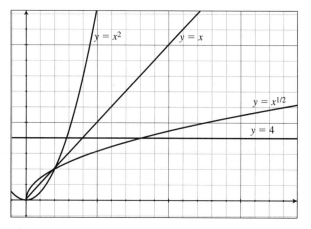

Figure 6.2 Which Represents the Period of a Pendulum?

graph, then the corresponding relationship should appear in your final equation. Which of the following relationships is consistent with your data? (*T* = period, *L* = length of the pendulum, and *m* = mass of the pendulum. The other factors are constants.)

(a) $T = 2\pi g \sqrt{m/L}$, (b) $T = \dfrac{2\pi m \sqrt{L}}{g}$

(c) $T = 2\pi g L m$, (d) $T = 2\pi \sqrt{\dfrac{L}{g}}$,

(e) $T = L^2 m^2 / 2\pi g$

ACTIVITY 6.2.2 *Developing a Periodic Table by Inductive Reasoning (Chemistry)*

Materials: Paint chips (available from a home improvement or paint store)

The pioneering Russian chemist Dmitri Mendeleyev analyzed data of the elements and found that when arranged according to their atomic weight, properties repeated at predictable intervals. Mendeleyev developed a table in which he arranged elements with similar properties in columns of ascending atomic mass. His table provided a general summary of the elements, had tremendous predictive value, and is widely used in its revised form, the periodic table of the elements (Figure 6.3).

In this activity, you will engage in an analogous process as you arrange paint color chips into an organized "periodic table." Your instructor will provide you with an envelope containing paint chips of a variety of colors and intensities. Apply the following rules as you arrange the chips.

• *The basic color of a paint chip represents its "chemical" properties.* For example, all blue paint chips can be considered to have similar properties, significantly different from those of red chips. The basic color of a chip is analogous to melting point, ionization energy, conductivity, or some other periodic property.

• *The shade of a paint chip is analogous to "atomic mass."* Thus, a light blue paint chip represents an element of lower atomic mass while a dark blue paint chip represents an element that has similar properties as the light blue chip, but with higher atomic mass.

Arrange all chips with similar colors in the same column (family) and all colors with similar intensity (shade) in the same row (series). In the real Periodic Table of the Elements, properties gradually change from metallic to nonmetallic as you proceed through a series from the left to the right across the table. You may illustrate this concept by arranging your columns in the sequence of the visible spectrum: red-orange-yellow-green-blue-violet. Place the reddest colors on the left of your table and the most violet colors on the right (Figure 6.4).

ACTIVITY 6.2.3 *Making Inferences About the Cell Cycle from Photographs (Biology)*

Materials: microscope and onion root tip slides, or the data provided.

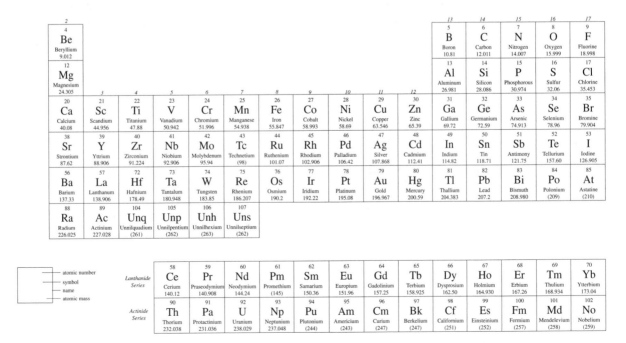

Figure 6.3 Periodic Table of the Elements

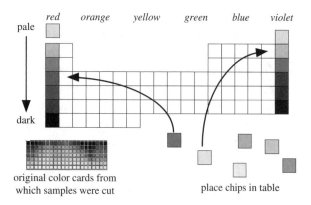

Figure 6.4 Constructing a "Periodic Table of Paint Chips"

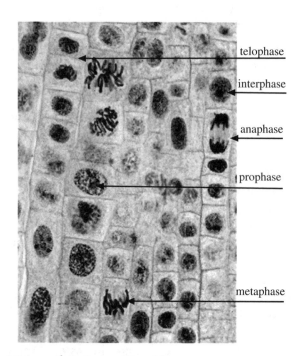

Figure 6.5 Onion Root Tip

An *inference* is a conclusion drawn inductively from evidence and reasoning. Inferences may be wrong, but if done logically from sound data, they provide a great wealth of useful ideas. Scientists make inferences when they are unable to make direct observations. Paleontologists make inferences about extinct organisms from fossils, climatologists make inferences about past climates by examining tree rings in petrified wood, and physicians make inferences about patient health from blood pressure, pulse, and other vital signs.

In this activity, you will make inferences about a dynamic process, the cell cycle, from static photographs. Figure 6.5 is a photograph of an onion root tip showing cells in various stages of the cell cycle. Learn to classify the stages of mitosis

in onion cells by examining Figure 6.5, and then count the number of onion cells in each stage in one or more prepared microscope slides. Collect classroom data and report in a table such as Table 6.5. If you are unable to gather class data, use the table provided in Table 6.5. Examine the data, and make generalizations or hypotheses, or both, about the cell cycle in onion root tips. Identify all assumptions you have made in developing your hypotheses.

Table 6.5 Onion Root Data

Sample	Interphase	Prophase	Metaphase	Anaphase	Telophase
1	45	15	5	3	5
2	89	23	5	4	9
3	101	17	6	2	8
4	67	27	3	1	7
5	88	34	6	0	8
6	77	33	3	2	5
7	89	24	5	3	7
8	45	12	3	3	3
9	68	12	4	5	6
10	99	29	5	3	9

ACTIVITY 6.2.4 *Finding Patterns in Seismic and Volcano Data (Earth Science)*

It is hard to imagine a world without petroleum. Much of our modern life, particularly transportation, revolves around the combustion of gasoline and other petroleum products. Many geologists believe we have passed the time of peak production, however, and that each year we will produce less than previous years, despite the fact that the demand for oil is growing as the Earth's population and economies grow. Although there is much research into alternative energy, the reality is that our societies will be dependent on petroleum for years to come. Geologists are continually searching for new oil reserves, but how do they find them? Drilling is expensive and occurs only after geologists can draw a reasonable inference that oil exists.

Exploration geologists are successful because they can predict the likelihood of oil on the basis of geological features. They understand patterns and know that they will not find oil in igneous rock, but may find it in sedimentary formations, particularly in regions once occupied by ancient seas and accompanied by features known as salt domes. Exploration geologists infer the presence of oil on the basis of patterns they observe, even though they are not certain until they drill. Although they are not always correct, their ability to see patterns and drill in areas where they find these patterns enables them to find oil. Geologists, like all other scientists, develop generalizations when they see repeated patterns in the data.

In this activity, you will use the same type of inductive reasoning to see patterns and develop generalizations and hypotheses regarding volcano and earthquake activity. On a world map, plot the distribution of the world's most famous volcanoes (Table 6.6) and the largest earthquakes since 1900 (Table 6.7). Place a world map on the wall, and use map pins or adhesive colored dots to identify the volcanoes in red and the earthquakes in blue. Each student can plot a few points until all are plotted. You may need to use an almanac or perform an Internet search to locate your features. Alternatively, each student can plot all of the events on a small world map. On the same chart, plot the epicenters of earthquakes from the past week or month as reported by the U.S. Geological Survey (look online at *sciencesourcebook.com*, earthquake. usgs.gov., or search "USGS recent earthquakes").

1. Explain the relationship between the distribution of volcanoes and earthquakes, if any.
2. Explain the relationship between the distribution of volcanoes and earthquakes, and any geographical features, if any.
3. Explain the relationship of the distribution of current earthquakes with ones from the past.
4. Generate one or more hypotheses about the occurrence of earthquakes or volcanoes, or both, on the basis of this information.
5. Perform an Internet search for a map showing tectonic plate boundaries. Is there any correlation between the location of earthquakes and volcanoes, and plate boundaries? If so, explain. (See *sciencesourcebook.com* or image search "plate tectonics map.")

Table 6.6 Notable Volcanoes

Kilauea, Hawaii	Nyiragongo, Congo	Hekla, Iceland
Mount St. Helens, Washington	Santorini, Greece	Taal, Philippines
Vesuvius, Italy	Ruapehu, New Zealand	Colima, Mexico
Fuji, Japan	Agung, Indonesia	Lassen Peak, California
Merapi, Indonesia	Mayon, Philippines	Yellowstone, Wyoming
Pelee, Martinique	Sakurajima, Japan	White Island, New Zealand
Arenal, Costa Rica	Mauna Loa, Hawaii	Rabaul, Papua New Guinea
Stromboli, Italy	El Chichon, Mexico	Long Valley, California
Krakatau, Indonesia	Ruiz, Colombia	Lamington, Papua New Guinea
Etna, Italy	Popocatepetl, Mexico	Paricutin, Mexico
Santa Maria, Guatemala	Katmai, Alaska	Tambora, Indonesia

Table 6.7 Notable Earthquakes

Location	Date	Magnitude	Latitude	Longitude
Chile	1960	9.5	−38.2	−73.1
Prince William Sound, Alaska	1964	9.2	61.0	−147.7
Off northwest coast of Sumatra	2004	9	3.3	95.8
Kamchatka	1952	9	52.8	160.1
Off coast of Ecuador	1906	8.8	1.0	−81.5
North Sumatra, Indonesia	2005	8.7	2.0	97.0
Rat Islands, Alaska	1965	8.7	51.2	178.5
Andrean of Islands, Alaska	1957	8.6	51.6	−175.4
Assam, Tibet	1950	8.6	28.5	96.5
Kuril Islands	1963	8.5	44.9	149.6
Banda Sea, Indonesia	1938	8.5	−5.1	131.6
Kamchatka	1923	8.5	54.0	161.0

6.3 Deductive Reasoning

Whereas inductive reasoning draws general principles from specific instances, *deductive reasoning* draws specific conclusions from general principles or premises. A *premise* is a previous statement or proposition from which another is inferred or follows as a conclusion. Unlike inductive reasoning, which always involves uncertainty, the conclusions from deductive inference are certain provided the premises are true. Scientists use inductive reasoning to formulate hypotheses and theories and deductive reasoning when applying them to specific situations. The following are examples of deductive reasoning:

Physics: Electric Circuits

First premise: The current in an electrical circuit is directly proportional to the voltage and inversely proportional to the resistance ($I = V/R$).

Second premise: The resistance in a circuit is doubled.

Inference: Therefore, the current is cut in half.

Chemistry: Element Classification

First premise: Noble gases are stable.
Second premise: Neon is a noble gas.
Inference: Therefore, neon is stable.

Biology: Plant Classification

First premise: Monocot flower parts are in multiples of three.
Second premise: Apple flowers have five petals.
Inference: Therefore, apple trees are not monocots.

Astronomy: Planetary Motion

First premise: The ratio of the squares of the periods of any two planets is equal to the ratio of the cubes of their average distances from the Sun. $T_1^2/R_1^3 = T_2^2/R_2^3$

Second premise: Earth is closer to the Sun than Mars.

Inference: Therefore, Earth orbits the Sun faster than Mars.

ACTIVITY 6.3.1 *Deducing the Wavelength of Sound (Physics)*

Materials needed: tuning forks, 1 L graduated cylinder or equally deep sink or container, 1" or 2" diameter PVC or glass pipe; or use the sample data provided.

The following premises apply to a pipe that has one open end and one sealed end:

Premise 1: A resonant "standing wave" is established when two sound waves of the same amplitude and wavelength travel in opposite directions.

Premise 2: Sound waves reflect off the sealed end of a tube.

Premise 3: A tube with one open end resonates when its length is one quarter the wavelength of sound (1/4λ).

Inference: The wavelength of sound is four times the shortest length of pipe that resonates. We can therefore determine the wavelength of sound by finding the shortest length of pipe in which the sound will resonate and multiplying its length by four.

Use a hacksaw to cut a section (length 50 cm or more) of Plexiglas, PVC, or ABS pipe (diameter 2.5 cm or more), and immerse it in an upright position in a large graduated cylinder or other deep container. Hold a vibrating middle C (261.6 Hz) tuning fork above the cylinder (Figure 6.6), and slowly raise the pipe until it resonates and the amplitude of the sound increases significantly. The shortest length at which the pipe resonates is known as the *fundamental mode* and is one-quarter the length of the sound wave. Measure the length of the air-filled pipe and multiply by four to determine the wavelength (λ) of sound generated by the tuning fork. Continue raising the pipe, and

Table 6.8 Tube Lengths and Wavelengths (m)

Note	L	λ (4 × L)	Note	L	λ (4 × L)
C			G		
D			A		
E			B		
F			C		

note that the volume decreases before it increases again at the third harmonic. Record the length of the third harmonic. Is it three times the length of the first harmonic? Repeat this process using other tuning forks in the octave scale and record your results in Table 6.8.

ACTIVITY 6.3.2 *Chemistry Deducing the Relative Sizes of Atomic Radii*

Chemical reactions occur as outermost (valence) electrons of different atoms are shared or exchanged. Electrons are easily lost if the atomic radius (distance between the nucleus and the outermost electron) is large relative to the nuclear charge and are held tightly if the atomic radius is small relative to the nuclear charge. Atomic radius is a useful tool in predicting ionization energy, electron affinity, and many other properties of the elements. Although it is necessary to consult a reference to know the precise atomic radii, it is possible to estimate relative atomic radii given the following premises:

Premise 1: Atomic radii increase within a family.

Premise 2: Atomic radii decrease within a series.

Inference: Using this information, one can draw a graph of relative atomic radii versus atomic number.

The first premise (atomic radii increase within a family) implies that atoms get larger as one proceeds from the top of a column (group, family) in the periodic table to the bottom. This is a consequence of the increasing number of electron shells. For example, in group 8, helium is the smallest because it has only one shell, while neon is larger because it has two shells, and argon is larger still because it has three shells. The second premise

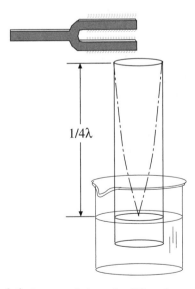

1/4λ

Figure 6.6 Determining the Wavelength of Sound

is based on the fact that opposite charges attract. The nucleus is positively charged and electrons are negatively charged, and the force of the attraction between these is proportional to the product of the charges and inversely related to the square of the distances between them $F = k(q_1q_2)/r^2$. As one proceeds across a row (series) in the periodic table, the number of protons increases, causing the force of attraction on the valence electrons to be greater. This reduces the radius as the electrons are pulled more strongly by the nucleus. Using the premises stated above, sketch a graph of atomic radius (y-axis) as a function of atomic number (x-axis). This will be an approximate graph and only represents major trends.

ACTIVITY 6.3.3 *Deducing the Sources of Communicable Diseases (Biology)*

Epidemiologists study the origin and spread of diseases. Communicable diseases are passed from one person to another as pathogens travel through air, fluids, or direct contact between individuals. Table 6.9 lists the leading cause of death in developed and developing nations. The italicized items are communicable diseases. Note that the third, fourth, and eighth leading causes of death in developing nations are communicable disease, while only one of the top 10 causes of death in

Table 6.9 Leading Causes of Death, 2001

Developed Nations	Developing Nations
1. Heart disease	1. Heart disease
2. Stroke	2. Stroke
3. Lung cancer	3. *Lower respiratory infections*
4. *Lower respiratory infections*	4. *HIV/AIDS*
5. Chronic obstructive pulmonary disease	5. Fetus/newborn (perinatal) conditions
6. Colon cancers	6. Chronic obstructive pulmonary disease
7. Alzheimer's disease	7. Diarrhea
8. Diabetes	8. *Tuberculosis*
9. Breast cancer	9. Malaria
10. Stomach cancer	10. Road traffic accidents

developed nations are in this category. This is an indication that epidemiologists, physicians, and public health specialists have done a good job of identifying the sources of disease and the ways to control them.

Epidemiologists often use survey data and deductive reasoning to determine the sources of disease. In this activity, you will collect your own data (or use the data in Table 6.10 if you are unable to do the activity) in an effort to determine the source of a "disease."

Each person is provided with two test tubes that are placed upright in clear plastic cups. Each pair of test tubes is marked with an identifying number and labeled C (for control) or E (for experimental). For example, student number 5 has two identical test tubes labeled 5C and 5E. All test tubes contain an equal amount of water, with the exception of one pair that contains an equal volume of dilute solution of sodium hydroxide (0.01 N; made by adding 0.4 g of sodium hydroxide to 1 L of water). Avoid spilling fluids; if you contact the fluid, rinse the area with water.

The test tubes containing dilute sodium hydroxide represent a person with a communicable disease. All other tubes represent healthy people. No one except the teacher knows who received the "infected" tubes, and it is the goal of the class to find out. At the teacher's command, pair up with another member of the class, record that person's number, and exchange a couple milliliters of fluid with each other using a Beral pipette or eyedropper. Alternatively, you pour a little from your container to theirs and visa versa. This is time 1 (T_1). Repeat this process twice when instructed by the teacher (T_2, T_3). After the third (for classes of 20 or fewer) or fourth (for classes of 40 or fewer) exchange, the teacher will place a drop of phenolphthalein solution in all of the experimental test tubes. A pink color indicates "infection" because phenolphthalein turns pink in basic solutions such as the one containing sodium hydroxide and all other cups contaminated by it. Create a table on the board or an overhead transparency, and indicate the people who exchanged at each interval as shown in Table 6.10. Put boxes around the names or numbers of the people who are

Table 6.10 Data for Communicable Diseases

Person	T₁	T₂	T₃	Person	T₁	T₂	T₃
1	19	16	2	11	9	14	17
2	20	7	1	12	7	15	10
3	14	19	20	13	17	8	14
4	18	5	8	14	3	11	13
5	6	4	16	15	16	12	19
6	5	20	7	16	15	1	5
7	12	2	6	17	13	9	11
8	10	13	4	18	4	10	9
9	11	17	18	19	1	3	15
10	8	18	12	20	2	6	3

"infected" as indicated by pink coloration (final column, Table 6.10). Using the following premises, deduce the possible sources of the disease. You should be able to narrow to two possibilities.

- Premise 1: A clear tube has not mixed with any "infected" tubes.
- Premise 2: A pink tube has mixed with "infected" tubes (or is the source).

Using logic, you can identify tubes that could not have been the source. You can deduce that if a test tube is clear after the final exchange, then none of the tubes that it mixed with could have been the source. For example, in Table 6.10, test tube 3 is clear, and therefore you can deduce that tubes 14, 19, and 20 could not have been the source. Tube 2 is infected but cannot be the source because it exchanged with tube 20, which is still clear at the end. Tube 20 would have been pink had tube 2 have been the source. Using deductive reasoning, identify the two possible sources of the disease.

Once all of the students have predicted the source of the disease, the teacher will place an equal amount of phenolphthalein in each of the control tubes. Only the tube representing the source of the disease will turn pink. The control tubes represent abstinence (in the case of sexually transmitted diseases like HIV/AIDS or syphilis), vaccination (in the case of measles of tetanus), or masks (in the case of respiratory illnesses).

ACTIVITY 6.3.4 *Determining the Epicenter of an Earthquake by Deduction (Geology)*

Seismologists determine the epicenter (the point on the earth's surface directly above the focus of a seismic event) of an earthquake by deductive reasoning. Earthquakes propagate p waves and s waves that can be measured on seismographs distant from the epicenter. Figure 6.7 shows that p waves travel faster and reach the seismograph sooner than s waves:

Premise 1: Earthquakes release compression waves (P waves) that travel at 7 km/s in Earth's crust (this value varies depending upon crust composition)

Premise 2: Earthquakes emit shear waves S-waves) that travel at 58 percent the speed of P waves, or 4 km/s.

Inference: The distance to the epicenter can be calculated by the formula:

$$d = \frac{(t_2 - t_1)(r_s r_p)}{r_p - r_s}$$

This can be deduced using the following algebra: Since distance is the product of rate and time ($d = rt$), the distance from the epicenter, d, can be represented using the primary wave (indicated with a subscript of p) as $d = r_p t_p$, and with the secondary wave (indicated with a subscript of s) as $d = r_s t_s$. Once the primary wave hits the seismograph, t_1 seconds have elapsed since the

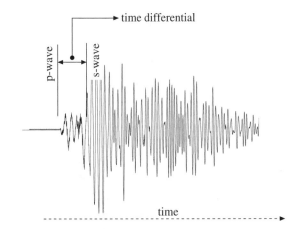

Figure 6.7 P Waves and S Waves

earthquake, and by the time the slower S wave hits the seismograph, t_2 seconds have elapsed. So $t_2 - t_1$ represents the elapsed time, or $(d/r_s - d/r_p)$:

$$t_2 - t_1 = d/r_s - d/r_p$$

$$t_2 - t_1 = \frac{r_p d - r_s d}{r_s r_p}$$

$$t_2 - t_1 = \frac{d(r_p - r_s)}{r_s r_p}$$

$$d = \frac{(t_2 - t_1)(r_s r_p)}{r_p - r_s}$$

Therefore, you can calculate the distance from the epicenter, d, if you know the velocities of the P wave and S wave, and the elapsed time between them $(t_2 - t_1)$. Assuming speeds of 7 km/s for P waves, and 4 km/s for S waves, we can calculate the distance as:

$$d = \frac{(t_2 - t_1)(7\,km \cdot s^{-1})(4\,km \cdot s^{-1})}{(7\,km \cdot s^{-1} - 4\,km \cdot s^{-1})} = (t_2 - t_1)9.3\,km \cdot s^{-1}$$

Thus, using the principles of algebra and the two premises of earthquake waves, we deduced that the distance to the epicenter can be calculated by multiplying the time differential $(t_2 - t_1)$ between the P-wave and the S-wave by 9.3 km/s.

In Figure 6.7, the difference between the S and P waves at Northridge, California, was recorded as 26.5 seconds. Therefore, the distance to the epicenter was

$$26.5\ s \times \frac{9.3\ km}{s} = 246\ km$$

Knowing the scale on the map, one can draw a circle with a center at Northridge and a radius of

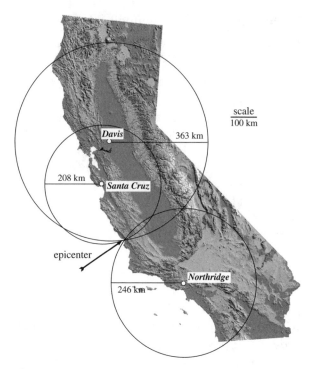

Figure 6.8 Determining the Epicenter of an Earthquake
Source: United States Geological Survey. Shaded relief map of California. Retrieved February 12, 2008, from http://education. usgs.gov/california/resources.html.

246 km (Figure 6.8). The epicenter is somewhere on this circle. By examining the seismographs at Davis and Santa Cruz, we find that the epicenter was 363 and 208 km from each of these locations, respectively. By drawing the circles on the map, you can see that they all intersect in one point near Moro Bay, California, and can deduce that this is the epicenter of the earthquake.

Table 6.11 records the time difference between the p wave and s wave for five hypothetical earthquakes. Determine the distance to the epicenter from each of the three stations in kilometers (km),

Table 6.11 Data Table for Determining the Epicenter of Earthquakes

Earthquake→	1			2			3			4			5		
↓seismograph	s	km	mm	s	km	mm	s	km	mm	s	km	mm	s	km	mm
Davis	57			12			11			35			32		
Santa Cruz	43			16			10			50			19		
Northridge	4			62			57			95			29		

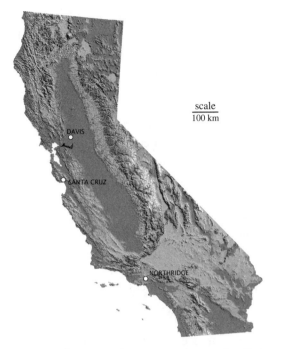

scale
100 km

Figure 6.9 Map for Determining the Epicenter of Earthquakes

and using the scale on Figure 6.9, determine the scaled distance in millimeters (mm) for the map. Using a ruler, set your compass for the appropriate radii from each seismograph location, and draw circles. Deduce the epicenter by looking for the place where the three circles intersect. You may need to look at a more detailed map of California to locate the cities closest to these epicenters. Complete Table 6.11.

6.4 Lateral Thinking

Lateral thinking is the ability to approach problems from a variety of perspectives rather than only from the single most obvious approach. Consider the following question:

> Example 1: On January 5, 2006, a jet traveled east from Quito, Ecuador, at 800 km/hour. How far did it travel in 3 hours?

The standard way to approach this question is to calculate the distance relative to a point on the Earth's surface by multiplying the speed of the jet (800 km/h) by the time in flight (3 hours). Alternatively, you could calculate the speed relative to the Earth's center by factoring in the rotational speed of the earth at the equator (1675 km/h) on which Quito sits. Another way to approach this question is to include the speed relative to the Sun, in which case you would also need to consider the Earth's orbital speed of 107,826 km/h. Finally, you could consider other variables such as the directions and magnitudes of winds on January 5, 2006.

Although such solutions may seem silly given the context in which such a question is traditionally asked, the ability to analyze the question from different perspectives is not. Lateral thinking exercises, such as those that follow, are used to help executives, engineers, planners, and designers think of alternative solutions to the problems they face. Not all alternatives are of equal merit, and although it is important to think of alternative ways of doing things, it is also important to evaluate the relative merit of each. Many lateral thinking exercises are expressed as riddles, such as the one that follows:

> Example 2: An explorer travels 1 km due south, then 1 km west, followed by 1 km north to arrive at the place he started. Where is this explorer?

This question seems impossible. Everyone knows that to return to the same location, the explorer must complete the fourth side of the square and travel 1 km east. This question can only be solved by thinking outside the box to an environment unlike your own. An explorer to the North Pole (such as Robert Perry or Matthew Henson) could accomplish this task by leaving the North Pole, traveling 1 km south, 1 km west, and then return 1 km north. This is possible because all longitudes (north-south meridians) converge at the North Pole.

ACTIVITY 6.4.1 *Lateral Thinking*
Edward deBono, a cognitive psychologist who popularized lateral thinking activities, argues that such exercises help us become more creative and

insightful. Many problems in science are solved only when researchers drop their assumptions and adopt a novel approach. For example, vitamins were discovered only after researchers stopped looking for a pathogenic cause for beriberi and started looking for the absence of some essential material.

The following riddles can be solved only by dropping standard assumptions and approaching the question from different perspectives. Some of following are adapted from widely circulated riddles whose original authorship is unknown. Provide plausible solutions for each, noting that there may be more than one way to solve each riddle:

1. A chemistry stockroom technician is 188 cm (6'2") tall. What does he weigh?
2. A rope ladder is hung over the side of research vessel in the Bay of Fundy so that the bottom rung just reaches the water. If the rungs are 20 cm apart, how many rungs will be under water when the tide rises 3 m?
3. A research ecologist drank heavily from the punchbowl at a research picnic in the Himalayan Mountains. He left the party early and was surprised to find that all of his team came down with giardiasis (a waterborne disease) the next day, even though nothing was added to the punch after he left and no one had drunk anything since the party.
4. The younger of two twins celebrates her birthday 2 days before her older twin. How can this be if both twins are celebrating their birthdays on the calendar days on which they were born?
5. A mineralogist examines seven crystals that are identical except that one has slightly less mass than the other six. How can the mineralogist determine which is the smallest crystal using just a double pan balance and two measurements?
6. Why do civil engineers design round manhole covers rather than square ones?
7. A botanist is growing plants in three sealed, windowless growth chambers, but can't remember which of three light switches controls the light in chamber C, 100 m away. To minimize disturbance to the plants, he can open the chamber only once for 5 seconds. How can he determine which switch controls the light in chamber C?
8. How far can an elk run into the woods?
9. A boat is floating in the lock of a canal. What will happen to the water level in the lock if an anchor is thrown overboard?
10. Following is a list of newspaper headlines that can be interpreted in different ways. Give the probable intended meaning and a humorous alternative interpretation.
    - safety experts say school bus passengers should be belted
    - teacher strikes idle kids
    - squad helps dog bite victim
    - miners refuse to work after death
    - juvenile court to try shooting defendant
    - stolen painting found by tree
    - killer sentenced to die for second time in 10 years
    - milk drinkers are turning to powder
    - dealers will hear *Car Talk* at noon
    - man struck by lightning faces battery charge

Answers to Chapter Activities

6.1.1   Classification of biology questions: (1) comprehension, (2) synthesis, (3) application, (4) evaluation, (5) analysis, (6) knowledge.

6.1.2   Classification of chemistry questions: (1) comprehension, (2) analysis, (3) synthesis, (4) evaluation, (5) knowledge, (6) application.

6.1.3   Classification of earth science questions: (1) comprehension, (2) synthesis, (3) knowledge, (4) evaluation, (5) application, (6) analysis.

6.1.4   Student responses will vary.

6.2.1   The only equation consistent with the data is $T = 2\pi\sqrt{L/g}$. Note that mass (m) does not appear in the equation because period is independent of mass (the plot of period versus mass is a horizontal line). Note that the graph of period versus length resembles the square root function ($y = x^{1/2}$), so T must be a function of $\sqrt{L}$. Answer d is the only one that fills this criterion. With more effort, students could figure out the entire equation, but for our purposes, it is sufficient to infer that the period is independent of the pendulum mass, but directly proportional to the square root of the length.

6.2.2   Students use inductive reasoning to develop a periodic table of paint chips from the data before them (color, shade). When Mendeleyev developed his original table, he noticed that there were gaps and predicted the presence and properties of elements not yet discovered.

You may wish to omit one or more chips and ask students to determine which ones are missing.

6.2.3 Students may infer that cells spend more time in interphase than in mitosis (prophase, metaphase, anaphase, telophase). They may also conclude that dividing cells spend the most time in prophase, followed by telophase, metaphase, and anaphase. Students should identify the assumptions they have made when drawing these inferences.

6.2.4 Students may make a variety of generalizations including:

(1) The distribution of earthquakes is similar to the distribution of volcanoes.

(2) Earthquakes and volcanoes appear to occur in lines and are more common on the boundaries of continents than in the centers.

(3) Recent earthquakes are distributed in much the same way as older events.

(4) The east and west edges of the Pacific Ocean are particularly active.

Scientists used these observations, along with seafloor spreading and continental drift, when they developed the theory of plate tectonics using inductive logic. Students may hypothesize that there is a relationship between earthquakes, volcanoes, and plate boundaries if they are familiar with the concepts of plate tectonics.

(5) Earthquakes and volcanoes are distributed close to the plate boundaries. After the students have plotted the data, show them the plate boundaries (Figure 6.10) and discuss how seismic data is used to identify plate boundaries.

6.3.1 The wavelength of a fundamental tone (lowest resonant frequency) is approximately 4 times the length of a closed tube ($\lambda: = 4 \times L$) as shown in Table 6.12.

Experimentation, however, shows that the diameter of the tube also influences the frequency. When the diameter of the tube is considered, the equation becomes: $\lambda: = 4(L - 0.4d)$. Use this formula for more precise measurements and predictions.

6.3.2 Given the premises, students may deduce a graph of relative atomic radii versus atomic number such as the one shown by the dashed line in Figure 6.11. If students can generate a graph similar to this, they have demonstrated the understanding necessary to predict other properties, such as ionization energy and electron affinity. Although a graph drawn by deduction (dashed line) will not have all of the nuances of the real values (solid line), it shows that students understand the basic factors determining atomic radii.

6.3.3 Students should be able to deduce that one of two people was the source of the disease. The bold type in the final column indicates people that were "infected" at the time of testing (Table 6.13). You can narrow the list of candidates for the source of the disease to either person number 7 or 12. Note that the boxes for 7 and

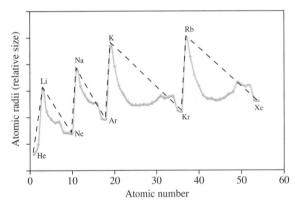

Figure 6.11 Deducing Atomic Radii Versus Atomic Number

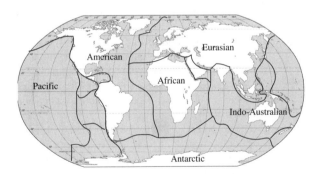

Figure 6.10 Tectonic Plate Boundaries

Table 6.12 Tube Lengths and Wavelengths (m)

Note	L	λ (4 × L)	Note	L	λ (4 × L)
C	0.235	0.94	G	0.178	0.71
D	0.200	0.80	A	0.158	0.63
E	0.188	0.75	B	0.140	0.56
F	0.168	0.67	C	0.125	0.50

Table 6.13 Disease Data Interpreted

Person	T_1	T_2	T_3	Person	T_1	T_2	T_3
1	19	16	**2**	11	9	14	17
2	20	**7**	**1**	**12**	7	15	**10**
3	14	19	20	13	17	8	14
4	18	5	8	14	3	11	13
5	6	4	16	15	16	**12**	**19**
6	5	20	**7**	16	15	1	5
7	12	2	**6**	17	13	9	11
8	10	13	4	18	4	10	9
9	11	17	18	19	1	3	**15**
10	8	18	**12**	20	2	6	3

Table 6.14 Locations of Epicenters

seismograph	Fillmore		Inverness		San Francisco		Arcata		Coalinga	
	s	km	s	km	s	km	s	km	s	km
Davis	57	526	12	109	11	104	35	327	32	294
Santa Cruz	43	402	16	145	10	95	50	468	19	176
Northridge	4	40	62	580	57	527	95	886	29	270

12 extend all the way to the left of the table, indicating that these individuals remain candidates after all data has been considered). Because all individuals exchanged at T_1, it is impossible to identify the true source until the controls are tested. The size of the data table will depend on the number of students in your class. For example, a class of 36 will have 36 rows. If there are an odd number of students in your class, one person will have to pass on each exchange.

6.3.4   The epicenters for the earthquakes were Fillmore, Inverness, San Francisco, Arcata, and Coalinga as shown in Table 6.14. All of these are located near the San Andreas Fault system, the largest fault in North America.

6.4.1   The following lists possible responses.

(1)   Possible solution: chemicals

(2)   Possible solution: None. The boat rises with the tide, and so does the rope ladder.

(3)   Possible solution: The punch was cooled with ice cubes from a local water supply. The protozoan that causes giardiasis was released to the punchbowl as the ice melted. Since the researcher left the party early, there was insufficient giardia in the water to give him the disease.

(4)   Possible solution: The mother of the twins was on a Pacific cruise at the time she delivered her twins. The older one was born in the Eastern Hemisphere on March 1, just before the boat crossed the international dateline. The younger twin was born minutes later on February 28 in the Western Hemisphere. On leap years, the younger twin will celebrate her birthday two days earlier because of the introduction of February 29.

(5)   Possible solution: The mineralogist should put three crystals on one side of the balance and three on the other side. If the masses are equal, the crystal still on the table is the smaller one. If they are not equal, the smaller crystal is on the side with less mass, and the

mineralogist should clear the pans, take two from this side, and place them on opposite pans. If these two crystals are of equal mass, the smaller crystal is the third member from this group. If the masses are unequal, the crystal on the pan that registers less mass is the smaller one.

(6)   Possible solutions: This question is often given during job interviews to see how candidates reason with novel problems. Round manhole covers will not fall in the hole, while square ones can if they are tilted diagonally. Round manhole covers do not need to be aligned as they are put in place, while square ones do. Round manhole covers can be easily rolled to and from their destination, while square ones must be carried. In addition, round manhole covers are easier to manufacture than rectangular or square ones.

(7)   Possible solution: The botanist can turn on switch 1 for a couple of minutes, then turn it off and turn on switch 2 and go immediately to chamber C. If the light bulb is off and the bulb is warm, the light is controlled by switch 1. If the light is on, the light is controlled by switch 2, and if the light is off and the bulb is cool, the light is controlled by switch 3.

(8)   Possible solution: Halfway, because after that it is running out of the woods.

(9)   Solution: The water level will fall slightly. While the anchor is on board, it displaces an amount of water equivalent to its weight, but when submerged, it displaces only an amount of water equivalent to its volume. Since iron is 7.8 times denser than water, it will displace 7.8 times as much water when onboard than when submerged.

(10)   Most of the potential problems in this question are due to truncation or lack of punctuation. Students should give a humorous interpretation as well as the probable intended meaning.

Chapter Seven

Thinking Critically and Resolving Misconceptions

For the Teacher 125

7.1 Critical Thinking 126

7.2 Evaluating Claims 129

7.3 Using a Decision-Making Matrix 131

7.4 Misconceptions in Physics 132

7.5 Misconceptions in Chemistry 135

7.6 Misconceptions in Biology 137

7.7 Misconceptions in Earth and Space Science 139

Answers to Chapter Activities 142

For the Teacher

Critical thinking is the process of analyzing and evaluating information to determine its veracity or plausibility. There is no set pattern to critical thinking, but it often involves the following:

Identification of premises and conclusions. Critical thinkers break arguments into basic statements and draw logical implications.

Clarification of arguments. Critical thinkers locate ambiguity and vagueness in arguments and propositions.

Establishment of facts. Critical thinkers determine if the premises are reasonable and identify information that has been omitted or not collected. They determine if the implications are logical and search for potentially contradictory data.

Evaluation of logic. Critical thinkers determine if the premises support the conclusion. In deductive arguments, the conclusions must be true if the premises are true. In inductive arguments, the conclusions are likely if the premises are true.

Final evaluation. Critical thinkers weigh the evidence and arguments. Supporting data, logic, and evidence increase the weight of an argument. Contradictions and lack of evidence decrease the weight of an argument. Critical thinkers do not accept propositions if they think there is more evidence against them or if the argument is unclear, omits significant information, or has false premises or poor logic.

There are numerous misconceptions in science that spread when people repeat what they have heard without thinking critically of the issues. Francis Bacon, one of the founders of scientific thought, said that "the ill and unfit choice of words wonderfully obstructs the understanding." For example, people often use the word *weight* when they mean *mass* and vice versa, causing others to think that they are the same thing. We often propagate misconceptions because we do not use precise language. We prefer "everyday language," yet often it is not precise enough to describe or differentiate scientific concepts. By deferring to colloquial speech everyday analogies, and relying heavily on visible effects and changes, it is easy to communicate misunderstandings.

Misconceptions often arise through the use of common sense or casual observation and reasoning. For example, many people believe that venous blood is blue based on the premise that the veins in forearms and legs have a bluish tint. A hasty conclusion is that veins appear blue because the blood within them is blue. Diagrams in books support this conclusion by coloring systemic veins blue and systemic arteries red. However, a critical analysis reveals problems in the blue-blood conclusion. Veins do appear to have a blue or purple coloration when viewed from outside the body, but it does not necessarily follow that this coloration is due to the color of the blood within. Perhaps overlying tissues affect their appearance, or perhaps these vessels are pigmented differently from the blood they contain. The implication is that venous blood samples should appear blue, but those who have given blood know that it is dark red, even when it is not exposed to the air. This evidence suggests that we should reject the blue-blood conclusion.

Many preconceptions and misconceptions in science are persistent. For example, studies show that large percentages of chemistry graduate students believe that the bubbles in boiling water are composed of air (nitrogen and oxygen, for example) rather than vaporized water. The visual similarity of water vapor bubbles to air bubbles is very strong and may explain why this misconception is so persistent. Other studies have shown that large numbers of astronomy graduate students hold a fundamental misconception regarding the reason for seasonality, believing that seasons are caused by the elliptical path of the Earth around the Sun rather than the tilt of the Earth's axis. They incorrectly conclude that summer occurs at perigee and winter at apogee, forgetting that seasons in the Southern Hemisphere are opposite those in the Northern Hemisphere at any point in time.

The first activity in this chapter focuses on the development of critical thinking skills, and the remaining activities use critical thinking to reveal and correct common misconceptions in science. In these later activities, you will find lists of the most common misconceptions in physics, chemistry, biology, and earth and space science. For the first five in each series, we have stated a misconception, contradictory data, and finally a corrected statement. Your students should use this same pattern to correct the misconceptions you assign.

7.1 Critical Thinking

Critical thinkers draw conclusions only after they have defined their terms, distinguished fact from opinion, asked relevant questions, made detailed observations, and uncovered assumptions. They make assertions based on solid evidence and sound logic. In relying on evidence, critical thinkers:

- Examine problems carefully.
- Ask pertinent questions.
- Identify assumptions and biases.
- Define criteria.
- Look for evidence.
- Identify missing information.

And in relying on logic, critical thinkers:

- Assess statements and arguments.
- Analyze data.
- Consider a variety of explanations.
- Reject information that is incorrect or irrelevant.

- Admit a lack of understanding or information when necessary.
- Suspend judgment until all facts have been gathered and considered.
- Weigh evidence and draw reasoned conclusions.
- Adjust opinions when new facts are found.

The following activities are designed to help develop critical thinking skills. Each of these activities uses some of the strategies listed above.

ACTIVITY 7.1.1 *Constructing Data Comparison Tables*

Every year voters go to the polls to cast their ballots for candidates and initiatives. Unfortunately, most voters base their decisions on limited and biased data. Scientists cannot afford to do their research in this way and must rely on evidence and logic. One of the simplest ways to compare evidence is through a data comparison table. Figure 7.1 is a comparison table that illustrates the similarities and differences of two types of flowering plants, monocots and dicots. Note how the tabular approach helps make comparisons easy.

Create a similar comparison table for a topic in your curriculum such as one of those listed in Table 7.1. Your table should list similarities and differences as illustrated.

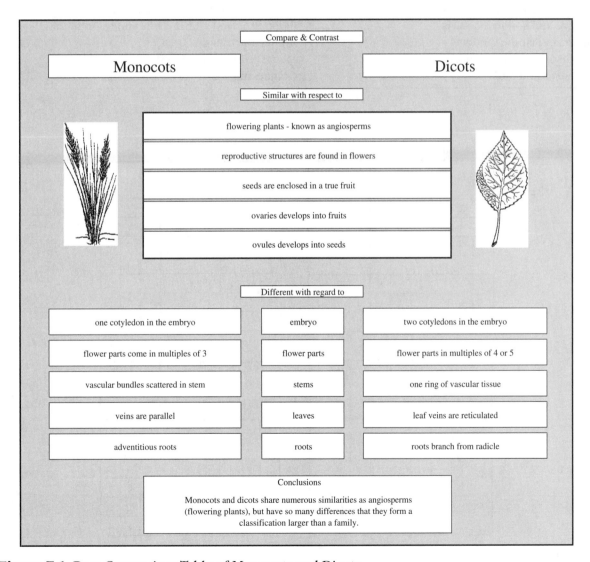

Figure 7.1 Data Comparison Table of Monocots and Dicots

Table 7.1 Topics for Comparison Tables

Physics	Chemistry
Inertial and noninertial frames of reference	Noble gases and halogens
Newtonian and relativistic physics	Standard and benfry periodic tables
Parallel and series circuits	Nuclear fusion and nuclear fission
Particle and wave theories of light	Bohr and Schrödinger models of the atom
Strong and weak nuclear forces	Ionic and covalent bonds
Gravity and electrostatic attraction	Metals and nonmetals
Red and blue lasers	Colloidal suspensions and solutions
Refracting and reflecting telescopes	Oil and coal

Biology	Earth and Space Science
Plant cells and animal cells	Inner and outer planets
Transcription and translation	One-time and recurring comets
Reptiles and amphibians	Richter Scale and Mercali Index
Photosynthesis and chemosynthesis	NASA's *Voyager* 1 and *Voyager* 2 missions
Mojave and Sonoran deserts	Barometric and global positioning systems altimeters
Arctic and alpine tundra	Arctic and Antarctic
Angiosperms and gymnosperms	Mount Rainier and Mount Fuji
Mammals and birds	Granite and basalt

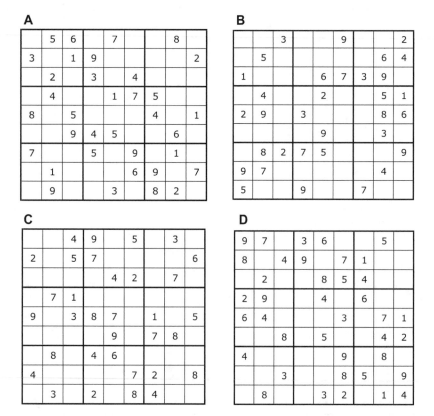

Figure 7.2 Sudoku Puzzles

ACTIVITY 7.1.2 *Evaluating Solutions: Sudoku Puzzles*

Scientists often evaluate many possible solutions before coming to a conclusion. If a proposed solution contradicts evidence, they set it aside in favor of one that is consistent with the evidence. Mathematical puzzles require this same logic and can be used to develop critical reasoning skills.

Number puzzles were introduced in the United States in 1979, but later gained tremendous popularity in Japan, where they became known as *sudoku* puzzles, before being reintroduced to America. Each sudoku puzzle is composed of nine boxes, each containing nine cells, as shown in Figure 7.2. To solve the sudoku puzzle, numbers must be placed in empty cells such that all nine of the nine-celled boxes have all of the numbers from 1 to 9. In addition, each row and column in the complete table of 81 cells must have all of the numbers from 1 to 9. Solve the puzzles in Figures 7.2A to 7.2D, and identify the critical thinking skills necessary to do so from the list above.

You can continue to build your skills by solving sudoku puzzles found in newspapers or on the Internet (at *sciencesourcebook.com* or search "sudoku").

7.2 Evaluating Claims

Advertisement is the promotion of goods and services with the goal of increasing sales and revenue. Without critical thinking skills, consumers can fall for a variety of false claims. For example, in the nineteenth century, stores sold Bonnore's Electro Magnetic Bathing Fluid, which claimed to cure cholera, neuralgia, epilepsy, scarlet fever, necrosis, mercurial eruptions, paralysis, hip diseases, chronic abscesses, and "female complaints." Many consumers purchased the product with hopes that it would cure their ailments, but others rejected the claims after using one or more of the following critical thinking strategies:

Identification of biases. The Bonnore Company had a vested interest in selling this fluid and therefore might have been biased in the presentation of its claims.

Examination of evidence. There were no medical reports on Bonnore's Electro Magnetic Bathing Fluid. If it had cured any of these conditions, one would have expected published reports by nonbiased researchers.

Assessment of statements and claims. It is unlikely that any medical treatment could cure such a wide range of maladies. Cholera is caused by bacteria and affects the digestive tract. Neuralgia is generally caused by viruses and affects the cranial nerves of the nervous system. Hip diseases may be caused by metabolic disorders or skeletal system diseases. "Female complaints" are a vague collection of problems, but likely caused by hormones affecting the reproductive system. It is highly unlikely that a single medicine could cure diseases with such different causes that affect such different systems.

Evaluation of evidence. The evidence suggests that the medicinal claims for Bonnore's Electro Magnetic Bathing Fluid were false or grossly exaggerated.

ACTIVITY 7.2.1 *Evaluating Tobacco Advertisements*

Early cigarette advertisements made many unsubstantiated claims. It was common to read that smoking could improve your disposition, reduce indigestion, ease tension, keep you slender, or simply provide a "lift" (see *sciencesourcebook.com,* or search "chesterfield cigarette ads"). One 1946 ad said, "24 hours a day, your doctor is on duty . . . a few winks of sleep, a few puffs of a cigarette . . . and he's back at the job again." Others made claims such as these: "More doctors smoke Camels than any other Cigarette," "For digestion's sake—smoke Camels," or "Just what the doctor ordered."

Today it is difficult to make such blatantly bogus claims since the Federal Trade Commission requires that advertisers have evidence to back up their claims. Additional legislation requires that all cigarette advertisements and packages marketed in the United States carry prescribed warnings such as: "Smoking causes lung cancer, heart disease, emphysema, and may complicate pregnancy"; "Quitting smoking now greatly reduces serious risks to your health"; "Smoking by pregnant women may result in fetal injury, premature birth, and low birth weight"; and "Cigarette smoke contains carbon monoxide." Despite such regulations, tobacco companies continue to advertise heavily, relying primarily on imagery and slogans rather than direct claims. Many cigarette companies have slogans that create an image but don't necessarily say anything false:

Camel: "Where a man belongs; I'd walk a mile for a Camel."

Kool: "Come all the way up to Kool."

Marlboro: "Come to Marlboro Country. Come to where the flavor is!"

Newport: "Alive with pleasure!"

Pall Mall: "Wherever particular people congregate."

Virginia Slims: "It's a woman's thing; You've come a long way, baby!"

Winston: "Winston tastes good like a cigarette should!"

Critically analyze five or more recent cigarette advertisements. Describe the visual messages associated with the advertisements, and identify the inferences advertisers probably want consumers to make. Evaluate these unwritten claims in the light of evidence. For example, an advertisement may show business executives smoking around a conference table, creating the impression that smoking is a way to be successful in the business world. Evidence, however, shows that large numbers of major corporations are smoke free and even subsidize clinics and support groups to assist employees to kick the habit.

There is significant medical evidence showing adverse effects of smoking on the respiratory system (throat, larynx, trachea, bronchi, lungs), skeletal system (bones), muscular system (muscles, joints), circulatory system (heart, arteries), urinary system (kidneys, bladder), digestive system (stomach, intestines), nervous system (brain, eyes, nerves), endocrine system (thyroid, hormones), reproductive system (reproductive organs), immune system (T cells, antibodies), and integumentary system (skin, nails). Research these effects as they pertain to the advertisements you evaluate. For example, if a cigarette advertisement portrays an athlete, discuss how smoking injures the respiratory and

muscular systems on which the athlete depends, or if it pictures a model, discuss the adverse effects of smoking on the skin and nails.

ACTIVITY 7.2.3 *Evaluating Alcohol Ads*

The primary goal of advertisements is not to inform the public but to increase sales. Consumers should be aware of this bias and critically evaluate explicit and implicit advertising claims. Alcohol advertisers rarely provide factual information; rather, they create images of lifestyles they hope consumers may associate with their products.

Identify the unspoken message of five or more alcohol advertisements, and contrast these with evidence. Develop a parody advertisement for one product. Your advertisement should resemble the original but reflect the adverse effects associated with overconsumption. The following summary of the health and social problems commonly associated with excessive alcohol consumption will help you develop your satirical advertisement:

Physical Effects Related to Excessive Alcohol Consumption

- *Impaired judgment:* Alcohol consumption can lead to impaired judgment, reduced reaction time, slurred speech, and difficulty walking.
- *Effect on body systems:* When alcohol is consumed rapidly and in large amounts, it can result in coma and death. Alcohol may interact with medications and intensify their effect. Excessive alcohol consumption is associated with liver diseases, including cirrhosis and liver cancer.
- *Hangovers:* Hangover symptoms such as flushing, nausea, and dizziness are common following excessive drinking.
- *Fetal alcohol syndrome:* Alcohol use by pregnant women can cause serious damage to the developing fetus.

Social Issues Related to Excessive Alcohol Consumption

- *Alcohol-related deaths:* In 2000, there were approximately 85,000 deaths in the United States attributable to alcohol consumption, making it the third leading cause of death.[1]

- *Crime:* In 1997, approximately 40 percent of all crimes in the United States were committed under the influence of alcohol.[2]
- *Child abuse:* It is estimated that nearly half of the cases of child abuse and neglect are associated with parental alcohol or drug abuse.[3]
- *Suicide:* Approximately one-fourth of all suicide deaths are committed under the influence of alcohol.[4]
- *Risky behaviors:* People who abuse alcohol are more likely to engage in dangerous behaviors, such as unsafe sexual activity and illegal drug use.[5]
- *Traffic arrests:* In 2003, approximately 1.4 million arrests were made for driving under the influence of alcohol or narcotics.[6]
- *Motor vehicle deaths:* In 2004, more than 17,000 people in the United States died in alcohol-related motor vehicle crashes, accounting for 41 percent of all traffic-related deaths.[7]
- *Binge drinking:* Binge drinking (periods of intense alcohol consumption) is highly correlated with violence (homicide, suicide, child abuse, domestic violence), injuries (motor vehicle accidents, falls, burns, drownings, and hypothermia), and medical hazards (sudden infant death syndrome, fetal alcohol syndrome, alcohol poisoning, hypertension, sexually transmitted diseases, and meningitis).[8]

ACTIVITY 7.2.3 *Evaluating Claims of Diets, Herbal Supplements, and Medication*

Apply your critical thinking skills to evaluate the health-related claims of a diet (Atkins, South Beach, Jenny Craig, Weight Watchers, Slim-Fast), herbal supplement (stevia, ephedra, ginkgo biloba, ginseng), or over-the-counter medication (antihistamines, decongestants, antacids, analgesics).

Construct a table to compare and contrast evidence for the positive and negative effects. Discuss potential benefits, side effects, costs, practicality, alternatives, and other relevant issues.

7.3 Using a Decision-Making Matrix

Many decisions require the review and consideration of a variety of options and variables. One way of organizing issues is through the use of a decision-making matrix: a rectangular array of information that allows a quick comparison of features of competing alternatives.

To develop a matrix, determine the criteria for comparison, select the alternatives to be compared, and generate scores based on established criteria. Table 7.2 compares three brands of a field instrument such as a global positioning system (GPS) device or portable pH probe. The products are rated on a variety of criteria, with 5 being the highest and 0 the lowest score possible. Totaling the number of points for each option yields a score that will help in the decision-making process. In this activity, product B appears to be the best option because it received the most points. Decision-making matrices are a critical thinking tool for complex comparisons. Evaluators must choose an appropriate weighting scale to give appropriate emphasis to each criteria.

ACTIVITY 7.3.1 *Determining the Best Alternative Energy Sources (Earth Science)*

Energy shortages are a reality in modern industrial societies. In World War II there was a significant oil shortage, and many countries imposed rationing. In 1973 there was a major energy crisis when

Table 7.2 Sample Decision-Making Matrix

	Cost	Durability	Accuracy	Size	Weight	Score
Product A	5	2	2	3	2	14
Product B	3	4	4	4	3	18
Product C	4	3	3	2	1	13

Arab members of the Organization of Petroleum Exporting Countries (OPEC) announced that they would not ship petroleum to the United States, Western Europe, or other countries that supported Israel in its conflict with Egypt and Syria. Soaring prices, long lines at gasoline pumps, and closed service stations were common. In 1979 another energy crisis occurred during the Iranian Revolution, and the U.S. Department of Energy, fearing a severe fuel shortage, printed gasoline-rationing coupons, although it never distributed them.

Most nations are dependent on imported petroleum, and it is only a matter of time before there is another production or distribution crisis, or supplies simply run out. Governments and energy companies are actively pursuing alternative energy sources to reduce dependency on petroleum. Unfortunately, each energy source has problems, so there is no clear choice regarding a replacement for petroleum. Energy officials must use critical reasoning skills to determine the best options to pursue. Table 7.3 is a decision-making matrix that compares and contrasts the costs and benefits associated with a variety of energy sources. Assign relative values for each cell on a 1 to 5 scale, as illustrated in Table 7.2, and total each row to determine which energy source you think is most promising. Write a persuasive essay encouraging the development of the energy source that rates highest in your decision-making matrix. Defend your choice using data from the matrix and other sources.

ACTIVITY 7.3.2 *Using a Decision-Making Matrix for Environmental Issues*

The decision-making matrix is useful for a wide range of scientifically based decisions, particularly in the field of environmental policy and law. Select one of the following issues or an issue of your choice. Then determine the criteria for comparison (some possibilities are shown in parentheses for each issue), develop a decision-making matrix, assign values, and come to a conclusion regarding the best option. Defend your argument using data collected from the decision-making matrix and other sources.

- Industrial pollution control policies (pollution credits, pollution penalties, pollution tax)

- Land use policies for your region (preservation, conservation, free market)
- Solid waste management (incineration and energy recovery, composting, exporting, sanitary land fills, open dumping, ocean dumping)
- Techniques for increasing supplies of freshwater (dams, groundwater, desalination, towing glaciers, cloud seeding)
- Population distribution effects on the environment (urbanization, distributed population)
- Types of grazing (continuous, intensive, rotational)
- Logging (clear-cut, patch clear-cut, group selection, single tree selection, thinning, shelterwood, salvage cutting)
- Wildland forest fire policies for western North America (total suppression, natural burn, prescribed burn)

Table 7.4 is a sample decision-making matrix for industrial pollution control policies. To determine which policy is best, government officials might look at the revenue generated, the effectiveness in reducing pollution, and the impact on industrial production on the local economy. By assigning scores from 1 to 5 for each cell and then totaling each row, public policymakers might be able to come to a conclusion on the best policy.

7.4 Misconceptions in Physics

All of us have misconceptions about the way the world works. We acquired many of these early in life by inadequate observation and false assumptions, but others are spread by inexact textbooks and movies that do not reflect reality. For example, movies may show visible laser beams (laser beams are not visible unless reflected by dust or other matter), exploding cars (cars don't explode on impact), conversations in outer space (sound does not travel in a vacuum), and guns that do not recoil (a violation of conservation of momentum). Most misconceptions can be identified by careful observation and use of critical thinking strategies. Consider the following misconceptions and how

Table 7.3 Decision-Making Matrix for Alternative Energy Sources

	Description	Abundance	Accessibility	Costs	Safety and Environment	Ease of Use
Oil	Nonrenewable fossil fuel; formed by compression of ancient organisms	Worldwide resources being depleted; U.S. has small reserve	Locating oil is getting more difficult as the more accessible oil fields have already been tapped	Existing technologies for extraction, refinement, storage, shipment, and use keep prices down	Flammable, toxic, and carcinogenic; major source of air pollution in urban areas	Portable and easy to use in motor vehicles
Natural gas	Nonrenewable gaseous fossil fuel; methane	U.S. has large reserves	Located in places that are difficult to develop, such as northern Alaska	Does not require refinement; distribution systems are extensive, keeping costs reasonable	Explosive gas, but relatively clean burning	Difficult to use in vehicles; good home distribution network
Coal	Nonrenewable fossil fuel from metamorphosed vegetation	U.S. has 25% of world's supply; more abundant than oil	Over 40% is currently mined from deep mines; most of the reserves are less accessible	Requires no refinement; shipped by railroad to power plants; use in homes is minimal	Mining very hazardous; major cause of acid rain; strip mines destroy landscape	Not useful for vehicles; good for generating electricity
Nuclear	Nonrenewable energy derived from fission of uranium	U.S. reserves can power current reactors for 30 years	Uranium ore is low yield, requiring large mines	Extremely expensive to mine, build reactors, and meet safety and environmental standards	Safety record good, radioactive waste extremely hazardous and difficult to store	Must be converted to electricity for home use
Geothermal	Semirenewable; productivity falls if gradient drops due to overuse	Plentiful because the Earth's mantle is made of hot magma	Requires a significant temperature gradient that generally occurs only deep in the earth's crust	Expensive to develop new technologies and wells that tap deep gradients; energy is free once facilities built	Very few safety or environmental concerns	Not portable; can't be used in cars and trucks
Wind	Renewable; turbines in dams produce electricity	Abundant, depending on topography	Windy areas, such as oceans and mountains, are difficult to exploit	Cost of turbines is very high; energy is essentially free after installation	Safe; large windmill farms consume much land	Useful for homes, but not for transportation
Hydro-electric	Renewable; turbines in dams produce electricity	Larger rivers tend to be in flatter areas	New sites are remote or protected in parks and wilderness areas	Dams are very expensive to build; energy is essentially free thereafter	Safe; dams destroy habitats and eventually fill with silt	Useful for home use, but not for transportation
Solar	Energy from the sun is tapped by solar panels and solar cells	Abundant in portions of the country with clear skies	Widespread but diffuse source of energy	Solar cells are very expensive, but energy is free once they are installed	Safe; large solar collectors occupy land	Useful for homes but not industry

Table 7.4 Sample Decision-Making Matrix for Pollution Control Policies

	Revenue Generated	Reduction in Pollution	Effect on Local Economy	Score
Credit				
Penalties				
Tax				

a review of contradictory data is used to identify them:

Misconception: An object at rest has no energy

Contradictory data: Automobiles at rest can accelerate with no outside force.

Correct explanation: An object at rest has no kinetic energy, but it may have energy in other forms, such as thermal, gravitational potential or, in this case, chemical potential energy in the gasoline.

Misconception: Doubling the speed of an object doubles its kinetic energy

Contradictory data: The braking distance for a car traveling at 20 miles per hour is 6 m, while the braking distance at twice the speed (40 mi per hour) is 24 m, four times as far.

Correct explanation: The kinetic energy of an object increases as the square of the velocity ($E_k = 1/2\ mv^2$).

Misconception: Rockets accelerate as expanding gases push on matter behind them

Contradictory data: Rockets adjust the orbits of satellites in the vacuum of space.

Correct explanation: Rockets accelerate in the direction opposite of expanding exhaust gases according to the law of the conservation of momentum.

Misconception: Weight is the same thing as mass

Contradictory data: Astronauts in space are weightless but still have inertia, a property of mass.

Correct explanation: Weight is a measure of the force of gravity on mass. An object can have mass and be weightless if the net force acting on it is 0. Unfortunately, people confuse the terms and state their "weight" in kilograms (a unit of mass) rather than in newtons (a unit of force).

Misconception: Acceleration always occurs in the same direction as an object is moving

Contradictory data: Newton's second law states that $F = ma$, where F represents force, m represents mass, and a represents acceleration. The force of friction on tires during braking is opposite the direction of motion; therefore, the acceleration must also be in the opposite direction.

Correct explanation: Acceleration is always in the direction of the net force, which may or may not be in the direction of movement.

ACTIVITY 7.4.1 *Clarifying Misconceptions in Physics*

Note to teacher: Following is a list of common misconceptions in physics. Give one misconception to each student, and instruct the class to research the misconception, explain why it is wrong by reasoning from observed facts and experiences, and provide a correct explanation:

The first item is an example:

1. *Misconception:* Electrical charge is used up as it flows through a circuit. *Correct explanation:* Many analogies are made between plumbing systems and electrical systems, and this may create some confusion if the analogies

are taken too far. In plumbing systems, water is consumed and must be replenished, but in circuits, the electrons remain in the wire and cycle when an electromotive force is applied.

2. *Misconception:* Charge flows through circuits at the speed of light.
3. *Misconception:* Red light is most energetic, and blue light is least energetic.
4. *Misconception:* We are running out of energy.
5. *Misconception:* Sonic booms occur only at the moment when the sound barrier is punctured.
6. *Misconception:* Centrifugal force pushes riders into the walls of turning cars or banking roller coasters.
7. *Misconception:* The sky is blue because it reflects the color of the ocean.
8. *Misconception:* Vacuum cleaners suction (pull) up debris from the carpet.
9. *Misconception:* Warmer objects have more heat than cooler objects.
10. *Misconception:* Rays of sunlight that hit the Earth are parallel.
11. *Misconception:* Electric companies sell electric charge that flows to consumers.
12. *Misconception:* The primary colors of light are red, blue, and yellow.
13. *Misconception:* When white light passes through a colored filter, the filter adds color to the light.
14. *Misconception:* Gravity is a strong force.
15. *Misconception:* Infrared light is a kind of heat radiation.
16. *Misconception:* Energy and force are the same thing.
17. *Misconception:* Velocity is another word for speed.
18. *Misconception:* If an object has zero velocity, it has zero acceleration
19. *Misconception:* The effects of light are instantaneous.
20. *Misconception:* Gamma rays, x-rays, ultraviolet light, visible light, infrared light, microwaves, and radio waves are all very different entities.
21. *Misconception:* When two pulses or waves that are traveling in opposite directions meet, they bounce off each other.
22. *Misconception:* More massive objects fall faster.
23. *Misconception:* The more mass in a pendulum bob, the faster it swings.
24. *Misconception:* All metals are attracted to a magnet.
25. *Misconception:* As waves move, matter moves along with them.

7.5 Misconceptions in Chemistry

People's perception of chemistry is influenced by the media. Movies have often pictured chemists as mad scientists (*Dr. Jekyll and Mr. Hyde,* 1931) or as crazy professors (*Absent-Minded Professor,* 1961, *Flubber,* 1997). Unfortunately, very few people can accurately explain what chemistry is or what chemists do. It is no wonder, therefore, that misconceptions about chemical principles abound.

Following are a few common misconceptions, each with contradictory data that can be used to disprove the misconception and arrive at the correct explanation:

Misconception: Fluid pressure acts only downward

Contradictory data: You feel pressure in both ears when swimming deep in the water, regardless of the way your head is positioned.

Correct explanation: This misconception probably comes from diagrams with arrows showing the downward pressure of the atmosphere or ocean on objects below. According to Pascal's principle, all points at the same depth in a fluid experience the same pressure. If, for example, you release a Styrofoam cup from a bathyscaphe deep in the ocean, it will not flatten like a pancake; rather, it will shrink equally in all dimensions so that it is a tiny replica of the original.

Misconception: Ice is always at zero degrees Celsius (32 °F)

Contradictory data: The coldest temperature recorded on Earth is -129 degrees Fahrenheit at Vostok, Antarctica. How can ice in Vostok remain a warm 32°F (161 degrees warmer) without an external heat source?

Correct explanation: Although the temperature of ice can vary widely, the temperature of ice water (where solid ice is in equilibrium with liquid water) is stable at 0°C. The temperature of ice water is widely known, and scientists calibrate temperature probes to 0°C by placing them in ice water. This familiarity with ice water probably leads to the misconception about ice. Solid ice, however, can be colder than 0°C if the environment is colder.

Misconception: Heat rises

Contradictory data: Heat is defined as a form of energy arising from the random motion of the molecules of bodies. It is not matter and therefore cannot rise or fall.

Correct explanation: Heat can be transferred by conduction, convection, or radiation. Warmer fluids rise above cooler fluids, carrying heat energy with them. The molecules in warmer fluids are more energetic and widely spaced than those in cool fluids. As a result, cooler fluids are denser and sink below warmer fluids (warmer fluids rise).

Misconception: Organic farmers use organic chemicals

Contradictory data: Organic growers market their produce as "all natural," but organic chemicals, such as synthetic fertilizers, pesticides, and herbicides, are manufactured.

Correct explanation: The adjective *organic* indicates that something was derived from living matter. Organic farmers use fertilizers derived from living matter such as manure and fish meal and manage pests using biological controls. The term *organic chemistry* refers to carbon-based chemistry. This term was derived from the fact that nearly all synthetic carbon-based chemicals are derived from petroleum, a product of decayed, compressed vegetation. Organic farmers, however, do not use synthetic organic chemicals.

ACTIVITY 7.5.1 *Clarifying Misconceptions in Chemistry*

Note to teacher: Following is a list of common misconceptions in chemistry. Give one misconception to each student, and instruct the class to research the misconception, explain why it is wrong by reasoning from observed facts and experiences, and provide a correct explanation.

The first item is an example:

1. *Misconception:* Objects float because they are lighter than water. *Correct explanation:* Objects float if they are buoyed up by a force greater than their own weight (Archimedes principle). Some barges are made of concrete and float well because they displace a greater weight of water than their own weight. Fluids of lower density than water (not lower weight) float on top of water.
2. *Misconception:* Wood floats, and rocks sink.
3. *Misconception:* Liquids in straws and pipettes rise due to suction.
4. *Misconception:* The maximum temperature that water can be is 100°C.
5. *Misconception:* The bubbles in boiling water are made of air or oxygen.
6. *Misconception:* Electrons flow at the speed of light in copper wires.
7. *Misconception:* Cations are positive because they have gained protons
8. *Misconception:* Iron and steel are the only strongly ferromagnetic materials.
9. *Misconception:* The faster a fluid moves, the higher its pressure is.
10. *Misconception:* All radioactivity is man-made.
11. *Misconception:* Thermal expansion is due to the expansion of particles of matter.
12. *Misconception:* Electrons orbit the nucleus like planets around the Sun
13. *Misconception:* The metric system is more accurate than the other measurement systems.
14. *Misconception:* Heat and temperature are the same.
15. *Misconception:* There are 92 naturally occurring elements on Earth.
16. *Misconception:* Solids are completely solid and contain no space.
17. *Misconception:* Air has no mass.
18. *Misconception:* Rusting iron does not change weight.
19. *Misconception:* Drops on the outside of a cold container are due to leakage.

20. *Misconception:* Chemical reactions continue until all the reactants are exhausted.
21. *Misconception:* Endothermic reactions are never spontaneous.
22. *Misconception:* Combustion reactions are endothermic because energy must be added before they will occur.
23. *Misconception:* The space between electrons and the nucleus is composed of air.
24. *Misconception:* Oxidation is the addition of oxygen in a reaction.
25. *Misconception:* Reduction is the removal of oxygen in a reaction.
26. *Misconception:* Electrons enter an electrolytic cell at the cathode, travel through the solution, and exit at the anode.
27. *Misconception:* Energy is released when bonds are broken.

7.6 Misconceptions in Biology

Misconceptions can kill you. One common misconception is, "If a little is good, more is better." A little medicine, painkiller, or sedative can relieve symptoms, but too much may cause complications and even death. For example, an excess of sleeping pills (barbiturates) has led to the death of many celebrities, including rock and roll stars Elvis Presley, Jimi Hendrix, and Brian Jones (Rolling Stones) and movie star Marilyn Monroe.

Many misconceptions are propagated because they seem logical. For example, many believe that you can treat frostbite (injury to fingers, toes, ears, and other body tissues due to exposure to extreme cold) by drinking alcohol, smoking cigarettes, and not drinking water. This seems logical since alcohol makes one feel warm, cigarettes bring hot air into the lungs, and water is generally cool. However, medical experts say that alcohol reduces shivering (the body's way of generating friction to keep tissues warm), nicotine (the addictive substance in tobacco) slows circulation, and dehydration (insufficient body water) reduces blood flow to endangered tissues. Thus, a person suffering frostbite, a person *should* drink water but *should not* smoke or drink alcohol.

Following are a few common misconceptions, each with contradictory data that can be used to disprove the misconception and arrive at the correct explanation:

Misconception: Cold, wet weather causes the flu

Contradictory data: Influenzas are caused by viruses. Viruses live and reproduce within the cells of host organisms, not within cold, wet rain.

Correct explanation: People believe that cold, wet weather causes the flu because people often get sick during this type of weather. It is true to say that influenza is correlated with this type of weather but incorrect to say that it is caused by it. People tend to stay inside more during this type of weather and therefore are more likely to come in contact with others, who may be infected. Although the weather does not cause the flu, people may be more susceptible if they are chilled.

Misconception: Plant mass comes from the water and minerals that plants obtain from the soil

Contradictory data: One would expect plants to sink into the soil if their entire mass was drawn from the minerals and water withdrawn from the soil. However, there are not depressions around trees or bushes, suggesting that this explanation is flawed.

Correct explanation: Although plants absorb and retain water and minerals from the soil, the majority of plant mass is made of cellulose and other carbon-based molecules. Most plant mass is obtained from atmospheric carbon dioxide as carbon is fixed into sugars during the process of photosynthesis.

Misconception: People use only 10 percent of their brains

Contradictory data: Positron emission tomography (PET scan) and functional magnetic resonance imaging (fMRI) show activity in all parts of the brain, although not simultaneously.

Correct explanation: The 10 percent myth is frequently quoted by psychics and other who exploit people's ignorance and offer ways of tapping into the "unused 90 percent" of the brain. We use different portions and pathways of the brain for different functions, so it is impossible to say precisely what percentage of the brain we use at any time.

Misconception: Only meat, fish, and eggs have protein

Contradictory data: DNA is transcribed to RNA, which is translated into proteins. All life is based on DNA; therefore, all living systems must produce proteins.

Correct explanation: All cells manufacture protein. Proteins provide structure and serve as enzymes and hormones essential for biological processes. Certain foods have a higher percentage of proteins than other foods. For example, meats have a high percentage of proteins because they come from muscular tissue, which is composed primarily of two proteins, actin and myosin.

Misconception: There is a start and an end to the food chain

Contradictory data: If this were true, all nutrients would end up at the end of the food chain and there would be none available for new life.

Correct explanation: Decomposers, primarily fungi and bacteria, break down all life forms, including those at the top of the food web, and return nutrients to the soil, water, and air, where they are used by primary producers. If there were no decomposers, the vast majority of carbon and other nutrients would be locked up in dead organisms and unavailable for further life.

ACTIVITY 7.6.1 *Clarifying Misconceptions in Biology*

Note to teacher: Following is a list of common misconceptions in biology. Give one misconception to each student, and instruct the class to research the misconception, explain why it is wrong by reasoning from observed facts and experiences, and provide a correct explanation.

The first item is an example:

1. *Misconception:* Worry and stress turn hair gray. *Correct explanation:* The graying of hair is a genetic phenomenon. Melanocytes, the cells that produce the pigments in the hair, stop producing pigments at different times in different people as a result of genetics, not stress.
2. *Misconception:* If you cross your eyes, they may get stuck.
3. *Misconception:* Your heart stops when you sneeze.
4. *Misconception:* Heartburn is in your heart.
5. *Misconception:* Chemicals are bad for you.
6. *Misconception:* Plants respire only at night.
7. *Misconception:* Daughters inherit their physical characteristics from their mothers and sons from their fathers.
8. *Misconception:* All deciduous trees are angiosperms.
9. *Misconception:* The most abundant phenotype in a population represents the dominant trait.
10. *Misconception:* All plant shoots are phototropic (they grow toward light).
11. *Misconception:* When lemmings are overpopulated, they commit suicide by running off cliffs into the ocean.
12. *Misconception:* Anaerobic respiration takes place only when there is no air.
13. *Misconception:* The heart is on the left side of the body.
14. *Misconception:* All plants are photosynthetic.
15. *Misconception:* The stomach occupies most of your abdomen.
16. *Misconception:* Food enters the blood stream from the stomach.
17. *Misconception:* Alcohol is a stimulant.
18. *Misconception:* The cornea is simply a window to the eye, and the lens alone focuses light.
19. *Misconception:* Arteries carry oxygenated blood, and veins carry deoxygenated blood.
20. *Misconception:* Muscles contract and expand to cause motion.
21. *Misnomers:* A misnomer is a misleading name. Explain why the following are misnomers. *Example:* juvenile diabetes: Both children and adults may have either type 1 ("juvenile") or type 2 diabetes.

a. adult stem cells
b. peanuts
c. coconut
d. poison oak
e. seagrass
f. pinenuts
g. abscissic acid
h. dark reactions
i. century plant
j. koala bear
k. starfish
l. bald eagle
m. fireflies
n. heartburn
o. killer whale
p. sea monkey
q. seahorse
r. jellyfish
s. junk DNA
t. spongy bone
u. fast metabolism

7.7 Misconceptions in Earth and Space Science

What is wrong with this sentence?

"At *sunset* we sat *motionless,* pondering the mysteries of the *dark side* of the Moon, when a *shooting star* passed *by* the *evening star.*"

Although this statement is easily understood, it is filled with error. We can never be motionless because we are on the surface of the Earth, which is spinning rapidly on its axis as it orbits the Sun, which is itself in motion. The Sun never sets but simply disappears from view as the Earth rotates. There is no "dark side" to the Moon. We never see the far side of the Moon because the Moon rotates on its axis at the same rate it orbits the Earth so that the same side always faces us. The "dark side" is exposed to sunlight whenever the side facing us is dark. Shooting stars (meteors) are glowing pieces of rock and dust and bear no resemblance to stars other than that they emit light. The evening star is actually the planet Venus, not a star

at all. Finally, the meteor was millions of miles in front of the evening star and did not pass "by" it.

Many of our misconceptions are rooted in experience. From our frame of reference, it makes sense to talk about sunrise and sunset, for we have no sensation of the Earth's rotation. It certainly seems as if we are standing still because we don't experience any wind or feeling of acceleration or movement. Figure 7.3 is a photograph I took while backpacking in California's Sierra Nevada Mountains. The shutter was left open for a few hours, allowing starlight to expose Mount Lyell. The stars appear to be moving in an arc from right to left, and in the absence of other knowledge of astronomy, it is fair to conclude that the stars, like the Sun, rotate around the Earth. In reality, the Earth is spinning on its axis, creating the apparent motion of the stars. The line traveling at right angles to the stars was created by a satellite, and it is the only object in the photograph that is orbiting the Earth.

Research studies have shown that many people share the same misconceptions about the universe. For example, a large percentage of people believe that we experience summer at the point in our

Figure 7.3 Time Exposure of Stars

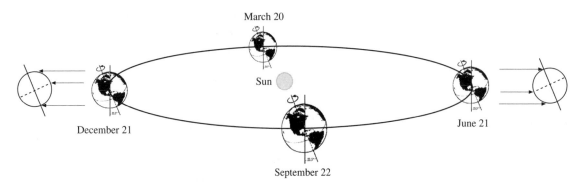

Figure 7.4 Earth's Orbit Around the Sun

orbit where we are closest to the Sun (perihelion) and winter when we are farthest from the Sun (aphelion). This makes sense based on our experience with other luminous objects. We feel warmer when we approach a campfire and colder when we move away from it. However, our concept is challenged when we look at additional data. For example, the Southern Hemisphere experiences winter when the Northern Hemisphere experiences summer. How can two parts of the world experience different seasons if seasonality is based solely on proximity to the Sun?

Diagrams can help clarify misconceptions but may also be the source of misconceptions. Figure 7.4 is designed to show the reasons for the seasons. The earth is tilted 23.5 degrees on its axis, so on December 21, relatively little light hits the Northern Hemisphere, while much hits the Southern Hemisphere. December 21 is the shortest day of the year in the Northern Hemisphere and the longest in the Southern Hemisphere. These factors explain why it is colder in the Northern Hemisphere on this day than it is in the Southern Hemisphere. Although the diagram helps explain seasons, it can also lead to some confusion. For example, the scale of the diagram is very misleading and does not represent the relative size of the Earth and Sun or the distance of the Earth from the Sun. If it were drawn to scale, the Earth would appear as a tiny spec on the ellipse.

Following are a few common misconceptions in earth and space sciences, each with contradictory data that can be used to disprove the misconception and arrive at the correct explanation:

Misconception: Space is a zero-gravity environment

Contradictory data: The Moon is in space, and yet gravity is sufficient to cause it to orbit the Earth.

Correct explanation: Astronauts experience weightlessness not because they are in space but because they are in orbit around the Earth. They are in a continual state of free fall toward the center of the Earth, but because they also have a tangential velocity, they orbit the Earth rather than plunge toward it.

Misconception: Gravity is a strong force

Contradictory data: A small magnet can raise a paper clip against the force of gravity, even though the Earth is far more massive than the magnet.

Correct explanation: The gravitational attraction between protons is a factor of $1/10^{36}$ the strength of electromagnetic repulsion. The gravitational attraction or repulsion of protons and electrons is negligible compared to electrostatic attraction or repulsion. Although gravity is such a weak force, it is the main force between celestial bodies, because planets and stars do not carry any net charge and are therefore electrically neutral. Gravity dominates the universe, although it is an extremely weak force. If the strong nuclear force is assigned a strength of 1, the strength of the electromagnetic force is 1×10^{-2}, and the strength of the weak nuclear force is 1×10^{-13}, then the strength of gravity is 1×10^{-38}.

Misconception: The "greenhouse effect" is a bad thing

Contradictory data: Without greenhouse heating, the Earth's average temperature would be about −73°C (−100°F), cold enough to freeze even the oceans.

Correct explanation: The greenhouse effect is the process in which the atmosphere warms a planet. Infrared radiation emitted from the Earth is captured by greenhouse gases, warming the atmosphere and keeping temperatures reasonable for life. Although the greenhouse effect is essential for life, the release of excessive greenhouse gases by human activity, particularly carbon dioxide released from the combustion of fossil fuels, is believed to contribute to global warming, a potentially devastating trend.

Misconception: The Coriolis effect causes water in drains to rotate clockwise in the Northern Hemisphere and counterclockwise in the Southern Hemisphere

Contradictory data: In the same house, water in a kitchen sink may run one way, while water in a bathroom sink runs the other.

Correct explanation: Although the Earth rotates eastward (toward the Sun) with constant angular velocity, points on Earth have very different linear speeds. The North and South Poles have a linear speed of 0, while points on the equator travel at nearly 0.5 km per second. A point on the equator travels 40,075 km (24,900 mi) per day, while points at the poles travel nowhere. When an object moves north or south from the equatorial regions and is not firmly connected to the ground, it maintains some of its initial eastward velocity as it moves. Objects moving away from the equator veer relative to the more slowly moving Earth beneath them. The reverse happens moving from northern or southern regions (low linear velocity) toward the equator (high linear velocity). This causes currents to move clockwise in the Northern Hemisphere and counterclockwise in the Southern Hemisphere (Figure 7.5), but is too small to affect water

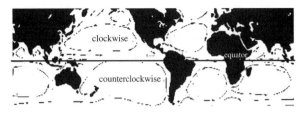

Figure 7.5 Ocean Currents Caused in Part by the Coriolis Effect

running down a drain. Surface features, drain geometry, and initial conditions affect the direction of a vortex in a drain.

Misconception: A tsunami is a "tidal wave"

Contradictory data: The tides are caused by the gravitational pull of the Moon on the waters in the oceans. Tsunamis, however, occur at random intervals and are not correlated with the position of the Moon.

Correct explanation: A tsunami is a series of waves formed when a massive amount of water is displaced by an earthquake or volcano. Tsunamis are frequently called tidal waves because they resemble a violent rushing tide as they approach land. But they are not related to the Moon or to tides, so oceanographers say that the term *tidal wave* is very misleading and should not be used.

ACTIVITY 7.7.1 *Clarifying Misconceptions in Earth and Space Science*

Note to teacher: Following are a few common misconceptions, each with contradictory data that can be used to disprove the misconception and arrive at the correct explanation:

The first item is an example:

1. *Misconception:* The Great Wall of China is the only man-made object that can be seen from the Moon. *Correct explanation:* No manmade objects are visible from the Moon, and astronauts note that the Great Wall of China disappears from view earlier than more massive man-made structures such as highways, cities, and large ships. The Great Wall of China is much narrower than modern highways, and

if such roads cannot be seen from space, then neither would the Great Wall of China.

2. *Misconception:* It is possible to balance eggs on end on the vernal equinox.

3. *Misconception:* There is a dark side of the Moon.

4. *Misconception:* Stars twinkle because they are on fire.

5. *Misconception:* The tail of a comet travels behind it as it moves.

6. *Misconception:* Planets traveling closest to the Sun travel slowest because they have the smallest orbits.

7. *Misconception:* The Moon orbits the center of mass of the Earth.

8. *Misconception:* Raindrops are shaped like teardrops.

9. *Misconception:* Polaris (the North Star) has always been in the direction of true north.

10. *Misconception:* A magnetic compass always points north.

11. *Misconception:* The north end of a compass needle points to the Earth's magnetic North Pole.

12. *Misconception:* Rivers flow south.

13. *Misconception:* There is a "up" and "down" in space.

14. *Misconception:* Black holes are empty holes in space.

15. *Misconception:* All of the planets have solid surfaces.

16. *Misconception:* The Sun is directly overhead at noon.

17. *Misconception:* The Sun does not rotate.

18. *Misconception:* Shadows don't exist on overcast days because the Sun is not bright enough.

19. *Misconception:* Clouds, fog, and steam are water vapor.

20. *Misconception:* The phases of the Moon are due to the shadow of the Earth.

21. *Misconception:* The stars of a constellation are near each other.

22. *Misconception:* The Sun rises in the east and sets in the west.

23. *Misconception:* Small earthquakes prevent big ones from happening.

24. *Misconception:* Underground streams flow just like streams above ground.

Answers to Chapter Activities

7.1.1   Students will construct data comparison tables.

7.1.2   Sudoku puzzles require many of the critical thinking skills on the list. Players must examine problems carefully, look at all evidence, reject incorrect information, and suspend judgment until sufficient facts have been considered. Encourage students to explain specific strategies with their peers through a pair-share activity. Answers are found in Figure 7.6.

7.2.1–7.2.3 Student projects and responses will vary.

7.3.1   Students complete the decision-making matrix and write a persuasive essay for the fuel source that ranks highest. You may wish to encourage students to use additional resources as they write their essays.

7.3.2   Students will generate decision-making matrices. Some categories may be much more important than others, and students should be encouraged to weight the scores of the more important columns more heavily.

7.4.1   Clarifying misconceptions in physics: The misconception is followed by the correct explanation.

1. Electrical charge is used up as it flows through a circuit. Correct explanation: Answer provided in activity section.

2. Charge flows through circuits at the speed of light. Correct explanation: Electric fields propagate at nearly the speed of light in electric circuits as electrons begin to move. The electrons themselves move rather slowly. The theory of relativity ($E = mc^2$, where $c = 3.0 \times 10^8$ m/s) indicates that far too much energy is required to move electrons at the speed of light.

3. Red light is most energetic and blue light least energetic. Correct explanation: Students grow up associating red with hot and blue with cold. Labels on faucets and diagrams reinforce this association. The energy of electromagnetic radiation is proportional to frequency $E = hf$, $i h$ is Planck's constant 6.6×10^{-34} Js. Blue light (7×10^{14} Hz) has a higher frequency than red light (4×10^{14} Hz), and therefore higher energy.

4. We are running out of energy. Correct explanation: Energy is not destroyed but converted to less useful forms, such as heat and sound. As a civilization, we are depleting usable energy sources, notably the chemical potential energy within fossil fuels. As these fuels are burned, energy is released in less usable forms as heat, light, sound, and motion.

5. Sonic booms occur only the moment when the sound barrier is punctured. Correct explanation: Sonic booms are heard whenever an object is exceeding the speed of sound. Stationary observers hear it only once as the shock wave moves past them.

6. Centrifugal force pushes riders into the walls of turning cars or banking roller coasters. Correct explanation: Centrifugal force (meaning "center fleeing") is a fictitious force that appears when one is in a rotating frame of reference like a roller coaster or a turning car. It appears as though there is a force pushing the rider away from the center of rotation. However, when viewed from an inertial frame of reference, one sees

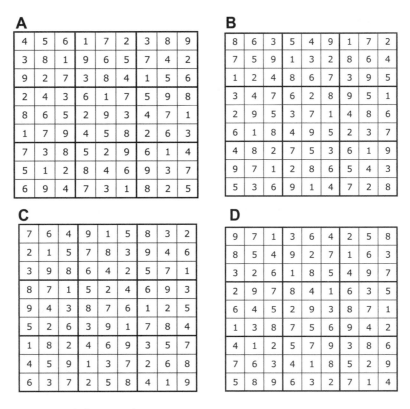

Figure 7.6 Solutions to Sudoku Puzzles

that the passenger's inertia resists acceleration, and the walls of the car push on the passenger.

7. The sky is blue because it reflects the color of the ocean. Correct explanation: The sky appears blue because gases in the atmosphere scatter blue light more than the other colors (Rayleigh scattering). Oceans and lakes appear blue on sunny days as they reflect the color of the sky. Note that the ocean and lakes appear gray on overcast days.

8. Vacuum cleaners suction (pull) up debris from the carpet. Correct explanation: Suction is a fictitious force. Vacuum cleaners create a low-pressure zone, and atmospheric pressure outside pushes debris into them. Suction implies pulling, but there is no medium to pull with. Solids can be pulled; gases cannot be.

9. Warmer objects have more heat than cooler objects. Correct explanation: Temperature is a measure of the intensity of energy, and heat is a measure of the extent of energy. A cold ocean has much more energy than a warm cup of coffee even though the coffee has a higher temperature. This misconception arises because people use the terms interchangeably in everyday language. We say "it is a hot day" or that "we don't enjoy the heat." Instead, we should say "the temperature is high today" or that "we don't enjoy high temperatures."

10. All rays of sunlight that hit the Earth are parallel. Correct explanation: Light rays from distant stars are essentially parallel because they emanate from point sources, but light rays from the Sun are not because the Sun has observable dimensions. Light rays from one side of the Sun cross those emanating from the other side. Most textbooks describe light rays from the Sun as parallel, and they are close enough to parallel for purposes of focusing light to a small dot with a hand lens.

11. Electric companies sell electric charge that flows to consumers. Correct explanation: Electric companies sell energy delivered by alternating current (AC). In AC, the electrons move back and forth over small distances, generating an electric field the length of the wire. Electric companies charge per kilowatt-hour, which is a measure of energy, not a measure of charge. If electric companies sold charge, they would charge per coulomb, not per kilowatt-hour.

12. The primary colors of light are red, blue, and yellow. Correct explanation: The primary colors of light are red, green, and blue. All computer monitors and TV monitors are composed of red, green, and blue pixels that can be used to create a variety of colors when stimulated to varying degrees. The retinas in our eyes contain photoreceptive cones that detect red, green, and blue light, and hence these are the primary colors for purposes of human vision. Students often think that blue, red, and yellow are the primary colors because they learned in art class that you can make all colors

by mixing these pigments in varying degrees. Actually, cyan, magenta, and yellow are the three primary colors of pigments, as reflected in the c/m/y toner and ink cartridges of printers. Cyan (a bluish color), magenta (a reddish color), and yellow pigments can be mixed to give a variety of colors in print media. However, pigments act in a subtractive manner to produce new colors, whereas light acts in an additive fashion.

13. When white light passes through a colored filter, the filter adds color to the light. Correct explanation: Filters remove all colors but the ones they transmit or reflect. A red filter removes all light but red.

14. Gravity is a strong force. Correct explanation: Gravity is an extremely weak force, but it is significant because there is so much mass through which it acts. The comparative weakness of gravity is demonstrated by the ease with which a small magnet using electromagnetic force can lift an iron nail against the full gravitational pull of the Earth.

15. Infrared light is a kind of heat radiation. Correct explanation: Infrared light was discovered when William Herschell noticed that the zone beyond red light in a spectrum could heat surfaces. In fact, all forms of visible lights, not just infrared, can heat surfaces. People link infrared with heat because objects at room temperature emit radiation in the mid-infrared region. Electric heaters feel hot because they are "extremely bright" in the red and infrared portion of the spectrum.

16. Energy and force are the same thing. Correct explanation: Energy is the capacity to do work, and work is the application of a force through a distance, so energy and force are related, but not synonymous.

17. *Velocity* is another word for *speed*. Correct explanation: Speed is the rate of movement measured in distance per unit of time, whereas velocity is the speed in a given direction. Velocity is a vector quantity; speed is scalar quantity. Students confuse these terms because they often hear them incorrectly used interchangeably.

18. If an object has zero velocity, it has zero acceleration. Correct explanation: Acceleration is the rate of change of velocity. A thrown football experiences an acceleration of 1 g (9.8 m/s^2) toward the Earth from the moment it is thrown. At the top of its parabolic flight it has a vertical velocity of 0 m/s but is still accelerating toward the Earth at 9.8 m/s^2.

19. The effects of light are instantaneous. Correct explanation: Light has a measurable speed (3.0×10^8 m/s in a vacuum) but travels so fast that its effects appear instantaneous over short distances. It takes light approximately 8.3 seconds to travel 93 million miles from the Sun to Earth.

20. Gamma rays, X-rays, ultraviolet light, visible light, infrared light, and microwaves and radio waves are all very different entities. Correct explanation: All of these are forms of electromagnetic radiation and vary only in their frequency ($f = \lambda^{-1}$). People regard them as different entities because they have such different applications. For example, radio waves are used for communication, light for vision, and X-rays for medical diagnostics. Nonetheless, they are all variations of the same phenomenon.

21. When two pulses or waves, traveling in opposite directions meet, they bounce off each other. Correct explanation: Waves reflect off surfaces, leading some to believe that they reflect off each other. However, sound, light, water, and mechanical (on a string or rope) waves travel through each other, unaffected by one another.

22. More massive objects fall faster. Correct explanation: All objects accelerate under gravity at the same rate in a vacuum. However, less dense objects are generally affected more by air resistance than denser or more streamlined objects, and hence they fall slower in the atmosphere. Misconceptions arise when one does not define the environmental parameters.

23. The more mass in a pendulum bob, the faster it swings. Correct explanation: The period (T) of a pendulum is dependent on length (L) but independent of mass (m). $T = 2\pi(L/g)^{1/2}$. People often think that more massive pendulums fall faster for the same reason that they believe heavier objects fall faster than lighter objects. The timing of grandfather clocks is adjusted by changing the length of the pendulum rather than changing its mass.

24. All metals are attracted to a magnet. Correct explanation: Not all metals are attracted to magnets. Aluminum, copper, lead, gold, and silver are examples of metals that are not attracted to a magnet.

25. As waves move, matter moves along with them. Correct explanation: This misconception is derived by watching the surf at the ocean. It appears as though water from far out in the ocean is pushed ashore. Although currents move water laterally, waves do not, except when they crash on the shore. Waves transmit energy without transmitting matter. The energy released in an earthquake is transmitted through the Earth to seismographs around the world without the transmission of matter. Similarly, energy is transmitted by light without the transmission of matter.

7.5.1 Clarifying misconceptions in chemistry: The misconception is followed by the correct explanation:

1. Objects float because they are lighter than water. Correct explanation: Answer provided in activity section.

2. Wood floats and rocks sink. Correct explanation: Some woods have a density greater than water (1.00 g/ml) and sink: lignum vitae (1.37g/ml), desert ironwood (1.15 g/ml), and ebony (1.12 g/ml) are examples. Some rocks, such as pumice (a volcanic rock with trapped gases), have a density less than water and float.

3. Liquids in straws and pipettes rise due to suction. Correct explanation: Suction does not exist. Liquids and gases cannot be pulled because they do not have tensile strength. Straws and pipettes work because a person or bulb creates a low-pressure zone. Atmospheric pressure outside pushes the fluid up the tube because of this pressure differential.

4. The maximum temperature that water can be is 100°C. Correct explanation: The boiling point is the

temperature at which vapor pressure is equal to the surrounding air pressure. The boiling point can be raised far above 100°C by sealing the container, as is done in a pressure cooker in which liquid water reaches temperatures far in excess of 100°C.

5. The bubbles in boiling water are made of air or oxygen. Correct explanation: A liquid boils when its vapor pressure is equal to the surrounding atmospheric pressure. The bubbles in boiling water are gaseous water, not air or oxygen.

6. Electrons flow at the speed of light in copper wires. Correct explanation: Electrons travel only a few millimeters per second in copper wires. When a switch is opened or closed, the change in potential difference moves at nearly the speed of light.

7. Cations are positive because they have gained protons. Correct explanation: Cations are positive because they have lost negatively charged electrons. Losing a negative charge leaves the atom with a net positive charge.

8. Iron and steel are the only strongly ferromagnetic materials. Correct explanation: Strong permanent magnets can be made of neodymium, cobalt-samarium, and other materials.

9. The faster a fluid moves, the higher its pressure is. Correct explanation: Bernoulli's principle states that a decrease in pressure occurs simultaneously with an increase in velocity. The faster a fluid moves, the lower its pressure is.

10. All radioactivity is man-made. Correct explanation: Natural radioactivity is common in the rocks and soil that makes up our planet, water, and oceans (deuterium and tritium), and in building materials and buildings themselves.

11. Thermal expansion is due to the expansion of particles of matter. Correct explanation: Atoms do not expand when heated, but the spacing of atoms does increase according to the kinetic theory. The energy and speed of atoms or molecules increase as the temperature rises, causing them to spread out.

12. Electrons orbit the nucleus like planets around a sun. Correct explanation: The solar system model is inconsistent with principles of quantum mechanics. Chemists prefer to discuss electron clouds as zones where electrons are likely to be.

13. The metric system is more accurate than the other measurement systems. Correct explanation: The metric system is easier to use than the customary (English) system but not more accurate or precise.

14. Heat and temperature are the same. Correct explanation: Temperature is an intrinsic property of matter (dependent only on intensity), while heat is an extensive property (dependent on the extent or amount of matter). The ocean may have the same temperature as a glass of water, but it has much greater energy.

15. There are 92 naturally occurring elements on Earth. Correct explanation: Since uranium (element 92) is the largest naturally occurring element, many people

assume that elements 1 to 91 also occur in nature. However, there are no stable isotopes of technetium (element 43) and promethium (element 61).

16. Solids are completely solid and contain no space. Correct explanation: Atoms are mostly space, and so all liquids, solids, and gases must also be mostly space. It is estimated that if the space between electrons and the nucleus of atoms could be removed, the entire mass of the Earth would collapse to size of a basketball.

17. Air has no mass. Correct explanation: Air is made of matter (nitrogen, oxygen, carbon dioxide, argon, and so forth) and therefore has mass. The density of air at sea level is approximately 1/800th the density of water (1.25 kg/m^3).

18. Rusting iron does not change weight. Correct explanation: Iron combines with oxygen to produce iron oxide or rust. The addition of oxygen causes the mass and weight to increase.

19. Drops on the outside of a cold container are due to leakage. Correct explanation: The drops on the outside of a cold container are the result of the condensation of atmospheric water vapor. The higher the relative humidity is, the greater the condensation.

20. Chemical reactions continue until all the reactants are exhausted. Correct explanation: Chemical reactions reach equilibrium when the rate of the forward reactions is equal to the rate of the reverse reactions. In some reactions, the initial forward rate may greatly exceed the reverse rate, giving the misimpression that all of the reactants are exhausted.

21. Endothermic reactions are never spontaneous. Correct explanation: Change in free energy (ΔG), not the change in enthalpy (ΔH), determines the spontaneity of a reaction. Reactions are spontaneous whenever there is a release in free energy (ΔG is negative); Gibbs free energy is composed of enthalpy and entropy as seen in the equation $\Delta G = \Delta H - T\Delta S$. Endothermic reactions are spontaneous when the increase in entropy (ΔS) is sufficiently large. In other words, a reaction is spontaneous when ΔG is negative, which occurs in endothermic reactions only when the magnitude of $T\Delta S$ is greater than ΔH.

22. Combustion reactions are endothermic because energy must be added before they will occur. Correct explanation: A reaction is exothermic whenever there is a net release of energy. Activation energy must be used to initiate combustion reactions, but more energy is released than consumed, so they are considered to be exothermic.

23. The space between electrons and the nucleus is composed of air. Correct explanation: There is nothing in the space between electrons and the nucleus of an atom or between atoms or molecules in matter.

24. Oxidation is the addition of oxygen in a reaction. Correct explanation: Oxidation is a reaction in which the oxidation number increases. Oxygen is an excellent oxidizing agent because it removes electrons and causes the oxidation number to increase. Iodine, fluorine, and bromine are also good oxidizers, but they are less common than oxygen.

25. Reduction is the removal of oxygen in a reaction. Correct explanation: Reduction occurs whenever the oxidation number is decreased. This may take place when oxygen is removed, but it also takes place in many other equations in which oxygen is not involved.

26. Electrons enter an electrolytic cell at the cathode, travel through the solution, and exit at the anode. Correct explanation: Although the movement of electrons causes a current within metals, the movement of ions causes a current within solutions.

27. Energy is released when bonds are broken. Correct explanation: Energy is always required to break bonds. Energy is released in a reaction if the sum of the bond energies of the products is less than the sum of the bond energies of the reactants.

7.6.1 Clarifying misconceptions in biology: The misconception is followed by the correct explanation.

1. Worry and stress turn hair gray. Correct explanation: Answer provided in activity section.

2. If you cross your eyes, they may get stuck. Correct explanation: Crossing the eyes is a voluntary motion, and the muscles will fatigue and return to their normal positions as other voluntary muscles do.

3. Your heart stops when you sneeze. Correct explanation: Intrathoracic pressure increases while sneezing. This may decrease venous blood flow to the heart, resulting in a slight change of the breathing rate, but it does not stop the electrical and muscular activity of the heart.

4. Heartburn is in your heart. Correct explanation: Heartburn is a form of indigestion that causes a burning sensation in the chest. It is the result of acid regurgitation from the stomach into the esophagus.

5. Chemicals are bad for you. Correct explanation: Many chemicals are bad for you, but many are essential. Your body is composed of myriad chemicals, including carbohydrates, lipids, proteins, and nucleic acids.

6. Plants respire only at night. Correct explanation: Plants, like animals, respire continuously to produce adenosine triphosphate (ATP) for use in growth, and development.

7. Daughters inherit their physical characteristics from their mothers and sons from their fathers. Correct explanation: A child receives half of his or her genes from each parent. The expression of these genes (phenotype) depends on the ratio of dominant and recessive alleles inherited.

8. All deciduous trees are angiosperms. Correct explanation: Some gymnosperms, notably the metasequoia and larch, are deciduous. Most people see only evergreen gymnosperms such as pine, fir, cypress, and spruce, hence, the misconception that all gymnosperms are evergreens.

9. The most abundant phenotype in a population represents the dominant trait. Correct explanation: Dominance refers to the expression of a gene, not its abundance. A good example of a rare dominant characteristic is pseudoachondroplasia, a type of dwarfism. Although the gene is rare, it is dominant and phenotypically expressed in all offspring who contain the gene.

10. All plant shoots are phototropic (grow toward light). Correct explanation: The tendrils of vines are negatively phototropic. This causes them to grow toward walls, rocks, and branches for support.

11. When lemmings are overpopulated, they commit suicide by running off cliffs into the ocean. Correct explanation: Lemming populations, like those of many other rodents, periodically exhibit dramatic growth and decline, but this is due primarily to migration and disease. The lemming myth was probably created to explain population cycles and was popularized in Walt Disney's 1958 movie *White Wilderness* in which moviemakers induced lemmings to jump.

12. Anaerobic respiration takes place only when there is no air. Correct explanation: Anaerobic respiration occurs whenever there is insufficient oxygen for complete aerobic respiration. The product of anaerobic respiration in humans is lactic acid, which may trigger muscle contractions and cramping.

13. The heart is on the left side of the body. Correct explanation: The heart is located in the center of the chest, but its left side is larger. The left ventricle pumps to the entire body and is therefore more muscular than the right side, which pumps only to the lungs.

14. All plants are photosynthetic. Correct explanation: A few hundred plant species lack chlorophyll, are parasitic, and obtain their energy from their hosts.

15. The stomach occupies most of your abdomen. Correct explanation: The stomach is located immediately below the diaphragm. Most of the space in the abdomen is occupied by the intestines.

16. Food enters the bloodstream from the stomach. Correct explanation: Food is chemically and mechanically digested in the stomach, but the absorption of nutrients takes place in the intestines.

17. Alcohol is a stimulant. Correct explanation: Alcohol is a sedative and depresses central nervous system functions.

18. The cornea is simply a window to the eye, and the lens alone focuses light. Correct explanation: The cornea is the main lens of the eye. It is more curved than the lens and plays a significant role in focusing light on the retina.

19. Arteries carry oxygenated blood, and veins carry deoxygenated blood. Correct explanation: Arteries carry blood away from the heart, and veins carry blood toward the heart. Pulmonary arteries (those going to the lungs) carry deoxygenated blood, while systemic arteries (those supplying the rest of the body) carry oxygenated blood. Pulmonary veins (those bringing blood from the lungs to the heart) carry oxygenated blood, while systemic veins (those bringing blood from the rest of the body to the heart) carry deoxygenated blood.

20. Muscles contract and expand to cause motion. Correct explanation: All motion is caused by muscle contraction, not expansion. Muscles are paired in agonist/antagonist pairs. Agonists contract to cause flexion or extension, and antagonist muscles contract to counter these motions with extension or flexion.

21. Misnomers. A misnomer is a misleading name. Explanations of the misnomers follow each term.

a. adult stem cells: Adult stem cells are cells that reside in developed tissue but can also be found in infants and children.

b. peanuts: Peanuts are legumes, not nuts.

c. coconut: Coconuts are fruits, not nuts.

d. poison oak: Poison oak is not an oak but a member of the sumac family.

e. seagrass: Seagrasses do not belong to the grass family.

f. pinenuts: Pinenuts are seeds, not nuts.

g. abscissic acid: Abscissic acid is not involved in abscission, but rather the maintenance of dormancy in buds and seeds.

h. dark reactions: The "dark reactions" of photosynthesis (carbon fixation) occur during the daytime but do not require light. It is preferable to use the term *Calvin cycle reactions*.

i. century plant: The life cycle of a century plant (Agave) is closer to 35 years than to 100 years.

j. koala bear: Koalas belong to the Phascolarctidae, not to the Ursoidae (bear family).

k. starfish: Starfish are echinoderms, not fish.

l. bald eagle: Bald eagles are not bald; they have white feathers on their head.

m. fireflies: Fireflies are beetles, not flies.

n. heartburn: Heartburn is due to indigestion and has nothing to do with the heart.

o. killer whale: Killer whales (orcas) are members of the dolphin family.

p. sea monkey: Sea monkeys are a hybrid form of brine shrimp.

q. seahorse: Seahorses are not horses but members of the Syngnathidae.

r. jellyfish: Jellyfish are coelenterates, not fish.

s. junk DNA: Noncoding DNA may be spacer material that allows enzyme complexes to form around functional elements more easily. Many other proposed functions have been proposed.

t. spongy bone: Spongy bone is actually hard, although it appears spongy in appearance.

u. fast metabolism: Metabolism is the sum of catabolism (building up) and anabolism (breaking down). It is better to refer to the speed of catabolic or anabolic processes.

7.7.1 Clarifying misconceptions in earth and space science: The misconception is followed by the correct explanation:

1. The Great Wall of China is the only man-made object that can be seen from the Moon. Correct explanation: Answer provided in activity section.

2. It is possible to balance eggs on end on the vernal equinox. Correct explanation: The vernal equinox (generally March 20) and autumnal equinox (generally September 22) are two days of the year when there is an equal length of day and night, but this has no effect on balancing eggs. With considerable practice, it is possible to balance an egg on end any day of the year.

3. There is a dark side of the Moon. Correct explanation: The Moon rotates on its axis as it orbits the Earth such that the same side always faces the Earth. Although we never see the far side of the Moon from Earth, it receives just as much sunlight as the side that faces us.

4. Stars twinkle because they are on fire. Correct explanation: Light bends, or refracts, when it passes between media of differing optical densities such as the layers of the atmosphere. Turbulence in the atmosphere repositions parcels of air, causing changes in the refraction of light and the consequent twinkling we see when viewing from Earth. Stars do not appear to twinkle when viewed from space because there is no atmosphere.

5. The tail of a comet travels behind it as it moves. Correct explanation: Although the smoke from a locomotive travels behind a train, the "tail" of a comet always flows away from the Sun. The trail of smoke from a train is affected by wind resistance, while the "tail" of a comet is directed by solar wind and light. Solar wind is composed of charged particles that direct the fluorescing ion tail away from the Sun. Simultaneously, solar radiation exerts a pressure on reflective particles in the dust tail, pushing them away from the Sun (Figure 7.7).

6. Planets traveling closest to the Sun travel slowest because they have the smallest orbits. Correct explanation: Kepler's second law states that an imaginary line drawn from the center of the Sun to the center of the planet will sweep out equal areas in equal intervals of time. Thus, the closer a planet is to the Sun, the faster it travels. Mercury, the planet closest to the Sun, has the highest orbital speed among the planets. Mercury derived its name because of its speed (in mythology, Mercury was the messenger of the gods).

7. The Moon orbits the center of mass of the Earth. Correct explanation: The Moon and the Earth orbit a point of common gravity that is approximately 1000 km below the Earth's surface on a line between the center of mass of the Moon and Earth.

8. Raindrops are shaped like teardrops. Correct explanation: The shape of a raindrop is determined by the interaction of surface tension of water and the pressure of the air as it falls. In small droplets (1 mm or smaller), raindrops assume a spherical shape, while larger droplets become indented. Water droplets over 4 mm in diameter tend to assume a parachute shape before breaking into smaller drops. The only place one finds the teardrop shape is when water lands on a surface and starts to slide, as on a windshield (Figure 7.8).

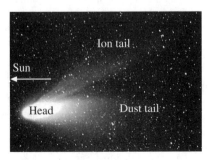

Figure 7.7 Comet Tails

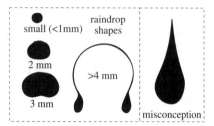

Figure 7.8 Raindrops

9. Polaris (the North Star) has always been in the direction of true north. Correct explanation: The Earth precesses like a wobbling, spinning top. Currently Polaris is within 1 degree of true north, but at other times Thuban, Vega, and Alpha Cephei have held this position.

10. A magnetic compass always points north. Correct explanation: It is believed that the Earth's magnetic field is produced by electric currents in the liquid part of the core. The magnetic pole wanders about 40 m per day, and you may wish to have students plot its movement given these historic data: 1831 96.5° W 70.1° N; 1904 96.2° W 70.5° N; 1948 101.1° W; 73.8° N; 1973 101.3° W 76.1° N; 1994 104.0° W 78.5° N. True north, however, is on the imaginary line extending from the axis of the Earth and is fixed at 90.0° N.

11. The north end of a compass needle points to the Earth's magnetic north pole. Correct explanation: The north end of a compass needle is defined as a north magnetic pole. Opposite magnetic poles attract, and the north pole of the compass is attracted to the Earth's south magnetic pole, which happens to be located near the geographical North Pole. We do, however, refer to this as the Magnetic North Pole because it is close to the true North Pole, so confusion is justified.

12. Rivers flow south. Correct explanation: Many of the world's largest rivers, most notably the Nile, flow north. Rivers flow downhill, regardless of the direction.

13. There is an "up" and "down" in space. Correct explanation: The definitions of *up* and *down* are based on our frame of reference. Since we live on the surface of the Earth, "down" is toward the geometric center of the Earth, and "up" is in the opposite direction. In space, these definitions are meaningless.

14. Black holes are empty holes in space. Correct explanation: A black hole is an extremely small region of space-time with a gravitational field so strong that not even light can escape. Black holes are the densest objects in the universe and thought to have formed from the collapse of larger stars.

15. All of the planets have solid surfaces. Correct explanation: The inner planets (Mercury, Venus, Earth, and Mars) are rocky. Jupiter, Saturn, Uranus, and Neptune are gaseous giants, composed primarily of hydrogen and helium and do not have solid surfaces.

16. The Sun is directly overhead at 12 noon. Correct explanation: The Earth is tilted 23.5° on its axis, so the Sun will never appear directly overhead north of the tropic of Cancer (23.5° N) or south of the Tropic of Capricorn (23.5° S). Even within this region, it will appear directly overhead at noon on only one or two days a year, and then only if you are in the exact middle of the time zone. Each time zone has a reference longitude where the Sun appears in line with both poles at noon. By definition, this is in the middle of the time zone.

17. The Sun does not rotate. Correct explanation: The Sun does rotate, but not like a solid planet. The Sun's rotational period is about 25 days at the equator and about 35 days near the poles.

18. Shadows don't exist on overcast days because the Sun is not bright enough. Correct explanation: Shadows are cast by directional lighting. On cloudy days, sunlight is very diffuse, reflected off water droplets in the clouds. Lighting is much more uniform, and as a result, shadows are faint or nonexistent.

19. Clouds, fog, and steam are water vapor. Correct explanation: Water vapor is made of molecules too small to be seen. Clouds, fog, and steam are composed of tiny droplets of liquid water. The bubbles of gas in boiling water are water vapor. When water vapor hits cooler air, some condenses as steam.

20. The phases of the Moon are due to the shadow of the Earth. Correct explanation: The phases of the Moon are due to the relative positions of the Sun, Earth, and Moon. A full Moon occurs when the Moon is on the opposite side of the Earth as the Sun. The Moon reflects its light back to the Earth. A new moon occurs when the Moon is between the Earth and the Sun. The Moon still reflects light, but back toward the Sun, not toward the Earth.

21. The stars of a constellation are near each other. Correct explanation: A constellation is a group of stars visible from Earth that forms a distinctive pattern. Although the stars appear in the same portion of the sky to us, they are often extremely far from each other and simply in the same direction when viewed from Earth.

22. The Sun rises in the east and sets in the west. Correct explanation: The apparent directions of sunrise and sunset are a function of latitude and the season. On the summer solstice, the Sun never sets when viewed from the North Pole and never rises when viewed from the South Pole.

23. Small earthquakes prevent big ones from happening. Correct explanation: Small earthquakes may relieve stress on a fault line but do not prevent large ones from happening. The energy released in a single magnitude 6 earthquake is nearly 27,000 times as great as in a magnitude 3 earthquake. As a result, it would require many small earthquakes to release the energy that causes a large one.

24. Underground streams flow just like streams above ground. Correct explanation: Many underground streams seep through permeable rocks and sands rather than flowing through stream-like underground channels.

Part Three

Developing Scientific Understanding

Chapter Eight

Organizing Science Information and Concepts

For the Teacher 151

8.1 Advance Organizers 153

8.2 Orders of Magnitude: The Universe in Powers of Ten 154

8.3 Organizational Hierarchy in Biology 157

8.4 Organization of the Chemistry Curriculum 161

8.5 Organization of the Physics Curriculum 161

8.6 Earth Systems Interactions 162

Answers to Chapter Activities 165

For the Teacher

Many educators use advance organizers to introduce students to new material. An *advance organizer* is information presented prior to the main lesson that the learner uses to organize and interpret new information. David Ausubel, a prominent educational researcher in the 1960s, believed that the most important determinant of learning is *what a learner already knows.*[1] He encouraged teachers to introduce new concepts by connecting them to prior knowledge and the new material. Advance organizers can be helpful in the development of such connections by providing an outline in which learners can place new material in context with existing information and see how it will relate to future learning. Much research supports Ausubel's contention that advance organizers aid understanding and retention.

Teachers routinely use a variety of advance organizers, even if they are unfamiliar with the term. Lesson outlines, KWL charts, SQ3R charts, concept maps, skimming, and gapped handouts are but a few of the advance organizers routinely used in education. Learners organize information in *schemas,* conceptual patterns in their minds, and advance organizers help structure these schemas so learners can assimilate new information efficiently.

Shopping mall maps are a type of advance organizer. They illustrate the structure of the mall and indicate a shopper's current position with a "you are here" marker. The shopper is familiar with his or her immediate surroundings (prior knowledge) and uses the map (advance organizer) to see how shops of interest (new knowledge) are geographically related to their current position and to one another (interrelation). Similarly, textbook authors often include chapter outlines and highlights at the beginning of chapters, providing students with a map of what they will be learning and how it relates to what they already know. Unfortunately many novice readers ignore such tips, classifying them as superfluous information akin to similarly formatted enrichment information that is often sprinkled through their books. Shoppers who use the mall maps are routinely more efficient with their use of time and gain a better understanding of the mall for future reference. Similarly, students who study advance organizers will be more efficient in their studies and have a better understanding of the big picture and the interrelatedness of its components.

Teachers are encouraged to use advance organizers in their curriculum, reading, projects, and lessons to help students develop sound schemata into which new material can be assimilated. In the activities that follow, students are provided opportunities to use classic advance organizers for entire subjects. Advance organizers should be used not only in advance of a lesson but also during the lesson, in much the same way a traveler refers to a map during a trip. Midtrip references to a map ensure that the traveler stays on course, and midstream references to advance organizers ensure that learners don't lose sight of the big picture. Two advance organizers that are commonly used in science education are KWL charts and the SR3R technique.

KWL Charts

A popular advance organizer that can be applied to any science class is the KWL chart. With this approach, students work in small groups to complete a chart similar to the one shown in Table 8.1. They first discuss what they already know (K) about the topic (column 1 in the table). By discussing this among themselves, they are given the opportunity to share their existing knowledge and bring others to a similar point of understanding. Next, they discuss what they want (W) to learn about this topic (column 2). The teacher surveys students' knowledge and interest and adapts the lesson accordingly. After completing the activity or lesson, students report what they have learned (L, column 3). The KWL chart is a good metacognitive activity in which students think about their thinking.

SQ3R Charts

Textbooks are structured entirely differently from novels, and yet most students read textbooks in a serial fashion, from the first page in a chapter to the last, the same way they would read a novel. This approach is relatively ineffective because it ignores the organizational structure and study clues given by the author. The SQ3R technique (**S**urvey, **Q**uestion, **R**ead, **R**ecite, **R**eview) is an

Table 8.1 KWL Charts

K What do you _K_now?	W What do you _W_ant to Know?	L What have you _L_earned?
Earthquakes occur in California, Japan, and Mexico.	Where are earthquakes likely to occur?	
The center of an earthquake is known as the epicenter.	How can you tell where the epicenter of an earthquake was?	
Earthquake intensity is measured on the Richter scale.	What do Richter scale values mean?	
Earthquakes result from movement in the Earth's crust.	What causes earthquakes?	
No one seems to know when earthquakes will occur.	Can anyone predict earthquakes?	

active approach to reading that helps students get the most out of reading science texts by developing a framework prior to reading. Unlike pleasure reading, which by nature is relatively passive, the SQ3R technique is a active approach that requires the readers to apply their mental energies to grasp the concepts.

Survey: Survey the chapter to see its organization and themes before reading.
- Record the title of the chapter and predict what will be included.
- Read the introduction or chapter objectives, and jot down the key concepts to be discussed.
- Note the main ideas, which are marked with boldface type or are underlined.
- Read the summary to understand the relationship between the main ideas.
- Read the questions at the end of the chapter. These reveal what the author thinks are the most important concepts.
- Review graphics, charts, and diagrams.

Question: You learn and remember best when actively engaged in searching for answers to questions.
- Turn headings and subheadings into questions.
- Develop questions for small sections.
- Add more questions as you proceed to new sections.

Read: Read the chapter once you have developed a framework by the preceding activities.
- Read one section at a time.
- Read selectively, focusing your attention on material related to questions you developed.
- Read small sections at a time.

Recite: Although the second **R** in the SQ3R technique stands for "recite," the goal is to be more active than during normal recitation. Rather than reciting what the textbook says, readers should try to answer the questions in their own words.
- Answer questions in your own words.
- Focus on small sections at a time.
- Answer questions for the section you have just read.
- "Recite" as you read.

Review: Repetition is a valuable teacher. The review stage of SQ3R gives students the opportunity to review key concepts and build long-term memory.
- Review all your questions.
- Test yourself for memory

8.1 Advance Organizers

ACTIVITY 8.1.1 *Concept of Advance Organizers*

Traffic engineers and transportation agencies have the responsibility of moving traffic efficiently and safely. In order to do this, they have developed a series of standard sign shapes, colors, and designs to notify motorists of upcoming hazards and resources. The signs are advance organizers, helping motorists understand things to come and make their plans accordingly. Unfortunately, many people do not pay attention to road signs or memorize their basic shapes, and this may lead to inefficient or dangerous driving. How many of the basic traffic sign designs can you identify? Match the letters of the shapes in Figure 8.1 with the meanings in Table 8.2.

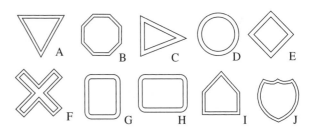

Figure 8.1 Traffic Sign Shapes

Table 8.2 Traffic Signs as Advance Organizers

Mileage	No Parking
Interstate highway	School zone
No passing zone	Stop
Railroad	Warning ahead
Railroad crossing	Yield

ACTIVITY 8.1.2 *Advance Organizers in Your Science Text*

Textbook authors and publishers use "traffic signs" to inform readers about the structure and content of the book. Research has shown that these advance organizers help students learn and remember new material by developing structures or schemas into which new information can be placed. Sadly, many students ignore these signs and spend much more time reading than necessary, yet with minimal understanding and retention.

Before reading a textbook, you should study its structure and features. Complete the following activity for a chapter that your science instructor assigns. By understanding the structure of the text, you will understand the structure of the discipline and be better able to integrate new ideas into your existing mental outline.

Organization of the Book

Special features: What are the unique or special features of this book? Most authors write a preface to explain their purpose in writing and describe the special features of their work.

Themes: What are the major themes of your textbook? Most authors group chapters in units with names that reflect the major themes of the book.

Topics: What are the main topics of the unit you are studying? This can generally be deduced from the chapter titles.

Organization of the Chapter

Objectives: What are the goals or objectives of the chapter you are studying? These are frequently listed at the beginning of the chapter.

Subtopics: What are the subtopics of the chapter? The subtopics are the division headings within chapters, often shown in **BOLDFACE CAPITALS**.

Major points: What are the major points of the section you are now studying? The major points are generally shown in **lowercase bold letters**.

Key terms: What are the key terms of the section you are now studying? In most textbooks, the key terms are shown in *italics* or **bold** letters.

8.2 Orders of Magnitude: The Universe in Powers of Ten

"How wide is the Milky Way galaxy?" "How small is a carbon atom?" These questions may sound simple, but their answers are virtually impossible to comprehend since nothing in our realm of experience approximates either of these measures. To grasp the magnitude of such dimensions is perhaps impossible, but it is relatively easy to express such dimensions by scaling up or down (expressing them in orders of magnitude greater or smaller) from things with whose dimensions we are familiar. An order of magnitude is the number of powers of 10 contained in the number and gives a shorthand way to describe scale. An understanding of scale allows us to organize our thinking and experience in terms of size and gives us a sense of dimension within the universe.

ACTIVITY 8.2.1 *Understanding Powers of Ten*

Note: This is an Internet-based activity.

To simplify the expression of very large and small numbers, scientists often use *scientific notation.* Scientific notation involves writing a number as the product of two numbers. The first one, the digit value, is always more than 1 and less than 10. The other, the exponential term, is expressed as a power of 10. Table 8.3 compares decimal and scientific notation.

The diameter of the Milky Way Galaxy is believed to be about 1,000,000,000,000,000,000,000 meters. By contrast, the diameter of the nucleus of a carbon atom is only approximately 0.000 000 000 000 01 meters. In scientific notation, the diameter of the Milky Way is 1×10^{21} m, and the diameter of the carbon nucleus is 1×10^{-14} m. The Milky Way is therefore approximately 10^{35} times (35 orders of magnitude) larger than the carbon atom. Calculators and computers may express the dimensions of the Milky Way and the carbon nucleus as 1.0E21 and 1.0E-14, where E stands for the exponential term. The speed of light, approximately 300 million (299,792,458) m

Table 8.3 Decimal and Scientific Notation

Decimal Notation	Scientific Notation	Order of Magnitude	Decimal Notation	Scientific Notation	Order of Magnitude
.001	1×10^{-3}	-3	10	1×10^{1}	1
.01	1×10^{-2}	-2	100	1×10^{2}	2
.1	1×10^{-1}	-1	1,000	1×10^{3}	3
1	1×10^{0}	0	10,000	1×10^{4}	4

per second, is expressed in scientific notation as approximately 3.0×10^{8} m/s (3.0E8). Avogadro's number, the number of molecules in a mole (602 21367000000000000000), is expressed as 6.02×10^{23} (6.02E23).

Scientific notation is particularly helpful when trying to express the scale of the universe. In 1957, Dutch educator Kees Boeke published *Cosmic View: The Universe in 40 Jumps,* in which he helped readers visualize the size of things in the known universe with reference to a square meter $(10^{0}$ m$^{2} = 1$ m$^{2})$.[2] In this book, Boeke showed successively smaller pictures, each one a tenth the dimension of the previous $(10^{-1}$ m, 10^{-2} m, 10^{-3} m, and so on) as well as successively larger pictures, each ten times larger than the previous $(10^{1}$ m, 10^{2} m, 10^{3} m, and so on). A number of moviemakers[3] and Web developers have followed Boeke's idea in an effort to help people understand the scale of things in the universe. After examining "powers of ten" resources online (look on *sciencesourcebook. com* or www.powersof10.com, or search "powers of ten"), perform the following investigation.

Figure 8.2 displays millimeter graph paper. The tiny black square in the upper left corner is 1 mm on a side, $(10^{-3}$ meters). The sides of the gray square in the upper left corner are an order of magnitude greater than the black square (10 mm per side, 10^{-2} m). Finally, the sides of the entire sheet, with 100 mm per side $(10^{-1}$ m), are two orders of magnitude greater than the black square and one order of magnitude greater than the gray square.

Working with your classmates, create a square meter (1000 mm on a side) by taping 100 of these squares together in a 10×10 square. This is 1 square meter with sides and

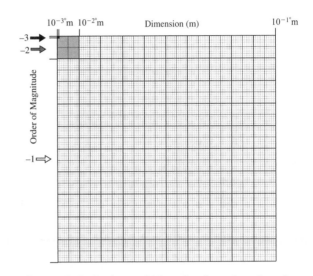

Figure 8.2 Orders of Magnitude $-3, -2, -1$

area three orders of magnitude greater than the square millimeter represented by the tiny black box. Measuring with a meter stick, place markers at the four corners of a 10 m square in one corner of your school's football field. This is four orders of magnitude greater than the original black square (1×10^{4} times larger). If space permits, mark out a 100 m square as shown in Figure 8.3. This square has sides that are five orders of magnitude larger (1×10^{5}) than the original black square.

You may continue to increase the order of magnitude by using satellite photos of your campus that are available on the Internet (look on *sciencesourcebook.com,* satellite view at maps. google.com, or earth.google.com). By zooming out of the satellite photo such that the football field represents approximately only one-tenth of

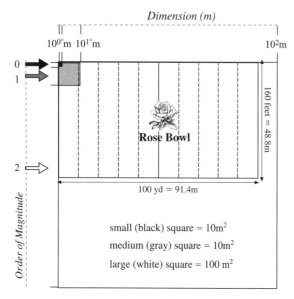

Figure 8.3 Orders of Magnitude 0, 1, 2

the field of view (Figure 8.4), you have reached the sixth order of magnitude.

Some mapping programs may allow you to zoom out to the diameter of the Earth, approximately 1.3×10^{10} mm, or ten orders of magnitude greater than the 1 m square you started with. If you have a digital microscope, continue the process in the reverse direction by viewing a leaf to 1×10^{-5} m (one-hundredth of a millimeter). Now that you have experienced a range in orders of magnitude, identify one or more common items for each of the sizes listed in Table 8.4.

ACTIVITY 8.2.2 *Making a "Powers of Ten" Poster*

Note: This is an Internet-based activity.

Table 8.4 Orders of Magnitude in Length: Common Items

Item	Length (m)	Item	Length (m)
	1×10^{-3}		1×10^{1}
	1×10^{-2}		1×10^{2}
	1×10^{-1}		1×10^{3}
	1×10^{0}		1×10^{4}

Each student in the class will be assigned one or more of the items in Table 8.5. In the upper left corner of a standard 8.5" × 11" sheet of paper, write in large or bold characters the approximate dimension of your object in scientific notation. For example, if you are assigned the Earth, you will write "10^{8} m" In the upper right corner, identify the object ("the Earth"). In the center of the sheet, place a picture of the object. Internet-based image search engines (see *sciencesourcebook.com* or google.com) may be useful in acquiring pictures that can be copied or drawn. Below the image, give a brief description of the object. As a class, arrange the photographs around the room from smallest to largest, as shown in Figure 8.5.

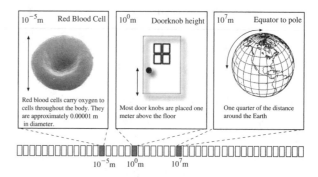

Figure 8.5 Powers of Ten Posters

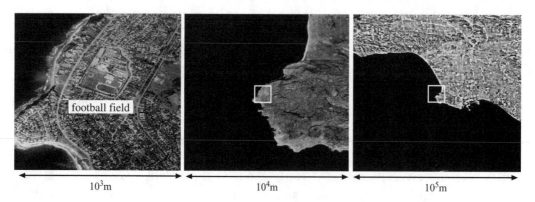

Figure 8.4 Orders of Magnitude 3, 4, 5

Table 8.5 Items to Illustrate When Making Powers of Ten Posters

Distance	Comparison (Approximate)	Distance	Comparison (Approximate)
10^0 m	Distance from floor to door knob	10^{26} m	Radius of observable universe
10^{-1} m	Width of hand	10^{25} m	Distance to the 3C273, brightest quasar
10^{-2} m	Width of fingernail on smallest finger	10^{24} m	Distance to the nearest large supercluster
10^{-3} m	Thickness of a U.S. dime		
10^{-4} m	Length of a dust mite	10^{23} m	Distance to galaxies beyond our local group
10^{-5} m	Diameter of human red blood cells		
10^{-6} m	Diameter of small bacteria	10^{22} m	Distance to Andromeda galaxy
10^{-7} m	Length of a virus	10^{21} m	Diameter of the disc of the Milky Way
10^{-8} m	Thickness of bacteria flagellum	10^{20} m	Diameter of the Small Magellanic Cloud
10^{-9} m	Width of DNA helix	10^{19} m	Approximate thickness of the Milky Way
10^{-10} m	Width of ice or quartz cell	10^{18} m	Diameter of a typical globular cluster
10^{-11} m	Radius of a hydrogen atom	10^{17} m	Distance from Earth to Vega
10^{-12} m	Wavelength of X-rays	10^{16} m	Inner radius of Oort cloud
10^{-13} m	Wavelength of an electron	10^{15} m	100 × diameter of the solar system
10^{-14} m	Diameter of a nucleus	10^{14} m	10 × diameter of the solar system
10^{-15} m	Diameter of a proton	10^{13} m	Diameter of solar system
10^{-16} m	One-tenth the diameter of a proton	10^{12} m	Distance from Sun to Saturn
10^{-17} m	One-hundredth the diameter of a proton	10^{11} m	Distance from Sun to Venus
		10^{10} m	One half the distance light travels in a minute
10^{-18} m	Radius of an electron		
		10^9 m	Diameter of the Sun
		10^8 m	Diameter of Saturn
		10^7 m	North Pole to equator
		10^6 m	Length of California (north to south)
		10^5 m	Length of Connecticut (north to south)
		10^4 m	Depth of Mariana Trench, deepest point
		10^3 m	One kilometer; 2.5 times around a track
		10^2 m	One side of a running track
		10^1 m	Distance for a first down in football
		10^0 m	Distance from floor to door knob

(Increasing Size ↑ — annotation at left of the right-hand column)

8.3 Organizational Hierarchy in Biology

Biology is a complex science with many levels of organization, and an understanding of these levels is essential to an understanding of biology. The following description of the organizational hierarchy starts with the smallest and most basic item and works toward the largest and most complex:

• *Fundamental particles:* We now believe that there are two basic types of fundamental, structureless particles of which all matter is made: *quarks* (up, down, charm, strange, top, bottom) and *leptons* (electron neutrino, electron, muon neutrino, muon, tau neutrino, tau). Future research may show that even these particles, with radii less than 10^{-19} m, are themselves composed of smaller particles.

• *Subatomic particles: Protons* and *neutrons* are made of quarks. Electrons are a type of lepton, and hence also considered to be fundamental particles. Acids are substances that can donate protons, and bases are electron pair donors. All living systems contain water, the pH of which is controlled by the presence of acids or bases.

• *Atoms* are composed of protons, neutrons, and electrons. Currently there are 116 known elements. The following is a list of the most important elements for living systems, easily remembered by the acronym *C HOPKINS CaFe Mg NaCl*: *"C. HOPKINS CaFe is Mighty good, but needs salt (NaCl)."* *Note that the underlined portions represent the element symbols: C(carbon), H(hydrogen), O(oxygen), P(phosphorous), K(potassium), I(iodine), N(nitrogen), S(sulfur), Ca(calcium), Fe(Iron), Mg(Magnesium), Na(sodium), Cl(chlorine).*

• *Micromolecules* are the building blocks from which macromolecules are made, and are themselves made of atoms. Glucose, ribose, glycerol, and fatty acids are made of C, H, and O, and amino acids and nucleotides are made of C, H, O, N, P, and S.

• *Macromolecules* are large molecules consisting of many subunits. For example, *starch* is composed of many glucose units, *proteins* are composed of many amino acids, *lipids* are composed of glycerol and fatty acids, and *nucleic acids* are composed primarily of nucleotides and ribose.

• *Molecular assemblies* are large, organized sets of molecular units. For example, *microtubules* (involved in cilia, flagella and the cytoskeleton) are polymers of the protein (tubulin), and *membranes* (providing structure and boundaries to organelles and cells) are composed of lipids and proteins.

• *Organelles* are "little organs," or specialized structures of the cell. They are composed of molecular assemblies and molecules of all sizes. *Mitochondria* (ATP-generating stations) are organelles composed of numerous membranes, while *centrioles* (organelles organizing the spindle fibers in cell division) are composed of microtubules.

• *Cells* are the simplest unit of biological organization. They are bounded by plasma membranes and composed of numerous organelles. For example, a *neuron* is a membrane bound structure, powered by mitochondria.

• *Tissues* are groups of similar cells that carry out specific sets of functions. For example, *nervous tissue* is composed of neurons and is specialized for the conduction and transmission of nerve impulses. In animals, there are four basic tissue types: nervous, muscular, epithelial, and connective.

• *Organs* are composed of tissues that are organized to perform specific functions. For example, the *brain* is composed of different nervous, connective, and epithelial tissues and functions to govern the body.

• *Organ systems* are groups of organs that conduct a wide set of functions. For example, the *nervous system* is composed of the brain, spinal cord, and cranial and spinal nerves. It receives information from external and internal environments, processes data, and responds appropriately to the stimuli.

• *Organisms* are individuals with their own distinct, unique existence. They range in complexity from single-celled organisms such as *paramecium* or *amoeba*, to complex multisystem organisms like humans. Humans, tigers, squirrels, and other mammals are composed of 11 major systems: nervous, integumentary, circulatory, endocrine, lymphatic, digestive, urinary, skeletal, muscular, respiratory, and reproductive. Organisms belong to a species, which is defined as a type of organism that can interbreed, and shares common traits.

• *Populations* are groups of individuals of the same species that are capable of interacting and interbreeding. Due to transportation and communication, the boundaries of human populations are flexible, but one can still talk loosely about the "population of the United States" or the "Tucano (tribal) population of the Amazonian Basin." Populations are often composed of smaller groups. For example, the ant population on an island may be composed of many *colonies,* and the wolf population in Yellowstone is composed of different *packs.* Other collective names for animal groups are *herd* (elephants, sheep, buffalo), *pod* (whales, seals), *school* (fish), *troop* (kangaroos, monkeys), *flock* (birds), and *pride* (lions).

• *Community:* A community is composed of populations of different species that live in the same region and interact with one another. For example, one can talk about the *riparian* (streamside) *community* along the Salt River in Arizona.

This encompasses all of the plant and animal species living along this river.

• *Ecosystem:* An ecosystem is an integrated association of biological and physical resources existing in the same region. Ecosystems result from the interaction of biological, geochemical, and geophysical systems. *Ponds, forests,* and *estuaries* are examples of ecosystems. The boundaries between ecosystems are ill defined.

• *Biome:* Biomes are the world's major life zones, classified according to the predominant vegetation and climate. They are composed of many similar and related ecosystems. For example, *tropical rain forests* are dominated by trees and are characterized by plants and animals that live in its warm, humid climate.

• *Biosphere:* The biosphere is the region in which life exists on *Earth,* reaching from the deepest oceanic trenches where thermophilic bacteria are the dominant life-forms, to regions high in the atmosphere where microbes and spores are carried aloft by strong winds.

ACTIVITY 8.3.1 *Visualizing the Levels of Organization*

Create a poster showing the levels of biological organization. Using a graphic search engine (such as the ones at *sciencesourcebook.com* or images.google.com), find one or more images of a representative of each level to include on the chart. For example, you can show pictures of mitochondria, chloroplasts, or nuclei to illustrate the organelle level and pictures of tundra and tropical rain forest to illustrate the biome level. Alternatively, you may choose to draw representative items for each level. Be creative!

ACTIVITY 8.3.2 *Identifying the Levels of Organization*

When addressing a letter, the sender identifies the recipient's first name, last name, street number, street name, city, state, zip code, and country. This information uniquely specifies the recipient out of more than 6 billion people in the world. Table 8.6 illustrates a similar method of identifying the position of an item such as a textbook, which could be located anywhere in the world. For example, you could identify a specific book by saying it is the biology *book* on the third *desk,* in the fifth *row,* of the second *room,* on the east *hall* of the north *wing,* of the third *floor,* of the science *building,* on the CSUN *campus,* in the *community* of Northridge, in the *city* of Los Angeles, in the *county* of Los Angeles, of the *state* of California, in the *country* of the United States, on the *continent* of North America,

Table 8.6 Levels of Organization in Biology

Level of Organization	Example Set 1	Example Set 2	Analogy	
Fundamental particles			Book	Biology book
Subatomic particles			Desk	Third desk
Atoms			Row	Fifth row
Micromolecules			Room	Second room
Macromolecules			Hall	East hall
Molecular assemblies			Wing	North wing
Organelles			Floor	Third floor
Cells			Building	Science building
Tissues			Campus	CSUN
Organs			Community	Northridge
Organ systems			City	Los Angeles
Organisms			County	Los Angeles County
Populations			State	California
Communities			Country	United States
Ecosystems			Continent	North America
Biomes			Hemisphere	Western Hemisphere
Biosphere			Planet	Earth

located in the Western *Hemisphere,* of the *planet* Earth. The sequence of levels listed (*book, desk, row, room, hall, wing, floor, building, campus, community, city, county, state, country, continent, hemisphere, planet*) represents an organizational hierarchy analogous to the biological hierarchy as shown in Table 8.6: fundamental particles, subatomic particles, atoms, micromolecules, macromolecules, molecular assemblies, organelles, cells, tissues, organs, organ systems, organisms, populations, communities, ecosystems, biomes, and biosphere. For the terms that follow, identify the appropriate level of organization by placing the term in the correct cell of Table 8.6.

Set 1: alpine, brain, carbon, Earth, fatty acid, gray matter, lipid, marmot, meadow, nervous system, neuron, nuclear membrane, nucleus, protons, quark, tundra, Tuolumne pack

Set 2: chloroplast, deciduous forest, Earth, glycine, leaf, maple tree, neutrons, nitrogen, Ohio hardwood forests, palisade, parenchyma, plasmalemma, protein, quark, riparian, stand, vegetative system

ACTIVITY 8.3.3 *Organizing the Many Disciplines of Biology*

Biology is a vast field of study that includes many disciplines, each with a unique focus at one or more levels of organization. For example, an ornithologist studies birds (organism level), and a cytologist studies cells (cellular level). Some fields of study cover many areas. For example, anatomy studies the structure and parts of the body. One can talk about the anatomy of an organelle, cell, tissue, organ, system, or organism, as represented by the cells in Table 8.7 with an X in them. By contrast,

Table 8.7 The Domains of Various Biological Disciplines

	Molecule	Organelle	Cell	Tissue	Organ	System	Organism	Population	Community	Ecosystem	Biome
Anatomy		x	x	x	x	x	x				
Biochemistry	x										
Biology	x	x	x	x	x	x	x	x	x	x	x
Biophysics											
Botany											
Cardiology											
Community ecology											
Cytology											
Dermatology											
Ecology											
Ecosystem ecology											
Epidemiology											
Forestry											
Genetics											
Histology											
Microbiology											
Molecular genetics											
Neurology											
Oncology											
Ornithology											
Physiological ecology											
Physiology											
Population ecology											
Taxonomy											
Zoology											

biochemistry deals specifically with the molecular level, while biology studies all levels from molecular through biome. Complete Table 8.7 by noting with an X the main levels of organization each discipline studies. Your teacher may assign a discipline to individuals, and request them to report to the class after completing their research. Note that some boundaries are less distinct than others.

8.4 Organization of the Chemistry Curriculum

Chemistry is the study of the composition, structure, properties, and reactions of matter. There are a variety of ways to organize the study of chemistry, and three are presented here: (1) the pattern followed by many introductory chemistry classes, (2) the outline used by the College Board's Advanced Placement Chemistry program, and (3) the way most colleges departmentalize chemistry.

ACTIVITY 8.4.1 *Developing an Outline for Chemistry*

Develop an outline for your chemistry textbook, and compare it with the three outlines listed here. Which of the models does your chemistry book most closely resemble? Give a one-sentence definition for each item in your outline as illustrated in model 3. Your outline will serve as a road map as you study chemistry. Refer to it often to develop an understanding of the scope and organization of chemistry.

Model 1: Introductory Chemistry
1. Basic Principles
   - Atomic theory
   - Chemical bonds and molecular structure
   - Conservation of matter
2. States of Matter
   - Kinetic theory and gases
   - Solutions
   - Acids, bases, and salts
3. Reaction Dynamics
   - Chemical thermodynamics
   - Kinetics and equilibrium
4. Specialized Chemistry
   - Organic chemistry and biochemistry
   - Nuclear chemistry

Model 2: College Board's Advanced Placement Chemistry
1. Structure of Matter
   - Atomic theory and atomic structure
   - Chemical bonding
   - Nuclear chemistry
2. States of Matter
   - Gases
   - Liquids and solids
   - Solutions
3. Reactions
   - Reaction types
   - Stoichiometry
   - Equilibrium
   - Kinetics
   - Thermodynamics

Model 3: Departmentalization of Chemistry at Many Colleges
1. Inorganic Chemistry (freshman class): Properties and reactions of substances that are not carbon based
2. Organic Chemistry (sophomore class): Study of the structure, properties, composition, reactions, and synthesis of carbon-based compounds
3. Physical Chemistry (upper-division class): Discovery and description of the theoretical bases for the behavior of matter
4. Biochemistry (upper-division class): The chemistry of living things, including the structure and function of biological molecules and the mechanisms and products of their reactions
5. Analytical Chemistry (upper-division class): The separation, identification, and measurement of components of matter
6. Nuclear Chemistry (upper-division class): The chemistry of radioactivity, nuclear processes, and nuclear properties

8.5 Organization of the Physics Curriculum

The term *physics* is derived from the Greek word *physis*, meaning "nature." Today we define *physics* as the natural science that studies the properties, changes, and interactions of matter and

Table 8.8 Organization of the Physics Curriculum

I. Newtonian Mechanics
  A. Kinematics
  B. Laws of motion
  C. Work, energy, power
  D. Momentum
  E. Circular motion and rotation
  F. Oscillations
  G. Gravitation

II. Fluid Mechanics and Thermal Physics
  A. Fluid mechanics
  B. Temperature and heat
  C. Kinetic theory and thermodynamics

III. Electricity and Magnetism
  A. Electrostatics
  B. Conductors, insulators, capacitors
  C. Electric circuits
  D. Magnetostatics
  E. Electromagnetism

IV. Waves and Optics
  A. Waves
  B. Sound
  C. Optics

V. Modern Physics
  A. Atomic physics
  B. Nuclear physics
  C. Relativity

energy—from subatomic particles to the universe (see powers of ten, section 8.2). Although physics is a large and diverse field of study, most textbook authors and physics teachers organize it in a manner similar to that shown in Table 8.8. The outline of your book or class will be your road map for physics. Study the outline that follows (or the one used by your teacher or textbook), and review it throughout the course.

ACTIVITY 8.5.1 *Using the "Road Map" for Physics*

Use your reasoning skills to match each of the following activities with the subtopics listed in the physics outline in Table 8.8, making logical guesses if necessary. *Note:* There is a one-to-one correspondence between the activities and the items outlined in Table 8.8. Note that the key physics concept appears in *italics.*

a. Plotting the *path* of a football from quarterback to receiver
b. Calculating the *acceleration* of a skydiver toward Earth
c. Determining the *efficiency* of a motor
d. Predicting the *impulse* of a baseball hit by a bat
e. Studying the *spin* of the Earth on its axis
f. Adjusting the *period* of the pendulum in a grandfather clock
g. Explaining how the *pull* of the Moon is responsible for the tides

h. Measuring the *buoyancy* of a submarine in the ocean
i. Determining the *energy* (caloric content) in a candy bar
j. Explaining the theory of steam *engines*
k. Understanding why carbon is *attracted* to paper in a photocopier
l. Selecting materials that will *conduct* currents
m. Comparing the voltage of *parallel and serial* circuits
n. Measuring the magnetic *field* of the earth
o. Comparing the energy of visible *light, X-rays,* and *radio* waves
p. Studying *tsunamis, light,* and *sound*
q. Determining the *harmonic frequencies* of guitar and piano strings
r. Designing the *lens* arrangement for a telescope
s. Using the *photoelectric effect* to make photo-voltaic cells
t. Comparing *fission* and *fusion* reactions.
u. Discussing the implications of the frame independence of the *speed of light*

8.6 Earth Systems Interactions

Environmental science studies the interactions of the physical, chemical, and biological components of the environment, including their effects on all types of organisms. *Earth science* (also known as *geoscience*) is an inclusive term for all sciences related to Earth (geology, meteorology, and oceanography, for example). Although environmental and earth science cover essentially the same material, environmental science places greater emphasis on the biological realm, while earth science places greater emphasis on the physical realm.

Environmental and earth science study the interactions of four major systems or spheres (Figure 8.6):

- The *geosphere* consists of the core, mantle, and crust of the Earth.
- The *atmosphere* contains all of the Earth's air and is divided into troposphere, stratosphere, mesosphere, thermosphere, and ionosphere.
- The *hydrosphere* contains all of the solid, liquid, and gaseous water on Earth, extending from the depths of the sea to the upper reaches of the troposphere where water is found. Ninety-seven percent of the hydrosphere is found in salty oceans, and the remainder is found as vapor or droplets in the atmosphere and as liquid in groundwater, lakes, rivers, glaciers, and snowfields.
- The *biosphere* is the collection of all Earth's life forms, distributed in major life zones known as biomes: tundra, boreal forest, temperate deciduous forest, temperate grassland, desert, savanna, tropical rain forest, chaparral, freshwater, and marine.

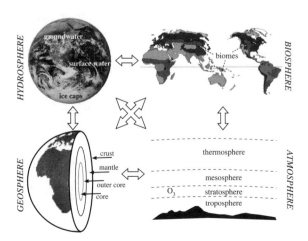

Figure 8.6 Interaction of the Four Spheres of Earth Science

Although the four systems have their unique identities, there is substantial interaction among them. Environmental scientists study the effects of events in one sphere on the other spheres. For example, a volcanic eruption in the geosphere may cause profound direct and indirect effects on the hydrosphere, atmosphere, and biosphere. The following examples of a volcano and fire illustrate these relationships.

Example 1: Volcano

On May 18, 1980, Mount Saint Helens, in the state of Washington, erupted. This event altered the surrounding environment and provided scientists with an opportunity to study the effects of volcanic eruptions on the geosphere, hydrosphere, atmosphere, and biosphere. Such studies are vital because volcanic eruptions will continue to occur and will have increasing impact on humans as people continue to settle closer to dormant volcanoes. The following are but a few of the myriad of interactions resulting from a volcanic eruption.

Volcano → geosphere → atmosphere → hydrosphere → biosphere

• Volcanoes (an event in the geosphere) release a large amount of particulate matter into the atmosphere. These particles serve as nuclei for the formation of water droplets (hydrosphere). Rainfall (hydrosphere) often increases following an eruption, stimulating plant growth (biosphere). Particulate matter in the air (atmosphere) falls out, initially smothering plants (biosphere) but ultimately enriching the soil (geosphere) and thereby stimulating plant growth (biosphere).

Volcano → geosphere → hydrosphere → biosphere

• Volcanoes (events in the geosphere) may release a substantial amount of hot lava (geosphere), which causes mountain glaciers (hydrosphere) to melt. Mud flows (geosphere) and flooding may occur downstream from volcanoes and may inundate streamside communities (biosphere).

Volcano → geosphere → atmosphere → biosphere → geosphere

• Volcanoes (events of the geosphere) release a large amount of carbon dioxide (atmosphere), the raw material for sugar production in plants (biosphere). This may increase photosynthetic production and eventually increase the amount of biomass, which, after a very long time, forms coal and oil deposits (geosphere).

Volcano → complex interactions

• Volcanoes (geosphere) may emit large quantities of sulfur dioxide (atmosphere). When atmospheric sulfur dioxide combines with water (hydrosphere), sulfuric and sulfurous acid form. Rain (hydrosphere) may bring these acids to the Earth, acidifying soils (geosphere), lakes, and rivers (hydrosphere). Acidic water leaches nutrients from the soil (geosphere) into the water table (hydrosphere), making the soil less fertile for plants (biosphere) and the subterranean water supply (hydrosphere) less potable for humans (biosphere). Acid rain falling on lakes and streams reduces the pH of the water (hydrosphere), which may result in a decrease in phytoplankton and zooplankton growth (biosphere). If photosynthesis is reduced, atmospheric concentrations of carbon dioxide can build up and stimulate global warming (atmosphere), which may contribute to increased melting of glaciers (hydrosphere).

Example 2: Fire

Forest fires are a common occurrence in the western United States. A prolonged drought at the turn of the twentieth century sparked many forest fires and many heated debates on how to reduce the risk to human and natural resources. Following are a few of the many system interactions resulting from large forest fires:

Fire → biosphere → hydrosphere → geosphere → biosphere

• Forest fires (event) remove much of the biomass and expose the soil (geosphere) to rainfall (hydrosphere). The resulting sheet, rill, and gully erosion may remove topsoil (geosphere) from the affected area. The lack of sufficient topsoil reduces the carrying capacity (biosphere) of the region. As silt erodes into streams (hydrosphere), turbidity increases, decreasing the amount of sunlight available to plankton (biosphere) and other species that live in the stream. Reduced productivity by these plants results in a decrease in the animal species (biosphere) that depend on them.

Fire → biosphere → geosphere → biosphere

• Plant biomass contains many minerals that are released into the soil (geosphere) following a fire (event). In addition, fire removes the canopy of vegetation (biosphere), allowing more light to penetrate to the soil (geosphere). Plants (biosphere) that require bare, mineral-enriched soil thrive in this new environment, initiating the first step in succession.

Fire → biosphere → atmosphere → biosphere

• Fire (event) transforms wood (biosphere) into carbon dioxide and water vapor (atmosphere). Increased levels of carbon dioxide may contribute to global warming (atmosphere) and promote plant growth (biosphere) because photosynthesis is dependent upon atmospheric carbon dioxide.

ACTIVITY 8.6.1 *Earth Science Systems Interactions*

Describe the direct and indirect influence of the following events on all four spheres: geosphere, hydrosphere, atmosphere, and biosphere. For each, draw one sequence of interactions as illustrated in examples 1 and 2 above:

- *Comet strike:* On June 30, 1908, a comet fragment approximately 80 m in diameter entered the Earth's atmosphere and exploded in the air above the Tunguska Valley in Siberia, Russia. Research the Tunguska event, and describe the Earth systems interactions.
- *Use of CFCs:* Chlorofluorocarbons were introduced in 1928 as nontoxic, nonflammable refrigerants. Research the effect of CFCs on ozone, and describe potential Earth systems interactions.
- *Burning of fossil fuels:* Fossil fuels (oil, coal, natural gas) provide much of the energy for modern civilization. Describe Earth systems interactions that may have resulted from the increased use of fossil fuels.

- *Deforestation policies in tropical rainforests:* An increasing demand for agricultural and range land has prompted dramatic deforestation in tropical rain forests. Describe the Earth systems interactions that may result from massive deforestation of the tropical rain forests.

- *Hunting predators:* In 1906, President Theodore Roosevelt established Grand Canyon National Game Preserve to preserve the mule deer from overhunting. Although it was illegal to kill mule deer, hunters could still kill mountain lions, bobcats, and wolves. Research the Earth systems interactions of a policy that allows hunting predators but not their prey.

The Earth systems interactions approach to teaching environmental and Earth science requires students to tie together knowledge in an integrated, nonlinear fashion. You may wish to create some of your own questions using things that involve more than one sphere, such as illustrated in Table 8.9. Earth systems interactions is a problem-based approach to learning and is best done with teams. You may wish to create electronic news groups (see *sciencesourcebook.com*) to promote this interaction outside class time.

Answers to Chapter Activities

8.1.1 See Table 8.10.

8.1.2 Students will develop an advance organizer for their text as outlined in the assignment description.

8.2.1 To understand lengths, it is important to have a common referent, something students can refer to when estimating length. For example, doorknobs are generally 1 meter from the ground. When asked to visualize 0.05 m or 3 m, students can do so by reference to the height of a doorknob. Student responses will vary considerably depending upon the student's experience. Table 8.11

Table 8.9 Additional Ideas for Earth Systems Interactions Projects

air pollution	globalization	photosynthesis
aquifer reduction	hurricane	tectonics
change in Earth's polarity	Ice Age	tornadoes
drought	La Niña	transgenic crops
El Niño	melting ice caps	tsunamis
erosion	nuclear war	urban sprawl
floods	overpopulation	volcanoes
fossil fuel consumption	ozone production	wave action

Table 8.10 Answers Traffic Signs as Advance Organizers

H	Guide signs (e.g., mileage signs)	G	Regulatory signs (e.g., no parking)
J	Interstate highway	I	School zone
C	No passing zone	B	Stop
D	Railroad advance warning	E	Warning sign (e.g., curves)
F	Railroad crossing	A	Yield

Table 8.11 Answers Orders of Magnitude in Length: Referent Items

Item	Length (m)	Item	Length (m)
Thickness of U.S. dime, width of a pencil lead	1×10^{-3}	First down, volleyball net length	1×10^{1}
		One side of a track, length of soccer field	1×10^{2}
Width of smallest fingernail	1×1^{-2}	Kilometer, four laps around a track	1×10^{3}
Width of hand, width of small paperback book	1×1^{-1}	10K race, 6.2 miles	1×10^{4}
Width of door, meter stick, height of a typical four year old	1×10^{0}		

lists some common items that are approximately the lengths listed. You may want to tell your students that many measurement units were originally derived from natural measurements. The inch represented the width of an average thumb; the foot, the length of a human foot; the yard, the distance from the tip of the nose to the end of the middle finger of an outstretched arm; the fathom, the distance from one fingertip to the other; and the cubit, the length of the forearm.

8.2.2 The "powers of ten" posters can become a permanent display in your classroom. Students can compare the size of things they are currently studying with references on the wall. Many students are intrigued with computers and are familiar with computer jargon. You may therefore wish to point out the orders of magnitude used to quantify computer memory:

byte (1; 1×10^0)—*a single character*
kilobyte (1000; 1×10^3)—*half a printed page*
megabyte (1,000,000; 1×10^6)—*small book*
gigabyte (1,000,000,000; 1×10^9)—*1,000 books*
terabyte (1,000,000,000,000; 1×10^{12})—*a college research library*

8.3.1 Student posters can make good room decorations. You may wish to provide students with additional ideas at each level so that their posters look different from one another. For example, you may tell them that they can illustrate the biome level with any of the following biomes: desert, tundra, taiga, temperate deciduous forest, mixed coniferous forest, chaparral, savanna, or tropical rain forest.

8.3.2 See Table 8.12.

8.3.3 Table 8.13 shows the main levels that each of these biological disciplines is concerned with. Note that there are other legitimate answers depending on the definitions one adopts. The purpose of this question is not to achieve an absolute answer but to show that the disciplines of biology focus on different levels or combinations of levels.

8.4.1 The three models illustrate a variety of ways a curriculum can be logically arranged. Note that the curricular structure of your textbook or course might be different from any of these models. Post the curricular outline you are using on your classroom wall and on your class Web site so students can refer to it as they progress through the course. The curriculum outline provides students a schema into which new information can be organized. Many states, provinces, and countries have adopted content standards. If this is true where you teach, use these content standards as an outline.

8.5.1 The answers that follow use titles from the physics outline in this chapter. The chapter titles from your textbook might be slightly different. I suggest that you use this activity near the beginning, middle, and end of your course to encourage students to develop and use a schema for understanding physics.

a. Plotting the *path* of a football from quarterback to receiver. *Kinematics*

b. Calculating the *acceleration* of a skydiver towards earth. *Laws of Motion*

c. Determining the *efficiency* of a motor. *Work, Energy, Power*

d. Predicting the *impulse* of a baseball hit by a bat. *Momentum*

e. Studying the *spin* of the earth on its axis. *Circular Motion and Rotation*

f. Adjusting the period of pendulum in a grandfather clock. *Oscillations*

Table 8.12 Examples of Items at Each Level of Organization

Level of Organization	Example Set 1	Example Set 2	Analogy	
Fundamental particles	Quark	Quark	Book	Biology book
Subatomic particles	Protons	Neutrons	Desk	Third desk
Atoms	Carbon	Nitrogen	Row	Fifth row
Micromolecules	Fatty acid	Glycine	Room	Second room
Macromolecules	Lipid	Protein	Hall	East hall
Molecular assemblies	Nuclear membrane	Plasmalemma	Wing	North wing
Organelles	Nucleus	Chloroplast	Floor	Third floor
Cells	Neuron	Palisade	Building	Science building
Tissues	Gray matter	Parenchyma	Campus	CSUN
Organs	Brain	Leaf	Community	Northridge
Organ systems	Nervous system	Vegetative system	City	Los Angeles
Organisms	Marmot	Maple tree	County	Los Angeles County
Populations	Tuolomne pack	Stand	State	California
Communities	Meadow	Riparian	Country	United States
Ecosystems	Alpine	Hardwood forests	Continent	North America
Biomes	Tundra	Deciduous forest	Hemisphere	Western Hemisphere
Biosphere	Earth	Earth	Planet	Earth

Table 8.13 Answers: The Domains of Various Biological Disciplines

	Molecule	Organelle	Cell	Tissue	Organ	System	Organism	Population	Community	Ecosystem	Biome
Anatomy		X	X	X	X	X	X				
Biochemistry	X										
Biology	X	X	X	X	X	X	X	X	X	X	X
Biophysics	X										
Botany		X	X	X	X	X	X				
Cardiology					X	X	X				
Community ecology									X		
Cytology		X	X								
Dermatology				X	X	X					
Ecology							X	X	X	X	X
Ecosystem ecology										X	
Epidemiology							X	X			
Forestry							X	X	X	X	
Genetics	X						X	X			
Histology				X							
Microbiology			X				X				
Molecular genetics	X										
Neurology				X	X	X	X				
Oncology			X	X							
Ornithology							X				
Physiological ecology				X	X	X	X			X	
Physiology			X	X	X	X	X				
Population ecology								X			
Taxonomy							X				
Zoology							X				

g. Explaining how the *pull* of the Moon is responsible for the tides. *Gravitation*

h. Measuring the *buoyancy* of a submarine in the ocean. *Fluid Mechanics*

i. Determining the *energy* (caloric content) in a candy bar. *Temperature and Heat*

j. Explaining the theory of steam *engines*. *Kinetic Theory and Thermodynamics*

k. Understanding why carbon is *attracted* to paper in a photocopy machine. *Electrostatics*

l. Selecting materials that will *conduct* currents. *Conductors, Insulators, Capacitors*

m. Comparing the voltage of *parallel and serial* circuits. *Electric Circuits*

n. Measuring the magnetic *field* of the earth. *Magnetostatics*

o. Comparing the energy of visible *light*, *X-rays*, and *radio* waves. *Electromagnetism*

p. Studying *tsunamis, light,* and *sound*. *Waves*

q. Determining the *harmonic frequencies* of guitar and piano strings. *Sound*

r. Designing the *lens* arrangement for a telescope. *Optics*

s. Using the *photoelectric effect* to make photovoltaic cells. *Atomic Physics*

t. Comparing *fission* and *fusion* reactions. *Nuclear Physics*

u. Discussing the implications of the frame independence of the *speed of light*. *Relativity*

Chapter Nine

Graphic Organizers for Science

For the Teacher 168

9.1 Conceptual Grids 169

9.2 Venn Diagrams 172

9.3 Flowcharts 174

9.4 Mind Maps 176

9.5 Concept Maps 178

Answers to Chapter Activities 182

For the Teacher

Metacognition is the awareness of one's thinking processes and strategies and the ability to modify them to optimize learning. Teachers should have an awareness of their own mental processes and be able to monitor, regulate, and direct them so they can help students do the same and thereby maximize learning. For example, teachers and learners should be able to identify and differentiate rote learning from meaningful learning. In *rote learning*, students memorize information without necessarily understanding or applying concepts. It is a mechanical form of learning, reliant on memorization and practice drills. By contrast, *meaningful learning* takes place when learners relate new knowledge to existing concepts. Rote learning may be useful in reciting information, but it is of little value in problem solving. By contrast, meaningful learning may not produce excellent recitation, but it will be of much greater value in assisting problem solving, analysis, and evaluation.

Educators influence the type of learning that occurs through instruction and assessment. If teachers introduce new concepts without relating them to familiar ones and if they deliver tests that require verbatim recall of information, students will most likely engage in rote learning. If, however, teachers introduce new concepts in relation to existing ones and deliver assessments that require understanding, students will be more likely to engage in meaningful learning.

Graphic organizers are a means of introducing and assessing concepts in a manner that encourages meaningful learning. Graphic organizers are diagrams or maps that show the relationship between new and existing concepts, thereby facilitating integration of new and familiar ideas. *Conceptual grids, Venn diagrams, flowcharts, mind maps,* and *concept maps* are some of the more common graphic organizers used to introduce science concepts and assess student learning, and they form the basis of this chapter.

Problem solving is dependent on the quantity and quality of concepts stored in one's long-term memory. Before new concepts can be stored in long-term memory (see Chapter Eleven), it is necessary to first encode them in short-term, or working, memory. Since working memory can process only five to nine items at any moment, it is necessary to organize larger bodies of information in logical ways that can be easily encoded as new information is received. Graphic organizers, particularly concept maps and outlines, facilitate meaningful learning by serving as a template by which knowledge is structured and encoded. It appears that the mind organizes knowledge in hierarchical frameworks, and learning techniques that present material in organized, integrated frameworks facilitate long-term memory.

Graphic organizers are valuable for instruction, study, and assessment. When teachers introduce material using graphic organizers, they present information in a logical manner to facilitate encoding into short- and long-term memory. In addition, they present a model of meaningful learning in which new concepts are integrated with familiar ones. Students can learn from such modeling and review and study subject matter by developing their own graphic organizers that show the relationship between relevant concepts using categories, position, and propositions (connections between two or more concepts). Teachers can then assess student understanding by evaluating student-generated graphic organizers. Although much more difficult to assess than objective rote-based questions, graphic organizers provide a valuable window to view student understanding and misconceptions.

9.1 Conceptual Grids

Many real-world decisions depend on a number of variables. For example, the decision to attend a particular college may be dependent on cost, quality of education, impact on future career, availability of student housing, and proximity to family and friends. Making complex decisions can be simplified by creating a conceptual grid such as shown in Table 9.1. By filling in the key variables, the user can make quick comparisons.

Conceptual grids are helpful when comparing and contrasting scientific concepts. For example, Table 9.2 compares Earth with its nearest neighbors, Venus and Mars, with respect to some important physical characteristics. This table normalizes all values with respect to Earth. In other words, the value for Earth is defined as 1 for each quantity, and the values for Venus and Mars are compared to it. For example, Venus has 81.5 percent the mass (0.815) of Earth, while Mars has only 10.7 percent (0.107). The conceptual grid allows us to make a simple comparison of values as shown in Table 9.2 and graphed in Figure 9.1.

Conceptual grids provide structure by organizing data as records (a row of information related to the same entity) and fields (a column of features that are compared). Table 9.3 is a conceptual grid comparing three classes of fish, Agnatha, Chondrichthyes, and Osteichthyes, according to temperature regulation, fins, respiration, skeleton, swim bladder, and mouth. When this grid is constructed, it becomes clear that 21 cells must be filled in to complete the comparison. Blank cells are an instant visual reminder that more data must be supplied. When the grid is

Table 9.1 Conceptual Grid for College Decision

	Cost	Quality of Education	Impact on Future Career	Availability of Housing	Proximity to Family
College 1	$$$	+++	⇧ ⇧ ⇧	🏠	Ⓟ
College 2	$$	++++	⇧ ⇧	🏠🏠	ⓅⓅⓅ
College 3	$	++	⇧	🏠🏠🏠	ⓅⓅⓅ

Table 9.2 Comparison of Venus and Mars to Earth

	Venus	**Earth**	**Mars**
Mass	0.815	1	0.107
Diameter	0.949	1	0.533
Density	0.951	1	0.713
Gravity	0.907	1	0.377
Escape velocity	0.926	1	0.45
Distance from sun	0.723	1	1.52
Perihelion	0.731	1	1.41
Aphelion	0.716	1	1.64
Orbital period	0.615	1	1.88
Orbital velocity	1.180	1	0.81
Axial tilt	0.113	1	1.07
Number of moons	0	1	2

completed, the similarities and differences of the records become evident. For example, note that all three classes of fish have fins, gills, and are ecto-therms. Both Chondrichthyes and Agnatha have cartilaginous skeletons and swim bladders, while both Chondrichthyes and Osteichthyes have jaws. A quick scan of the table reveals similarities and differences that might otherwise be overlooked.

Conceptual grids are essentially simple data-bases, comparing records (items compared) across fields (topics of comparison). The problems presented in this section illustrate a wide range of applications in science and should be assigned as research projects for individuals or teams. Once students have completed a table, they can be asked to summarize their findings. For example,

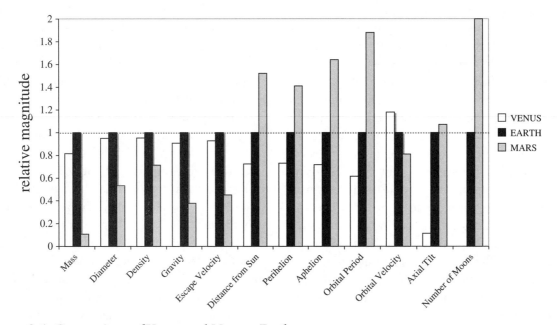

Figure 9.1 Comparison of Venus and Mars to Earth

Table 9.3 Conceptual Grid Comparing Three Classes of Fish

	Temperature Regulation	**Fins**	**Respiration**	**Skeleton**	**Swim Bladder**	**Mouth**	**Examples**
Agnatha	ectotherm	yes	gills	cartilage	no	sucker	lamprey, hagfish
Chondrichthyes	ectotherm	yes	gills	cartilage	no	jaw	shark, ray, skates
Osteichthyes	ectotherm	yes	gills	calcified	yes	jaw	salmon, perch, tuna

Table 9.4 Conceptual Grid for Four Forces

	Strength	Range	Particle
Strong nuclear	1	10^{-15} m	gluon
Electromagnetic	7×10^{-3}	infinite inverse square law applies	photon
Weak nuclear	1×10^{-6}	10^{-18} m 0.1% diameter of a proton	intermediate vector bosons
Gravity	6×10^{-39}	infinite inverse square law applies	graviton?

after completing a conceptual grid comparing the four known forces with respect to strength, range, and particles involved (Table 9.4), students may note that gravity is approximately 39 orders of magnitude weaker than the strong nuclear force, yet its range is believed to be infinite, while the range of strong nuclear force is only one-millionth of one-billionth of a meter! The astounding differences between these forces that might be quite easily lost in a paragraph become evident in a conceptual grid. Teachers are encouraged to develop their own conceptual grids, consistent with their specific needs, with the hope that students will eventually employ such techniques without prompting. Student answers will vary.

ACTIVITY 9.1.1 *Developing Conceptual Grids for Biology*

Virtually any type of comparison can be placed in a conceptual grid. Collect data from your textbook, the Internet, or the library, and develop a conceptual grid for one of the following, or for a topic specified by your instructor.

- *Arthropods:* Arthropods make up over 75 percent of the world's animal species. Arthropods include animals such as insects, crustaceans, and arachnids. Compare and contrast these three classes with respect to skeleton, legs, body systems, body parts, antennae, eyes, appendages, and examples.

- *Monocots and dicots:* Botanists classify all flowering plants as monocots or dicots. Develop a conceptual grid to compare monocots and dicots with respect to the number of cotyledons, pollen structure, number of flower parts, leaf venation, stem vascular arrangement, roots, secondary growth, and examples.
- *Biomolecules:* Develop a conceptual grid that compares and contrasts the four types of biological macromolecules—carbohydrates, proteins, lipids, and nucleic acids—with respect to elemental composition, structure, and function.
- *mRNA, tRNA, rRNA:* Develop a conceptual grid that compares and contrasts the three most common forms of RNA with respect to chemical composition, structure, location, and function.

ACTIVITY 9.1.2 *Developing Conceptual Grids for Chemistry*

Collect data from your textbook, the Internet, or the library, and develop a conceptual grid for one of the following, or for a topic specified by your instructor.

- *Family similarities:* Develop a conceptual grid that compares members of a family (e.g., alkali metals, halogens, noble gases) according to such key features as mass, electronegativity, melting point, and first ionization potential.
- *Differences between families:* Using a conceptual grid, compare and contrast the general

characteristics of any two families of elements according to criteria of your choice.

- *Metals, nonmetals, metalloids:* The elements of the periodic table can be classified as metals, nonmetals, and metalloids. Develop a conceptual grid that distinguishes these three groups of elements with respect to luster, malleability, electrical conductivity, heat conductivity, pH of oxides, and the nature of ions in solution.
- *Nuclear fusion and fission:* People often confuse nuclear *fusion* and *fission*. Develop a conceptual grid that shows the similarities and differences between these two nuclear processes with respect to reactants, products, conditions, controllability, and amount of energy released.

ACTIVITY 9.1.3 *Developing Conceptual Grids for Earth and Space Science*

Collect data from your textbook, the Internet, or the library, and develop a conceptual grid for one of the following, or for a topic specified by your instructor.

- *Inner versus outer planets:* Astronomers have noted substantial differences between the four inner planets (Mercury, Venus, Earth, and Mars) and the four large outer planets (Jupiter, Saturn, Uranus, and Neptune). Develop a conceptual grid to compare and contrast these two sets of planets with respect to size, composition, rings, orbital speed, density, and temperature.
- *Hurricanes and tornadoes:* Hurricanes and tornadoes are potentially destructive storms. Using a conceptual grid, compare and contrast these storms with respect to wind direction, wind speed, life span, storm width, prediction time, and location.
- *Types of rocks:* Geologists classify rocks as igneous, sedimentary, or metamorphic. Develop a conceptual grid that compares these rocks with respect to origin, crystal size, abundance, and location within the Earth.
- *Short- versus long-term comets:* Compare and contrast short- and long-term comets with respect to orbit, aphelion, nucleus, coma, and composition.

ACTIVITY 9.1.4 *Developing Conceptual Grids for Physics*

Collect data from your textbook, the Internet, or the library, and develop a conceptual grid for one of the following, or for a topic specified by your instructor.

- *Heat transfer:* Heat is transferred from one location to another by convection, conduction, and radiation. Develop a conceptual grid that compares and contrasts these forms of heat transfer with respect to the mechanism of transfer and the direction of transfer.
- *Forces:* Our current understanding is that there are four fundamental forces in the universe: gravity, nuclear weak force, electromagnetic force, and nuclear strong force. Develop a conceptual grid to compare the nature of these forces, their relative strength, the range over which they act, and the particles involved.
- *DC and AC circuits:* Electrical appliances run on direct current (DC) or alternating current (AC) circuits. Develop a conceptual grid to compare and contrast AC and DC circuits with respect to method of generation, polarity, equipment powered, and power transmission.
- *Waves:* A wave is a disturbance that travels through a medium, transporting energy without transporting matter. Waves can be longitudinal, transverse, or superficial. Use a conceptual grid to compare and contrast these waves with respect to particle movement, and give examples of each.

9.2 Venn Diagrams

One of the best-known ways of comparing and contrasting information is the Venn diagram, developed by mathematicians to show the relationship between sets of numbers. Circles are drawn to represent sets, and the areas in which these circles intersect illustrate the items held in common by both sets. Venn diagrams are useful in science, providing a quick summary of the similarities and differences between items compared. Figure 9.2A shows a Venn diagram for biology and chemistry. The intersection between biology and chemistry is

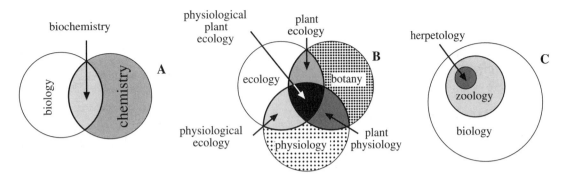

Figure 9.2 Venn Diagrams

the domain of biochemistry, a topic that is generally addressed in both biology and chemistry texts but is also a defined field of study. Figure 9.2B illustrates a more complex situation, looking at the intersection of physiology, botany, and ecology. The intersection between botany and physiology is plant physiology, the intersection between botany and ecology is plant ecology, and the intersection between physiology and ecology is physiological ecology. The science at the intersection of all three is known as physiological plant ecology. Figure 9.2C illustrates a situation in which one field of study is a subset of another. Herpetology (the study of reptiles) is a field within zoology, and zoology is a field within biology.

Figure 9.3 is a Venn diagram to show the similarities and differences of three classes of animals.

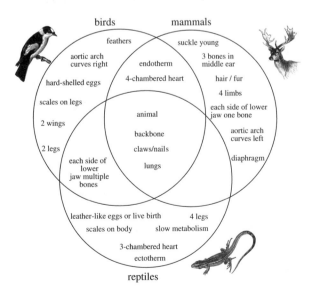

Figure 9.3 Venn Diagrams of Three Classes of Animals

A glance shows that all three classes are animals that have backbones, lungs, and claws or nails. It shows that only birds and mammals are endotherms with three-chambered hearts, while birds and reptiles share a similar jaw structure unlike that of mammals. The diagram also shows that each class has its own unique characteristics as well. Using the Internet or traditional print resources, research a set of topics selected by your teacher or one of the sets listed in the activities.

ACTIVITY 9.2.1 *Develop Venn Diagrams for Biology*

Develop a two- or three-circle Venn diagram for one of the biological topics listed below. Select just two or three items from each set for comparison.

- *Photosynthesis:* C3, C4, CAM
- *Single-celled organisms:* archaebacteria, eubacteria, protozoans
- *Tissue types:* nervous, muscular, epithelial, connective
- *Grasslands:* tundra, savanna, steppe, prairie

ACTIVITY 9.2.2 *Develop Venn Diagrams for Chemistry*

Develop a two- or three-circle Venn diagram for one of the chemistry topics listed below. Select just two or three items from each set for comparison.

- *Chemical bonds:* ionic, covalent, nonpolar covalent
- *Chemical reactions:* single replacement, double replacement, composition, decomposition

- *Chemical families:* I, II, III, IV, V, VI, VII, VII, VIII
- *Branches of chemistry:* inorganic, organic, biochemistry, physical, analytic

ACTIVITY 9.2.3 *Develop Venn Diagrams for Physics*

Develop a two- or three-circle Venn diagram for one of the physics topics listed below. Select just two or three items from each set for comparison.

- *Physical properties:* momentum, mass, inertia
- *Forces:* gravity, electromagnetism, strong nuclear force, weak nuclear force
- *Branches of physics:* nuclear, high energy, condensed matter
- *Levers:* first-, second-, or third-class levers

ACTIVITY 9.2.4 *Develop Venn Diagrams for Earth and Space Science*

Develop a two- or three-circle Venn diagram for one of the Earth and space science topics listed below. Select just two or three items from each set for comparison.

- *Rock types:* igneous, sedimentary, metamorphic
- *Faults:* normal, reverse, strike-slip faults
- *Stars:* neutron stars, white dwarfs, red giants, super novae, black hole
- *Cloud types:* cumulus, stratus, cirrus, nimbus

9.3 Flowcharts

A flowchart is a pictorial representation of a process, with all of its steps and decisions. Flowcharts are frequently used in computer science and business, and a standard set of symbols has been developed to represent specific stages (Figure 9.4). Traditionally the beginning of a process is indicated with a rounded rectangle, and an action is marked with a squared rectangle. Decisions are indicated with diamonds, documents with rectangles with a wavy side, and outputs marked with a rhombus. These symbols are helpful but not necessary to flowcharting.

Figure 9.4 Flowchart Symbols

The scientific method is a process that is generally presented as a list, such as the one that follows:

1. Make observations and identify the problem.
2. Form a hypothesis.
3. Test the hypothesis by performing experiments.
4. Organize and analyze data.
5. Draw conclusions.
6. Communicate results.

Although this list is helpful, it does not reflect the variety of problem-solving routes scientists use, which may be more accurately represented with a flowchart (Figure 9.5). The flowchart illustrates features that are difficult to describe in a list.

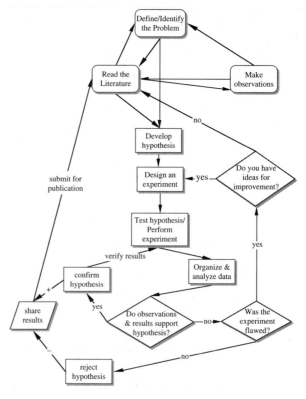

Figure 9.5 Flowchart for "Scientific Method"

For example, if the results of an experiment are not consistent with the hypothesis, the researcher can ask if the experiment was flawed. If it is concluded that the experiment is not flawed, then the hypothesis may be rejected, but if it is flawed, the researcher searches for ways to improve the experiment by consulting the literature or proposing an alternative design, or both. Although this is difficult to explain with words, it is succinctly communicated on the flowchart as shown in Figure 9.5.

ACTIVITY 9.3.1 *Developing Your Own Taxonomic Flowchart*

Taxonomy is the science of classification. Geologists classify rocks, astronomers classify stars, botanists classify plants, zoologists classify animals, musicians classify music, artists classify art, and even hardware manufacturers classify hardware. Figure 9.6 is a flowchart that leads to the classification of screws commonly used in construction. The diamonds represent decisions that must be made in order to identify a screw.

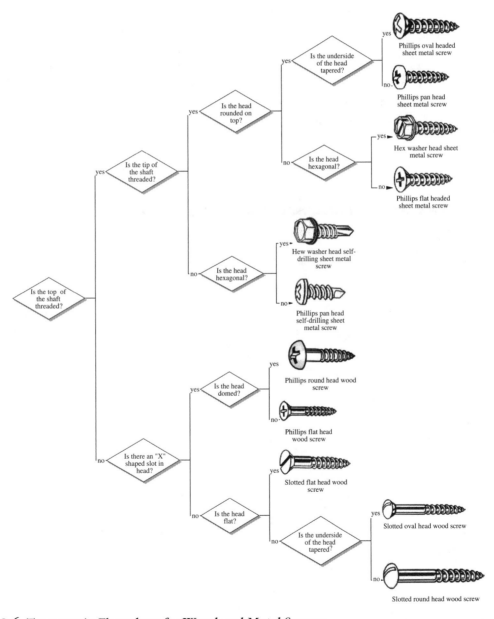

Figure 9.6 Taxonomic Flowchart for Wood and Metal Screws

After studying Figure 9.6, develop your own taxonomic flowchart for items of your choosing. You may classify flowers, rocks, fabrics, leaves, wood, assorted junk, or a collection of hardware (nails, screws, washers, bolts, hinges, clasps). Alternatively, you may classify photographs (cut from magazines or printed from the Internet) of cars, jewelry, foods, or other subjects of your choosing. You may develop a taxonomic chart on poster board or electronically using software (available at *sciencesourcebook.com*). Each decision should be a dichotomy (only two choices) as shown in the taxonomy of the wood and metal screws (Figure 9.6).

9.4 Mind Maps

Mind mapping is a brainstorming technique in which a radial "map" is developed showing the relationship of a central idea to supporting facts and concepts. The idea to be investigated is placed in the center, surrounded by series of supporting ideas (branches), which are themselves surrounded, by supporting information (twigs). Figure 9.7 is a mind map for "energy." Note that four major ideas (units, uses, laws, forms) are connected to "energy," and numerous secondary ideas are connected to these. This mind map provides a picture of what we know about energy and allows us to add new information and ideas by adding additional branches and twigs. Memory experts urge users to embellish their mind maps by grouping with colors or adding drawings.

Although football is wildly popular in the United States, it is relatively unknown in many other nations around the world. In fact, when "football" is mentioned, most internationals think of the sport Americans call *soccer*. To describe American football to someone outside the

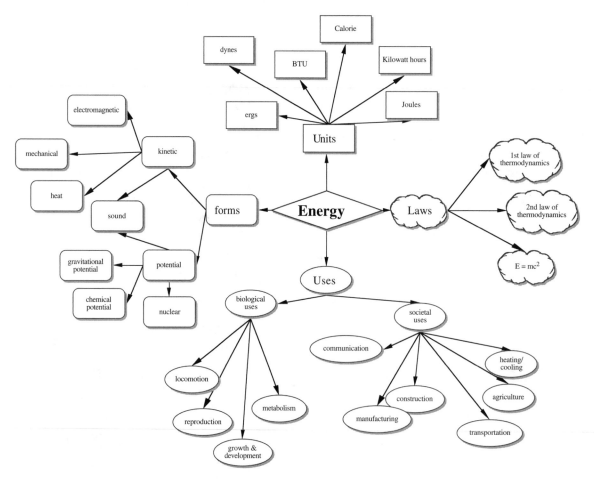

Figure 9.7 Mind Map of Energy

United States or Canada, it may be helpful to compare it with things with which they are familiar. For example, one could explain that football is played on a field similar to a soccer field, with a ball shaped somewhat like a rugby ball, by players wearing helmets similar to those worn by motorcyclists, and shoes with spikes similar to those worn by sprinters. Such comparisons can help someone visualize the game but only if he or she is already familiar with the other sports mentioned. If the other person knows nothing of rugby, soccer, motorcycling, or running, such descriptions would be useless, but for avid sports fans, such comparisons would be very helpful in understanding football. This illustrates the point that the more one knows, the easier it is to acquire new information, providing the learner actively establishes links between the old and new information.

Unfortunately, many students have not learned to make meaningful links between new and existing information, and therefore they are unable to benefit from information they previously learned when studying new material. Students may unwittingly compartmentalize knowledge, thereby reducing their ability to make meaningful connections to new concepts. This is due in part to the compartmentalized instruction they may have received. Unlike science education in many other countries, American science education has historically been segmented into discrete topics, such as chemistry, physics, biology, and geology. Students therefore may get the false impression that physics has nothing to do with biology and not search for useful connections between these two domains. Such linear thinking limits creativity and insight.

Most educational strategies train students to think in a linear fashion through a series of singular associations. However, cognitive psychologists argue that the brain operates in a radiant fashion, not a linear one, thinking from one image center out to others. Mind mapping is a technique that tries to imitate radiant thinking with the hope of engaging both sides of the brain: tapping the right side of the brain for images, dimension, size, and color and the left side for words, numbers, analysis, and logic.[1] Mind mapping is a technique that may assist learners in the acquisition of new

information into an existing cognitive structure and assist in the growth of the knowledge infrastructure so more information can be acquired. As students learn new information in an integrated manner, their mental schemas develop, making it ever easier for them to acquire yet more information. Student mind maps will vary depending on the connections they have made.

ACTIVITY 9.4.1 *Embellishing Mind Maps*
If you were to look through the journals or notes of Leonardo da Vinci, Albert Einstein, or Ludwig von Beethoven, you would see mind maps with colors, symbols, arrows, and pictures to augment the written notes. Memory experts encourage the use of these embellishments to promote better understanding and memory. Embellish the mind map for energy or the circulatory system (Figures 9.7 and 9.8) by adding color, symbols, diagrams, or pictures. When possible, use meaningful colors, and always make drawings or diagrams that relate to the topics listed. You may wish to transfer these mind maps, or portions of them, to large posters so you have sufficient room for embellishments.

ACTIVITY 9.4.2 *Organizing Information in a Mind Map*
Table 9.5 contains terms and ideas associated with *water*. Organize this information into a logical mind map with at least three tiers, using as many terms as you can. You may wish to use some of the following terms for main branches: chemical characteristics, common properties, biological uses, composition, locations in nature, and human uses. Feel free to add additional branches and twigs.

ACTIVITY 9.4.3 *Developing Your Own Mind Maps*
Develop a mind map for a topic of your choice or one assigned by your instructor. The idea to be investigated should be placed in the center of a blank page, connected to four or five major related topics. Each of these topics should then be connected to additional subtopics. Write down everything you know prior to starting your research, illustrating concepts with simple diagrams and

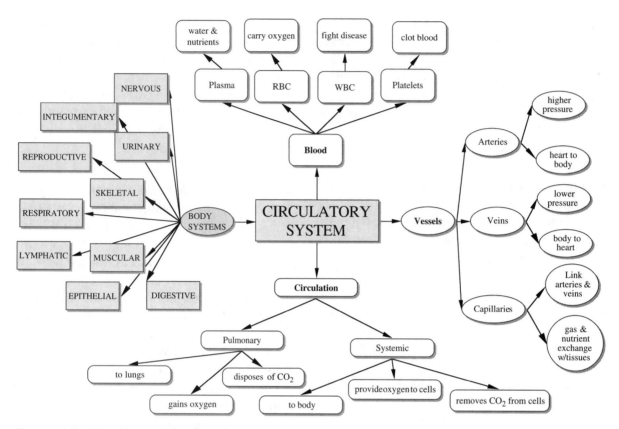

Figure 9.8 Mind Map of the Circulatory System

Table 9.5 Concepts and Terms for Developing a Mind Map on Water (Activity 9.4.2)

adhesion	estuaries	ice	polar
albedo	evaporation	ice caps	precipitation
aquifers	geysers	irrigation	runoff
bond angle	glaciers	lakes	solvent
cell structure	groundwater	life	springs
cohesion	high heat of fusion	liquid	steam
colorless	high heat of vaporization	Mars	streams
coolant	high specific heat	ocean	tasteless
cooling	hot springs	odorless	water cycle
density	hydrogen	oxygen	wells
Earth	hydrolysis	perspiration	

color-coded branches. Add branches and twigs as you conduct your research. Alternatively, you may wish to develop your mind map using software (available at *sciencesourcebook.com,* inspiration. com, or search "mind map software").

9.5 Concept Maps

A concept map is way to visualize the relationship between different concepts and propositions. Figure 9.9 is a concept map of the cell cycle.

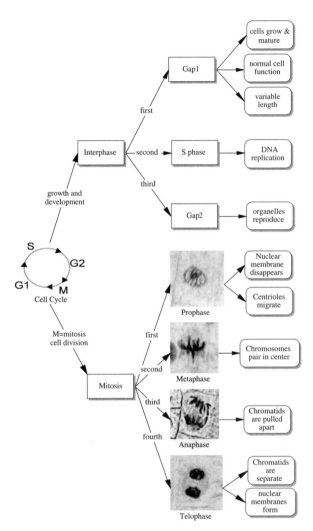

Figure 9.9 Concept Map of the Cell Cycle

A quick glance at the map reveals that the cell cycle is divided into two portions, (1) a growth and development phase and (2) a division phase. The growth and development phase is subdivided into three parts, and the division phase is subdivided into four. The map shows the sequence of phases and what each accomplishes. Although the same information could be described just with words, a concept map, which employs pictures, groupings, connections, and brief descriptions, may be a more economical and effective way to accomplish the same goals. It is easier to visualize a concept map, with an organized array of entries representing stages, than it is to visualize the same concept using only text.

Figure 9.10 is a more complex concept map, showing the relationship of various forms of energy. The rectangles identify different forms of energy, and the arrows identify the processes by which energy is transformed from one form to another. The ovals represent uses of this energy once it is distributed to homes by electricity. Note the many ways that energy may flow from the Sun to power homes, industry, and appliances.

Both of these concept maps summarize complex processes and represent them in the form of a map. Concept maps have been shown to aid learning and memory, but learners realize the real value of concept mapping when they develop their own maps. Concept maps can provide a foundation for writing reports, developing laboratory procedures, or brainstorming relationships within our complex world. Note that concept maps are not linear; they are branched and intertwined because the real world is interconnected.

Spatial memory is the portion of memory responsible for recording information about one's environment and its spatial orientation. We use spatial memory to navigate familiar territory and visualize the world around us. Spatial memory can be used to help visualize concepts and reduce cognitive load while enhancing learning. Concept mapping is a technique that capitalizes on spatial memory to store and analyze information that is not necessarily spatial in nature.[2] Concept mapping in science was popularized by Joseph Novak, based on the theories of David Ausubel, who stressed the importance of prior knowledge in the acquisition of new concepts.[3] Novak argued that meaningful learning involves the assimilation of new concepts and propositions into existing cognitive structures and suggested that this could best be done through mapping strategies that capitalize on spatial memory and intelligence.

Concept maps help us visualize relationships between concepts through labeled arrows (Figures 9.9 and 9.10). Concept maps are frequently used to stimulate and organize idea generation and are a popular brainstorming activity used to promote creativity. The concept maps shown in Figures 9.9 and 9.10 are well thought out and can be helpful in understanding related concepts. It is best to

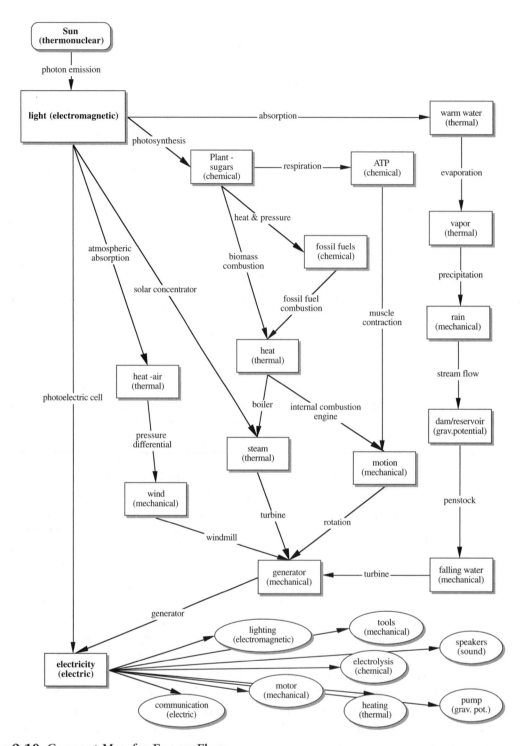

Figure 9.10 Concept Map for Energy Flow

use clear, well-thought-out concept maps during instruction. If students do not understand the concepts better with the aid of a concept map than without one, then the concept map is probably not well designed and should be discarded.

Student-generated concepts maps provide teachers with a window into their pupils' cognitive maps or schemas. Student-generated concept maps are often highly personalized and idiosyncratic and may therefore have little use in the instruction of others. Teachers should employ well-structured concept maps during direct instruction but encourage students to develop their own concept maps when brainstorming new ideas or representing established ones. Student concept maps in this activity will vary depending on student knowledge and schemas.

James Burke, a well-known historian of technology, stated that scientific discoveries or technological advances occur when people make connections between previously unrelated topics, creating new applications for novel situations. Burke has published numerous books and movies on creativity and invention.[4] He asks his readers and viewers seemingly bizarre questions such as: "How was Napoleon important to the development of the modern computer?" Through his books and movies, Burke shows how scientists and inventors make connections between many seemingly unrelated things in the process of making new inventions. You may wish to encourage your students to develop concept maps of such stories from such books and movies. Concept mapping is a great way to illustrate the interconnectedness of science and technology and may help students understand the importance of developing their own mental webs.

ACTIVITY 9.5.1 *Developing a Concept Map for a Complex Concept: Nuclear Winter*

Researchers have proposed that the climate of the Earth could become inhospitably cold in the event of a large-scale nuclear war. Nuclear explosions create a huge amount of dust and initiate numerous building, forest, and brush fires. These events could propel vast amounts of smoke and dust into the stratosphere, an otherwise stable layer of the atmosphere. Dust and smoke in the stratosphere could reflect much sunlight before it reaches Earth. Winds in the stratosphere could distribute the dust evenly around the Earth, causing surface temperatures to drop as much as 20°C due to the increased reflection of light back into space. The lack of sunlight and resulting decrease in global temperature could reduce the amount of photosynthesis, and thereby reduce available food and

oxygen supplies, disrupting all life that depends on plants. Nitrogen oxides produced during nuclear explosions could lead to a rapid degradation of the ozone layer and a dramatic increase in the amount of ultraviolet light reaching the surface of the Earth. Increased ultraviolet radiation could kill sensitive phytoplankton in the oceans, upsetting oceanic food chains that are dependent on them. The complex implications of a nuclear winter are better understood with the use of a concept map. Reread this paragraph, and draw a concept map showing the relationship between variables and processes.

ACTIVITY 9.5.2 *Developing a Concept Map for a Food Web*

Develop a concept map for a terrestrial food web with the organisms listed below. Arrows should point from food to the consumer, showing the flow of energy and nutrients.

- *Primary producers:* grasses, shrubs, trees
- *Primary consumers:* rabbits, squirrels, mice, seed-eating birds, herbivorous insects
- *Secondary, tertiary, and quaternary consumers:* spiders, predaceous insects, insectivorous birds, toads, snakes, foxes, hawks, owls
- *Detritivores:* millipedes, collembola, detritivore beetles
- *Decomposers:* fungi, bacteria

ACTIVITY 9.5.3 *Developing Concept Maps to Trace the Invention of New Technologies*

History records that Thomas Edison invented the light bulb, Alexander Graham Bell the telephone, and Jonas Salk the polio vaccine. Although they deserve credit for their inventions, it should be noted that they were successful only because they were able to connect the ideas of others. For example, to invent the light bulb, Edison had to connect the technologies and findings of many who preceded him, as the following paragraph details.

At the base of a light bulb are two *electrodes* that connect to opposite ends of a thin metal *filament* suspended in a *glass bulb* filled with an *inert gas,* such as argon. When the bulb is connected to a *power supply,* an electric *current* flows through the thin filament, which heats up due to its small width and high resistance. The filament glows when it reaches a certain temperature but does not ignite because of the inert atmosphere in the bulb. To invent the light bulb, it was necessary to tie together the following inventions and discoveries: *electricity, battery* or *power supply, electrical conductors, glass, argon or other inert gas,* and a *carbon or tungsten filament.*

Develop a concept map that shows how prior discoveries or inventions were essential to the development of the light bulb or other invention.

ACTIVITY 9.5.4 *Developing Your Own Concept Maps*

Develop a concept map for a topic of your own interest or one of the options that follows. Choose a theme that has many possible connections:

Life Sciences	Physical and Earth Sciences
heart rate regulation	carbon cycle
blood sugar regulation	nitrogen cycle
human life cycle	energy balance of Earth
cellular respiration	recycling
artificial selection	electricity—sources
gene sequencing	and uses
alternation of	from oil to plastics
generations	petroleum refining
temperature regulation	rock cycle
genetic engineering	water purification
PCR (polymerase chain	and treatment
reaction)	storm development

Answers to Chapter Activities

9.1.1–9.1.4 Student conceptual grids will vary.

9.2.1–9.2.4 Venn diagrams are a good activity to encourage student research. Figure 9.11 shows a Venn diagram for four sets of numbers, and diagrams for larger sets are even more unwieldy. A series of potential Venn diagram ideas is provided in the student section, but teachers and students are encouraged to develop their own comparisons from material in their curriculum. Student diagrams will differ from one another depending on the items compared. If you wish to standardize Venn activities for easy, consistent grading, we suggest that you place a list of potential words and phrases outside of the diagram so that students can simply move them into the appropriate cells. Figure 9.12 is a sample diagram for a rather complex comparison of the three photosynthetic pathways, C3, C4, and CAM, that could be derived from student Internet or library research (Activity 9.2.1). Venn diagrams are easy for two or three dimensions, but get increasingly complex and less useful when comparing larger sets of numbers.

9.3.1 This section introduces students to the standard flowcharting symbols. It should be clarified that flowchart symbols are conventional but not universal. For example, Figure 9.13 is a valid flowchart for classifying matter, although it does not use standard flowchart conventions. Student flowcharts will vary.

9.4.1–9.4.3 Student mind maps will vary depending on the connections they have made.

9.5.1–9.5.4 Student concept maps will vary.

Figure 9.11 Venn Diagrams for Two, Three, and Four Comparisons

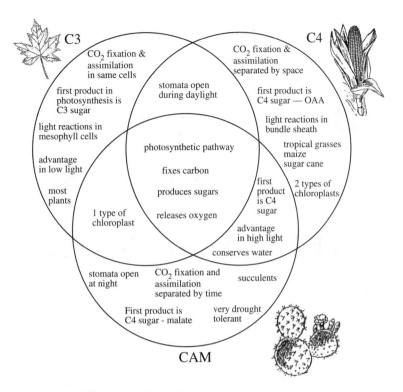

Figure 9.12 Venn Diagrams of Photosynthetic Pathways

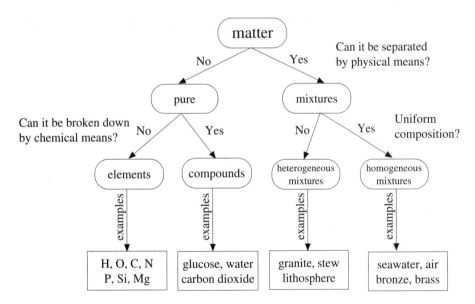

Figure 9.13 Flow Diagram for Classifying Matter

Chapter Ten

Learning Science Concepts with Analogies

For the Teacher 184

10.1 Extended Science Analogies 187

10.2 Analogies for Learning Physics 195

10.3 Analogies for Learning Chemistry 197

10.4 Analogies for Learning Biology 198

10.5 Analogies for Learning Earth and Space Science 199

Answers to Chapter Activities 200

For the Teacher

Constructivist theory suggests that learning is a continuous process in which learners take information and construct personal interpretation and meaning based on prior knowledge and experience.[1] According to this theory, effective learning takes place as the learner makes connections between new information and preexisting knowledge. Analogies are one of the major tools learners and teachers use in the process of making these connections. Analogical reasoning is therefore a key process in human cognition.

An analogy is a comparison between two different things that demonstrate a similarity in one or more key aspects. Analogies help learners understand new concepts by highlighting similarities to familiar ones. Learners understand the new concept more easily if they can relate it to something with which they are familiar. For example, most students find it difficult to visualize the structure of DNA when it is described as "a double helix in which the complementary spiral strands are connected by base pairs," but they can readily grasp the basic structure when it is analogized to a spiral staircase. The spiral staircase analogy allows the student to conceptualize the structure of DNA by relating this new concept to one with which he or she is familiar.

An analogy is similar to a metaphor, but while metaphors are implicit, analogies are explicit. A metaphor is the use of a word or phrase to make an implicit comparison between two things. Metaphors are frequently used in literature but may also appear in science texts. For example, a *building* is often used as a metaphor for a theory: "A theory should have a *good foundation* and provide a *framework* for understanding new knowledge.

If it is *built on shaky* assumptions rather than *solid* data, it will *collapse*. To *stand* the test of time it must be *supported* and buttressed with experimental results." The reader understands that metaphors make implicit comparisons and are not to be taken literally. Similarly, the reader must understand that an analogy is an explicit comparison with definite limitations and should not be extended too far. We use metaphors and analogies in our understanding of unfamiliar facts and phenomena, grasping abstract ideas, creative thinking, and communicating our ideas to others.

The prior knowledge in an analogy is known as *analogue,* source, base, or anchor, and the new information or situation is known as the *target.* Analogical reasoning requires a mapping of relational structure and involves the identification and transfer of structural information from a known system to a new and relatively unknown system.

Analogies are frequently used in science textbooks as well as in classrooms as an aid to the teaching-learning process. Many science teachers generate analogies spontaneously in order to facilitate students' perception and understanding. Analogies may be very helpful in the learning process, but they must be handled with care, or they can lead to misconceptions. For example, many teachers analogize the structure of an atom to that of the solar system. Both have a center (sun or nucleus) about which revolve smaller structures (planets or electrons), which rotate on their own axes (electron spin or planetary rotation). Although this analogy is helpful, its limitations must be clear. For example, planets vary in size, but electrons do not, and planets follow prescribed paths, whereas electrons occupy nebulous orbitals.

Students must learn to generate and use analogies but avoid the temptation to reason by analogy. For example, it may be useful to draw an analogy between Newton's universal law of gravitation (the analogue) and Coulomb's law of electrical force (the target). In both laws, the force generated is directly related to the product of the objects (mass or charge) involved and inversely related to the square of the distance between them. The similarity of the equations (Figure 10.1) helps illustrate that there are some common underlying

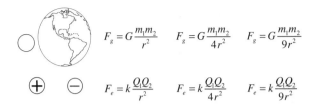

$$F_g = G\frac{m_1 m_2}{r^2} \qquad F_g = G\frac{m_1 m_2}{4r^2} \qquad F_g = G\frac{m_1 m_2}{9r^2}$$

$$F_e = k\frac{Q_1 Q_2}{r^2} \qquad F_e = k\frac{Q_1 Q_2}{4r^2} \qquad F_e = k\frac{Q_1 Q_2}{9r^2}$$

Figure 10.1 Analogy Between Newton's and Coulomb's Law

principles of geometry and physics. However, it is inappropriate to reason that because masses always attract each other, charges therefore always attract. A naive learner who reasons by analogy often develops such a misconception. Like any other analogy, the analogy between Newton's law and Coulomb's law has strict limitations, and it is important that learners understand such limitations so they can benefit from analogies without drawing false conclusions.

Teaching with Analogies

Teachers use analogies throughout their lessons, especially when responding to student questions. When a teacher says phrases such as "similarly," "likewise," "in the same way as," "in comparison to," and "just like," he or she is generally using analogies to help students grasp a concept. But if those analogies are not well chosen or applied systematically, they may be ineffective or cause confusion.

To maximize the benefit of analogies while minimizing the dangers, we suggest that educators employ the teaching with analogies (TWA) strategy introduced by Glynn, Duit, and Thiele.[2] This strategy models what expert teachers and authors employ when using analogies. In the TWA strategy, shared attributes between the analogue and target are known as *mappings*. The goal is to transfer ideas from a familiar concept (the analogue) to an unfamiliar one (the target) by mapping their relationship. The TWA model consists of six operations:

1. Introduce the target concept.
2. Review the analogue concept.

3. Identify the relevant features of target and analogue.
4. Map similarities between the target and analogue.
5. Indicate the limitations of the analogy.
6. Draw conclusions.

The following example illustrates the use of the TWA strategy when introducing the concept of a pulsar by analogizing it to the rotating lamp in a lighthouse:

1. *Introduce the target concept.* A pulsar is a rotating neutron start that emits radio waves in a narrow beam at regular intervals.
2. *Review the analogue concept.* A lighthouse contains a lamp that rotates on an axis and emits light beams to viewers at regular intervals.
3. *Identify the relevant features of target and analogue.* The relevant features are the source of electromagnetic radiation, the axis of rotation, the rotating source, the distant observer, and the appearance of pulsating energy.
4. *Map similarities between the target and analogue.* The neutron star at the core of the pulsar is analogous to the lamp in a lighthouse since both emit electromagnetic radiation. The spinning of the pulsar is analogous to rotation of the lamp. The earthbound astronomer who observes pulsating energy from a pulsar is analogous to the seafarer who observes pulsating light from the lighthouse.
5. *Indicate the limitations of the analogy.* The pulsar rotates at a rate of perhaps 30 times per second, while the lighthouse light rotates much more slowly. The energy emitted from the pulsar is primarily in the form of radio waves, while the energy from the lighthouse is primarily in the form of visible light. While the beam of light from a lighthouse is at right angles to the lamp's axis of rotation, the beam of energy from the pulsar may be at various angles depending on the alignment of the magnetic pole relative to the axis of rotation.
6. *Draw conclusions.* The student develops a basic understanding of the pulsar by analogy to the lamp in a lighthouse.

When student understanding does not match teacher expectation, it is often because there has been a failure at steps 2, 4, or 5, as the following example illustrates. Over the years, many biology teachers and texts have described mitochondria as the *powerhouses of the cell.* The question is, How many students have ever been to a powerhouse or know what it does? The analogy, although potentially a good one, adds little to student understanding because there is insufficient understanding of the analogue, much less the mappings between it and the target. The analogy is useful if the teacher first makes certain that students understand that a powerhouse is a place where energy is converted from a readily available but unusable form into an easily usable form. For example, the powerhouse at the base of a hydroelectric dam converts the kinetic energy of falling water into electricity that can then be distributed through power lines to homes and businesses, where it can be used to power various devices. Similarly, the powerhouse at a coal-burning power plant converts the chemical potential energy in coal to thermal energy in the boiler rooms, and ultimately to electrical energy that can once again be distributed and used.

Understanding the analogue, we are now able to map similarities between it (the powerhouse) and the target (mitochondria). The primary function of mitochondria is to convert energy from the chemical bonds in glucose molecules into the bonds of ATP, a form of energy that can be distributed and used throughout the cell. This is analogous to the function of a powerhouse, which converts energy from an available but impractical form, such as nuclear energy (nuclear reactor), kinetic energy (windmills or hydroelectric plants), or chemical bond energy (coal power generation plant), into electricity, a form of energy that can be easily distributed and used. In this analogy, coal or other raw energy source is analogous to glucose, ATP is analogous to electricity, the mitochondria are analogous to the powerhouse, the cell is analogous to a municipality, and the processes that consume ATP in the cell are analogous to all of those processes in the city that rely on electricity. Although this analogy is an excellent one, it has limitations. For example, unlike a powerhouse that can distribute energy almost immediately through conducting wires, the mitochondria distribute ATP slowly through the process of diffusion to surrounding organelles. And unlike a powerhouse that converts energy from one form to a totally different form (say, from nuclear energy to electrical energy), the mitochondria simply convert it from one type of chemical bond energy to another more usable form.

Analogies are a tool to help learners develop meaning as they relate new concepts (targets) to familiar ones (analogues). If, however, teachers don't recognize when students' existing concepts are flawed, then analogies may confuse the situation. For this reason, it is important that the teacher and student hold a common view of the analogue before mapping begins.

In the activities in this chapter, learners are introduced to a variety of classic and new analogies that can be used when teaching or learning biology, chemistry, physics, and earth and space science. After reading the analogies, the students will be asked to generate and explain analogies of their own. I suggest that teachers carefully read and introduce each example using the TWA strategy, adding further explanation as necessary.

10.1 Extended Science Analogies

Some analogies can be extended much further than others because of intrinsic similarities between the target and analogue concepts. In this section are three extended analogies to illustrate the length to which analogies can be developed. Teachers are encouraged to develop their own analogies and direct students to do the same. When introducing new concepts by analogy to previously learned concepts, teachers must clearly state the limitations so students do not begin to reason by analogy and draw false conclusions.

ACTIVITY 10.1.1 *Electrical Circuit/Plumbing Analogy*

Electricity is an important topic in physics and a vital feature of everyday life, yet it is difficult to understand because it cannot be seen or handled. To conceptualize electricity, it is helpful to draw an analogy between DC electric circuits and plumbing systems. In such an analogy, electricity is the primary *target*, and the plumbing system is the primary *analogue*, but there are numerous other targets and analogues that will be discussed as the analogy is developed. Like all other analogies, the relationship between the target and analogue is limited to the features discussed. No conclusions should be drawn about the nature of electricity by extending the analogy.

Target concept: In a direct current (DC) circuit, the *voltage* (V, volts) of a *battery* is a measure of the available *energy per unit charge*, which drives the electric *current* (I, amperes) around a *closed circuit*. An increase in electrical *resistance* (R, ohms) results in a decrease in *current*.

Analogue concept: In a plumbing system, the *pressure difference* (ΔP, kPa) generated by a *pump* is a measure of the *energy per unit volume*, which drives the *flow* of water (F, cm^3/s) through the *pipes*. An increase in the magnitude of a *restriction* results in a decrease in *flow*.

Relevant features/and mapping: Refer to Table 10.1 and Figure 10.2. The numbers in parentheses in the list that follows refer to the numbers in Figure 10.2:

battery $\leftrightarrow$ *pump:* A *battery* (1) converts chemical energy to electrical energy to drive an electric current through a conductor, just as an electric *pump* (1) converts electrical energy to kinetic energy to move water through a conduit. The strength of a battery is measured in volts (V), while the strength of a pump is measured in kilopascals (kPa). A battery takes in charge at low voltage (4), performs work on it, and releases it at high voltage (3). This is analogous to a pump that takes in water at low pressure (4), performs work on it, and releases it at high pressure (3).

voltage (potential difference) $\leftrightarrow$ *pressure:* Voltage (3) is a measure of the energy per unit charge available to drive charges through a circuit. This is analogous to fluid *pressure* (3), which is a measure of the energy per unit volume available to drive water through a plumbing circuit (see Figure 10.2). If all other factors are held constant, an increase in voltage causes

Table 10.1 DC Circuit/Plumbing Analogy

DC Circuit	Water System
voltage	**pressure**
energy/charge	energy/volume
joule/coulomb	joule/m^3
volt	pascal
battery	**pump**
chemical → electrical	electrical → kinetic
drives current in dc circuit	drives water in plumbing
takes in charge at low voltage	takes in water at low pressure
releases charge at high voltage	releases water at high pressure
current	**volume flow rate**
coulombs/s (amps)	m^3/s
conductor	**conduit (pipe)**
↓diameter ↓current	↑diameter ↑flow
conductive material	open pipe
nonconductive material	clogged pipe
closed circuit	**closed loop**
switch	valve
closed switch	open valve
resistance	**resistance**
small wire	restriction
electrical appliance	water-powered appliance
voltage drop	pressure drop
ammeter	flowmeter
ammeter placed in series	flowmeter placed in series

an increase in current just as an increase in pressure causes an increase in the flow of water. Voltage is measured in volts (joule/coulomb) while pressure is measured in kilopascals (kilojoules/cubic meter).

current ↔ flow rate: Current is a measure of the flow of electric charge through a conductor, just as *flow rate* is a measure of the flow of fluid through a conduit (pipe). Current is measured in coulombs/s (amps), while volume flow is measure in m^3/s.

conductor ↔ conduit: The flow of charge in an electrical *conductor* (2) is analogous to the flow of water in a *conduit* or pipe (2). As the names imply, *conductors* and *conduits conduct* things from one region to another. Increasing the *diameter of a conducting wire* (11,10) increases the *flow of electricity,* just as increasing the *diameter of a pipe* (11,10) increases the *flow of water.* Electricity will flow through a wire made of conductive material but not through a wire made of an *insulating material* (12) such as plastic or nylon. Similarly, water will flow through an open pipe but not through a *clogged pipe* (12).

closed circuit ↔ closed loop: Breaking a *circuit* with a *switch* (9) is analogous to breaking the *flow* of water in a pipe by closing a *gate valve* (9). A *closed switch* is analogous to an *open valve* in the plumbing analogy. An open circuit has voltage but no current because it has "infinite" resistance, just as a closed faucet has pressure but no flow due to high resistance.

resistance ↔ restriction: Electrical resistance is the opposition to the flow of electricity. Appliances such as lights, toasters, and refrigerators offer resistance and are referred to as "loads" on the circuit. *Resistance* (5) to electric current by an appliance is analogous to the *restriction* (5) in a plumbing line. A thin wire (11) restricts flow and is analogous to a narrow pipe (11).

voltage drop ↔ pressure drop: The electrical resistance of an appliance or resistor is so great compared to the copper wire that delivers the current that the *voltage drop* for a circuit is seen primarily across the appliance (5). This is analogous to the *pressure drop* across a pipe restriction or turbine (5).

ammeter ↔ flowmeter: An *ammeter* (7) is placed in series in a circuit to measure the current (6) just like a *flowmeter* (7) is placed in series in a pipe to measure the flow rate (6).

electrical ground ↔ reservoir: A *ground* wire (8) supplies charge to a circuit while holding the voltage of the adjacent wires steady at the voltage of the earth. This is analogous to a *reservoir* (8) that supplies water to a plumbing system while holding the pressure of the adjacent pipes at the pressure of the reservoir. A ground provides a voltage reference for a system but is not part of the circuit, just

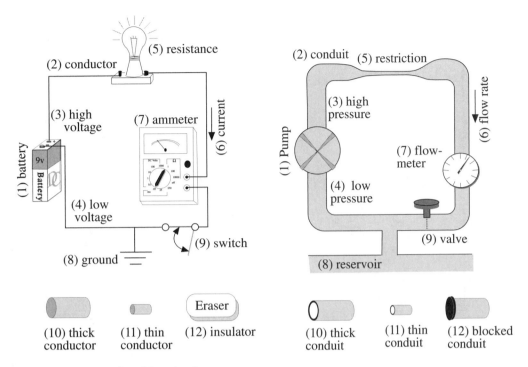

Figure 10.2 DC Circuit Plumbing Analogy

as a reservoir provides a pressure reference for a plumbing loop but is not part of that loop.

speed of electricity ↔ speed of water: When you flip a light switch, lights immediately glow, even though electrons move rather slowly. Similarly, when you open a spigot, water immediately flows, even though water travels rather slowly. In a conductor, electrons "push" adjacent electrons down the length of the wire and produce an immediate effect. Similarly, in pipes, water molecules "push" adjacent water molecules to produce an immediate effect.

Limitations of analogy: Although this is an excellent and time-tested analogy, it has many limitations. For example, if a pipe is cut, water will flow out, but if a wire is cut, electrons will not flow out. In addition, the current in a pipe results from the flow of the contents of that pipe. By contrast, the atoms of copper stay in a copper wire, even though electricity flows through it.

Student project: Illustrate and explain this analogy with a poster, Web page, PowerPoint, or model.

ACTIVITY 10.1.2 *Electron Energy Diagram/Parking Structure Analogy*

An understanding of electron energy is foundational to the study of chemistry, yet it is difficult to develop because both electrons and energy are abstract concepts. An analogy to a parking structure can facilitate understanding.

Target concept: Each electron in an atom has a unique energy address. When identifying an electron, we specify the (1) principal quantum number, n, indicating distance from the nucleus; the (2) angular momentum quantum number, l, indicating the shape of the orbital; the (3) magnetic quantum number, m_l, indicating the orientation of the orbital; and the (4) spin quantum number, m_s, indicating if the electron is spinning clockwise or counterclockwise (these terms have meaning only as opposites to each other in the same atom). The combination of the first three quantum numbers gives the probability of finding an electron in a given region (atomic orbital) while the fourth specifies the spin of the electron on its axis (clockwise or counterclockwise). Figure 10.3 shows an electron energy diagram.

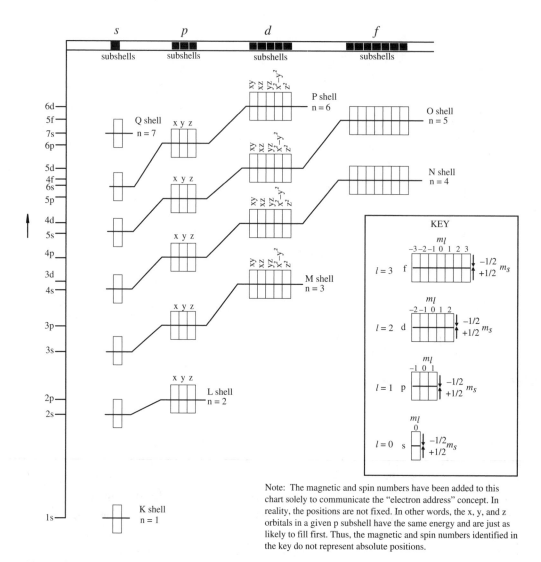

Figure 10.3 Electron Energy Diagram

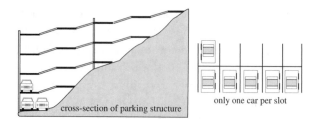

Figure 10.4 Electron Energy Diagram Analogy

Analogue concept: An electron energy diagram is analogous to a parking structure built on a hill (Figure 10.4). On the ground floor there are relatively few parking spots, but as you drive higher, there are progressively more spaces. Just as cars tend to fill the lowest spots in a parking structure first, so electrons fill the lowest energy positions first.

Relevant features and mapping: Features of the electron energy diagram can be mapped to the parking structure in these ways:

electron ↔ car: Electrons in an atom are analogous to cars of the same make and model in a parking structure. Just as the cars in our analogy have identical mass, so all electrons have identical mass. The energy of a car in our parking structure analogy is a function of its position. The higher a parking space, the higher the car's energy. Similarly, the energy of an electron is a function of the orbital it occupies within the atom.

electron energy ↔ *energy of car:* The energy address of an electron is determined by its distance from the nucleus, shape of its orbital, orientation of its orbital, and the direction of its spin. The "address" of a car in a parking structure is a function of the level where it is parked, the row, the position within the row, and the direction in which it is pointing. A car parked in the uphill side of the top row of the top level of a parking structure has much more potential energy than a car on the downhill side of the first row of the first level. Similarly, an electron at a higher level with a complex orbital has more energy than one at a lower level with a simpler shape.

electrostatic attraction ↔ *gravity:* Electrons are negatively charged particles and are attracted to the positively charged nuclei around which they orbit. The attraction between electrons and the protons of the nucleus is analogous to the pull of gravity on the cars in a structure. Just as it takes more energy to drive to the top of a parking structure, so it takes more energy to move an electron to a higher shell.

electron states ↔ *parking structure:* According to the principles of quantum mechanics, electrons in an atom can occupy only specific energy levels. In the same way, cars entering a parking structure can park only in specific spaces demarcated by white lines. Just as the hillside parking structure has more space as you increase levels, so an atom has more orbitals as you get farther from the nucleus.

Pauli exclusion principle ↔ *one car per space:* The Pauli-exclusion principle states that no two electrons can have the same quantum numbers, just as no two cars can occupy exactly the same parking space.

energy address ↔ *position of car:* We can identify the energy of an electron by a unique address, just as we can identify the location of car by giving a specific address. For example, the outermost electron in carbon is located in the second level, where it is found in a p-orbital with an x-orientation and a clockwise

spin. Similarly, we could say that a car is located on the second level of a parking structure, where it is found in the second section, in the second row, facing north.

principal quantum number, n ↔ *level in the parking structure:* The principal quantum number for an electron designates the energy of the shell and is related to the average distance of the electron from the nucleus. The higher the level, the more energetic the electron. This is analogous to the levels of a parking structure. An electron with a higher principal quantum number has more energy than one with a lower number, just as a car at a higher level in the garage has more potential energy than one at a lower level.

subsidiary quantum number orbitals, l (s,p,d,f) ↔ *position in level:* The subsidiary quantum number, describing the shape of the subshell (s,p,d,f) that the electron occupies is a secondary feature related to the energy of electrons. Large parking structures have sloped floors, and cars in spaces in the region closer to the entrance ramp have less energy than those farthest from it. Similarly, electrons in the first regions within a shell, such as *s* and *p*, have less energy than those in the last regions within a shell, such as *d*, and *f*.

magnetic quantum number, m ↔ *parking row:* The magnetic quantum number designates the orientation of the charge cloud in space. This is analogous to the parking rows in a garage, each of which may have a different angle.

spin quantum number, s ↔ *direction parked:* The spin quantum number specifies the direction of spin of the electron on its own axis. An electron can spin clockwise or counterclockwise. For every possible combination of *n*, *l*, and *m*, there can be two electrons, one spinning clockwise and the other counterclockwise. This is analogous to parking spaces in which cars park in opposite directions as they head into opposing slots.

electron positions ↔ *order the garage is filled:* Electrons in a stable atom occupy the lowest possible energy levels or orbitals. This is analogous to the way most parking garages fill. The first spots to fill are those closest to the entrance because they require the least energy to reach.

energy release by falling electrons ↔ energy released by rolling car: If an electron is at a higher energy address, it may spontaneously fall to a lower energy address and release light in the process. This is analogous to a car that occupies a space at the top of a parking structure that may roll to a lower level, releasing energy to charge the battery and heat the brakes.

Limitations: Like all other analogies, this has many limitations, a couple of which are mentioned here. In the parking lot analogy, the energy differences in cars resulted from differences in height above the ground. By contrast, the energy differences in an atom are due to a variety of factors other than distance, including the shape of the orbital, the orientation of the orbital, and the direction of electron spin. In addition, electrons are in constant motion, whereas the cars in this analogy are fixed in parking spaces.

Student activity: The best way to learn something is to teach another. Students should explain the electron energy diagram to a partner using this extended analogy. Read the analogy first, and then put it in your own words as you explain it to another student.

ACTIVITY 10.1.3 *Cell/Factory Analogy*

The cell is the basic unit of living systems. Although it is relatively easy to visualize the components of cells, it is difficult to conceptualize how these components function together to sustain life within the cell. To develop an understanding of the functional processes that take place in a cell, it is helpful to draw an analogy to an automobile factory.

Target concept: The dictionary defines a cell as "the smallest independently functioning unit in the structure of an organism, usually consisting of one or more nuclei surrounded by cytoplasm and enclosed in a membrane." Although this is a relatively accurate description, it is not an intuitive description that students can readily relate to. Because cells are microscopic, difficult to visualize in three dimensions, and exceedingly complex in function, most teachers draw analogies to help students grasp their significance. It is common to hear teachers draw analogies between cells and

cities, schools, and factories. In this example, we are illustrating an analogy between a cell and a factory, but others can be equally well developed.

Analogue concept: An analogy is helpful only when people are familiar with the analogue concept, in this case, a factory. Relatively few students have visited factories, and so it is helpful to review the organization of a factory as the analogy is developed. A factory is a facility where goods are manufactured for export. It consumes raw materials and energy in an effort to sustain its workers and provide resources to others. This is analogous to the functioning of a cell (Figure 10.5), as the following mapping explains.

Relevant features and mapping:

cell ↔ factory: A cell (in a multicellular organism) is an identifiable unit that is part of a larger organism, just as a factory is an identifiable unit that is part of society. A cell uses material and energy resources and produces products, just as a factory does.

cell products ↔ factory products: Cells do not work in isolation; they provide and receive resources from other cells or the surrounding environment. Factories produce products so that they may be sold and earn money for the corporation. Similarly, cells produce products that may be used by surrounding cells and in turn receive resources from surrounding cells. For example, cells in the beta islets of Langerhans in the pancreas produce insulin that surrounding cells use. Simultaneously, these same cells receive oxygen and nutrients provided by the red blood cells and plasma that flow in their neighborhood.

organelle membranes ↔ walls: In factories, walls are used to separate regions with different functions. For example, the paint room is separated from the upholstery shop so each can carry on its functions without interference from the other. Similarly, organelle membranes separate organelles from the cytoplasm, allowing them to have different functions than the cytoplasm in which they are immersed.

nucleus ↔ headquarters: The nucleus of a cell controls the operations of a cell. In a similar manner, factory headquarters controls the operations

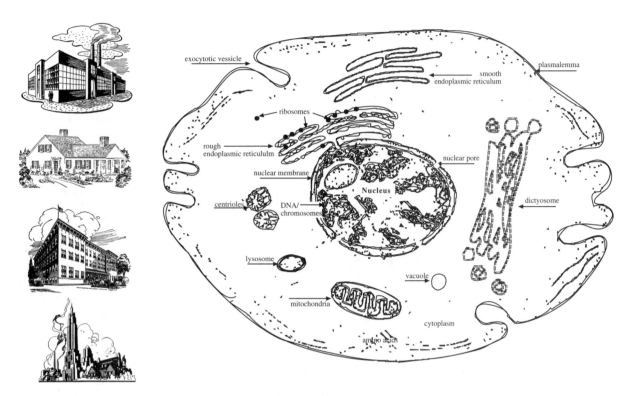

Figure 10.5 Some of the Many Analogies for a Cell

of a factory. The nucleus is separated from the rest of the cell by a nuclear membrane that allows it to function without interruption from surrounding organelles, just as the office walls of the headquarters allow planners and managers to direct the operations of the factory without being distracted by surrounding operations.

nuclear pore ↔ doors: Communication is essential to the proper functioning of a factory. Doors allow people from different departments to visit and communicate. In a similar manner, nuclear pores allow information and resources to flow between the nucleus and the cell it manages.

DNA/chromosome ↔ plans: Each factory has plans that govern the production and development of their products, as well as plans that govern the day-to-day operation of the factory. DNA is analogous to such plans, providing the code not only for all cell products but also the proteins that govern daily operations within the cell.

smooth endoplasmic reticulum ↔ hallways: Factories have hallways through which information from the office travels to the workers in all departments. Similarly, the cell has smooth endoplasmic reticulum through which it is believed that messenger RNA (mRNA) travels from the nucleus to places where it is decoded.

ribosome ↔ worker: Factory workers translate instructions from headquarters into products. In an analogous fashion, ribosomes are the site where m-RNA is translated into proteins.

rough endoplasmic reticulum ↔ assembly line: Workers gather in regions of the factory where assembly takes place. Similarly, ribosomes are positioned on rough endoplasmic reticulum, where the proteins are assembled.

protein ↔ product: Factories produce products for internal and external use. Similarly, cells produce proteins for internal use and for export. Proteins result when DNA code has been transcribed into RNA and translated into polypeptide chains. Similarly, factory products result when plans from the office are copied and distributed to workers, who combine various components to assemble a product.

cytoplasm ↔ stockroom: A factory needs a stockroom from which parts can be taken for use on the assembly line. Similarly, resources are distributed through the cytoplasm until they are used by surrounding organelles.

mRNA↔photocopy: Although the master plans of a company may be protected in the factory headquarters, individual plans may be photocopied from these plans and distributed to workers as needed. mRNA is like a photocopy of DNA that accurately transmits data from the nucleus to the ribosomes, where it is translated into useful proteins.

tRNA ↔ stockroom helpers: Stockroom helpers bring components to the assembly line where they can be combined into products. Similarly, tRNA (transfer RNA) brings amino acids from the cytoplasm to the ribosomes where assemblage of proteins may take place.

mitochondrion ↔ powerhouse: A powerhouse converts energy from one form to another. For example, the powerhouse at a hydroelectric dam converts the kinetic energy of falling water into electrical energy for distribution to homes and businesses. In a similar manner, mitochondria convert energy from the bonds in glucose to the phosphate bonds of ATP.

ATP ↔ electricity: Electricity is a flexible energy source that can be easily distributed to homes and businesses. Similarly, ATP is a flexible energy source that is used to power the growth, movement, and metabolism of the cell.

Golgi apparatus ↔ warehouse: Products from a factory are generally stored in a warehouse before exporting. The Golgi apparatus may serve as a warehouse where proteins are stored prior to export.

Limitations: This analogy should not be extended to cell division. Whereas industries grow by the addition of new factories, cells grow by the splitting and growth of existing cells. Thus, students should not try to find analogues for such things as asters, centrioles, and spindle fibers.

Student activity: Working in a team, develop a new analogy for a cell. You may wish to analogize a cell to a city, your school, your home, or another entity of your choice.

ACTIVITY 10.1.4 *Granite/Ice Cream Analogy*

Granite is a coarse to medium-grained intrusive igneous rock. It contains much quartz and feldspar and is the most common rock in the Earth's crust. It is a plutonic rock, forming as magma cools inside the Earth. Granite is frequently used to build monuments, face buildings, and cover kitchen counters. Yosemite's famed Half Dome (Figure 10.6) and many other mountain peaks are made entirely of granite.

Target concept: Although there are many variations of granite, all contain large percentages of quartz and feldspar. Granite is classified by the presence of schlieren, xenoliths, embedded minerals, and key additives.

Analogue concept: There are a variety of ice creams, just as there are a variety of quartz rocks. Although there are many types of ice cream, all share some common ingredients. By analogy, there are different varieties of granites, but all share some common minerals.

Relevant features and mapping:

rock composition ↔ ingredients: Both rocks and ice cream contain a few basic components. Ice cream contains milk, cream, and sugar, and granite contains feldspars and quartz.

Figure 10.6 Granite: A Common Plutonic Igneous Rock

rock formation ↔ *ice cream formation:* Both granite and ice cream start out as liquids that solidify when the temperature is decreased sufficiently. Both are crystalline solids that soften as they warm.

variation ↔ *flavor:* The three basic flavors of ice cream are chocolate, strawberry, and vanilla. The three basic types of granite are peralkaline, peraluminous, and metaluminous, indicating high concentrations of sodium and potassium, aluminum, or intermediate concentrations of each.

xenoliths ↔ *candies:* Some ice creams contain candy bars or cookies that are of quite different origin from the ice cream. These are analogous to xenoliths, rocks from the outside that became embedded at the time granite was forming.

shapes ↔ *forms:* Granite forms as dikes (upright sheets), batholiths (large round masses), and other shapes. Similarly, ice cream is formed into cones, cups, sandwiches, and other shapes.

biotite and hornblende ↔ *chips and nuts:* Many ice creams contain embedded chocolate or mint chips or nuts. Hornblende and biotite are common minerals embedded in granite.

schlieren ↔ *swirls:* Ice creams may have swirls of different flavors of ice cream. These are analogous to schlieren, layers of dark minerals that occur within the granite.

Limitations: Ice cream freezes at temperatures slightly below 0°C, while granite solidifies at temperatures of approximately −650°C. All granite can be categorized as peralkaline, peraluminous, or metaluminous, but not all ice cream can be categorized as chocolate, strawberry, or vanilla. These are a few of the many limitations of this analogy.

Student activity: Create your own analogy for sedimentary or metamorphic rock.

10.2 Analogies for Learning Physics

Following are some classic analogies in physics. Read through these before trying to generate your own analogies. Note that graphs and figures may be helpful in making an effective analogy:

• *Angular velocity is analogous to linear velocity.* Linear velocity is the rate of change in position with respect to time. This is analogous to angular velocity, which is defined as the change in angle with respect to time. Both angular and linear velocity are vector quantities:

$$\omega = \frac{\Delta \theta}{\Delta t} \text{ is analogous to } v = \frac{\Delta d}{\Delta t}$$

• *Coulomb's law of electrical force is analogous to Newton's universal law of gravitation.* The electrical force created by two charges is proportional to the product of their charges but inversely proportional to the square of the distance between these charges. Similarly, gravitational force is proportional to the product of two masses and inversely proportional to the square of the distances between them:

$$F_c = k \frac{q_1 q_2}{d^2} \text{ is analogous to } F_g = G \frac{m_1 m_2}{d^2}$$

• *Electromagnetic waves are analogous to water waves.* Although water waves and electromagnetic waves are vastly different in nature, both transmit energy without transmitting matter. Both are disturbances that move from one region to another and demonstrate refraction, reflection, diffraction, and interference. One of the best ways to illustrate these features of electromagnetic radiation (e.g., X-rays, ultraviolet, visible, radio) is by analogy to water waves. A wave tank can be made from a large glass cake pan and placed on an overhead projector. Wave fronts can be generated by moving a short plastic ruler in and out of the water, and point sources can be generated by touching the water with the blunt end of a pencil. Figure 10.7 demonstrates the patterns that can be projected on the screen to explain various wave interactions of electromagnetic radiation by analogy to water waves.

• *Reflection of light is analogous to the bounce of a ball.* When light reflects off a mirror, the angle of reflection is equal to the angle of incidence. This is analogous to the bounce of a ball off a backboard in which the angle of reflection is equal to the angle of incidence (Figure 10.8).

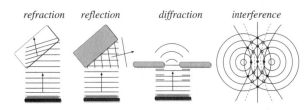

Figure 10.7 Electromagnetic Waves: Analogy to Water Waves

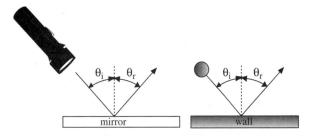

Figure 10.8 Reflection Analogy

• *The refraction of light passing from air into a glass is analogous to the movement of a skateboard rolling from pavement to grass.* When light passes obliquely from air into glass, it slows down and bends toward the normal. Similarly, a skateboard will slow down when it passes at a similar angle from a concrete sidewalk to grass. Glass has a higher optical density than air, causing a wave front of light to slow and bend. Similarly, grass has a higher coefficient of friction than concrete, causing the first wheel of a skateboard to

slow, thereby changing the angle of refraction (Figure 10.9).

• Red shift in stars is analogous to the Doppler shift of sound. Astronomers have noted that the light from distant stars is shifted toward the red end of the spectrum (lower frequency), indicating that they are moving away from us. This is analogous to the lower pitch (lower frequency) of a siren on a car moving away from us (Figure 10.10).

ACTIVITY 10.2.1 *Developing Analogies in Physics*

Develop analogies by explaining the similarities between the analogue and the target for each of the following:

1. Angular acceleration is analogous to linear acceleration.

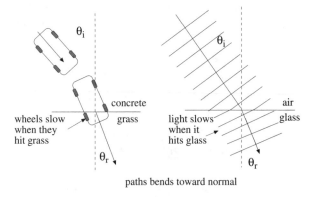

Figure 10.9 Analogy for the Refraction of Light

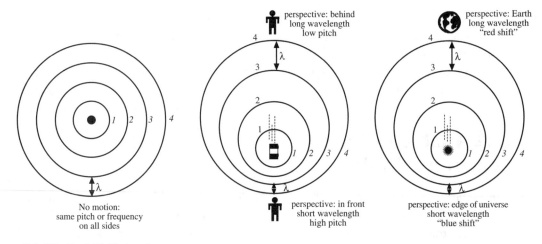

Figure 10.10 Red Shift Analogy

2. A mirror is analogous to a breakwater.

3. Optical density is analogous to the shallowness of water.

4. Sound waves are analogous to compression waves on a Slinky.

5. The wave mechanical model of the atom is analogous to a powerboat.

6. The emission of energy from a quasar is analogous to the heat generated at the entrance to a stadium.

7. Develop an analogy for your own topic.

10.3 Analogies for Learning Chemistry

The following are analogies in chemistry. Read through these before developing your own analogies. Note that graphs and figures may be helpful in making an effective analogy.

• *Entropy is analogous to the state of your room.* Entropy is a measure of the disorder that exists in a system. A messy room has "high entropy" because there are many possible ways to be messy. A neat room has "low entropy" because there are fewer ways to be organized and neat. The second law of thermodynamics states, "Whenever a spontaneous event takes place in the universe, it is accompanied by an overall increase in entropy." In other words, the entropy of the universe is increasing, just as a room will become progressively messier unless energy is expended to reverse the trend.

• *A diffusion gradient is analogous to a ball cage.* Substances diffuse from a region of higher concentration to lower concentration. This is analogous to a ball cage found at carnivals and fast food restaurants. The cage in which children play is filled with small, hollow plastic balls. Piling the balls on one side of the cage creates a gradient, which with time, will return to an equilibrium situation in which the balls lie at uniform depth.

• *Bonding is analogous to a man-on-man defense in basketball.* In a man-on-man defense in basketball, both players in a pair desire to get and keep the basketball. If both get their hands on it but neither one controls it, they are bonded by their mutual attraction for the basketball. This is analogous to a covalent bond in which atoms are held together by a mutual attraction for shared electrons. If one of the basketball players has the ball, his defender will follow him around the court, "attracted" by the basketball. This is analogous to an ionic bond in which one of the species has an extra electron and is therefore negatively charged, while the other is positively charged and thereby attracted to the first. Finally, a polar covalent bond is analogous to a situation in which both players have their hands on the basketball, but one player has it against his chest while the other is trying to retrieve it. In polar covalent bonds, the shared electrons are closer to one nucleus than the other but still under the attractive influence of both nuclei.

• *Surface tension of water is analogous to the tension on a drumhead.* Both a drumhead and the surface of water will resist deformation as they minimize surface area. The surface tension of water can be broken with soap and the tension of a drumhead broken with a knife.

• *A nuclear chain reaction is analogous to falling dominos.* Arrange dominoes to simulate a nuclear chain reaction. Stand dominoes upright as illustrated in Figure 10.11 such that if the first falls, it will strike two, and each of these will strike two more when they fall. The falling dominos are analogous to a nuclear chain reaction in that one reaction stimulates more than one additional reaction, which in turn stimulates more than one reaction each, and so forth.

• *An activated complex is analogous to a windowsill.* A firefighter entering a building by a ladder must first climb to the top of the sill before he or she can jump down to the floor. Similarly, on leaving the building, the firefighter must again climb up to the top of the sill before descending the ladder. Reacting molecules interact to produce high-energy intermediates known as *activated complexes*. These complexes have higher potential energy than either the reactants or products and are analogous to windowsills, which are higher than either the floor or the ground.

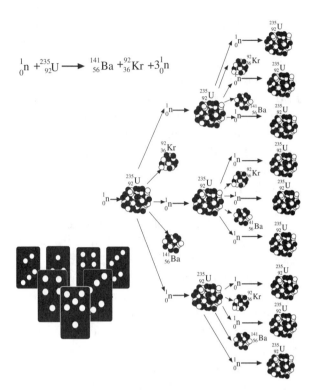

$$_0^1n + _{92}^{235}U \longrightarrow _{56}^{141}Ba + _{36}^{92}Kr + 3_0^1n$$

Figure 10.11 Chain Reaction Analogy

ACTIVITY 10.3.1 *Developing Analogies in Chemistry*

Develop analogies by explaining the similarities between the analogue and the target for each of the following:

1. Atomic spectra are analogous to fingerprints.
2. Phases of matter are analogous to stages of a school day.
3. Chemical reactions are analogous to dances.
4. Reactions are analogous to factory production.
5. Collision geometry is analogous to a jigsaw puzzle.
6. The mean free path is analogous to the movement of bumper cars.
7. Develop a chemistry analogy for a topic of your choice.

10.4 Analogies for Learning Biology

The following are some analogies in biology. Read through these before developing your own analogies.

• *Semipermeable membrane is analogous to a chain-link fence.* Small objects like water and dust can cross the fence, while larger particles like trash and leaves are stopped by it. This is analogous to semipermeable membranes, which allow small or appropriately charged molecules through while blocking others.

• *An enzyme is analogous to a baseball mitt.* A baseball mitt facilitates catching a fly ball, just as an enzyme facilitates a chemical reaction. A baseball mitt conforms around a baseball but not a basketball, just as an enzyme conforms to fit only specific substrate molecules but not others. The pocket of the glove fits the substrate like the active site of an enzyme fits the substrate molecules.

• *Homeostasis is analogous to a thermostat.* Homeostasis is the tendency of an organism to maintain optimal internal conditions (e.g., pH, temperature, oxygen concentration) by regulating behavior or internal processes. If the temperature is too high, a thermostat turns on the air conditioning, and if it is too low, it turns on the heater. Similarly, a person whose body temperature exceeds 37°C may cool down by sweating or walking to the shade, and if it drops below 37°C, the person may warm up by shivering (spontaneous muscle contraction) or by putting on a coat.

• *Gel electrophoresis is analogous to movement through a crowd.* Small children can move through a crowd faster than large adults because they can readily slip between openings in the crowd. Similarly, small strands of DNA move more rapidly around the obstructions in a gel during electrophoresis. Thus, movement through a crowd can separate small people from large people just like electrophoresis can separate small strands from large ones. One way to illustrate this in the classroom is to have individual students walk through an array of desks and then have a string of three people who are holding hands traverse the same path. The chain of people will travel more slowly due to the obstructions. Similarly, longer chains move more slowly through gels than short chains.

• *Transcription and translation of genetic material are similar to the transcription and translation of a book written in a different language from a reference library.* Just as a reference volume remains in the library, so DNA remains in the nucleus.

To be useful, however, both the reference and DNA must be transcribed, taken out of the library or cell, and translated into something meaningful. For example, to use a Russian text, a worker transcribes text from Cyrillic (the Russian alphabet) to Roman letters (used in English). Similarly, DNA in the nucleus is transcribed from DNA into RNA, a form that is readable in the cell. Once transcribed, text can be taken from the library to workers who translate it into English. Similarly, RNA exits the nucleus and binds to the ribosomes, where it may be translated to form proteins.

• *Biochemical reactions are analogous to the manufacturing process.* Reactants are analogous to raw materials in a manufacturing process, while products are analogous to the manufactured goods. Enzymes are like the workers that facilitate the assembly of the goods. Both enzymes and workers facilitate the bonding or unbonding of component parts. For example, if the demand for finished cabinets is high, a cabinetmaker will facilitate the construction of cabinets, but if the demand is low, he or she may reduce output and even disassemble existing stock to save room in the warehouse. Similarly enzymes facilitate the assemblage of products from reactants if the "demand for products is high" (the concentration of products is low relative to the reactants), but may facilitate the reverse reaction if the opposite conditions are true.

ACTIVITY 10.4.1 *Developing Analogies in Biology*

Develop the following analogies by explaining the similarities between the analogue and the target:

1. Binomial nomenclature is analogous to human names.
2. Blood vessels are analogous to a road system.
3. The immune system is analogous to a security guard.
4. The eye is analogous to a television camera.
5. Electron transport chains are analogous to balls rolling down staircases.
6. The movement of an action potential along an axon is analogous to the movement of a spectator "wave" at a sports stadium.

7. Develop a biology analogy for a topic of your choice.

10.5 Analogies for Learning Earth and Space Science

The following are analogies in earth and space science. Read these before developing your own analogies:

• *Heating rock is analogous to heating cheese.* When cheese is heated it melts. Similarly, when rock is heated, it melts. If heated to higher temperatures, the cheese bubbles as gases form inside the cheese. Similarly, rock bubbles if heated sufficiently as various gases form in the molten material.

• *Convection currents in the Earth's crust are analogous to convection currents in heated water.* Hot water rises in the center of a pot above the flame and sinks on the cooler sides. This is analogous to convection centers in the mantle, where rock rises at the oceanic ridge and then sinks in subduction zones at trenches.

• *Volcanic eruption is analogous to opening a soda that has been shaken.* When the lid is on, the pressure in a soda can is sufficient to keep the carbon dioxide dissolved in the liquid, but when the cap is removed, the pressure drops, carbon dioxide bubbles form, and a froth escapes. This is analogous to a magma chamber in which the pressure of the overburden rock prevents the rock from frothing, but when a vent develops, the magma froth forms and expands through the vents, expelling large quantities of shattered rock. Pumice, a lightweight volcanic rock marked with numerous gas chambers, is evidence of this reaction.

• *Sedimentary rock is like a club sandwich.* A club sandwich, like sedimentary rock, is made from the bottom up. The top layer of both is the most recent, and the bottom layer is the oldest.

• *The behavior of compressing or expanding gases is analogous to playing pool on a contracting or expanding pool table.* Temperature is a function of the average kinetic energy of molecules. A pool ball reflected off the wall of a pool table will return with approximately the same speed it had prior to the collision. If, however, the walls are contracting (moving toward the center) the billiard balls will rebound with greater speed. Analogously, molecules in a compressing environment will rebound with greater speed, and hence a greater temperature. If the pool table walls are expanding (moving away from the center) at the time of collision, the reflected pool balls will rebound with a significantly lower speed. This is analogous to molecules in an expanding environment. As molecules rebound, they do so with lesser speed, and hence lower kinetic energy and temperature.

• *The retrograde motion of planets is analogous to viewing a pedestrian from a passing car.* The planets beyond Earth appear to move backward as the Earth passes through the same angle from the sun. This is analogous to the appearance of a pedestrian walking the same direction as a moving car. The pedestrian appears to move backward against the distant horizon as the car speeds by. Although both the driver and pedestrian are moving in the same direction, the pedestrian appears to be moving backward with reference to the horizon when viewed by the passing driver.

ACTIVITY 10.5.1 *Developing Analogies in Earth and Space Science*

Select and develop some of the following analogies by explaining the similarities between the analogue and the target as well as the limitations of the analogy:

1. The relative dimensions in a cross-section of the Earth are analogous to the relative dimensions in the cross-section of a peach.
2. Rocks are analogous to Silly Putty.
3. The formation of spiral galaxies is analogous to the formation of pizza crust from raw dough.
4. Pulsars are analogous to lights on emergency vehicles.
5. Space-time is analogous to a trampoline.
6. The expanding universe is analogous to a rising loaf of raisin bread.
7. Develop an Earth or space science analogy for a topic of your choice.

Answers to Chapter Activities

10.1.1–10.1.4 The problems in section 10.1 require students to discover relationships within a set of established parameters. Many students will find this activity challenging and may not come up with the relationships described in the answer section. They should be rewarded for the accuracy of their reasoning, even if they find different relationships from those presented below. Many of the analogies described here have been used for years by science teachers. The teacher is encouraged to review them and use or modify those that meet their instructional needs.

10.2.1 Developing analogies in physics:
1. *Angular acceleration is analogous to linear acceleration.* Linear acceleration is the rate at which linear velocity changes. This is analogous to angular acceleration, which is the rate at which angular velocity changes.

$$\alpha = \frac{\Delta \omega}{\Delta t} \text{ is analogous to } a = \frac{\Delta v}{\Delta t}$$

2. *A mirror is analogous to a breakwater.* The reflection of a water wave from a flat breakwater is analogous to the reflection of light from a mirror. In both instances, the angle of incidence is equal to the angle of reflection.
3. *Optical density is analogous to the shallowness of water.* The refraction of light from air (lower optical density) into glass (higher optical density) is analogous to the refraction of water waves from deep to shallow water. Light travels faster in air than in glass, just as water waves travel faster in deep water than in shallow water (Figure 10.7). High optical density is analogous to shallow water and low optical density is analogous to deep water.
4. *Sound waves are analogous to compression waves on a Slinky.* Stretch a Slinky spring flat on the floor, and secure both ends. Gather together a set of coils at one end and release them. This creates a compression pulse that travels down the spring and reflects off the other end. The compression (longitudinal) waves of the Slinky are analogous to sound waves (Figure 10.12). Just as the coils are closer together in the compression pulse, so air molecules are closer together in the compression portion of a sound wave. Just as the compression wave reflects at the end of the Slinky, so sound waves echo off a fixed surface.
5. *The wave mechanical model of the atom is analogous to a powerboat.* As a boat moves, waves are greatest near the boat and decrease in amplitude moving away from the boat. You can locate the most probable location of the boat by analyzing the amplitude and energy of the waves. This is analogous to the wave mechanical model of the atom, which visualizes the atom as a positive nucleus surrounded by vibrating electron waves. The Shrödinger wave equation describes the amplitude of the waves associated with moving electrons and therefore also describes the relative location of these electrons.

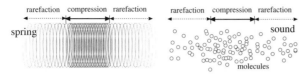

Figure 10.12 Sound/Longitudinal Wave Analogy

6. *The emission of energy from a quasar is analogous to the heat generated at the entrance to a stadium.* Quasars release an enormous amount of energy and may be thousands of times brighter than average galaxies. Some astronomers theorize that there are black holes at the centers of quasars. As matter falls into a black hole, it is squeezed and heated by friction with adjacent particles, making it extremely hot so that it gives off light. This is analogous to crowds entering a stadium. Fans get closer together as they funnel through the entrance gate, causing the heat to rise due to the proximity of one to the other and the friction caused by walking and rubbing shoulders as they move toward the gate.

7. Students generate their own analogies.

10.3.1 Developing analogies in chemistry:

1. *Atomic spectra are analogous to fingerprints.* Elements and molecules produce unique patterns of spectral lines. These spectra can be used to identify the presence of a particular element or molecule in an unknown substance, just as a fingerprint can be used to identify a unique individual (Figure 10.13).

2. *Phases of matter are analogous to stages of a school day.* The particles in a solid have a regular arrangement and limited range of movement. This is analogous to a classroom in which students are sitting in chairs. The shifting or turning of students in their seats is analogous to the vibratory motion that takes place in solids. When the bell rings, students flow easily from one class to another but contained by the schoolyard fence. This is analogous to a liquid phase in which molecules have limited translational motion that allows them to move among one another and through the halls but are still constrained by the container. At the end of the day, students are free to exit the school and leave the campus. This is analogous to the gas phase in which molecules have unrestricted translational movement, allowing for rapid diffusion.

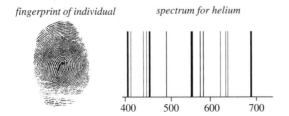

Figure 10.13 Atomic Spectrum Analogy

3. *Chemical reactions are analogous to dances.* A synthesis reaction is analogous to a couple who gets together to dance. The men and women in the dance are analogous to the cations and anions in a solution. A decomposition reaction is similar to the end of a dance, when the couple separates. A double replacement reaction is analogous to two couples who switch partners in the middle of the dance. A single replacement reaction is analogous to a dance in which someone cuts in on a couple and continues to dance with one of them.

4. *Reactions are analogous to factory production.* A reaction rate is the rate at which a product is produced or a reactant consumed. This is analogous to the rate of car production in an automobile factory. The rate of car production can be measured by the number of cars produced per day or the number of transmissions that are installed. If the factory runs out of transmissions, automobile production comes to a halt. This is analogous to the limiting reagent in a chemical reaction. When a reagent is exhausted, the reaction comes to a standstill. Chemical reactions can be accelerated by catalysts, which assist the reaction but are themselves not changed by it. This is analogous to robotic welders, which accelerate the rate at which cars are assembled but are not themselves changed by the assembly process.

5. *Collision geometry is analogous to a jigsaw puzzle.* Two molecules must collide with the correct collision geometry for bonds to form. This is similar to a jigsaw puzzle in which pieces must be oriented correctly so that pieces will interlock.

6. *The mean free path is analogous to the movement of bumper cars.* The mean free path is the average distance a molecule travels between collisions with other molecules. This is similar to riding bumper cars at a carnival. The more cars in the rink, the shorter the distance, or free path, prior to hitting another car. Smaller cars exhibit longer mean free paths. Similarly, smaller molecules exhibit longer free paths and higher rates of diffusion.

7. Students generate their own analogies.

10.4.1 Developing analogies in biology:

1. *Binomial nomenclature is analogous to human names.* Our surname (family name) indicates relatedness, just as a genus name indicates a level of similarity. Our given name differentiates us from other related people, just as a species name differentiates from others in the genus.

2. *Blood vessels are analogous to a road system.* Just as a road system is used to deliver food and consumer items while removing waste, so the vascular system is used to deliver food and oxygen while removing excess carbon dioxide and other toxins. Arteries and veins are analogous to major freeways, delivering massive amounts or resources quickly. Arterioles and venules connect arteries to capillaries, just as highways connect freeways to city streets. Capillaries are used to deliver nutrients and remove waste from individual cells, just as city streets

are used to deliver goods and remove waste from individual homes.

3. *The immune system is analogous to a security guard.* A security guard at a bank must be able to let in customers while keeping out criminals, just as the immune system must be able to determine self-proteins from non–self proteins. A security guard can be fooled by a false alarm and apprehend innocent citizens. Similarly, the immune system can be fooled by tissue damage or pollen, resulting in inflammation or an allergic response.

4. *The eye is analogous to a television camera.* Both the eye and a television camera convert light into electrical impulses that are viewed and interpreted remotely. The lens of a camera focuses and inverts the image on the charged coupled device or similar device that turns light signals into electrical signals that travel to the monitor for viewing. Similarly, the lens and cornea of the eye focus light and create an inverted image on the retina, which converts the light signal into a nerve impulse, which travels to the brain for interpretation. The diaphragm of the camera opens or closes to regulate the light into the camera, just as the iris muscles contract or relax to regulate the size of the pupil and the amount of light that enters the eye. The inside of a camera is painted black to prevent the reflection of light and confusion of the image, just as the inside of the eye is dark to prevent internal reflection.

5. *Electron transport chains are analogous to balls rolling down staircases.* A bowling ball perched at the top of a staircase has potential energy that may be released in a single event if it slips under the banister or in many small events if it rolls down the staircase. Although the amount of energy released is the same regardless of the direction it moves in, it is much easier to manage if it rolls down the staircase. Similarly, electron transport chains release energy in small, manageable portions as electrons are transferred through a series of carriers rather than as bursts of energy that cannot be tapped.

6. *The movement of an action potential along an axon is analogous to the movement of a spectator "wave" at a sports stadium.* Spectators in a stadium sit until signaled to rise by the rising of their neighbors and return to their seats shortly after their neighbors do the same. Similarly, a portion of an axon maintains a negative polarity until stimulated to reverse by a neighboring portion. In both the stadium and the axon, the reversal is moving and transient. Just as the wave is short-lived at any point in the stadium, so polarity reversal is short-lived. Although a signal is sent in both cases, in neither situation is anything physically transmitted. Because spectators sit immediately after standing, the spectator wave goes only in one direction. Similarly, the refractory period of membrane repolarization ensures that the action potential travels in only one direction.

7. Student responses will vary.

10.5.1 Developing analogies in earth and space science:

1. *The relative dimensions in a cross-section of the Earth are analogous to the relative dimensions in the cross-section of a peach.* The proportions of the Earth are similar to the proportions of a peach. The core of the Earth is analogous (in relative size) to the seed, the mantle is analogous to the meat, and the crust is analogous to the skin.

2. *Rocks are analogous to Silly Putty.* Silly Putty will shatter if hit by a hammer but will slowly mold to a table if allowed to stand. Similarly, rocks break when subjected to intense stresses but slowly bend over geological time if the constant stress of gravity is applied.

3. *The formation of spiral galaxies is analogous to the formation of pizza crust from the dough.* A pizza chef spins a lump of dough until it is flattened in a pizza disk. Inertia tends to pull the lump of dough into a disc, and electrostatic attraction within the dough holds it together. Similarly, inertial forces may tend to pull a spinning galaxy into a disc, while gravitational attraction holds it together.

4. *Pulsars are analogous to lights on emergency vehicles.* Pulsars emit energy, but not equally in all directions. Strong magnetic fields concentrate the energy in two opposite directions. Pulsars spin like the emergency light on a police car or ambulance. Distant observers see pulses of energy at regular intervals.

5. *Space-time is analogous to a trampoline.* Space-time involves four dimensions, so any three-dimensional analogy is limited. The space-time continuum is analogous to the surface of a trampoline on which a number of people are standing. The gravitational attraction on each person warps the trampoline in the area surrounding their feet. If all but one of the people converge at one point on the trampoline, its surface will become dramatically warped. Balls (analogous to light or other radiation) can still be rolled from the remaining individual to the group, but balls rolled from the group to the individual are less likely to succeed due to the curvature of the trampoline (space-time). If many people gather at the center, the trampoline bends so that the group is surrounded by it, at which point balls (representing light) cannot exit. A black hole is thought to warp space-time completely around itself, like the group of people at the same point on the trampoline. If space-time is warped sufficiently, no light will escape, hence the term *black hole*.

6. *The expanding universe is analogous to a rising loaf of raisin bread.* In the 1920s, Edwin Hubble made the discovery that all distant galaxies are moving away from us. This is analogous to baking a loaf of raisin bread in which the raisins represent galaxies. As the loaf rises, the raisins in the loaf move farther from each other. Similarly, as the universe expands, galaxies are always moving farther from each other.

7. Students develop their own analogies.

Chapter Eleven

Tools for Improving Memory in Science

For the Teacher 203

11.1 The Primacy and Recency Effect 211

11.2 Expanding Short-Term Memory by Chunking 211

11.3 Science Acronyms and Abbreviations 215

11.4 Acrostics for Memorizing Lists 216

Answers to Chapter Activities 219

For the Teacher

"Is the primary goal of science instruction to encourage the development of higher order-reasoning, or to ensure mastery of specific science content?" This question is frequently debated by curriculum specialists and science educators and has led to periodic shifts in curricular plans in schools and districts throughout the country. I believe that this oscillating and schizophrenic approach to curriculum planning can be eliminated if educators agree that the development of reasoning skills and mastery of science content are complementary rather than competing objectives. Students with a solid understanding of basic facts are better able to engage in higher-order reasoning, and students who can reason well are better able to memorize and recall basic information.

This chapter emphasizes strategies and techniques for memorizing science principles and facts, with the understanding that such memory is foundational to the development of higher-order reasoning skills. To better understand how to improve memory, it is helpful to understand the basics of *cognitive science*, the study of the acquisition and use of knowledge.

Cognitive scientists describe three basic types of memory: sensory, short term, and long term. Sensory memory is immediate perceptual memory and lasts only 1 second or less. When we attend to stimuli, items acquired in sensory memory can be stored in short-term memory, where they either forgotten or maintained by rehearsal. From short-term memory, information is encoded into long-term memory by more elaborative rehearsal and encoding. During retrieval, information passes from long-term memory back into short-term memory, where we become conscious of it and can use it in solving problems.

Sensory memory has a large capacity but is very short-lived. We perceive images, sounds, and other sensory input for a brief moment, but this information is quickly lost if not encoded in short-term memory. By contrast, short-term memory has a very small capacity of seven (plus or minus two) chunks of information but can hold that information for up to half a minute or more. Short-term memory stores information for a brief period in preparation for encoding into long-term memory. During the 30 seconds or less that an item is stored in short-term memory, it may be maintained through rehearsal. For example, a science student may say an equation repeatedly to maintain it in short-term memory until it can be stored in long-term memory. There is no known limit to the capacity of long-term memory, and long-term memory may store items indefinitely when encoded with appropriate organization and meaning. A summary of the basic facts of human memory is illustrated in Figure 11.1 and summarized in Table 11.1.

Although the brain is exceedingly more complex than any manufactured computer, an analogy between a personal computer and the human mind may help explain certain aspects of human memory. In a personal computer, the central processing unit conducts the logical and mathematical operations. The computer has primary memory (working memory, also known as random access memory, RAM), which stores data for immediate use by the microprocessor. Data in primary memory are available for

processing but are lost when a computer is turned off unless the information has first been encoded in secondary memory (storage memory, in forms such as DVD, CD, or magnetic disc).

Human working memory (also known as short-term memory) is analogous to the primary memory of the microcomputer. We load information from long-term memory or from sensory memory into short-term memory before we perform operations with it in our mind, just as a computer loads data from a secondary storage media or input devices into RAM before performing operations.

When we stop concentrating, data in our working memory are lost unless we have first stored this information in long-term memory. In a similar manner, abruptly turning off the power to a computer causes all data in RAM to be lost unless it has first been saved to secondary memory. Distraction and interference can cause a loss from human short-term memory, just as power surges and electrical failure can cause a loss of information in the primary memory of a computer.

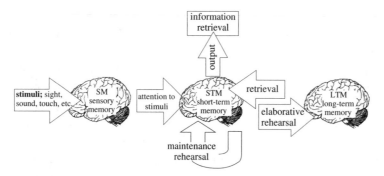

Figure 11.1 Memory Theory

Table 11.1 Forms and Stages of Memory

	Sensory Memory	**Short-Term Memory**	**Long-Term Memory**
Capacity	very large	7 ($\pm$2) chunks of data	no known limit
Maximum duration	1 second	30 seconds	permanent
Method of maintenance	not possible	maintenance rehearsal	elaborative rehearsal and organization
Method of retrieval	perception	serial, exhaustive search	search with retrieval cues
Chief cause of forgetting	decay	interference and decay	interference
Major information code	sensory	acoustic	semantic, meaning

Information that is stored in human long-term memory is relatively permanent but can be lost through physical trauma or chemical interactions, just as data on storage media may be lost by demagnetization, heat, or physical damage. Just as individuals encode information in different ways, so different computer operating systems encode files in different manners.

If the operating system of a computer fails to store file information accurately in the directory, the user may lose access to the files. Similarly, unless we properly encode our memories in elaborate and effective ways, we may lose access to them. Just as the files remain in the secondary memory of the computer and yet inaccessible due to a lack of appropriate directory information, so memory traces may remain inaccessible in our brain due to an inability to find an appropriate path to them. As the number of files in a computer grows, indexing and cross-referencing become more critical. Similarly, as we present students with more information, it becomes increasingly important to help them index this information in a manner that will facilitate retrieval. Nowhere is the knowledge explosion more dramatic than in the sciences, and educators should help students develop the logic necessary to encode and cross-reference data for easy retrieval.

Cognitive psychologists refer to working memory as short-term memory since it is ephemeral in nature. Traditionally the extent of short-term memory is measured by digit span: the number of random digits an individual can keep in short-term memory. Research indicates that most people have digit spans of five to nine and are unable to increase this span significantly. Although we may be unable to expand short-term memory, we can learn to use it more efficiently through techniques such as primary rehearsal and chunking, which we discuss in this section.

Long-term memory is more flexible than short-term memory, and there is a substantial amount of research on techniques to improve it, including multiple modalities, semantic depth, acrostics, acronyms, transfer appropriateness, unanticipated events, context effects, nonverbal memory, and retrieval practice. The student activities following the discussion of these memory techniques use these techniques to help build memory of science facts and concepts.

Memory Technique 1: Maintenance Rehearsal

The brain's cerebral cortex (center of short-term memory) receives messages from the eyes, ears, and touch sensors. It is necessary to pay attention to such stimuli for a few seconds to provide sufficient time for such information to be encoded into short-term memory. Interference at this stage can displace newly acquired information from the consciousness. Teachers should make certain their lectures and discussions have sufficient wait times to allow students to encode new information into short-term memory.

Primary rehearsal (a conscious mental reiteration of information), also known as *maintenance rehearsal* or *rote cycling*, maintains a memory trace in short-term memory. Primary rehearsal is useful when one must apply the knowledge immediately, as when remembering information from a lecture while writing it in one's notes. Research shows that one mechanism of primary rehearsal is an articulatory loop (one that involves speaking). Electromyographic studies have detected action potentials in the sublabial muscles (those below the lip) when subjects were asked to silently memorize random digit sequences, indicating that the subjects were subvocalizing the sequences in an effort to keep the memory traces alive in short-term memory.[1] Since a memory must be kept alive in short-term memory before it can be encoded into long-term memory, it is to our advantage to capitalize on the articulatory loop. *Science teachers may ask students to repeatedly vocalize important information to be remembered.* For example, if you are introducing the Ideal Gas Law, have your class chant "$PV = nRT$" periodically throughout the class. Memory is improved by pronouncing the names of the items out loud, especially if they are grouped rhythmically. Grouping items into threes or fours also seems to aid recall. The repetition of important terms, phrases, and equations will keep them in short-term memory until they can be transferred to long-term memory.

Memory Technique 2: Chunking

If short-term memory storage is limited to seven (plus or minus two) items, one might wonder how complex situations can be memorized quickly. Blind chess players, for example, must keep the positions of 32 pieces on a chessboard in working memory. Expert players overcome this problem by chunking information in recognizable units. For example, knowing that your opponent has a king's side castle defense requires only one "digit" of your memory span yet identifies the position of four or more pieces.

Figure 11.2A shows a random setup for a chessboard. If this diagram is shown briefly to both novice and expert players, neither will be able to remember the entire setup because it is far too complex to quickly memorize. By contrast, Figure 11.2B shows a standard opening that an expert will recognize and remember, while the novice will be unable to. The expert may recognize the entire opening as one or more chunks of information, while the novice simply sees a series of individual pieces. Novices can't memorize complex chess positions because they don't have relevant chunks of data in their long-term memory to draw upon.

To show the value of the chunking strategy, write the following sequence of letters on the board; after 30 seconds, cover it up and ask students to write it from memory:

pneumonoultramicroscopicsilico-
volcanoconiosis

Those who do not chunk the sequence will remember nine or fewer letters, but those who recognize chunks of information will be able to

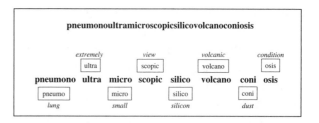

Figure 11.3 Chunking by Roots, Prefixes, and Suffixes

recall significantly more. This sequence of letters is the longest word in the English language and can be chunked into the following prefixes, roots, and suffixes: the prefix *pneumo-* means lung. Next, are *ultra-*, meaning extreme, *micro-* meaning small, and *scopic-* meaning to view. These are followed by *silico-*, which refers to silicon, and *volcano-*, which refers to the mineral particles that make up a volcano. Next there is *coni-*, a derivative of the Greek word *konis* meaning dust, and the suffix *-osis*, which refers to a condition. Thus, this word, referring to a disease of the lungs caused by extremely small particles of ash and dust, is made of eight chunks of information (Figure 11.3) and may be kept in short-term memory. Some people might use larger chunks (perhaps *ultramicroscopic*) and thereby use less of their memory span. Once this term has been committed to long-term memory, it consumes only a single chunk in the short-term memory span. Activity 11.2 presents some chunking exercises designed to help students develop this important memory skill.

Short-term memory has significant acoustic and articulatory components. In other words, people keep things in short-term memory best if they hear (acoustic) and speak (articulation) them. Thus, when you want students to keep information in short-term memory so they may be processed for long-term memory, it is helpful to say the items and have students repeat them out loud, or say them silently to themselves so they can hear them in their minds.

Memory Technique 3: Multiple Modalities

The human mind is capable of storing images in short-term memory, but research suggests that this imagery system is based on spatial orientation

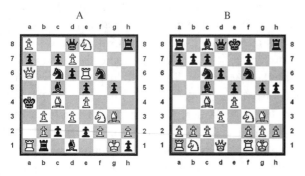

Figure 11.2 (A) Random and (B) Nonrandom Arrangements on a Chess Board

as well as visual information. As a result, students develop better short-term memory traces of images through kinesthetic and visual experiences than purely visual experiences. Thus, when a student handles a rock specimen or titrates a solution, the image trace is much richer than when he or she simply looks at the rock or watches the instructor perform a titration. Given that the primary trace is stronger, there is greater likelihood that the experience will be encoded into long term memory.

An old proverb says, "Tell me and I will forget; show me and I may remember; involve me and I will understand." This proverb describes a basic pedagogical principle: *teachers should present material in multiple modalities (auditory, visual, and kinesthetic) to provide optimal conditions for encoding into memory.* Laboratory activities are generally a good way to involve all three modalities, but many concepts are not practically introduced with a laboratory experience, and with these concepts, the teacher needs to be particularly creative. For example, most students are introduced to the bones of the wrist and hand by showing them a chart or diagram. An introduction to such material can be enhanced if the student is asked to use one hand to palpate and draw the apparent bone structure of the other. This kinesthetic and visual experience can then be augmented auditorily and visually as the teacher explains the structure of the hand using a diagram. The activities throughout involve multiple learning modalities. You should always be thinking of ways to present your lessons that require the use of vision, hearing, and touch.

Memory Technique 4: Semantic Depth

Research indicates that individuals can develop their long-term recall and recognition significantly by using deeper encoding mechanisms when learning new material.[2] Cognitive scientists identify the depth of encoding as the degree of semantic involvement. The more meaning (semantic depth) attributed to an item during the encoding process, the better the memory trace is. Researchers describe four levels of encoding. These levels, in order of increasing depth, are (1) *structural* (the actual sequence of letters and shape of the

word), (2) *phonemic* (the sounds generated when the word is pronounced), (3) *categorical* (the relationship of the word to known taxonomies), and (4) *sentence* (the contextual relationship of the word in language usage). When study time and method of testing are kept constant, subjects who are asked deeper-level (semantic) questions while learning vocabulary words perform significantly better on subsequent recall and recognition tests than those asked less semantically deep questions. Thus, if you want your students be able to recall and recognize information at a later date, you will be wise to employ techniques that require deeper-level processing. For example, if you are giving a vocabulary list that includes new terms, it is more advantageous to ask students to create new sentences that demonstrate their understanding of the meaning of these words rather than simply having them transcribe glossary definitions. When students are asked to create meaningful sentences using new vocabulary words, they must analyze semantic relationships and integrate new words into appropriate context, and this deeper encoding promotes subsequent recall. This is commonly known as the *generation effect.*

Given that it is beneficial for students to generate semantically rich sentences from new vocabulary words, it is logical to assume that they will also benefit by discovering the meanings of the roots from which scientific words are composed. Fortunately, nearly all scientific terms are derived from meaningful Latin and Greek root words, providing a rich semantic environment in which to learn vocabulary. Students should be challenged to analyze the meanings of the roots of every new vocabulary word in an effort to establish a root word vocabulary list (see Chapter One) from which they can discover new words. For example, you might ask your students to generate a name for the shallow muscle that "bends the fingers." Looking at the root word lists, the student may see such associations as *flex*-bend, *digit*-finger, and *superficial*-surface, and derive or identify the term: *flexor digitorum superficialis.* To avoid misleading conclusions and confusing detours, initially guide the class through a collective discovery exercise. Once students correctly associate a concept with a term, they will have a richer understanding of the word and see how it relates to other concepts. For example, *flexor digitorum superficialis* is semantically related to "flexing muscles" (both involve bending a joint), the "digital system" (both our number system and the hands have ten digits), and "superficial arguments" (a superficial muscle is located near the surface, while a superficial argument is a shallow one). After you lead the class through the process of discovering terms from logical root words, have them employ these terms in meaningful new sentences to benefit from the generation effect.

In conclusion, to develop long-term recall and recognition of terms, concepts, or processes, strive to present new material in a semantically deep manner, and create study activities that require students to learn in a manner that stresses meanings and relationships. Such an approach to teaching and learning may require more time initially but will lead to a better understanding and a longer memory.

Memory Technique 5: Acronyms

Memory technique 4 stresses the importance of semantic depth in the memory and recall of new concepts, terms, and processes. One way in which to apply this principle is to explain the meaning of acronyms when introducing them in the curriculum. An acronym is a word or collection of letters formed by the first letters of words of a particular concept, organization, or principle. For example, the term *scuba* is an acronym for "**s**elf-**c**ontained **u**nderwater **b**reathing **a**pparatus." Most people simply memorize the term without understanding its origins, and therefore do not benefit from the semantics inherent in the term. We suggest that you explain the meanings of acronyms when introducing them. Students will not only benefit from a deeper understanding of what the acronyms represent, but will be much more likely to remember them long term. Activity 11.3 can be used in the classroom to help students understand the value of acronyms.

Memory Technique 6: Acrostics

There are many situations in which science students must memorize lists of information. An acrostic is a memory strategy for memorizing ordered and nonordered lists for which there is no apparent organization in the items themselves. Unlike acronyms, which take the first letters of words in a series or phrase to form a single summarizing word (the acronym), acrostics take the first letters of a series of words to form a memorable phrase (the acrostic). By memorizing the acrostic, students may be better able to recall the list of items the phrase represents. For example, students may become frustrated memorizing the major elements necessary for human life because there is no apparent reason that some are necessary and others are not. They may see no a priori reason that the list should contain carbon, hydrogen, oxygen, phosphorous, potassium, iodine, nitrogen, sulfur, calcium, iron, magnesium, sodium, and chlorine but exclude boron, silicon, and lithium. To simplify the memorization of the this list, introduce an acrostic using the elemental symbols for the items in the list:

C. HOPKINS CaFe Mg NaCl

Carbon, **H**ydrogen, **O**xygen, **P**hosphorous, potassium (**K**), **I**odine, **N**itrogen, **S**ulfur, **Ca**lcium, iron (**Fe**), magnesium (**Mg**), sodium (**Na**), chlorine (**Cl**)

This acrostic, pronounced "C. Hopkins Café, "Mighty Good, needs NaCl (salt)," is easy to memorize if said out loud to the class. Once memorized, the acrostic helps the student remember the items it represents. For example, when asked if phosphorous is an essential element, a student can immediately say yes because of the "P" in the acrostic. Activity 11.3 will help students learn to employ acrostics when memorizing lists for science class.

Memory Technique 7: Transfer Appropriateness

Memory research shows that items are easier to recall if the cues at the time of retrieval match those at the time of encoding. This principle, referred to as *transfer appropriateness*, may be helpful for a specific memory task. For example, if you need to recall some childhood memory, it is advantageous to return to your childhood home where that memory was encoded. In a similar although less dramatic, manner, science students may benefit by studying for a science test in the same room in which they will be examined, because the environment at the time of retrieval will match the environment at the time of encoding.

In real life, however, retrieval cues generally don't match encoding cues. Students may do well on an assessment of memory but be unable to transfer the concepts they have learned to novel environments or situations. Thus, although memory experts suggest matching encoding and retrieval cues to promote recall, I believe that efforts to do so may simply be teaching to the test and give students a false sense of accomplishment. Nevertheless, an understanding of the principle of transfer appropriateness may help science teachers see how and why some recall problems develop and suggest ways to address such problems.

The principle of transfer appropriateness is clearly seen in the application of algebraic principles to chemistry. Introductory chemistry uses many algebraic principles, yet students often have difficulty applying these previously learned concepts to chemistry. For example, students will generally have no difficulty solving for b in the equation $ab = cde$, while being unable to solve for wavelength (λ) in the equation $n\lambda = 2d(\sin\theta)$. Although the algebra in both situations is similar, the cues are different. The first uses variable names frequently seen in an algebra class; the second equation does not.

Fortunately, most recent mathematics textbooks include problems that employ variable symbols commonly used in chemistry and physics. Science teachers are advised to encourage their colleagues in the math department to use such problems so that students will be better able to transfer math skills to science. Similarly, science teachers should stress the interrelationships of science to other fields of study so that students use the concepts they learned in science in other fields. Later we discuss the importance of transfer appropriateness when teaching science classes.

Memory Technique 8: Discrepant Scenes and Events

Research by cognitive scientists indicates that when initial visual processing is relatively easy, effortless,

and "automatic," subsequent memory for an event is typically poor, but when processing is difficult, extensive, or elaborate, retention is relatively high.[3] For example, people remember unexpected visual images better than common visual images because they require a greater degree of analysis and invoke more semantic processing. Advertisers frequently use this principle when promoting a product. For example, an advertiser may hide the company logo of the product in a relatively abstract scene. The viewer, by struggling to determine the meaning of the scene, discovers the logo and remembers it well.

Science teachers can also employ discrepant scenes and events to promote memory of important principles. For example, students expect wood to float and rocks to sink when placed in water. When a piece of ebony wood is placed in a container of water, students are surprised to see it sink, and when a chunk of pumice rock is placed in the same container, they are surprised to see it float. The discrepant visual images of sinking wood and floating rock can help students remember Archimedes' principle, which describes the conditions under which a substance will sink or float. Science teachers should employ many discrepant events because they trigger more elaborate processing and better memory. (For examples of discrepant events, see Chapter Five, as well as *Hands-On Chemistry Activities with Real-Life Applications* and *Hands-On Physics Activities with Real-Life Applications*.)[4]

Memory Principle 9: Integration of Visual and Verbal Information

Cognitive science suggests that humans have a dual memory system, with some memories stored in a spatial-visual system and others in a temporal-verbal system. Since item-for-item storage capacity is greater for pictorial than verbal material and since individuals can use learned equivalences to transfer between visual images and verbal concepts, science educators should employ spatial-visual materials to improve memory of both visual and verbal information.

Unfortunately, some educators do not recognize the significance of linking visual and verbal information, as reflected in purely verbal lectures or curricula that separate form from function. For example, many colleges teach anatomy and physiology as two separate classes, causing a dichotomy between the spatial-visual rich information of anatomy and the temporal-verbal rich material of physiology. When students learn function in the context of form, they develop meaningful relationships between the two, thereby improving understanding and memory. Form and function should be taught in a unified manner to help forge important connections between data in spatial-visual and temporal-verbal memory systems.

Although science educators are not able to illustrate all concepts in graphic form, they should strive to do so whenever possible. Even if it is not feasible to draw a picture or a diagram, a teacher can explain material in a way that helps students generate images in their minds. For example, rather than simply stating that biceps brachii is a muscle of the upper arm, you should explain that the term itself can be used to generate a mental picture of the muscle. Since *bi* means "two," *cep* means "head," and *brachii* refers to the upper arm, the *biceps brachii* must be a two-headed muscle of the upper arm. Students can picture this in their mind and immediately distinguish it from the triceps brachii (three-headed muscle of the upper arm) or the biceps femoris (two-headed muscle of the upper leg). Although no physical picture has been drawn, the description of the muscles based on the meanings of their roots is sufficient for students to draw a picture in their mind, thereby linking the spatial-visual information with the temporal-verbal knowledge and improving understanding and memory.

Memory Principle 10: Retrieval Practice

Memory researcher Robert Bjork stated, "The typical college student spends too much time reading and underlining and far too little time summarizing, paraphrasing, and testing his or her ability to retrieve what has been studied."[5] Professors, teachers, and students tend to spend much more time and energy on the process of inputting and encoding information than on the retrieval and outputting of this information. This imbalance is unfortunate, particularly since all of testing instruments directly assess the ability to retrieve and output rather than the ability to input and encode. Although effective input and encoding are essential for a strong memory, they must be coupled with effective retrieval and output.

As educators, we should encourage retrieval practice (the outputting of information stored in long-term memory) in ways that resemble the exam on which a student is assessed. Students should learn to quiz themselves and each other, simulating testing situations as closely as possible. When individuals learn to practice output or retrieval techniques, they generally see a marked improvement in their test scores. But few students study in such output-oriented modes, spending the vast majority of their study time passively reading the book, reviewing their notes, and listening to recordings of the lecture.

As science educators, one of the ways we can encourage an output-oriented approach to learning is by modeling such an approach in the classroom. The Socratic method of instruction is one such approach that is effective in encouraging student output and participation. The instructor asks leading questions of the class to guide the students in review and discovery. Students in such classes eventually learn to ask questions of themselves in a similar manner and thus become self-monitoring, output-oriented learners. In addition, the instructor can use various team games (see Chapter Thirteen) to encourage retrieval practice in preparation for exams. Rather than offering traditional review sessions in which the teacher once again presents material and students try to input it, it is more effective to employ games that will motivate students to practice retrieving and outputting what they have already learned. Throughout this book are activities that can be used to encourage the retrieval and output of information just learned, thereby building student memory. I encourage you to monitor your own teaching to ensure that you model output-oriented learning while providing ample opportunities for student retrieval and output practice.

11.1 The Primacy and Recency Effect

Short-term memory is brief in duration (approximately 30 seconds or less) and small in capacity (five to nine items), while long-term memory may last indefinitely and has unknown capacity. Memory researchers believe that memories must first be formed in short-term memory before they can form in long-term memory. The experiment in Activity 11.1.1 tests the concepts of primacy and recency as students analyze the ability of people to recall a series of unrelated terms. *Primacy* refers to the idea that the first items presented will be remembered better than later items because data have more time in which to move from short-term to long-term memory. *Recency* refers to the idea that items presented most recently should remain in short-term memory better than ones presented earlier because of the temporal nature of short-term memory. Thus, one might predict that when given a long list of items to remember, a student may remember well the first (*primacy* effect) and last items (*recency* effect) but not the ones in the middle. To test this hypothesis, conduct this memory experiment with five or more of your fellow students.

ACTIVITY 11.1.1 *Memory Experiment*
Tell the participants that you will read a list of 20 words at a rate of 1 per second:

(1) energy	(11) momentum
(2) volcano	(12) cell
(3) experiment	(13) whale
(4) photosynthesis	(14) comet
(5) gravity	(15) combustion
(6) fault	(16) microscope
(7) force	(17) fungus
(8) mitosis	(18) radiation
(9) eclipse	(19) geyser
(10) carbon	(20) titanium

At the end of the time, they are to write down as many words as they can recall. On graph paper, place 20 marks on the *x*-axis, numbered from 1 to 20, to indicate the number of each word presented in sequence. The *y*-axis should be labeled to indicate the percentage of the participants that recalled each term. Thus, if four out of five people recalled the first term, you would indicate that 80 percent of the people recalled the first term. Plot the results of your experiment. Do your data support the primacy (early terms have been encoded into long-term memory) and recency (latest items are still in short-term memory) hypotheses? What other factors may explain why some terms are remembered better than others?

11.2 Expanding Short-Term Memory by Chunking

Cognitive scientists have determined that human short-term memory can hold five to nine items simultaneously. In other words, most people can remember between this number of unrelated pieces of information in short-term memory but are unable to hold longer sequences. For example, you can probably look at a phone book and remember the seven-digit telephone number of your insurance company long enough to make a call, but cannot glance at your family's seventeen-digit vehicle identification number (a unique number that identifies each vehicle) and give it to your insurance representative without first writing it down or committing it to long-term memory.

Although cognitive scientists say that our short-term memory has a digit span of seven plus or minus two, some people are known to be able to keep long lists of information in short-term memory. Although they appear to have extraordinary short-term memory, their talent is not due to some physiological or psychological superiority but rather to their trained ability to organize large amounts of information into a short number of recognizable "chunks." *Chunking* is the process of breaking down a complex sequence or concept into nine or fewer independently recognizable units that can all be stored simultaneously in short-term memory. For example, people cannot place the sequence 18005551212 into short-term memory unless they have chunked the data into a smaller number of recognizable units. An astute individual may see that this resembles a telephone number that can be represented as four meaningful chunks 1–800–555–1212 (international dialing code—area code—prefix—number). Radio announcers know the importance of chunking, and they break down telephone numbers into recognizable units as they are spoken, making it easier for listeners to remember the numbers. For example, a radio announcer would say that the telephone number starts with "1–800," a recognizable prefix for U.S. toll-free long distance. Thus, the first four digits are represented as just one chunk in the memory span.

The two most important factors in encoding information into short-term memory are *meaningfulness* (informational value) and *chunking* (combining stimuli to reduce memory load). To improve short-term memory, it is vital to look for meaning and chunk data into logical subsets whenever possible. Increasing short-term memory is an important step to increasing long-term memory, because information must pass through short-term memory before it can be stored as a long-term memory.

I already noted that it is not possible to keep the seventeen-character sequence of a vehicle identification number (VIN) in short-term memory, yet auto insurance adjusters (people who estimate the cost of repairing damaged vehicles) seem to do so with little effort. Although the sequence of numbers (generally found on the dashboard next to the windshield and on the engine block and other parts) appears random and meaningless to most people, it is packed with information to those who understand the code. Each character represents something about the car. The first character identifies the country where it was assembled, the second the company that manufactured it, and so on. Thus, a VIN that starts with the number 1G belongs to a vehicle made in America (1 = USA) by General Motors (G = General Motors), whereas a VIN that starts with JT belongs to a vehicle made in Japan (J = Japan) by Toyota (T = Toyota). The rest of the characters in the VIN identify such things as engine size, model year, and color of paint, making it easy for the adjuster to match a VIN with a car. To an insurance adjuster, a sequence such as 1G or JT is

simply one meaningful chunk of information and takes up only one space in short-term memory.

Nothing enters long-term memory without first passing through short-term memory, so to improve long-term memory, it is essential to improve the capacity of short-term memory. To increase your short-term memory capacity, it is necessary to chunk information into meaningful and recognizable units.

Memorizing new vocabulary terms for a science class can prove to be a daunting task because many terms are lengthy and have unusual sounds. Fortunately, most scientific terms are very descriptive once you understand the roots, prefixes, and suffixes. Each of these components is a meaningful chunk that can be used to hold the terms in short-term memory until they can be committed to long-term memory. Knowledge of root words (see Chapter One) is extremely useful in chunking terms. For example, the term *sternocleidomastoid* is a difficult term to memorize unless it is chunked as *sterno-* (related to the sternum), *cleido* (related to the clavicle), and *mastoid* (related to the mastoid process of the temporal bone.) The term *sterno-cleido-mastoid* can be held in short-term memory with just three chunks of information. The fact that these chunks are meaningful helps us eventually condense this into one chunk of information as "the muscle that joins the sternum and clavicle with the side of the head."

Activities 11.2.1 to 11.2.4 present a variety of lengthy and probably unfamiliar scientific terms. Students will chunk each term into meaningful roots, prefixes, and suffixes using the roots provided in Chapter One or online (go to *sciencesourcebook.com* or search "dictionary"). They will specify the meanings of each chunk (root) and then provide the definition of the entire term.

ACTIVITY 11.2.1 *Chunking New Vocabulary: Biology*

Break the following muscle names into meaningful chunks as illustrated in the first example. Define each term on the basis of its roots (see the root world list in section 1.1). After identifying the chunks and their meanings, attempt to identify

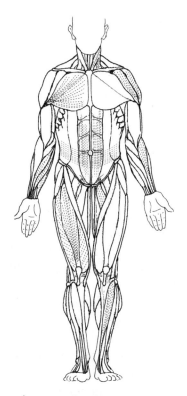

Figure 11.4 Muscular System

the location of each on Figure 11.4 without referring to your book or other diagrams.

Term	Chunks and Their Meanings
adductor longus	*adductor*—muscle that adducts (pulls toward the midline) *longus*—the longest of a set of muscles The *adductor* longus is the longest muscle that pulls legs inward.
brachioradialis deltoid flexor carpi pectoralis major quadriceps femoris rectus abdominus sternocleidomastoid tibialis anterior transversus abdominis	

ACTIVITY 11.2.2 *Chunking New Vocabulary: Chemistry*

Break the following terms related to air pollution into meaningful chunks as illustrated in the example. Define each term on the basis of its roots (see the root world list in section 1.2).

Term	Chunks and Their Meanings
photochemical	*photo*—light; *chemical*—chemical A *photochemical* reaction is one that is induced by light.
hydrocarbon chlorofluorocarbon infrared ultraviolet catalytic converter tetrachloroethylene trichlorofluoromethane spectrophotometer biogeochemical	

ACTIVITY 11.2.3 *Chunking New Vocabulary: Physics*

Break the following physics terms into meaningful chunks as illustrated in the example. Define each term on the basis of its roots (see the root world list in section 1.3).

Term	Chunks and Their Meaning
semiconductor	*semi*—half; *conductor*—transmits electricity A *semiconductor* is a partial conductor of electricity.
antiparticle calorimeter kilogram voltmeter aerodynamics thermodynamics electromagnetism chromosphere geosynchronous spectrogram	

ACTIVITY 11.2.4 *Chunking Earth and Space Science Vocabulary*

Break the following geology terms into meaningful chunks as illustrated in the example. Define each term on the basis of its roots (see the root world list in section 1.4).

Term	Chunks and Their Meanings
geomorphology	geo—earth; *morph*—form; *-ology*—study of *Geomorphology* is the study of the development of landforms.
geothermal	
microrelief	
supraglacial	
lithosphere	
asthenosphere	
geochemistry	
lichenometry	
lithification	
mineralization	
metaconglomerate	

ACTIVITY 11.2.5 *Chunking and Short-Term Memory*

The following activities require working in pairs.

a. *Chunking in phonemes:* Write the following sequence on a blank sheet of paper and show it to your partner for 3 seconds before removing it. Ask your partner to write down everything he or she can remember.

> u e i g l r t d r c o n

Repeat the same exercise with the following sequence:

> c o u r t r e d l i n g

On which task did your partner perform better? Why? Both are meaningless sequences, but the second is easier to remember because it is arranged in one pronounceable (although nonsensical) chunk rather than 12 unrelated chunks as the first sequence. Examine data from the rest of the class to see if this phenomenon is generalizable.

b. *Chunking in logical units:* Write the following sequence on a blank sheet of paper, and show it to your partner for 3 seconds before removing it and asking your partner to write down everything he or she can remember:

> 1492177618651969

Repeat the same exercise with the following sequence:

> 1492 1776 1865 1969

On which task did your partner perform better? Why? Both represent the same sequence, but the second has been broken into four chunks, each of which may represent just one item in the memory span, particularly if your partner recognizes these sequences as significant dates in American history (1492, Columbus landed in the New World; 1776, the colonies declared their independence from Britain; 1865, the American Civil War ended; 1969, the United States landed a man on the Moon). Instead of memorizing 16 unrelated pieces of information, your partner needed to remember only four meaningful dates.

c. *Series and chunking:* Write the following sequence on a blank sheet of paper and show it to your partner for 5 seconds before removing it and asking your partner to write down everything he or she can remember:

> G8E7A1F10C19DB56

Next, repeat the same exercise with the following sequence:

> 5A6B7C8D9E10F11G

On which task did your partner perform better? Why? Both series contain the same characters, but the second is arranged in a manner that can be memorized as a single chunk: the numbers 5 to 11 interspersed with letters from A to G.

d. *Organization and chunking:* Show Figure 11.5 to your partner for 3 seconds before removing it. Then ask your partner to sketch what he or she saw. Repeat the same exercise with Figure 11.6. On which task did your partner perform better? Why? Although both contain the same figures, the second is much easier to remember because it is displayed in a way that promotes chunking.

This activity illustrates the importance of organization in the process of chunking for

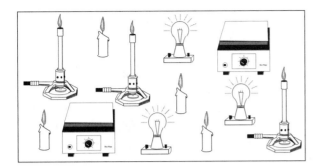

Figure 11.5 Items Arranged Randomly

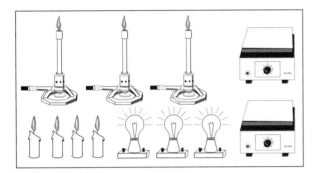

Figure 11.6 Items Arranged to Facilitate Chunking

short-term memory. Whether you organize data when problem solving or your equipment when conducting a laboratory experiment, you will find a dramatic improvement in your ability to chunk larger amounts of information if the data has been preorganized.

11.3 Science Acronyms and Abbreviations

An *acronym* is a word or collection of letters formed by the first letters of words of a particular term. For example, *NASA* stands for **N**ational **A**eronautics and **S**pace **A**dministration. An abbreviation is a shortened form of a word or phrase. For example, *smog* is an abbreviation for "**sm**oke and f**og**." Acronyms or abbreviations help save time and energy when explaining concepts, but they are meaningless to those unfamiliar with their origin.

Most students of biology know that DNA is a substance that carries the genetic code, yet do not understand why it is called DNA, or what the name says about the substance. Someone who knows that DNA stands for *deoxyribonucleic acid* can reasonably infer that DNA is found in the nucleus (deoxyribo**nucle**ic acid), is acidic in nature (deoxyribonucleic **acid**), contains the sugar ribose (deoxy*ribo*nucleic acid), and differs from RNA (ribonucleic acid) by lacking oxygen on one of the carbons in the ribose (*deoxy*ribonucleic acid). Some acronyms become used so frequently that they become accepted words in the English language. For example, *laser* (note that it is in lowercase letters because it has become accepted as a standard word) is an acronym for **l**ight **a**mplification by **s**timulated **e**mission of **r**adiation. In a laser, light (**l**aser) is amplified (l**a**ser) as atoms emit (las**e**r) visible *radiation* (lase**r**) when atoms in the laser crystal are stimulated (la**s**er) by an external power source. Understanding the origin of acronyms and abbreviations helps in understanding and remembering what they represent.

I encourage you to always investigate the origin of scientific acronyms (refer to *sciencesourcebook. com* or search "acronym dictionary") and abbreviations, and determine what can be known from the terms they represent.

ACTIVITY 11.3.1 *Biology Acronyms and Abbreviations*

Using traditional dictionaries, online acronym databases, or other resources, identify the original terms represented by each of the following acronyms or abbreviations, and explain what can be learned about each.

(1) AIDS	(6) ECG	(11) PCR
(2) BAL	(7) GI	(12) RBC
(3) CDC	(8) LD50	(13) REM
(4) CPR	(9) LDL	(14) RNA
(5) CVA	(10) MRI	(15) TB

ACTIVITY 11.3.2 *Chemistry Acronyms and Abbreviations*

Using traditional dictionaries, online acronym databases, or other resources, identify the original terms represented by each of the following acronyms or abbreviations, and explain what can be learned about each.

(1) ACS	(6) DDT	(11) ppm
(2) alnico	(7) MSDS	(12) PSI
(3) canola	(8) MTBE	(13) R&D
(4) CFC	(9) OSHA	(14) redox
(5) CO	(10) PVC	(15) smog

ACTIVITY 11.3.3 *Physics Acronyms and Abbreviations*

Using traditional dictionaries, online acronym databases, or other resources, identify the original terms represented by each of the following acronyms or abbreviations, and explain what can be learned about each.

(1) AC	(6) MASER	(11) UV
(2) CRT	(7) quasar	(12) VHF
(3) DC	(8) Rf	(13) WIMP
(4) IR	(9) EM	(14) parsec
(5) laser	(10) UHF	(15) VOM

ACTIVITY 11.3.4 *Earth and Space Science Acronyms and Abbreviations*

Using traditional dictionaries, online acronym databases, or other resources, identify the original terms represented by each of the following acronyms or abbreviations, and explain what can be learned about each.

(1) EPA	(6) NGS	(11) radar
(2) GEOS	(7) NOAA	(12) scuba
(3) GMT	(8) NRAO	(13) sonar
(4) GPS	(9) NSF	(14) USGS
(5) JPL	(10) NWS	(15) UTC

11.4 Acrostics for Memorizing Lists

An acrostic is a strategy for memorizing ordered and nonordered lists for which there is no apparent organization in the names themselves. Unlike acronyms, which take the first letters of words in a series to form a word, acrostics take the first letters of a series of words to form a memorable phrase. For example, the ordered list of classification terms in biology (**k**ingdom, **p**hylum, **c**lass, **o**rder, **f**amily, **g**enus, **s**pecies) can be represented by the acrostic *King Philip came over for great spaghetti.* Because the

acrostic must be said in one order and make sense, it helps students remember the correct sequence. Note that in the example, *Kingdom* precedes *phylum* in classification, just as *King* precedes *Philip* in the acrostic. In the activities that follow, you will see a series of acrostics for many ordered and nonordered lists of information in science. Select one acrostic for each, and use it to memorize the series or list.

ACTIVITY 11.4.1 *Using Acrostics to Memorize Lists in Biology*

The first group of words contains the list of scientific information. It is followed by one or more acrostics. Select one acrostic for each, and use it to memorize the series or list.

Biological Classification
Kingdom, **P**hylum, **C**lass, **O**rder, **F**amily, **G**enus, **S**pecies
King **P**hilip **C**ame **O**ver **F**or **G**reat **S**paghetti
Kings **P**lay **C**hess **O**n **F**unny **G**reen **S**quares

Cranial Nerves
(I) **O**lfactory, (II) **O**ptic, (III) **O**culomotor, (IV) **T**rochlear, (V) **T**rigeminal, (VI) **A**uditory, (VII) **F**acial, (VIII) **V**estibulocochlear, (IX) **G**lossopharyngeal, (X) **V**agus, (XI) **A**ccessory, (XII) **H**ypoglossal
On **O**ld **O**lympus's **T**owering **T**op, **A** **F**at, **V**ery **G**luttonous **V**ulture **A**te **H**ikers

Stages of Mitosis
Interphase—**P**rophase—**M**etaphase—**A**naphase—**T**elophase
I **P**assed **M**y **A**lgebra **T**est

Essential Elements for Plants
C, H, O, P, K, N, S, Ca, Fe, Mg, B, Mn, Cu, Zn, Mo, Ni, Cl
C HOPKNS CaFe Mg B Mn CuZn MoNiCl
(Phonetically speaking: C Hopkins café managed by mine cousin Monicl)

Major Essential Elements for Animals
C, H, O, P, K, I, N, S, Ca, Fe, Mg, Na, Cl
C HOPKNS CaFe Mg NaCl

(Phonetically speaking: **C HOPKINS CaFe** is Mighty Good, but needs salt (**NaCl**))

Major Nutrients of Life
Carbon Hydrogen Oxygen Nitrogen
C H O N

Elements in Proteins
Sulfur, Phosphorous, Oxygen, Nitrogen, Carbon, Hydrogen
S P O N C H

Taxonomic Classification for Humans
Animalia   Chordata   Mammalia   Primata Hominidae Homo Sapiens
Animals Can Make People Horrendously Home Sick

The Krebs Cycle
Citric Acid, Isocitric, Ketoglutaric, Succinyl, Succinic, Fumaric, Malic, Oxaloacetic
Can Intelligent Karl Solve Some Formidable Math Operations?

Treatment of Muscle Injury
Rest, Ice, Compress, Elevate
R I C E

ACTIVITY 11.4.2 *Using Acrostics to Memorize Lists in Physics and Chemistry*
The first group of words contains the list of scientific information. It is followed by one or more acrostics. Select one acrostic for each, and use it to memorize the series or list.

Colors of the Spectrum
Red Orange Yellow Green Blue Indigo Violet
ROY G. BIV (pronounce as a man's name, Roy G. Biv)
Richard Of York Gave Battle In Vain

Color Codes on Resistors
Black, Brown, Red, Orange, Yellow, Green, Blue, Violet, Gray, and White.
Color-code sequence for electronic resistor value numerals:
(Black-0, Brown-1, Red-2, Orange-3, Yellow-4, Green-5, Blue-6, Violet-7, Gray-8, White-9)

Betty Brown Runs Over Your Garden But Violet Grey Walks

Metric System Prefixes
kilo-, hecto-, deka-, meter, deci-, centi-, milli-
King Henry Died Monday Drinking Chocolate Milk

Solving Word Problems
W—What is the question?
I—Identify the knowns and givens
M—Math equation
P—Plug-in and solve

The Orbital Names for Electrons
S–P–D–F–G–I–K
Sober Physicists Don't Find Giraffes In Kitchens

Oxidation/Reduction
"Lose Electrons Oxidation" and "Gain Electrons Reduction"
LEO says **GER**

Diatomic Molecules
I_2–Br_2–C_2–F_2–$O2$–N_2–H_2
I Bring Clay For Our New Home

ACTIVITY 11.4.3 *Using Acrostics to Memorize Lists in Earth and Space Science*
The first group of words contains the list of scientific information. It is followed by one or more acrostics. Select one acrostic for each, and use it to memorize the series or list.

Planets in Our Solar System
Mercury, Venus, Earth, Mars, Jupiter, Saturn, Uranus, Neptune, Pluto
My Very Educated Mother Just Served Us Nine Pizzas
My Very Easy Method Just Speeds Up Naming Planets
(Note: In 2006 the International Astronomical Union demoted Pluto to "dwarf planet" status.)

Constellations of the Zodiac

Aries, Taurus, Gemini, Cancer, Leo, Virgo, Libra, Scorpio, Sagittarius, Capricorn, Aquarius, Pisces

A **T**ense **G**rey **C**at **L**ay **V**ery **L**ow, **S**neaking **S**lowly, **C**ontemplating **A** **P**ounce

(The zodiac is a band in the sky through which the planets, Sun, and Moon appear to move.)

Geological Eras

Cambrian, Ordovician, Silurian, Devonian, Carboniferous, Permian, Triassic, Jurassic, Cretaceous, Paleocene, Eocene, Oligocene, Miocene, Pliocene, Pleistocene, and Recent

Camels **O**ften **S**it **D**own **C**arefully. **P**erhaps **T**heir **J**oints **C**reak. **P**ersistent **E**arly **O**iling **M**ight **P**revent **P**ermanent **R**heumatism.

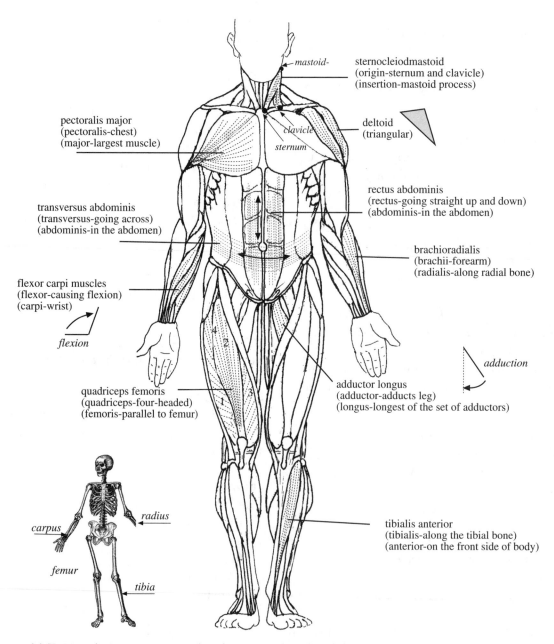

Figure 11.7 Muscle Names Are Made of Meaningful Chunks

Points of a Compass
North, East, South, West
Never Eat Shredded Wheat

Hardness Scale for Minerals
Talc, Gypsum, Calcite, Fluorite, Apatite, Orthoclase feldspar, Quartz, Topaz, Corundum, Diamond
Terrible Giants Can Find Alligators Or Quaint Tigers Conveniently Digestible.

Galilean Moons of Jupiter
Io, Europa, Ganymede, Callisto
I Eat Good Cake

ACTIVITY 11.4.4 Making Your Own Acrostics
Generate your own acrostics for the following ordered and nonordered lists.

a. Elements in the first two series (as an ordered list): Hydrogen, helium, lithium, beryllium, boron, carbon, nitrogen oxygen, fluorine, and neon.

b. Systems in the human body (nonordered list): circulatory, immune, nervous, reproductive, lymphatic, respiratory, urinary, muscular, digestive, integumentary, and endocrine.

c. Select one of the lists in Activities 11.4.1 to 11.4.3, and make your own acrostic.

Answers to Chapter Activities
11.1.1 Students will probably, but not always, confirm the recency and primacy effects. It is suggested that they analyze the class data by plotting the information with a spreadsheet program. Students may wish to make their own word or object lists.

11.2.1 Biology terms (muscles). Figure 11.7 illustrates how the muscles got their names. Students who chunk difficult terms into meaningful units will find it much easier to retain these terms in short-term memory and will develop much longer memories of them due to the greater semantic depth at the time of encoding.

11.2.5 (a) Class results typically show that recall is much stronger when common phonemes are in the nonsense

Term	Chunks and Their Meanings
adductor longus	*adductor*—muscle that adducts (pulls toward the midline) *longus*—the longest of a set of muscles The *adductor longus* is the longest muscle that pulls legs inward.
brachioradialis	*brachi*—arm *radialis*—radius The *brachioradialis* is a muscle on the radial side of the forearm.
deltoid	*delt*—delta or triangle *oid*—resembling The *deltoid* muscle has a triangular shape.
flexor carpi muscles	*flexor*—muscle that causes bending *carpi*—wrist The *flexor carpi* bend the wrist.
pectoralis major	*pectoralis*—of the chest *major*—largest The *pectoralis major* is the largest of the muscles of the chest.
quadriceps femoris	*quadriceps*—four-headed muscle *femoris*—in the region of the femur The *quadriceps femoris* is a four-headed muscle near the femur.
rectus abdominus	*rectus*—upright *abdominis*—in the abdominal region The fibers of the *rectus abdominis* are arranged vertically in the abdomen.
sternocleidomastoid	*sterno*—associated with the sternum; *cleido*—associated with the clavicle *mastoid*—associated with the mastoid process of the temporal bone The *sternocleidomastoid* has origins in the sternum and clavicle, and an insertion in the mastoid process of the temporal bone.

(Continued)

Term	Chunks and Their Meanings
tibialis anterior	*tibialis*—pertaining to the tibia *anterior*—front The *tibialis anterior* is located on the front side of the tibia.
transversus abdominis	*transversus*—arranged in a lateral manner *abdominis*—pertaining to the abdomen The *transversus abdominis* goes across the abdomen.

11.2.2 Chemistry Terms (Air Pollution Chemistry)

Term	Chunks and Their Meanings
photochemical	*photo*—light; *chemical*—chemical A *photochemical* reaction is one that is induced by light.
hydrocarbon	*hydro*—containing hydrogen; *carbon*—containing carbon. *Hydrocarbons* are made of hydrogen and carbon.
chlorofluorocarbon	*chloro*—chlorine; *fluoro*—fluorine; *carbon*—carbon *Chlorofluorocarbons* are hydrocarbons containing chlorine and fluorine.
infrared	*infra*—below; *red*—red *infrared* radiation (IR) has lower energy than red light.
ultraviolet	*ultra*—beyond; *violet*—violet *Ultraviolet* (UV) light has higher energy than violet light.
catalytic converter	*catalytic*—acting as a catalyst; *converter*—something that causes change *Catalytic converters* speed the change of pollutants to safe chemicals.
tetrachloroethylene	*tetra*—four; *chloro*—chlorine; *ethylene*—ethylene *Tetrachloroethylene* (TCE) is ethylene with four chlorines ($Cl_2C = CCl_2$).
trichlorofluoromethane	*tri*—three, *chloro*—chlorine; *fluoro*—fluorine, *methane*—CX_4 *Trichlorofluoromethane* has three chlorines, and one fluorine (CCl_3F).
spectrophotometer	*spectro*—spectrum; *photo*—light; *meter*—to measure *Spectrophotometery* is the quantitative study of light spectra.
biogeochemical	*bio*—life; *geo*—earth; *chemical*—chemical *Biogeochemical* cycles involve living and nonliving systems.

11.2.3 Physics terms (general terms)

Term	Chunks and Their Meanings
semiconductor	*semi*—partial; *conductor*—transmits electricity A *semiconductor* is a partial conductor of electricity.
antiparticle	*anti*—against; *particle*—particle The mass, spin, or charge of an *antiparticle* have the same magnitude, but opposite sign of an elementary particle.
calorimeter	*calor*—heat, *meter*—measure A *calorimeter* measures heat.
kilogram	*kilo*—thousand, *gram*—gram A *kilogram* is 1000 grams.
voltmeter	*volt*—unit of electric potential; *meter*—measure A *voltmeter* measures electrical potential.
aerodynamics	*aero*—air, *dynamics*—movement *Aerodynamics* is the study of the movement of objects in air.

thermodynamics	*thermo*—heat; *dynamics*—motion, work *Thermodynamics* focuses on the relationship between heat and work.
electromagnetism	*electro*—electricity; *magnetism*—magnetism *Magnetism* caused by an electric field is known as electromagnetism.
chromosphere	*chromo*—color, *sphere*—sphere The *chromosphere* is the colorful envelope around the Sun's photosphere.
geosynchronous	*geo*—earth, *synchronous*—synchronized with *Geosynchronous* satellites orbit Earth at the same rate the Earth rotates.
spectrogram	*spectro*—spectrum, *gram*—picture A *spectrogram* is a representation or photograph of a spectrum.

11.2.4 Earth science terms (geology)

Term	Chunks and Their Meanings
geomorphology	*geo*—earth; *morph*—form; *-ology* study of *Geomorphology* is the study of the development of land forms.
geothermal	*geo*—earth; *thermal*—heat *Geothermal* events are heated by the Earth.
microrelief	*micro*—small; *relief*—topography *Microrelief* refers to small topographic details.
supraglacial	*supra*—on top of; *glacial*—pertaining to glaciers *Supraglacial* materials are found on top of glaciers.
lithosphere	*lith*—rock; *sphere*—sphere, Earth The *lithosphere* is the rocky, solid crust of the Earth.
asthenosphere	*asthen*—weak; *sphere*—sphere, Earth The *asthenosphere* is the less rigid portion below the lithosphere.
geochemistry	*geo*—earth; *chemistry*—chemistry *Geochemistry* is the study of the Earth's chemistry.
lichenometry	*lichen*—lichens; *metry*—process of measuring *Lichenometry* is the process of measuring time by lichen growth.
lithification	*lith*—rock; *tion*—process of During *lithification* rocks are made by compression of sediment.
mineralization	*mineral*—mineral; *-ion* process of *Mineralization* is the conversion of something to a mineral substance.
metaconglomerate	*meta*—change; *conglomerate*—combination *Metaconglomerates* have undergone metamorphosis.

words. It is suggested that the students examine data from the entire class. (b) Students will find the grouped numbers much easier to remember even if they are unfamiliar with the significance of the specific dates or number sequences. The grouping allows students to chunk more easily. (c) Students should be able to keep the second option in short-term memory better, but only if they see the pattern. Once they recognize the series, they can store the sequence as a single chunk of data. (d) Students will be able to memorize the organized picture much more easily than the random picture.

11.3.1 Biology acronyms and abbreviations

(1) AIDS	**Acquired Immune Deficiency Syndrome**	AIDS is a disease of the immune system caused by infection with the HIV retrovirus.
(2) BAL	**Blood Alcohol Level**	BAL is a measure of the amount of alcohol in blood, recorded as milligrams alcohol per 100 ml of blood.
(3) CDC	**Centers for Disease Control**	CDC is a federal agency for protecting the health and safety of society by monitoring diseases and other health concerns.
(4) CPR	**CardioPulmonary Resuscitation**	CPR is an emergency procedure to restore normal breathing and circulation after cardiac arrest or other trauma.
(5) CVA	**CerebroVascular Accident**	CVAs result in the impairment of brain function due to substantial reduction in blood flow or bleeding in the brain.
(6) ECG	**ElectroCardioGram**	An ECG is a trace of the electric current generated by the heart muscle.
(7) GI	**GastroIntestinal**	The GI system includes the digestive tract, particularly the stomach and intestines.
(8) LD50	**Lethal Dose (50%)**	LD50 is a measure of toxicity, recorded as the dosage of a substance at which 50% of test animals die.
(9) LDL	**Low Density Lipoprotein**	LDL is "bad" cholesterol that can slowly build on walls of arteries, thereby contributing to atherosclerosis.
(10) MRI	**Magnetic Resonance Imaging**	MRI is a technique to produce images of the inside of the body from the resonance of electrons in hydrogen atoms.
(11) PCR	**Polymerase Chain Reaction**	PCR is a laboratory technique for making numerous copies of a specific segment of DNA quickly and accurately.
(12) RBC	**Red Blood Cell**	RBCs, also known as erythrocytes, are oxygen-carrying cells in the bloodstream.
(13) REM	**Rapid Eye Movement**	REM is a stage of sleep characterized by rapid movement of the eyes.
(14) RNA	**RiboNucleic Acid**	RNA is a nucleic acid containing ribose and is essential for the manufacture of proteins.
(15) TB	**TuBerculosis**	TB is an infectious disease caused by several species of tubercle bacillus bacteria.

11.3.2 Chemistry acronyms and abbreviations

(1) ACS	**American Chemical Society**	The ACS is a professional society of chemists and chemistry educators.
(2) alnico	**ALuminum + NIckel + CObalt**	Alnico is a powerful permanent magnetic alloy containing aluminum, nickel, cobalt, and other elements.
(3) canola	**CANada Oil + Low Acid**	Canola is a variety of the rapeseed plant that yields a low-acid, high-nutritional value oil.
(4) CFC	**ChloroFluoroCarbon**	CFCs are hydrocarbons containing chlorine and fluorine, and are known to break down stratospheric ozone.
(5) CO	**Carbon monOxide**	CO is a molecule made of one carbon atom and one oxygen atom. It is a toxic substance in car exhaust and cigarette smoke.
(6) DDT	**Dichloro Diphenyl Trichloroethane**	DDT was originally used to kill mosquitoes in ponds, but became a major environmental pollutant.
(7) MSDS	**Material Safety Data Sheet**	A MSDS is a safety information sheet that must accompany chemicals sold in the United States.
(8) MTBE	**Methyl Tertiary Butyl Ether**	MTBE is a gasoline additive that is intended to make gas burn cleaner, but is also known to be a health hazard.
(9) OSHA	**Occupational Safety and Health Administration**	OSHA is a federal organization that oversees health and safety conditions in schools and workplaces.
(10) PVC	**PolyVinyl Chloride**	PVC is a hard vinyl chloride polymer used in flooring, piping, and clothing.

(11) ppm	**Parts Per Million**	ppm is a measure of the concentration of pollutants and other substances in a gas or liquid.
(12) PSI	**Pounds per Square Inch**	PSI is a customary measure of pressure, frequently used to indicate pressure in automobile tires.
(13) R&D	**Research and Development**	Chemical companies must have an R&D department if they hope to introduce new products.
(14) redox	**RED**uction + **OX**idation	Redox reactions are ones in which one substance is oxidized while another is reduced.
(15) smog	**SM**oke + **FOG**	Smog originally referred to a mixture of smoke and fog, but now refers to all types of air pollution.

11.3.3 Physics acronyms and abbreviations

(1) AC	**Alternating Current**	AC regularly reverses direction, and is the form of electricity delivered through power lines to homes.
(2) CRT	**Cathode Ray Tube**	CRTs emit a stream of electrons from a cathode. They were the functional elements in early computer monitors.
(3) DC	**Direct Current**	DC flows in only one direction, and is produced by batteries and appliance transformers.
(4) IR	**Infra-Red**	IR is a form of electromagnetic radiation that has lower energy than red or other visible light.
(5) laser	**Light Amplification by Stimulated Emission Radiation**	Lasers emit a highly focused beam of single wavelength radiation, and are used in numerous electronics devices to read and record data.
(6) MASER	**Microwave Amplification by Stimulated Emission Radiation**	A MASER is a device used in radar and radio astronomy to boost the strength of microwaves.
(7) quasar	**QUAS**i-stell**AR**	Quasars resemble stars, but are located in deep space and emit huge amounts of energy.
(8) Rf	**Radio Frequency**	RF includes any frequency between 10 kHz and 300 kHz, RF is used for radio and TV transmission.
(9) EM	**ElectroMagnetic**	The EM spectrum is created by oscillating electromagnetic fields, and includes light, radio, X-rays, and other radiation.
(10) UHF	**Ultra High Frequency**	UHF is a radiofrequency that is higher than VHF and is used for transmitting mobile phone signals.
(11) UV	**UltraViolet**	UV light is more energetic than violet light and can cause sunburns, mutations, and skin cancer.
(12) VHF	**Very High Frequency**	VHF includes high-frequency radio waves used for the transmission of FM radio signals.
(13) WIMP	**Weakly Interacting Massive Particle**	WIMPs are a hypothetical form of dark matter thought to compose much of the matter in the universe.
(14) parsec	**PAR**allax **SEC**ond	A parsec is a unit of measure equal to the distance of an object having a parallax of one second (326 light-years).
(15) VOM	**Volt-Ohm Millimeter**	A VOM is a multimeter used to measure potential (volts), resistance (ohms), and other features.

11.3.4 Earth and space science acronyms

(1) EPA	**Environmental Protection Agency**	The EPA is a federal agency charged with monitoring and protecting the environment.
(2) GEOS	**Geodetic and Earth Orbiting Satellite**	GEOS is a satellite designed for making precise measurements of the Earth's surface.
(3) GMT	**Greenwich Mean Time**	GMT is the mean solar time of the longitude (0°) of the former Royal Observatory at Greenwich, England.

(Continued)

(4) GPS	**Global Positioning System**	GPS is a system of satellites that transmit signals used to determine one's precise position.
(5) JPL	**Jet Propulsion Laboratory**	JPL was originally a laboratory for jet and rocket engines, and is now the center for U.S. unmanned space missions.
(6) NGS	**National Geodetic Survey**	The NGS is a survey to determine and publish latitude, longitude, elevation, and gravity data.
(7) NOAA	**National Oceanic and Atmospheric Administration**	NOAA provides details on weather, oceans, satellites, fisheries, climate, navigation, and coasts.
(8) NRAO	**National Radio Astronomy Observatory**	NRAO operates powerful, advanced radio telescopes spanning the Western Hemisphere.
(9) NSF	**National Science Foundation**	NSF supports basic research and education in the sciences, mathematics, and engineering.
(10) NWS	**National Weather Service**	The NWS predicts and reports weather conditions throughout the United States.
(11) radar	**RAdio Detection And Ranging**	Radar is used for locating and tracking objects by transmitting radio waves and observing the echoes.
(12) scuba	**Self-Contained Underwater Breathing Apparatus**	Scuba is an apparatus with a portable air supply, used for breathing while swimming underwater.
(13) sonar	**SOund Navigation And Ranging**	Sonar is a technology for locating objects in water by means of reflected sound waves.
(14) USGS	**United States Geological Survey**	The USGS gathers and shares information about the Earth's resources, natural hazards, and environment.
(15) UTC	**Universal Time Coordinated**	UTC is the international basis of civil and scientific time, implemented in 1964.

11.4.1–11.1.4 Students will memorize a series of terms using the acrostics provided or ones they develop on their own.

Chapter Twelve

Structure and Function in Science

For the Teacher 225

12.1 Form and Function in Machines 226

12.2 Structure and Function in Anatomy and Physiology 229

12.3 Structure and Function in Plants 233

12.4 Structure and Function at a Molecular Level 235

12.5 Model Building 238

Answers to Chapter Activities 239

For the Teacher

Anatomy is the study of the bodily structure of humans, animals, and other living systems. By contrast, *physiology* is the study of the functions of these organisms and their component parts. In many schools and colleges, anatomy and physiology are taught as separate subjects, so students learn structure apart from function or function apart from structure. Although it may be convenient to teach anatomy and physiology as separate disciplines, it is not wise to do so. The structures of organisms and their component systems, organs, tissues, cells, organelles, and molecules are directly related to their physiological functions. For example, the *structure* of red blood cells is best understood in the light of their *function,* and vice versa. Red blood cells (erythrocytes) carry oxygen from the lungs to body tissues and carbon dioxide from body tissues to the lungs. The relationship between structure and function in red blood cells is illustrated as follows.

1. Red blood cells must travel through tiny capillaries (*function*) to exchange oxygen with surrounding tissues and must therefore be small, smooth, and flexible (*structure*). Figure 12.1A is a scanning electron micrograph illustrating their small, smooth shape, and it is easy to imagine how they flex when traveling through capillaries.

2. Red blood cells exchange gases (*function*) with surrounding tissues by diffusion. Oxygen diffuses to body tissues, while carbon dioxide diffuses from these tissues to the red blood cells. The rate of diffusion is related to the ratio of surface area to volume of the cells. Note that the unique biconcave shape (*structure*) of red blood cells dramatically increases this ratio, thereby increasing the rate of diffusion.

3. Hemoglobin (the oxygen-carrying protein in red blood cells) must bind and hold oxygen (*function*) in order to carry it through the bloodstream. The iron-centered porphyrin ring

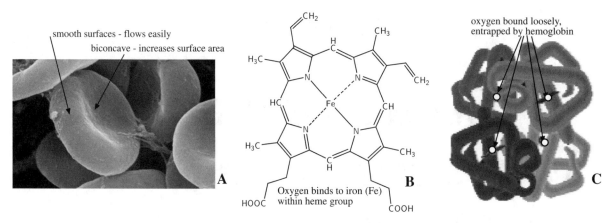

Figure 12.1 Erythrocyte (A), Porphyrin Ring (B), and Three-Dimensional View of Hemoglobin (C)

(*structure*) of hemoglobin enables such binding. Oxygen is bound by electrostatic attraction to the central iron atom (Fe) and is protected from competing forces by the surrounding organic ring (Figure 12.1B).

4. Oxygen binds tightly to iron, and if two iron-containing heme molecules come together in the presence of oxygen, the molecules will bind irreversibly, preventing further uptake or release. However, oxygen must be easily acquired in the lungs and easily released in respiring tissues (*function*) to sustain life. This is facilitated by the globin chains that prevent irreversible binding by folding around the oxygen binding site (*structure*), protecting it from the attractive forces of other heme groups (Figure 12.1C).

Many teachers introduce the *structures* of the heme group, hemoglobin molecule, or red blood cells apart from their *functions,* depriving students of the opportunity for true comprehension. *Whenever possible, discuss structure and function at the same time, showing how structure determines function.* This chapter provides a variety of activities that can be used to demonstrate the relationship between *structure* and *function* in living and nonliving system.

The anatomy and physiology activities in this chapter involve much terminology, so remind students that by understanding component root words, they can learn a great deal about the

structure or function of the entities they describe. This is clearly seen in the names of muscles as illustrated in Table 12.1. These names may refer to region, origin and insertion, shape, location, or function. For example, flexor digitorum superficialis is a shallow (position) muscle that flexes (action) the fingers (region). Table 12.1 is helpful in remembering the names of muscles and other organs. (Refer to Chapter One for activities designed to build a general knowledge of root words and an understanding of scientific terminology.)

12.1 Form and Function in Machines

Engineers apply the principles of science and mathematics to develop new products. Following is a list of engineering professions and their functions:

- *Aerospace engineers* design and test aircraft and spacecraft.
- *Biomedical engineers* design equipment to improve health, including artificial limbs, monitoring equipment, and assistive devices such as pacemakers and insulin pumps.
- *Chemical engineers* integrate the principles of chemistry and engineering to develop machinery to manufacture chemicals or use

Table 12.1 Understanding the Meaning of Muscle Names

Direction, Position	Region	Action
anterior (front)	abdominis (abdomen)	abductor (move away)
externus (superficial)	anconeus (elbow)	adductor (move toward)
extrinsic (outside)	auricularis (outer ear)	depressor (bring down)
inferioris (below)	brachialis (upper arm)	flexor (reduce angle)
internus (deep)	capitis (head)	levator (raise up)
intrinsic (inside)	carpi (wrist)	pronator (turn in)
lateralis (to the side)	cervicis (neck)	rotator (to rotate)
medialis (toward middle)	cleido (clavicle)	supinator (turn up)
oblique (on an angle)	costalis (ribs)	
posterior (back)	digitorum (fingers, toes)	**Description**
profundus (deep)	femoris (femur, upper leg)	alba (white)
rectus (straight)	genio (chin)	brevis (short)
superficialis (toward surface)	glosso (tongue)	gracilis (slender)
transversus (across)	hallucis (great toe)	lata (wide)
	illio (illium, hip)	latissimus (widest)
Shape	lumborum (lumbar)	longus (long)
deltoid (triangular)	nasalis (nose)	longissimus (longest)
orbicularis (circular)	nuchal (back of neck)	magnus (large)
pectinate (comblike)	oculo (eye)	major (larger)
piriformis (pear shape)	oris (mouth)	maximus (largest)
pyramidal (pyramid)	pollicis (thumb)	minor (smaller)
rhomboideus (rhomboid)	psoas (loin)	vastus (great)
serratus (serrated, teeth)	radialis (radii of forearm)	biceps (two heads)
teres (long and round)	scapularis (scapula)	triceps (three heads)
trapezius (trapezoidal)	temporalis (temples of head)	quadriceps (four heads)
	thoracis (thorax, chest)	
	tibialis (tibia, shin)	
	ulnaris (ulna)	
	uro (urinary)	

chemicals for energy, electronics, food, clothing, and other purposes.

- *Civil engineers* design roads, bridges, buildings, airports, tunnels, water supply systems, and other basic structures.
- *Electronic and computer engineers* design and develop communications devices, computers, and other electronics equipment.
- *Environmental engineers* develop solutions to environmental problems by applying the principles of chemistry, engineering, and biology.
- *Mechanical engineers* design tools, machines, engines, and other mechanical devices.

Engineers design structures so they will perform specific functions. The following activities examine the relationship between structure and function for some well-known products of engineering.

ACTIVITY 12.1.1 *Structure and Function: Bicycles*

Engineers develop and refine products to meet specific needs. The structure of each product is designed to meet the required functions. Although the five types of bicycles shown in Figure 12.2 have the same basic structure, each is equipped with components whose structural features make it well suited for a specific application.

Figure 12.2 illustrates five popular styles of bicycle: mountain, road racing, touring, hybrid,

Figure 12.2 Structure Determines Function in Bicycles

and beach cruiser. Discuss the relationship between structures and functions for the bicycles listed in Table 12.2 following the example of mountain bikes illustrated in Table 12.3.

- *Mountain bikes*—designed for rough terrain, rocks, and hill climbing
- *Road racing bicycles*—designed for speed and distance competitions such as the world-famous Tour de France
- *Touring bicycles*—designed for long-distance riding on paved roads and highways
- *Hybrid bicycles*—designed for riding on paved roads and well-graded dirt or gravel roads

- *Beach cruisers*—designed for riding on flat boardwalks and roads near beaches and other level areas

ACTIVITY 12.1.2 *Structure and Function: Tools*

Mechanical engineers design tools to meet specific needs. The *structure* of a tool reflects and determines its *function*. Examine the structure of the individual tools in the Leatherman tool illustrated in Figure 12.3, and match functions with tools. Explain the relationship between tool structure and function.

(a) cutting wire
(b) opening tin cans
(c) gripping small objects
(d) cutting
(e) cutting through wood
(f) whittling wood
(g) filing
(h) turning single notch screws
(i) measuring
(j) turning small notch screws

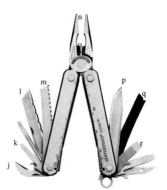

Figure 12.3 Match the Structure with the Function

Table 12.2 Comparison of Five Types of Bicycles

	Mountain	**Road Racing**	**Touring**	**Hybrid**	**Beach**
Tire width	2.20 in	1.00 in	1.50 in	1.95 in	2.00 in
Tire tread	heavy knobs	linear, smooth	light	medium knobs	medium
Handlebars	wide	dropped	dropped	wide	wide
Gears	21–27	10	15	15	1
Weight	30 lb	16 lb	24 lb	30 lb	35 lb

Table 12.3 Mountain Bikes Are Designed for Riding on Rough Terrain

Mountain bikes are equipped with wide tires (*structure*) to provide stability (*function*) and support on uneven trail conditions.

The tires have heavy, knobby tread (*structure*) to grip rock, sand, and gravel (*function*).

Mountain bike frames must be stronger and heavier (*structure*) than others because they are designed to be ridden on rough terrain (*function*) including logs, rocks, bumps, and jumps.

Mountain bikes are equipped with a wide range of gears (*structure*) so riders can find appropriate gear ratios to ride in varied terrain (*function*).

Mountain bikes have wide, upright handles (*structure*) that provide riders with significant leverage to maintain control (*function*) when encountering ruts, holes, and other obstacles.

12.2 Structure and Function in Anatomy and Physiology

Personal fitness centers typically have a variety of specialized exercise equipment: free weights, pull-up bars, treadmills, ellipticals, handcycles, stationary bikes, rowing machines, leg pulleys, and squat handlebars. Each device is designed to exercise a specific muscle or collection of muscles. The design and structure of a machine determines its function for personal fitness training. Just as each piece of equipment has a specific structure and corresponding function, so each of the more than 650 muscles and 206 bones in the human body has a specific *structure* and corresponding function.

ACTIVITY 12.2.1 *Structure and Function: Muscles*

To fully understand the function of a muscle, it is necessary to understand its anatomy, particularly its origin and insertion. The origin of a muscle is defined as the less moveable point of attachment, while the insertion is defined as the more moveable point. For example, the sternocleidomastoid has its origin on the tops of the sternum and clavicle and its insertion on the mastoid process of the skull (Figure 12.4). When the left sternoclediomastoid muscle contracts, the left side of the skull is pulled, causing the skull to rotate and tilt sideways

to the left. Similarly, if the right sternoclediomastoid contracts, the right side is pulled, rotating and tilting the skull sideways to the right. Note that this muscle gets its name from its origins, *sterno-* (sternum), *cleido-* (clavicle), and insertion, *mastoid* (mastoid process of the skull), while other muscles acquire their names from shape, location, or function (Table 12.4). Remember that nearly all scientific terms are descriptive and can be understood if one knows the component roots (see Chapter One).

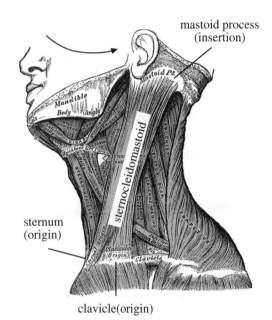

mastoid process (insertion)

sternum (origin)

clavicle(origin)

Figure 12.4 Origin and Insertion

Table 12.4 Muscle Names Derived from Origin and Insertion, Shape, Location, or Function

Origin and insertion	*sternocleidomastoid*	origin at sternum (*sterno*) and clavicle (*cleido*), and insertion in the mastoid (*mastoid*) process
	sternohyoid	origin in the sternum (*sterno*), insertion in the hyoid bone (*hyoid*)
	styloglossus	origin at styloid process (*stylo*), insertion in the tongue (*glossus*)
Shape	*gastrocnemius*	large belly (*gastro*) that narrows to a threadlike (*nemius*) tendon
	deltoid	shaped like (*-oid*) the Greek letter delta, Δ (*delt*)
	trapezius	shaped like a trapezoid (*trapezius*)
Location	*lattissimus dorsi*	widest (*latissimus*) muscle of the back (*dorsi*)
	biceps femoris	two(*bi*)-headed (*ceps*) muscle of the femur (*femoris*)
	rectus abdominis	straight (*rectus*) muscle of the abdomen (*abdominis*)
Function	*adductor magnus*	large (*mag*) muscle that adducts (*adductor*) (pulls toward body)
	flexor digitorum	muscles that bend (*flexor*) the fingers (*digitorum*)
	extensor digitorum	muscles that extend (*extensor*) the fingers (*digitorum*)

Muscles contract but do not extend unless pulled by an outside force such as an antagonistic muscle that pulls the opposite direction. Under most situations, when a muscle contracts, the bone of insertion moves toward the bone of origin. For example, the origin of the biceps brachii is the scapula and upper humerus, and the insertion is the radius of the forearm. When the biceps contract, they flex the lower arm (Figure 12.5A). The antagonist to the biceps is the triceps brachii, with origin in the scapula and upper humerus, and insertion in the elbow of the ulna. When the triceps contract, the lower arm extends (Figure 12.5B).

Table 12.5 shows the origin and insertion of some notable muscles of the body. Figure 12.6 indicates the attachments of 10 significant muscles. Examine the origin and insertion, and predict the key action of each muscle, remembering that the insertion moves toward the origin. Determine one or more sports or activities that rely heavily on this muscle for a particular motion, and record your ideas in Table 12.5. As you complete this activity, you are using knowledge of *structure* to predict *function*.

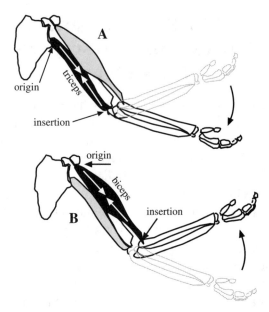

Figure 12.5 Motion of the Triceps and Biceps

ACTIVITY 12.2.2 *Structure and Function: Bones*

The skeletal system provides structure and protection and supports movement of the body. In many anatomy classes, students memorize numerous

Table 12.5 Structure and Function of Muscles

	Muscle	Location	Origin	Insertion	Key Action	Activity/Sport
1	deltoid	shoulder	clavicle, spine of scapula	humerus	raise arm, pull it forward or back	swimming, pitching, javelin, shot-put
2	rectus abdominis	front of torso	pubis, front of pelvic bones	lower ribs		
3	gastrocnemius	back of lower leg	lower femur	calcaneus (heel bone)		
4	gluteus maximus	back of the hip	back of hip, sacrum	femur		
5	pectoralis major	chest	sternum, clavicle	humerus		
6	quadriceps femoris	front of upper leg	front, top of femur	tibia		
7	biceps brachii	front of upper arm	scapula, upper humerus	radius (radial tuberosity)		
8	triceps brachii	back of upper arm	scapula, upper humerus	elbo (ulna)		
9	latissimus dorsi	sides of back	lower vertebrae	humerus		
10	biceps femoris	back of femur	ischium and top of femur	fibula		

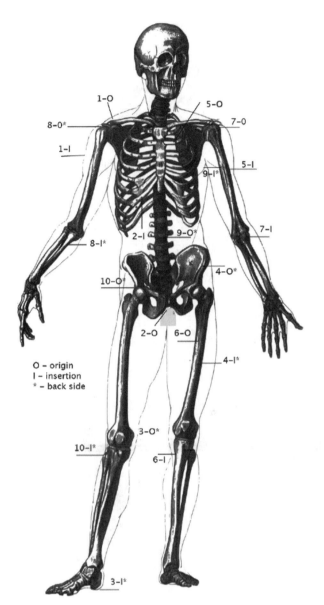

Figure 12.6 Origins and Insertions of Muscles

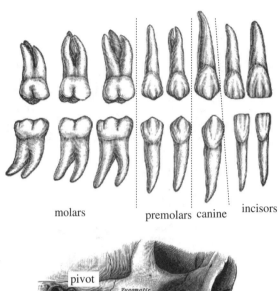

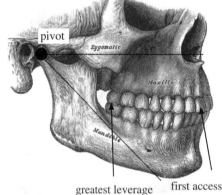

Figure 12.7 The Structure of Teeth

features of bones without realizing their function. If, however, they know the *structure* of a bone feature, they can predict the *function*. For example, examine the teeth in the human jaw (Figure 12.7). Note that the *molars* are positioned in the rear of the jaw, where leverage is greatest. Molars have a broad crown and base and multiple roots that allow them to withstand the great forces that occur when crushing and grinding food. The term *molar* means "millstone," reflecting the role of these teeth in grinding food. The *premolars* are in front of molars and are also know as *bicuspids* because of

the two (*bi-*) cusps, or bumps, on their surfaces. The bicuspids are positioned between the canines and the molars, and are transitional teeth that chew food and move it back to the molars for grinding. The *canines* are the sharpest teeth and derive their name from a word for *dog* (canine) because they resemble the sharp teeth wild dogs use to catch and tear their food. The front teeth are in the best position to cut food off and are named *incisors* because they function much like scissors as they cut up food. Note that they are the thinnest and most planar of the teeth, a design that facilitates cutting.

The structure and position of a tooth determines its function, illustrating the importance of understanding structure in the light of function and vice versa. The same can be said for every bone in the body.

Figure 12.8A shows a side view of the vertebral column, and Figures 12.8B to 12.8G are enlarged

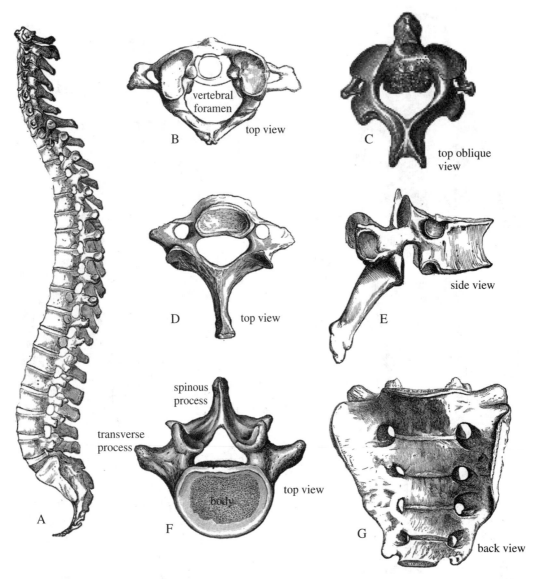

Figure 12.8 Structure of the Skeletal System

views of specific vertebrae. Examine each of the vertebrae, and answer the following questions by analyzing the structure and predicting its function. Match the letters of the appropriate bones with each statement.

1. These vertebrae have the largest bodies because they must support the most weight.
2. This vertebra has the smallest body because it supports the least weight.
3. These vertebrae transmit the weight of the upper body to the hips through fused joints.
4. This vertebra has the largest foramen (opening) because the spinal cord is larger here than anywhere else in the spinal column.
5. These vertebrae have additional foramen (openings) in their transverse processes to protect the cranial nerves that parallel the spinal cord.
6. This vertebra has a bony axis about which the uppermost vertebra rotates when one swivels the head.
7. These vertebrae have numerous facets (small, smooth surfaces) where ribs articulate.

8. This vertebra supports the skull and has two large facets (smooth surfaces) on its upper surface where it articulates with the base of the skull.
9. This vertebra rotates on the bone below it and has an additional hole through which the process of the bone below it penetrates.
10. These vertebrae are inflexible.

12.3 Structure and Function in Plants

Cross-pollination is the fertilization of ovules on one plant with pollen from another. The seeds that are produced have a genetic makeup distinct from either parent. Pollination is critical to the survival of flowering plants, and flowers are structured to facilitate pollination. For example, bees see particularly well in the yellow, blue, and ultraviolet portions of the spectrum, and bee-pollinated flowers are generally yellow or blue and often have ultraviolet markings (invisible to humans) so that they are easily seen by their pollinators.

ACTIVITY 12.3.1 *Structure and Function: Flowers and Pollinators*

Note: This activity is best performed when plants are flowering in your region.

Examine five or more flowers in your neighborhood, and predict pollinators by referring to the flower and pollinator characteristics in Table 12.6. The flowers of many trees and grasses

Table 12.6 Flower Structure, Pollinator Characteristics, and Pollination

Flower Characteristics	Pollinator Characteristics
Bee-pollinated flowers are often blue or yellow with ultraviolet markings.	Bees see well in the yellow, blue, and ultraviolet portions of the spectrum.
Bee-pollinated flowers produce sticky pollen.	Bees have numerous hairs on their surface to which pollen may stick.
Butterfly-pollinated flowers are often red and orange.	Butterflies see well in the red and orange portions of the spectrum.
Butterfly-pollinated flowers have long tubes.	Butterflies have long probosci to extract nectar from long tubes.
Moth-pollinated flowers are often pale or white and open at night.	Moths fly at night when reflectivity, not color, makes flowers visible.
Moth-pollinated flowers emit a sweet odor.	Moths are attracted to the sweet smell of nectar which serves as a food source.
Fly-pollinated flowers emit a rotten odor.	Flies lay their eggs on dead animals and are attracted to rotten smells.
Bird-pollinated flowers are often red or yellow.	Birds see well in the red and yellow portions of the spectrum.
Bird-pollinated flowers produce a fluid nectar in large quantities.	Birds consume nectar and lap it up with their tongues.
Hummingbird-pollinated flowers have long, tubular corolla.	Hummingbirds have very long beaks to access tubular flowers.
Beetle-pollinated flowers often produce strong odors.	Beetles are attracted to many strong odors.
Beetle-pollinated flowers are dull or white.	Beetles do not see color but can see the light reflected off white objects.
Wind-pollinated flowers have stamens and feathery stigma exposed to the wind.	Wind is not focused or consistent, so flowers must maximize the likelihood of fertilization.
Wind-pollinated flowers are small, numerous, and often green.	Wind is inanimate and indiscriminate of size or color.

Figure 12.9 Digital Photography of Pollinators

are small and green, so you may need to look very carefully. If possible, photograph flowers with a digital camera (Figure 12.9), and identify any pollinators that you see. Record the names and descriptions of each flower and the pollinator you observed or predicted. Identify the structures and features of the flowers that serve specific functions in attracting pollinators.

ACTIVITY 12.3.2 *Form and Function: Seed Dispersal*

Unlike animals, plants are unable to move to new environments and must rely on seed and spore dispersal to deliver their offspring to new regions favorable for growth and development. Plants may rely on gravity, mechanical devices, wind, water, or animals to distribute seeds. Many species of conifers rely on gravity. Heavy cones fall from pine, fir, cedar, and other conifers, dispersing seeds on impact (Figure 12.10A). Some plants rely on mechanical expulsion to spread their seeds (Figure 12.10B).

Stork's bill, oxalis, spurges, and many other weedy plants produce pods that explode, sending seeds to new environments. Wind is a particularly useful mechanism of seed dispersal for terrestrial plants. Wind-dispersed seeds are generally very light and may contain parachute-like devices such as those commonly found on dandelion seeds (Figure 12.10C). Water is a useful distribution medium for plants that live in or near aquatic or marine environments. For example, coconut palms found on islands in the South Pacific produce large, buoyant fruits that can float for thousands of miles and still germinate once washed ashore (Figure 12.10D). Some plants disperse seeds by attaching to the fur of passing animals (Figure 12.10E), while others produce edible fruit that animals harvest (Figure 12.10F). Such plants produce seeds with a tough seed coat that protects them as they pass through the digestive tract before being deposited at some distance from the parent plant. Many trees produce nuts that squirrels or other rodents bury so they will have food during the winter (Figure 12.10G). Finally, others, such as the peanut (Figure 12.10H), bury their own seeds as stalks grow and push fruits underground. Many of these nuts are never found and eventually germinate.

Photograph five or more plants in your neighborhood that are producing cones or fruits. Tape photographs of these plants and their fruit to heavy cardstock. Tape seeds of each plant next to the appropriate photograph. Predict the method of seed dispersal, and explain the features that lead

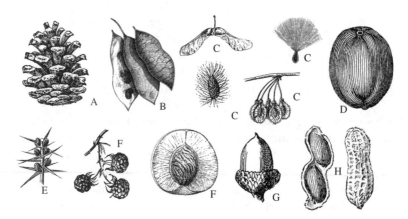

Figure 12.10 Seed and Fruit Structure Determines the Mechanism of Dispersal

you to this prediction. In other words, analyze the structure of the seeds and fruits to predict their function in seed dispersal.

12.4 Structure and Function at a Molecular Level

The relationship between structure and function is found everywhere in the natural world, even at the atomic and molecular levels. Knowledge of the structure of a molecule helps in understanding how it functions. For example, carbon can exist in a variety of forms, including graphite (Figure 12.11A), diamond (Figure 12.11B), and nanotubes (Figure 12.11C). Carbon forms four bonds, and the nature of the bonding patterns (structure) determines the properties (functions) it will display.

Each carbon in graphite bonds with three other carbons in a plane to form a hexagonal grid, as shown in Figure 12.11A (each junction represents a carbon). The fourth bond (dashed line) connects one plane with another. Although the three planar bonds are very strong, the fourth is relatively weak because it is so long. The electrons in this bond are free to move throughout the structure between the planes, making graphite a good conductor of electricity. The weakness of the bonds between planes allows them to slide across one another, making graphite slippery and an excellent lubricant. Graphite is used in pencil "lead," and as the tip of the pencil moves across the page, a layer of carbon is left behind, which we recognize as handwriting, drawing, or scribbling.

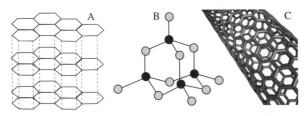

Figure 12.11 Carbon in Various Forms: (A) Graphite, (B) Diamond, (C) Nanotubes

Contrast the structure of diamond with graphite (Figure 12.11B). In the diagram, the black circles represent atoms as they are positioned in diamond, each with four bonds. The gray circles indicate carbons to which more will bond (four per carbon) to extend to the diamond's edges. In diamond, all four carbon bonds are of equal length and strength. All of the electrons are tightly bound, so there are no free electrons, and diamond therefore does not conduct electricity. The tetrahedral array makes diamond very strong (it is the hardest substance known) and gives it a very high melting point (much energy is required to break the bonds so it will flow).

Carbon can also exist as nanotubes, which consist of graphite cylinders closed at either end with caps containing pentagonal rings (Figure 12.11C). Carbon's fourth electron forms looser bonds with adjacent nanotubes, making nanotubes electrically conductive, as is graphite. The tubular shape gives nanotubes great tensile strength and many potential applications. By examining the structure of graphite, diamond and nanotubes, we can see that the bonding pattern of a molecule determines its properties and potential applications.

ACTIVITY 12.4.1 *Structure and Function: Proteins (Online)*
Proteins perform a wide variety of biological functions. Some proteins provide structure for cells and organisms, while others serve as enzymes to catalyze biological reactions or provide immunity to disease. Proteins are high-molecular-weight substances formed by the bonding of amino acids. The structure of each protein is determined at four levels:

- The *primary structure* of a protein is the sequence of amino acids.
- The *secondary structure* refers to patterned substructures, such as sheets or helices.
- The *tertiary structure* of a protein refers to its overall shape, formed primarily by hydrogen bonds, ionic interactions, and disulfide bonds.
- The *quaternary structure* is determined by the bonding of protein subunits to form a protein complex.

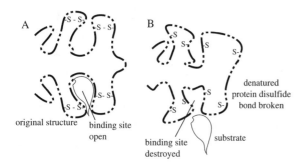

Figure 12.12 The Structure of a Protein Determines Its Function

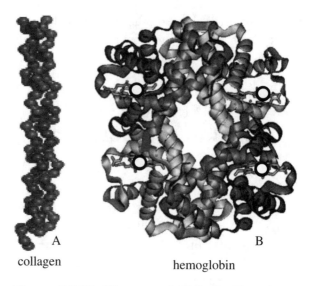

Figure 12.13 Fibrous and Globular Proteins

Proteins, like tools, have a specific structure and a corresponding function. If the structure is altered, the function will be altered or destroyed. Figure 12.12A shows the structure of an imaginary enzyme whose tertiary structure is determined by disulfide bonds. When heated, these bonds break; the protein loses its shape, becomes denatured, and ceases to function as an enzyme. Before heating, the enzyme could interact with a substrate, but after heating, the enzyme's shape is altered so that no interaction can occur (Figure 12.12B). Clearly the structure of a protein determines its properties and functions.

Protein structure can be categorized as fibrous or globular. Figure 12.13A illustrates the structure of collagen, the most abundant protein in mammals and the main component of cartilage, ligaments, tendons, and skin. Collagen is fibrous and ropelike, has great tensile strength, and provides support and integrity for a variety of connective tissues. By contrast, hemoglobin (Figure 12.13B) is a globular protein, whose structure envelops and bonds four oxygen atoms that it carries to respiring tissues as it travels in red blood cells. In general, structural proteins are fibrous, and functional proteins are globular.

The diagrams in Figures 12.13A and 12.13B were generated by a molecular visualization program that portrays the three-dimensional structure of molecules. Many free software tools and protein data files are available on the Internet from the Research Collaboratory for Structural Bioinformatics' Protein Data Bank and other sources. Download the appropriate software so you can

visualize any of the thousands of proteins available online. (To find it, go to *sciencesourcebook.com* or www.rcsb.org, or search "rcsb, pdb, protein data bank.")

The following are lists of a few common proteins and their functions:

Structural Proteins

- Collagen (primary structural component in bone and skin)
- Keratin (main structural component of hair and nails)
- Fibrin (primary structural component in blood clots)
- Elastin (a major structural component of ligaments)

Functional Proteins

- Hemoglobin (transport protein that carries oxygen in the blood)
- DNA polymerase (enzyme that assists in DNA replication)
- ATPase (enzyme that breaks ATP to ADP to release energy for cell use)
- Amylase (digestive enzyme that breaks down polysaccharides such as starch)
- Alcohol dehydrogenase (enzyme that breaks down toxic alcohol molecules)

- Insulin (hormone to regulate blood sugar levels in the body)
- Ferritin (storage protein that stores iron in the liver)
- Actin and myosin (contractile proteins that enable muscle contraction)

Select a structural protein and a functional protein from the lists above. (a) Research the protein on the Internet, and write a summary of its structure, function, and importance. (b) Download each protein's database file from an online protein data bank, and display the protein on your computer. Rotate the protein so you can view it from different angles, and print out representative views for your report. (c) In general, structural proteins are long and fibrous, connecting tissues with one another, while functional proteins are globular, with highly specific shapes that allow them to carry out specific functions. Does this relationship between structure and function apply for the molecules you have selected? Explain your answer.

ACTIVITY 12.4.2 *Structure and Function: Water*

The structure of a molecule determines its properties. The relationship between structure and function is clearly seen in water, the most abundant molecule on the surface of the Earth and in living systems. Although water is commonplace, its properties are unlike any other molecule and vastly different from those with similar molecular weight. Water demonstrates a collection of unique properties that make it essential for life.

The hydrogen-oxygen bond in water is polar covalent, such that the hydrogens acquire a partial positive charge and the oxygens a partial negative charge. The angle between the two hydrogens and the oxygen is 104.45 degrees, creating a bent molecule in which the partial negative charge is on the side with the oxygen and the partial positive side is on the end with the two hydrogens. The structure of this bond makes water polar, and the positive end of one water molecule is attracted to the negative end of another (Figure 12.14A). This attraction is known as *hydrogen bonding* and gives water a high surface tension as each molecule is attracted to others.

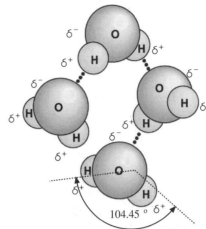

A   The δ⁺ and δ⁻ signs indicate partial charge.

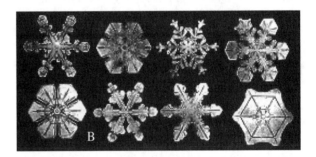

Figure 12.14 (A) The Structure of the Water Molecule Determines Its Properties. (B) Ice Crystals

From the following list of properties that result from the structure of the water molecule (104.45 degree bond angle), select one or more properties and research their significance. (Your teacher may assign different members of the class different properties and ask you to report back to the entire class.) (a) Write a paragraph explaining the importance of the property you selected to life on earth, and (b) explain what would happen if water did not have its unusual structure, and consequently did not exhibit this characteristic.

1. High specific heat (1 cal/°C; 75 J/mole K)
2. High surface tension
3. Strong cohesion (sticks to itself)
4. Strong adhesion (sticks to other things)
5. Excellent solvent (dissolves many things)
6. Exists in three states (solid, liquid, gas) on Earth.

7. High boiling point (100°C)
8. High melting point (0°C)
9. Expands on freezing
10. Highest heat of vaporization (540 cal/g; 40.6 KJ/mole)
11. Forms hexagonal-based crystals (snowflakes) upon freezing (Figure 12.14B)

12.5 Model Building

In his classic work on the theory of multiple intelligences,[1] Howard Gardner argues that visual/spatial intelligence is one of the basic forms of intelligence. *Visual/spatial intelligence* is the capacity to think in images and pictures and to visualize accurately and abstractly. Architects and engineers generally excel in this dimension. To communicate and test their concepts, they often make models or prototypes, thereby using their kinesthetic intelligence.

Model building is an excellent activity for exercising visual/spatial and kinesthetic intelligence, and understanding the relationship between form and function. The following model-building activities can be used as individual or group projects and competitions.

ACTIVITY 12.5.1 *Bridge Building*
The goal of this competition is to build the bridge that supports the greatest weight before collapsing. The guidelines for the competition are:

Materials
- Materials—1 pack of dry spaghetti
- Modifications—noodles can be cut, notched, steamed, or boiled
- Adhesive—1 bottle of white glue
- Restrictions—no paint, varnish, or shellac

Specifications
- Mass—250 g or less
- Length—between 43 and 45 cm
- Width—between 4.5 and 7.0 cm
- Height—25 cm or less
- Roadbed—unobstructed so that a model car 3.5 cm wide can pass

- Opening—1 cm diameter hole in the center to insert the loading device

Contest
- Loading device—a board 3.5 cm × 2 cm × 10 cm, with a 1 cm hole in middle
- Setup—align the hole in the loading device with the hole in the bridge
- Testing—insert the hook from below the roadbed, fasten with a threaded wing nut from above, and add weights to the hook until the bridge fails
- Failure—if the bridge collapses or bends 5 cm or more
- Winner—the team whose bridge supports the most weight before failing

You may also wish to perform this competition using popsicle sticks (craft sticks) or balsa wood instead of spaghetti. In such cases, you may need to adjust the specifications appropriately. What design features are correlated with the strongest bridges?

ACTIVITY 12.5.2 *Egg Drop*
The goal of this egg drop competition is to design a device that will prevent a raw egg from breaking when dropped from successively greater heights. The team whose egg sustains the greatest fall without breaking is declared the winner.

Construct a device to protect a raw egg. The competition starts from a height of 2 m and increases by ½ m each round. If your egg survives a drop without cracking, it qualifies for the next round.

Impulse ($F\Delta t$) is defined as the product of a force (F) and the time interval (Δt) during which it acts. It is equal to the change in momentum $m\Delta v$, where m is the mass and Δv represents the change in velocity. Thus:

$$F\Delta t = m\Delta v$$

The egg is broken by the forces it encounters on impact. Solving for force, we have:

$$F = \frac{m\Delta v}{\Delta t}$$

The impact force can be reduced by increasing the time over which the impact takes place (Δt) by cushioning its fall. Boxers increase the time of impact and decrease the force by rolling with the punches. Baseball catchers, skydivers, and stuntmen do the same. The impact force can also be reduced by decreasing the change in velocity (Δv) as the egg hits. This is accomplished by reducing the speed at which it hits the ground. Devices such as parachutes and wings may increase wind resistance, slow the egg, and thereby decrease the impact force. You therefore want to design a device that slows the descent while cushioning the impact.

You may construct your device using any or all of the following materials:

10 plastic drinking straws	white glue	1 m of yarn
10 popsicle sticks	10 large paper clips	1 plastic grocery bag
5 rubber bands	3 pipe cleaners	10 cotton puffs
3 sheets of paper	2 m of masking tape	staples

ACTIVITY 12.5.3 *Water Bottle Rocket*

Design a water rocket according to the plans outlined in Activity 16.5.1 (Observing High-Speed Activities). The rocket that travels the greatest distance (given identical launch pressures) is declared the winner.

ACTIVITY 12.5.4 *Reconstructing a Skeleton*

Note to teacher: This activity uses sterilized owl pellets, which can be ordered from most scientific curriculum supply companies. Owls eat small rodents and birds. Several hours after eating, the indigestible parts (fur, bones, teeth, and feathers) are compressed into a pellet that the owl regurgitates and expels. This "owl pellet" often contains all of the bones of the animal that the owl ate.

Order sterilized owl pellets from a scientific supply company (search "owl pellet"). Wear latex gloves, and dissect the pellet with dissection tools. Reassemble the skeleton, and identify the organism by comparing it with pictures of skeletons of mice, voles, shrew, lizards, and birds available on the Internet.

ACTIVITY 12.5.5 *Cell Model*

Make a three-dimensional model of a plant or animal cell illustrating as many of the following features as possible: cell membrane, cell wall, cytoplasm, nucleus, nucleolus, DNA, ribosomes, endoplasmic reticulum, Golgi apparatus, lysosomes, mitochondria, chloroplasts, and vacuoles. You may use gelatin, fruit, beans, seeds, candies, plastic bags, pasta, pipe cleaners, and anything else you wish. Be creative. Include a key to identify each organelle.

ACTIVITY 12.5.6 *Anatomical Models*

Scientific supply companies provide models of the human body, skeleton, brain, heart, eye, knee, and other features. Your teacher will provide a fully disassembled model, which you will reconstruct.

ACTIVITY 12.5.7 *Robotics*

Many schools offer classes and clubs in robotics in which students design, build, and program robots for various tasks. There are a variety of robotics competitions in which teams from various schools compete. For example, the FIRST (For Inspiration and Recognition of Science and Technology) robotics competition challenges teams to solve a common problem in a 6 week time frame using a standard set of parts. Teams compete to design a robot that will accomplish the task most efficiently and effectively. Robotics programs help students develop preengineering skills as they learn computer-aided design, pneumatics, motors, electronics, gears, fabrication, structures, and programming. Search online for robotics programs and competitions at *sciencesourcebook.com* or search "robotics competitions."

Answers to Chapter Activities

12.1.1 *Structure and function:* Bicycles: *Road racing bicycles* have extremely narrow tires and smooth linear tread to reduce rolling resistance on paved surfaces. Handlebars are dropped so as to force the rider into a crouched position to minimize wind resistance. *Road race bikes* are extremely light to reduce inertia for quick starts and reduce the amount of work that must be done against friction during races. *Touring bikes* are for long-distance road rides. Their tires are wider than road racing bikes to ensure stability on a variety of paved surfaces. Touring bikes often have 15 gears, giving them a range of gear ratios without excessive weight. The frames are heavier and stronger than road racing bikes but lighter than mountain bikes whose strength is critical due to rugged terrain. *Hybrid bikes* are designed for casual on- and off-road riding. They have relatively wide tires to allow them to move on dirt roads, but only medium-knobbed tread to give sufficient traction on dirt without excessive rolling resistance on pavement. Hybrids are relatively heavy bikes because speed is not a primary issue. *Beach cruisers* have very wide tires so they can ride on the wet sand and boardwalks. Beach cruisers are not designed for speed or hills, so they can be heavy and equipped with a single gear.

12.1.2 *Structure and function:* Tools

(a) cutting wire	(6) wire cutters
(b) opening tin cans	(1) tin can opener
(c) gripping small objects	(5) needle nose pliers
(d) cutting	(3) serrated knife
(e) cutting through wood	(4) saw
(f) whittling wood	(7) smooth knife blade
(g) filing	(8) file
(h) turning single notch screws	(9) flathead screwdriver
(i) measuring	(10) ruler and straight edge
(j) turning small single notch screws	(2) small flathead screwdrivers

12.2.1 Structure and Function: Muscles

12.2.2 *Structure and function:* Bones (1) F-lumbar, (2) B-atlas, (3) G-sacral, (4) B-atlas, (5) D-cervical, (6) C-axis, (7) E-thoracic, (8) B-atlas, (9) B-atlas, (10) G-sacral.

12.3.1 *Structure and function:* Flowers and pollinators. Student answers will vary. Students may wish to present a digital slide show using photographs they have taken of various flowers. The teacher can guide a discussion regarding the relationship between floral structure and function. Alternatively, the teacher may download photographs of flowers from a graphic library on the Internet and use them to discuss the relationships between flowers and pollinators.

12.3.2 *Structure and function:* Seed dispersal. Student answers will vary. Teachers may wish to provide students access to digital video microscopes so they may take detailed photographs of seed or fruit features that may help dissemination.

12.4.1 *Structure and function:* Proteins. Student answers will vary, but they should all note that structural proteins tend to be long and fibrous while functional proteins are globular.

12.4.2 *Structure and function:* Water. Student answers will vary, but the following information may be included in student responses.

1. *High specific heat:* Water has a very high specific heat (1 cal/g°C). Since it requires a large amount of energy to change the temperature of water, substances containing water resist rapid changes in temperature. Water can absorb a lot of heat energy before it begins to get hot, which is why it is a valuable coolant in industrial

	Muscle	Location	Origin	Insertion	Key Action	Activity or Sport
1	deltoid	shoulder	clavicle, scapular spine	humerus	raise arm, pull it forward or back	swimming, pitching, tennis, shot put
2	rectus abdominis	front of torso	pubis, front of pelvis	lower ribs	flexes spine	sit-ups, wrestling
3	gastrocnemius	back of lower leg	lower femur	calcaneus (heel bone)	points toes down	walking, running, hiking
4	gluteus maximus	back of the hip	back of hip, sacrum	femur	extends upper leg	bicycling, climbing
5	pectoralis major	chest	sternum, clavicle	humerus	flexes shoulder horizontally	pushing, punching, throwing, basketball
6	quadriceps femoris	front of upper leg	front, top of femur	tibia	extend tibia	jumping, running, climbing, skiing
7	biceps brachii	front of upper arm	scapula, upper humerus	radius	flexes lower arm	chinning, lifting weights with arms
8	triceps brachii	back of upper arm	scapula, upper humerus	elbo (ulna)	extend lower arm	pushing, throwing, tennis
9	latissimus dorsi	sides of back	lower vertebrae	humerus	pulls arms down and to sides	rowing, kayaking, canoeing
10	biceps femoris	back of femur	ischium and top of femur	fibula	flexes knees, extends hips	sprinting, running

processes and in automobile radiators. Seventy-one percent of the Earth's surface is covered by water, stabilizing the temperature of the planet. Regions near oceans enjoy a much more equable climate (less variation in temperature) than those inland. Nearly 60 percent of the mass of our bodies is composed of water. Since water has a high specific heat, body temperatures remain much more constant than if they were composed of a solvent other than water. *If water did not have its unusual structure and resulting high specific heat,* the temperature of organisms and the planet would vary too much and too quickly for organisms to survive.

2. *High surface tension:* Water has a very high surface tension, as the positive ends of one molecule are attracted to the negative ends of others. This high surface tension reduces the amount of evaporation that occurs from oceans, lakes, and streams. *If water did not have its unusual structure and resulting high surface tension,* it would evaporate more readily and be less available for consumption by animals. In addition, insects would sink when landing on water, thereby altering the aquatic food chain.

3. *Strong cohesion:* Water molecules are attracted to each other by electrostatic attraction. As water molecules ascend the xylem of plants, others follow, creating a coherent stream of water. *If water did not have its unusual structure and resulting cohesiveness,* it could not be pulled up within xylem vessels, and terrestrial plants could not exist.

4. *Strong adhesion:* Water is polar and adheres to substances that have polar regions. The xylem (water conducting tubes) of plants is made of cellulose (the main component of wood), a macromolecule with polar regions. *If water did not have its unusual structure and resulting adhesiveness to substances like cellulose,* then it would drain out of terrestrial plants and we would not have any trees, shrubs, or crops.

5. *Excellent solvent:* The 104.45 degree bond angle of water makes it an excellent solvent. Minerals, carbohydrates, nucleic acids, and most proteins easily dissolve in water. Essential minerals, such as calcium, iron, magnesium, and sodium, dissolve in water as positively charged ions known as cations. Once dissolved, they can be transported in the xylem of plants or in the bloodstreams and interstitial fluids of animals to the cells where they are required. All cells of all organisms are based on water. *If water did not have its unusual structure and resulting solvent properties,* no life could exist, as there would be no medium for molecules and nutrients to interact or be delivered.

6. *Exists in three states (solid, liquid, gas) on Earth:* Water is the only natural substance that is found in solid, liquid, and gaseous form on the surface of the Earth. If water did not have its unusual structure and exist in a gaseous phase in the atmosphere, there would be no evaporation from the oceans, no rain would fall on the continents, and the continents would be massive deserts. *If water did not exist as a solid,* there would be no snow and no glaciers. Runoff would be much more rapid, and streams and rivers would be much less predictable in many regions of the world.

7. *High boiling point (100°C):* Water boils at 100°C, while methane, a similarly sized molecule (MW_{water} = 18 g/mole; $MW_{methane}$ = 16 g/mole), boils at −162°C. Methane is a symmetrical molecule, while water is polar. As a polar molecule, water adheres to itself and resists a phase change. *If water did not have its unusual structure and resulting high boiling point,* life could not exist at common temperatures on Earth because it would be gaseous rather than liquid.

8. *High melting point (0°C):* The melting point of water is approximately 100°C higher than what one would predict based on comparison with other group-6 hydrides. In ice, all water molecules participate in four hydrogen bonds (two as donor and two as acceptor) and are held relatively static. This is due to the unusual structure of the water molecule. Thus, ice is stable at temperatures below 0°C. Ice is an important reservoir of fresh water, particularly for mountainous regions in Central Asia and other places that rely on glacial melt for much of their water. In addition, ice sculpts the landscape through glacial action, carving such features as Yosemite Valley and the numerous lakes that are scattered over Canada and the northern United States. *If water did not have its unusual structure and resulting high melting point,* ice would not exist in sufficient quantity to sculpture the landscape and fracture rocks. Soils would be scarcer, and there would be less vegetation.

9. *Expands on freezing:* Most liquids contract as they are cooled because molecules slow down, and the attractive intermolecular forces draw them closer to each other. As most substances solidify, they form tightly packed crystalline solids, with a density greater than that of the liquid phase. Water, like other substances, gets denser as it cools, but only until 4°C. As it is cooled below this temperature, water expands until its final volume is approximately percent larger than an equivalent quantity of liquid water. This property of water is due to the polar structure of the bent water molecule. There is a strong tendency to form a network of hydrogen bonds, where each hydrogen atom is in a line between two oxygen atoms. The resulting structure is much more open than the liquid phase and therefore has lower density. As water freezes in cracks of rocks, it expands and fractures the rocks, helping to create the soil that is vital for terrestrial plant life. *If water did not have its unusual structure and thus expand on freezing,* ice would sink and eventually cover the floors of many lakes and much of the oceans. Ice would build up, leaving small layers of melted water on the surface. Fish and other aquatic and marine life would not be as protected from seasonal variations in temperature, and thus would be less able to survive.

10. *Highest heat of vaporization (540 cal/g; 40.6 KJ/mole) of any liquid*: The bent molecular shape of water makes the water molecule polar and leads to hydrogen bonding. Even at the boiling point (100°C), approximately 75 percent of all water molecules are engaged in hydrogen bonds with other molecules. To overcome this bonding and release water molecules to the gaseous phase, much energy must be applied. Each gram of water requires 540 calories of energy to vaporize. Evaporative cooling occurs whenever water is vaporized from the surface of an organism. As animals sweat, they lose heat energy. Sweating is an extremely important form of temperature regulation, particularly when environmental temperatures exceed body temperature and one can no longer lose heat by contact or radiation to the local environment. *If water did not have its unusual structure and resulting high heat of vaporization,* animals could not cool themselves by sweating or panting, and many would get sick or die when ambient temperatures exceeded 40°C.

11. *Water forms hexagonal crystals (snowflakes) on freezing:* Water molecules form a hexagonal lattice that grows into a snowflake with sixfold symmetry, as shown in Figure 12.14B. Snowflakes have a very high ratio of surface area to volume and thus fall very slowly. They have sharp, planar surfaces that reflect light, making snow appear white and brilliant. Snow and ice reflect light from the Earth's surface, helping to keep the global climate constant and the environment suitable for life. *If water did not have its unusual structure and resulting hexagonal crystalline shape,* ice would not be as reflective, much more light would be absorbed on ice fields, and the Earth's temperature would increase. Some scientists are concerned that the rate of global warming will increase as polar ice caps melt because less light will be reflected from the surface of the Earth, and consequently, more energy absorbed.

Chapter Thirteen

Games for Learning Science

For the Teacher 243

13.1 Science Jeopardy 244

13.2 Science Taboo 247

13.3 Science Bingo 248

13.4 Science Pictionary 248

13.5 Science Bowl 250

13.6 Science Baseball 252

13.7 What in the World? 252

13.8 Twenty Questions 255

13.9 Logic Games 256

For the Teacher

Science teachers employ classroom games to review course work, stimulate interest, and promote teamwork.[1] This chapter discusses the potential uses of classroom games and provides detailed instructions on a variety that are well suited for secondary school science classrooms.

Classroom games provide an active alternative to traditional review sessions, which are often passive, teacher-centered events that require minimal student involvement. Reviews that simply tell students what will be on the exam, present information in a repetitive manner, or require little student involvement are largely ineffective and should be replaced by activities centering on students and requiring their participation. Active learning events such as classroom games are more effective in promoting student learning than teacher-centered review sessions.[2] Students are likely to study in preparation for the game and again for the test, particularly if the game has highlighted their areas of weakness.

All games are more interesting when teams are of equal ability. Fans pour out of baseball stadiums during the seventh inning if there is a wide margin in the score but stay and cheer if the score remains close. In a similar manner, students lose interest if teams are mismatched in ability and performance. The losing team has a tendency to give up and the winning team a tendency to slack off. For this reason, it is best to arrange teams so that all have roughly equivalent abilities.

Students join sports teams not only for love of the game but also for the camaraderie that develops among team members. A team's performance is based on the dedication and skill of all its players, and members encourage one another to excel for the collective good. Unfortunately, there are relatively few team activities in the academic arena. Students compete for grades and class rank and may be hesitant to help one another for fear that their efforts might "raise the curve." By contrast, games promote teamwork, an attitude and skill that are invaluable in every aspect of life. Teachers should assemble teams, appoint captains, and allow members to create team names consistent with course content. For example, biology students may create team names such as the Phosphorylators, Catabolists, or Active Transporters, and chemistry students may chose names such as the Catalysts, Ionizers, or Solutions.

We often think of peer pressure as negative, but it can also be a positive tool, particularly in classroom management. Students understand that the performance of a team is dependent on the cooperation and performance of all of its members. When they understand that disorderly conduct adversely affects the team score, members are likely to hold teammates accountable for their behavior. It may be wise to use the same teams for laboratory experiments and group activities so as to further promote teamwork and discipline. Instructors should use simple cues to remind students of the behavior expectations. For example, you may wish to keep an overhead transparency with team names on it. Whenever there is a discipline problem, move the transparency to the projector and students will understand that you are about to subtract points from a disorderly team. Students will recognize the cue and quickly get their teams in order. Such student-centered management approaches are generally much more effective than teacher-centered techniques, such as raising one's voice or calling out specific individuals.

Because of the benefits in classroom management that may accompany the use of games, it is generally a good idea to maintain team composition long enough to build camaraderie and accountability. When team organization remains constant throughout a semester, it is possible to develop leagues (different class periods), rankings (team placement within a period), all-star games (competitions between the best players from different periods), and superbowls (competitions between the best teams). Ranking can be based on a win-loss record or the cumulative percentage of questions answered correctly, or both. Enthusiasm grows when the games are well developed and well executed. This enthusiasm can be shared with the school by holding all-star and superbowl contests during lunch break or after school in the auditorium or school quad. Many teachers offer an extra-credit incentive for teams that win games or championships but find that the need for extra credit diminishes as enthusiasm grows. With time, students may be more motivated by the game than by any extra-credit points they might earn by winning the game.

Benjamin Franklin said, "Trouble springs from idleness, and grievous toil from needless ease." Guard against idleness by designing games so all students are engaged in the learning process. Whenever possible, games should involve the entire class, and questions or tasks should rotate among team members.

You may ask students to submit questions to be entered in a database for future use. Screen all questions for accuracy and appropriateness. If you maintain them in a database file, you may print them in tabular form so they may be easily cut up and drawn from a hat. There should be a judge (generally you) who rules on all game activities. The judge should be impartial and accurate, and his or her rulings should stand. Grievances should be dealt with after the game and outside class so as not to distract from academic tasks.

13.1 Science Jeopardy

Science Jeopardy is a classroom game patterned after the popular television game show *Jeopardy.* In most games, tests, or classroom drills, students provide answers to questions posed by their teachers. In Science Jeopardy, students create questions to answers provided by teachers. The example illustrates this difference:

Traditional Method: Question Precedes Answer
Teacher: What biome is found north of the taiga?
Student: Tundra.

Jeopardy: Answer Precedes Question

Teacher: The answer is "tundra."

Student: What biome is found north of the taiga?

Student: What cold-weather biome is dominated by grasses?

Student: What biome is found in northern Alaska, Canada, and Russia?

Student: What biome has permafrost and short growing seasons?

Because Science Jeopardy requires students to generate questions in response to answers rather than answers in response to questions, it assesses comprehension in addition to knowledge. There is often more than one correct question for each answer. Figure 13.1 illustrates a jeopardy board prior to a game. The numbers represent point values and hide answers written beneath. The game board can be made on an overhead transparency. Each answer is covered by a sticky note that is removed when the item is selected. Alternatively, an electronic version can be made using PowerPoint slides or a Word document in which answers are placed in a table and covered by opaque rectangles made with the drawing tool (see *sciencesourcebook.com* or search "jeopardy template").

As with any other classroom game, adjust the organization and rules to meet the specific needs of the class. A team of five is suggested, one of whom is selected as captain. A different captain is selected for each game. Table 13.1 is a sample game with questions to show possible responses.

ACTIVITY 13.1.1 *Play Science Jeopardy*

The teacher conducts Science Jeopardy according to the following rules. The categories and answers are chosen to relate to current class content:

- *Opening:* The lowest-ranked team starts first. If both teams have equal rank, the order is determined by flipping a coin. (Ranking is based on win and loss record or the total number of points earned in previous games.)

- *Selecting answers:* The team captain selects an answer (e.g., "Cells for 300") for which all lower values in the category have already been selected. For example, Cells 100 and Cells 200 must be selected before Cells 300 may be selected. All teams try to generate a question that has the given answer.

- *Response:* During the first 30 seconds, only the team that made the selection can respond. If they have not drafted a question within the first 30 seconds, any other team captain can raise his or her hand. If two captains raise their hands simultaneously, the answer is given to the lower-scoring team.

- *Providing the question:* The team captain selects an individual to read the team's question. The same individual cannot be selected more than once in a row.

- *Scoring:* Points are awarded for a well-phrased question that has the specified answer. No points are taken off for incorrect answers, except in Final Jeopardy. The harder the question, the higher its point value.

- *Next answer:* The first team with a correct question is given the privilege of choosing the next answer. A team is not allowed to select more than two answers in a row. After that, the lowest-scoring team is given that privilege.

- *Ending the game:* Jeopardy is completed when all answers have been revealed or at the discretion of the teacher. The teams now proceed to Final Jeopardy, the closing round in which

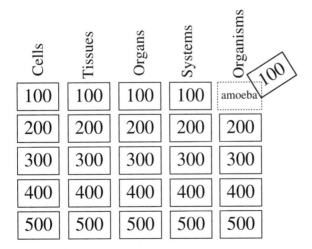

Figure 13.1 Science Jeopardy Board

Table 13.1 Sample Jeopardy Answers and Possible Questions

Points	Biology	Chemistry	Physics	Earth and Space Science
100	*Answer:* prokaryote *Question:* What kingdom does not have membrane-bound organelles?	*Answer:* calorie *Question:* What is the amount of heat required to raise 1 gram of water 1 degree Celsius?	*Answer:* Newton *Question:* What is the unit of force equal to one kilogrammeter per second squared ($kg \cdot m \cdot s^2$)	*Answer:* light-year *Question:* What is the distance light travels in space in one earth-year?
200	*Answer:* mutualism *Question:* What is the name for a mutually beneficial association between different kinds of organisms?	*Answer:* double displacement *Question:* What is an ionic reaction in which ion pairs are switched?	*Answer:* $E = hf$ *Question:* What is the equation that describes the energy of a photon in terms of the frequency of light?	*Answer:* Proxima-Centauri *Question:* What is the name for the star that is closest to our Sun?
300	*Answer:* ATP *Question:* What compound is aptly known as the "energy currency" of the cell?	*Answer:* alpha particle *Question:* What is a helium nucleus that is emitted by certain radioactive substances?	*Answer:* capacitance *Question:* What is the ability to store electric charge known as?	*Answer:* umbra *Question:* What is the part of a shadow or eclipse in which all light is eliminated?
400	*Answer:* auxins *Question:* Which plant hormones stimulate the elongation of cells in shoots?	*Answer:* $1s^2 2s^2 2p^6$ *Question:* What is the electron configuration of neon?	*Answer:* inverse square law *Question:* What law describes the attenuation in radiating forces as a function of distance?	*Answer:* pulsar *Question:* What are cosmic objects that emit extremely regular pulses of radio waves?
500	*Answer:* CAM *Question:* Which photosynthetic pathway predominates in succulents and cacti?	*Answer:* Bose-Einstein condensate *Question:* What is the state of matter formed by bosons cooled to temperatures near absolute zero	*Answer:* kilogrammeter squared per second cubed ($kg \cdot m^2 \cdot s^{-3}$) *Question:* What is a watt, or joule per second?	*Answer:* lateritic soil *Question:* What are the leached soils characteristic of the tropics?

teams have the opportunity to wager any or all of their points with the hope of winning.

- *Wagers:* The teacher announces the category of the Final Jeopardy answer before wagers are made. Each team may wager any or all of its points. Each captain must write the team's wager on paper and give it to the teacher.

- *Final Jeopardy:* The teacher reads the Final Jeopardy answer, and all teams write their questions within 2 minutes. Teams use this time to build consensus and compose a question on paper that they submit to the instructor.

- *Final Jeopardy points:* If the team has a correct question, it receives as many points as wagered, but if the question is incorrect, they lose this number of points.

- *Winning:* The team with the highest score wins.

13.2 Science Taboo

In 1771 the British explorer James Cook visited the Pacific Island of Tonga and made insightful observations of its native Polynesian culture. In particular, he noticed that the Tongans had many rules, based on ritualistic distinctions, that prohibited certain actions. The Tongans referred to such forbidden behaviors as *taboo*. It was taboo to touch tribal chiefs, travel in certain areas of the forest, and engage in various other seemingly harmless activities. The punishment for doing something taboo was often quite serious.

The Hasbro Company played on the taboo concept when it introduced a popular party game by the same name. In Taboo, players must describe a target term to their partners without using any taboo terms (forbidden words) frequently associated with it. For example, a team representative may have to explain gravity without mentioning "Earth," "apple," "Newton," "attraction," or "fall." The team scores if they guess "gravity" within the allotted time.

Science Taboo is a classroom game based on the party game. It is designed to test student understanding of scientific concepts. A representative of one team draws a card such as shown in Figure 13.2 and must explain the target term without using any of the five taboo terms below it. For example, a team representative who drew the term "telescope" would have to explain this concept so teammates could guess it but would have to do so without using any of the taboo terms: "star," "astronomer," "observatory," "planet," or "look."

Science Taboo tests the ability of the representative to explain science concepts in his or her own words. In traditional settings, a student could "explain" by parroting a glossary definition. By contrast, in Taboo, the person must convey concepts in his or her own words. A student who is able to explain a term without using taboo terms probably has a good understanding of the target term.

Figure 13.2 illustrates some sample Taboo cards. The target word is in bold at the top of the column, and the taboo terms appear below it. The student cannot use any of these words, or their derivatives, when explaining the concept to teammates. Following are sample explanations that a team representative might use to explain the target term without using the taboo terms:

- *Telescope:* This instrument is used to observe cosmic objects.
- *Photosynthesis:* This plant process fixes carbon dioxide into sugars.
- *Earthquake:* A sudden, violent, movement of the earth.
- *Convection:* The transference of thermal energy by the movement of a fluid.

ACTIVITY 13.2.1 *Play Science Taboo*

The teacher conducts Science Taboo as described below. The topics and terms should relate to current class content.

- *Make Taboo cards:* Make taboo cards using target terms relevant to the curriculum. I suggest selecting taboo terms (the forbidden words) from those found in glossary or dictionary definitions of the target term (Figure 13.3). The teacher may ask students to make cards for competitions in other classes.
- *Teams:* Split the class into two or more teams, and select a captain for each. The captain determines the order in which team members will serve as the referee and representative.
- *Game play:* The first team chooses a representative to explain target terms. The representative

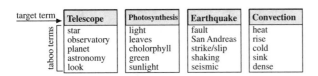

Figure 13.2 Taboo Cards

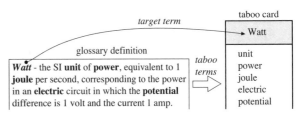

Figure 13.3 Constructing Taboo Cards from Glossary Definitions

gives an explanation for the term without using use any of the taboo words or their derivatives. The representative has 1 minute to explain as many target terms as his or her team can guess.

- *Referee:* A referee from the next team is chosen to ensure none of the taboo words are used. If any are used, the referee sounds a buzzer or bell, and the remainder of the turn is forfeited.

- *Transition:* After the 1 minute turn has expired, the student who served as referee becomes the representative for the team and draws a new target term. Students serve as referees immediately prior to serving as representatives. There should always be a representative and a referee in front of the class.

- *Team response:* Team members shout answers in response to the clues given by their representative. The teacher awards points whenever a correct answer is given and immediately gives the team representative a new card until the 1 minute turn has expired. No points are given if a team guesses a term after the 1 minute buzzer.

- *Scoring:* Three points are awarded for each target term that is guessed. If a taboo term is used, the representative's turn is immediately ended. The representative may elect to pass a term for at a cost of 1 point. The representative is then given another taboo card.

- *Illegal techniques:* The representative cannot say "sounds like" or use physical movements to explain the term. If such actions are used, the team's turn is forfeited.

- *Winning:* The teacher determines the number of rounds that are played. The team with the most points at the end of the game wins.

13.3 Science Bingo

Science students memorize large numbers of new terms, many of them abstract and difficult to understand. To assess student understanding, teachers often ask students to define terms. Unfortunately students may be able to memorize definitions and repeat them on tests or quizzes, but have no real understanding of their meaning or significance. To ensure that students truly understand

definitions, teachers can turn to Science Bingo or a similar activity that assesses their understanding rather than mere memorization. Unlike the popular Bingo game, Science Bingo is based on skill and understanding rather than chance.

ACTIVITY 13.3.1 *Play Science Bingo*

- *Vocabulary list:* The teacher develops a list of 25 or more words for the game (Figure 13.4).

- *Setup:* Students construct a five-by-five grid on a sheet of paper and fill the grid with terms from the list, as shown in Figure 13.4. Each term may appear only once.

- *Definitions:* The teacher reads definitions and their corresponding numbers. For example, if the first term to be identified is *cellulose*, the teacher should say, "Number 1: The main component of cell walls."

- *Identifying terms:* When students hear a definition and associate it with a term on their grid, they put the clue number in the appropriate cell.

- *Winning:* Students say "Bingo!" when they have identified five terms in a row, column, or diagonal. The teacher must look at the student's card to ensure that the numbers associated with the terms match the numbers of the definitions read. Continue reading terms until at least five students have achieved Bingo.

13.4 Science Pictionary

It has been said that a picture is worth a thousand words, and yet many educators do not take full advantage of diagrams and drawings in their instruction. Winn and Holiday summarized the benefits of using diagrams in instruction as follows:

(1) Diagrams help learners because they direct attention to important information, replacing critical verbal information with graphic devices such as lines and arrows; (2) diagrams help low-verbal learners overcome some of their difficulty with language by providing information in a form they can handle more easily; (3) through the use of normal left-right, top-bottom layout, arrows and other graphic

Card made by student 1

Bingo!

absolute zero 12	anode	ductility	gizzard	joule 3
homo-zygous 10	impulse	taiga 2	energy	diamond 4
cellulose 18	glycogen 9	diode 5	meso-derm 13	torr 1
codon	electron 17	halite	monocot	zygote 8
vector 15	ampere	dielectric 6	enzyme 16	synapse 11

possible terms

absolute zero	gizzard
allotrope	glycogen
ampere	halite
anode	homozygous
cellulose	impedance
codon	impulse
community	joule
diamond	mesoderm
dielectric	monocot
diode	olfaction
ductility	synapse
electron	taiga
endothermic	torr
energy	vector
enzyme	zygote

Card made by student 2

cellulose 18	joule	diamond 4	ductility	absolute zero 12
zygote 8	monocot	anode	energy	homo-zygous 10
synapse	olfaction	diode 5	impulse	dielectric 6
cellulose	glycogen 9	imped-ance	synapse 11	ampere
codon	taiga 2	allotrope	enzyme 16	vector 15

The teacher reads the definitions. Students put the numbers of each definition in the cell with the corresponding term. The definitions of 19–26 would be read if Bingo had not been reached.

(1) A unit of pressure equal to 1 mm Hg.
(2) Boreal forest; subarctic coniferous forest.
(3) Chamber in a bird specialized for grinding food.
(4) A colorless form of carbon that is extremely hard.
(5) A semiconductor device with two terminals.
(6) An electrical insulator.
(7) An energy-consuming process.
(8) A fertilized egg.
(9) A storage form of carbohydrates in animals.

(10) Having two identical alleles of a particular gene.
(11) The junction between two neurons.
(12) –273.15 °C.
(13) The middle layer of three primary germ layers.
(14) The effective resistance to alternating current.
(15) An animal that transmits a pathogen.
(16) An organic catalyst.
(17) The primary carrier of electricity in solids.
(18) The main constituent of cell walls.

Figure 13.4 Bingo Cards, Terms, and Definitions

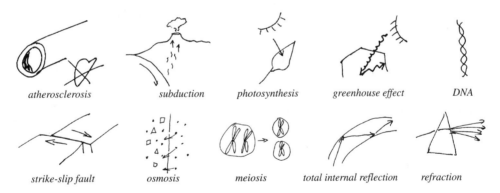

atherosclerosis · subduction · photosynthesis · greenhouse effect · DNA

strike-slip fault · osmosis · meiosis · total internal reflection · refraction

Figure 13.5 Sample Science Pictionary Drawings and Corresponding Terms

devices, diagrams can teach sequences of events effectively; [and] (4) the addition of study questions to diagrams helps learners by directing their attention to critical information.[3]

Students as well as teachers need to develop the skill of diagramming concepts rather than simply copying those developed by others. Science Pictionary is a game that helps develop such skills.

Science Pictionary is patterned after the popular party game invented by Pictionary Incorporated in which team members communicate concepts and terms through drawings that do not use standard letters, numbers, or other common symbols. Students with a good understanding of a concept can diagram it in a way that others can recognize without the use of written or spoken words. Figure 13.5 illustrates some sample Science Pictionary drawings and the terms they describe. Note that drawings should be simple and represent key ideas. For example, the atherosclerosis diagram shows a clogged artery and indicates it might lead to a heart attack, and the sub-duction diagram shows downward-moving rock and the corresponding formation of volcanoes. The goal is to illustrate key concepts as simply as possible.

ACTIVITY 13.4.1 *Play Science Pictionary*

- *Teams:* The class is divided into teams, and captains are assigned or elected. The teacher determines the number and size of teams.
- *Lineup:* The team captain determines the sequence in which students from his or her team will draw. The opportunity to draw alternates between teams.
- *Drawing:* The drawer is given a science term or concept that he or she must represent on the overhead, whiteboard, or blackboard. The drawer may not say anything, make any gestures, or draw any letters or common symbols other than arrows.
- *Team response:* As the student draws, his or her team members shout out terms they think the diagram represents. The drawer cannot say anything except to knowledge a correct guess.
- *Scoring:* When a correct term is guessed, the team is awarded a number of points equivalent to the number of seconds it took teammates to guess the term. If the student's team has not guessed the term correctly after 60 seconds, they get 60 points and the other team is given 10 seconds to guess the term. If the other team is correct, 10 points are subtracted from their score. A student may pass a difficult term for a 10 point penalty.
- *Completion of the game:* The instructor determines an appropriate number of questions for the game. The team with the fewest points (least time to communicate concepts through drawing) wins the game.

13.5 Science Bowl

Since 1953 the College Bowl Company has been producing College Bowl as a live event for television and radio. More recently, the company introduced High School Bowl and international versions of College Bowl. The company has received an Emmy, as well as congressional and presidential citations for promoting academics through the popular media. Science Bowl, a modified version of the academic game, can be used to stimulate learning and enthusiasm for science while promoting class spirit. Students from basic to Advanced Placement courses have enthusiastically received Science Bowl. The instructor plays the role of a game show host and sports announcer, emceeing the game and building enthusiasm through "play-by-play" analysis. This activity assesses knowledge and comprehension of scientific facts and may be used prior to examinations so students have basic facts before they encounter higher-order questions on examinations.

ACTIVITY 13.5.1 *Play Science Bowl*

- *Team size:* Science Bowl can be conducted with teams of any size, depending on the needs and the time available. If you have an entire class period, you may wish to have numerous small teams and run three or four games. If you have less than half an hour, it is better to split the class in two and conduct just one game. I suggest that you keep team composition the same for at least one quarter to foster the development of team camaraderie and accountability.
- *Assigning teams:* Games are much more interesting to watch and play if they are evenly matched. It is therefore good to make teams as equal as possible. Each member should be assigned a number and a letter as shown in Figure 13.6. Note that the numbering and lettering are done so that no two students have the same coordinates. This allows the teacher

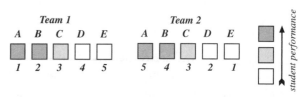

Figure 13.6 Coordinates of Team Members

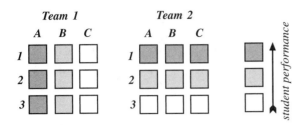

Figure 13.7 Arrangements for Larger Teams

to pair up different individuals. A question asked of A's will match student A1 on team 1 with student A5 on team 2, and a question asked of 1's will match student A1 on team 1 with student E1 on team 2. Figure 13.7 illustrates how to arrange students in larger groups so that you can better match scores to keep games competitive. For example, if team 1 is behind, the teacher might ask questions of A's favoring team 1. By contrast, if team 2 is behind, the teacher might ask questions of 1's, thereby favoring team 2. The teacher should not disclose the rationale for the seating arrangements.

- *Questions:* The teacher maintains a bank of questions pertinent to the curriculum. These questions may be developed by former students and kept in a database file for ease of access.

    Designated questions—1 point: When the teacher calls C, only students with a C designation can answer. Similarly, when the instructor calls "3's," only those with a designation of 3 can answer. Sometimes two or more sets can be identified, such as "1's and D's." If no one answers the question in the allotted time (generally 10 seconds), you can open it up to other combinations. Students will remain alert if there is always a chance that their number or letter will be called.

    Toss-up questions—1 point: These questions can be answered by any team member.

    Team questions—3 points: The time limit is tripled (30 seconds) for these questions because they require consultation. They are more difficult or multipart questions and must be answered by the team captain or his or her designee after consensus has been reached.

- *Sample questions for genetics:*
    "What is the sequence of nucleotides in a start codon?" (designated or toss-up question, 1 point)
    "When does synapsis of homologous chromosomes occur?" (designated or toss-up question, 1 point)
    "In what stage does DNA synthesis occur?" (designated or toss-up question, 1 point)
    "Describe three steps of the Sanger process for gene sequencing." (team question, 3 points)
    "How many different gametic genotypes are possible for an individual heterozygous at 5 loci?" (team question, 3 points)
    "Give the correct names for the following symbols: A, C, G, T, U, DNA, RNA." (team question, 3 points)

- *Scoring:* The first eligible student to raise his or her hand or press the buzzer after the question has been asked must answer the question. A student who raises his or her hand before the question has been completed must answer immediately, without the benefit of whatever else might have been said. If the student is correct, his or her team scores and the teacher poses another question. If the student is incorrect, his or her opponents are read the remainder of the question and given the full time to respond. There are no penalties for wrong answers. If a student raises his or her hand or hits the buzzer out of turn, it is an automatic forfeit, and the opposing team has the opportunity to answer the question without competition.

- *Ranking:* Teams are ranked on the basis of their win-loss record. If two teams have identical records, their rankings will then be based on the total percentage of points that their team has earned throughout the year.

- *Special awards:* Although this game is designed as a team sport, you may wish to record individual scores and recognize the most valuable players (MVPs).

- *Special games:* If you have multiple sections of a class, you may wish to hold all-star or superbowl games in which the best students or team from one class compete with the best students or team from another. These games can be held at lunch or after school. When held in a public place like the gymnasium or quad, the games may draw a crowd and build interest in your program among future students.

13.6 Science Baseball

Every science class has students with a range of abilities and interests. Students have differences in prior knowledge, interest, and motivation yet rarely are given individual assignments tailored to their abilities and needs. This lack of individualization is true in many classroom games as well: all students are asked the same questions and assigned the same tasks. In contrast to most other games, Science Baseball offers a degree of individualization by providing the option to select the level of difficulty of the question asked.

Science Baseball may hold interest for sports-minded students because of the analogy with America's pastime. Students will be enthusiastic if the teacher is enthusiastic. A teacher who comes to class in an umpire's shirt, announces plays and scores like a sportscaster, and decorates the classroom with baseball paraphernalia will generate much greater interest than one who does nothing extra. Enthusiasm is contagious, but so is apathy.

ACTIVITY 13.6.1 *Play Science Baseball*

- *Questions:* Develop a set of questions, and categorize them in four groups (singles, doubles, triples, and home runs) according to difficulty. Students may be asked to develop questions for use in other classes.
- *Recording play:* Project a baseball diamond on the screen, or draw a replica on the board. Record the scores and names of the players as illustrated in Figure 13.8.
- *Lineups:* Split the class into two teams and determine a lineup sequence for each, or appoint team captains and allow them to make the lineups. Each student "comes to bat" according to position in the lineup and selects the difficulty of the question to be asked. Singles are easiest and home runs the most difficult. The teacher

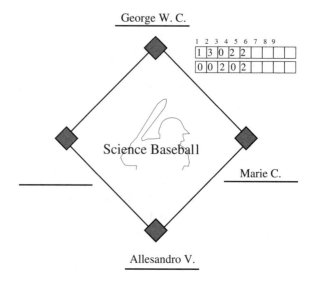

Figure 13.8 Science Baseball Diamond

reads a question aloud from the appropriate category and gives the "batter" a standard amount of time to respond.
- *Scoring:* If the "batter" answers the question correctly, the instructor writes his or her initials by the appropriate base (Figure 13.8). Wrong answers are considered an "out." Each team is allowed three outs per inning. The game is scored like baseball, with points given for each "runner" who crosses home plate. Play as many innings as time permits.

13.7 What in the World?

Science concepts are often best represented graphically, and teachers assess understanding by requiring their students to draw or label diagrams. For example, it is common to ask biology students to label the bones or organs on a diagram of the body or the organelles on a stylized model of a cell. Unfortunately, such tests are often more an indicator of a student's ability to memorize a particular diagram than an indicator of his or her level of understanding. For example, students may be able to accurately label all of the bones on a diagram of the skeleton from their textbook but unable to identify the same bones on a model or disarticulated skeleton.

Students need to learn to identify salient features in the objects studied so that they can develop a general understanding that will allow them to recognize and identify the same objects in different settings. For example, a student who truly understands the anatomy of the femur will not only be able to identify it on the diagram from which he or she studied but also from X-rays or photographs taken from different angles and diagrams drawn from different perspectives. In addition, this student will be able to locate the bone on himself or herself, or identify it from a model when blindfolded.

It is the teacher's responsibility to stress the significant features of the objects studied and provide a rich learning environment in which students will be exposed to examples from a variety of sources. What in the World? is a game that requires students to identify familiar objects in unfamiliar views and thereby assesses their ability to generalize, transfer, and extrapolate.

Select a series of images related to your lesson using a graphic search engine (see *sciencesource book.com* or images.google.com). To encourage the development of transference skills (the ability to recognize similar features in dissimilar environments), select images that portray the objects of interest from new perspectives. For example, if your textbook illustrates chloroplasts diagrammatically, then obtain images of chloroplasts taken with a scanning or transmission electron microscope. In order to identify novel images of familiar objects, students must be able to differentiate relevant from irrelevant information. Although the diagram in the book may show the chloroplast as a green structure, the micrograph from a transmission electron microscope will display it in black and white. Students must recognize that color is not a key feature in this situation because transmission electron microscopes use electrons rather than light to create images. Similarly, the diagram in the text may present the chloroplast in a three-dimensional manner, while the micrograph shows only a thin section through the center of the organelle. Students must therefore look for distinctive features, such as grana stacks, that will appear in both diagrams and micrographs.

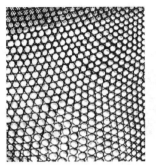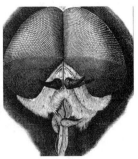

Figure 13.9 Extrapolation Exercise: The Compound Eye of a Fly

What in the World? can also be used to develop extrapolation skills: the ability to get the big picture from small portions of a picture. Collect large digital images of things you have studied. Using a graphics-editing program such as PhotoShop or your digital photo album software, select a closeup view of just a portion of the image, and incorporate this into your game. For example, if you have been studying flies, display just a portion of the compound eye of a fly (Figure 13.9)[4] to see if students can extrapolate from this to identify the organ or organism from which it was taken. Locate and download images to your personal computer, and reference their sources as outlined in Chapter Three. Import these graphics in an appropriate sequence into an electronic slide sorter or presentation manager such PowerPoint.

ACTIVITY 13.7.1 *Play What in the World?*

- *Create a game:* Create a slide show using PowerPoint, slide viewer software, or a presentation manager (find images at *sciencesource book.com* or images.google.com). The images and questions should be related to your curriculum. Figure 13.10 shows a sample game, the answers to which are (1) transistors, (2) scanning tunneling microscopy, (3) metal crystals (tin, Sn), (4) optic fiber, (5) magnetic storage media, (6) stress, (7) ATP, (8) composite volcano, (9) plant meristematic tissue, (10) about 4 hours, (11) below the picture, and (12) thermophilic bacteria.

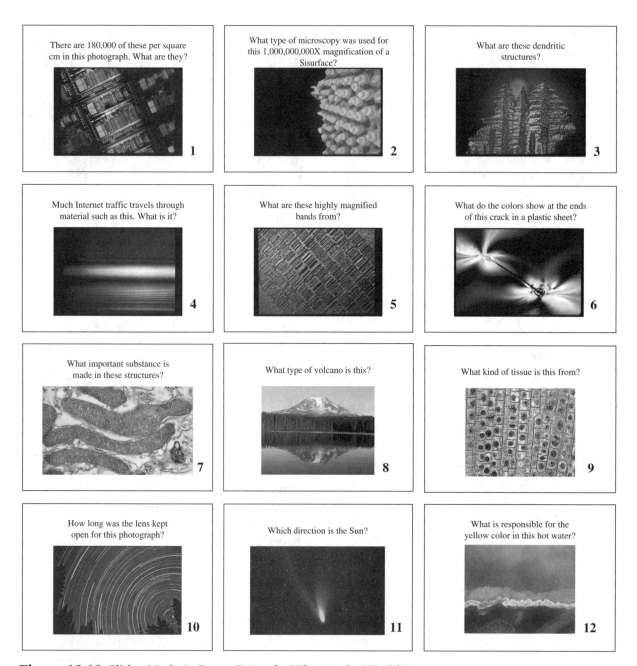

Figure 13.10 Slides Made in PowerPoint for What in the World? Game

Source: Lucent Corporation (2004). Microscapes. Retrieved January 2004 from http://www.lucent.com/minds/innovating/microscapes. html (first six images).

- *Teams:* Divide the class into two or more teams, and select a captain for each. The team captain is responsible for building consensus among team members when asked to identify features of a novel image.
- *Conference:* Present the images using a data projector or overhead projector. Ask the first team in the lineup a question about the image.

Other teams should also try to answer the question because they will be asked it if the first team fails. Provide a set amount of time for the team members to share their ideas and reach consensus. The team captain must develop consensus among the team and appoint a member to answer the question. The team must respond within the allotted time or forfeit its turn.

- *Scoring:* A team that gets the correct answer scores 1 point, and the next team in line is given the opportunity to answer a new question. If a team does not get the correct answer, the next team is given the same question, thereby ensuring that all teams will work on all questions, even when they are not up. After giving each team an equal and predetermined number of questions, the team with the highest score is declared the winner.

13.8 Twenty Questions

A dichotomous key is a tool for classifying plants, animals, bacteria, fungi, protozoans, rocks, or other natural items or features. The trick is to ask dichotomous questions: questions in which there are only two possible responses. After answering a series of dichotomous questions, the object is "keyed out" or classified. Figure 13.11 illustrates a simplified dichotomous key for classifying the general appearance of plants. Twenty Questions is a classroom game, based on a popular radio and television game series, and spoken parlor game. It helps build keying skills and deductive reasoning.

Taxonomists classify organisms according to common characteristics. Table 13.2 illustrates the classification of *Magnolia grandiflora*, a broadleaf tree native to the southeastern United States. Each level in the classification can be reached by asking specific questions in a similar fashion to

Table 13.2 Classification of *Magnolia grandiflora*

Kingdom	*Plantae*—all plants
Division	*Magnoliophyta*—flowering plants
Class	*Magnoliopsida*—dicots
Subclass	*Magnoliidae*—subclass for Magnolia-like plants
Order	*Magnoliales*—order for Magnolia-like plants
Family	*Magnoliaceae*—family for Magnolia-like plants
Genus	*Magnolia*—genus that includes all
Species	*Magnolia grandiflora*—specific epithet

that illustrated above. It should be noted that the word endings (see boldfaced portions) are generally associated with the level of classification. For example, Magnoli*aceae* can refer only to a family because of the -*aceae* suffix.

Classification is extremely important in science, yet not all classification schemes are equally valuable. The popular game of Twenty Questions can provide an excellent introduction to the concept of dichotomous keying and illustrate the importance of asking good questions, and in a logical sequence, when developing a taxonomic key.

ACTIVITY 13.8.1 *Play Twenty Questions*
- *Target:* The teacher writes a relevant concept, structure, process, or organism on an overhead

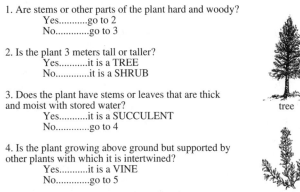

1. Are stems or other parts of the plant hard and woody?
  Yes...........go to 2
  No.............go to 3

2. Is the plant 3 meters tall or taller?
  Yes...........it is a TREE
  No.............it is a SHRUB

3. Does the plant have stems or leaves that are thick and moist with stored water?
  Yes...........it is a SUCCULENT
  No.............go to 4

4. Is the plant growing above ground but supported by other plants with which it is intertwined?
  Yes...........it is a VINE
  No.............go to 5

5. Is the base of the leaf wrapped around the stem?
  Yes...........it is a GRASS
  No.............it is a HERB

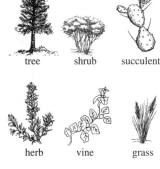

Figure 13.11 Dichotomous Key for the Physiognomy of Plans

transparency and covers it with a piece of paper. For example, in a biology class, a teacher might write a concept (Hardy-Weinberg equilibrium, cryptic coloration, founder effect), structure (lungs, alveoli, sternum), process (gene flow, respiration, transcription), or organism (paramecium, baleen whale, retrovirus).

- *Questioning:* Students try to determine what the teacher has written by asking yes or no questions. Since every question must be answered with a yes or no, students are effectively classifying the mystery item using a dichotomous key. Many students try to circumvent the keying process and immediately guess a specific item. Each time they do this, they waste a question, and since only 20 questions are allowed, they decrease their chances of determining the unknown.

- *Developing a dichotomous key:* With time, students should learn that dichotomous keys work best when each question divides the remaining domain into two approximately equal subdomains. If each question splits the remaining domain exactly in half, then the number of items that can be keyed out will increase as a power of 2. One dichotomous question can key out two items (2^1), two questions can key out four items (2^2), three questions can key out eight items (2^3), and so on. Theoretically, one can key out 2^{20} items ($2^{20} = 1,048,576$) with 20 dichotomous questions. In reality, the number is much smaller because it is difficult to divide the remaining domains exactly in half. Nonetheless, the process shows how the dichotomous key is a powerful tool for classifying a large set of objects.

- *Playing with multiple teams:* You may wish to separate the class into different teams and give each an identical series of terms to solve through the questioning process. Separate the groups sufficiently so they will not be able to hear the questioning process of the other groups. Select knowledgeable and impartial students to serve as game hosts, and appoint one to work with each team. Team members should write down each question that is asked and its answer on a sheet of paper or their

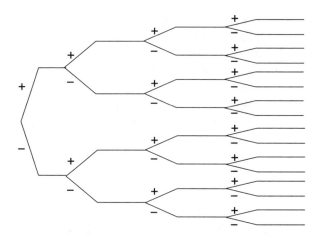

Figure 13.12 Template for a Dichotomous Key

science notebooks (see Chapter Three). This becomes their dichotomous key for the mystery item. The game host reveals the mystery term only after the puzzle has been solved. The team that solves the puzzle with the fewest number of questions is declared the winner.

ACTIVITY 13.8.2 *Developing a Taxonomic Key*

Once students have learned the value of asking the right questions and sequencing them in a logical fashion, give them the opportunity to develop a taxonomic scheme for a set of miscellaneous objects such as hardware (assorted nails, washers, bolts, nuts, cotter pins, dowels) or desk items (assorted pens, pencils, paper clips, rubber bands, tacks). Give each group a jar containing a similar assortment of items, and ask them to develop a logical classification scheme. Students should draw a dichotomous decision tree (Figure 13.12) on a large sheet of paper. Each branch should be numbered and identified with a yes-no question. The objects should be placed on the appropriate branches and the key photographed and shared with the class.

13.9 Logic Games

Numerous games can be used to introduce or reinforce scientific principles and develop logical reasoning. Many of these have been made into computer games and can be accessed or downloaded from the Internet (see *sciencesourcebook.com* or search "science shareware" or "logic games"). In this section we introduce Mastermind, Kakuro, Bridges, Sudoku, and Puzzle Loops. There are many other logic games that may be of use in building scientific and spatial reasoning, including Tower of Hanoi, Tetris, Wordcross, Concentration, Othello, Gridlock, and Chess. All of these, and many more, may be found online. Teachers can model the problem-solving process by illustrating how these puzzles are solved. Games may be played for homework or extra credit.

ACTIVITY 13.9.1 *Mastermind (Code Breaker)*

Many games have relevance to the science classroom even though they may not deal directly with science content. For example, logic games can be used to introduce scientific reasoning. One such game is Mastermind (Figure 13.13), a computer game copied from the popular Milton Bradley board game by the same name. The objective in Mastermind is to guess a hidden code of four or more colors selected by the opponent (the computer in this case). Each time the player guesses a sequence of colors, the computer returns pegs. Each gray peg indicates that the guess includes a correct color in an incorrect location, and each black peg indicates that the guess includes a correct color in a correct location. The position of the gray and black pegs is unrelated to the actual position within the code.

Mastermind provides a great introduction to "black box" science in which scientists must use probes to measure an unseen object and can see the only response of probes since the object is too small or too difficult to be seen. For example, Ernest Rutherford determined the basic structure of the atom through a classic black box experiment in which he shot alpha particles at a thin sheet of gold foil. Although he could not see the atoms in the foil, he concluded that they must be composed primarily of space since most of the alpha particles went straight through the opaque foil, while only a small percentage were reflected or deflected by particles within the foil.

In the same way, students playing a strategy game like Mastermind must work with probes to determine a code that they are not allowed to see. The black and gray pegs returned by their opponent (computer) are analogous to outputs from a probe, such as the deflected or reflected alpha particles in the Rutherford experiment, giving evidence of the hidden code or structure, and allowing the experimenter (student) to draw inferences about the unseen. In Mastermind, it may be necessary to discard an assumed sequence if it does not fit the new data, just as a scientist must revise or discard previous hypotheses that don't fit new data. Mastermind games can be downloaded from, or played on, the Internet (go to *sciencesourcebook.com* or search "Mastermind" or "code-breaker game").

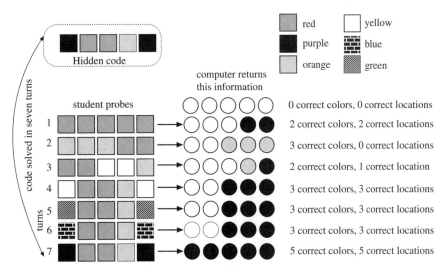

Figure 13.13 Mastermind (Code Breaker) Logic Game

ACTIVITY 13.9.2 *Kakuro: Cross Sums*

Kakuro is a numerical crossword game in which the player fills all of the blank squares in a grid with the numbers from 1 to 9. Each horizontal or vertical block of digits must add up to the number given to the left or above, respectively. All the digits in each such block must be different. Numbers can be repeated on a line as long as they are in different blocks. Figure 13.14 shows a Kakuro puzzle and its solution. Kakuro puzzles can be found on the Internet (go to *sciencesourcebook.com* or search "Kakuro" or "cross sums").

ACTIVITY 13.9.3 *Bridges: Hashiwokakero*

The circles in Figure 13.15 are "islands," and the enclosed numbers are the quantity of "bridges" that touch each "island." The goal is to connect all of the islands by drawing the specified number of "bridges" (lines). The bridges may run vertically or horizontally but not diagonally. No more than two bridges (double lines) can connect two islands. Solving a Hashiwokakero puzzle requires advanced planning and attention to procedure.

Building a bridge often restricts the placement of subsequent bridges. Bridges puzzles can be found on the Internet (see *sciencesourcebook.com* or search "bridges puzzle" or "Hashiwokakero").

ACTIVITY 13.9.4 *Sudoku*

The objective in Sudoku is to complete the grid such that every row, column, and the nine 3 3 3 blocks contain the digits from 1 to 9, as illustrated in Figure 13.16. Sudoku puzzles can be found on the Internet (see *sciencesourcebook.com* or search "Sudoku").

ACTIVITY 13.9.5 *Puzzle Loops*

The objective of Puzzle Loops is to make one continuous loop such that each number is bordered by the specified number of line segments, as shown in Figure 13.17. Crossings, Ts, branches, and loose ends are not allowed. Each number indicates exactly how many lines should be drawn around it. Cells that do not have numbers inside can be surrounded by any number of lines. Puzzle Loops games can be found on the Internet (see *sciencesourcebook.com* or search "puzzle loops").

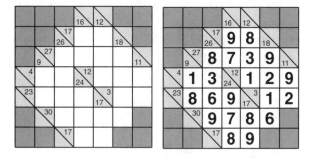

Figure 13.14 Kakuros (Cross-Sums) Game

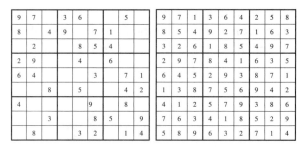

Figure 13.16 Sample Sudoku Puzzle

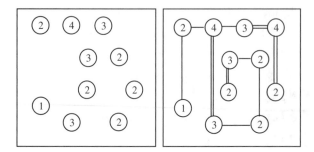

Figure 13.15 Bridges (Hashiwokakero) Logic Game

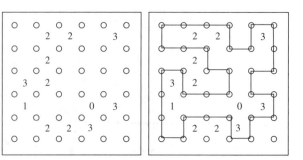

Figure 13.17 Sample Puzzle Loops Game

Part Four

Developing Scientific Problem-Solving Skills

Chapter Fourteen

Science Word Problems

For the Teacher 261

14.1 Translating Common Words into Mathematical Symbols 263

14.2 Translating Natural Language into Algebraic Expressions 264

14.3 Translating Algebraic Expressions into Natural Language 266

Answers to Chapter Activities 268

For the Teacher

"Mathphobia" is a national problem. Negative attitudes toward mathematics hinder learning and may limit students' options in school and the workplace. Many students are dismayed when they learn that science classes require a knowledge of math, and it is not uncommon for teachers to hear students say, "But I thought this was a science class, not a math class!" when word problems are introduced.

Unfortunately many mathphobic students develop a corresponding fear of science when word problems are introduced. Their fears are heightened by well-intentioned teachers who use phrases such as, "It's easy," "The answer is obvious," or "It is intuitively clear," when illustrating the solutions to word problems. To students who find such tasks difficult, such statements only reinforce negative views of their own abilities.

Although word problems may be easy for the teacher and some advanced students, they are not easy for most. It is unfortunate that students develop a dislike for word problems because these problems (also known as story problems) are at the heart of scientific problem solving. In the real world, problems do not show up in symbolic or arithmetic form. Rather, they must be translated from natural language into mathematical symbols to be solved.

Solving word problems is often a complex activity requiring the integration of numerous concepts, facts, and strategies. Unlike symbolic arithmetic problems that are highly standardized and require uniform application of specific algorithms, word problems are highly variable and can often be solved in a variety of ways. Despite this variability, a task analysis of expert problem solvers reveals similarities in their approaches. This chapter introduces a few of these common strategies related to problem translation, and the following chapters discuss a number of additional strategies, including dimensional analysis.

Translation is one of the most difficult aspects of solving word problems, but it is also the most important; without it, no one can use mathematics to solve any real-world problems. In natural language, learners first learn how to recognize terms, then phrases, and finally sentences. In developing mastery of word problems, the approach is similar. Students first learn vocabulary (Chapter One) before they can decode phrases and ultimately make sense of sentences.

The English language is exceedingly complex, and there are many words for the same concept.

Table 14.1 shows words that generally imply specific mathematical operations, and you may wish to provide your students with a copy of this list to assist them in decoding word problems. Context affects the meaning of words, and it is important to understand this when translating word problems. For example, to "take 40 percent of something" means to multiply by 0.40. However, to calculate the percentage of something means to divide a part by the whole and multiply by 100 percent. Similarly, the term *increase* generally implies addition (e.g., the value increased by 5; $x + 5$) but can imply multiplication in other phrases (e.g., the product increased by a factor of

Table 14.1 Terms in Word Problems That Imply Specific Mathematical Operations

+	−	×	÷
add	change in	by	cut
addition	debt	by a factor of	divide
also	decreased by	double[a]	each
and	deduct	fold	half of[a]
combined	delete	multiply	into
exceeds	difference of	of	over
increased by	diminish	percent of[a]	part
including	less	product of	per
increment	lose	quadruple[a]	percent
more	minus	repeat	quarter of[a]
more than	negative	times	quotient of
plus	remove	triple[a]	ratio of
sum	subtract	twice[a]	reciprocal
together	take away	each[a]	separate into
total of	take from		split
with			third of[a]

x^y	?	=	( )
cubed (x^3)[a]	answer	amounts to	all
exponent	how far?	are	distributed over
order of magnitude	how many?	be	grouped
power of	how much?	equals	quantity of
raised to the ...	solution	gives	taken together
scientific notation[a]	to what extent?	is	
square root $(x^{0.5})$[a]	what?	the same as	
squared (x^2)[a]	what value?	was	
	when?	were	
		will be	
		yields	

[a]Indicates a specific form. For example, twice indicates a multiplication by two.

five: 5*x*). When reviewing Table 14.1 with your students, show them that some terms refer to specific types of a particular operation. For example, the inverse of a number is simply the quotient of 1 and that number. You may want to make a large poster of Table 14.1, and place it on the bulletin board for students to reference.

Some students will experience anxiety when exposed to the problems in this part of the book. Remind your students that these exercises focus on aspects of translation and do not require knowledge of the underlying scientific principles. It is beneficial to work through sample problems with your students so that they can see that the strategies they are learning are universal and will be of help whenever they face word problems, particularly when they are unfamiliar with the underlying scientific principles.

14.1 Translating Common Words into Mathematical Symbols

One of the greatest challenges in working with science word problems is translating them into symbolic form. The lists that follow include a variety of words often found in science word problems. Identify each of the terms as addition $(+)$, subtraction $(-)$, multiplication $(\times)$, division $(\div)$, power (x^y), unknown $(?)$, equal $(=)$, or parentheses $(\ )$ by placing the appropriate symbol after the term. Some terms may imply a specific type of the process. For example, *triple* implies "multiplication by three," not just "multiplication." Other terms have different meanings depending on the way in which the sentence is written. For example, if the problem says to "calculate percent," then division of the part by

the whole and multiplication by 100 is implied, while if the problem says to "take the percent of something," then multiplication by a decimal is implied.

Always look at the context when interpreting a word problem, as there is not always a one-to-one correspondence between math words and symbols. The following activities use the most common meaning of the word. Figure 14.1 shows how the Ideal Gas Law can be mapped from natural language to symbolic form. Note how much simpler the symbolic form is than the natural language form.

ACTIVITY 14.1.1 *Translating Words into Mathematics Symbols: Part 1*

Translate each of the following words into its most likely mathematical meaning, and indicate with the appropriate symbol: addition $(+)$, subtraction $(-)$, multiplication $(\times)$, division (4), power (x^y), unknown $(?)$, equal $(=)$, or parentheses $(\ )$.

add	deduct	how far?
addition	delete	how many?
all	difference of	how much?
also	diminish	including
amounts to	distributed over	increased by
and	divide	increment
answer	double	into
are	each	is
be	each	less
by	equals	lose
by a factor of	exceeds	minus
combined	exponent	more
cubed	fold	more than
cut	gives	multiply
debt	grouped	negative
decreased by	half of	of

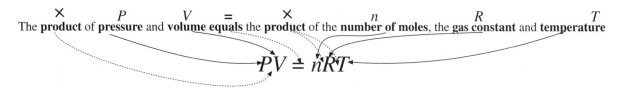

Figure 14.1 Mapping the Ideal Gas Law from Natural Language to Mathematical Symbols

ACTIVITY 14.1.2 *Translating Words into Mathematics Symbols: Part 2*

Translate each of the following words into its most likely mathematical meaning and indicate with the appropriate symbol: addition ($+$), subtraction ($-$), multiplication ($\times$), division (4), power (x^y), unknown (?), equal ($=$), or parentheses ( ).

order of	reciprocal	third of
magnitude	remove	times
over	repeat	to what extent?
part	scientific	together
per	notation	total of
percent	separate into	triple
percent of	solution	twice
plus	split	was
power of	square root	were
product of	squared	what?
quadruple	subtract	when
quantity of	sum	will be
quarter of	take away	with?
quotient of	take from	yields
raised to the	taken together	
ratio of	the same as	

14.2 Translating Natural Language into Algebraic Expressions

Arithmetic is the most basic branch of mathematics, and algebra is a tool used to present arithmetic in a generalized form. Algebra simplifies problem solving by providing a pattern that can be followed for an unlimited number of related arithmetic calculations. For example, the distance that light travels through space in a given period can be represented by the algebraic relationship:

$$d = ct$$

where d = distance, c = speed of light in a vacuum, and t = time.

This relationship holds true regardless of the time period involved. The calculation of specific distances involves substitution of specific values. For example, to calculate the distance light travels

in 60 seconds, we substitute values into the algebraic expression and then perform the arithmetic:

$$c = 3.0 \times 10^8 \text{ m/s (speed of light in a vacuum)}$$
$$t = 60 \text{ s (time)}$$
$$d = ct$$
$$d = ct = \left(3.0 \times 10^8 \text{ m/s}\right) 60 \text{ s} = 1.8 \times 10^{10} \text{ m}$$

We can use the same algebraic expression to solve related arithmetic problems. For example, to determine the distance light will travel in 2 seconds, we substitute the new value for t ($t = 60$ s) into the algebraic expression and again perform the arithmetic.

$$c = 3.0 \times 10^8 \text{ m/s (speed of light in a vacuum)}$$
$$t = 2 \text{ s (time)}$$
$$d = ct$$
$$d = ct = \left(3.0 \times 10^8 \text{ m/s}\right) 10 \text{ s} = 3.0 \times 10^9 \text{ m}$$

Algebra simplifies problem solving by providing general relationships in a simplified manner. For example, the equation

$$d = ct$$

is a simplified way of stating that "the distance light travels in a year is the product of the speed of light in a vacuum and the elapsed time."

Algebra is an indispensable tool for problem solving in science, and although algebraic expressions are simplified expressions of natural language, the process to convert natural language to algebraic expressions is not so simple. Figure 14.2 shows how natural language can be mapped to mathematical symbols. Note how much simpler the symbolic form is. To become a good problem solver, one must learn how to translate verbal descriptions into algebraic expressions.

The following activities provide practice translating phrases into algebraic expressions. The better students become at translating phrases in algebraic expressions, the better they will be at solving word problems. Activity 14.2.1 provides natural language phrases and algebraic expressions.

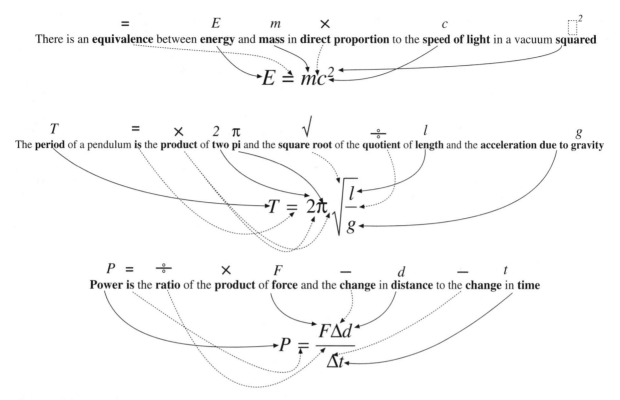

Figure 14.2 Mapping Sentences to Symbolic Equations for Relativity, Pendulums, and Force

ACTIVITY 14.2.1 *Matching Natural Language with Algebraic Expressions: Part 1*
Read the phrase on the left, and then match it with the corresponding algebraic expression on the right. The first expression is given as an example.

Natural Language	Algebraic
1. Sum of five and the mass maps to $5 + m$	$(7 + L)/L$
2. Four less than the unknown	$(d_2 + d_1) - 15$
3. Quotient of 3 and the temperature	$(L_1 \times L_2)^2$
4. Difference of first and second trial times	$(x + y)^{1/3}$
5. Ratio of seven more than the length to the length	$\boxed{5 + m}$
6. Fifteen less than the total of the two distances	$3/T$
7. The square of the product of two lengths	$5h$
8. The cube root of the quantity $x+y$	m/V
9. Ratio of mass to volume	$t_1 - t_2$
10. Height increased by a factor of five	$x - 4$

ACTIVITY 14.2.2 *Matching Natural Language with Algebraic Expressions: Part 2*
Read the phrase on the left, and then match it with the corresponding algebraic expression on the right. The first expression is an example.

Natural Language	Algebraic
1. Difference of area and distance squared maps to a $-d^2$	$(d_2 - d_1)/(t_2 - t_1)$
2. Order of magnitude greater than x^3	$(Fd)^2$
3. Fivefold increase in energy	$1/f$
4. Difference in distances over difference in time	$5E$
5. Pressure is increased by a factor of 7	$7P$
6. Volume per capita	$\boxed{a - d^2}$
7. Half of the mass	$m/2$
8. Power divided by time	i
9. Square of the product of force and distance	V/N
10. Reciprocal of frequency	x^4

ACTIVITY 14.2.3 *Developing Algebraic Expressions from Natural Language*

Figure 14.2 illustrates how algebraic expressions can be developed from natural language descriptions. Develop algebraic expressions for each of the following. You may wish to refer to Table 14.1 to see the correlation between terms and mathematical operations.

1. Work (W) is the product of the force (F) and the distance (d) through which the force is applied.
2. The coefficient of friction (F_c) is equal to the ratio of the force of friction (F_f) to the normal force (F_N).
3. Density (d) is the ratio of mass (m) to volume (V).
4. Force (F) is equal to the product of mass (m) and acceleration (a).
5. The final velocity (v_f) is equal to the sum of the initial velocity (v_i) and the product of acceleration (a) and the difference in time (t).
6. Pressure (P) is the ratio of force (F) to area (A).
7. The ratio of the height (h_i) of an image to the height of its object (h_o) is equal to the ratio of the distance from the lens to the image (d_i) and the distance from the lens to the object (d_o).
8. The change in Gibbs free energy (G) is equal to the change in enthalpy (H) minus the product of the temperature (T) and the change in entropy (S).
9. The force between two point charges (F) is equal to the product of a proportionality constant (k) and the two charges (Q_1, Q_2) divided by the square of the distance (d) between them.
10. The energy of a photon (E_p) is equal to the product of Planck's constant (h) and the frequency (f).

14.3 Translating Algebraic Expressions into Natural Language

The ancient Egyptians wrote in hieroglyphics, pictorial symbols illustrated in the Papyrus of Ani (Figure 14.3). Can you interpret what is written on the papyrus? Well, neither can I! The problem

The Papyrus of Ani - (public domain image)

Figure 14.3 Ancient Egyptian Hieroglyphics

is that we lack an interpreter. Fortunately, there are Egyptologists who have deciphered the ancient code and can translate such writings into English, but I certainly am not one of them!

Unfortunately, many of us look at the equations in a science book and see hieroglyphics! Look at the equations listed below. Perhaps these look as confusing as what is written on the Papyrus of Ani. Fortunately, however, we can learn to interpret such equations and the properties they represent. All of the equations listed below are algebraic expressions involving addition, subtraction, multiplication, division, powers, and/or roots. The problem is that the variable names are not the same as the *a*, *b*, *c* or *x*, *y*, *z* found in traditional algebra books with which you may be familiar.

When given the equation $PV = nRT$, and asked to solve for P, many students are stumped, but if they are given the equation $ab = cde$ and asked to solve for a, they can readily do so. The problem is that most are familiar with the algebraic variable names *a*, *b*, *c*, *d*, and *e*, but not with *P*, *V*, *n*, *R*, and *T*. But although the symbols are different, the principles and operations are the same. Translators are fluent in translating ideas between languages. To be fluent in science requires the ability to translate concepts from natural language into algebraic expressions and translate algebraic expressions into natural language.

This activity focuses on the second skill: translating algebraic expressions into natural language. For example, the equation $d = ct$ (where d is distance, c is the speed of light in a vacuum, and t is time) can be expressed in natural language as follows: *The distance light travels in a vacuum is equal to the product of the speed of light and the elapsed time.*

ACTIVITY 14.3.1 *Translating Algebraic Expressions into Natural Language*

This activity is designed to provide practice translating relationships from algebra to natural language. You need not be familiar with any of the following equations, but you will need to make logical inferences when translating them. Don't panic if these equations are new to you. The algebraic principles are the same even though the scientific principles vary. For each equation, there are two statements in natural language: one is correct, and the other is incorrect. Interpret the algebraic expressions, make logical inferences about variable names, and circle the correct statements. In most instances variable symbols are the first letters of the variables they represent.

1 $a_{av} = \dfrac{v_f - v_i}{t_f - t_i}$

(a) As the difference in velocity between final and initial times increases, acceleration decreases.
(b) Average acceleration is determined by dividing the difference of final and initial velocities by the difference of final and initial times.

2 $E = mc^2$

(a) A little bit of matter represents a huge amount of energy.
(b) As the mass increases, the energy decreases.

3 $T = 2\pi\sqrt{\dfrac{l}{g}}$

(a) The period of a pendulum (T) is independent of the mass of the pendulum.
(b) The period of the pendulum decreases as the length increases.

4 $F = G\dfrac{m_1 m_2}{d^2}$

(a) The force of gravity between two objects is proportional to the product of their masses.
(b) The force of gravity between two objects decreases as the cube of distance between their centers of mass.

5 $E = hf$

(a) The energy of a wave is directly proportional to its frequency.
(b) Energy is an order of magnitude greater than frequency.

6 $p = \dfrac{F\Delta d}{\Delta t}$

(a) Power is equal to the quantity of force and distance divided by time.
(b) Power is the product of force and distance traveled, divided by the change in time.

7 $F\Delta t = m\Delta v$

(a) The force of an impact increases if the mass increases while the change in time and velocity are held constant.
(b) The product of force and time is the same as the quotient of mass and velocity.

8 $V = \dfrac{4}{3}\pi r^3$

(a) If the radius of sphere is tripled, volume increases 27-fold.
(b) The volume of a sphere is the sum of 4/3 and the product of pi times the radius cubed.

9 $d = \dfrac{m}{V}$

(a) Density is independent of volume and mass.
(b) Density is the ratio of mass to volume.

10 $\dfrac{A_{surface}}{V} = \dfrac{4\pi r^2}{\left(\frac{4}{3}\pi r^3\right)}$

(a) The surface area to volume ratio of a sphere is quotient of 3 and the radius.
(b) The surface area to volume ratio of a sphere increases with increasing radius.

11 $\dfrac{R_1}{R_2} = \sqrt{\dfrac{d_2}{d_1}}$

(a) As the density of a gas decreases, so does the rate of diffusion.
(b) As the density of a gas increases, the rate of diffusion decreases.

(continued)

12	$E_p = mgh$	(a) Doubling the height will reduce the potential energy. (b) Potential energy is the product of mass, the acceleration due to gravity and the height.
13	$E_k = \dfrac{1}{2}I\omega^2$	(a) The kinetic energy of a rotating mass is equal to half of the product of its rotational inertia and its squared rotational velocity. (b) Rotational inertia is inversely proportional to kinetic energy.
14	$\beta = 10\log\dfrac{I}{I_0}$	(a) The decibel rating (b) of a sound is independent of its intensity. (b) When the intensity of sound (I) is equal to the intensity of the threshold of human hearing (i), the decibel rating (b) is zero.
15	$PV = nRT_k$	(a) The pressure of an ideal gas is equal to the product of the number of moles, the gas constant (R) and the temperature. (b) In a closed system at constant temperature, the pressure increases as the volume is decreased.
16	$F = k\dfrac{Q_1 Q_2}{d^2}$	(a) The force of attraction between two oppositely charged objects increases as the product of their charges. (b) Electrostatic attraction is independent of the distance between the objects.
17	$R = r_0 N\dfrac{(K - N)}{K}$	(a) The rate of population growth (R) depends on the number of organisms present (N). (b) When the number of organisms (N) reaches the carrying capacity (K), the rate of population growth (R) increases by a factor of r_0.
18	$Q = I^2 Rt$	(a) The heat energy generated in an electric circuit increases proportionate to the cube of the current (I). (b) The amount of heat generated in a circuit is proportional to the square of the current (i).
19	$R_f = \dfrac{d_{pigment}}{d_{solvent}}$	(a) The retention factor in chromatography can be calculated as the quotient of the distance the pigment travels and the distance the solvent travels. (b) The retention factor is zero when the pigment travels the same distance as the solvent.
20	$K_{eq} = \dfrac{[NO][CO_2]}{[NO_2][CO]}$	(a) The equilibrium constant of a reaction is independent of the concentrations of reactants and products. (b) The equilibrium constant is dependent on the concentrations of reactants and products.

Answers to Chapter Activities

14.1.1

add ($+$)	cubed (x^y)	each ($\div$)	increased by ($+$)
addition ($+$)	cut ($\div$)	equals ($=$)	increment ($+$)
all ( )	debt ($-$)	exceeds ($+$)	into ($\div$)
also ($+$)	decreased by ($-$)	exponent (x^y)	is ($=$)
amounts to ($=$)	deduct ($-$)	fold ($\times$)	less ($-$)
and ($+$)	delete ($-$)	gives ($=$)	lose ($-$)
answer (?)	difference of ($-$)	grouped ( )	minus ($-$)
are ($=$)	diminish ($-$)	half of ($\div$)	more ($+$)
be ($=$)	distributed over ( )	how far? (?)	more than ($+$)
by ($\times$)	divide ($\div$)	how many? (?)	multiply ($\times$)
by a factor of ($\times$)	double ($\times$)	how much? (?)	negative ($-$)
combined ($+$)	each ($\times$)s	including ($+$)	of ($\times$)

14.1.2

order of magnitude (x^y)	quarter of ($\div$)	square root (x^y)	together ($+$)
over ($\div$)	quotient of ($\div$)	squared (x^y)	total of ($+$)
part ($\div$)	raised to the (x^y)	subtract ($-$)	triple
per ($\div$)	ratio of ($\div$)	sum ($+$)	twice
percent (4)	reciprocal ($\div$)	take away ($-$)	was ($=$)
percent of ($\times$)	remove ($-$)	take from ($-$)	were ($=$)
plus ($+$)	repeat ($\times$)	taken together ( )	what (?)
power of (x^y)	sci. notation (x^y)	the same as ($=$)	when (?)
product of ($\times$)	separate into (4)	third of (4)	will be ($=$)
quadruple ($\times$)	solution (?)	times ($\times$)	with ($+$)
quantity of ( )	split (4)	to what extent? (?)	yields ($=$)

14.2.1 (1) $5 + m$, (2) $x - 4$, (3) $3/T$, (4) $t_1 - t_2$, (5) $(7 + L)/L$,
   (6) $(d_2 + d_1) - 15$, (7) $(L_1 \times x L_2)^2$, (8) $(x + y)^{1/3}$, (9) m/V,
   (10) $5h$

14.2.2 (1) $a - d^2$, (2) x^4, (3) $5E$, (4) $(d_2 - d_1)/(t_2 - t_1)$, (5) $7P$,
   (6) V/N, (7) $m/2$, (8) P/t, (9) $(Fd)^2$, (10) $1/f$

14.2.3

(1) Work (W) is the product of the force (F) and the distance (d) through which the force is applied.	Work	$W = F\Delta d$
(2) The coefficient of friction (F_c) is equal to the ratio of the force of friction (F_f) to the normal force (F_N).	Coefficient of friction	$F_c = \dfrac{F_f}{F_N}$
(3) Density (d) is the ratio of mass (m) to volume (V).	Density	$d = m / V$
(4) Force (F) is equal to the product of mass (m) and acceleration (a).	Newton's second law	$F = ma$
(5) The final velocity (v_f) is equal to the sum of the initial velocity (v_i) and the product of acceleration (a) and the difference in time (t).	Uniformly accelerated motion	$v_f = v_i + a\Delta t$
(6) Pressure (P) is the ratio of force (F) to area (A).	Pressure	$P = F/A$
(7) The ratio of the height (h_i) of an image to the height of its object (h_o) is equal to the ratio of the distance from the lens to the image (d_i) and the distance from the lens to the object (d_o).	Law of lenses	$\dfrac{h_i}{h_o} = \dfrac{d_i}{d_o}$
(8) The change in Gibbs free energy (G) is equal to the change in enthalpy (H) minus the product of the temperature (T) and the change in entropy (S).	Free energy equation	$\Delta G = \Delta H - T\Delta S$
(9) The force between two point charges (F) is equal to the product of a proportionality constant (k) and the two charges (Q_1, Q_2) divided by the square of the distance (d) between them.	Coulomb's Law of electrostatics	$F = k\dfrac{Q_1 Q_2}{d^2}$
(10) The energy of a photon (E_p) is equal to the product of Planck's constant (h) and the frequency (f).	Energy of a photon	$E_p = hf$

14.3.1 (1) b, (2) a, (3) a, (4) a, (5) a, (6) b, (7) a, (8) a, (9) b,
   (10) a, (11) b, (12) b, (13) a, (14) b, (15) b, (16) a, (17) a,
   (18) b, (19) a, (20) b.

Chapter Fifteen

Geometric Principles in Science

For the Teacher 270

15.1 Developing Measurement Scales 271

15.2 Indirect Measurement in Science 273

15.3 Ratios for Solving Problems in Science 275

15.4 Surface Area to Volume Ratios 277

15.5 Surface Area to Volume Ratios in Living Systems 279

15.6 The Inverse Square Law in the Physical Sciences 283

15.7 Scientific Applications of Conic Sections 287

Answers to Chapter Activities 290

For the Teacher

At most colleges and universities, students can earn a degree in mathematics with few or no science courses. As a result, many mathematics teachers are not prepared to discuss the scientific application of mathematical principles, and their students learn mathematics apart from its scientific applications. To compound the problem, many science teachers avoid using mathematics because of their own insecurities with math or because their students lack sufficient mathematical skills.

If math teachers do not incorporate science problems and science teachers avoid problems requiring math, students will fail to see the relevance of math to science, and vice versa. When students fail to integrate math and science concepts, both their understanding and abilities will be severely limited. We encourage math teachers

to talk about the scientific origins and applications of mathematics, and science teachers to incorporate mathematics as a tool for teaching and understanding science.

The histories of mathematics and science are tightly interwoven. Scientific problems have led to major advances in mathematics, and the development of new techniques in mathematics has led to the foundation of new branches in science. Recent archeological finds have shown that people living as early as 3000 B.C. made use of mathematical rules to survey land, construct buildings, and measure storage containers. In the sixth century B.C., the Greeks gathered and extended this practical knowledge in a subject now known as *geometry*, a word derived from the Greek words *geo* ("Earth") and *metron* ("measure"). Geometry is often taught as an abstract body of knowledge, but it had its origins in the practical measurements

---

270

necessary for commerce. Similarly, other branches of mathematics had their origin in scientific or practical problems. It is helpful to review the history of science and mathematics to illustrate why it is important to teach math with a view toward scientific applications and science with an application of mathematical principles.

Have you ever wondered why there are 360 degrees in a circle rather than 100, or 60 minutes in an hour rather than 10? Wouldn't it be more consistent to have 10 seconds in a minute, 10 minutes in an hour, and 10 hours in a day? We owe our odd measures of direction and time to the ancient Babylonians, who used a base 60 system rather than the base 10 system with which we are familiar. In their early work in astronomy, the Babylonians divided a circle into 360 parts so they could chart celestial bodies and predict the daily positions of the planets. Similarly, ancient Egyptians used geometric principles to calculate the areas of fields, the volumes of granaries, and the numbers of bricks for proposed buildings. These ancient peoples gave us accurate and consistent measurement systems, an essential element in the development of empirical research.

In the sixth century B.C., the Greek mathematicians Thales of Milets and Pythagoras of Sámos developed a system of deductive geometric proofs. Their systems of deductive proof laid the foundation for deductive reasoning, a key tool in scientific problem solving. Using deduction, the early Greek geometer Eratosthenes accurately estimated the circumference of the earth in the third century B.C. Archimedes, another great Greek mathematician and scientist, produced theorems to calculate complex volumes and employed such calculations in his studies on buoyancy. Later the Greek astronomer Hipparchus developed Tables of trigonometric ratios, which he used to determine distances between cities, the circumference of the Earth, and the distance to the Moon.

The seventeenth-century founders of modern science, Copernicus, Kepler, Galileo, and Newton, made huge strides in astronomy and optics as they sought to find mathematical laws in the natural world. To deal with previously insoluble problems in astronomy and motion, Sir Isaac Newton invented calculus, a branch of mathematics that subsequently revolutionized virtually every science by providing tools to deal with rates of change for continuous functions.

More recently mathematician Hermann Minkowski contributed the notion of the space-time continuum, with time as the fourth dimension, a concept essential to the development of Einstein's theory of relativity, and mathematician John von Neumann developed a branch of algebra that has been an invaluable tool in the development of quantum mechanics. Today the new frontiers of science are increasingly dependent on mathematics, and the push for mathematics research is made by scientists who need new tools to solve their problems.

Although all branches of mathematics have application in science, we focus on geometry and trigonometry in this chapter. Both of these fields involve graphic representations that can be used to help visualize and solve real-world problems. Although you may initially encounter resistance from your students as you emphasize mathematical applications in science class, we encourage you to stay the course and show students how math is a tool that simplifies, rather than complicates, science. Mathematical equations and geometric relations are simplified representations of scientific problems, and students who understand this will be better prepared to understand the underlying principles.

15.1 Developing Measurement Scales

On August 10, 1519, the Portuguese navigator Ferdinand Magellan embarked with a fleet of five ships and 230 men with a goal to be the first to sail around the world. Magellan and his crew became the first to sail past the southern tip of South America and the first to cross the Pacific Ocean, but Magellan was later killed by natives in the Philippines. The Basque navigator Viscaya Guetaria assumed leadership, and in September 1522, he returned home with just one ship and only 18 of the original crew. The Magellan/Guetaria voyage was a grueling adventure with significant loss of life, but it opened the way for further exploration, communication, and commerce.

In addition to finally proving that the world was spherical, a notion proposed centuries before by ancient mathematicians and geographers (see section 15.3), the crew charted new lands and seas. Although crude by modern mapmaking standards, the Magellan/Guetaria maps were drawn to scale and thereby allowed later navigators to estimate distances between ports. Today, with the help of satellite-based global positioning systems (GPS), maps are drawn to precise scale, allowing motorists, sailors, pilots, and hikers to accurately calculate distances.

Scientists make use of scales when drawing or interpreting diagrams and photographs. For example, a radiologist may determine the length of a fracture by applying a scale to an X-ray of a bone, and a geneticist may determine the distance between two genes by applying a scale to the chromosome. In the following activities, students asked to develop scales to determine distances.

ACTIVITY 15.1.1 *Developing Measurement Scales*

The map provided in Figure 15.1A shows a hypothetical lunar landing site and four experimental research sites. Table 15.1 includes only the distance between the landing site (1) and a research site (2). Use this information to develop a scale for the map by dividing the real distance (measured in kilometers) by the map distance (measured in millimeters). This ratio is your scale. Include this value in Table 15.1, and use it to estimate the distance between the research station (point 1) and the other research sites (points 3, 4, and 5).

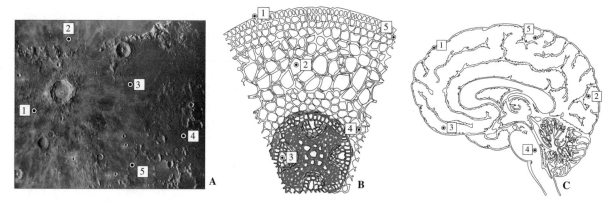

Figure 15.1 Developing Scales of Measurement for (A) the Moon, (B) a Dicot Stem, and (C) the Brain
NASA. (1973). Surface of the moon. Retrieved June 11, 2007, from http://nix.nasa.gov.

Table 15.1 Determining Distances with Measurement Scales

	Moon		Plant Stem (xs)		Brain (ls)	
	Scale 1 mm = ____ km		Scale 1 mm = ____ mm		Scale 1 mm = ____ mm	
	Map Distance	**Actual Distance**	**Map Distance**	**Actual Distance**	**Map Distance**	**Actual Distance**
1→2		15 km		2 mm		130 mm
1→3						
1→4						
1→5						

Develop scales for plant tissue (Figure 15.1B) and the brain (Figure 15.1C), and use these scales to estimate the distances to points 2, 3, 4, and 5.

15.2 Indirect Measurement in Science

A science almanac states that the average distance to the Sun is 1.50×10^{11} m, while the distance between hydrogen and oxygen atoms in a water molecule is only 9.6×10^{-11} m. How can such distances be measured? There is no tape long enough to measure astronomical distances or any scale precise enough to measure bond lengths. Although it *is* impossible to directly measure such distances, it *is* possible to determine them indirectly by comparing them with distances that can be measured. For example, if a skyscraper casts a shadow 50 times as far as an adjacent house of known height, we can assume that it is 50 times as tall, even though we have not made a direct measurement of its height. Scientists determine many values indirectly.

ACTIVITY 15.2.1 *Direct and Indirect Measurements*

The following is a list of unusual facts, some of which were determined by direct measurement and others by indirect measurement. Identify those that must have been made indirectly because they could not have been measured directly.

1. The average surface temperature of Mars is 210 K.
2. The wingspan of a Boeing 747-400 jetliner (231.85 ft) is greater than the distance of the Wright brother's first flight (120 ft).
3. Bamboo can grow up to 36 in. in a day.
4. A flea can jump 350 times its own body length.
5. The length of a carbon-aluminum bond is double the distance of a carbon-hydrogen bond.
6. Fingernails grow nearly four times faster than toenails.
7. Rain falls at 11 km per hour (7 mph).
8. The oldest living plants, bristlecone pines, are approximately 4600 years old.
9. Beans and pepper were cultivated in Peru starting about 6000 B.C.
10. The Sun is composed of 91.2 percent hydrogen, 8.7 percent helium, and 0.1 percent other elements.
11. The mass of the Moon is 7×10^{22} kg.
12. The highest recorded "sneeze speed" is 165 km per hour.
13. The surface temperature of Pluto is 40 K.
14. In 2000, Americans ate an average of 18 acres of pizza every day.
15. An ant can survive up to 2 days underwater.

ACTIVITY 15.2.2 *Determining the Diameter of the Moon by Indirect Measurement*

Astronomers have estimated the average distance from the surface of the Earth to the Moon to be 385,000 km. Given this value, we can calculate its diameter. With a partner, take turns holding a washer of any size at arm's length (Figure 15.2). Sight the Moon with one eye, keeping the other closed, such that the Moon is visible in the center of the washer hole. Slowly bring the washer closer until the Moon's circular surface appears to just touch the inside rim of the washer. Your partner should measure the distance between the washer and your eye. The triangle formed by the diameter of the Moon and the distance to the Moon is a similar triangle to that formed by the diameter of the washer hole and the distance to the washer hole so that the following ratio holds:

$$\frac{diameter\ of\ Moon}{distance\ to\ Moon} = \frac{diameter\ of\ washer\ hole}{distance\ from\ eye\ to\ washer}$$

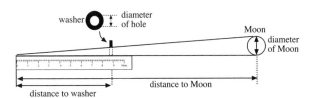

Figure 15.2 Estimating the Diameter of the Moon

Once you have made these measurements, convert them to kilometers (100,000 cm = 1 km), and calculate the diameter of the Moon:

$$diameter\,of\,Moon =$$
$$(385{,}000\,km) \times \frac{diameter\,of\,washer\,hole}{distance\,from\,eye\,to\,washer}$$

According to your calculations, what is the diameter of the Moon? Look up the accepted value and determine the percent error between your calculated value (observed) and the accepted value. Percent error is defined as:

$$percent\,error = \frac{(observed - accepted)}{accepted} \times 100\%$$

ACTIVITY 15.2.3 *Determining Height by Indirect Measurement*

The tallest mountain in the world is Mount Everest in the Himalayas of Nepal (8849 m). Mount Everest was determined to be the highest point on Earth in 1856 by a British survey team and was named in honor of the man who had led the survey team from 1830 to 1843. The British survey team never climbed Everest but determined its height indirectly using ratios and other mathematics principles.

In this activity, you will employ some of the same principles to determine the height of a tall tree (you can do this same activity with a building or other structure). Place a rod in the soil such that the shadow cast by the rod falls to the same point as the shadow cast by the tall object (Figure 15.3). Measure the height of the rod, the length of the rod's shadow, and the length of the tree or building's shadow. The triangle formed by the tree or building and its shadow is similar to the triangle formed by the rod and its shadow. In other words, the ratio of the tree (or building) height to the length of its shadow is identical to the ratio of the rod's height to the length of the rod's shadow. Stated in equation form:

$$\frac{height\,of\,tree}{length\,of\,tree\,shadow} = \frac{height\,of\,rod}{length\,of\,rod\,shadow}$$

Solving for the unknown height of the tree, we have:

$$height\,of\,tree = (length\,of\,tree\,shadow)$$
$$\times \frac{height\,of\,rod}{length\,of\,rod\,shadow}$$

According to your calculations, what is the height of the tree (or building)?

ACTIVITY 15.2.4 *Determining the Thickness of a Sheet of Paper*

The preceding activities used ratios to measure objects too large to measure directly. In this activity, you will use indirect measurement to measure things too small to measure directly (Figure 15.4). The thickness of a piece of paper is too small to measure with a ruler, but it can be determined indirectly.

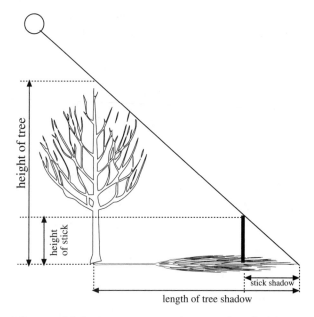

Figure 15.3 Determining the Height of a Tree

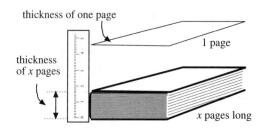

Figure 15.4 Determining the Thickness of a Page

Open a book, and determine the number of pages by adding the numbered pages with the introductory and closing pages. Determine the number of sheets by dividing by two (there are generally two pages, front and back, per sheet). Close the book, and measure the thickness from the first sheet to the last sheet. Divide this distance by the number of sheets to determine the thickness of a sheet of paper:

$$thickness\,of\,a\,sheet = \frac{thickness\,of\,all\,sheets}{number\,of\,sheets}$$

15.3 Ratios for Solving Problems in Science

Mathematics has been an essential tool to scientists throughout the ages. In 240 B.C. the Greek mathematician, geographer, and astronomer Eratosthenes became the first to accurately estimate the circumference of the Earth. Obviously Eratosthenes could not directly measure the Earth's circumference, so he used some basic mathematics principles to arrive at a reasonable estimate.

Eratosthenes knew that the summer solstice (June 20–21) is the longest day of the year. He noted that at noon on this day, the Sun cast no shadows in the city of Syene, Egypt. On another summer solstice, Eratosthenes noticed that the Sun cast a shadow of 7.2 degrees in Alexandria, a city 800 km (497 mi) north of Syene. He reasoned that the difference in the angles of the shadows was a result of a difference in the positions of the two cities on the surface of a spherical earth (Figure 15.5) and that a 7.2 degree difference indicated that Alexandria was 7.2 degrees (out of a 360 degree circle) north of Syene. Eratosthenes concluded that the distance from Syene to Alexandria represented 2 percent (7.2°/360°) of the circumference of the Earth. He then set up the following ratio to determine the Earth's circumference:

$$\frac{angle\,around\,Earth}{angle\,between\,cities} = \frac{360°}{7.2°}$$

$$= 50$$

$$= \frac{circumference\,of\,Earth}{distance\,between\,cities}$$

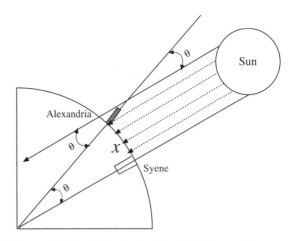

Figure 15.5 Calculating Earth's Circumference

$$\therefore \frac{circumference}{of\,Earth} = 50\,(distance\,between\,cities)$$

$$= 50\,(800\,km) = 40,000\,km$$

ACTIVITY 15.3.1 *Calculating the Circumference of the Earth*

In this activity, you will calculate the circumference of the Earth using Eratosthenes' technique. This is best done on either the winter or summer solstices (December 21–22, June 20–21) or the spring or fall equinoxes (March 20–21 or September 22–23). The Earth is tilted 23.5 degrees, and on the winter equinox it is positioned such that the Sun is at its lowest point above the horizon as viewed from northern latitudes, but directly overhead when viewed form the Tropic of Capricorn, an imaginary line around the globe at 23.5 degrees south latitude (Figure 15.6). On June 21, the Earth is positioned so that the Sun appears directly overhead at noon along the Tropic of Cancer, an imaginary band circling the Earth at 23.5 degrees north latitude. On the fall and spring equinoxes, the Sun appears directly overhead at noon along the equator.

This activity should be performed at noon on or close to one of the equinoxes or solstices. Data for a few major cities appear in Table 15.2, and data for hundreds more can be found online at sciencesourcebook.org.

Pound a pole into the ground, and check to make sure it is vertical using a carpenter's level. At solar noon on the selected day (when the shadow points directly north), record the length of the

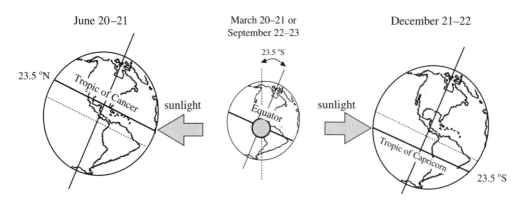

June 20–21

March 20–21 or
September 22–23

December 21–22

Figure 15.6 Where the Sun Is Directly Overhead on the Solstices and Equinoxes

Table 15.2 Distance (km) North of Key Latitude (Tropics of Capricorn or Cancer, and Equator) on Winter (W) and Summer (Su) Solstices, and the Spring and Fall Equinoxes (S, F)

	°N	°W	W	Su	S,F
Fairbanks, AK	64.8	147.9	4592	9815	7203
Phoenix, AZ	33.4	112.0	1104	6327	3716
Los Angeles, CA	33.9	118.4	1159	6383	3771
San Francisco, CA	37.6	122.4	1569	6792	4180
Denver, CO	39.8	104.9	1806	7029	4418
Washington, DC	38.9	77.0	1706	6929	4318
Miami, FL	25.8	80.3	256	5479	2867
Atlanta, GA	33.7	84.4	1128	6351	3740
Honolulu, HI	21.3	157.9	−241	4982	2371
Chicago, IL	42.0	87.9	2054	7277	4666
Lexington, KY	38.0	84.6	1615	6838	4227
Boston, MA	42.4	71.0	2097	7320	4708
Minneapolis, MN	44.9	93.2	2376	7600	4988
St. Louis, MO	38.8	90.4	1695	6918	4306
Helena, MT	46.6	112.0	2567	7790	5179
New York, NY	40.8	74.0	1921	7144	4532
Raleigh, NC	35.9	78.8	1374	6598	3986
Cleveland, OH	41.4	81.9	1989	7213	4601
Portland, OR	45.6	122.6	2456	7679	5068
Pittsburgh, PA	40.5	80.2	1889	7113	4501
Memphis, TN	35.1	90.0	1284	6507	3895
Dallas, TX	32.9	96.9	1039	6262	3651
Houston, TX	30.0	95.4	719	5942	3330
Seattle, WA	47.7	122.3	2684	7907	5296

shadow and the length of the pole, and calculate the angle of the shadow by taking arc tangent $(\tan^{-1})$ of the ratio of these values (Figure 15.7):

$$\tan^{-1}\left(\frac{length\,of\,shadow}{length\,of\,pole}\right) = shadow\,angle$$

Determine the distance to the key latitude for the day on which you make your measurements. The key latitude is the position where the Sun appears directly overhead at noon. The Sun is overhead at noon along the Tropic of Cancer (23.5° N) on the summer solstice (June 21),

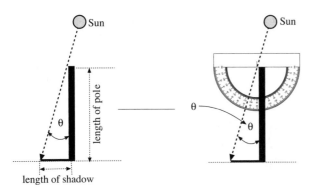

Figure 15.7 Determining the Angle of the Shadow of the Sun

Tropic of Capricorn (23.5° S) on the winter solstice (December 21), and on the equator (0°) for the equinoxes (March 21 and September 21). The ratio of the angle of the shadow to the full angle of the Earth (360 degrees) is proportional to the ratio of the distance to the key latitude compared to the circumference of the Earth:

$$\left(\frac{shadow\ angle}{360°}\right) = \left(\frac{distance\ to\ key\ latitude}{circumference\ of\ Earth}\right)$$

We can calculate the circumference of the Earth:

$$circumference\ of\ Earth = \left(\frac{360°}{shadow\ angle}\right) \\ \times distance\ to\ key\ latitude$$

The accepted value for the circumference of the Earth is 40,008 km. Calculate the percentage error in your calculations using the following formula:

$$\substack{percentage \\ error} = \left(\frac{(observed - accepted)}{accepted}\right) \times 100\%$$

$$\substack{percentage \\ error} = \left(\frac{\left(\dfrac{calculated}{circumference} - 40{,}008\ km\right)}{40{,}008\ km}\right) \\ \times 100\%$$

15.4 Surface Area to Volume Ratios

Humans can survive up to 40 days without food, 3 to 5 days without water, but only 4 to 6 minutes without oxygen. Plants produce the food and oxygen we need through a process known as *photosynthesis*. Approximately one-third of the world's oxygen production comes from microscopic algae known as phytoplankton that live in the surface waters of the world's oceans. These phytoplankton must be near the surface, where light intensity is great enough for photosynthesis to occur. Ironically, phytoplankton are considerably denser than water, so what keeps these tiny plants near the surface where they can capture light and produce the oxygen we breathe?

The force of gravity is proportional to an object's mass ($F = mg$), while drag (resistance to sinking) is proportional to its surface area. Given constant density, the mass of an object is directly proportional to its volume. If an object has a low surface area to volume ratio, then the force of gravity acting on it may exceed the drag, causing it to sink. If, however, the surface area to volume ratio is high, the forces may balance, preventing sinking.

Phytoplankton remain suspended in the upper layers of the ocean because they have very high surface area to volume ratios. Figure 15.8 shows that most have projections that dramatically increase surface area. Would phytoplankton stay suspended or sink if they were scaled up in

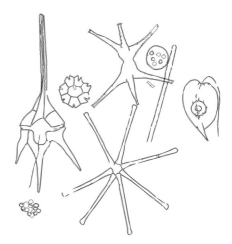

Figure 15.8 Phytoplankton

size? In other words, would they stay suspended if they were macroscopic (large enough to be seen without a microscope)?

In this activity, you will investigate how the surface area to volume ratio of an object changes as a function of its size and why the small size of plankton is important to their survival, and to ours! Phytoplankton have diverse and complex shapes, which makes calculations of surface area and volume difficult, so to simplify matters, we will investigate the relationship between surface area and volume using simpler shapes: cubes and spheres.

ACTIVITY 15.4.1 *Surface Area to Volume Ratios in Cubes and Spheres*

How does a change in the linear dimension of a cube affect its surface area and volume? Using sugar cubes, construct the series of composite cubes shown in Figure 15.9. For each cube constructed, measure the length of a side, compute the surface area and the volume, and write your answers in a data table such as illustrated in Table 15.3. In addition, determine the mass of each object using a scale or balance. You may wish to stack the cubes directly on the balance, or glue them together with white glue and place them on the balance when you are done.

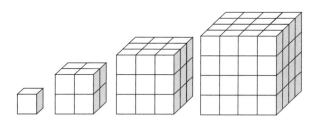

Figure 15.9 Surface Area to Volume Ratio of Cubes

Table 15.4 Geometric Ratios of a Sphere

Radius (r)	Surface Area ($4\pi r^2$)	Volume ($4/3\ \pi r^3$)	radius volume	surface area mass
cm	cm^2	cm^3	cm^{-2}	cm^{-1}
cm	cm^2	cm^3	cm^{-2}	cm^{-1}
cm	cm^2	cm^3	cm^{-2}	cm^{-1}
cm	cm^2	cm^3	cm^{-2}	cm^{-1}

Use your measurements and calculations to compute the ratios of length to volume, mass to volume, and surface area to volume. Prepare separate plots of the following (1) length/volume versus length, (2) surface area/mass versus length, and (3) surface area/volume versus length.

Although it is easy to directly measure the dimensions of a cube, it is not so easy to directly measure the dimensions of a sphere, much less irregular shapes such as phytoplankton. In the natural world, many things, such as water droplets and soap bubbles, assume a spherical shape. To see if the relationships between surface area and volume hold true for spheres, perform the calculations specified in Table 15.4.

1. As a cube increases in size, does the ratio of surface area to volume increase or decrease?
2. As the cube grows larger, does the ratio of surface area to mass increase or decrease?
3. Do these relationships hold true for spheres as well? Explain your answer.
4. Phytoplankton are very small and often contain numerous spines (Figure 15.8). Explain how these features help keep them near the surface, where they can receive sufficient light to conduct photosynthesis.

Table 15.3 Geometric Ratios of a Cube, Where L = Length of One Side of a Cube

length of edge (L)	surface area ($6L^2$)	volume (L^3)	mass	length volume	surface area mass	surface area volume
cm	cm^2	cm^3	g	cm^{-2}	cm^3/g	cm^{-1}
cm	cm^2	cm^3	g	cm^{-2}	cm^3/g	cm^{-1}
cm	cm^2	cm^3	g	cm^{-2}	cm^3/g	cm^{-1}
cm	cm^2	cm^3	g	cm^{-2}	cm^3/g	cm^{-1}

5. In animals, heat production is proportional to mass, while heat loss is proportional to surface area. If all other factors are equal, will a baby or an adult be more susceptible to getting chilled?

6. If the amount of heat lost through the skin of an animal is directly proportional to its surface area, what might you conclude about the relative heat loss of a very small animal compared to a very large animal? Which size animal would find it easier to keep warm in the winter, and which animal would find it easier to keep cool in the summer?

15.5 Surface Area to Volume Ratios in Living Systems

The idea of giants and dwarfs has fascinated authors and moviemakers through the years. In 1726, the British author Jonathan Swift wrote his classic work, *Gulliver's Travels*. Although written as a political satire, the book became enshrined in adolescent literature for its fanciful depictions of a man held hostage by people only 6 in. (15 cm) tall. In 1865, Lewis Carroll wrote *Alice in Wonderland*, an imaginative children's story in which a little girl grew to gigantic size and then shrank to a fraction of her original height after following a white rabbit into a dreamlike world. In 1933, RKO Radio Pictures released *King Kong*, the classic tale of a giant gorilla that terrorized New York City. The theme of abnormally large and small creatures has continued to be popular in books and movies. Giants and dwarfs make great science fiction, but a look at the principles of geometry and their applications to science shows why such stories can indeed be science *fiction*.

Movie aficionados estimate that the giant ape in the original King Kong movie was 150 ft tall, and therefore a 30 times enlargement of a standard 5 ft tall ape. Could such a gigantic creature stand on its feet or cling to a skyscraper? A geometric analysis will help in the investigation. The strengths of animal bones are proportional to their cross-sectional areas. If King Kong were a 30 times

enlargement of an ape, then the cross-sectional radii of his bones would have been 30 times larger and their cross-sectional areas 900 times greater ($A = \pi r^2$). Since strength is proportional to cross-sectional area, the bones of King Kong would have been approximately 900 times stronger than those of the standard ape. Although the strength of King Kong's bones would have been proportional to the cross-sectional area of his bones, his body weight would have been proportional to his volume. In Activity 15.4.1 we learned that the volume of a sphere increases as the cube of its radius ($v = (4/3)\pi r^3$) and the volume of a cube increases as the cube of its length ($v = l^3$).

Although the shape of an ape is more complex than a sphere or cube, its body volume also increases as approximately the cube of its linear dimensions. If an ape is scaled up 30 times to the height of King Kong, then its volume is scaled up as a function of the cube of his height ($30^3 = 27,000\times$). Thus, although King Kong's bones would have been approximately 900 times stronger than a standard ape's bones, his volume, and thus his mass, would have been nearly 27,000 times greater! By scaling an ape up 30 times to King Kong's size, the strength to weight ratio decreases to only 3 percent of its original value ($900/27,000 = 0.03$). As a result, King Kong's bones would have collapsed under his massive weight, and he could never have walked, much less climbed, the Empire State Building.

You might wonder how a tiger can support its weight since it appears to be a scaled-up version of a house cat. (The apparent similarity between house cats and tigers has led to "Tiger" being the most popular name given to house cats.) If you compare the dimensions of tigers with house cats, you will notice that tigers are not a scaled-up model of house cats. The leg bones of tigers are proportionately wider than what would be expected by simply scaling up. Tigers must have proportionately wider bones than house cats in order to support their disproportionately greater weight. Moviemakers generally don't take these principles into account when creating movies. For example, the gigantic spider in the movie classic *The Lord of the Rings* appears thousands of times the size of a normal spider but could never survive in the real world because its legs would be crushed under its own weight. The cross-sectional area of its legs would be insufficient to support its enormous weight.

Surface area to volume ratio is indeed one of the most important geometric principles in science. Many biological functions are determined or regulated by surface area and others by volume, so the surface area to volume ratio often dictates what an organism can and can't do. One of the first biologists to examine the importance of size and surface area to volume ratio was J.B.S. Haldane, who in 1928 published an often quoted essay, "On Being the Right Size."[1] In this essay, Haldane discussed the importance of size:

> To the mouse and any smaller animal it [gravity] presents practically no dangers. You can drop a mouse down a thousand-yard mine shaft; and, on arriving at the bottom, it gets a slight shock and walks away, provided that the ground is fairly soft. A rat is killed, a man is broken, a horse splashes. For the resistance presented to movement by the air is proportional to the surface of the moving object. Divide an animal's length, breadth, and height each by ten; its weight is reduced to a thousandth, but its surface only to a hundredth. So the resistance to falling in the case of the small animal is relatively ten times greater than the driving force.

> An insect, therefore, is not afraid of gravity; it can fall without danger, and can cling to the ceiling with remarkably little trouble. It can go in for elegant and fantastic forms of support like that of the daddy-longlegs. But there is a force which is as formidable to an insect as gravitation to a mammal. This is surface tension. A man coming out of a bath carries with him a film of water of about one-fiftieth of an inch in thickness. This weighs roughly a pound. A wet mouse has to carry about its own weight of water. A wet fly has to lift many times its own weight and, as everyone knows, a fly once wetted by water or any other liquid is in a very serious position indeed. An insect going for a drink is in as great danger as a man

leaning out over a precipice in search of food. If it once falls into the grip of the surface tension of the water—that is to say, gets wet—it is likely to remain so until it drowns. A few insects, such as water-beetles, contrive to be unwettable; the majority keep well away from their drink by means of a long proboscis.

Consider another issue relating to scale. "Warm-blooded" animals lose heat primarily through their external surfaces, and it can be shown that the rate of heat loss is proportional to surface area, all other factors being constant. Since food provides the energy necessary for an animal to keep warm and mobile, food requirements for heat balance are proportional to surface area. Consequently, smaller animals, with their greater surface area to weight ratios, require proportionally more food to survive. The Lilliputians in *Gulliver's Travels* are approximately one-tenth the height of Gulliver and would therefore require a volume of food approximately 1/100 as great as Gulliver, even though they have only 1/1000 his weight. Hence, proportionate to their body size, the Lilliputians would have to eat 10 times as much food as Gulliver. To do this, the Lilliputians would spend much of their time eating, which is what hummingbirds and other small warm-blooded animals do.

The most significant thing about scaling up or down in size is the resulting change in the ratios between length, area, and volume. If a cubic object doubles in length (l) its area (l^2) quadruples and its volume (l^3) increases by a factor of 8. This has a host of effects on living and nonliving systems, one of which is heat transfer. If a person were to be scaled up two times so his or her new height, h, was two times as great as the original, his or her surface area would increase by a factor of 4 ($h^2 = 4$), while his or her volume would increase by a factor of 8 ($h^3 = 8$). Features dependent on surface area, such as heat transfer, would increase by a factor of approximately 4, while factors dependent on volume, such as heat production, would increase by a factor of approximately 8. Thus, the person who was scaled up two times would generate heat faster than he or she could release it and would probably overheat. By contrast, if a person is scaled down to one-half his or her original size ($h = 1/2$), his or her surface area would decrease to one-fourth ($h^2 = 1/4$) while his or her volume and mass would decrease to one-eighth ($h^3 = 1/8$) of the original values. Although such a person would lose heat only one-fourth as fast, he or she would produce it only one-eighth as fast and therefore would get cold faster. (Young animals are not scale models of older animals, and shorter people are not scale models of taller people. When we refer to scaling, we refer to multiplying all dimensions by the same factor, which is not what occurs during normal growth and development.)

ACTIVITY 15.5.1 *Characteristics of Large and Small Animals*

Although large animals are not scale models of small ones, there is a tendency for larger animals to have a small surface area to volume ratio and small animals to have a large surface area to volume ratio. Examine each of the statements in Table 15.5, and determine if it is a characteristic of large (L) or small (S) animals.

ACTIVITY 15.5.2 *Calculating Your Personal Surface Area to Volume Ratio*

What is your personal surface area to volume ratio? How does it compare to classmates who are taller or shorter than you? Although it is difficult to directly measure the surface area or the volume of a human body, it is relatively easy to estimate. The surface area of your body is roughly 100 times as great as the surface area of your handprint.

Measure the surface area of your hand by drawing an outline on a sheet of graph paper and counting the number of cells covered by your hand, not including your wrist (Figure 15.10A). Multiply this number by the area of a single square to estimate the surface area of your hand, then by 100 to obtain a rough estimate of the surface area of your body. A more accurate estimate of your surface area can be derived from the nomograph in Figure 15.10B, or by solving for *SA* in the formula: $lnSA = a_0 + a_1 lnH + na_2 lnW$, in which $a_0 = -3751$, $a_1 = 0422$, and $a_2 = 0515$ if height (*H*) is

Table 15.5 Identify as a Characteristic of Large (L) or Small (S) Animals

1   Gravity is frequently a dangerous force.
2   Electrostatic charge can be a dangerous force.
3   Getting wet can be dangerous because proportionately greater weight is carried.
4   The heart has to service proportionately more body mass, so it must work harder.
5   It is difficult to do a somersault.
6   Keeping cool is a bigger problem than keeping warm.
7   They may "shut down" when they can't stay warm.
8   They can jump proportionately farther and move proportionately faster.
9   They can live in colder climates because they hold their heat better.
10 They can run up trees and may hang on glass or from a smooth ceiling.
11 They can take a water bath to cool off.
12 They carry proportionately less weight and lose proportionately more body heat.
13 They have proportionately little water reserve.
14 They lose heat quickly, so they have to eat frequently to stay warm.
15 They must actively move air inside, and oxygen to all cells.
16 They pant or sweat to lose excess water.
17 Surface absorption is a major source of oxygen.

measured in centimeters, weight (*W*) in kilograms, and surface area in square meters.[2]

Express the surface area of your body in square centimeters (cm²). To estimate your body volume, first obtain your weight in pounds and convert to kilograms by multiplying by 0.454 kilograms per pound. One kilogram of water has a volume of 1 L, but the body is denser than water due to bones and various other dense tissues. To determine the volume of your body, multiply its mass in kilograms by 0.9 L per kilogram. Now calculate the surface area to volume ratio (cm²/L) of your body. Plot surface area to volume ratios as a function of height for the members of your class. Plot student heights on the *x*-axis, and the corresponding surface area to volume ratios on the *y*-axis. Is there a general relationship between height and surface area to volume ratio? Explain your answer.

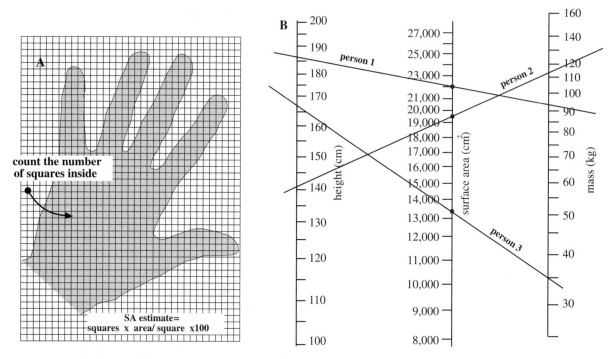

Figure 15.10 Estimating the Surface Area of the Body from (A) Hand Area and (B) a Nomograph

ACTIVITY 15.5.3 *Surface Area to Volume Ratio in Real Life*

The surface area to volume ratio of an organism or object has a profound influence on what it interacts with in its environment. For example, the world's largest animal, the blue whale, can attain a length of 110 ft and live comfortably in the ocean. If such a whale were to be beached, its ribs would likely collapse under its immense weight. As the world's largest animal, the blue whale has an extremely low surface area to volume ratio. The strength of its bones (proportional to the cross-sectional area of its bones) is not great enough to support its mass (proportional to its volume) once it is no longer supported by water.

The surface area to volume ratio also affects the way freshly baked cookies cool. You may have noticed that smaller cookies cool much faster than larger ones. Small cookies have a much higher surface area to volume ratio than do large cookies. Since the rate of heat loss is proportional to the surface area of the cookie while its heat content is proportional to its mass, and consequently its volume, a small-scale cookie cools much faster than

a large-scale one. Use similar logic to explain the following phenomena. Include in your explanations the role of surface area and volume as well as the processes, which are listed in italics.

1. A hot car in the summer time is more dangerous for infants than adults. (*cooling by sweating, dehydration*)
2. It is proportionately less expensive per item in inventory to build a superstore or warehouse store than it is to build a small store. (*cost of construction, value of store contents*)
3. Larger organisms are made of many small cells rather than a few large cells. (*diffusion of nutrients, need for nutrients*)
4. Powdered sugar dissolves faster than an equal mass in the form of a sugar cube. (*solubility*)
5. Elephants have proportionately much larger ears than mice, and this prevents overheating. (*heat loss*)
6. Microvilli are small finger-like convolutions in the walls of cells. They are found lining the small intestines. (*nutrient absorption, water absorption*)

7. Larger organisms have respiratory systems, while smaller organisms such as protozoans and insects rely on diffusion. (*oxygen absorption, oxygen demand*)

8. Cacti are less likely to overheat in hot desert climates than plants with traditional leaves. (*heat absorption, changes in temperature*)

9. Some very small mammals eat more than three times their body weight each day. (*heat loss*)

10. Small animals such as insects can walk up walls and across ceilings with ease, while larger animals cannot. (*gravity, mass*)

11. Crushed ice melts faster than block ice. (*heat exchange*)

15.6 The Inverse Square Law in the Physical Sciences

Imagine what life would be like without electricity. No lights, no dishwashers, no hair dryers, no toasters, no air conditioning, no computers, no power tools, no electric motors, and so on. Although we are indebted to many scientists and engineers for the luxuries that electricity provides, we are particularly indebted to Danish scientist Hans Christian Ørsted, who in 1820 showed that an electric current could deflect a magnetic needle. This simple observation showed that electricity and magnetism are related and opened the door for studies that led to the development of the electrical generator (a device that converts mechanical energy into electrical energy by electromagnetic means) and the electric motor (a device that converts electrical energy into mechanical energy by electromagnetic means). Without generators we would have no electricity in our homes or business (except for battery driven devices), and without electric motors we would have few electrically powered machines.

Although Ørsted's experiments showed that electricity and magnetism are related phenomena, he was not the first to suggest this relationship. Others had suspected this because magnetic poles, like electric charges, attract and repel with a force that is dependent on the inverse square of the distance between them. Scientists reasoned that this inverse square relationship was based on a fundamental relationship of the forces, and by the mid-nineteenth century, James Clerk Maxwell and others developed the field theory of electromagnetism. In the early part of the twentieth century, Albert Einstein developed the field theory of gravitation and attempted to construct a unified field theory in which electromagnetism and gravity would emerge as different aspects of a single fundamental field. Although physicists have failed to demonstrate a unified field, many are still interested because of the similarities shared by gravity and electromagnetism.

Just as electricity and magnetism display an inverse square relationship in the strength of forces, so gravity falls off as an inverse square of the distance between two objects. The inverse square relationship, which electricity, gravity, and magnetism demonstrate, has emerged as one of the most important principles of physics, and one that is based primarily on geometry. A basic understanding of geometry helps in understanding the influence of distance on electric force, magnetic force, gravitational forces, light intensity, sound intensity, radiation intensity, and others. Although different in many ways, all of these phenomena share a common geometric principle: they generate a field or a wave front in all directions, and the intensity of this field or wave diminishes as it spreads out over more and more area.

Imagine throwing a rock into a glassy-smooth pond. Waves emanate in all directions from the point where the rock hits the surface of the pond. As a wave moves from the point of impact, the same energy is spread over an increasingly large area. Initially the waves are tall, but as the waves get farther from the source, they get longer but shorter. What is true of the water wave along the surface of the pond is similar to what happens to any point source that spreads its influence equally in all directions. Although the water waves are confined to the surface of the water, point sources, such as gravitational force, electric field, light, sound, and radiation, display a similar attenuation with distance. Some simple geometry will help in understanding the interconnectedness of these phenomena.

Figure 15.11A shows a point source (of light or sound, for example) at *S*. The energy from this point source radiates out as a sphere. The energy that was initially concentrated at *S* is now spread over the surface of a spherical shape. To determine the intensity of the energy at this time, we need to divide the total energy by the surface area of the sphere to which it is now distributed. Since the surface area of a sphere can be calculated as $A = 4\pi r^2$, the intensity at any point can be calculated as $I_{1r} = \dfrac{S}{4\pi r^2}$. As the energy continues to radiate, the intensity will decrease as a function of the inverse square ($1/r^2$) of the radius, even though the amount of energy (*S*) remains constant. Figure 15.11B shows that if the intensity of the energy at $r = 1$ is defined as I_{1r}, then the intensity at $r = 2$ will be $I_{2r} = \dfrac{1}{4}I_{1r}$, and the intensity at $r = 3$ will be $I_{3r} = \dfrac{1}{9}I_1$. The intensity falls off as

the inverse square of the distance from the source simply because the spherical front on which it resides increases as a function of the surface area.

The intensity of anything that radiates uniformly from a point source will consequently decrease as a function of the inverse square of the distance from the source. If the distance doubles, the total energy remains constant, but is spread over four times as much space, and consequently the energy is only one fourth as intense. Understanding the basic geometry of a sphere, we can predict that the intensity of anything that radiates from a point sphere will consequently decrease as the inverse square of the distance from the point source.

Since it is purely geometric in its origin, the inverse square law applies to diverse phenomena. Point sources of gravitational force, electric field, light, sound, or radiation obey the inverse square law (Figure 15.12).

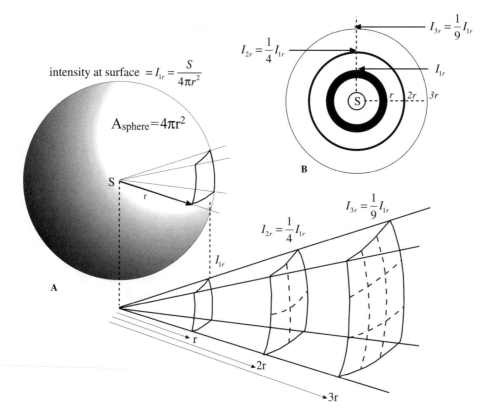

Figure 15.11 (A) Inverse Square Law and (B) Its Effect on Intensity

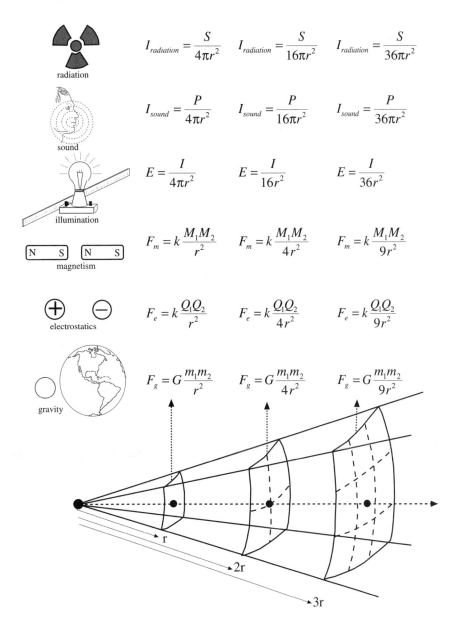

Figure 15.12 Applications of the Inverse Square Law

ACTIVITY 15.6.1 *Illumination and the Inverse Square Law*

Photocopy graph paper onto a piece of stiff card stock paper. Using a craft knife, cut out a window as shown in Figure 15.13, and record its size. Place the card stock vertically at a distance r (10–20 cm works well) from a candle, and record the distance. Place a second piece of graph paper as shown at a distance of $2r$ from the candle. Light the candle, turn off the lights, and count the number of squares illuminated on the second sheet. Move this sheet to a distance of $3r$, $4r$, and $5r$, and record the number of illuminated squares. Graph the number of squares illuminated on the y-axis and the distance from the candle on the x-axis. If possible, repeat this activity using a light sensor and appropriate probeware for your calculator or computer.

1. What happens to the surface area on which the light is projected as the distance from the light source increases?

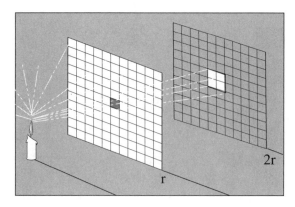

Figure 15.13 Illumination and the Inverse Square Law

2. Record the intensity of light at *r, 2r, 3r, 4r,* and *5r*. What is the relationship of intensity to distance from the light source? Plot intensity versus distance.

3. Express your finding for intensity as an equation.

ACTIVITY 15.6.2 *Sound, Magnetism and the Inverse Square Law*

Many people suffer from tinnitus, partial deafness, and other hearing-related problems as a result of listening to music with earphones. Although the power (energy released per unit time) of such devices may be very small, the distance of the sound source from the eardrum is very short, dramatically increasing the volume.

Place an electronic buzzer (available at electronic supply stores) at one end of a meter stick and a sound meter at the other. Make certain the environment is quiet, and then turn on the buzzer. Record the sound level at 20 cm intervals and plot sound level (in decibels) as a function of distance from the source. If you have access to a magnetometer, repeat the process to see the relationship between magnetic field strength and distance. A magnetometer is a device used to measure the strength of a magnetic field. A compass is essentially a magnetometer but does not record in useful units. The best option is to use sound and magnetometer probes and probeware with your computer (see *sciencesourcebook.com*). Such devices provide continuous readouts and are generally accurate.

1. What is the relationship between sound level (intensity) and distance from the sound source?

2. Compare the graph of sound intensity as a function of distance with the graph of light intensity and magnetism as a function of distance (above). Are the intensities of light, sound, and magnetism all functions of the inverse square of the distance from the source? Explain your answer.

ACTIVITY 15.6.3 *Agriculture on Other Planets?*

With the exception of chemosynthetic bacteria, all life is dependent on sunlight. Plants are *autotrophic,* meaning that they produce their own food through the process of photosynthesis. Animals, however, are *heterotrophic,* dependent on plants or other animals for their energy. All civilizations are dependent on agriculture, and therefore dependent on the light of the Sun. Many science-fiction writers have imagined the colonization of other planets, but how practical would such an endeavor be even if we could deliver people and materials to these faraway worlds?

According to the inverse square law, the intensity of light decreases as the inverse square of the distance from the light source. Doubling the distance from the Sun results in a fourfold reduction in light intensity. We know that the average light intensity on Earth is adequate for agriculture, but how about on distant planets? Table 15.6 shows the relative distance between the planets and the Sun.

The average distance from the Sun to Earth is 149,597,870 km (92,955,807 miles), a distance

Table 15.6 Solar Intensity Relative to Earth

Planet	AU	I_{planet}/I_{Earth}
Mercury	0.387	
Venus	0.723	
Earth	1.000	1.000
Mars	1.523	
Jupiter	5.202	
Saturn	9.538	
Uranus	19.181	
Neptune	30.057	

that astronomers call *1 astronomical unit,* or 1 AU. Since the average distance between the Sun and the Earth is defined as 1 AU, planets closer to the Sun have distances less than 1 AU, while planets farther from the Sun have distances greater than 1 AU. How does the intensity of the light on these planets compare with the intensity of light on Earth, knowing that intensity is a function of the inverse square of distance from the Sun? Complete Table 15.6; then create a graph with the distance of the planets from the Sun measured in AUs on the *x*-axis (independent variable), and the intensity of light on these planets, measured relative to the intensity on earth (I_{planet}/I_{Earth}) on the *y*-axis (dependent variable).

1. Do you think that it would be possible to grow food in planetary greenhouses on any of the inner rocky planets: Mercury, Venus, or Mars?
2. In the summer of 1989, NASA's *Voyager 2* became the first spacecraft to observe the planet Neptune, its final planetary target during its 12 month voyage from Earth. What was the intensity of light from the sun at this point?

ACTIVITY 15.6.4 *Applications of the Inverse Square Law*

The following are true statements. Explain each using the inverse square law.

1. The largest antennae in the world are radio telescopes, detecting radio waves from distant galaxies.
2. Immunotherapy is used to treat cancer. Scientists find antibodies that attack specific cancer cells, then separate the antibodies in the laboratory and derive millions of copies. The antibodies are doped with radioactive molecules and given to the patient. The radioactivity kills the cancerous cells to which the antibodies cling but has little effect on surrounding tissues.
3. Pseudoscientists have warned of the dire gravitational effects associated with the alignment of Jupiter, Mars, and the Moon. Although these are massive objects, the combined force of attraction of these objects causes no noticeable effects on Earth.

4. There is no such thing as a position around the Earth in which there is zero gravity. Astronauts orbiting the earth are simply in a continual state of free fall and therefore experience zero gravity, even though they are well within the gravitational field of the Earth.

15.7 Scientific Applications of Conic Sections

In 1977, NASA launched *Voyager 2,* an unmanned craft that collected a tremendous number of data as it flew past Jupiter, Saturn, and Uranus before reaching Neptune in 1989. For this interplanetary travel to be successful, scientists had to calculate the precise position of the planets in their elliptical orbits around the Sun, as well as predict the hazards posed by the elliptical orbits of asteroids and the elliptical, parabolic or possibly hyperbolic paths of comets. The craft collected data on the circular rings around Saturn and discovered the circular rings around Uranus. Data from numerous scientific instruments were sent back to Earth using parabolic transmitting antennas and received by large parabolic receiving antennae in NASA's Deep Space Network.

Although *Voyager 2* was perhaps the most advanced scientific and engineering feat ever accomplished to that time, it was dependent on an understanding of geometric principles discovered more than 2000 years earlier. In approximately 200 B.C., the great mathematician Apollonius of Perga wrote a treatise entitled *Conics,* in which he discussed the mathematics of circles, ellipses, parabolas, and hyperbolas—shapes created when a plane intersects a cone (*conic sections,* Figure 15.14). Apollonius's work was forgotten for many years but was rediscovered during the Renaissance and helped lay the mathematical foundation for the scientific revolution.

Conic sections have proven to have many scientific and technological applications, which we discuss following a brief introduction of the mathematics. Figure 15.14 shows two cones that

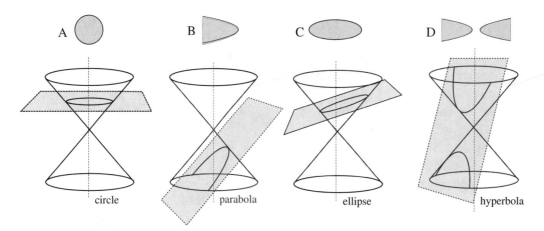

Figure 15.14 Conic Sections Are Determined by the Plane of Intersection

share the same axis of symmetry and the same vertex but are positioned in opposite directions. A *circle* is formed if a plane perpendicular to the cone axis intersects one of the cones at any point but the vertex (Figure 15.14A). A *parabola* is formed when a cone is intersected by a plane parallel to the surface of the cone (Figure 15.4B). An *ellipse* is formed when a plane intersects a cone at an angle between the angle perpendicular to the cone axis and the angle parallel to the surface of the cone (Figure 15.14C). A *hyperbola* is formed when the plane intersects both parts of the cone (Figure 15.14D).

Variations of these shapes are formed when different shapes of cones are used. Each of the conic sections can be described by a unique equation (Table 15.7). For any of the equations with a center (j, k) instead of $(0, 0)$, replace each *x term* with $(x − j)$ and each *y term* with $(y − k)$.

The circle, and its three-dimensional rotation, the *sphere*, are characterized by a constant radius. Anything that radiates evenly from a source will assume a spherical shape. For example, the sound waves emanating from a firecracker travel in a spherical fashion when it is detonated, and the light from a candle proceeds in a spherical wave front

Table 15.7 Equations for Conic Sections

	Circle	**Ellipse**	**Parabola**	**Hyperbola**
Equation (horizontal vertex)	$x^2 + y^2 = r^2$	$x^2/a^2 + y/b^2 = 1$	$4px = y^2$	$x^2/a^2 − y^2/b^2 = 1$
Equation (vertical vertex)	$x^2 + y^2 = r^2$	$y^2/a^2 + x^2/b^2 = 1$	$4py = x^2$	$y^2/a^2 − x^2/b^2 = 1$
Variables	r = circle radius	i = major radius (= 1/2 length major axis) i = minor radius (= 1/2 length minor axis)	p = distance from vertex to focus (or directrix)	a = 1/2 length major axisi = 1/2 length minor axis
Definition	distance to the origin is constant	sum of distances to each focus is constant	distance to focus = distance to directrix	difference between distances to each focus is constant

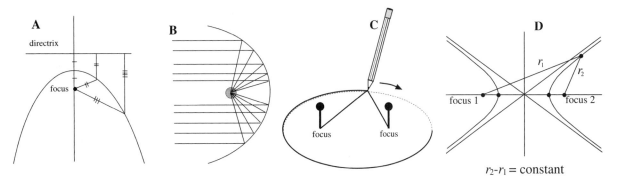

Figure 15.15 (A) Definition of a Parabola. (B) Rays in a Parabola. (C) Drawing an Ellipse. (D) A Hyperbola.

until it is interrupted by a barrier. A basketball, volleyball, or soccer ball becomes spherical when inflated as air presses uniformly on the inner walls of the ball.

The parabola, and its three-dimensional rotation, the *paraboloid,* are open curves such that the path to the focus and the path to a horizontal line known as the *directrix* are equal (Figure 15.15A). Anything that enters a parabola as parallel rays will concentrate at the focus, and anything emanating from the focus will exit the parabola as parallel rays. Figure 15.15B shows how parallel rays emanating from a light bulb reflect off the parabolic surface and exit as parallel rays.

The ellipse, and its three-dimensional rotation, the *ellipsoid,* are similar to the circle and sphere but have one axis that is longer than the other. Although the radii may differ in length, the sum of the radii is constant. An ellipse can be drawn by placing two pins (foci) in cardboard and connecting them by a string longer than the distance between the pins. When a pen is constrained by the string, an ellipse will be drawn (Figure 15.15C). The length of the string and the distance between the pins will determine the shape of the ellipse. Planets travel in elliptical paths around the Sun, with the Sun at one focus. The axis between *perigee* (the position where Earth is closest to the Sun) and *apogee* (the position where the Earth is farthest from the Sun) is the major axis of the ellipse.

The hyperbola, and its three-dimensional rotation, the *hyperboloid,* are open, two-branched curves. These are defined as the surface created by points such that the difference of the distances between two fixed points (*foci*) is constant (Figure 15.15D).

ACTIVITY 15.7.1 *Scientific and Technological Examples of Conic Sections*
Following is a list of the practical applications of conic sections (circle, parabola, ellipse, and hyperbola) or their three-dimensional rotations (sphere, paraboloid, ellipsoid, and hyperboloid). Identify each of the following as a circle, parabola, ellipse, hyperbola, sphere, paraboloid, ellipsoid, or hyperboloid.

1. The celestial equator is a(n) _____ projection into space of the Earth's equator. Astronomers use the celestial equator to reference the position of stars and other celestial objects.

2. If a source of sound is placed at one focus of a(n) _____ room, the sound converges on the other focus. For this reason, concert halls do not have this shape.

3. *Loran* is an acronym for *long-range navigation,* a technology developed during World War II to identify the location of ships at sea. Two transmitters (A1, A2) beam radio signals from fixed points at land. Upon analyzing the time difference between the two signals, the onboard Loran system determines the specific _____ curve on which the boat must be located (Figure 15.15D). This process is repeated with a different set of transmitters (B1, B2), and the intersection of the resulting _____ curves identifies the boat's precise location.

4. The high-beam lamp in an automobile headlight is placed at the focus of a(n) _____ reflecting surface, such that the emanating light reflects off the curved surface and leaves in parallel rays, lighting the distant road.

5. The Moon orbits the Earth in a(n) _____ path with the Earth at one focus.

6. The International Space Station and other artificial satellites travel in _____ orbits with the Earth at one focus.

7. A free throw in basketball, a line drive in baseball, and a long bomb in football all follow a(n) _____ path (neglecting air friction).

8. A returning comet follows a(n) highly eccentric _____ path with the Sun at one focus. As the comet approaches perihelion (the closest it gets to the Sun), solar winds (high-energy particles from the Sun) lengthen the tail of the comet and sunlight illuminates it, making it long and visible. As the comet approaches the other focus deep in the solar system, the tail shrinks, and the comet becomes invisible to the Earth-bound observer.

9. To intensify the light from faint, distant objects, _____ telescope mirrors collect and focus parallel beams of light.

10. Water from a hose, sprinkler, drinking fountain, or decorative fountain travels in a(n) _____.

11. Sportscasters eavesdrop on the conversations of coaches and players by using microphones placed at the focus of _____ reflectors.

12. The Le Four Solaire at Font-Romeur is an eight-story-high _____ solar reflector in the mountains of France. It is made of 8000 mirrors arranged so that light reflects to one focus, generating temperatures up to 6000°F.

13. To create a weightless condition, NASA flies training astronauts in planes with an upward _____ trajectory. Using this technique, astronauts can train in a weightless environment for approximately 30 seconds at a time.

14. The light cast on a wall, above and below a lampshade, forms a(n) _____.

15. Three-lobed _____ cylinders are used to concentrate light at a common focus.

16. In the absence of gravity, bubbles, water droplets, and flames assume a(n) _____ shape.

17. Although the Earth appears to be a sphere, it is actually more nearly a(n) _____. The flattening of the ellipse of the Earth is only about 1 part in 300 but is significant enough to become a necessary part of calculations in plotting accurate maps at a scale of 1:100,000 or greater.

18. When a rock is thrown in a pond, it generates _____ surface waves.

19. The surface waves from an earthquake expand in a(n) _____ fashion.

20. A(n) _____ ball-and-socket joint allows for rotary motion.

21. The _____ radiocarpal joint in the wrist allows front-back movement along the short axis but limited movement along the long axis.

22. The curve of cables in a suspension bridge form a(n) _____.

23. When two rocks are dropped in the water at the same time, they create radiating rings. When the peak of one wave hits the peak of another, the wave doubles in height, but when the peak of one hits the trough of another, the waves cancel. These patterns of constructive and destructive interference form a(n) _____.

24. Microwave antennae are _____ and can therefore collect and concentrate signals at the focus.

25. The heating element of a radiant heater is placed at the focus of a(n) _____ such that the infrared rays will project evenly and warm the room in which it is placed.

Answers to Chapter Activities

15.1.1 Scales depend on the degree to which the original is enlarged.

15.2.1 1-direct (the Mars Exploration Rover and other Martian probes have made direct measurements of the surface temperature of Mars), 2-direct, 3-direct, 4-direct, 5-indirect (bond lengths are too small to measure directly), 6-direct, 7-direct, 8-indirect (we can infer the age of the bristlecones by examining tree rings and other evidence, but cannot measure their age directly), 9-indirect, 10-indirect, 11-indirect (it is impossible to weigh the Moon or any other celestial body, so measurements must be made indirectly), 12-direct, 13-indirect (no space probes have ever landed on Pluto, so measurements of its surface temperature must have been made indirectly), 14-indirect (such a conclusion is made on the basis of statistical data of a small sample size, and not on direct measurement of the entire population), 15-direct.

15.2.2 The accepted diameter of the Moon is 3476 km. Student answers will vary.

15.2.3 Student answers will vary.

15.2.4 Student answers will vary.

15.3.3 The accepted circumference of the Earth is 40,008 km. Student answers will vary, but most should calculate a percentage error less than 10 percent.

15.4.1 (1) The surface area to volume ratio decreases as the size of the cube increases. (2) The surface area to mass ratio decreases as the size of the cube increases. (3) Yes. (4) Phytoplankton are small, and thus have a higher surface area to volume ratio than if they were larger. The spines also increase the surface area to volume ratio. Since drag increases with increasing surface area, spiny phytoplankton will not sink even though they may be denser than the ocean water. (5) A baby is more susceptible to chilling because it has a high surface area to volume ratio and loses heat faster relative to its mass than does an adult. (6) Very small animals lose heat faster than very large animals. It is easier for large animals to stay warm in the winter and for small animals to stay cool in the summer, all other factors being equal.

15.5.1 1(L), 2(S), 3(S), 4(L), 5(L), 6(L), 7(S), 8(S), 9(L), 10(S), 11(L), 12(S), 13(S), 14(S), 15(L), 16(L), 17(S).

15.5.2 Answers will vary, but students should notice that the surface area to volume ratio decreases as height increases.

15.5.3 (1) Small children have a high surface area to volume ratio. They therefore heat up more rapidly in a hot car. They cool readily due to sweating that takes place over their proportionately large surface area, but may dehydrate more rapidly because they have relatively low body volumes, and consequently low reservoirs of water. (2) The cost of construction for a warehouse is more highly correlated with surface area (walls) than volume (empty space inside). Large stores have a high volume to surface area ratio, meaning they can store lots of goods with relatively little construction cost. (3) For cells to survive, nutrients must diffuse in and out. Diffusion rates are increased by large surface areas but decreased by long diffusion paths. Diffusion is much more efficient in small cells because they possess a higher surface area to volume ratio. (4) Dissolution requires direct contact between the solute (sugar) and the solvent (water). In powdered form, the surface area to volume ratio is high, increasing the rate at which sugar dissolves. (5) Elephants are large and have a very low surface area to volume ratio. The large ears of elephants are radiators, dissipating heat through their large surface area and thereby preventing overheating. (6) Nutrient absorption is a major

issue for large organisms due to their low surface area (absorption surface) to volume (nutrient demanding tissue) ratio. Microvilli increase the surface area and increase nutrient and water absorption. (7) Absorption of oxygen from the surrounding environment is no problem for single-celled organisms because absorption is a function of surface area and they have high surface area to volume ratios. By contrast, larger organisms have an oxygen demand due to high volume to surface area ratios. To provide sufficient oxygen for the disproportionately large volume and mass of tissues, larger organisms have lungs that dramatically increase the absorptive surface area. (8) Cacti have large stems and no leaves. They also have a large volume of water relative to their surface area. Since they have low surface area to absorb heat and high volume of water that acts as a heat sink, cacti rarely overheat. (9) Small animals have a large surface area to volume ratio. Since heat is lost through the surface and since heat production is a function of volume, they must eat more regularly to deal with the proportionately greater heat loss. (10) The force of gravity is a function of the mass and, indirectly, the volume of an organism. The adhesion between an organism and a surface is a function of the area of the surface in contact. The high surface area to volume ratio of insects maximizes the adhesive properties while minimizing the force of gravity. (11) Heat is a function of mass and therefore indirectly a function of volume. Heat exchange is a function of surface area. Consequently crushed ice, which has a very high surface area to volume ratio, melts more rapidly than block ice.

15.6.1 (1) The surface area increases as a square of the distance from the light source. (2) Intensity is a function of the inverse square of the distance from the light source. Figure 15.16 is a plot of intensity as a function of distance. (3) $I = \dfrac{Energy_{source}}{r^2}$.

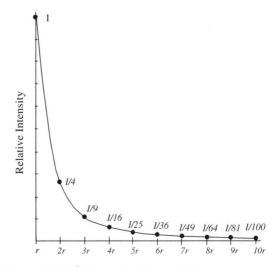

Figure 15.16 Intensity Versus Distance

15.6.2 Students will develop a graph for sound and magnetism that resembles Figure 15.16. (1) Sound intensity is a function of the inverse square of the distance from the sound source. (2) Yes. The inverse square law is a geometric principle and applies to anything that radiates from a point source.

15.6.3 Students should calculate values as shown in Table 15.8 and draw a graph such as illustrated in Figure 15.17. (1) The light intensity on Mercury and Venus is very high, and greenhouses would have to reduce the

Table 15.8 Solar Intensity Relative to Earth

Planet	**(AU)**	$(I_{planet}/I_{Earth})\%$
Mercury	0.387	667.7%
Venus	0.723	191.3%
Earth	1.000	100.0%
Mars	1.523	43.1%
Jupiter	5.202	3.7%
Saturn	9.538	1.1%
Uranus	19.181	0.3%
Neptune	30.057	0.1%

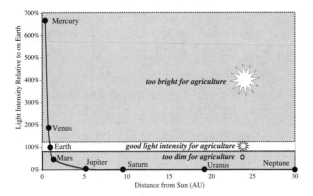

Figure 15.17 Intensity of Sunlight on Planets

amount of light. The greater challenge would be the temperature and atmosphere of these planets, both of which are extremely hostile for life. On Mars, the light intensity is only about 43 percent that on Earth, so crops could not flourish unless the light intensity was boosted with mirrors and the atmosphere in greenhouses controlled to match that on Earth. (2) The light intensity on Neptune is approximately 0.1 percent the intensity here on Earth.

15.6.4 (1) Radio signal strength drops off as the inverse square of the distance from the source. Radio waves produced in distant galaxies are extremely faint due to the inverse square law and the great distances from Earth. Large antennae are necessary to gather signals large enough to analyze. (2) The radioactively tagged antibodies selectively bind to the cancerous cells. Since radiation emanates from these uniformly in all directions, the intensity of the radiation will fall off as a function of the inverse square of distance from the antibody. The cancerous cells to which the radioactive antibodies bind are destroyed, while only minimal damage is inflicted on surrounding tissues, which receive much less radiation due to their distance from the radioactive source and the inverse square law. (3) Since gravity is a function of the inverse square of the distance from the center of mass, the attractive force of Mars and Jupiter will be extremely small in comparison with the smaller but much closer Moon. (4) The universal law of gravitation incorporates the inverse square law: $F_g = G\dfrac{m_1 \cdot m_2}{r^2}$. The Earth exerts gravity on the spacecraft and everything else in the universe, but its effect diminishes rapidly as distance increases. As distance, r, approaches infinity, the force of the Earth's gravity becomes negligible.

15.7.1 (1) circular, (2) elliptical, (3) hyperbolic, (4) parabolic, (5) elliptical, (6) elliptical, (7) parabolic, (8) elliptical, (9) parabolic, (10) parabolic, (11) parabolic, (12) parabolic, (13) parabolic, (14) hyperbola, (15) elliptical, (16) spherical, (17) ellipsoid, (18) circular, (19) circular, (20) spherical, (21) ellipsoid, (22) parabola, (23) hyperbola, (24) parabolic, (25) parabolic.

Chapter Sixteen

Diagramming and Visualizing Problems in Science

For the Teacher 293

16.1 Vector Diagrams 295

16.2 Interpreting Scientific Diagrams 298

16.3 Pictorial Riddles 301

16.4 Analyzing Photographs 304

16.5 Digital Movies and Animations 310

16.6 Extrapolation 316

16.7 Interactive Scientific Simulations 318

Answers to Chapter Activities 319

For the Teacher

Bloodhounds have a sense of smell that is approximately 100 million times more sensitive than that of humans. A bloodhound is able to follow the trail of a fugitive or missing person even 2 or 3 days after the person has left. Bloodhounds learn well by olfaction (smell) and can identify people, plants, animals, and objects by the unique odors they emit. Although humans also learn by smell (olfaction) and taste (gustation), we learn primarily through vision, hearing, and touch. Learners acquire information through all modalities but often exhibit preferences. *Visual learners* learn best by pictures, charts, diagrams, movies, and illustrated procedures. *Auditory learners* learn best by listening to directions, explanations, and lectures and by talking with and explaining to others. *Kinesthetic learners* learn best by doing: moving, manipulating, and gesturing.

Although studies have shown that visual learners represent the largest portion of the population, many teachers fail to use visual learning techniques, relying on lectures, discussion, and other nonvisual modes of instruction. Since it is easier to talk about something than it is to illustrate it, many people default to verbal descriptions, neglecting the benefits that visual instruction provides. Teachers should strive to incorporate visual, auditory, and kinesthetic components in their instruction. This chapter focuses on visual techniques.

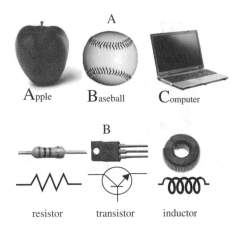

Figure 16.1 (A) Learning the Alphabet.
(B) Electronic Components.

Source: (A) Anonymous. (no date). X-ray of lung cancer. Image courtesy of the *National Cancer Institute.* Retrieved April 2007 from http://visualsonline.cancer.gov. (B) Anonymous. (no date). Breast cancer cells viewed with a light microscope. Image courtesy of the National Cancer Institute. Retrieved April 2007 from http://visualsonline.cancer.gov. (C) Anonymous. (no date). PET scan of a brain tumor. Image courtesy of the National Cancer Institute. Retrieved April 2007 from http://visualsonline.cancer.gov.

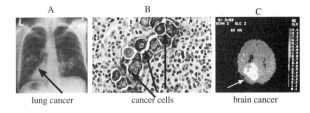

Figure 16.2 Different Views of Cancer

Pictures, photographs, and diagrams are invaluable tools at every level of education and profession. Preschoolers learn the alphabet by associating symbols with pictures (Figure 16.1A), while physics and engineering students learn circuit elements by associating electronic components with schematic symbols (Figure 16.1B). Informational graphics are foundational for learning science, making new discoveries, and applying scientific principles to real-life problems.

Consider the pictures in Figure 16.2. Each illustrates cancer, but in different ways. Figure 16.2A is a chest X-ray that shows a tumor in the left lobe of the lung. Figure 16.2B is a microscope slide of normal and cancerous cells from a patient with breast cancer. Figure 16.2C is a PET (positron emission tomography) scan of a patient with

a brain tumor. Initially each type of imaging technology was simply a curiosity, but as researchers learned to perfect and interpret the images, these technologies became invaluable diagnostic tools.

Imaging technologies have revolutionized not only medicine but also astronomy, biology, chemistry, physics, and every other branch of science, enabling scientists to understand the structure and order of the natural world. Scientists use diagrams, photos, and graphics on a daily basis, and science teachers should do so as well to communicate the concepts and relationships in teaching.

Although graphics, charts, diagrams, and photos are essential tools in science education, many students do not make good use of them. Often students memorize graphics rather than spending time to understand what they represent. To ensure understanding, teachers should use a variety of graphics for the same topic so students learn to abstract basic principles and transfer concepts, regardless of the form in which they are presented. Fortunately, it is easy to obtain alternative diagrams and photographs with the aid of a graphic search engine. Search the Internet for alternative images of the concepts you are teaching, and present them in class to help students develop generalized understandings. For example, students learn human anatomy primarily by studying line diagrams of the human body. Teachers should augment this instruction with a variety of images: photographs, microscope slides, X-rays, PET scans, CAT scans, and electron micrographs. Search for the Internet for such images, download them to your computer, cite your sources, and project them so all students can see.

Organize your photos and diagrams in folders and subfolders within your photo management software so you can easily access them as needed. Most photo management software provides previews so you can scroll through the library of images and select just the relevant ones to project (Figure 16.3). Help your students recognize features in these images and correlate them with diagrams or photographs of the same structures in their textbooks. The use of images will make your presentations more interesting and relevant, and help students develop better analytical skills.

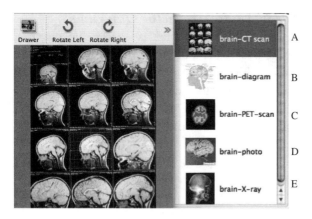

Figure 16.3 Photo-Viewing Software

It is critical that science students learn to read and interpret photographs, diagrams, and pictures. The activities in this chapter are designed to facilitate the development of observational and interpretive skills. Samples of various types of exercises are provided, and I encourage you to develop additional exercises that meet your curricular needs.

16.1 Vector Diagrams

Physics is the most basic science and is essential for understanding chemistry, biology, geology, meteorology, and the other sciences. Unlike other sciences, however, most of what is studied in physics cannot be seen. While geologists photograph rocks and minerals and biologists photograph cells and organisms, no one has ever taken a photograph of force, electricity, magnetism, heat, gravity, time, torque, inertia, or momentum! How can you study something that cannot be seen?

Although the properties of physics are invisible, they can be measured and quantified with various instruments. It is impossible to photograph the force with which the Earth pulls on your body, for example, but you can quantify it by standing on a scale. If a property can be quantified, it can be made visible through the use of a diagram. Force, for example, is traditionally illustrated by an arrow known as a vector (Figure 16.4). The length of a vector is proportional to its magnitude or strength, and the bearing reflects its direction.

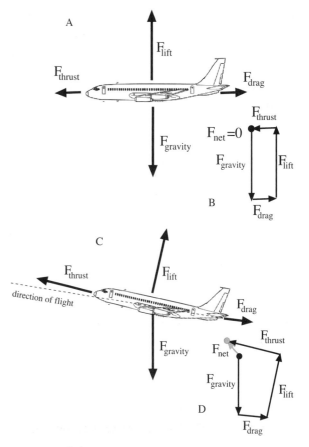

Figure 16.4 Force Vectors Acting on a Plane in Flight

Scientists and engineers use vectors to visualize and communicate force.

Figure 16.4 is a vector diagram that illustrates the four basic aerodynamic forces that act on an airplane in flight. Although none of these forces can be seen, they can be visualized by four vectors. Studying these vectors enables understanding and predicting the motion of the airplane. Gravity acts to pull the plane down and is the weight of the aircraft ($F_{gravity}$ = weight). If the vertical component of the lift (F_{lift}) created by the wings is equal to the weight of the aircraft ($F_{gravity}$), the plane will remain at the same elevation. If the lift is greater, the plane will climb, and if it is less, the plane will descend. Thrust (F_{thrust}) is the force produced by the engine and is directed forward along the axis of the engine. Thrust is countered by air resistance or drag (F_{drag}), which acts opposite to the direction of flight. If these forces are balanced (vectors are equal in length but opposite in direction), the plane will fly forward at constant velocity (no acceleration). If the thrust vector is longer than the drag vector, the plane will accelerate, and if the drag vector is longer than the thrust vector, the plane will decelerate.

To determine the net force on an object, add all of the vectors head to tail, such that the head (tip of the arrow) of one vector is touching the tail (base of the arrow) of the next vector. The sum of the vectors can be represented by one vector that starts at the tail (base) of the first vector and ends at the tip (head) of the last vector. This vector is known as the *resultant* and illustrates the net force acting upon the object.

Figure 16.4A shows the force vectors acting on a plane that is maintaining constant elevation and velocity. When the vectors are added head to tail, they perfectly balance, showing that there is no net force or acceleration (Figure 16.4B). Note that the resultant vector is zero because the head of the last arrow ends at the tail of the first. By contrast, Figure 16.4C illustrates a situation in which the vectors do not balance. Note that the engines are exerting more thrust, and the plane is angled slightly up. This changes the directions of the lift, thrust, and drag forces, and if one adds the vectors head to tail as before, there is a resultant vector, illustrating a net force acting up and forward (Figure 16.4D). This indicates that the plane must be accelerating in this direction.

ACTIVITY 16.1.1 *Vector Diagrams*

Vector diagrams enable visualizing the invisible. In Figures 16.5A and 16.5B, the vectors represent forces, while in Figure 16.5C, they represent velocities. Each of the vector diagrams in Figure 16.5 tells a story. Analyze each of the vector diagrams, and match it to one of the stories listed.

1. *Force vectors:* The following is a series of stories. Match each story with a force vector diagram illustrated in Figure 16.5A. *Neglect friction.*
   (a) A tug-of-war in which no team wins
   (b) A jet being pushed by a strong tailwind
   (c) The wind pushing a sailboat forward
   (d) A jet encountering a strong headwind
2. *Force vectors:* Friction always acts opposite to the direction of an applied force. Each of the following stories involves friction. Match each story with a vector diagram in Figure 16.5B.
   (a) A mountain biker rides through deep sand.
   (b) A tow truck is unable to pull a car out of the sand.
   (c) A skydiver is falling at constant speed after the chute has opened.
   (d) A skydiver is accelerating before the chute has opened.
3. *Velocity vectors:* Velocity has magnitude and direction and therefore can be illustrated with vectors. By convention, upward arrows indicate north, or away from the Earth, and downward arrows indicate south, or toward the Earth.

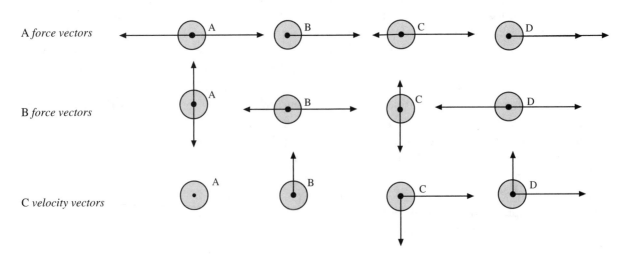

Figure 16.5 Force and Velocity Vectors

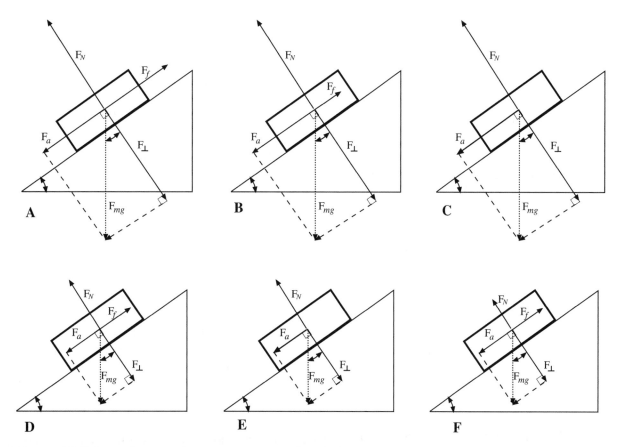

Figure 16.6 Force Vectors for a Box on an Inclined Plane

Match each story with a vector diagram in Figure 16.5C.

(a) A bicyclist travels east in a strong south (north-heading) wind.

(b) A motorboat crosses the Mississippi River from Arkansas to Tennessee.

(c) An apple hangs on a tree.

(d) The space shuttle lifts off the launch pad.

4. *Force vectors:* Figure 16.6 displays vector diagrams that describe conditions for a box on an inclined plane. Match each of the following stories with a vector diagram. Note that gravitational force is resolved into a force acting downhill (the accelerating force parallel to the surface, F_a) and a force acting at right angles toward the surface (perpendicular force, $F_\perp$). A description of the component forces follows:

F_{mg}—gravitational force; product of the mass, m, and the acceleration due to gravity, g

$F_\perp$—perpendicular force; component of gravity acting at right angles to surface

F_a—parallel force; component of gravity acting parallel to surface

F_N—normal force, acting at right angles away from the surface; equal and opposite to $F_\perp$

F_f—frictional force, acting opposite the direction of motion

(a) A box bends the ramp.

(b) A heavier box accelerates down a frictionless ramp.

(c) A lighter box rests on a ramp at an angle where it is just about to slide.

(d) A lighter box accelerates down a frictionless ramp.

(e) A heavier box rests on a ramp at an angle where it is just about to slide.

(f) A heavier box accelerates down a ramp, generating heat from friction.

16.2 Interpreting Scientific Diagrams

A diagram is a simplified drawing that represents the appearance, structure, workings, or relationships of something. Learning to "read" diagrams is an essential skill in science. Diagrams explain without using sentences, and we can usually make reasonable inferences even in the absence of explanatory text. The following activities are about a series of diagrams that explain certain phenomena. Answer the questions by analyzing the diagrams, even if you are unfamiliar with the content.

ACTIVITY 16.2.1 *Ray Diagrams*

Figure 16.7 shows how a single biconvex lens can create a variety of images depending on its location relative to the object it is imaging. If the object is at a great distance away, so that the light rays coming from it are parallel, all light will condense at one spot, named the *focal point, F* (Figure 16.7A). If, however, the object (solid arrow) is relatively close to the lens but beyond the focal length, the light rays emanating from it will not be parallel when they reach the lens and will converge on the other side to make real images (Figures 16.7B–16.7E). Match the following phrases (place in the first blank in questions 1 to 6) and the correct part of Figure 16.7 (16.7A–16.7F;

place in the second blank) with the corresponding written descriptions. Note that this activity does not require knowledge of physics, but it does require you to analyze and interpret the diagrams.

Possible Phrases for First Blank

at the focal length
at two times the focal length
between the focal length and two times the focal length
beyond two times the focal length
far from the lens
inside the focal length

1. When an object is _____, as in example _____, no real image is formed, but the viewer sees an enlarged, virtual image on the same side as the object. This is used in hand lenses such as those used by field biologists, geologists, or jewelers.
2. When an object is _____, as in example _____, the image is the same size but inverted. Inverting lenses are used in telescopes so that images appear upright after they have been enlarged by other lenses.
3. When an object is _____, as in example _____, the image will be larger and inverted. Enlarging lenses are used by photographers to create photographic enlargements.

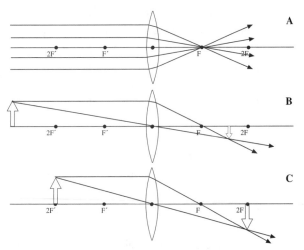
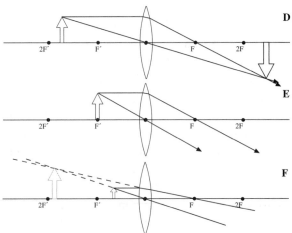
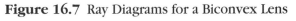

Figure 16.7 Ray Diagrams for a Biconvex Lens

4. When an object is _____, as in example _____, the image will be inverted and reduced. This is used in cameras to place real images on film or photo sensors.

5. When an object is _____, as in example _____, all rays will be emitted parallel, and no image will be formed. This arrangement is found in flashlights and searchlights.

6. When an object is _____, as in example _____, all of the rays converge at the focal point. This arrangement is used when starting a fire in the sunlight with a magnifying lens.

ACTIVITY 16.2.2 *Interpreting Scientific Diagrams*

If a diagram is clear, it should be possible to interpret it with minimal written explanation. Examine Figures 16.8A to 16.8D, and answer the following questions based solely on the information provided in the questions and the diagrams. You do not need to have knowledge of the subjects presented.

1. The Earth slowly precesses so that its axis points at different stars at different times. Currently Polaris is aligned with the Earth's

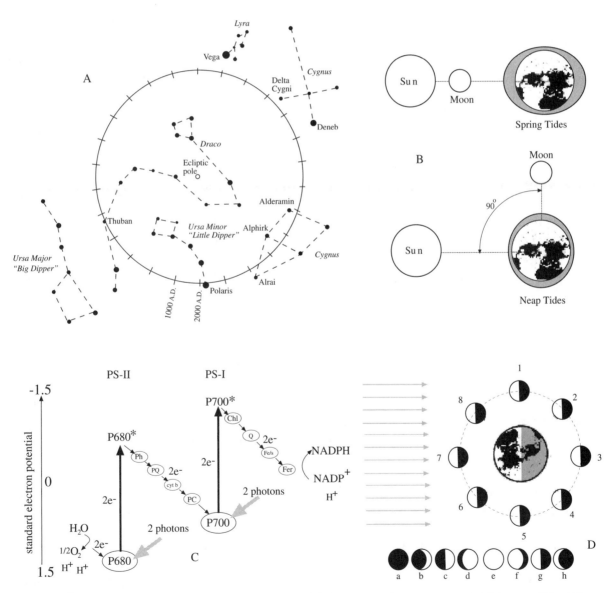

Figure 16.8 Diagrams showing (A) Precession, (B) Tides, (C) Light Reactions, (D) Phases of the Moon

axis above the North Pole and is therefore known as the North Star or Pole Star (Figure 16.8A). What will probably be the "north star" in (a) 4000 A.D.? (b) 7000 A.D.? (c) 12,000 A.D.?

2. Figure 16.8B correlates tides with positions of the Sun and Moon. The gray color represents water in the oceans. (a) Which has a greater influence on the tides, the Sun or Moon? (b) Under what conditions are tides the highest? (c) Under what conditions are tides the lowest?

3. Figure 16.8C shows the "Z-scheme" of the light reactions of photosynthesis. (a) What energizes electrons? (b) What is the most energetic species in the Z-scheme? (c) The Z-scheme is an electron transport scheme. What is the symbol for electrons? (d) Where is water broken into hydrogen and oxygen? (e) Is photosystem I or photosystem II more sensitive to light of 700 nm wavelength?

4. Figure 16.8D shows how the Sun illuminates the Earth and Moon as the Moon travels around the Earth. The moon will orbit the Earth in a lunar month of approximately 28 days. At the bottom of the diagram are the phases of the Moon as viewed from Earth. Correlate the positions of the Moon (numbers) with the phases of the Moon (letters).

ACTIVITY 16.2.3 *Developing Your Own Diagrams*

Drawing diagrams can help you conceptualize problems and communicate them to others without the need for lengthy explanations. Consider the following situation:

Copper and iron electrodes are placed in a solution of copper sulfate and connected by wires to a battery. When they are subjected to an electric field, sulfate ions move toward the positively charged copper electrode, while copper ions move toward the negatively charged iron electrode where they form a copper plate.

Although this description is accurate, many people, particularly those with limited English proficiency, will find Figure 16.9 much easier to understand and conceptualize. Combining a

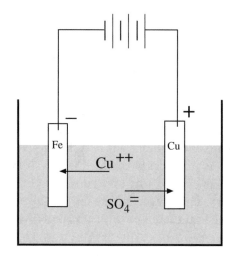

Figure 16.9 Electroplating Diagram

written explanation with a diagram and spoken explanation provides a much better learning environment than any one or two approaches alone.

It has been said that the best way to learn is to teach another. Developing diagrams to explain concepts is a way of sharing your ideas with others, and in the process you will learn them better yourself. Develop diagrams as directed by your teacher, and write accompanying explanations. The following list presents possible ideas, but it may be better to select ones from what you are working on in class as directed by your teacher. Study relevant chapters or sections as necessary, but do not copy existing diagrams.

- *Environmental science:* succession, food web, water cycle, carbon cycle, groundwater pollution, photochemical smog production
- *Chemistry:* titration, distillation, bright line spectrum, electroplating, electrolysis, ionization, fusion, fission
- *Biology:* electrophoresis, gene splicing, DNA replication, transcription, enzyme function, biological magnification
- *Earth science:* rock cycle, cloud formation, seasonal overturn, Coriolis effect, subduction, star formation
- *Physics:* forces acting on a car, magnetic field around a wire, electromagnetic radiation, components of velocity of a thrown football, nuclear decay

16.3 Pictorial Riddles

A *riddle* is a question or statement posed so that it requires ingenuity to determine its answer or meaning. Consider the following riddle: "What appears to lie at your feet in the morning, follow you all day long, nearly vanish at noon, and disappear at night?" The riddle is phrased in such a way that you might first think of a pet, but this does not fit the last two clues. To solve the riddle requires "thinking outside the box" and consider inanimate objects as well, in which case you might realize that your shadow meets the criteria of the riddle. Riddles are engaging and demand creative thinking.

Pictorial riddles are riddles in graphic form. Ingenuity is required to analyze the pictures and arrive at reasonable solutions. In the activities that follow, students will work with a variety of types of pictorial riddles.

ACTIVITY 16.3.1 *Time-Series Pictorial Riddles*

Figures 16.10 to 16.14 are time-series riddles. The first pictures in a series represent earlier times, and later pictures represent later times. To solve such riddles, you must supply a process or activity that occurs between the various pictures that can adequately explain why the pictures have changed over time. For example, Figure 16.10 shows a series of pictures of a magnetic compass. What can explain the different orientations of the compass needle from the first moment to the final moment? A geologist might explain that there is a tremendous amount of time between each event, and the directionality of the compass reflects the changing magnetic field of the Earth. At some times in geological history, the magnetic north pole was near the geographic North Pole (Figures 16.10A, 16.10C), while at other times the polarity of the Earth's magnetic field was reversed such that the magnetic North Pole was near the geographic South Pole (figures 16.10B, 16.10D). By contrast, a physicist might suggest that the compass needle spins because of a changing magnetic field induced by a local magnet. For example, if you move a magnet around a compass, the needle will follow it. Riddles may therefore have more than one reasonable solution. Provide reasonable solutions for pictorial riddles 16.10 to 16.14.

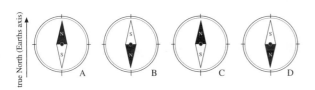

Figure 16.10 Time-Series Riddle: Compass

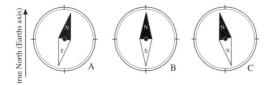

Figure 16.11 Time-Series Riddle: Compass

1. Figure 16.11 represents magnetic compasses. Suggest processes or events that explain the change from A to C.
2. Figure 16.12 shows magnetic compasses surrounding a wire. Suggest a process or event that can explain the changes from A to C.

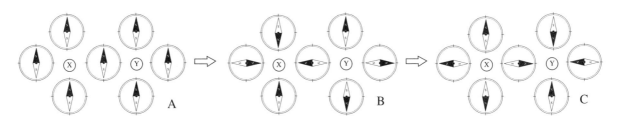

Figure 16.12 Times Series Riddle: Compasses Surrounding Electric Wires

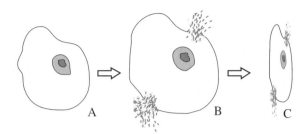

Figure 16.13 Times-Series Riddle of a Cell

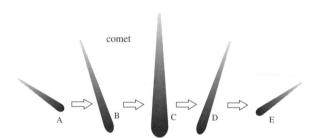

Figure 16.14 Times-Series Riddle of a Cell

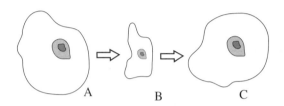

Figure 16.15 Comet

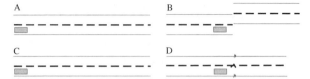

Figure 16.16 Times-Series Riddle: Highway

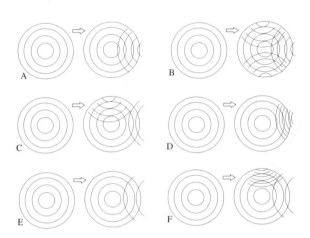

Figure 16.17 Times-Series Riddle: Motion Detector

3. Figure 16.13 represents a single cell. Suggest processes or events that explain the change from A to C.

4. Figure 16.14 represents a single cell. Suggest processes or events that explain the change from A to C.

5. Figure 16.15 represents a comet at different times from A to E. Suggest processes or events that explain the changes. The comet is orbiting the Sun, which is out of the picture below the diagram.

6. Figure 16.16 represents a two-lane highway. Suggest processes or events that explain the change from A to B and from C to D.

7. Figure 16.17 represents radio waves emanating from a motion detector. Examine the patterns of reflected waves, and match the following descriptions with the appropriate diagrams.
   - One nearby stationary object
   - One object moving away from the source
   - One object moving toward the source and one moving away from it
   - One object that is moving toward the source
   - Three nearby stationary objects
   - Two nearby stationary objects, one of which is closer than the other

8. Figure 16.18 shows electrocardiograms, made from a device that monitors the electrical activity of the heart. Offer explanations for each of the changes seen at the time of the arrow.

9. Figure 16.19 shows an elephant and dog on the same beam. Offer an explanation for the movement of the beam from A to C.

10. Figure 16.20 is a human skeleton. Offer an explanation for the sequence.

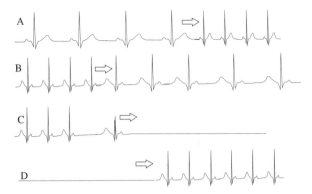

Figure 16.18 Times-Series Riddle: Electrocardiogram

Figure 16.19 Times-Series Riddle: Balancing Beam

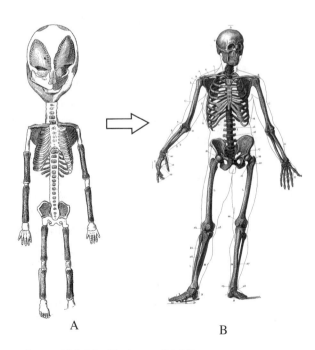

Figure 16.20 Skeleton Riddle

ACTIVITY 16.3.2 *Analyzing Diagrams for Similarities and Differences*

On January 28, 1986, the NASA Space Shuttle *Challenger* launched from Kennedy Space Center in Florida. Seventy-three seconds into flight the *Challenger* exploded, killing all seven crew members. Engineers pinned the disaster on a faulty O-ring seal in the right solid rocket booster. When the seal failed, a flame leaked from the booster and damaged the adjacent propellant tank. Although the O-ring looked like other ones produced by the manufacturer, apparently it was different in at least one critical aspect. Unfortunately, this difference was not detected prior to lift-off.

Scientists, engineers, and manufacturers frequently analyze things for similarities and differences. Manufacturers employ quality control technicians to ensure that all products meet specifications. Quality control technicians protect the public from defective products and employers from lawsuits. They must develop good analytical skills so they can determine which products are good and which are not. The ability to analyze things for similarities and differences is vital to science and industry.

In this activity, you will exercise this skill as you analyze sets of plants and animals for similarities and differences. For example, in Figure 16.21A the penguin does not fit with the others. Although all five are large marine animals, four are mammals, while the penguin is a bird. Examine each of the sets in Figure 16.21 and determine which one does not belong with the others.

ACTIVITY 16.3.3 *What's Wrong with This Picture?*

"What's wrong with this picture?" is a popular game found in children's magazines. An otherwise normal picture has odd things hidden in it that the reader must discover. These games are popular and challenging, and they require the analytical skills used in scientific reasoning. Examine Figures 16.22A to 16.22M, and determine what's wrong with each picture. Explain in complete sentences.

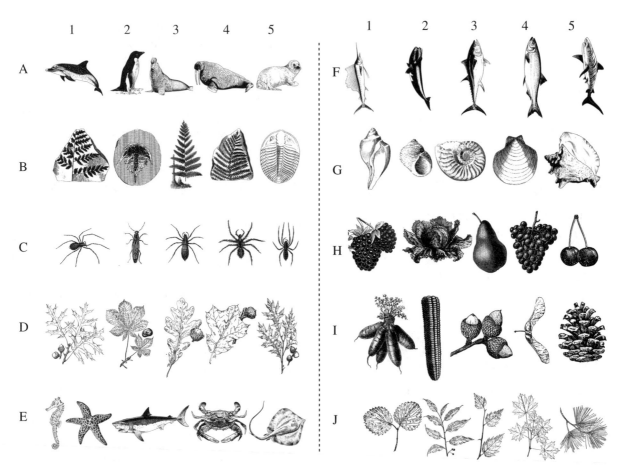

Figure 16.21 Analyzing for Similarities and Difference
Source: Anonymous. (various dates). Images from *Desk gallery compact dsc.* Images distributed on CD by Zedcor (Dover Publications). Used by permission.

16.4 Analyzing Photographs

Figure 16.23 is a copy of what is perhaps the first permanent photograph ever taken. The image was recorded in 1826 by French inventor Nicéphore Niépce. Despite the graininess of the photo, a viewer can make observations and inferences about the environment in which the camera was sitting at the time the film was exposed. For example, the shadows indicate that the photograph was taken when the Sun was above and to the right of the camera. The gray and black shapes are probably roofs, eaves, walls, and windows, and it appears as though the camera was resting on a wall or windowsill above a courtyard. It is likely that the photograph was taken in the country, as there appear

to be a tree and field in the distance. Photographs provide a tremendous amount of information that is useful to historians, physicians, scientists, and other professionals.

Photography enables us to study environments, events, and processes and to share our findings with others. Every photograph contains information, and photography has become a universal tool in scientific research. Today, scientists use photographs to study giant events such as storms on Earth (Figure 16.24A) and Jupiter (Figure 16.24B), or infinitesimal structures such as the viruses that cause polio (Figure 16.24C) or Ebola fever (Figure 16.24D).

Drawings and photographs give us the ability to study phenomena over time. In 1665 Italian astronomer Giovanni Cassini drew diagrams showing

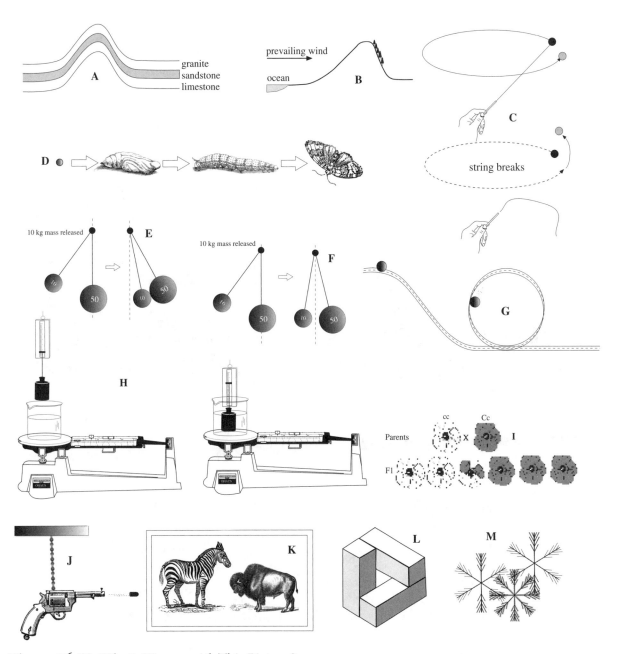

Figure 16.22 What's Wrong with This Picture?

a speck on the surface of Jupiter. Two centuries later, Wilhelm Tempel's scale drawings demonstrated that this speck was two to three times the diameter of the Earth, and in 1979, the American space probes *Voyager 1* and *Voyager 2* sent back photographs (Figure 16.25) demonstrating that Cassini's speck, now known as the Great Red Spot, is actually a massive, centuries-old storm. Drawings and photographs give us information to help us understand the dynamics of phenomena throughout the universe.

ACTIVITY 16.4.1 *Examining Photographs for Evidence*

Figures 16.26A to 16.26C are images from the surface of the Earth, space, and the surface of the Moon. Each image contains clues about the environment it represents. Support each of the following statements with observations from one of the photographs.

1. Earth is a suitable environment for life.
2. There is no atmosphere on the Moon.
3. Gravity is a significant force on Earth.
4. Astronauts in orbit around the Earth experience weightlessness.

5. There is little or no atmosphere in space.
6. The surface of the Moon does not support life.
7. There is no rain on the Moon.
8. The force of gravity on the Moon is less than on Earth.
9. Earth has an atmosphere.

Figure 16.23 First Photograph Ever Taken, 1826
Source: Niépce, N. (1826). First permanent photograph. The original photograph is owned by the University of Texas at Austin, Gernsheim Collection.

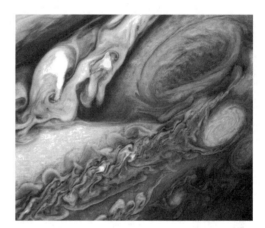

Figure 16.25 Great Red Spot
Source: National Aeronautics and Space Administration. (1979). View of Jupiter's great red spot from Voyager II spacecraft. Image courtesy of NASA. Retrieved August 2006 from http://www.nasa.gov/multimedia/imagegallery.

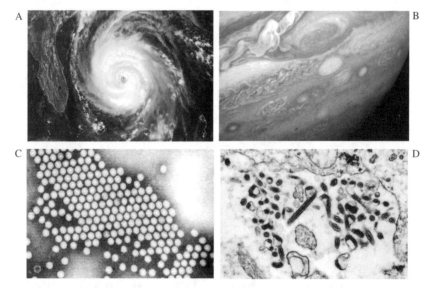

Figure 16.24 Photography: An Invaluable Tool in Science
Source: (A) National Oceanic and Atmospheric Administration. (no date). Satellite photograph of a hurricane. Image courtesy of the NOAA. Retrieved April 2007 from http://www.photolib.noaa.gov. (B) National Aeronautics and Space Administration. (1979). View of Jupiter from Voyager II spacecraft. Image courtesy of NASA. Retrieved August 2006 from http://www.nasa.gov/multimedia/imagegallery. (C) Esposito, J., & Murphy, F. (no date). Polio virus. Public Health Image Library. Image courtesy of the Centers for Disease Control (CDC). Retrieved March 2007 from http://phil.cdc.gov. (D) Goldsmith, C. (no date). Ebola virus. Public Health Image Library. Image courtesy of the Centers for Disease Control (CDC). Retrieved August 2006 from http://phil.cdc.gov.

Figure 16.26 Images from (A) Earth, (B) Space, (C) the Moon
Source: National Aeronautics and Space Administration. (various dates). Images courtesy of NASA. Retrieved August 2006 from http://www.nasa.gov/multimedia/imagegallery.

ACTIVITY 16.4.2 *Making Inferences from Photographs*

An inference is a tentative conclusion that is reached on the basis of evidence and reasoning. Scientists must frequently make inferences, but inferences are only as good as the evidence and reasoning behind them. Figure 16.27 is a photograph of the stars that I took. Examine it, and answer each of the following questions, supporting your conclusions with evidence and reasoning.

1. This photo was taken looking (a) east, (b) northeast, (c) north, (d) northwest, (e) west.
2. The shutter on the camera was kept open for (a) 10 seconds, (b) 2 minutes, (c) 5 minutes, (d) 1 hour, (e) 6 hours.
3. The photograph was taken in (a) the mountains, (b) the city, (c) the desert, (d) the tropics, (e) a planetarium.

Figure 16.27 Photograph of the Stars

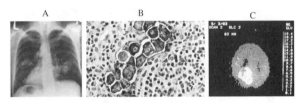

Figure 16.28 Identify the Cancerous Tissue in the Three Views

ACTIVITY 16.4.3 *Making Inferences from Medical Images*

Physicians rely heavily on images to diagnose injuries, illness, and disease. Oncologists (doctors who treat cancer patients) hope to identify cancers in their earliest stages so that they can treat patients before cancer spreads. It is difficult to determine if a patient has cancer simply by interview or external appearance, so oncologists rely heavily on medical imaging techniques such as X-rays (Figure 16.28A), microscope photographs from tissue samples (Figure 16.28B), and PET (positron emission tomography) scans (Figure 16.28C) to detect the presence and location of cancerous tissues. Cancer is a collection of diseases characterized by rapid, uncontrolled cell division of abnormal cells. These cells may interfere with normal-functioning cells. Oncologists analyze images for abnormal growths and tissues. Pretend that you are an oncologist as you analyze the evidence from the following images:

1. Figure 16.28A is a chest X-ray of a patient with lung cancer. Identify the location where you think the cancerous tissue is.

2. Figure 16.28B is a photograph of cells from a patient with breast cancer. Identify the cells that you think are cancerous.

3. Figure 16.28C is a PET scan of the brain of a patient with a brain tumor. Identify where you think the tumor is located.

ACTIVITY 16.4.4 *Identifying Structures from Medical Images*

Assume you are a medical doctor, and a patient complains of frequent headaches. You must make a diagnosis, but you know that headaches may be caused by narcotics, migraines, pressure in the meninges, swelling of blood vessels, eyestrain, electrolyte imbalance, low blood sugar, neck pain, head trauma, cancer, or many other possibilities. To make an accurate diagnosis, you need more information, much of which can be obtained by medical imaging technologies such as X-rays, CT scans, PET scans, sonograms, and MRI scans (Figures 16.29A to 16.29E). These technologies, explained below, allow you to visualize things

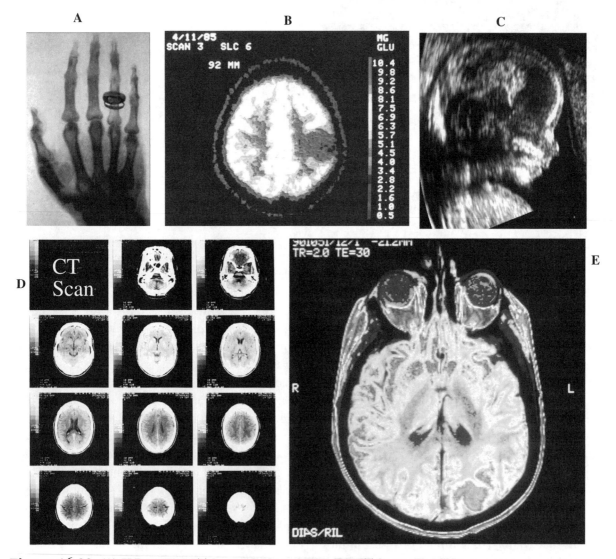

Figure 16.29 (A) X-Ray, (B) PET Scan, (C) Sonogram, (D) CT Scan, (E) MRI

Source: (A) Roentgen, W. (1896). X-ray picture of the hand of Alfred von Kolliker. Image courtesy of Radiology Centennial, Pennsylvania State University. (B, C, E) Anonymous (no date). Miscellaneous medical images. Public Health Image Library. Image courtesy of the Centers for Disease Control (CDC). Retrieved August 2006 from http://phil.cdc.gov. (D) Bartlett, L. (no date). CT scan of brain. Image courtesy of the Centers for Disease Control (CDC). Retrieved August 2006 from http://phil.cdc.gov.

that are otherwise invisible to the observer. Read about the different medical imaging technologies; then label as many structures as you can identify in each of the images. You may use other diagrams and pictures to help you identify the structures.

- X-*rays:* X-rays are high-energy electromagnetic radiation that penetrate soft tissues but are blocked by bone and other dense structures. They provide silhouettes of bones and other structures, and are immensely valuable in orthopedics and other medical professions. Figure 16.29A is one of the earliest X-rays recorded. It was made by Wilhelm Roentgen, the inventor of X-ray imaging, in 1896.
- *Positron emission tomography (PET scan):* Patients are injected with a short-lived radioactive isotope that is incorporated in a metabolically active molecule such as sugar. Once absorbed by tissues, positrons (the antiparticles of electrons) are emitted and detected by the scanner, providing an image of the tissues that have absorbed the carrier molecule. Figure 16.29B is a PET scan showing a cancerous tumor in the brain.
- *Sonography:* Sonography is the imaging of structures with ultrasonic sound waves. Sound waves in excess of 20,000 Hz are projected into the body and reflect off muscles, tendons, and other internal organs. The reflected sound waves are received and interpreted graphically, as shown in Figure 16.29C. Sonographs (known commonly as ultrasound images) are used to track fetal development. Figure 16.29C is a sonogram of a 14-week-old human embryo.
- *Computed tomography (CT scan):* Computed tomography generates images of virtual "slices" of the body. CT scans integrate X-ray data from a variety of angles to generate a series of sectional images (Figure 16.29D). With CT scans, the physician can see what the body looks like at a series of elevations or levels.
- *Magnetic resonance imaging (MRI):* Magnetic resonance imaging allows physicians to examine soft tissues. Images are created from the resonating magnetic fields of the hydrogen atoms within the water molecules of the body.

Computer-generated images allow medical personnel to visualize soft tissues, such as the brain shown in Figure 16.29E.

ACTIVITY 16.4.5 *Correcting Misconceptions in Science*

In 2001 a popular television network aired a program *Conspiracy Theory: Did We Land on the Moon?* This pseudodocumentary concluded that NASA faked the moon landing by taking pictures in the Nevada desert. Each of the following accusations was based on NASA photographs such as Figure 16.30. Examine each of the following claims in the light of Figure 16.30, and offer a plausible explanation to rebut those who say the Moon landing was staged.

1. There is no atmosphere on the Moon, and therefore no wind, yet Figure 16.30 shows the flag flying, indicating that the photograph was taken on Earth.

Figure 16.30 Astronaut Buzz Aldrin on the Moon, 1969

Source: Armstrong, N. (1969). Astronaut Edwin E. Aldrin Jr., lunar module pilot of the first lunar landing mission, poses for a photograph beside the deployed United States Flag during an Apollo 11 extravehicular activity (EVA) on the lunar surface. July 20, 1969. Image courtesy of NASA. Retrieved August 2006 from http://www.nasa.gov/multimedia/imagegallery.

2. The flag is fluttering rather than hanging flat. If a horizontal crossbeam supported the flag, the fabric would hang straight, but it appears to be fluttering as it would in a breeze. There is no atmosphere on the Moon, so there are no breezes, indicating that the photograph was taken on Earth.

3. The shadows in the photograph are not parallel. Shadows are caused when objects intercept light. Since the Sun is very far from the Moon, the rays reaching the Moon are essentially parallel, and thus the shadows should be parallel as well. The nonparallel shadows must be caused by the presence of additional lighting sources, such as those on a movie set.

4. No stars are visible even though the sky is black. Since there is no atmosphere on the Moon, there is no light and therefore no scattering of the light rays. The sky is therefore black during the daytime, and stars are visible even when the Sun is up. Since no stars are visible, the photograph could not have been taken on the Moon.

ACTIVITY 16.4.6 *Detecting Hoaxes*

Photographs can be misleading, particularly since the advent of digital photography and associated software such as Photoshop. A skillful graphic artist can easily alter photographs, so you should be particularly skeptical about unusual photographs you receive by e-mail or see on the Internet and in magazines. It used to be said that "photographs don't lie," and although this statement was more accurate in the predigital era than now, photographs have long been used to mislead and trick.

Following is a list of classic hoaxes that fooled millions. Select one of the following images, and locate it on the Internet using a graphic search engine. You may need to enter the name of the location or photographer, or both, in addition to the name of the photograph. Critique the photograph and suggest how it may have been made.

1. *Sea Serpent:* A long marine serpent found in Ballard, Washington, in 1906.

2. *Jackalopes:* A cross between jackrabbits and antelopes, popularized on postcards from Colorado and Wyoming starting in 1950.

3. *Loch Ness Monster:* A reclusive animal resembling a plesiosaur; photographed by R. K. Wilson in 1934 in the Scottish lake Loch Ness.

4. *Brown Lady of Raynham Hall:* A 1936 photograph in *Country Life Magazine* that was purported to be the ghost of Lady Townshend, imprisoned in Raynham Hall.

5. *Sympsychograph:* A machine purported to transfer images from the mind onto film. Photographs were first published in 1896 in *Popular Science Monthly* by David Starr Jordan.

6. *Bigfoot:* A large apelike animal living in the woods of northern California, photographed by Roger Patterson and Robert Gimlin in 1967.

7. *Venusian spacecraft:* A photograph of a flying saucer by George Adamski who claimed that he was visited by aliens from Venus in 1952.

16.5 Digital Movies and Animations

Movies are an extremely useful tool in science and engineering. Figure 16.31 shows frames from the famous 1940 movie of the collapse of the Tacoma Narrows Bridge. The bridge, over 1 mi in length, collapsed during a 42 mph windstorm just four months after construction was completed. Scientists and engineers from the state of Washington and around the rest of the world intently studied this movie to understand the causes of the disaster. As a result of their findings, designs for suspension bridges were forever altered, and there has been no comparable disaster with suspension bridges since.

Movies such as those made of the Tacoma Narrows Bridge collapse, the *Challenger* space shuttle explosion, the World Trade Center towers attack, and the assassination of John F. Kennedy have been studied extensively, and they have yielded information that has helped engineers and decision makers in their attempts to avert similar calamities. Scientists have realized the value of movies, and today, digital video cameras are used in thousands of laboratories to record experiments and make observations.

Figure 16.31 Scenes from the Tacoma Narrow Bridge Disaster, 1940

Source: Elliot, B. (1940). Tacoma Narrows bridge disaster. Movie courtesy of the Tacoma Fire Department. Retrieved December 2006 from http://www.archive.org.

Video editing software allows users to examine videos in great detail. Slow motion, single-frame viewing, and time-lapse photography are a few of the many techniques scientists use to study their subjects. NTSC video (the most common format in the United States) is shot at approximately 30 frames per second. Therefore, each new frame represents the passing of an additional 1/30 of a second of time. PAL and SECAM formats shoot 25 frames per second, so if you use these formats, each frame represents an additional 1/25 of a second. Studies of motion and process are greatly simplified with the use of digital video. In this section students use a couple of powerful techniques to study scientific phenomena.

ACTIVITY 16.5.1 *Observing High-Speed Activities*

Many interesting scientific phenomena take place so fast that observers cannot fully appreciate or understand the process. Digital video technology allows users to record such events and replay them at greatly reduced speeds so they can be studied and understood.

A favorite activity in the study of motion is the water rocket, pictured in Figure 16.32. This activity requires two 2 L plastic bottles, a launch mechanism (available from many scientific supply companies), and a bicycle pump. Water is placed in the rocket and the opening sealed with a one-way valve. A pump is used to increase the air pressure inside the container. Eventually the trigger string is pulled, releasing the water from the bottle. As the water is forced out, the bottle flies up, as one would predict by Newton's law of interaction: for every action, there is an equal and opposite reaction. Following is a set of instructions for constructing and videotaping a water rocket.

Using scissors, cut the top off a plastic 2 L soda bottle, as shown in Figure 16.32A. Place this end over the bottom of another empty bottle, packing the space between with old rags or similar material to provide weight in the front of the rocket (16.32B). Tape this junction, and place a rubber stopper in the head of the bottle (16.32C). The rags and the stopper weight the tip and help the rocket fly straighter. Carefully cut three fins out of the sides of the first bottle, and seal them firmly to the sides of the rocket (Figure 16.32D) using duct tape or other strong adhesive. The plastic fins will maintain some of their original curvature, and all three fins should be mounted so that the curves go in the same direction. It is easiest to mount the fins by first bending the bases 90 degrees and sealing them to the bottle using duct tape. The fins will cause the rocket to spin along the vertical axis. This same spinning motion is used to stabilize footballs and rifle bullets in flight.

Fill the rocket partially with water, and seal the mouth with a one-hole stopper fitted with

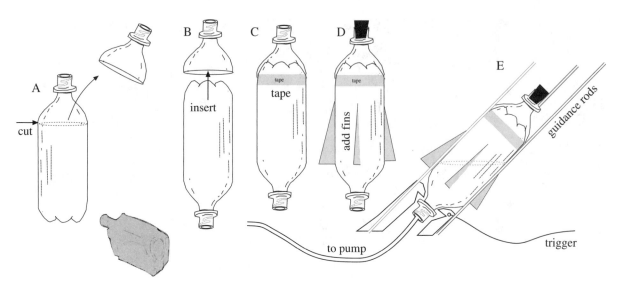

Figure 16.32 Using Digital Movies to Analyze Water Rockets

a one-way ball valve, available through many supply companies (look on *sciencesourcebook.com*, or search "soda bottle rocket launcher"). Firmly secure the guidance rods (wooden dowels or PVC pipe) around the rocket so it cannot tip over when the trigger is pulled (Figure 16.32E). Make certain everyone leaves the launch site.

Set the video camera on a tripod a long distance from the launch site so it will be able to capture the entire flight without panning. Make sure that something of known or measurable height is in the field of view close to the rocket so that you will be able to make distance and height measurements. Set the video camera to Record. Put on goggles. Connect the valve using tubing to a tire pump. Stand to the side of the rocket, and pump to the desired pressure. Start with low pressure, and work up once you have an understanding for how far the rocket will fly. Stand behind a tree, wall, or other form of protection, and pull the trigger line. The water will rush out of the mouth of the bottle, propelling the rocket along a parabolic trajectory. *Caution:* The bottle can easily fly more than 100 m, so this activity should be performed under the supervision of an experienced teacher, and only in very large areas where no one else is around.

Import the video into a computer equipped with video editing software. Examine the frames

in which the rocket was airborne. Measure the horizontal distance (d_x) and the vertical distance (d_y) from the launch site for each frame. Such measurements can be made by comparing lengths with other things of known height or length, such as a tree, building, or the hash marks on a football field. Plot vertical and horizontal distance as a function of time, remembering that each frame represents 1/30 of a second. Next, plot the vertical distance as a function of the horizontal distance. Does the rocket follow a parabolic trajectory? Use this setup to study the effect of reaction mass (the amount of water used), air pressure (the amount of pumping performed), rocket design (presence or absence of fins and nose cone), or elevation (the angle from which the rocket launched).

Following is a list of high-speed processes that can be studied with the use of digital video. Some require a video-microscope. Specific information on each of the following can be accessed on the Internet by searching for key terms.

- *Biology:* Cytoplasmic streaming in Elodea (aquarium pondweed), heart rate in Daphnia (water flea), fertilization in sea urchins, muscle action in a running dog, cilia movement in paramecium, blood flow in the tail of a goldfish, phagocytosis in amoeba

- *Chemistry:* End point of a titration, fast chemical reactions, crystal formation in supercooled environments, flame tests, combustion reactions
- *Physics:* Acceleration and deceleration of automobiles, acceleration of falling objects, collisions of rolling or gliding objects, center of mass in a thrown hammer or other irregular object, air track collisions
- *Earth and space science:* Movement of leaves in a whirlwind or "dust-devil," ocean wave behavior, movement of dust in a wind tunnel

ACTIVITY 16.5.2 *Time-Lapse Photography of Slow Processes*

Digital video provides the opportunity to analyze slow processes as well as fast ones. Time-lapse photography is the process of taking frames less frequently so that the process appears more rapid when played back. Figure 16.33 illustrates the growth of crystals as observed under a video microscope. Figure 16.33A illustrates how such videos are captured at a rate of 30 frames per second. If, however, frames are taken only three times a second (Figure 16.33B), the resulting movie will compress the real action into one-tenth the time when it is played back (Figure 16.33C). Many video cameras, especially those used for microscopic photography, have time-lapse options. See your camera manual (available on the manufacturer's Web site) for details.

Make a time-lapse recording of a slow process such as one of those listed below. Select an appropriate time-lapse frame rate. The frame rate should be much slower for lengthy processes, such as seed germination or fruit rotting. Set the camera on a tripod where it is protected from wind, weather, and vibrations. It is often helpful to place

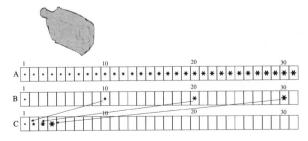

Figure 16.33 Time-Lapse Photography for Analyzing Low-Speed Processes

an analogue clock in the field of view to record the time of each frame. Study the movie when it is played back at normal speed and report what you learn from this movie that you would not have noticed without time-lapse photography.

Subjects for Time-Lapse Photography

- *Biology:* Rotting fruit, bacterial growth in a petri dish, seed germination, phototropism in lupines or sunflowers, flower opening, caterpillar or snail movement, tunneling in an ant farm, tendril movement in peas, motion of *Mimosa pudica* ("sensitive plant"), insect molting, hatching of insect or bird eggs, growth of mold on bread
- *Chemistry:* Slow chemical reactions, condensation on the outside of a cold cup, boiling of water, formation of salt or sugar crystals by evaporation of salt or sugar water, combustion of wood in a fireplace, evaporation of water from a glass, crystal formation (alum, ammonium phosphate, Epsom salt, sodium thiosulfate, copper sulfate pentahydrate, nickel sulfate, ferrous sulfate, potassium sodium tartrate, potassium chromate, potassium dichromate, silver from silver nitrate and copper, potassium ferrocyanide)
- *Physics, and earth and space science:* Moon rise, phases of the Moon, cloud formation, ocean tides, patterns in visible air pollution, soil erosion in a stream flow experiment, apparent rotation of stars around the North Star

ACTIVITY 16.5.3 *Making and Editing Science Videos*

Digital video editing software allows users to integrate video, text, still images, narration, and music into a dynamic movie (Figure 16.34). Develop a brief video of an experiment, activity, science project, field trip, or interview. Include explanatory sound and subtitles. Here are some ideas:

- *Biology:* Biology experiment, introduction to a local ecosystem, highlights of a local zoo or botanical garden, field trip to a local biotech laboratory or university biology lab, behavior of a pet or wild animal, interview with a biologist concerning his or her profession

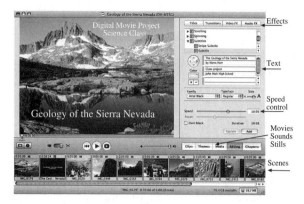

Figure 16.34 Digital Video Editing Provides Opportunities for Science Projects

- *Chemistry:* Chemistry experiment, field trip to a refinery or chemical production facility, documentary of a chemical pollution problem in your region, interview of a chemist or chemical engineer about his or her profession
- *Physics:* Physics experiment, field trip to an engineering firm or university physics research laboratory, interview with a physicist or engineer about his or her profession, documentary about a recent development or application in physics.
- *Earth and space science:* Local geology; current weather patterns and analysis; field trip to a water treatment facility, weather station, landfill, or construction site; interview with a geologist, astronomer, environmental scientist, oceanographer, or meteorologist about his or her profession.

ACTIVITY 16.5.4 *Using Digital Video for Science Instruction*

Nielsen Media Research reported that in 2005, the average American watched an average of 4 hours and 32 minutes of television per day.[1] Put another way, in 2005 the average American spent 28 percent of his or her waking life watching TV and videos. Even if the programming were decent or educational, which it rarely is, the sheer investment of time poses serious social, mental, and health threats to the "couch potatoes" and "vidiots" who so indulge. Researchers have linked excessive television watching with obesity,[2] poor academic performance, and social dysfunction.[3] Students who spend large amounts of time in the passive environment of television are less likely to eat, exercise, study, and socialize appropriately. It is very clear that students do not need any more entertainment. Unfortunately, many students view videos in the classroom the way they use them at home: as entertainment, rather than as a learning experience. Students and teachers need to master the remote control so they can use appropriate sections of videos for student-taught lessons or interactive instruction. Figure 16.35 shows standard video controllers for digital media. Develop and present a 5- to 10-min lesson with excerpts from a digital movie. Add your own dialog and questions to tie the clips together. You may use a movie designed to teach science or a popular movie that incorporates science themes such as *October Sky* (an inspirational story of youth excelling in science), *Blue Planet* (the natural history of the

Figure 16.35 Numerous Features of Digital Viewers for Use in Instruction

world's oceans), *Planet Earth* (the natural history of terrestrial and aquatic biomes), *Apollo 13* (the heroic story of the crew of a Moon mission that ran into serious trouble), *March of the Penguins* (the behavior and ecology of Antarctica's emperor penguins), or *An Inconvenient Truth* (the evidence of climate change). Your lesson should demonstrate mastery of the techniques listed below.

- *Minimize:* The movie can be minimized to reveal other relevant documents or Web sites.
- *Movie:* Videos can be shown full screen or a portion thereof. It is often useful to show the video in partial screen so other applications can be viewed simultaneously. For example, you can write and display notes in a word processor adjacent to the movie being viewed.
- *Time:* You can reference the precise time of a particular scene or sequence.
- *Play/Pause:* Use the Pause button to discuss important scenes or concepts and engage students in predictions. During the pause, students can make measurements or plot positions of items on the screen.
- *Stop:* Stop the video when you have dealt with the key issues. Do not feel compelled to show the entire movie.
- *Previous chapter/scan backward:* It may be advantageous to show a scene multiple times to make sure that students understand key events and concepts.
- *Next chapter/scan forward:* Skip through material that is not relevant to your lesson.
- *Volume:* Turn off the sound so the teacher or students can narrate a clip.
- *Slow motion:* Use slow motion to analyze rapidly occurring events such as a beating heart or a rocket launch.
- *Step frame:* This allows you to view key scenes one frame at a time, which is particularly valuable for critical sequences such as cell division or a collision. Each frame represents 1/30 of second of real time.
- *Subtitles/closed captioning:* Turn on the closed captioning for hearing-impaired individuals or English learners. Closed captioning allows English learners to see and hear words

simultaneously, helping them to associate spoken and written language.

- *Audio/alternate languages:* Many videos are recorded in more than one language. Use this feature if you want learners to hear explanations in their native tongue so they can better understand the English explanations.
- *Bookmark:* This feature allows you to reference a specific frame within the video. Bookmark key frames, and label and organize them in folders associated with your lessons.
- *Video clips:* The video clip feature defines start and end times for video clips. These may be labeled and organized in the same manner as bookmarks so as to provide easy access for future lessons.

ACTIVITY 16.5.5 *Electronic Presentations*

The most effective way to learn something is to prepare a lesson and teach it. In this activity, students teach their peers with the aid of electronic presentation tools. Software such as PowerPoint makes it possible to integrate photos, text, movies, sound, and animation in electronic presentations (Figure 16.36). Although such presentations are potentially very helpful in science instruction, they are often overused or abused. Many students have

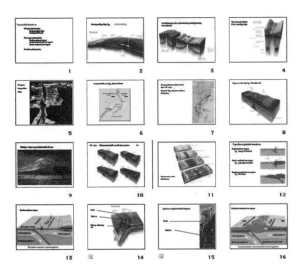

Figure 16.36 Digital Slide Show for Science Topics

suffered "death by PowerPoint" by being subjected to unending sequences of digital text with cute but useless transitions and special effects. Fortunately, electronic presentations can be very helpful if the following guidelines are adhered to. Prepare a presentation on a topic relevant to your curriculum, taking the following points into consideration.

Guidelines for Preparing Electronic Presentations

- *Use only key terms and phrases.* Use a limited amount of text. Single words and brief phrases are easier to read, take notes on, and remember than sentences or paragraphs.
- *Make all text readable.* The text should be large enough that everyone in the class can read and should be in a color that is easily seen against the background.
- *Reveal text progressively.* Animate text so it appears only when you are ready to discuss it. This allows your audience to track with your thoughts. Revealing all of the text at once may prevent you from asking relevant questions because the answers are already on the screen.
- *Use clear graphics.* Use graphics that illustrate your points and are large and clear enough that everyone in the class can see the details you describe.
- *Resize graphics to conserve memory.* Resize graphics so they are appropriate for the size of your display. Digital cameras and scanners produce files many times larger than necessary for projection. Large files require extra memory and may slow your computer.
- *Provide notes.* Provide users with notes that show the contents of your slides. Encourage students to add their own notes to the framework you have provided.
- *Employ multimedia.* Electronic presentations should make use of text, graphics, movies, sounds, animations, and Web links. Such resources should be relevant to your topic.
- *Interact with your audience.* The main cause of "death by PowerPoint" is that presenters do not interact with their audiences as they proceed dutifully from one slide to the next. Invite student comments, and write down key

ideas on the screen, whiteboard, or overhead as you go. Master the navigation controls so you can access any slide, Web page or document as appropriate. Do not be constrained by the linear sequence in which your slides are arranged.
- *Use the appropriate technology.* Your electronic presentation is not the teacher. You are! Use it as a tool to illustrate your points. Skip slides that are unnecessary, and use other media as appropriate. The overhead, whiteboard, chalkboard, and digital visual presenter are generally better than electronic presentations when illustrating equations and solving problems. Such media allow a more flexible presentation and enable your students to see your thought processes as they develop rather than those you used when you made the slide show hours before.

16.6 Extrapolation

An extrapolation is an inference based on the assumption that trends continue beyond the set of data collected. Scientists often extrapolate from laboratory data to the real world. For example, cancer researchers cannot perform experiments on human subjects but can do so on laboratory rats and other animals. Such researchers may conclude that chemicals are carcinogenic to humans based solely on data collected from other laboratory animals. To make such conclusions, it is necessary to extrapolate from the animals to the human population.

ACTIVITY 16.6.1 *Extrapolation Game*
Extrapolations can also be made from graphics or pictures. Figures 16.37A to 16.37X show common items viewed at 50 to 100 times magnification. Each of these photographs contains clues (evidence) of its source. Search each photograph for clues, and extrapolate to the item photographed by matching with the objects listed below. Students or teachers can make their own extrapolation games or exercises with a handheld digital microscope.

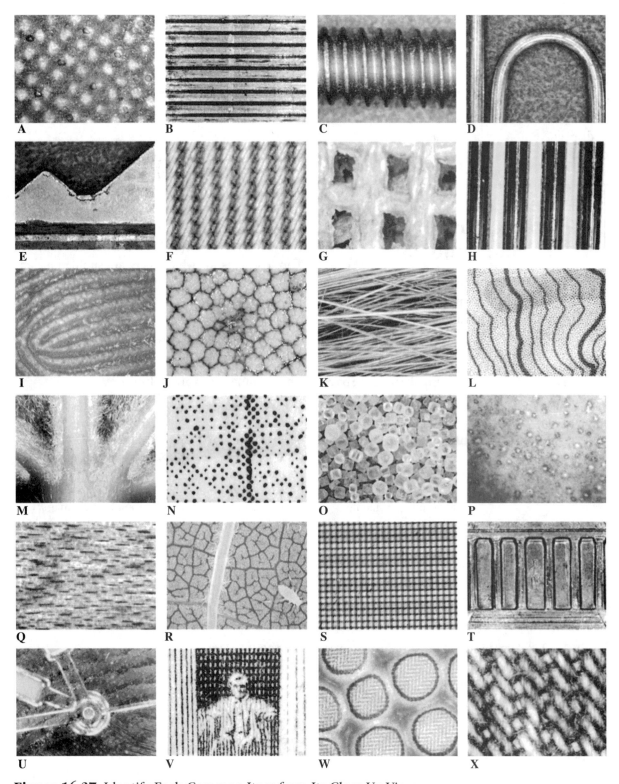

Figure 16.37 Identify Each Common Item from Its Close-Up View

aphid on leaf	finger	salt
apple	football	screw
Band-Aid	hair	stalk (petiole)
Chex cereal	jeans	of leaf
comb	key	staples
plasma display	newspaper photograph	topographic map
cotton shirt	paper clip	watch
daisy	penny	wood

16.7 Interactive Scientific Simulations

An interactive simulation is one in which the user can experiment by manipulating input variables. A variety of software is available to design interactive simulations, and many science simulations are available on the Internet. Interactive simulations are particularly useful in science because they allow students to visualize, manipulate, and experiment with concepts that cannot easily be observed.

ACTIVITY 16.7.1 *Teaching and Learning Science Concepts with Simulations*

Locate a simulation of a scientific concept assigned by your teacher, and teach your study group or class the concept using the simulation and a data projector. Tables 16.1 to 16.4 list a few of the many science concepts for which there are simulations and animations on the Internet (see *sciencesourcebook. com* or search for a "simulation" or "animation" of your topic).

Table 16.1 A Few of the Many Earth and Space Science Animations on the Internet

aurora borealis	Foucault's pendulum	ocean currents	seasons
carbon cycle	geyser eruption	ocean mapping	seismographs
cloud formation	glacier movement	oil formation and trapping	soil porosity
coastal winds	greenhouse effect		star spectra
Coriolis effect	hurricane motion	orbital motion	subduction
crystallization	Kepler's Laws	phases of the moon	tides
eclipse	locating an epicenter	plate tectonics	topographical maps
Eratosthenes measurement	Milankovitch cycles	process of folding	volcano formation
erosion	mineral growth	red shift	water cycle
	motions of the planets	rock cycle	water pollution
fault types and motion	nitrogen cycle	seafloor spreading	weather maps

Table 16.2 A Few of the Many Biology Animations on the Internet

cardiac cycle	food web	lytic cycle	perception
cell cycle	fruit formation	meiosis	photophosphorylation
cell energy cycle	gas exchange	migration	photosynthesis
countercurrent exchange	genetics	mitosis	pollination
dehydration synthesis	germination	mutation	population dynamics
diffusion	Hardy-Weinberg equilibrium	natural selection	protein synthesis
digestion		nerve transmission	reflexes
DNA replication	hearing	nutritional analysis	respiration
electrophoresis	homeostasis	osmosis	translocation in plants
enzyme action	hormone action	PCR (polymerase chain reaction)	transpiration
epidemiology	karyotyping		vision

Table 16.3 A Few of the Many Chemistry Animations on the Internet

acid-base equilibrium	covalent bonding	ionic bonding	pH analysis
Archimedes principle	dehydration synthesis	kinetic theory	phase changes
Bohr model	density determination	limiting reactants	photoelectric effect
boiling point elevation	distillation	mass spectroscopy	reduction
Boyle's Law	double replacement	molecular kinetics	Rutherford experiment
calorimetry	dry cell	nitrogen fixation	single replacement
Charles Law	electron configuration	nuclear decay	solubility
chemical analysis	electron orbitals	nuclear fission	spectral analysis
chromatography	equation balancing	nuclear fusion	stoichiometry
colligative properties	freezing point	nuclear magnetic	titration
collision theory	depression	resonance	X-ray crystallography
condensation	half-life determination	oxidation	

Table 16.4 A Few of the Many Physics Animations on the Internet

additive colors	freefall	nuclear fusion	satellite motion
air tracks	frequency	parallel circuits	series circuits
Archimedes principle	Galileo's experiments	pendulum motion	simple harmonics
ballistic pendulum	harmonic oscillation	photoelectric effect	simple machines
black holes	inclined planes	potential and kinetic	sound generation
chromatic aberration	interference	energy	subtractive pigments
collisions	Kepler's laws	precession	superposition
Coulomb force	lightning	prismatic	torque
diffraction	longitudinal waves	decomposition	trajectories
Doppler shift	magnetic induction	pulleys	transverse waves
electromagnetic fields	Millikan's experiment	ray tracing	vector addition
fan carts	moment of inertia	reflection	
fiber optics	nuclear fission	refraction	

Answers to Chapter Activities

16.1.1 (1a) A, (1b) D, (1c) B, (1d), C; (2a) B, (2b) D, (2c) A, (2d), C; (3a) D, (3b) C, (3c) A, (3d), B; (4a) F. Note that the perpendicular force into the ramp exceeds the force exerted by the ramp on the box. Since the forces are unbalanced, the ramp will bend (accelerate) in the direction of the greater force. (4b) C. This is considered a heavier box because the gravitational force, as represented by the F_{mg} vector, is greater than it is for the lighter boxes, D, E, and F. Note that there is no frictional force acting to counter the accelerating force, F_a. (4c) D. This is considered a lighter box because the gravitational force, represented by the F_{mg} vector, is less than it is for the heavier boxes, A, B, and C. The accelerating and frictional forces are balanced, and the perpendicular and normal forces are balanced. (4d) E. One can see that the ramp is frictionless because there is no vector to counter the accelerating force, F_a. (4e) A. This is considered a heavier box because the gravitational force, represented by the F_{mg} vector, is greater than it is for the lighter boxes, D, E, and F. The accelerating and

frictional forces are balanced, and the perpendicular and normal forces are balanced. (4f) B. This box will accelerate because the accelerating force, F_a, exceeds the frictional force, F_f. Frictional forces, F_f, generate heat.

16.2.1 (1) Inside the focal length, as in Figure 16.7F. (2) At two times the focal length, as in Figure 16.7C. (3) Between the focal length and two times the focal length, as in Figure 16.7D. (4) Beyond two times the focal length, as in Figure 16.7B. (5) At the focal length, as in Figure 16.7E. (6) Far from the lens, as in Figure 16.7A.

16.2.2 (1a) Alrai. (1b) Alderamin. (1c) Delta Cygni. (2a) Moon. (2b) Spring tides, when the Sun and Moon are aligned with the Earth. (2c) Neap tides, when the Sun and Moon are at right angles to the Earth. (3a) photons. (3b) P700. (3c) e^-. (3d) P680. (3e) PS-I. (4) 1c, 2d, 3e, 4f, 5g, 6h, 7a, 8b.

16.2.3 Student diagrams will vary, but should succinctly and accurately illustrate the key concepts.

16.3.1 (1) The compass is mounted to the dashboard of a car driving east across the United States. The compass needle always points to magnetic north, which is in northern Canada, rather than to the true North Pole, which is in the middle of the polar ice cap. The first picture could represent a location on the West Coast (e.g., San Francisco, declination 14.7°); the second a position in the middle of the country where the declination is essentially zero because the car, magnetic pole, and geographic pole are on the same meridian (e.g., Cedar Rapids, Iowa, declination 0.2°); and the third a city on the East Coast (e.g., Boston, declination −15.4°). Alternatively, the movement of the compass needle could be the result of a magnet that is brought near to compass.

(2) The wire is viewed in cross section and is part of a loop. X and Y represent the cross section of a wire that comes out of the plane of the paper, at X makes a U-turn, and then reenters the plane at Y. A magnetic field is produced when an electric current flows through the wire. The field is always oriented the same way with respect to the wire. It is oriented opposite if the wire is bent and the current flows in the opposite direction. The circuit is open in the first picture, so no current flows and no magnetic field is generated. The circuit is closed in the second picture, allowing electricity to flow in one direction and opposite magnetic fields to be generated in the two portions of wire that are going different directions. The current is reversed (as in an AC current) in the final picture, causing a reversal of magnetic fields.

(3) The cell is initially in an isotonic solution (A), but when placed in a hypotonic solution, the cell swells and breaks (B and C).

(4) The cell is initially in an isotonic solution (A), but when placed in a hypertonic solution, the cell shrinks (B) before it is again placed in the original solution and resumes its shape (C).

(5) The tail of the comet (A) grows under the influence of solar wind (B and C) as it approaches the Sun and shrinks as it moves away from the sun (D and E).

(6) Figures 16.16A and 16.16B represent an aerial view of a highway that experienced a massive earthquake on a strike-slip fault. Figures 16.16C and 16.16D represent a highway that experienced an earthquake along a reverse or compressional fault. The total distance has decreased due to compression.

(7) (A) one nearby stationary object. (B) three nearby stationary objects. (C) two nearby stationary objects, one of which is closer than the other. (D) one object that is moving toward the source. (E) one object moving away from the source. (F) one object moving toward the source and one moving away from the source.

(8) (A) A person is excited, startled, or starts to exercise, leading to an increase in heart rate. (B) A person is sedated or stops exercising, leading to a decrease in heart rate. (C) A person suffers a heart attack, causing the heart to stop beating. (D) A patient's heart is restarted following a heart attack.

(9) (A) The dog is positioned closer to the elephant so that the center of mass for the system is on the left of the fulcrum. (B) The dog moves backward until the center of mass is directly above the fulcrum and the animals are balanced. (C) The dog continues to move back until the center of mass is to the right of the fulcrum, causing a net torque so the plank rotates to the right.

(10) Growth and development occur between A and B. The first diagram (A) is a picture of a fetal skeleton scaled up to the size of an adult skeleton. The second skeleton (B) is a mature human skeleton.

16.3.2 Student answers may vary, depending on the criteria they select. The following are common answers, but the teacher should also give credit for other reasonable answers. (A) A penguin. (2) is a bird; the others are mammals. (B) The living fern (3) is not a fossil; the others are. (C) The insect (2) has six legs; the others are spiders with eight legs. (D) The buckeye (2) is not an oak and does not produce acorns. (E) The shark (3) has a backbone; the others do not. (F) The whale (2) is a mammal; the others are bony or cartilaginous fish. (G) The clamshell (4) is a bivalve shell; the others are helical (spiral). (H) The cabbage (2) is a vegetable; the others are fruits. (I) The carrots (1) are vegetative; the others are reproductive parts. (J) The pine (5) is a gymnosperm; the others are angiosperms.

16.3.3 (A) Granite is a plutonic, igneous rock and should be found at the bottom of the profile rather than the top.

(B) Mountains cause winds to rise, cooling air and causing precipitation. Forests are typically found on the windward rather than the leeward sides of mountain ranges, and rain shadow deserts are found on the leeward sides rather than the windward.

(C) The ball should travel straight (tangential to the movement) when the string is cut. When the string is cut, there is no remaining force to create a curved path.

(D) This illustrates the stages of metamorphosis in a moth. The larvae (caterpillar) and pupa stages (stages 2 and 3) should be switched.

(E) The 50 kg mass has much more inertia than the 10 kg mass. The 10 kg mass should therefore bounce backward off the more massive 50 kg mass.

(F) Conservation of momentum dictates that the momentum following a collision should be the same as the momentum preceding a collision. Since the heights of the balls are the same, one can assume they are moving at similar speeds away from each other; in fact, the smaller one should be moving much faster than the larger one for momentum to be conserved.

(G) In a frictionless system, a ball could roll to reach the same elevation it started from, but would have no remaining kinetic energy to complete the loop. A roller-coaster loop must always be lower than the starting point if it is driven only by gravity.

(H) Newton's law of interaction states that for every action, there is an equal and opposite reaction. When the mass is suspended in the beaker, its weight decreases, and the weight on the balance must therefore increase by an equal amount, but this is not shown in the picture.

(I) One parent is homozygous recessive, and the other is heterozygous. They can therefore produce white or colored flowers, but not flowers with alternating petal color.

(J) Newton's law of interaction states that for every action, there is an equal and opposing reaction. The gun should recoil to the left as the bullet flies to the right.

(K) Zebras are native to Africa, and bison are native to North America. They would not be seen in the same photograph unless in a zoo.

(L) The angles of the blocks appear to be right angles (90°), but it would be impossible for three such blocks to form a closed figure as shown since the sum of the angles would have to be 360°, when the sum of three right angles is only 270°.

(M) Snow crystals have six sides, but one of those illustrated has eight. It has been said that every snowflake has a unique shape. Although this cannot be proven, we do know that they are generally different, yet two in this picture have the same shape.

16.4.1 (1) The birds flying to the right of the space shuttle indicate the Earth can support living systems. (2) The sky is completely black even though the Sun is shining. This occurs because there is no atmosphere to scatter or refract light. (3) The huge exhaust clouds from the space shuttle engines and solid rocket boosters indicate great force is required for lift-off. (4) It appears as though the astronauts can float in any position. The tail fin of the space shuttle appears to be upside down, an orientation that makes sense only if the passengers are weightless. (5) Space appears dark black, indicating that there is no atmosphere to scatter light. (6) The astronauts are wearing protective suits that isolate them from the environment of the Moon, presumably because it is inhospitable for life. (7) The lunar surface appears devoid of life, and there are no visible erosion channels. (8) The astronaut is wearing a larger suit and carrying a larger backpack than he would be able to carry comfortably on Earth. (9) The sky is not black, indicating that there is an atmosphere to scatter or reflect light.

16.4.2 (1) North. The stars appear to be rotating around the North Star (Polaris), a star that is aligned with the Earth's axis or rotation. (2) One hour. The arcs left by the stars represent approximately 1/24 of a circle. Since there are 24 hours in a day, each 1/24 of an arc represents 1 hour. (3) Mountains. The trees appear to be conifers such as pines, firs, or spruces. Such trees are commonly found in the mountains, but not in the desert or tropics, or in a planetarium. Although conifers may be found in the city, it is unlikely that a photograph in the city would show so many stars due to light pollution.

16.4.3 (1) The white mass in the left lung is probably cancerous. (2) The stripe of larger cells is cancerous. (3) The white area in the back of the brain represents the tumor.

16.4.4 Following is a list of some of the prominent features that can be identified in the images: (1) X-ray: first and second metacarpals; proximal, middle, and distal phalanges. (2) PET scan: left cerebral hemisphere, right cerebral hemisphere. (5) sonogram: eyes, nose, mouth, teeth, forehead, brain, shoulder. (3) CT scan: ventricles, skull, cerebral hemisphere, convolutions of the cerebrum. (4) MRI scan: eyes, optic nerves, ventricles, cerebrum, central sulcus.

16.4.5 (1) The flag is supported by a horizontal beam to give the appearance of flying in the breeze.

(2) The flag is not made from cotton or other fabrics commonly found in flags on Earth. It is made of a stiff fabric that became crinkled when stored in a tube on the way to the Moon. Gravity on the Moon is only one-sixth that on Earth and is insufficient to straighten out the creases in the flag.

(3) Photographs are two-dimensional representations of a three-dimensional world. Flattening images causes distortions, and similar nonparallel distortions are found in photographs taken on Earth.

(4) The intensity of solar radiation on the Moon is very high due to the lack of an atmosphere. The lunar soil is reflective, as is the astronaut's spacesuit. To correctly expose the film, the aperture must be small and the shutter speed fast. Under such conditions, the surface of the Moon and the astronaut will be correctly exposed, but dim objects, like the stars, will be underexposed and not show in the picture.

16.4.6 Student answers will vary.

16.5.1–16.5.4 Students develop various digital multimedia projects.

16.6.1 (A) Band-Aid, (B) staples, (C) screw, (D) paper clip, (E) key, (F) cotton shirt, (G) Chex cereal, (H) comb, (I) finger, (J) daisy, (K) hair, (L) topographic map, (M) stalk (petiole) of leaf, (N) newspaper photograph, (O) salt, (P) apple, (Q) wood, (R) aphid on leaf, (S) plasma display, (T) penny, (U) watch, (W) football, (X) jeans.

Chapter Seventeen

Dimensional Analysis

For the Teacher 322

17.1 Unit Measures 326

17.2 Fundamental Quantities 329

17.3 SI and Non-SI Units 333

17.4 CGS and MKS Units 334

17.5 Discovering Physical Laws Using
Fundamental Units 335

17.6 Simplifying Calculations with
the Line Method 337

17.7 Solving Problems with Dimensional Analysis 339

Answers to Chapter Activities 346

For the Teacher

Many teachers tell their students to solve word problems by "thinking logically" and checking their answers to see if they "look reasonable." Although such advice sounds good, it doesn't translate into good problem solving. What does it mean to "think logically"? How many people ever get an intuitive feel for a coulomb, joule, volt, or amp? How can any student confidently solve problems and evaluate solutions intuitively when the problems involve such abstract concepts as moles, calories, or newtons?

To become effective problem solvers, students need to develop sound problem-solving techniques and strategies. The most useful problem-solving technique in science is *dimensional analysis,* also known as *factor-label method* and *unit analysis.* Dimensional analysis is a general problem-solving method that uses the dimensions (units) associated with numbers as a guide in setting up and checking calculations. It is a consistent and predictable technique, yet many teachers are not experienced enough with the technique to teach others. If you are not comfortable with your ability to use or teach dimensional analysis, work through the exercises in this chapter, paying particular attention to section 17.7, which has numerous sample problems. Students learn well by seeing patterns in examples, so you will be wise to photocopy the sample problems and give them to your students as a reference.

If teachers are not consistent in their use of units, students will not be either. Many teachers forget to use units when solving problems for their students, and this gives students license to do the same. To avoid this problem, consider awarding students extra credit for catching you each time you omit units in a measurement or calculation.

Dimensional analysis is predicated on the fact that all measurable quantities have dimensions (units). To specify that the speed of light is 3.0×10^8 is meaningless. Is it 3.0×10^8 miles/hour, 3.0×10^8 kilometers/second, or 3.0×10^8 fathoms/fortnight?! The number 3.0×10^8 has no inherent meaning. However, when we specify that the speed of light is 3.0×10^8 meters/second, we provide all the information necessary to compare it with the speed of other things and solve equations that involve the speed of light. Before solving a problem, make certain that all numbers have units, with the exception of the following: trigonometric functions (e.g., sine, cosine, tangent), logarithms, and certain special numbers such as e and π.

Just as a golfer searches for the flag of the next hole before teeing off, so the experienced problem solver determines the dimensions of the final answer (the *unknown*) before solving a problem. If you do not know the desired units of your answer, you will be like a golfer who tees off before determining the location of the next hole. The likelihood that either of you will achieve your goal is slight. Once you have identified the desired units of the answer (the *unknown*), list the values and units of all things that you do know (the *knowns*). If appropriate, draw a diagram of the problem, and label the parts with the appropriate units.

Examine the units of the knowns and unknown, and specify all relevant *conversion factors* and *formulas*. For example, if your answer has units that include hours and your known values are expressed only in minutes, you will need the conversion factor, 60 minutes = 1 hour. Without conversion factors, it may be impossible to express answers in the desired units. Conversion factors can be expressed as ratios with a value of 1. For example, since 60 minutes is the same time as 1 hour, the ratio or 60 minutes/hour or 1 hour/60 minutes is equal to 1:

$$1\,\text{hour} = 60\,\text{minutes}$$

$$\therefore 1 = \frac{60\,\text{minutes}}{\text{hour}} \quad \text{or} \quad 1 = \frac{\text{hour}}{60\,\text{minutes}}$$

According to the *identity property of multiplication*, anything can be multiplied by 1 without changing its value. Therefore, you can multiply by conversion factors as needed to adjust units, without concern of changing values.

Dimensional analysis uses what is known to determine what is unknown. It is necessary to establish an equation that shows how the unknown is related to the knowns. Customarily, one places the units of the unknown on the right side of the equation and manipulates the knowns on the left side to determine the value of the unknown. Conversion factors are used to ensure that the units on both sides of the equation are equal.

Before calculating the unknown, make certain that the units on the left side of the equation are equivalent to those on the right. If the units are not equivalent, the setup is either incomplete or incorrect, and you must reexamine the known side and manipulate the setup as necessary to get the desired units. When working to balance units, make certain to keep all conversion factors and formulas intact, even if inverted. For example, if an equation involves the use of the 60 min/hour conversion factor, you can multiply by (60 min/hr) or (hr/60 min), but not by (1/60 min/hr). Once the units on the left side equal those on the right, you may proceed with calculations.

An example from physiology illustrates dimensional analysis. If the average heart rate is 72 beats per minute, approximately how many times will a heart beat in a year (Figure 17.1)?

1. *Unknown:* An analysis of the problem shows that the unknown (the estimated average number of heartbeats per year) must have units of beats/year.
2. *Knowns:* We know that the average heart rate is 72 beats/min.
3. *Conversion factors and formulas:* To convert minutes to years, we will need the following conversion factors: 1 hour is equal to 60 minutes, 1 day is equal to 24 hours, and 1 year is equal

Unknown	Knowns	Conversion factors		

$$\frac{? \text{ beats}}{\text{year}} \qquad \text{heart rate} = \frac{72 \text{ beats}}{\text{min}} \qquad 1 = \frac{60 \text{ min}}{\text{hour}} \qquad 1 = \frac{24 \text{ hours}}{\text{day}} \qquad 1 = \frac{365 \text{ days}}{\text{year}}$$

Equation & Calculation

$$\frac{72 \text{ beats}}{\text{min}} \left| \frac{60 \text{ min}}{\text{hour}} \right| \frac{24 \text{ hours}}{\text{day}} \left| \frac{365 \text{ days}}{\text{year}} \right. = 3.78 \times 10^7 \frac{\text{beats}}{\text{year}}$$

Figure 17.1 Calculating How Many Times the Heart Beats Each Year

to 365 days. Since conversion ratios are always equal to one (1 = 60 min/h; 1 = 24 h/d; 1 = 365 d/y), you can multiply by them, or divide by them (invert and multiply) without changing values.

4. *Equation:* The units of the unknown (beats/year) are the target units and are placed on the right side of the equation. The left side of the equation is arranged so that units cancel, leaving an answer expressed in the target units.

5. *Calculation:* After the units are canceled, the equation yields the answer in beats/year.

Activity 17.1.1 (The Hazards of Not Using Units) illustrates the importance of using units. Students will struggle to complete part B because of the absence of units. Although they may be able to make reasonable inferences, they will experience difficulty and uncertainty due to the ambiguity inherent in dimensionless values.

Activity 17.2.1 (Different Units for the Same Quantity) can be performed as a pretest and posttest in a unit on problem solving. Most students have never heard of some of the units in this activity but can still make logical inferences. For example, since "candela" sounds like "candle," it may be inferred to be a measure of luminous (light) intensity. Similarly, "sidereal day" (the time it takes for the Earth to make one complete revolution in relation to a given star; equal to 23 hours, 56 minutes, 4.1 seconds), may be inferred as a measure of time because it contains the word *day*.

Many students experience difficulty with dimensional analysis because there are multiple units for the same quantity. For example, the quantity "length" can be measured in centimeters, nanometers, miles, inches, feet, fathoms, Ångstroms, microns, kilometers, yards, light-years, femtometers, mils, or astronomical units. Table 17.1 may be used to illustrate that the same quantity can be measured in many different units.

Table 17.1 Multiple Units to Express the Same Quantities

Quantity	SI Base Units	Other Units
distance	meters	centimeters, nanometers, miles, inches, feet, fathoms, Ångstroms, microns, kilometers, yards, light-years, femtometers, mils, astronomical units
mass	kilograms	grams, centigrams, kilograms, milligrams, micrograms, atomic mass units, carats, ounces, slugs, tons, metric tons
time	seconds	hours, days, minutes, centuries, decades, millennia, nanoseconds, milliseconds
temperature	kelvin	degrees centigrade, degrees Celsius, degrees Fahrenheit, degrees Rankine
volume	cubic meters	milliliters, cubic centimeters, liters, bushels, gallons, cups, pints, quarts, pecks, tablespoons, teaspoons, cubic yards, barrels, board feet
density	kilograms per cubic meter	grams per milliliter, grams per cubic centimeter, grams per liter, pounds per cubic foot, ounces per gallon
pressure	newtons per square meter	pascals, kilopascals, bars, millibars, dynes/cm^2, baryes, torrs, millimeters Hg, centimeters H_2O, atmospheres (atm), pounds per square inch (PSI)
energy	joules	kilojoules, ergs, dynes, Calories, kilocalories, kilowatt-hours, British thermal units, therms, electron volts

Activity 17.3.1 (Where Did the SI Base Units Come From?) helps students see the logic behind measurement conventions. The astute student may look at the answers to this activity and notice that the original SI definition of mass required a measurement of length (a kilogram is the mass of 1 cubic decimeter of water), and the original SI definition of length required a measurement of time (a meter is the length of a pendulum having a period of 1/2 second). The original SI unit of time, however, was not as intuitive, defined as 1/86,400 *of* the mean solar day.

To integrate history and science, you may wish to show that the customary (English) system measurements of length was rooted in natural dimensions of the adult human body. Although such measurements were approximate, they were easy to conceptualize. For example, the inch represented the average width of an adult thumb, the foot was the length of an average adult male foot, the yard approximated the distance from the tip of the nose to the end of the middle finger, the fathom was the total arm span, and the mile was the length of 1000 paces (where a pace was defined as two steps). If students are not familiar with a unit name, they may rush to a dictionary to identify it. I suggest that you first encourage them to talk in groups to see if they can figure out the answers based on their collective experience. English language learners may to do better if they realize that some of the terms have cognates (words with same etymological roots and similar sounds) in their native languages. For example, *kilometer* in English is *chilometro* in Italian, *kilómetro* in Spanish, *kilomètre* in French, and *Kilometer* in German.

Activity 17.4.1 (Converting CGS Units to MKS Units) illustrates the power of dimensional analysis in understanding important laws and principles. Dimensional analysis with fundamental units helps students see the simplicity and elegance of the physical world by showing that everything that is measurable can be expressed as a combination of just seven fundamental units. A manipulation of these units reveals numerous relationships and promotes a deeper understanding of science. Students who are adept at dimensional analysis

with fundamental units are able to understand and derive relationships that others blindly memorize. An analysis of the equations derived in this activity reveals important relationships in the physical world. For example, $C = Q/V$ is a definition of capacitance, $V = IR$ is a statement of Ohm's law of resistance, $P = W/t$ is a definition of power, and $P = I^2R$ is an expression of the power expended in a circuit. After deriving these equations by dimensional analysis, students will have a better understanding of the relationship between physical quantities.

Show your students that the final four equations in this activity are all expressions of energy: $E = Fd$; $E = W$; $E = mv^2$; $E = mad$. The product of force and distance has units of energy ($E = Fd$), indicating that energy is the capacity to move a force through a distance or, more specifically, energy is the capacity to do work ($E = W$). The product of mass and speed squared has units of energy ($E = mv^2$), which helps one understand why the kinetic energy of an object can be expressed as $1/2\ mv^2$ (where m is mass and v is velocity), while the energy obtained by the conversion of mass to energy in a nuclear reaction ($E = mc^2$, where c is the speed of light) has the same units. Energy is one of the central themes of science, and dimensional analysis of fundamental units can be used to show how and where it occurs in equations and relationships.

Activity 17.5.1 (Discovering Key Equations with Dimensional Analysis) encourages science teachers and students to communicate using standard *MKS-SI* units rather than *CGS-SI* or *customary* (English) units. Table 17.2 has been included to aid the conversion of cgs to mks units.

Activity 17.6.1 (Dimensional Analysis with the Line Method) introduces a simplified approach for dimensional analysis that reduces the amount of writing and the potential for error. Make certain students understand that the "line method" is simply a formatting technique and does not represent a difference in the mathematics.

Activity 17.7.1 (Solving Problems in Everyday Life with Dimensional Analysis) is the culminating activity in this chapter and stresses the importance of solving problems with this technique. The problems at the beginning of each set are simpler

Table 17.2 CGS and MKS Units

CGS Unit	Measuring	SI (MKS) Equivalent
barye (ba)	pressure	0.1 pascal (Pa)
biot (Bi)	electric current	10 amperes (A)
calorie (cal)	heat energy	4.1868 joule (J)
dyne (dyn)	force	10^{-5} newton (N)
erg (erg)	work, energy	10^{-7} joule (J)
franklin (Fr)	electric charge	3.3356×10^{-10} coulomb (C)
galileo (Gal)	acceleration	0.01 meter per second squared (m·s^{-2})
gauss (G)	magnetic flux density	10^{-4} tesla (T)
gilbert (Gi)	magnetomotive force	0.795 775 ampere-turns (A)
lambert (Lb)	illumination	104 lux (lx)
langley (Ly)	heat transmission	41.84 kilojoules per square meter (kJ·m^{-2})
maxwell (Mx)	magnetic flux	10^{-8} weber (Wb)
ørsted (Oe)	magnetic field strength	79.577 472 ampere-turns per meter (At·m^{-1})
poise (P)	dynamic viscosity	0.1 pascal second (Pa·s)

than those at the end. I have included problems from everyday life, biology, chemistry, earth and space science, and physics to illustrate the importance of dimensional analysis throughout the sciences.

Although it may be tempting to photocopy the solutions and project them during instruction, I encourage you to solve each problem in class from scratch. There are many potential sequences by which each problem may be solved, so don't be concerned if the sequences you use differ from those shown here. The important issue is that the units cancel to leave only the desired units.

Please note that some conversion values are precise and therefore have an unlimited number of significant digits. For example, there are precisely 10 millimeters in 1 centimeter, so the 10 mm/cm conversion ratio does not limit the number of significant figures in any calculation. Failing to clarify this issue can cause confusion among students who are trying to express answers in the right number of significant units. The following example may help clarify this situation:

The product of 25 cm and 2.000 cm is 50 cm^2, not 50.00 cm^2. Since there are only two significant digits in the first multiplier, there can be no more than two in the answer. By contrast, the product of 2.000 cm and 10 mm/cm

Figure 17.2 A Reminder to Use Dimensional Analysis

is 20.00 mm. Note that the conversion factor (10 mm/cm) is precise (based on the definition of a millimeter), has unlimited significant digits, and therefore does not reduce the number of significant digits in the answer.

Students may get lazy or overconfident and try to solve problems without dimensional analysis. To impress the importance of dimensional analysis, you may post a "warning" in your room such as illustrated in Figure 17.2.

17.1 Unit Measures

On September 24, 1999, the *New York Times* declared: "Mars Orbiting Craft Presumed Destroyed by Navigation Error."[1] The article explained, "A $125 million robotic spacecraft, the first ever dispatched especially to investigate weather on another world, was missing on Thursday and presumed destroyed just as it was supposed to go into an orbit around Mars." After extensive investigation, it was learned that the Mars Climate Orbiter was lost not due to system malfunction or collision with an asteroid but rather because a few engineers failed to include units with their calculations. Lockheed Martin Corporation in Colorado sent daily course adjustments to the Jet Propulsion Laboratory in Pasadena with numbers that should have included customary (English) units of pound-seconds to describe the impulse necessary to adjust the course of the spacecraft into orbit around Mars. Unfortunately the engineers at JPL assumed these numbers specified impulse in newton-seconds. "Since a newton-second is only 0.225 pound-second, the rocket motors were given only 22.5% the impulse needed to alter the orbit appropriately, and it is presumed that the craft plummeted into the Red Planet. If engineers had included or checked units, this disaster could have been avoided."

Using the correct units is important not only for scientists and engineers but for people in all walks of life. The Federal Food and Drug Administration (FDA) estimates that medication errors cause at least one death every day and injure approximately 1.3 million people annually in the United States. It cites errors in medical abbreviations or writing, including the absence of dimensions (units), as one of the chief causes for these problems. According to the National Academy of Sciences' Institute of Medicine, drug complications in the hospital are the leading cause of medical mistakes in America, accounting for nearly 20 percent of all errors. The institute's study, *To Err Is Human: Building a Better Health System,* reported that 2 out of every 100 hospital admissions experienced a "preventable adverse drug event."[2] The Institute of Medicine study estimated that the cost of prescription errors was $2 billion annually. Some of these costly errors can be avoided if physicians, pharmacists, and consumers indicate and check units.

ACTIVITY 17.1.1 *The Hazards of Not Using Units*

Much confusion is caused when measurements are reported without units, as you will see in the following incomplete statements. Examine each statement, and make your best guess of the correct units.

1. *Medication:* A typical adult prescription of the painkiller acetaminophen with codeine is 500 _____.

   (a) tablets, (b) grams, (c) milligrams, (d) ounces, (f) milliliters

   Consequences of being incorrect: Symptoms of overdose may include cold and clammy skin, extreme sleepiness progressing to stupor or coma, general bodily discomfort, heart attack, kidney failure, liver failure, low blood pressure, muscle weakness, nausea, slow heartbeat, sweating, and vomiting.

2. *Speed limit:* The speed limit in school zones in Canada is 30 _____.

   (a) miles/hour, (b) kilometers/hour, (c) feet/second, (d) meters/second, (e) yards/second

   Consequences of being incorrect: Speeding in a school zone may result in an accident or a significant fine.

3. *Bicycle tire pressure:* The recommended air pressure in many mountain bike tries is 60 _____.

   (a) pascals, (b) kilopascals, (c) pounds per square inch, (d) torr, (e) milimeters mercury

   Consequences of being incorrect: Underinflated tires puncture more easily, wear out faster, are more difficult to pedal, and don't stop as efficiently. Overinflated tires *may* blow out.

4. *Dietetics:* Many physicians recommend that pregnant women take no more than 10,000 _____ of vitamin A per day.

   (a) grams, (b) milligrams, (c) ounces, (d) international units, (5) microliters

   Consequences of being incorrect: Excess vitamin A may give rise to birth defects, dry skin, scaly skin, headaches, fatigue, painful bones, and loss of appetite.

5. *Food storage:* Food scientists recommend that produce companies store apples, cherries, apricots, and most berries at 2 _____.

   (a) degrees Fahrenheit, (b) kelvin,
   (c) degrees Celsius, (d) degrees Rankine,
   (e) degrees Reaumur

   Consequences of being incorrect: Storing these fruits at too high a temperature will result in ethylene production and early ripening. Storing them at too low of a temperature will damage the integrity of the fruit.

6. *Your example:* Develop a hypothetical problem that may arise when units are omitted in a field such as sportscasting, international trade, or an area of your choice.

ACTIVITY 17.1.2 *Units in Everyday Life*

In the statements that follow, you will find a variety of interesting facts, but each is missing a crucial piece of information: the units (dimensions)! All the statements are meaningless until supplied with the appropriate units. Complete the following statements using the units in Table 17.3, using whatever resources you wish. In most, you will need to draw logical inferences.

1. *Coldest place in the known universe.* The Boomerang Nebula, a cloud of dust and gas dispensed by a "white dwarf," is one of the coldest places in the known universe, with an estimated temperature of −521.6 _____.

2. *Deepest lake.* The deepest lake in the world is Lake Baikal, in Siberia, Russia. The lake has a depth of 15,371 _____, of which 3875 _____ are below sea level. Baikal contains one-fifth of all the world's fresh surface water. The lake has a surface area of 12,200 square _____.

3. *Highest G-force endured by an animal.* The click beetle (*Athous haemorrhoidalis*) moves its body in a snapping fashion to generate lift at a record-breaking acceleration of 400 _____. The beetle jumps this way to avoid predators and can leap up to 15 _____ high. By comparison, humans can endure brief periods of up to 6 _____.

4. *Fastest dive by a bird.* A peregrine falcon can reach a velocity of 350 _____ when diving toward its prey.

5. *Driest place on earth.* The meteorological station in Quillagua, in the Atacama Desert, Chile, records an average annual rainfall at just 0.5 _____.

6. *Greatest temperature range on Earth.* The greatest recorded temperature variation is in Verkhoyansk, Siberia. The temperature is as high as 105 _____ in the summer and as low as −68°C _____ to 37 _____ in the winter.

7. *Fastest avalanche.* The volcanic explosion of Washington State's Mount St. Helens on May 18, 1980, triggered an avalanche with a velocity of 250 _____.

8. *Farthest object visible by the unaided eye.* The most remote object visible with the unaided eye is the Great Galaxy in the constellation of

Table 17.3 Units for Activity 17.1.2

acre	inches	liters	ounces
centimeters	kilocalories (Cal)	megatons	pounds
degrees Celsius	kelvin	meters	square miles
degrees Fahrenheit	kilograms	miles	square kilometer
feet	kilometers	miles per hour	stories
G	kilometers/hour	milligrams	tons
grams/milliliter	kilowatt-hours	milliliters	yard
hectare	light-years	millimeters	

Andromeda. The Great Galaxy is composed of approximately 200,000,000,000 stars and is 2,200,000 _____ from Earth.

9. *Most powerful nuclear explosion.* The most powerful thermonuclear device ever tested was the Soviet Union's Tsar Bomba, with an explosive force equivalent to that of 57 of _____ TNT. The shock waves from the 1961 blast circled the Earth three times.

10. *Tallest living tree.* The tallest tree currently standing is the Mendocino tree, a coast redwood (*Sequoia sempervirens*) at Montgomery State Reserve, California. When measured, its height was determined to be 112.014 _____.

11. *Wood and paper use.* The average amount of wood and paper consumed per person each year in America is equivalent to a tree _____ tall and 16 _____ diameter.

12. *Largest forest.* The boreal forests of northern Russia, lying between latitude 55° N and the Arctic Circle, cover a total area of 2.7 billion _____.

13. *Longest venomous snake.* The king cobra (*Ophiophagus hannah*) from Southeast Asia and India grows to an average length of 3.6 to 4.5 meters (12–15 feet)! It is estimated that 2 fluid _____ of a king cobra's venom can kill 20 people.

14. *Largest bird.* The largest bird is the North African ostrich. It can grow to 2.75 _____ tall and weigh 156.5 _____. The ostrich is also the fastest bird on land, reaching speeds of 72 _____.

15. *Greatest snowfall for a snowstorm.* In February 1959, a single snowstorm dropped 480 _____ of snow at Mount Shasta Ski Bowl, California.

17.2 Fundamental Quantities

One of the greatest inventions of all time is the alphabet, a set of symbols representing the basic sounds (phonemes) of spoken words. English and many other languages use the Latin alphabet, which developed from the Greek alphabet

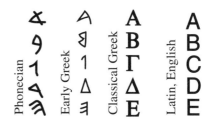

Figure 17.3 Origins of the Alphabet

(Figure 17.3), which in turn developed from the ancient Phoenician alphabet. A comparison of these alphabets illustrates a common heritage.

In an alphabetic writing system such as English, each letter represents a consonant or a vowel rather than a syllable or concept. Since alphabetic characters represent the most basic features of speech, only a small number are necessary to code the entire lexicon of a language. Although English has the largest vocabulary of any other language, the entire lexicon can be expressed using just the 26 characters of the alphabet. By contrast, languages that are based on larger units, such as syllables or concepts, are much more complex. Chinese, for example, employs a logographic writing system in which characters are used to represent the basic words of the Chinese language. There are approximately 40,000 Chinese characters, of which nearly 2000 must be memorized to be functionally literate.

The beauty and power of an alphabetic system is that it is based on the most fundamental linguistic units. From these fundamental units, one can derive any term in the spoken language. In a similar manner, there are fundamental units of measurement from which all other units of measurement are derived. Just as comprehension of the Latin alphabet is necessary to read and write English, so comprehension of the "scientific alphabet" is essential to understand the language of science.

There are seven "letters" in the "language of measurement" from which all units of measurement are derived: *distance, mass, time, electric current, temperature, amount,* and *luminous intensity* (see Table 17.4). These are known as the *fundamental quantities* because they cannot be expressed

Table 17.4 Physical Quantities and Their SI Units

Quantity	Symbol	SI Measurement Units	Symbol	Unit Dimensions
distance	d	meter	m	m
mass	m	kilogram	kg	kg
time	t	second	s	s
electric current	I	ampere	A	A
temperature	T	kelvin	K	K
amount	n	mole	mol	mol
luminous intensity	I	candela	cd	cd
acceleration	a	meter per second squared	m/s^2	m/s^2
area	A	square meter	m^2	m^2
capacitance	C	farad	F	$A^2 \cdot s^4/kg \cdot m^2$
concentration	[C]	molar	M	mol/m^3
density	D	kilogram per cubic meter	kg/m^3	kg/m^3
electric charge	Q	coulomb	C	$A \cdot s$
electric field intensity	E	newton per coulomb	N/C	$kg \cdot m/A \cdot s^3$
electric resistance	R	ohm	Ω	$kg \cdot m^2/A^2 \cdot s^3$
emf	ξ	volt	V	$kg \cdot m^2/A \cdot s^3$
energy	E	joule	J	$kg \cdot m^2/s^2$
force	F	newton	N	$kg \cdot m/s^2$
frequency	f	hertz	Hz	s^{-1}
heat	Q	joule	J	$kg \cdot m^2/s^2$
illumination	E	lux (lumen per square meter)	lx	cd/m^2
inductance	L	henry	H	$kg \cdot m^2/A^2 \cdot s^2$
magnetic flux	ϕ	weber	Wb	$kg \cdot m^2/A \cdot s^2$
potential difference	V	volt	V	$kg \cdot m^2/A \cdot s^3$
power	P	watt	W	$kg \cdot m^2/s^3$
pressure	p	pascal (newton per square meter)	Pa	$kg/m \cdot s^2$
velocity	v	meter per second	m/s	m/s
volume	V	cubic meter	m^3	m^3
work	W	joule	J	$kg \cdot m^2/s^2$

Note: Fundamental units are in **bold** type.

in a simpler fashion. All other measurable quantities are known as *derived quantities* because they can be derived by combining two or more fundamental quantities.

Length (distance) is a fundamental quantity because it can be expressed in no simpler terms than length. *Volume* is a derived quantity because it can be expressed as the *cube of length*. For example, when you measure the volume of a box, you multiply its length by its width by its height. The resulting measure is expressed as *length cubed* (*length³*) such as cubic feet or cubic centimeters. *Density* is considered a derived unit because it can be expressed in terms of the fundamental quantities of *mass* and *length* (*density = mass/length³*).

In 1960 the Eleventh General Conference on Weights and Measures adopted the *International System* of measurement (*SI*) and assigned base units for each physical quantity.[3] Table 17.4 shows some common physical quantities and their SI units. The first seven (bold type) are the seven fundamental units, and the remaining are derived

Table 17.5 Definitions of the Units of the Seven Fundamental Quantities

Quantity	SI Unit	Definition of Unit
distance	meter (m)	The meter is the length of the path traveled by light in vacuum during a time interval of 1/299 792 458 of a second.
mass	kilogram (kg)	The kilogram is equal to the mass of the international prototype of the kilogram.
time	second (s)	The second is the duration of 9 192 631 770 periods of the radiation corresponding to the transition between the two hyperfine levels of the ground state of the cesium 133 atom.
electric current	ampere (A)	The ampere is that constant current that, if maintained in two straight parallel conductors of infinite length, of negligible circular cross-section, and placed 1 meter apart in vacuum, would produce between these conductors a force equal to 2×10^{-7} newton per meter of length.
temperature	kelvin (K)	The kelvin is the fraction 1/273.16 of the thermodynamic temperature of the triple point of water.
amount of substance	mole (mol)	The mole is the amount of substance of a system that contains as many elementary entities as there are atoms in 0.012 kilogram of carbon 12.
intensity of light	candela (cd)	The candela is the luminous intensity, in a given direction, of a source that emits monochromatic radiation of frequency 540×10^{12} and that has a radiant intensity in that direction of 1/683 watt per steradian.

Source: 22nd General Conference on Weights and Measures. (2003). *The International System of Units (SI).* Paris: Organisation Intergouvernementale de la Convention du Mètre.

from these. Table 17.5 provides definitions of the fundamental units. Originally units were defined in more understandable terms but had to be redefined to acquire permanent and precise values. For example, originally a meter was defined to represent one ten-millionth of the circumference of the Earth, from the North Pole to the equator, through Paris. Although such definitions were easier to visualize than newer definitions—a meter is now defined as the length of the path traveled by light in a vacuum during a time interval of 1/(299 792 458) of a second—they were less precise and constant.

ACTIVITY 17.2.1 *Different Units for the Same Quantity*

Although there are only seven fundamental quantities, many ways have been developed to measure these quantities, making things seem much more complex than they really are. For example, Daniel Fahrenheit, the German physicist who invented the alcohol thermometer, developed a temperature scale that took as zero the temperature of an equal ice-salt mixture and selected the values of 30°F and 90°F for the freezing point of water and normal body temperature, respectively. (Later, the temperatures of freezing water and body temperature were revised to 32°F and 98.6°F.) In 1742 the Swedish astronomer Anders Celsius developed a competing temperature scale in which 0°C was defined as the freezing point and 100°C as the boiling point of water. In addition, Renè Reamur, William Rankine, and William Thompson (Lord Kelvin) developed temperature scales that now bear their names. Despite the different names

Table 17.6 Different Units for the Same Quantity

	Mass	Length	Time	Temperature	Luminous Intensity	Electric Charge	Quantity		Mass	Length	Time	Temperature	Luminous Intensity	Electric Charge	Quantity
A (ampere)								hour							
amu								inch							
biot								K (kelvin)							
bolt (of cloth)								kilogram							
Cd (candela)								league							
cubit								meter							
day								mole							
decade								neutron mass							
°C								oz (ounce)							
°F								pace							
°R (Rankine)								pica							
°Re (Reaumur)								pound ap							
dozen								pound							
dram ap								second							
earth mass								sidereal day							
football field								sidereal month							
fortnight								slug							
gross								UK mile							
hand								week							
hefner candle								yr (year)							

and ways of measuring, Fahrenheit, Celsius, Reamur, Rankine, and Kelvin simply provide different ways of expressing temperature, a single fundamental quantity.

Anyone who assumes that different unit names measure different physical quantities can become confused. The terms in Table 17.6 are units for measuring the seven fundamental quantities of length, mass, time, temperature, current, luminous intensity, and quantity. Examine the list, and classify each term as a measure of one of these seven fundamental quantities.

17.3 SI and Non-SI Units

Some of the most commonly measured quantities in science are distance, mass, time, temperature, volume, density, pressure, amount, concentration, energy, velocity, molarity, and electric charge. All of these quantities can be measured in a variety of ways. For example, distance can be measured in centimeters, nanometers, miles, inches, feet, fathoms, Ångstroms, microns, kilometers, yards, light-years, femtometers, and mils.

Specialized circumstances often call for specialized units. For example, interstellar distances are measured in light-years (the distance between our Sun and the next nearest star, Proxima Centurai, is 4 light-years) while intermolecular bond lengths are measured in Ångstroms (the distance between hydrogen and oxygen in water is 0.958 Å). Although light-years and Ångstroms are both measures of distance, many assume they are unrelated.

In an effort to minimize confusion, the International Union of Pure and Applied Chemists (IUPAC) recommended that all quantities be measured in SI units (e.g., meters) or multiples of SI units (e.g., femtometers, nanometers, micrometers, millimeters, centimeters, and kilometers). Despite growing acceptance of the SI system, many other measurement units continue to be used, among them miles, inches, feet, fathoms, Ångstroms, microns, yards, light-years, and mils.

ACTIVITY 17.3.1 *Where Did the SI Base Units Come From?*

During the nineteenth and twentieth centuries, great advances in science and technology led to a variety of overlapping systems of measurements as scientists and engineers improvised to meet the needs of their individual disciplines. To minimize the confusion of multiple systems of measurement, scientists called for a uniform international system of measurement, and over the years, conferences and committees were held to establish a set of standard units, the base units of which are found in Table 17.5. Although the definitions in Table 17.5 are precise, they are dissatisfying. Why, for example, should a meter be defined as the length of the path traveled by light in vacuum during a time interval of 1/299 792 458 of a second? It sounds like a rather random definition and is certainly difficult to conceptualize. Originally the definitions of the basic units were easier to conceptualize, but as time progressed, the definitions became more specific so as to avoid errors or circular reasoning. Nonetheless, it is interesting to see what the original definitions were.

a. *Definition of length:* Scientists wanted to ensure that the standard length of a meter was the same around the world and came up with a definition based on the motion of a pendulum. The period of a pendulum is the time it takes for a bob to complete one swing and return to its original location. The period of a pendulum is dependent only on its length, and so, scientists argued, a length of 1 m could be defined in terms of the period of a pendulum. What is that definition? Construct a 1 m pendulum by tying a weight to a 1 m length of string, and recording the time for 10 complete swings. Divide the time by 10 to determine the period of one pendulum swing. Repeat this process twice, take an average value, and complete the following definition.

A meter is the length of a pendulum having a period of _____ seconds.

b. *Definition of mass:* Originally scientists sought to define the standard measure of mass (the kilogram) as the mass of a known volume of water. Place a 1 or 2 L graduated cylinder on a balance, and determine its mass. Slowly add water until the mass has increased by precisely 1 kg. What volume of water has a mass of 1 kg? Remembering that 1 ml is identical to 1 cubic centimeter and that 1 cubic cm is equal one-thousandth of a cubic decimeter or one-millionth of a cubic meter, complete the following definition:

A kilogram is the mass of _____ cubic _____ of water.

Table 17.7 Different Units for the Same Quantities

Quantity	SI Base Units	Other Units
distance	meters (m)	
mass	kilograms (kg)	
time	seconds (s)	
temperature	kelvin (K)	
volume	cubic centimeters (cm^3)	
density	kg/m^3	
pressure	newtons per square meter (N/m^2)	
energy	joules	

Ångstroms (Å)
astronomical units (au)
atmospheres (atm)
atomic mass units (amu)
bars (bar)
barrels (bbl)
barye (ba)
board-feet (bd ft)
British thermal units (Btu)
bushels (bu)
calories (cal)
carats (ct)
centigrade (°C)
centigrams (cg)
centimeters (cm)
centuries
centimeters water (cm H$_2$O)
cubic centimeters (cm^3)
cubic yards (yd^3)
cups (c)
days (d)
decades
degrees Celsius (°C)
degrees Fahrenheit (°F)
degrees Rankine (°R)
dynes (dyn)

dyne per square meter (dyn/m^2)
electron volts (ev)
ergs (erg)
fathoms (fth)
feet (ft)
femtometers (fm)
gallons (gal)
grams per cubic cm (g/cm^3)
grams per liter (g/l)
grams per milliliter (m/ml)
grams (g)
hours (h)
inches (in.)
joules (J)
kilocalories (kCal)
kilograms (kg)
kilojoule (kJ)
kilometers (km)
kilopascals (kPa)
kilowatt-hours (kWh)
light-years (ly)
liters (L)
metric tons (mt)
micrograms (μMg)
microns (μMm)
mils (mm)

miles (mi)
milligrams (mg)
millennia
millibar (mb)
milliliters (ml)
milliseconds (ms)
minutes (min)
millimeters mercury (mm Hg)
nanometers (nm)
nanoseconds (ns)
ounces (oz)
ounces per gallon (oz/gal)
pascals (Pa)
pecks (pk)
pints (pt)
pounds per cubic foot (lb/ft^3)
pounds per square inch (lb/in^2)
quarts (qt)
slugs (slug)
tablespoons (tbsp)
teaspoons (tsp)
therms (therm)
tons (T)
torrs (torr)
yards (yd)

ACTIVITY 17.3.2 *Different Units for the Same Quantities*

The left column in Table 17.7 lists some of the most commonly measured quantities, and the middle column lists their SI units. The list after the table provides a list of other units that are used in the measurement of one of these eight quantities. Examine each of these terms, and try to determine which quantity it measures (e.g., distance, mass time). Place these units in the table adjacent to the quantity you believe they measure.

17.4 CGS and MKS Units

The metric system was introduced to simplify calculations and facilitate communication between scientists and engineers. Ironically, however, two separate approaches to metric measurements developed. Scientists working in laboratories preferred to work

Table 17.8 SI CGS and MKS Units

CGS Unit	Measuring	SI MKS Equivalent
centimeter (cm)	distance	.01 meter (m)
gram (g)	mass	.001 kilogram (kg)
second (s)	time	1 second (s)
barye (ba)	pressure	0.1 pascal (Pa)
biot (Bi)	electric current	10 amperes (A)
calorie (cal)	heat energy	4.19 joule (J)
dyne (dyn)	force	10^{-5} newton (N)
erg (erg)	work, energy	10^{-7} joule (J)
franklin (Fr)	electric charge	3.36×10^{-10} coulomb (C)
galileo (Gal)	acceleration	0.01 meter per second squared (m·s^{-2})
gauss (G)	magnetic flux density	10^{-4} tesla (T)
maxwell (Mx)	magnetic flux	10^{-8} weber (Wb)
phot (ph)	illumination	10^{4} lux (lx)
poise (P)	dynamic viscosity	0.1 pascal second (Pa·s)

with smaller measures of mass and length than those working in the field. For example, research chemists, working with small quantities of chemicals in the laboratory, preferred to measure masses in grams, while chemical engineers, analyzing production processes, preferred to measure production in kilograms. As a result, two metric systems of measurement arose: the CGS system (based on the **c**entimeter, **g**ram, and **s**econd), and the MKS system (based upon the **m**eter, **k**ilogram, and **s**econd). Table 17.8 compares the CGS with the MKS units.

In 1960, *the Eleventh General Conference on Weights and Measures* addressed this issue and set forth the *International System of Units (SI)*, using the meter, kilogram, second, ampere, kelvin, and candela as basic units. Since 1960, there has been a trend among scientists and engineers to report measurements in MKS units, but many continue to report them in CGS, and some still prefer to report measurements in customary English units. When comparing data reported in different systems, scientists generally convert all units to MKS values. To ensure that this conversion process is done accurately, scientists use dimensional analysis to convert all measures to MKS.

ACTIVITY 17.4.1 *Converting CGS Units to MKS Units*
Use Table 17.8 and dimensional analysis to convert the following *CGS* units to *MKS* units:

(1) 20 cm, (2) 150 g, (3) 25 ba, (4) 2 cal, (5) 100,000 dyn, (6) 10^{12} Fr, (7) 100 G

For example, to convert 1.5 biots to amperes, simply multiply

$$1.5 \text{Bi} \times \frac{10 \text{amp}}{\text{Bi}} = 15 \text{amp}$$

17.5 Discovering Physical Laws Using Fundamental Units

It is possible to construct all of the words in the English language using just 26 letters. In a similar way, with only seven quantities, it is possible to express all measurable quantities in science: length, mass, time, electric current, temperature, amount, and luminous intensity. These quantities are fundamental because they cannot be expressed in a simpler fashion. Examine Table 17.4, and note that all of the derived units can be expressed in terms of the seven fundamental units.

Time is a fundamental quantity, because it can be expressed in no simpler units than those of *time*. *Distance* is a fundamental quantity because it can be expressed in no simpler terms than distance. *Velocity,* however, is not fundamental, because it can be expressed as a ratio of two other units: distance and time ($v = d/t$). Because velocity can be derived from distance and time, it is known as a *derived unit.*

Just as all words can be expressed as a series of letters, so all measurable quantities can be expressed in terms of their fundamental quantities. Dimensional analysis of terms that are expressed in fundamental units can reveal many important relationships. For example, the farad (F) is a measure of *electrical capacitance* (*C,* the ability to store charge) and can be expressed in fundamental terms as:

$$F = \frac{A^2 \cdot s^4}{kg \cdot m^2}$$

where A represents amps (a measure of current or charge), s represents seconds (a measure of *time*), kg represents kilograms (a measure of *mass*), and m represents meters (a measure of *length*). An examination of Table 17.4 shows that the units of a farad,

$$F = \frac{A^2 \cdot s^4}{kg \cdot m^2}$$

are similar to the units of an inverse volt,

$$\frac{1}{V} = \frac{A \cdot s^3}{kg \cdot m^2}$$

If we multiply an inverse volt by current (amps, A) and time (seconds, s), the units are farads (F), a measure of capacitance:

$$\frac{A \cdot s^3 \cdot (A \cdot s)}{kg \cdot m^2} = \frac{A^2 \cdot s^4}{kg \cdot m^2} = F$$

In other words, a farad is equal to an amp·second divided by a volt:

$$F = \frac{A \cdot s}{V}$$

In Table 17.4 we notice that a coulomb (C, a measure of charge) is defined as an amp·second,

and we can therefore rewrite the equation to show the relationship of the units:

$$F = \frac{C}{V}$$

Since a farad is a unit of capacitance (*C*), a coulomb a measure of charge (*Q*), and a volt a measure of potential difference (*V*), the equation may be expressed in quantities as:

$$C = \frac{Q}{V}$$

Thus, by examining the fundamental units of capacitance, current, and potential difference, we have determined that capacitance is the ratio *of charge to potential difference* (*C = Q/V*), which is what we find in the dictionary: "capacitance is equal to the surface charge divided by the electric potential."

Important note: It is important to distinguish quantities (e.g., capacitance, *C;* charge, *Q;* potential difference, *V*) from the SI units used to measure these quantities (e.g., farads, F; coulombs, C; and volts, V). By convention, quantities are expressed in *italics,* while specific units are not. The use of similar letters for both quantities and units may lead to much confusion, particularly in a problem like this. Note, for example, that *C* (capacitance, measured in farads, F) is not the same as C (coulombs, a unit of charge, *Q*).

ACTIVITY 17.5.1 *Discovering Key Equations with Dimensional Analysis*

Table 17.4 showsthe most commonly used units and illustrates how they may be expressed in fundamental terms. The seven fundamental quantities are shown at the top of the table in bold print. Table 17.9 lists sets of physical quantities that are related. By examining the fundamental units of these quantities, determine their relationship and express it mathematically. Each quantity (second column) should be expressed in terms of the quantities listed in the final column, as illustrated in the example in the first line. It is not necessary to understand what each term means to discover relationships.

Table 17.9 Discovering Key Equations with Dimensional Analysis

Derived Unit	Quantity	Expressed as Fundamental Units	Complete the Equation . . .	In Terms of . . .
volt	(potential diff., V)	$\dfrac{\text{kg}\cdot\text{m}^2}{\text{A}\cdot\text{s}^3}$	$V = IR$	*current (I)* *resistance (R)*
watt	(power, P)	$\dfrac{\text{kg}\cdot\text{m}^2}{\text{s}^3}$	$P =$	*current (I)* *potential difference (V)*
watt	(power, P)	$\dfrac{\text{kg}\cdot\text{m}^2}{\text{s}^3}$	$P =$	*current (I)* *resistance (R)*
watt	(power, P)	$\dfrac{\text{kg}\cdot\text{m}^2}{\text{s}^3}$	$P =$	*work (W)* *time (t)*
joule	(energy, E)	$\dfrac{\text{kg}\cdot\text{m}^2}{\text{s}^2}$	$E =$	*force (F)* *distance (d)*
joule	(energy, E)	$\dfrac{\text{kg}\cdot\text{m}^2}{\text{s}^2}$	$E =$	*work (W)*
joule	(energy, E)	$\dfrac{\text{kg}\cdot\text{m}^2}{\text{s}^2}$	$E =$	*mass (m)* *velocity (v)*
joule	(energy, E)	$\dfrac{\text{kg}\cdot\text{m}^2}{\text{s}^2}$	$E =$	*mass (m)* *acceleration (a)* *distance (d)*
N·s	(impulse)	$\dfrac{\text{kg}\cdot\text{m}}{\text{s}}$	*Impulse =*	*force (F)* *time (t)*
farad	(capacitance, C)	$\dfrac{\text{A}^2\cdot\text{s}^4}{\text{kg}\cdot\text{m}^2}$	$C =$	*potential difference (V)* *charge (Q)*
Pa	(pressure, p)	$\dfrac{\text{kg}\cdot\text{m}}{\text{s}^2}$	$p =$	*force (F)* *distance (d)*

17.6 Simplifying Calculations with the Line Method

Which of the answers in Figure 17.4 is correct for the problem in the box? The problem is ambiguous, so any of them could be correct, depending on the assumptions made and the sequence of mathematical operations performed. If you assume that the problem is 3/2 divided by 5/7, then you could indicate this by extending the line between 2 and 5 and arrive at 2.10 (Figure 17.4A). If, however, you assume that the problem is 3/2 divided by 5 divided by 7, then you could indicate this by drawing the lines as illustrated in Figure 17.4B and

arrive at 0.043. Finally, if you assume the problem is 5/7 divided into 2, divided into 3, you could draw the lines as illustrated in Figure 17.4C and arrive at 1.07!

The traditional setup allows one to place fractions over fractions but requires that the solver specify the sequence of operations by the lengths of the dividing lines or by parentheses. Unfortunately, many teachers and students are not precise in their problem setup, leading to confusion and errors in calculation. Slight differences in line length may not be detected, resulting in different calculations. To avoid this and other problems, it is preferable to use the *line method*. The line method requires that the problem solver place all fractions

$$\frac{\dfrac{3}{2}}{\dfrac{5}{7}} = \frac{1.50}{0.571} = 2.10 \qquad \textbf{A}$$

$$\frac{\dfrac{3}{2}}{\dfrac{5}{7}} = ?$$

$$\frac{\dfrac{3}{2}}{\dfrac{5}{7}} = \frac{\dfrac{1.50}{5}}{\dfrac{.300}{7}} = 0.043 \qquad \textbf{B}$$

$$\frac{\dfrac{3}{2}}{\dfrac{5}{7}} = \frac{\dfrac{3}{2}}{0.714} = \frac{\dfrac{3}{2.80}}{} = 1.07 \qquad \textbf{C}$$

$$\frac{3}{2}\bigg|\frac{7}{5} = \frac{21}{10} = 2.10 \qquad \textbf{D}$$

$$\frac{3}{2}\bigg|\frac{}{5}\bigg|7 = \frac{3}{70} = 0.043 \qquad \textbf{E}$$

$$\frac{5}{7}\bigg|\frac{3}{2} = \frac{15}{14} = 1.07 \qquad \textbf{F}$$

Figure 17.4 Traditional (A–C) and Line (D–F) Methods

on one straight line so that there are no fractions over fractions. Since multiplication by the inverse of a fraction is the same thing as division by the fraction, all calculations can be reduced to a single line. For example, if the problem is 3/2 divided by 5/7, it can be illustrated on a straight line, as shown in Figure 17.4D. Figures 17.4E and 17.4F illustrate the straight line representation for the other two solutions. Note that there are no fractions over fractions, and hence no confusion regarding the operation to be performed.

In the line method, each vertical line represents multiplication, and the horizontal line indicates division. No fractions are placed over fractions. If a fraction exists in the numerator, its numerator is placed on top of the line and its denominator under the line beneath it. If, however, a fraction exists in the denominator, it is inverted so that the numerator is placed under the main line and its denominator immediately above it. Compare the traditional method (Example 1)

A traditional setup

$$PV = nRT \qquad T = \frac{PV}{nR} = \frac{2\ \text{atm} \cdot 5\text{L}}{3\text{moles} \cdot \dfrac{0.0821\ \text{L} \cdot \text{atm}}{\text{mole} \cdot \text{K}}}$$

B straight-line setup

$$T = \frac{PV}{nR} = \frac{2\ \text{atm}\,\big|\,5\text{L}}{\quad\big|\,3\text{moles}\,\big|\,0.0821\ \text{L} \cdot \text{atm}}\bigg|\,\text{mole} \cdot \text{K}$$

C

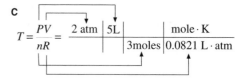

$$T = \frac{PV}{nR} = \frac{2\ \text{atm}\,\big|\,5\text{L}}{\quad\big|\,3\text{moles}\,\big|\,0.0821\ \text{L} \cdot \text{atm}}\bigg|\,\text{mole} \cdot \text{K}$$

Figure 17.5 Traditional (A) and Line (B, C) Methods

with the line method (Example 2) for the solution of the following problems:

Example 1: What is the approximate temperature of 3 mol of nitrogen gas contained in a 5 L flask at 20 atm (R = 0. 0821 L atm/mol K)? The traditional method requires that the universal gas constant, R, be placed as a fraction in the denominator (Figure 17.5A). By contrast, the line method requires that the universal gas constant, R, be inverted and multiplied so that there are no fractions in the numerator or denominator (Figure 17.5B). It is now easier to see how units cancel (Figure 17.5C).

Example 2: An ancient measurement of volume mentioned in the Bible is the ephah. Write an equation using the line format to express 1.00 ephah in liters using the following conversion factors (Figure 17.6):

1 ephah = 2.429 modium (a modium is an ancient Roman measure of volume)

1 modium = 0.7076 vedro (a vedro is an old Russian measure of volume)

$$\frac{1.00\ \text{ephah}}{} \bigg| \frac{2.429\ \text{modium}}{1\ \text{ephah}} \bigg| \frac{0.7076\ \text{vedro}}{1\ \text{modium}} \bigg| \frac{0.349\ \text{bushels}}{1\ \text{vedro}} \bigg| \frac{2150\ \text{cubic inches}}{1\ \text{bushel}} \bigg| \frac{0.01639\ \text{liters}}{1\ \text{cubic inch}} = 21.1\ \text{liters}$$

Figure 17.6 Line Setup for Unit Conversion Problem

1 vedro = 0.349 bushels (a customary measure of volume)

1 bushel = 2150 cubic inches

1 cubic inch = 0.01639 liters

The line method generally reduces the number of pen strokes and makes the problem setup less cluttered. Students should know how to solve a problem using both the traditional and line techniques, but I recommend the line method for most problems involving dimensional analysis.

ACTIVITY 17.6.1 *Dimensional Analysis with the Line Method*

Set up each of the following problems on a straight line. Note that it is not necessary to understand the context of the problems to set them up correctly. What are the final values and units in each case?

1. A *tsubo* is a Japanese unit of area. Write an equation using the line method to express 1 tsubo in m^2 given that 1 tsubo is equal to 5124 in^2, 1 in^2 is equal to 6.452 cm^2, and 1 cm^2 is equal to 0.0001 m^2.

2. Write an equation using the line method to express 1 light-year (the distance light travels in 365. 25 days) in meters, knowing that light travels at 3.0×10^8 m/s.

3. Write an equation using the line method to express 1.0 g in carats. Include all of the following conversion factors: 1 kg = 0.001 tonne, 1 g = 0.001 kg, 1 tonne = 0.9842 long tons, 1 long ton = 2240 lb, 1 pound = 16 oz, 1 oz = 138.3 carats.

4. A bit is a binary digit, the smallest element of computer storage. It is a single binary number represented by a 1 or a 0. The bit can be a transistor or capacitor in a memory cell, a magnetic domain on a hard disk drive, or a reflective dot on an optical disc. Write an equation in line format to express 1 terabyte of memory in bits given that there are 1024 gigabytes per terabyte, 1024 megabytes per gigabyte, 1024 kilobytes per byte, 1024 bytes per kilobyte, and 8 bits per byte.

Solve for force (*F*) in problems 5 to 7. A newton (N) = kgm/s^2

5. $F = \dfrac{m\Delta v}{\Delta t}$ where $m = 2\,kg$; $\Delta v = 50\dfrac{m}{s}$; $\Delta t = .01s$

$F_g = G m_1 m_2 / d^2$

where $G = 6.67 \times 10^{-11}\,N \cdot m^2 / kg^2$

6. $m_1 = 1.67 \times 10^{-27}\,kg$; $m_2 = 9.11 \times 10^{-31}\,kg$; $d = 1.00 \times 10^{-10}\,m$

7. $F_c = k\dfrac{Q_1 Q_2}{d^2}$ where $k = 8.987 \times 10^9\,N \cdot m^2 / C^2$; $Q_1 = 10^{-2}\,C$; $Q_2 = 10^{-2}\,C$; $d = 10m$

17.7 Solving Problems with Dimensional Analysis

Chess is one of the most popular board games in the world and also one of the most complex (Figure 17.7). White opens the game by selecting any of 20 possible opening moves. Black counters with 20 possible moves, bringing the number of variants to 400 at the end of two moves (one complete turn). The number grows rapidly as the game progresses: three moves, 8902; four moves (two complete turns), 197,281; five moves, 4,865,609; six moves (three complete turns), 119,060,324. Thus, at the end of just six moves, there are nearly 120 million possible variants of the game! Expert

Figure 17.7 Chess Players Use Heuristics

chess players often plan three or four moves ahead, but certainly they cannot ponder all of the options. Instead of considering all scenarios, they focus on logical ones, dramatically increasing their efficiency and effectiveness.

Chess masters develop *heuristics,* methods for directing their attention to reasonable options while ignoring unreasonable ones. Rather than considering all options, they concentrate only on those that are more likely to produce favorable results. Chess players will not advance in the game until they develop good heuristics that allow them to discard unlikely variants and focus only on the likely ones.

In a similar manner, scientists use problem-solving strategies that allow them to focus their attention on likely possibilities rather than all possibilities. Perhaps the most widely used problem-solving strategy is *dimensional analysis* (also know as *unit analysis* and *factor-label method*). Dimensional analysis allows you to set up the problem and check for logic errors before performing calculations and to determine intermediate answers en route to the solution. A student or scientist who does not use dimensional analysis is like a chess player who has not learned key strategies of the game. He or she will spend an inordinate amount of time checking illogical possibilities, with no assurance that the steps taken are correct. Dimensional analysis has five basic steps:

1. *Unknown:* Clearly specify the units (dimensions) of the desired product (the unknown). These will become the target units for your equation.
2. *Knowns:* Specify all known values with their associated units. It is often a good idea to draw a diagram of what you know about the situation, placing values with their units on the diagram.
3. *Conversion factors and formulas:* Specify relevant formulas and all conversion factors (with their units).
4. *Equation:* Develop an equation (using appropriate formulas and conversion factors) such that the units of the left side (the side containing the known values) are equivalent to the units of the right side (the side containing the unknown). If the units are not equal, the problem has not been set up correctly and further changes in the setup must be made.
5. *Calculation:* Perform the calculation only after you have analyzed all dimensions and are certain that both sides of your equation have equivalent units.

Example 1: Medicine

The label on a stock drug container gives the concentration of a solution as 1200 mg/mL. Determine the volume of the medication that must be given to fill a physician's order of 1600 mg of the drug (Figure 17.8).

1. *Unknown:* An analysis of the problem shows that the unknown (the volume of solution to be given) must have units of volume (mL medicine).
2. *Knowns:* We know that the solution has a concentration of 1200 mg drug/mL medicine and that we must obtain 1600 mg of the drug. Figure 17.8 illustrates what must be done.
3. *Conversion factors and formulas:* None necessary.

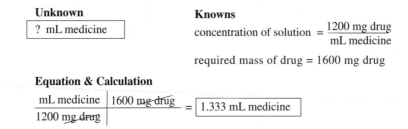

Figure 17.8 Determining How Much Medication Should Be Given

4. *Equation:* You must divide by concentration and multiply by mass of the drug in order to get the desired units (mg medicine).
5. *Calculation:* After the units are canceled, the equation yields 1.333 mL of medicine.

Example 2: Space Science

On June 19, 1976, the United States successfully landed *Viking 1* on the surface of the planet Mars. Twenty years later, on July 4, 1997, NASA landed another robotic probe, *Mars Pathfinder,* at a distance of 520 miles from the *Viking 1* landing site. Unlike the Viking mission, the Pathfinder mission included a surface rover known as Sojourner, a six-wheeled vehicle that was controlled by an Earth-based operator. Knowing that the distance between the landing site of the *Mars Pathfinder* and the *Viking 1* craft is 520 mi, what would be the minimum number of hours required to drive Sojourner to the Viking site assuming a top speed of 0.70 cm/s, and no obstacles (Figure 17.9).

1. *Unknown:* The number of hours to reach the *Viking 1* site.
2. *Knowns:* The distance is 520 mi, and the speed is 0.7 cm/s.
3. *Conversion factors and formulas:* The distance is measured in customary units (miles), and the speed of Sojourner is measured in metric units (cm/s). We will therefore need to use the following conversion ratios to obtain units with the correct dimensions: 2.54 cm/in., 12 in./ft, 5280 ft/mi.
4. *Equation:* The answer must have units of time. The only known factor that includes units of time is the speed of the rover (distance/time).

It is therefore evident that we must divide by speed to get units of time in the numerator where they are needed. To arrive at the desired units of time, it is necessary to cancel the units of distance by multiplying by the distance that must be traveled. It is now necessary to multiply or divide by the appropriate conversion ratios to ensure that all units of distance are canceled.

5. *Calculation:* After the units are canceled, the equation yields the answer in hours, as desired. The number is changed to two significant figures since one of the factors has only two significant figures, and you can have no greater accuracy than your least accurate factor.

Example 3: Physics

A 2.00 L tank of helium gas contains 1.785 g at a pressure of 202 kPa. What is the temperature of the gas in the tank in kelvin given that the molecular weight of helium is 4.002 g/mol and the universal gas constant is 8.29×10^3 L·Pa/mol·K (Figure 17.10)?

1. *Unknown:* The unknown is the temperature of the gas, expressed in kelvin.
2. *Knowns:* Volume of helium container (2.00 L), mass of helium (1.785 g), molecular weight (*MW*) of helium (He; 4.002 g/mol), pressure of helium (202 kPa), universal gas constant (8.29×10^3 L·Pa/mol·K). In addition, we know the number of moles ($n = 0.446$ mol) of helium since $n = m/MW$.
3. *Conversion factors and formulas:* This problem requires the use of the Ideal Gas Law equation ($PV = nRT$), which must be expressed in terms of temperature: $T = PV/nR$.

Unknown	Knowns	Conversion factors		
? h	distance = 520 miles	$1 = \dfrac{2.54 \text{ cm}}{\text{in}}$	$1 = \dfrac{12 \text{ in}}{\text{ft}}$	$1 = \dfrac{5280 \text{ ft}}{\text{mi}}$
	speed = $\dfrac{0.70 \text{ cm}}{\text{s}}$			

Equation & Calculation

$$\frac{s}{0.70 \text{ cm}} \left| \frac{520 \text{ miles}}{} \right| \frac{5280 \text{ ft}}{\text{mile}} \left| \frac{12 \text{ in}}{\text{ft}} \right| \frac{2.54 \text{ cm}}{\text{in}} \left| \frac{\text{min}}{60 \text{ s}} \right| \frac{\text{h}}{60 \text{ min}} = \boxed{33208 \text{ h} = 3.3 \times 10^4 \text{ h}}$$

Figure 17.9 Calculating the Time Required for a Specific Trip

Unknown	Knowns			Formulas
$?K$	$V = 2.00L$	$MW = 4.002g/mol$	$R = \dfrac{8.31 \times 10^3 \text{L·kPa}}{\text{mol·K}}$	$PV = nRT$
	$m = 1.785g$	$P = 202 \text{ kPa}$		$T = \dfrac{PV}{nR}$

Equation & Calculation

$$n = \frac{m}{MW} = \frac{1.785g}{} \frac{\text{mol}}{4.002 \text{ g}} = 0.446 \text{ mol}$$

$$T = \frac{PV}{nR} = \frac{202 \text{ kPa}}{} \frac{2.00L}{} \frac{}{0.446 \text{ mol}} \frac{\text{mol·K}}{8.31 \times 10^3 \text{L·kPa}} = \boxed{0.109 \text{ K}}$$

$n = \dfrac{m}{MW}$

Figure 17.10 Using Dimensional Analysis for Determining the Temperature of a Gas

Unknown	Knowns		Conversion factors	
$?g \text{ Ag}$	$I = 5.12A$	$Ag^+ + e^- \rightarrow Ag$	$1 = \dfrac{96{,}500 \text{ C}}{\text{mol } e^-}$	$1 = \dfrac{60 \text{ min}}{h}$
	$t = 2.00h$	$AW_{Ag} = 107.9 \text{ g/mol}$	$1A = \dfrac{1C}{s}$	$1 = \dfrac{60 \text{ s}}{\text{min}}$

Equation & Calculation

$$\frac{5.12A}{1A} \frac{1C}{s} \frac{\text{mol } e^-}{96{,}500 \text{ C}} \frac{1 \text{ mol Ag}}{1 \text{ mol } e^-} \frac{107.9 \text{ g Ag}}{1 \text{ mol Ag}} \frac{60 \text{ s}}{\text{min}} \frac{60 \text{ min}}{h} \frac{2.00 h}{} = \boxed{41.2 \text{ g Ag}}$$

Figure 17.11 Using Dimensional Analysis for Determining the Mass of Silver Electroplated

4. *Equation:* The equation must be set up so all units cancel except the desired units, kelvin (K).
5. *Calculation:* Once the equation is set up so that the units cancel to leave only the target units of K, calculations can be performed.

Example 4: Chemistry

Calculate the mass of silver metal that can be deposited if a 5.12 ampere current is passed through a silver nitrate solution for 2.00 hours. *Note:* There are 96,500 C per mole of electrons, and the gram atomic weight of silver is 107.9 g/mol (Figure 17.11).

1. *Unknown:* An analysis of the problem shows that the unknown (the mass of silver metal deposited) must have units of grams silver.
2. *Knowns:* We know that the current is 5.12 amps for a period of 2.00 hours. We also know that 1 mole of silver is deposited per mole of electrons from the fact that silver is a plus one cation ($Ag^+ + e^- \rightarrow Ag$). From the problem description, we know the experimental setup and can therefore draw a diagram. We also can acquire the gram-atomic weight of silver from the periodic table.

3. *Conversion factors and formulas:* This problem requires a number of conversion factors in order to get the appropriate units. One coulomb is 1 amp second. One mole of electrons is 96,500 coulombs. One hour is 60 minutes. One minute is 60 seconds. Because these are equalities, they can be represented as conversion factors, each of which is equal to one.
4. *Equation:* The units of the unknown become the target units and are set up on the right side of the equation. The left side of the equation is assembled so that units will cancel and leave only the target units.
5. *Calculation:* Once the equation is set up so that the units cancel to leave only the target units, calculations can be performed.

Example 5: Earth Science

The island of Greenland is approximately 840,000 mi^2, 85 percent of which is covered by ice with an average thickness of 1500 m. Estimate the mass of the ice in Greenland in kg (assume two significant figures). The density of ice is 0.917 g/mL, and $1 \text{ cm}^3 = 1 \text{ mL}$ (Figure 17.12).

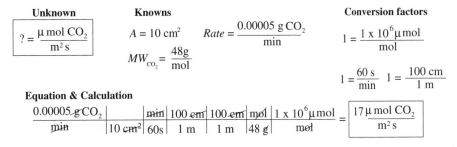

Figure 17.12 Using Dimensional Analysis for Determining the Mass of Ice in Greenland

Unknown

$? = \dfrac{\mu\,mol\,CO_2}{m^2\,s}$

Knowns

$A = 10\ cm^2$

$Rate = \dfrac{0.00005\ g\,CO_2}{min}$

$MW_{CO_2} = \dfrac{48g}{mol}$

Conversion factors

$1 = \dfrac{1 \times 10^6 \mu mol}{mol}$

$1 = \dfrac{60\ s}{min}$ $1 = \dfrac{100\ cm}{1\ m}$

Equation & Calculation

$$\dfrac{0.00005\ g\,CO_2}{min}\left|\dfrac{min}{10\ cm^2}\right|\dfrac{100\ cm}{60s}\left|\dfrac{100\ cm}{1\ m}\right|\dfrac{mol}{1\ m}\left|\dfrac{1 \times 10^6 \mu mol}{48\ g}\right|\dfrac{}{mol} = \dfrac{17\,\mu\,mol\,CO_2}{m^2\,s}$$

Figure 17.13 Using Dimensional Analysis for Determining Photosynthesis Rates

1. *Unknown:* An analysis of the problem shows that the unknown must have units of mass. Since the specific units of mass are not specified, we will use the MKS unit of kilograms.
2. *Knowns:* Since we know that the area of Greenland is 840,000 miles² and 85 percent of it is covered by ice, then 714,000 miles² must be covered by ice. We also know that the density of ice = 0.917 g/mL and the ice has an average depth (height) of 1500 m.
3. *Conversion factors and formulas:* Some measurements are in customary units, while others are in metric. We should always convert all units to metric unless otherwise specified. To do so, we will need to convert miles to meters using the following conversion factors: 5280 ft/mile, and 0.3048 m/ft. We also need to use conversion factors to obtain consistent metric units for mass and volume. Knowing that 1 cm = 0.01 m, then 1 cm³ = 0.000001 m³. We also know that 1 kg = 1000 g.
4. *Equation:* The units of the unknown become the target units and are set up on the right side of the equation (kg ice). The equation mass = (height × area) density is the basic

equation, and the conversion factors are inserted to make certain all units are consistent.
5. *Calculation:* Once the equation is set up so units cancel to leave only the target units of kilograms of ice, calculations can be performed.

Example 6: Biology

The rate of photosynthesis is often measured in the number of micromoles of carbon dioxide (CO_2) fixed per square meter of leaf tissue, per second ($\mu mol\ CO_2/m^2s$). What is the rate of photosynthesis in a leaf with an area of 10 cm² if it assimilates 0.00005 grams of carbon dioxide each minute (MW of CO_2 = 48 g/mol)? (Figure 17.13).

1. *Unknown:* We are trying to determine the rate of photosynthesis in units of $\mu mol\ CO_2/m^2s$.
2. *Knowns:* The rate of carbon dioxide assimilation by the leaf is 0.00005 g of carbon dioxide per minute. We also know that the leaf area responsible for this is 10 cm².
3. *Conversion factors and formulas:* The gram molecular weight of CO_2 = 48 g/mol. This

Table 17.10 SI and Customary Units of Conversion

Quantity	SI Unit	Symbol	Customary Unit	Symbol	Conversion
length	meter	m	foot	ft	1 m = 3.280 ft
area	square meter	m^2	square foot	ft^2	1 m^2 = 10.76 ft^2
volume	cubic meter	m^3	cubic foot	ft^3	1 m^3 = 35.32 ft^3
speed	meter per second	m/s	foot per second	ft/s	1 m/s = 3.280 ft/s
acceleration	meter/s/s	m/s^2	feet/s/s	ft/s^2	1 m/s^2 = 3.280 ft/s^2
force	newton	N	pound	lb	1 N = 0.2248 lb
work	joule	J	foot-pound	ft·lb	1 J = 0.7376 ft·lb
power	watt	W	ft-pound/s	ft·lb/s	1 W = 0.7376 ft·lb/s
pressure	pascal	Pa	lb per sq inch	lb/in^2	1 Pa = 1.450×10^{-4} lb/in^2
density	kg per cubic meter	kg/m^3	lb per cubic foot	lb/ft^3	1 kg/m^3 = 6.243×10^{-2} lb/ft^3

Table 17.11 Common Conversions

Quantity	Customary Unit	Metric Unit	Customary/Metric	Metric/Customary
Length	inch (in.)	millimeter (mm)	1 in = 25.4 mm	1 mm = 0.0394 in
	foot (ft)	meter (m)	1 ft = 0.305 m	1 m = 3.28 ft
	yard (yd)	meter (m)	1 yd = 0.914 m	1 m = 1.09 yd
	mile (mi)	kilometer (km)	1 mi = 1.61 km	1 km = 0.621 mi
Area	square inch (in^2)	square centimeter (cm^2)	1 in^2 = 6.45 cm^2	1 cm^2 = 0.155 in^2
	square foot (ft^2)	square meter (m^2)	1 ft^2 = 0.0929 m^2	1 m^2 = 10.8 ft^2
	square yard (yd^2)	square meter (m^2)	1 yd^2 = 0.836 m^2	1 m^2 = 1.20 yd^2
	acre (acre)	hectare (ha)	1 acre = 0.405 ha	1 ha = 2.47 acre
Volume	cubic inch (in^3)	cubic centimeter (cm^3)	1 in^3 = 16.39 cm^3	1 cm^3 = 0.0610 in^3
	cubic foot (ft^3)	cubic meter (m^3)	1 ft^3 = 0.0283 m^3	1 m^3 = 35.3 ft^3
	cubic yard (yd^3)	cubic meter (m^3)	1 yd^3 = 0.765 m^3	1 m^3 = 1.31 yd^3
	quart (qt)	liter (L)	1 qt = 0.946 L	1 L = 1.06 qt
Mass	ounce (oz)	gram (g)	1 oz = 28.4 g	1 g = 0.0352 oz
	pound (lb)	kilogram (kg)	1 lb = 0.454 kg	1 kg = 2.20 lb
	ton (ton)	metric ton (t)	1 ton = 0.907 t	1 t = 1.10 ton
Weight	pound (lb)	newton (N)	1 lb = 4.45 N	1 N = 0.225 lb

will be essential in determining the number of micromoles of carbon dioxide. We also know that there are 10^6 micromoles/mole, 100 cm/m, and 60 s/min. We may multiply or divide by these unit factors because each one is an identity (equal to 1).

4. *Equation:* Since the rate of photosynthesis is defined as the number of moles of carbon dioxide absorbed per square meter of tissue per second, the equation becomes: Rate = quantity of CO_2 per square area of tissue, per second.

5. Calculation: Once the equation is set up so that the units cancel to leave only the target units of μmol CO_2/m^2s, then calculations can be performed.

Tables 17.10 and 17.11 may be helpful in the activities that follows.

ACTIVITY 17.7.1 *Solving Problems in Everyday Life with Dimensional Analysis*

1. Convert the following:
   (a) 61.0 kilometers to miles
   (b) 2.7 quarts to liters
   (c) 56 grams to pounds
   (d) 17 pounds to kilograms
   (e) 1 million seconds to days
   (f) 21 feet/minute to miles/hour
   (g) 0.391 grams/mililiter to kilograms/liter
   (h) 85.5 meters/day to centimeter/minute

2. The food that the average American eats in one day provides 2000 calories of energy. How many calories per second is this?

3. Three people estimate the height of the Washington monument in Washington, D.C.: tourist, 555 feet; congressman, 158 yards; lobbyist, 0.173 km. Which is closest to the true height of 169.3 meters?

4. The EPA sticker on a car states that it will obtain 30 miles per gallon on the highway. How many liters of gasoline must the driver have to ensure that he or she can get home from college if there are 300 miles of highway driving between college and home?

5. You want to earn $600 to buy a new bicycle. You have a job that pays $6.75 per hour, but you can work only 3 hours each day. How many days before you will have enough to buy the bike?

6. Corn sells for $8.00/bushel. Your land's yearly yield is 25 bushels/acre. How many acres should you put in corn to make $1000 each year?

7. A landscaper charges $7 per square meter to plant sod. How much will it cost to plant a 1 acre lawn? (1 hectare = 10,000 square meters)

8. A chemist was traveling 2850 centimeters per second on his way to work. Could he be cited for speeding if the speed limit was 60 miles per hour?

9. Two of fastest cars ever built were the Lingenfelter Corvette 427 biturbo (which would accelerate from 0 kilometers per second to 100 kilometers per hour in 1.97 seconds) and the Hennessey Dodge Viper Venom 800 (0 miles per hour to 62 miles per hour in 2.40 seconds). Which car demonstrated greater acceleration?

ACTIVITY 17.7.2 *Solving Problems in Biology with Dimensional Analysis*

1. What is the net primary productivity ($kg/m^2 \cdot y$) of a field of wheat if an average of 2500 kg is harvested each year in a plot that is 10 m $\times$ 10 m?

2. Cheetahs are the fastest land mammals and are capable of sprinting at 27.8 m/s in short bursts. How long would it take a cheetah to run the length of a 100 yd football field running at this top speed (1 yd = 0.914 m)?

3. If an artificial heart is capable of pumping at least 57,000,000 pints of blood before failure, how long will it probably last in a patient whose average heart rate is 72 beats per minutes and average stroke volume (the amount of blood pumped with each stroke) is 70 mL?

4. The rate of respiration is often measured in the number of micromoles of CO_2 fixed per gram of tissue per second ($\mu mol\ CO_2/g \cdot s$). What is the rate of respiration in an organism with a mass of 1 g if it produces 0.002 g of carbon dioxide each minute (MW of CO_2 = 48 g/mol)?

5. A 125 lb patient is to receive a drug at a rate of 0.300 mg per 1.00 kg of body weight. If the drug is supplied as a solution containing 5.00 mg/mL, how many milliliters of drug solution should the patient receive?

6. A calcium report indicated 8.00 mg/dL of calcium ions in the blood. If we assume that the patient has 6.00 qt of blood, how many grams of calcium ions are in his or her blood? (1 dL = 0.1 L)

7. A large dose of an antileukemia drug is to be administered to a 190 pound patient by intravenous (IV) injection. The recommended dosage is 50.0 mg per kg of body weight, and the drug is supplied as a solution that contains 20.0 mg per mL. The IV has a flow rate of 3.00 mL/min. How long will it take to administer the recommended dose?

ACTIVITY 17.7.3 *Solving Problems in Earth Science with Dimensional Analysis*

1. Earth has an orbital velocity of 1.0 km/s. How far will it travel in 1 year?
2. When a 4.13 g chunk of rock is dropped into a graduated cylinder containing 8.3 mL of water, the water level rises to 9.8 mL. What is the density of the rock in grams per cubic centimeter? Is this rock more likely granite (2.7–2.8 g/cm3) or basalt (2.9 g/cm^3)?
3. The Atlantic Ocean is growing wider by about 1 in./yr. There are 12 in./ft and 5280 ft/mi. How long will it take for the Atlantic to grow 1 m in width?
4. The average distance between the Earth and Sun is approximately 93,000,000 miles. Express this distance in centimeters.
5. A chunk of the mineral galena (lead sulfide) has a mass of 12.4 g and a volume of 1.64 cm^3. What is its density? Will it float or sink in a pool of mercury (density Hg = 13,600 kg/m3)?
6. A solid concrete dam measures 50 GL. How many cubic meters of concrete are in this structure? 1 GL = 1 × 109 L; 1 L = 1000 cm3.
7. The mass of Earth is 5.97 × 10^{24} kg. What is its average density in g/mL if it has a radius of 6378 km (Vsphere = 4/3πr3)?

ACTIVITY 17.7.4 *Solving Problems in Chemistry with Dimensional Analysis*

1. Platinum has a density of 21.4 g/mL. What is the mass of 5.90 mL of this metal?
2. The mass of a proton is 1.67272 × 10^{-27} kg. What is its mass in μg?
3. What mass of silver nitrate must be used to make 2.00 dm^3 of a 1.00M solution? 1 dm = 0.1m, 1 dm^3 = 1L.
4. Calculate the mass of solute required to make 750 mL of a 2.50 M sodium chloride solution.
5. Calculate the molarity of a 1.50 × 10^3 cm^3 solution that contains 200.0 grams of $MgCl_2$.
6. What is the mass of solute in 300.0 mL of a solution if the solution is 85 percent water and has a density of 1.60 g/cm^3?
7. A copper refinery produces a copper ingot weighing 150 lb. If the copper is drawn into wire of diameter 8.25 mm, how many feet of copper can be obtained from the ingot? The density of copper is 8.94 g/cm^3.

ACTIVITY 17.7.5 *Solving Problems in Physics with Dimensional Analysis*

1. A beta particle travels at a speed of 112,000 miles per second. What is its speed expressed in centimeters per second? (Give three digits in your answer and use scientific notation.) 5280 ft = 1.00 mi; 12 in. = 1 ft; 2.54 cm = 1.00 in.
2. An object is traveling at a speed of 7.5 × 10^3 cm/s. Convert the value to kilometers per minute.
3. Traffic accident investigators often discuss reaction time when trying to determine liability for an accident. If a person's reaction time is 1.5 sec, how many meters will his or her car travel before the brakes are activated if the car is traveling at 70 mph?
4. The wavelength of visible light is 706 nm. What is its frequency in sec^{-1} (Hz)? The speed of light, c = 3.00 × 10^8 m/sec. 1 nm = 1 × 10^{-9} m.
5. The acceleration due to gravity on Earth is 9.8 m/s^2 and 3.7 m/s^2 on the surface of Mars. If you weigh 700 N on Earth, how many newtons would you weigh on Mars? 1 N = 1 kg·m·s^{-2}.
6. A light-year is the distance light (c = 3.0 × 10^8 m/s) travels in one Earth-year. Alpha Centauri C, the star closest to our Sun, is 4.22 light-years away. How far is this expressed in meters?
7. The escape velocity for earth is 11.2 km/s. How far will a spacecraft travel in an hour if it is traveling at 1.6 times the escape velocity?

Answers to Chapter Activities

17.1.1 (1) milligrams; (2) km/hour; (3) 60 PSI; (4) IU; (5) degrees Celsius.

17.1.2 (1) °F; (2) feet, feet, miles; (3) G, CM, G; (4) km/h; (5) mm; (6) °C; (7) miles/h; (8) light years; (9) megatons; (10) meters; (11) feet, inches; (12) acres; (13) ounces; (14) meters; (15) inches.

17.2.1 Units are classified correctly as measures of one of the seven fundamental quantities as shown in Table 17.12.

17.3.1 (a) A meter is the length of a pendulum having a period of one-half second. (b) A kilogram is the mass of one cubic decimeter of water.

17.4.1 (1) 0.20 m, (2) 0.150 kg, (3) 2.5 Pa, (4) 8.38 J, (5) 1 N, (6) 336 C, (7) 0.01 T

17.5.1 C = Q/V; V = IR; P = IV; P = I^{2}R; P = W/t; E = Fd; E = W; E = 1/2 mv^2; E = mad.

Table 17.12 Classification of Units

	Mass	Length	Time	Temperature	Luminous intensity	Electric Charge	Quantity		Mass	Length	Time	Temperature	Luminous intensity	Electric Charge	Quantity
A (ampere)						X		hour			X				
amu	X							inch		X					
biot						X		K (kelvin)				X			
bolt (of cloth)		X						kilogram	X						
Cd (candela)					X			league		X					
cubit		X						meter		X					
day			X					mole							X
decade			X					neutron mass	X						
°C				X				oz (ounce)	X						
°F				X				pace		X					
°R (Rankine)				X				pica		X					
°Re (Reaumur)				X				pound ap	X						
dozen							X	pound	X						
dram ap	X							second			X				
earth mass	X							sidereal day			X				
football field		X						sidereal month			X				
fortnight			X					slug	X						
gross							X	UK mile		X					
hand		X						week			X				
hefner candle					X			yr (year)			X				

17.6.1 Dimensional analysis with the line method

(1)
$$\frac{1 \text{ tsubo}}{} \left| \frac{5124 \text{ sq.inches}}{1 \text{ tsubo}} \right| \frac{6.452 \text{ square cm}}{1 \text{ sq. inch}} \left| \frac{0.0001 \text{ m}^2}{1 \text{ square cm}} \right. = 3.3 \text{ m}^2$$

(2)
$$\frac{3.0 \times 10^8 \text{ m}}{\text{s}} \left| \frac{60 \text{ s}}{\text{min}} \right| \frac{60 \text{ min}}{\text{h}} \left| \frac{24 \text{ h}}{\text{day}} \right| 365.25 \text{ day} = 9.47 \times 10^{15} \text{ m}$$

(3)
$$\frac{1.0 \text{ g}}{1 \text{ g}} \left| \frac{0.0010 \text{ kg}}{1 \text{ kg}} \right| \frac{0.001 \text{ tonne}}{1 \text{ tonne}} \left| \frac{0.9842 \text{ long tons}}{\text{long ton}} \right| \frac{2240 \text{ pounds}}{\text{pound}} \left| \frac{16 \text{ ounces}}{\text{ounce}} \right| 138.3 \text{ carats} = 4.9 \text{ carats}$$

(4)
$$\frac{1 \text{ TB}}{\text{TB}} \left| \frac{1024 \text{ GB}}{\text{GB}} \right| \frac{1024 \text{ MB}}{1 \text{ MB}} \left| \frac{1024 \text{ kB}}{\text{kB}} \right| \frac{1024 \text{ bytes}}{\text{byte}} \left| \frac{8 \text{ bits}}{} \right. = 8.8 \times 10^{12} \text{ bits}$$

(5)
$$F = \frac{2 \text{kg}}{} \left| \frac{50 \text{ m}}{\text{s}} \right| \frac{}{0.01 \text{ s}} = 1 \times 10^4 \text{ N}$$

(6)
$$F = \frac{6.67 \times 10^{-11} \text{ N m}^2}{\text{kg}^2} \left| \frac{1.67 \times 10^{-27} \text{ kg}}{} \right| 9.11 \times 10^{-31} \text{ kg} \left| \frac{}{1.00 \times 10^{-20} \text{ m}^2} \right. = 1.01 \times 10^{-47} \text{ N}$$

(7)
$$F = \frac{8.987 \times 10^9 \text{ N} \cdot \text{m}^2}{\text{C}^2} \left| 10^2 \text{ C} \right| 10^2 \text{ C} \left| \frac{}{100 \text{ m}^2} \right. = 9.0 \times 10^4 \text{ N}$$

17.7.1 Solving problems in everyday life with dimensional analysis

(1) (a) 61.0 kilometers = 37.9 miles   (e) 1.00 million seconds = 11.6 days
      (b) 2.7 quarts = 2.6 liters   (f) 21 ft/minute = 0.24 miles/hour
      (c) 56 grams = 0.12 pounds   (g) 0.391 grams/ml = 0.391 kg/liter
      (d) 17 pounds =7.7 kilograms   (h) 85.5 meters/day = 5.94 cm/minute

(2) $\dfrac{2000 \text{ Cal}}{1 \text{ day}} \cdot \dfrac{1 \text{ day}}{24 \text{ h}} \cdot \dfrac{1 \text{ h}}{60 \text{ min}} \cdot \dfrac{1 \text{ min}}{60 \text{ s}} = \dfrac{0.023 \text{ Cal}}{\text{s}}$

(3)   *tourist* $\dfrac{555 \text{ ft}}{} \cdot \dfrac{0.305 \text{ m}}{1 \text{ ft}} = 169 \text{ m}$ *congressman* $\dfrac{158 \text{ yd}}{} \cdot \dfrac{0.914 \text{ m}}{1 \text{ yd}} = 144 \text{ m}$

        lobbyist $\dfrac{0.173 \text{ km}}{} \cdot \dfrac{1000 \text{ m}}{1 \text{ km}} = 173 \text{ m}$ the tourist's estimate is closest

(4) $\dfrac{1 \text{ gal}}{30 \text{ miles}} \cdot \dfrac{300 \text{ miles}}{} \cdot \dfrac{4 \text{ qt}}{1 \text{ gal}} \cdot \dfrac{0.946 \text{ L}}{1 \text{ qt}} = 37.8 \text{ L}$

(5) $\dfrac{\$600}{} \cdot \dfrac{1 \text{ hour}}{\$6.75} \cdot \dfrac{1 \text{ day}}{3 \text{ hours}} = 30 \text{ days}$

(6) $\dfrac{\$1000}{} \cdot \dfrac{\text{bushel}}{\$8.00} \cdot \dfrac{\text{acre}}{25 \text{ bushels}} = 5 \text{ acres}$

(7) $\dfrac{\$7}{1 \text{ m}^2} \cdot \dfrac{10,000 \text{ m}^2}{1 \text{ ha}} \cdot \dfrac{1 \text{ ha}}{2.47 \text{ acres}} \cdot \dfrac{1 \text{ acre}}{} = \$28,340$

(8) $\dfrac{2850 \text{ cm}}{1 \text{ s}} \cdot \dfrac{\text{in}}{2.54 \text{ cm}} \cdot \dfrac{\text{ft}}{12 \text{ in}} \cdot \dfrac{\text{mile}}{5280 \text{ ft}} \cdot \dfrac{60 \text{ s}}{\text{min}} \cdot \dfrac{60 \text{ min}}{\text{h}} = \dfrac{63.7 \text{ miles}}{\text{h}}$

(9) $\dfrac{100 \text{ km}}{\text{h}} \cdot \dfrac{\text{h}}{1.97 \text{ s}} \cdot \dfrac{\text{min}}{60 \text{ min}} \cdot \dfrac{\text{min}}{60 \text{ s}} \cdot \dfrac{1000 \text{ m}}{\text{km}} = \dfrac{14.1 \text{ m}}{\text{s}^2}$ *Lingenfelter Corvette* $a = dv/dt$

       $\dfrac{62 \text{ miles}}{\text{h}} \cdot \dfrac{\text{h}}{2.40 \text{ s}} \cdot \dfrac{\text{h}}{60 \text{ min}} \cdot \dfrac{\text{min}}{60 \text{ s}} \cdot \dfrac{1.62 \text{ km}}{\text{mile}} \cdot \dfrac{1000 \text{ m}}{\text{km}} = \dfrac{11.6 \text{ m}}{\text{s}^2}$ *Dodge Viper*

17.7.2 Solving problems in biology with dimensional analysis

(1) $\dfrac{2500 \text{ kg}}{\text{yr}} \cdot \dfrac{}{10 \text{ m}} \cdot \dfrac{}{10 \text{ m}} = \dfrac{25 \text{ kg}}{\text{m}^2 \text{ yr}}$

(2) $\dfrac{100 \text{ yd}}{} \cdot \dfrac{0.914 \text{ m}}{\text{yd}} \cdot \dfrac{\text{s}}{27.8 \text{ m}} = 3.29 \text{ s}$

(3) $\dfrac{\text{min}}{72 \text{ beats}} \cdot \dfrac{\text{beat}}{70 \text{ mL}} \cdot \dfrac{1000 \text{ mL}}{\text{L}} \cdot \dfrac{0.946 \text{ L}}{\text{qt}} \cdot \dfrac{\text{qt}}{2 \text{ pt}} \cdot \dfrac{57,000,000 \text{ pt}}{} \cdot \dfrac{\text{h}}{60 \text{ min}} \cdot \dfrac{\text{day}}{24 \text{ h}} \cdot \dfrac{\text{y}}{365 \text{ day}} = 10.2 \text{ y}$

(4) $\dfrac{0.002 \text{ g CO}_2}{1 \text{ g tissue} \cdot \text{min}} \cdot \dfrac{\text{mol CO}_2}{48 \text{ g CO}_2} \cdot \dfrac{1 \times 10^6 \text{ } \mu\text{mol}}{\text{mol}} \cdot \dfrac{\text{min}}{60 \text{ s}} = \dfrac{0.7 \text{ } \mu\text{mol CO}_2}{\text{g tissue} \cdot \text{s}}$

(5) $\dfrac{\text{mL}}{5.00 \text{ mg}} \cdot \dfrac{0.300 \text{ mg}}{1.00 \text{ kg}} \cdot \dfrac{\text{kg}}{2.20 \text{ lb}} \cdot \dfrac{125 \text{ lb}}{} = 3.41 \text{ mL}$

(6) $\dfrac{8.00 \text{ mg calcium ions}}{\text{dL blood}} \Bigg| \dfrac{\text{dL}}{0.1 \text{ L}} \Bigg| \dfrac{0.946 \text{ L}}{\text{qt}} \Bigg| \dfrac{6.00 \text{ qts blood}}{} \Bigg| \dfrac{g}{1000 \text{ mg}} = 0.454 \text{g calcium ions}$

(7) $\dfrac{\text{min}}{3.00 \text{ mL solution}} \Bigg| \dfrac{\text{mL solution}}{20.0 \text{ mg drug}} \Bigg| \dfrac{50.0 \text{ mg drug}}{\text{kg body wt}} \Bigg| \dfrac{190 \text{ lb body wt.}}{} \Bigg| \dfrac{0.454 \text{ kg}}{1.00 \text{ lb}} = 71.9 \text{ min}$

17.7.3 Solving problems in earth and space science with dimensional analysis

(1) $\dfrac{1.0 \text{ km}}{s} \Bigg| \dfrac{60 \text{ s}}{\text{min}} \Bigg| \dfrac{60 \text{ min}}{\text{hr}} \Bigg| \dfrac{24 \text{ hr}}{\text{day}} \Bigg| \dfrac{365 \text{ day}}{y} = \dfrac{3.1 \times 10^7 \text{ km}}{y}$

(2) $\dfrac{4.13 \text{ g}}{1.5 \text{ mL}} \Bigg| \dfrac{\text{mL}}{\text{cm}^3} = \dfrac{2.8 \text{ g}}{\text{cm}^3}$ *it is probably granite*

(3) $\dfrac{y}{1 \text{ in}} \Bigg| \dfrac{\text{in}}{2.54 \text{ cm}} \Bigg| \dfrac{100 \text{ cm}}{\text{m}} \Bigg| \dfrac{1 \text{ m}}{} = 39 \text{ y}$

(4) $\dfrac{93,000,000 \text{ miles}}{} \Bigg| \dfrac{5280 \text{ ft}}{\text{mile}} \Bigg| \dfrac{12 \text{ in}}{\text{ft}} \Bigg| \dfrac{2.54 \text{ cm}}{\text{in}} = 1.4 \times 10^{13} \text{cm}$

(5) $\dfrac{12.4 \text{ g}}{1.64 \text{ cm}^3} \Bigg| \dfrac{1 \text{ cm}^3}{1 \text{ mL}} = \dfrac{7.56 \text{ g}}{\text{mL}}$ *galena*   *galena will float in mercury*

$\dfrac{13,600 \text{ kg}}{\text{m}^3} \Bigg| \dfrac{\text{m}^3}{1.0 \times 10^6 \text{cm}^3} \Bigg| \dfrac{1 \text{ cm}^3}{1 \text{mL}} \Bigg| \dfrac{1000 g}{\text{kg}} = \dfrac{13.6 g}{\text{mL}}$ *mercury*

(6) $\dfrac{50 \text{ GL concrete}}{} \Bigg| \dfrac{1 \times 10^9 \text{ L}}{\text{GL}} \Bigg| \dfrac{1000 \text{ cm}^3}{\text{L}} \Bigg| \dfrac{\text{m}^3}{1 \times 10^6 \text{ cm}^3} = 50,000,000 \text{ m}^3 \text{ concrete}$

(7) $\dfrac{5.97 \times 10^{24} \text{kg}}{} \Bigg| \dfrac{3}{4\pi(6378 \text{ km})^3} \Bigg| \dfrac{\text{km}}{1000 \text{ m}} \Bigg| \dfrac{\text{km}}{1000 \text{ m}} \Bigg| \dfrac{\text{km}}{1000 \text{ m}} \Bigg| \dfrac{\text{m}^3}{1.0 \times 10^6 \text{cm}^3} \Bigg| \dfrac{1 \text{ cm}^3}{\text{mL}} \Bigg| \dfrac{1000 \text{ g}}{\text{kg}} = \dfrac{5.5 \text{ g}}{\text{mL}}$

17.7.4 Solving problems in chemistry with dimensional analysis

(1) $\dfrac{21.4 \text{ g}}{1 \text{ mL}} \Bigg| \dfrac{1 \text{ mL}}{1 \text{ cm}^3} \Bigg| \dfrac{5.90 \text{ cm}^3}{} = 126 \text{ g}$

(2) $\dfrac{1.67272 \times 10^{-27} \text{ kg}}{} \Bigg| \dfrac{1000 \text{ g}}{\text{kg}} \Bigg| \dfrac{1,000,000 \text{ } \mu g}{g} = 1.67272 \times 10^{-18} \mu g$

(3) $\dfrac{170 \text{ g } AgNO_3}{\text{mole } AgNO_3} \Bigg| \dfrac{1.00 \text{ mole } AgNO_3}{\text{L}} \Bigg| \dfrac{1 \text{ L}}{1 \text{ dm}^3} \Bigg| \dfrac{2.00 \text{ dm}^3}{} = 340 \text{ g } AgNO_3$

(4) $\dfrac{58.4 \text{ g NaCl}}{\text{mole NaCl}} \Bigg| \dfrac{2.50 \text{ mole NaCl}}{\text{L}} \Bigg| \dfrac{\text{L}}{1000 \text{ mL}} \Bigg| \dfrac{750 \text{ mL}}{} = 110 \text{ g NaCl}$

(5) $\dfrac{\text{mole } MgCl_2}{95.1 \text{ g } MgCl_2} \Bigg| \dfrac{200.0 \text{ g } MgCl_2}{1.50 \times 10^3 \text{ cm}^3} \Bigg| \dfrac{1.00 \times 10^3 \text{ cm}^3}{\text{L}} = \dfrac{1.40 \text{ mole } MgCl_2}{\text{L}} = 1.40 \text{ M}$

(6) $\dfrac{15 \text{ g solute}}{100 \text{ g solution}} \Bigg| \dfrac{1.60 \text{ g}}{\text{cm}^3} \Bigg| \dfrac{\text{cm}^3}{\text{mL}} \Bigg| \dfrac{300.0 \text{ mL solution}}{} = 72.0 \text{ g solute}$

(7) $V = \dfrac{mass}{density}$ $\qquad density = \dfrac{mass}{V}$ $\qquad V_{wire} = V_{cylinder} = l(\pi r^2)$ $\qquad$ $\boxed{V = l\pi r^2}$

where $l = length$

$r = \dfrac{8.25 \text{ mm}}{} \Bigg| \dfrac{1 \text{ cm}}{10 \text{ mm}} \Bigg| \dfrac{1 \text{ inch}}{2.54 \text{ cm}} \Bigg| \dfrac{1 \text{ ft}}{12 \text{ inches}} = 0.0270 \text{ ft}$ $\qquad\qquad l = \dfrac{V}{\pi r^2} = \dfrac{mass}{density} \Bigg| \dfrac{1}{\pi r^2}$

$length = \dfrac{mass}{density} \Bigg| \dfrac{1}{\pi r^2} = \dfrac{150 \text{ lb}}{} \Bigg| \dfrac{\text{kg}}{2.20 \text{ lb}} \Bigg| \dfrac{1000 \text{ g}}{\text{kg}} \Bigg| \dfrac{\text{cm}^3}{8.94 \text{ g}} \Bigg| \dfrac{\text{in}^3}{16.4 \text{ cm}^3} \Bigg| \dfrac{\text{ft}^3}{1728 \text{ in}^3} \Bigg| \dfrac{1}{\pi \cdot 7.29 \text{ x } 10^{-4} \text{ ft}^2} = 118 \text{ ft}$

17.7.5 Solving problems in physics with dimensional analysis

(1) $\dfrac{112{,}000 \text{ miles}}{\text{s}} \Bigg| \dfrac{5280 \text{ ft}}{\text{mile}} \Bigg| \dfrac{12 \text{ in}}{\text{ft}} \Bigg| \dfrac{2.54 \text{ cm}}{\text{in}} = \dfrac{1.80 \text{ x } 10^{10} \text{ cm}}{\text{s}}$

(2) $\dfrac{7500 \text{ cm}}{\text{s}} \Bigg| \dfrac{60 \text{ s}}{\text{min}} \Bigg| \dfrac{\text{m}}{100 \text{ cm}} \Bigg| \dfrac{\text{km}}{1000 \text{ m}} = \dfrac{4.5 \text{ km}}{\text{min}}$

(3) $\dfrac{70 \text{ miles}}{\text{hr}} \Bigg| \dfrac{\text{hr}}{60 \text{ min}} \Bigg| \dfrac{\text{min}}{60 \text{ s}} \Bigg| \dfrac{1.5 \text{ s}}{} \Bigg| \dfrac{5280 \text{ ft}}{\text{mile}} \Bigg| \dfrac{0.305 \text{ m}}{\text{ft}} = 47 \text{ m}$

(4) $\dfrac{1}{706 \text{ nm}} \Bigg| \dfrac{1.0 \text{ x } 10^9 \text{ nm}}{\text{m}} \Bigg| \dfrac{3.0 \text{ x } 10^8 \text{ m}}{\text{s}} = 4.2 \text{ x } 10^{14} \text{ s}^{-1} = 4.2 \text{ x } 10^{14} \text{ Hz}$

(5) $\dfrac{700 \text{ kg m}}{\text{s}^2} \Bigg| \dfrac{\text{s}^2}{9.80 \text{ m}} \Bigg| \dfrac{3.70 \text{ m}}{\text{s}^2} = \dfrac{264 \text{ kg m}}{\text{s}^2} = 264 \text{ N}$

(6) $\dfrac{3.0 \text{ x } 10^8 \text{ m}}{\text{s}} \Bigg| \dfrac{3600 \text{ s}}{\text{h}} \Bigg| \dfrac{24 \text{ h}}{\text{d}} \Bigg| \dfrac{365 \text{ d}}{\text{y}} \Bigg| \dfrac{4.22 \text{ y}}{} = 3.99 \text{ x } 10^{16} \text{ m}$

(7) $\dfrac{11.2 \text{ km}}{\text{s}} \Bigg| \dfrac{1.6}{} \Bigg| \dfrac{60 \text{ s}}{\text{min}} \Bigg| \dfrac{60 \text{ min}}{\text{h}} \Bigg| \dfrac{1.0 \text{ h}}{} = 6.5 \text{ x } 10^4 \text{ km}$

Chapter Eighteen

Stoichiometry: Interactions of Matter

For the Teacher 351

18.1 Predicting Oxidation States and Ions 354

18.2 Predicting Polyatomic Ions, Reactants, and Products 360

18.3 Techniques for Balancing Equations 363

Answers to Chapter Activities 366

For the Teacher

Students should be proficient in stoichiometry and balancing equations if they are to comprehend the nuclear, chemical, geochemical, and biochemical interactions that undergird physics, chemistry, biology, and earth and space science. Unfortunately, many see *stoichiometry* (the quantitative relationships among the reactants and products in a reaction) as an irrelevant exercise in logic, and it is therefore important to give sufficient examples from each of the sciences to demonstrate how stoichiometry describes the interactions of matter and energy. The following are a few of the many important chemical and nuclear reactions foundational to physics, biology, and the earth and space sciences. Review these equations with your students so they may come to realize the importance of stoichiometry to all of the sciences, not just chemistry.

Physics

Fusion: Nuclear fusion is the process that fuels our Sun and other stars, producing the light necessary for life on Earth. One of the many fusion reactions that takes place in the sun is the fusion of hydrogen-1 and hydrogen-2 to form helium-3 and gamma radiation:

$$\,^1_1H + \,^2_1H \longrightarrow \,^3_2He + \gamma$$

Fission: Nuclear fission is a reaction in which a heavy nucleus splits into lighter nuclei with the release of a large quantity of energy that can be used to power or destroy civilizations. The first human-initiated nuclear fission reaction resulted from the bombardment of uranium-235 by neutrons:

$$\,^{235}_{92}U + \,^1_0n \longrightarrow \,^{141}_{56}Ba + \,^{92}_{36}Kr + 3\,^1_0n + energy$$

Electrolysis: In an effort to provide energy for society's needs and reduce dependence on petroleum, physicists and engineers are working to perfect fuel cell technology. Fuel cells are dependent on hydrogen, which can be produced in a process known as electrolysis.

$$2H_2O(l) \longrightarrow 2H_2(g) + O_2(g)$$

Biology

Photosynthesis: Plants use light energy to synthesize high-energy sugars (glucose) from carbon dioxide and water. Photosynthesis yields the sugars that are necessary for the survival of plants and animals, as well as the oxygen essential for respiration:

$$6CO_2 + 6H_2O \xrightarrow{light} C_6H_{12}O_6 + 6O_2$$

Respiration: Respiration is the process by which plants and animals transfer energy from the chemical bonds of sugar to the phosphate bonds of ATP, a form of energy necessary to the survival of all cells.

$$C_6H_{12}O_6 + 6O_2 + 38ADP + 38P_i$$
$$\longrightarrow 6CO_2 + 6H_2O + 38ATP$$

Nitrogen fixation: Proteins and nucleic acids have substantial amounts of nitrogen. Much of this nitrogen enters the food web when nitrogen-fixing bacteria produce ammonia from atmospheric nitrogen as represented in the following equation:

$$N_2 + 8H^+ + 8e^- + 16ATP$$
$$\longrightarrow 2NH_3 + H_2 + 16ADP + 16P_i$$

Earth and Space Science

Chemical weathering: Chemical weathering is an important geological process that breaks down granite, basalt, and other rocks to sands and soils. Without weathering, there would be no soils, no agriculture, and no human society.

One example of chemical weathering is the rusting of iron:

$$4Fe(s) + 3O_2(g) \longrightarrow 2Fe_2O_3(s)_{rust}$$

Element formation: The following equation is for a nuclear fusion reaction thought to take place in stars, where internal temperatures exceed 15 million degrees Kelvin. The element nitrogen is formed by the fusion of carbon and hydrogen, and without such processes, there would be no heavy elements.

$$^{12}_{6}C + ^{1}_{1}H \rightarrow ^{13}_{7}N + \gamma$$

Atmospheric pollution: The greenhouse effect is caused primarily by extensive burning of fossil fuels (natural gas, gasoline, coal, and oil), leading to an increase in the concentration of atmospheric carbon dioxide. In addition to retaining heat in the atmosphere, carbon dioxide acidifies rain. The following equation shows how carbon dioxide reacts with water to give carbonic acid, one of the components that lowers the pH of rainwater and contributes to another serious ecological problem known as acid rain.

$$CO_2 + H_2O \longrightarrow H_2CO_3$$

Mastering the Mechanics of Equation Balancing

People get lost in forests when they "can't see the forest because of the trees." To find their way, hikers may climb a mountain to gain perspective. Much of the confusion students experience in science is due to a lack of perspective. When trying to understand stoichiometry, it is particularly important for students to have perspective before focusing on mechanics.

Stoichiometry is concerned with the quantitative relationships among the reactants and products in a chemical or nuclear reaction. It involves more than equation balancing. It is important to know the numerical relationships between reactants and products and why a reactant or product has the formula it does. For example, why is water H_2O rather than H_3O? One could say, "This relationship exists because oxygen has a $+1$ oxidation state and hydrogen a -2 oxidation state, so the two electrons contributed by the two hydrogens fulfill the two oxidation state deficit of oxygen." Although this is accurate, it does not explain why the elements have the oxidation states they do. In this chapter we first focus on (1) the logic behind oxidation states, then (2) show how this determines the chemical formulas of reactants and products, before (3) introducing techniques for equation balancing that are based on these principles.

To understand the process of equation balancing, students must first understand the principle of the conservation of mass. The first law of thermodynamics (the law of conservation of mass and energy) states that during natural processes, matter and energy are neither created nor destroyed. The processes that change the chemical or physical properties of a substance in an isolated system do so without changing the mass. The law of the conservation of mass is one of a number of conservation laws that state that a particular property does not change over time in an isolated system. In addition to the *conservation of mass,* the *conservation of energy, momentum, angular momentum, electric charge,* and *magnetic flux* are principles that can be introduced to help students understand the interactions of matter.

An understanding of the conservation of mass and electrical charge is foundational to the process of equation balancing. The reactants are placed on one side of the equation and the products on the other, and the mass and charge on the left must equal the mass and charge on the right. In a chemical reaction, matter can be rearranged but never destroyed or created. Therefore, we can represent chemical reactions as equations. An equation is a mathematical statement of the equality of two things. In the case of chemical reactions, the equation shows that the total mass and charge of the *reactants* must equal the total mass and charge of the products. Thus, a chemical equation is similar to an algebraic equation. For example, the chemical equation for the hydrolysis of water can be represented in traditional algebraic fashion, where x represents hydrogen and y represents oxygen:

$$2H_2O \longrightarrow 2H_2 + O_2$$

$$2(2x + y) = 2(2x) + 2y$$

In both instances, one side of the equation has an equivalent number of each component as the right side, hence the term *equation*. The first law of thermodynamics is known as the law of conservation of energy and mass. Although matter can be converted to energy in nuclear reactions (the special theory of relativity illustrates that mass and energy are related: $E = mc^2$, where E = energy, m = mass, and c = speed of light), it always remains as matter in chemical reactions. Thus, not only must there be a balance of mass on both sides of a chemical equation, there must also be a balance in the quantity of each species. For example, if there are four hydrogen atoms on the left, there must be four hydrogen atoms on the right. Similarly, if there is no net charge on the left side of the equation, there will be no net charge on the right side either.

Balancing Redox Reactions in Acidic or Basic Solutions

In this chapter, students are introduced to a simple and effective technique for balancing equations. Although it can be used for the majority of problems, it will not be able to solve all. Redox reactions in acidic or basic solutions can be difficult to balance because there are often several reactants and several products. Table 18.1 lists the steps to follow to help balance equations for such reactions, and Table 18.2 contains a sample problem using this technique. Introduce this material only if you have an advanced class and the students have already mastered the simple approach introduced in the student section.

Consider the oxidation of iodide ion (I^-) by permanganate ion (MnO_4^-) in basic solution to produce molecular iodine (I_2) and manganese oxide (MnO_2). The skeleton equation is:

$$I^- + MnO_4^- \longrightarrow MnO_2 + I_2$$

Table 18.2 shows how to apply the steps introduced in Table 18.1 to balance the equation.

Table 18.1 Steps for Balancing Redox Reactions in Acidic or Basic Solutions

For Acidic Solutions

(1)   Write separate equations for the oxidation and reduction half-reactions.
(2)   For each half-reaction, balance all atoms except hydrogen and oxygen.
(3)   Balance oxygen using H_2O.
(4)   Balance hydrogen using H^-.
(5)   Balance the charge using electrons.
(6)   If necessary, multiply one or both half-reactions by an integer to equalize the number of electrons transferred in the two half-reactions.
(7)   Add the half-reactions, cancel identical species that occur on both sides, and reduce the coefficients to smallest integers.

For Basic Solutions

If the solution is basic, use steps 1 through 7 to balance the equation as if the reaction occurred in an acidic solution (containing H^- ions), then add these steps:
(8)   Note the number of H^- ions in the equation.
(9)   Add this number of OH^- ions to *both* sides of equation (to eliminate H^- ions by forming H_2O).
(10)   Cancel any H_2O molecules that occur on both sides of the equation and reduce the equation to simplest terms.

Table 18.2 Balancing an Equation Using Half-Reactions (Sample)

Step	Equation
$1_{(red)}$	$MnO_4^- \rightarrow MnO_2$
$1_{(ox)}$	$I^- \rightarrow I_2$
$2_{(ox)}$	$2I^- \rightarrow I_2$
$3_{(red)}$	$MnO_4^- \rightarrow MnO_2 + 2H_2O$
$4_{(red)}$	$MnO_4^- + 4H^+ \rightarrow MnO_2 + 2H_2O$
$5_{(red)}$	$MnO_4^- + 4H^+ + 3e^- \rightarrow MnO_2 + 2H_2O$
$5_{(ox)}$	$2I^- \rightarrow I_2 + 2e^-$
$6_{(red)}$	$2(MnO_4^- + 4H^+ + 3e^- \rightarrow MnO_2 + 2H_2O)$
$6_{(ox)}$	$3(2I^- \rightarrow I_2 + 2e^-)$
7	$2MnO_4^- + 8H^+ + 6I^- + 6e^- \rightarrow 2MnO_2 + 4H_2O + 3I_2 + 6e^-$
7	$2MnO_4^- + 8H^+ + 6I^- \rightarrow 2MnO_2 + 4H_2O + 3I_2$
9	$2MnO_4^- + 8H^+ + 6I^- + 8OH^- \rightarrow 2MnO_2 + 4H_2O + 3I_2 + 8OH^-$
9	$2MnO_4^- + 6I^- + 8H_2O \rightarrow 2MnO_2 + 4H_2O + 3I_2 + 8OH^-$
10	$2MnO_4^- + 6I^- + 4H_2O \rightarrow 2MnO_2 + 3I_2 + 8OH^-$

18.1 Predicting Oxidation States and Ions

Introductory chemistry students are often asked to memorize the common ions and their charges. Although it is helpful to have such information memorized, it will be soon forgotten if the logic for these charges is not understood. Why does aluminum generally have a $+3$ charge and barium a $+2$ charge? Why do you never see Al^{+4} or Ba^{+3} in nature? Memorization should not be done in a vacuum but with understanding of underlying principles.

If an ion is common, it is probably stable; otherwise it would transition to some other form. In general, elements are stable when they have eight valence electrons, such as the noble gases shown in Figure 18.1. This family was once known as the "inert gases" because of their amazing stability (lack of reactivity). Since chemical reactions are dependent on the sharing and exchange of electrons, stability indicates that the noble gases have a stable electron configuration. We now know that the stability of this family is due to a complete set of eight valence (outermost) electrons.

Chemical reactions are dependent on the sharing and exchange of electrons. The electrons that react the most readily are those farthest from the nucleus. These electrons come in contact with other atoms first and are therefore the ones involved in reactions and bonding. Figure 18.2A shows the Bohr model of the atom, with each small rectangle indicating the possible position of an electron. Note that there are two spaces in level 1, eight in level 2, eighteen in level 3, and so forth. One might think therefore that there are two valence (outermost) electrons in the first shell, eight in the second, and eighteen

in the third. Although this supposition is correct for the first two levels, it is not correct for the third and subsequent levels. This is because electrons fill spaces on an energy basis, with electrons occupying the lowest energy states first, even if these are not the closest to the nucleus. The energy of an electron is dependent on more than just its distance from the nucleus and is modified by the shape of the orbital, the axis of the orbital, and the spin of the electron.

Figure 18.2B shows an energy diagram, indicating that electrons fill the spaces at the bottom first and the top last. Note, however, that the 4s electrons are lower energy than the 3d electrons, even though they are farther (fourth shell) from the nucleus than the 3d electrons (third shell). Thus, the 4s electrons fill before 3d electrons, starting a new shell in which the valence electrons will reside. Because 4s electrons fill before 3d electrons and 5s before 4d, the number of valence electrons for these shells is capped at eight (the sum of s and p electrons for any shell). This trend is also true for higher levels, and elements therefore have a maximum of eight valence electrons (2 s-electrons plus 6 p-electrons).

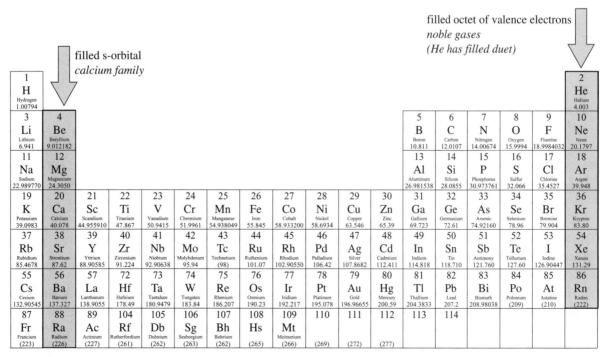

Figure 18.1 Noble Gases Have a Filled Valence Shell

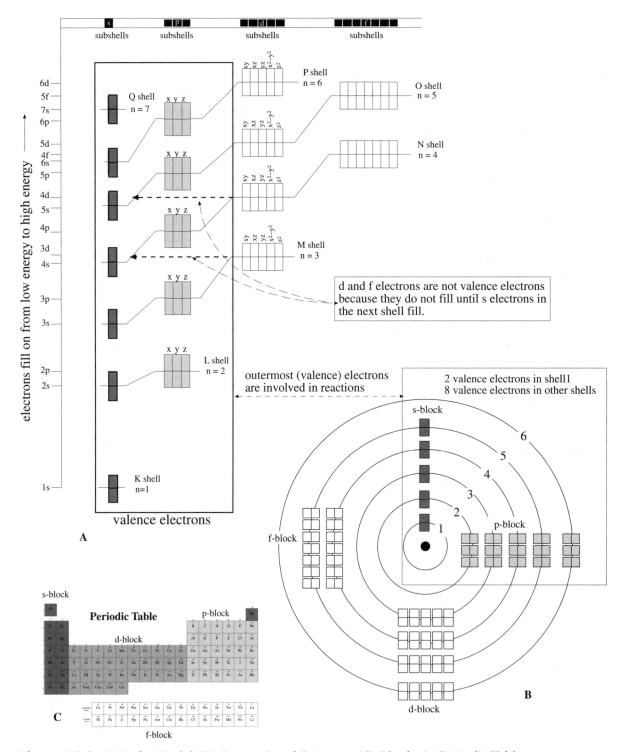

Figure 18.2 (A) Bohr Model. (B) Energy Level Diagram. (C) Blocks in Periodic Table

The first electron in a new shell is inherently reactive. It is far from the attractive forces of the nucleus and thus susceptible to the pull of surrounding atoms. By contrast, filling the final valence electron in a shell creates a stable situation in which the valence electrons are as close to the positively charged nucleus as they can get for elements in that shell. When the ratio of protons to radius is high, the relatively large attractive force (the electrostatic force between the oppositely charged protons in the nucleus and the orbiting electrons) is acting over a relatively short distance (radius to electrons) and therefore exerting a relatively large pull. Note that in Figure 18.3, the eighth family (noble gases) has the smallest radii, and the largest protons to radius ratio, and therefore the greatest stability.

To add an electron to any of the noble gases requires addition in a new outermost shell. Such an electron would be far away from the attraction of the positively charged nuclei, and thus easily lost. By contrast, the eight electrons in the outer shell of the noble gases represent a completed

shell in which the distance to the valence electrons is minimal relative to the attractive charge of the nuclei. Stability is conferred on the noble gases and elements that have the electron configuration of noble gases. For example, chlorine is a member of the seventh family. It has seven valence electrons and can acquire one more to complete its octet. Thus, chloride (Cl^-) is relatively stable and occurs frequently in nature. You will never see Cl^{--}, because the addition of two electrons requires the placement of an electron in the next higher energy level, an inherently unstable position. Similarly, it is common for barium, a member of the second family, to lose two electrons to become a Ba^{++} ion, which has a completed octet

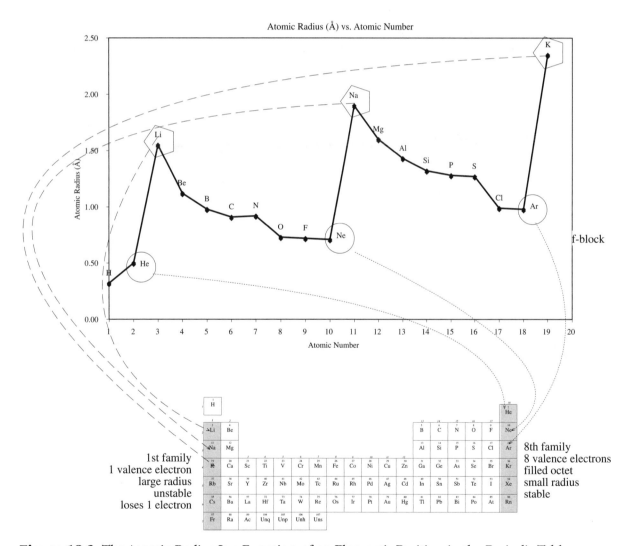

Figure 18.3 The Atomic Radius Is a Function of an Element's Position in the Periodic Table

with the electron configuration of xenon. The loss of a third electron, however, is extremely difficult because Ba^{++} has the stable configuration associated with a completed octet.

Examine Figure 18.4A. Note that neon has a filled octet of valence electrons. It has a relatively small radius, and is stable. By contrast, Ne^{-} has a very large radius (Figure 18.4B), with no additional protons to pull on the additional electron. The $3s^1$ electron of Ne^- is lost immediately because of the minimal attractive force of the nucleus. Sodium (Na) has the same electron configuration as Ne^- ($1s^2 2s^2 2p^6 3s^1$) but is more stable because it has an additional proton to exert force on it (Figure 18.4B). However, this electron is still far from the nucleus relative to the pull of the protons, and is therefore easily lost, to form the sodium cation (Na^+) (Figure 18.4A). This is a stable ion because it has a small radius

with no remote electrons. Thus, it is common to find Ne and Na^+ in nature, but rare to find Na. Ne^- may exist for a brief moment in some reactions but is not seen in nature.

Bookkeeping methods using oxidation numbers (also called *oxidation states*) have been devised to help keep track of electrons during chemical reactions. An *oxidation number* may be defined as the charge that an atom would have if both of the electrons in each bond were assigned to the more electronegative element (the element with greater attraction for electrons). The oxidation number reflects the extent to which an element has been oxidized or reduced. Each element in a reaction must be assigned an oxidation number.

In the case of monatomic ions that have undergone a complete exchange of electrons, the oxidation state is obvious. For example, Na^+ and Cl^- ions have oxidation states equivalent to their

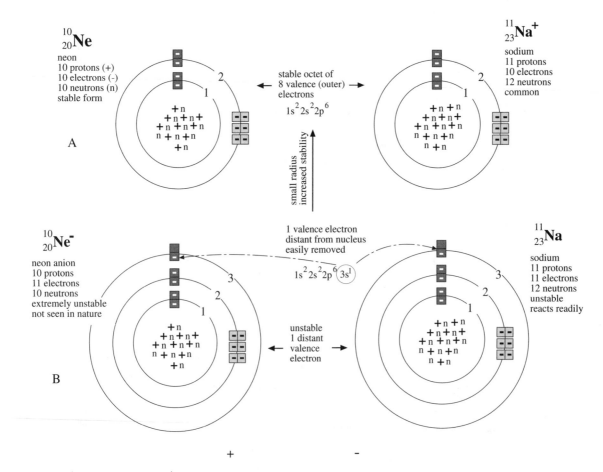

Figure 18.4 (A) Ne and Na^+ are Stable. (B) Ne^- and Na are Unstable

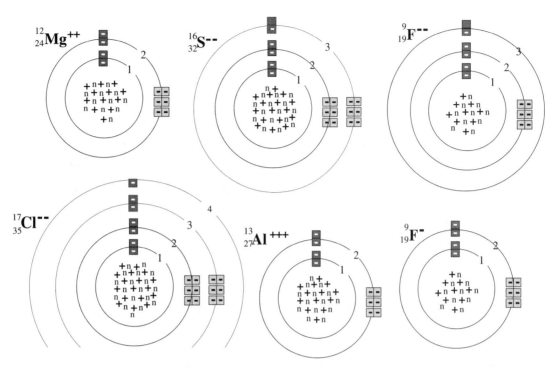

Figure 18.5 Which of These Ions Exist in Nature?

charges, $+1$ and -1. In other types of reactions, such as those in which electrons are shared, the assignment of oxidation numbers may not be so clear. Hence, guidelines have been established for assigning oxidation numbers. Note that for oxidation numbers, we write the sign before the number (e.g., $+1$) to distinguish oxidation numbers from actual electric charges, for which we write the number before the algebraic sign (e.g., $1+$). For example, in the following equation, the 0 below Fe, the $+2$ below Cu, the $+2$ below Fe, and the 0 below Cu indicate oxidation numbers. The $2+$ after Cu and the $2+$ after Fe indicate the actual charges on these ions.

$$\underset{0}{Fe(s)} + \underset{+2}{Cu^{2+}(aq)} \longrightarrow \underset{+2}{Fe^{2+}(aq)} + \underset{0}{Cu(s)}$$

ACTIVITY 18.1.1 *Predicting the Charge on Ions*

Using the reasoning introduced in this section and a periodic table (Figure 18.1), determine if the following ions are commonly found in nature:

(1–6) see Figure 18.5; (7) Kr^-; (8) Ca^{++}; (9) Na^{++}; (10) H^+.

ACTIVITY 18.1.2 *Predicting Oxidation States*

Chemists use oxidation states to describe the status of a particular element. The oxidation state shows the total number of electrons that have been removed from an element (positive oxidation state) or added to an element (negative oxidation state) to get to its present state. In a monatomic ion, it is simply the number of the charge on the element. In molecules, however, the oxidation number represents the number of electrons lost (or partially lost) or gained (or partially gained) to form bonds. An element assumes an oxidation state if the addition or removal of electrons will complete an octet (filled s and p orbitals in a shell) or an s-orbital (Figure 18.1). Many students memorize oxidation states, but such a process is time-consuming and may not involve much thinking.

In this activity, you will see that the common oxidation states for elements are a function of their position in the periodic table. Filled s or filled p orbitals add considerable stability to an element. Each of the elements in Table 18.3 has common oxidation states, some of which are shown. These oxidation states are predictable based on the position of the element in the periodic table. For example, a common oxidation state of iodine is -1 because it gains one electron (gaining a negative charge reduces the oxidation state) as it completes the p orbital and fills the octet of valence electrons. Look at the position of each element listed in Table 18.3 in the periodic table (Figure 18.1) and indicate if the oxidation state listed is a result of a filled octet or filled s-orbital. For example, place a mark

Table 18.3 Predicting Oxidation States on the Basis of Filled Orbitals

Element	Oxidation State	Filled Octet	Filled S-Orbital
Al	+3	*	
As	−3		
Ba	+2		
Br	−1		
Br	+5		
Br	+7		
C	+4		
Ca	+2		
Cl	−1		
Cl	+7		
Cl	−5		
Cr	+6		
F	−1		
K	+1		
Mg	+2		
Mn	+7		
N	+3		
N	+5		
O	−2		
P	+5		
P	+3		
S	+4		
S	+6		
Sb	−3		
Si	+2		
Si	+4		
V	+3		
V	+5		

in the "filled octet" space adjacent to aluminum, indicating that its $+3$ oxidation state results from the loss of three electrons, taking it to the electron configuration of neon, and a filled octet ($1s^2 2s^2 2p^6$).

18.2 Predicting Polyatomic Ions, Reactants, and Products

One of the reasons that English is a difficult language to learn is that it has the world's largest vocabulary, a large percentage of which is not spelled phonetically (including the term *phonetics*). In an effort to deal with the inconsistencies characteristic to natural languages like English, the Polish linguist L. L. Zamenhof developed an artificial language in which all verbs are regular, all grammar regular, and all spelling phonetic. The language, known as Esperanto, is extremely easy to learn because it is predictable and consistent.

Fortunately, chemistry, like Esperanto, is highly predictable for those who understand the underlying principles. In section 18.1 we learned how to predict the oxidation states of elements in the periodic table, and although there are some states that we cannot predict based on the rules introduced, the majority of the common ones are predictable. The formulas of many polyatomic ions and compounds can be predicted on the basis of oxidation numbers, which are themselves predictable based on the position an element occupies in the periodic table. Knowing this and the following rules, one can predict if a compound is logical:

- The oxidation state of an uncombined element is zero.
- The sum of the oxidation states of all the atoms or ions in a neutral compound is zero.
- The sum of the oxidation states of all the atoms in an ion is equal to the charge on the ion.
- The more electronegative element in a substance is given a negative oxidation state. The less electronegative one is given a positive oxidation state. Fluorine is the most electronegative element, with oxygen second most.

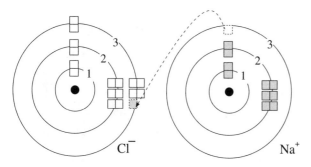

Figure 18.6 The Electron Lost by Na Is Gained by Cl

Table 18.4 Common Oxidation States of Select Elements		
Element	**Symbol**	**Common Oxidation States**
aluminum	Al	+3
antimony	Sb	−3,+3,+5
arsenic	As	−3,+3,+5
barium	Ba	+2
bismuth	Bi	+3,+5
bromine	Br	−1,+1,+3,+5,+7
calcium	Ca	+2
carbon	C	+2,+4,-4
chlorine	Cl	−1,+1,+3,+5,+7
chromium	Cr	+2,+3,+6
cobalt	Co	+2,+3
copper	Cu	+1,+2
fluorine	F	−1
gold	Au	+1,+3
hydrogen	H	−1,+1
iodine	I	−1,+1,+3,+5,+7
iron	Fe	+2,+3
magnesium	Mg	+2
manganese	Mn	+2,+3,+4,+6,+7
mercury	Hg	+1,+2
nickel	Ni	+2,+3
nitrogen	N	−1,+3,+5
oxygen	O	−2,−1
phosphorous	P	+3,+5
platinum	Pt	+2,+4
potassium	K	+1
silicon	Si	+2,+4
silver	Ag	+1
sodium	Na	+1
strontium	Sr	+2
sulfur	S	−2,+4,+6
tin	Sn	+2,+4
titanium	Ti	+2,+3,+4
tungsten	W	+6
zinc	Zn	+2

• Some elements almost always have the same oxidation states in their compounds: Group 1 metals (halogens) are +1; Group 2 metals (alkali metals) are +2; oxygen −2, and hydrogen +1.

For example, sodium chloride is logical because sodium is a group 1 metal and assumes an oxidation state of 11, while chlorine is a halogen and assumes an oxidation state of −1. The sum of the oxidation states is zero, indicating that one sodium (11) is matched with one chlorine (−1) to produce neutral sodium chloride (NaCl) (Figure 18.6). Similarly, calcium bromide must have the formula $CaBr_2$ because calcium is a group 2 metal, assumes an oxidation state of 12 in compounds and can pair with two bromine atoms, both of which have a −1 state. Thus, one of the electrons donated by calcium binds with one bromine, while the other binds with a second bromine atom. The resulting formula, $CaBr_2$ indicates that the product has zero net charge. By contrast, you would never see $CaBr_3$ in nature because the oxidation number of calcium (12) adds to three negatively charged bromines (−1) to give a net charge of −1, not zero as indicated by the formula $CaBr_3$.

ACTIVITY 18.2.1 *Using Oxidation Numbers to Predict Polyatomic Ions*

Table 18.4 shows common oxidation states of select elements. Use the data in this table to determine if the ions listed in Table 18.5 are logical or illogical. A substance is "illogical" if the oxidation numbers do not add up correctly. For each of the pairs in Table 18.5, add up the oxidation numbers to see if they match the ion charge. If an element has more than one oxidation number, select those that will most closely balance to give the indicated charge. Write the sum of the oxidation numbers in the column to the right of each ion, and highlight

Table 18.5 Which of the Following Are Logical?

CO_3^{2-}	-2	~~CO_4^{2-}~~	-4	HSO_4^-	$H_3SO_4^{-3}$
SO_3^{2-}		SO_3^{7-}		OH^-	OH^{-2}
ClO_3^{2-}		$Cl_2O_3^{2-}$		Cl_3O^-	ClO^-
ClO_2^-		ClO_2		NO_3^-	NO^-
CrO_4^{2-}		CrO_4^{4-}		NO_2^-	NO_2^{-4}
CN^{-2}		CN^-		ClO_4^-	$Cl_7O_4^-$
$Cr_2O_7^{2-}$		$Cr_3O_4^{3-}$		$Mn_5O_4^-$	MnO_4^-
$Fe(C_3N)_6^{4-}$		$Fe(CN)_6^{4-}$		PO_4^{3-}	$P_3O_4^{3-}$
$Fe(CN)_6^{3-}$		$Fe_5(CN)_6^{3-}$		SO_4^{2-}	$S_2O_4^{2-}$
HCO_3^{-2}		HCO_3^-		NH_4^+	$N_4H_4^+$

or circle the member of each pair that is a real compound based on your analysis, and strike through the one that is not as shown in the first example.

ACTIVITY 18.2.2 *Determining Element Ratios in Ionic Compounds*

Ionic compounds form as a result of the attraction between cations (positively charged ions) and anions (negatively charged ions). In ionic compounds, the total positive charge must equal the total negative charge. For example, the singly charged ammonium (NH_4^1) cation will combine in a one-to-one ratio with the singly charged bromide ($Br-$) anion to form ammonium bromide: $NH_4 Br$. By contrast, three bromide ions ($Br-$) are required to balance the chromium (III) cation Cr^{31} when forming chromic bromide ($CrBr_3$). Table 18.6 lists common cations and anions.

This activity is designed to help visualize the ratios in which ionic compounds form. Make four photocopies of Figure 18.7A, and cut all of the individual ion symbols apart. If possible, photocopy these onto overhead transparencies so that you can show others your work on the overhead projector. Cations (light circles) combine with anions (dark hexagons) in such a way that there is no net charge. For example, combine one aluminum (charge $+3$) with three nitrites (charge -1) to

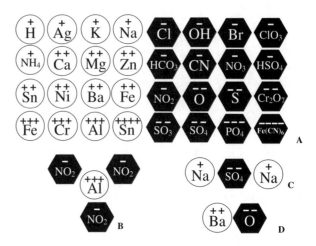

Figure 18.7 Determining and Visualizing Ratios in Ionic Compounds

produce neutral aluminum nitrite ($Al(NO_2)_3$) as shown in Figure 18.7B. Ratios other than 1:3 will not produce a neutral product, and therefore will not occur in nature. Now combine two sodiums ($+1$) with one sulfate (-2) (Figure 18.7C); and one barium ($+2$) with one oxygen (-2) as shown in figure (Figure 18.7D). Notice how the net charge in each case is zero.

You will notice in Table 18.4 that certain metallic elements form more than one ion. For example, iron may carry a $+2$ charge or a $+3$ charge. To differentiate these, we apply a Roman numeral after the metal ion for clarification. For example, Fe^{2+} is known as the iron (II) ion, and the Fe^{3+} ion is known as the iron (III) ion. In the following list, combine ion symbols to balance charge (net charge of zero), and determine appropriate formulas for the compounds listed:

a. ammonium nitrate (a common component of lawn fertilizers)
b. calcium carbonate (found in Carlsbad Caverns, Mammoth Caves, and other limestone caves)
c. hydrogen sulfate (also known as sulfuric acid, one of the most common industrial acids)
d. iron (III) oxide (ferric oxide; a form of rust, used as a red pigment in paints)
e. magnesium hydroxide (used in antacids and laxatives such as milk of magnesia)

f. silver chloride (a photochemical used in the development of film)

g. sodium hydrogen carbonate (sodium bicarbonate; baking soda, used to deodorize refrigerators and as a leavening agent to help bread rise)

h. calcium phosphate (one of the main components in bone; used in plant fertilizers to provide phosphorous)

i. sodium nitrite (kills bacteria; used to preserve such foods as frankfurters, corned beef, and tunafish)

j. ammonium phosphate (used by firefighters to retard the spread of forest fires)

18.3 Techniques for Balancing Equations

Does your car use regular-, extra-, or premium-grade gasoline (Figure 18.8)? The grade of a gasoline is based on its "octane rating." Octane ratings measure a gasoline's ability to resist engine knock, a pinging sound that results from premature ignition of the compressed fuel-air mixture in the cylinders. Most stations offer regular (87), extra (89), and premium (93) gasolines, and the pumps are marked with bright yellow stickers as shown in Figure 18.8.

At the refinery, many hydrocarbon chains are made from the cracking of crude oil. Hydrocarbons that are 7-carbons (heptane) or 8-carbons (octane) in length are particularly good for use in automobile engines. Octane resists knocking better than heptane, and a gasoline that is rated at 93 octane (premium grade) is made of 93 percent octane and 7 percent heptane, or some other combination of fuels that has the same performance. The combustion of octane in the cylinders of your car can be represented by the following equation:

$$2C_8H_{18}(g) + 25O_2(g) \longrightarrow 16CO_2(g) + 18H_2O(g)$$

The equation indicates that 25 oxygen molecules are required to combust 2 octane molecules and will produce 16 carbon dioxide molecules and 18 water molecules. The chemical equation is an

REGULAR	EXTRA	PREMIUM
MINIMUM OCTANE RATING (R+M)/2 METHOD	MINIMUM OCTANE RATING (R+M)/2 METHOD	MINIMUM OCTANE RATING (R+M)/2 METHOD
87	**89**	**93**

Figure 18.8 Gasoline Octane Ratings

algebraic expression describing the chemical reaction. In a chemical equation, the material to the left of the arrow indicates the reactants and the material on the right the products. The law of conservation of mass states that in a chemical reaction, no mass is lost or gained, so the total mass on the left side of the equation should equal the total on the right, and the total number of atoms of each element on the left must match the total number of atoms of the same elements on the right. Note that there are 16 carbons on the left and 16 on the right, 50 oxygens on the left and 50 on the right, and 36 hydrogens on the left and 36 hydrogens on the right. How are equations balanced?

The following is a powerful and proven technique that you can use to balance equations. Focus on the logic of each step, not just the results:

I. **Word Equation:** Identify the reactants and products.
   - Determine the reactants and products from experimental observations.
   - Express the reaction in words.

II. **Skeleton Equation:** Determine the formulas for the reactants and products.
   - Express reactants and products as formulas. Make certain the subscripts within polyatomic ions or subgroups are correct (see section 18.2; Table 18.6).
   - Adjust only subscripts of entire ions or subgroups (not the elements within a polyatomic ion or subgroup) to balance oxidation states within reactants and products (see section 18.2).

III. **Balanced Equation:** Determine the stoichiometric relationship of the reaction
   - Change only the coefficients of the reactants or products to balance the equation. The number of each element should be the same on both sides of the equation.

Table 18.6 Common Cation and Anions

Common Cations		Common Anions	
aluminum	Al^{3+}	acetate	$(C_2H_3O)_2^{-}$
ammonium	NH_4^{+}	bromide	Br^{-}
barium	Ba^{2+}	carbonate	CO_3^{2-}
calcium	Ca^{2+}	chlorate	ClO_3^{2-}
chromium(III)	Cr^{3+}	chloride	Cl^{-}
cobalt(II)	Co^{2+}	chlorite	ClO_2^{-}
copper(I)	Cu^{+}	chromate	CrO_4^{2-}
copper(II)	Cu^{2+}	cyanide	CN^{-}
hydronium	H_3O^{+}	dichromate	$Cr_2O_7^{2-}$
iron(II)	Fe^{2+}	fluoride	F^{-}
iron(III)	Fe^{3+}	hexacyano-	
lead(II)	Pb^{2+}	ferrate(II)	$Fe(CN)_6^{4-}$
magnesium	Mg^{2+}	hexacyano-	
mercury(I)	Hg_2^{2+}	ferrate(III)	$Fe(CN)_6^{3-}$
mercury(II)	Hg^{2+}	hydride	H^{-}
nickel(II)	Ni^{2+}	hydrogen	
potassium	K^{+}	carbonate	HCO_3^{-}
silver	Ag^{+}	hydrogen sulfate	HSO_4^{-}
sodium	Na^{+}	hydroxide	OH^{-}
tin(II)	Sn^{2+}	hypochlorite	ClO^{-}
tin(IV)	Sn^{4+}	iodide	I^{-}
zinc	Zn^{2+}	nitrate	NO_3^{-}
		nitrite	NO_2^{-}
		oxide	O^{2-}
		perchlorate	ClO_4^{-}
		permanganate	MnO_4^{-}
		peroxide	O_2^{2-}
		phosphate	PO_4^{3-}
		sulfate	SO_4^{2-}
		sulfide	S^{2-}
		sulfite	SO_3^{2-}

Do not change subscripts, because doing so would change the reactants or products that were already established in step II.

- Identify an element (not an ion or subgroup) that occurs in only one reactant and one product. Balance this element first because it establishes a ratio that must persist through the balancing process. *This is a key concept!*
- Repeat the procedure for any other elements that are found in only one reactant or one

product, proceeding from those found in the most complex compounds to those found in the simplest.

- Balance elemental substances (elements that are not bonded to other elements) last, using fractions if necessary.
- Multiply by the common denominator to remove any fractions.

Example 1: Ionic Double-Replacement Reaction

The ancient Egyptians used alum (aluminum sulfate) to purify water and dye fabrics. Today we use alum in a wide variety of applications, including the treatment of wastewater, production of paper, and manufacture of soaps.

I: Word Equation   One way to produce aluminum sulfate is by the reaction of aluminum nitrate with sulfuric acid, producing aluminum sulfate and nitric acid. From this empirically determined information, we can record the reactants (aluminum nitrate and sulfuric acid) and products (aluminum sulfate and nitric acid), and draft a word equation:

aluminum nitrate + sulfuric acid $\longrightarrow$

aluminum sulfate + nitric acid

II: Skeleton Equation   Constructing a skeleton equation requires knowing the formulas for the nitrate and sulfate ions (see the technique in section 18.2 and the data in Table 18.6). Second, one must adjust the subscripts of entire ions and subgroups to balance oxidation numbers within reactants and products (section 18.2). For example, charge is not balanced in our initial expression of aluminum nitrate (three positives and only one negative):

$$Al^{3+}(NO_3^{-})$$

We must therefore multiply the entire nitrate ion by three so that the three negative charges from the three nitrates will balance the three positive charges from the one aluminum:

$$Al^{3+}(NO_3^-)_3$$

Note that one does not change the subscript of oxygen or nitrogen within nitrate because that would indicate a different compound from what is specified. Using the same logic we arrive at the formula for aluminum sulfate,

$$Al_2^{3+}(SO_4^{2-})_3$$

and eventually the skeleton equation:

$$Al^{3+}(NO_3^-)_3 + H_2^+(SO_4^{2-}) \longrightarrow$$
$$Al_2^{3+}(SO_4^{2-})_3 + H^+NO_3^-$$

Since the charges are balanced and no reactant or product has a net charge, we can rewrite the equation without charges.

$$Al(NO_3)_3 + H_2(SO_4) \longrightarrow Al_2(SO_4)_3 + HNO_3$$

III: Balanced Equation   Now that we have the correct word equation and skeleton equation, we can proceed to balance the equation. No subscripts should be changed because we have already determined the ions and subgroups involved and have made certain they are internally balanced with respect to oxidation number. Now we have to apply the law of conservation of mass to make certain that the mass on the left side of the equation is equal to the mass on the right side of the equation. Since there is no transmutation of elements in chemical reactions, the number of atoms of any element should also be the same on both sides of the equation. We know that our reactants and products are correctly expressed, so the only thing we can change is the coefficients in front of each.

We should, if possible, start balancing with an element that occurs in only one reactant and one product. Since the element occurs in only one species on each side of the equation,

the ratio is fixed. For example, in this reaction, aluminum occurs only in aluminum sulfate and aluminum nitrate. To balance these, one must put a coefficient of 2 in front of the aluminum nitrate:

$$2Al(NO_3)_3 + H_2(SO_4) \longrightarrow 1Al_2(SO_4)_3 + HNO_3$$

This ratio is now fixed. Because aluminum occurs nowhere else in the reaction, the ratio must always be 2 aluminum nitrates to 1 aluminum sulfate. It is helpful to put the coefficient "1" in front of the aluminum sulfate as a reminder that it has been balanced. Now that this ratio between aluminum nitrate and aluminum sulfate has been determined and fixed, proceed from the most complex substance to the simplest, balancing others that are found in only one reactant and one product. In the sample reaction, three sulfurs are found in aluminum sulfate, so the coefficient "3" must be placed in front of sulfuric acid, the only place sulfur occurs on the reactant side of the equation:

$$2Al(NO_3)_3 + 3H_2(SO_4) \longrightarrow 1Al_2(SO_4)_3 + HNO_3$$

Nitrogen is also found in only one reactant and one product, so the coefficient 6 must be placed in front of nitric acid to balance.

$$2Al(NO_3)_3 + 3H_2(SO_4) \longrightarrow 1Al_2(SO_4)_3 + 6HNO_3$$

Now there are an equal number of atoms of each element on both sides of the equation: Al (2), N (6), S (3), H (6), and O (30). The last two steps of part III are not necessary in this equation since the reaction is balanced.

Example 2: Covalent Combustion Reaction

We now apply the equation balancing technique to a combustion reaction involving covalent reactants and products. Paraffin (C_nH_{2n+2}, where n ranges between 26 and 30) is a long chain hydrocarbon commonly referred to as candle wax. In addition to its well-known application in candles, it is used to seal containers in home canning and minimize melting in many chocolate candy bars. We examine the combustion of paraffin assuming a 30-carbon chain.

I: Word Equation   Experiments show that paraffin combusts in oxygen to produced carbon dioxide and water, so the word equation is:

paraffin + oxygen $\longrightarrow$ carbon dioxide + water

II: Skeleton Equation   Next, we need to express the reactants and products as formulas. Paraffin is a straight chain hydrocarbon with the formula C_nH_{2n+2} where *n* is equal to 30: $C_{30}H_{62}$. Oxygen (O_2), carbon dioxide (CO_2), and water (H_2O) are well known molecules, with the formulas as written. Hence, the skeleton equation becomes:

$$C_{30}H_{62} + O_2 \longrightarrow CO_2 + H_2O$$

III: Balanced Equation   Carbon and hydrogen are both found in just one reactant and one product. We will balance carbon first by multiplying carbon dioxide by 30.

$$1C_{30}H_{62} + O_2 \longrightarrow 30CO_2 + H_2O$$

Next, we balance the hydrogen by multiplying water by 31:

$$1C_{30}H_{62} + 91/2O_2 \longrightarrow 30CO_2 + 31H_2O$$

Oxygen is typically balanced last for the following reasons. First, it is highly reactive and is often found in more than one reactant or one product, so there are more variables to contend with. Second, most reactions take place in air, where oxygen is found in elemental form (O_2). Elemental forms can be adjusted with fractions without altering the ratios of other substances. Because there is no other element associated with oxygen in its elemental state, any coefficients in front of O_2 will change only oxygen and no

other elements. Thus, we can easily make final adjustments by multiplying elemental oxygen (or other elemental reactants or products) last. In this case, we have 91 oxygens on the right, so we must multiply O_2 by 91/2 to get 91 oxygens on the left.

$$1C_{30}H_{62} + 91/2O_2 \longrightarrow 30CO_2 + 31H_2O$$

Although this equation looks awkward, it accurately expresses the ratio of paraffin to oxygen necessary for a complete combustion to carbon dioxide and water. One mole of paraffin reacts with 45½ moles of oxygen to produce 30 moles of carbon dioxide and 31 moles of water. Although this ratio is accurate, it is not in standard form. To present it in standard form, it is necessary to remove all fractions by multiplying all coefficients by the common denominator, 2. Hence the final equation is:

$$2C_{30}H_{62} + 91O_2 \longrightarrow 60CO_2 + 62H_2O$$

There are 60 carbons, 124 hydrogens, and 182 oxygens on both sides, indicating the reaction is balanced. This ratio is easily obtained by this technique but could take an exceptionally long time if not attempted in a logical fashion. Many people avoid using fractions when balancing equations, but that greatly complicates the balancing process. I encourage you to use fractions wherever they are useful, but remember to reduce them before the final expression of the equation.

ACTIVITY 18.3.1 *Using Logic to Balance Equations*
Apply the logic described in this chapter to balance the skeleton equations in Table 18.7. Do not change any subscripts, because the formulas of each substance have already been determined. It is said that necessity is the mother of invention, but repetition is the mother of skill. The more problems you solve, the stronger skill you will develop.

Answers to Chapter Activities
18.1.1 (1) Mg^{+2} yes; (2) S^{-2} yes; (3) F^{-2} no; (4) Cl^{-2} no; (5) Al^{+3} yes; (6) F^{-1} yes; (7) Kr^{-1} no; (8) Ca^{+2} yes; (9) Na^{++} no; (10) H^+ yes. You may want to provide students with Table 18.8 to assist them in this activity.

Table 18.7 Skeleton Equations That Need to Be Balanced

Part 1 (1–20)	Part 2 (21–40)
1　$Na + NaNO_3 \rightarrow Na_2O + N_2$	21　$Al + S_8 \rightarrow Al_2S_3$
2　$Na + O_2 \rightarrow Na_2O$	22　$Al(NO_3)_3 + H_2SO_4 \rightarrow Al_2(SO_4)_3 + HNO_3$
3　$Na + O_2 \rightarrow Na_2O_2$	23　$Al(OH)_3 + H_2CO_3 \rightarrow Al_2(CO_3)_3 + H_2O$
4　$NaOH + H_2CO_3 \rightarrow Na_2CO_3 + H_2O$	24　$C_6H_{12}O_6 \rightarrow C_2H_5OH + CO_2$
5　$NH_3 + HCl \rightarrow NH_4Cl$	25　$C_6H_6 + O_2 \rightarrow CO_2 + H_2O$
6　$Al(OH)_3 + HBr \rightarrow AlBr_3 + H_2O$	26　$Ca_3(PO_4)_2 + SiO_2 + C \rightarrow CaSiO_3 + CO + P$
7　$C + O_2 \rightarrow CO_2$	27　$CH_4 + O_2 \rightarrow CO_2 + H_2O$
8　$C + S_8 \rightarrow CS_2$	28　$FeS_2 + O_2 \rightarrow Fe_2O_3 + SO_2$
9　$C + SO_2 \rightarrow CS_2 + CO$	29　$H_2 + O_2 \rightarrow H_2O$
10　$O_2 + C_6H_{12}O_6 \rightarrow CO_2 + H_2O$	30　$H_2 + O_2 \rightarrow H_2O_2$
11　$CO_2 + H_2O \rightarrow O_2 + C_6H_{12}O_6$	31　$H_3PO_4 + Ca(OH)_2 \rightarrow Ca_3(PO_4)_2 + H_2O$
12　$C_{10}H_{22} + O_2 \rightarrow CO_2 + H_2O$	32　$HCl + NaOH \rightarrow NaCl + H_2O$
13　$C_{18}H_{38} + O_2 \rightarrow H_2O + CO_2$	33　$KClO_3 \rightarrow KCl + O_2$
14　$C_2H_6 + O_2 \rightarrow CO_2 + H_2O$	34　$KOH + HBr \rightarrow KBr + H_2O$
15　$H_3PO_4 + KOH \rightarrow K_3PO_4 + H_2O$	35　$Li + AlCl_3 \rightarrow LiCl + Al$
16　$H_3PO_4 + Mg(OH)_2 \rightarrow Mg_3(PO_4)_2 + H_2O$	36　$Li + H_2O \rightarrow LiOH + H_2$
17　$NH_3 + O_2 \rightarrow N_2 + H_2O$	37　$Mg + Cl_2 \rightarrow MgCl_2$
18　$NH_4OH + H_3PO_4 \rightarrow (NH_4)_3PO_4 + H_2O$	38　$N_2 + H_2 \rightarrow NH_3$
19　$Al(OH)_3 + H_2SO_4 \rightarrow Al_2(SO_4)_3 + H_2O$	39　$N_2 + O_2 \rightarrow N_2O_5$
20　$C_3H_8 + O_2 \rightarrow CO_2 + H_2O$	40　$Na + Cl_2 \rightarrow NaCl$

Table 18.8 Rules for Oxidation Numbers

	Classification	Rule
1	Free elements	In free (uncombined) elements, each atom has an oxidation number of zero (0).
2	Monatomic ions	For ions composed of only one atom, the oxidation number is equal to the charge on the ion. The ions Na^+, Ba^{2+}, I^-, S^{-2}, and Al^{3+} have oxidation numbers of $+1$, $+2$, -1, -2, and $+3$, respectively.
3	Fluorine	Fluorine is the most electron-negative element and therefore always has an oxidation number of -1 in compounds. Each of the other halogens has an oxidation number of -1 in binary (compounds that contain only two elements), except when the other element is another halogen above it in the periodic table or when the other element is oxygen.
4	Oxygen	The oxidation number of oxygen in most compounds is y2. In peroxides the oxidation number of oxygen is -1.
5	Hydrogen	The oxidation number of hydrogen is $+1$ in all compounds except metallic compounds (hydrides), in which the oxidation state is -1.
6	Neutral compounds	The sum of all the oxidation numbers of all the atoms in a neutral compound is zero.
7	Polyatomic ions	For a polyatomic ion, the algebraic sum of the oxidation numbers must be equal to the ion's charge. For example, consider the ammonium ion, NH_4^+. The oxidation number of N is -3, and the oxidation number of H is $+1$. The sum of the oxidation numbers is: $-3 + 4 = +1$, which is equal to the net charge of the ammonium ion as required.
8	Position	Since oxidation states are related to the electron structure of the parent element, the position of an element in the periodic table is related to the possible oxidation state(s) for the element. Group 1 elements (alkali metals) have an oxidation number of $+1$ in compounds, while Group 2 elements (alkaline earth metals) have an oxidation number of $+2$.

18.1.2 All of the oxidation states can be explained by either a filled octet (filled s and p-orbitals in a particular shell) or a filled s-orbital as shown in Table 18.9.

18.2.1 Table 18.10 highlights the true polyatomic ions. The correct answers are in bold. Note that the sum of the oxidation numbers as listed in the right column adds up to the oxidation number attached to the ion. For example the sum of the oxidation states in CO_3^{2-} is -2 (1 C with and oxidation state of $+4$, plus three oxygens with a total charge of -6 for a net charge of -2), which matches the charge number attached to the species. We have not indicated the net oxidation numbers for the incorrect substances because in many situations, students may calculate a different number depending un the oxidation numbers they use for those elements with multiple oxidation numbers.

18.2.2 (a) NH_4NO_3; (b) $CaCO_3$; (c) H_2SO_4; (d) Fe_2O_3; (e) $Mg(OH)_2$; (f) $AgCl$; (g) $NaHCO_3$; (h) $Ca_3(PO_4)_2$; (i) $NaNO_2$; (j) $(NH_4)_3PO_4$

18.3.1 The answers are in Table 18.11 (part 1) and 18.12 (part 2).

Table 18.9 Predicting Oxidation States on the Basis of Filled Orbitals

Element	Oxidation State	Filled Octet	Filled S-Orbital
Al	+3	*	
As	-3	*	
Ba	+2	*	
Br	-1	*	
Br	+5		*
Br	+7	*	
C	+4	*	
Ca	+2	*	
Cl	-1	*	
Cl	+7	*	
Cl	-5		*
Cr	+6	*	
F	-1	*	
K	+1	*	
Mg	+2	*	
Mn	+7	*	
N	+3		*
N	+5	*	
O	-2	*	
P	+5	*	
P	+3		*
S	+4		*
S	+6	*	
Sb	-3	*	
Si	+2		*
Si	+4	*	
V	+3		*
V	+5	*	

Table 18.10 Answers to Activity 18.2.1

CO_3^{2-}	-2	CO_4^{2-}	
SO_3^{2-}	-2	SO_3^{7-}	
H_3O		H_3O^{1+}	+1
ClO_2^-	-1	ClO_2	
CrO_4^{2-}	-2	CrO_4^{4-}	
CN^{-2}		CN^-	-1
$Cr_2O_7^{2-}$	-2	$Cr_3O_4^{3-}$	
$Fe(C_3N)_6^{4-}$		$Fe(CN)_6^{4-}$	-4
$Fe(CN)_6^{3-}$	-3	$Fe_5(CN)_6^{3-}$	
HCO_3^{-2}		HCO_3^-	-1
HSO_4^-	-1	$H_3SO_4^{-3}$	
OH^-	-1	OH^{-2}	
Cl_3O^-		ClO^-	-1
NO_3^-	-1	NO^-	
NO_2^-	-1	NO_2^{-4}	
ClO_4^-	-1	$Cl_7O_4^-$	
$Mn_5O_4^-$		MnO_4^-	-1
PO_4^{3-}	-3	$P_3O_4^{3-}$	
SO_4^{2-}	-2	$S_2O_4^{2-}$	
NH_4^+	+1	$N_4H_4^-$	

Table 18.11 Skeleton Equations and Balanced Equations from Section 18.3, Part 1

	Skelton Equation	Balanced Equation
1	$Na + NaNO_3 \rightarrow Na_2O + N_2$	$10Na + 2NaNO_3 \rightarrow 6Na_2O + N_2$
2	$Na + O_2 \rightarrow Na_2O$	$4Na + O_2 \rightarrow 2Na_2O$
3	$Na + O_2 \rightarrow Na_2O_2$	$2Na + O_2 \rightarrow Na_2O_2$
4	$NaOH + H_2CO_3 \rightarrow Na_2CO_3 + H_2O$	$2NaOH + H_2CO_3 \rightarrow Na_2CO_3 + 2H_2O$
5	$NH_3 + HCl \rightarrow NH_4Cl$	$NH_3 + HCl \rightarrow NH_4Cl$
6	$Al(OH)_3 + HBr \rightarrow AlBr_3 + H_2O$	$Al(OH)_3 + 3HBr \rightarrow AlBr_3 + 3H_2O$
7	$C + O_2 \rightarrow CO_2$	$C + O_2 \rightarrow CO_2$
8	$C + S_8 \rightarrow CS_2$	$4C + S_8 \rightarrow 4CS_2$
9	$C + SO_2 \rightarrow CS_2 + CO$	$5C + 2SO_2 \rightarrow CS_2 + 4CO$
10	$O_2 + C_6H_{12}O_6 \rightarrow CO_2 + H_2O$	$6O_2 + C_6H_{12}O_6 \rightarrow 6CO_2 + 6H_2O$
11	$CO_2 + H_2O \rightarrow O_2 + C_6H_{12}O_6$	$6CO_2 + 6H_2O \rightarrow 6O_2 + C_6H_{12}O_6$
12	$C_{10}H_{22} + O_2 \rightarrow CO_2 + H_2O$	$2C_{10}H_{22} + 31O_2 \rightarrow 20CO_2 + 22H_2O$
13	$C_{18}H_{38} + O_2 \rightarrow H_2O + CO_2$	$2C_{18}H_{38} + 55O_2 \rightarrow 38H_2O + 36CO_2$
14	$C_2H_6 + O_2 \rightarrow CO_2 + H_2O$	$2C_2H_6 + 7O_2 \rightarrow 4CO_2 + 6H_2O$
15	$H_3PO_4 + KOH \rightarrow K_3PO_4 + H_2O$	$H_3PO_4 + 3KOH \rightarrow K_3PO_4 + 3H_2O$
16	$H_3PO_4 + Mg(OH)_2 \rightarrow Mg_3(PO_4)_2 + H_2O$	$2H_3PO_4 + 3Mg(OH)_2 \rightarrow Mg_3(PO_4)_2 + 6H_2O$
17	$NH_3 + O_2 \rightarrow N_2 + H_2O$	$4NH_3 + 3O_2 \rightarrow 2N_2 + 6H_2O$
18	$NH_4OH + H_3PO_4 \rightarrow (NH_4)_3PO_4 + H_2O$	$3NH_4OH + H_3PO_4 \rightarrow (NH_4)_3PO_4 + 3H_2O$
19	$Al(OH)_3 + H_2SO_4 \rightarrow Al_2(SO_4)_3 + H_2O$	$2Al(OH)_3 + 3H_2SO_4 \rightarrow Al_2(SO_4)_3 + 6H_2O$
20	$C_3H_8 + O_2 \rightarrow CO_2 + H_2O$	$C_3H_8 + 5O_2 \rightarrow 3CO_2 + 4H_2O$

Table 18.12 Skeleton Equations and Balanced Equations from Section 18.3, Part 2

	Skelton Equation	Balanced Equation
21	$Al + S_8 \rightarrow Al_2S_3$	$16Al + 3S_8 \rightarrow 8Al_2S_3$
22	$Al(NO_3)_3 + H_2SO_4 \rightarrow Al_2(SO_4)_3 + HNO_3$	$2Al(NO_3)_3 + 3H_2SO_4 \rightarrow Al_2(SO_4)_3 + 6HNO_3$
23	$Al(OH)_3 + H_2CO_3 \rightarrow Al_2(CO_3)_3 + H_2O$	$2Al(OH)_3 + 3H_2CO_3 \rightarrow Al_2(CO_3)_3 + 6H_2O$
24	$C_6H_{12}O_6 \rightarrow C_2H_5OH + CO_2$	$C_6H_{12}O_6 \rightarrow 2C_2H_5OH + 2CO_2$
25	$C_6H_6 + O_2 \rightarrow CO_2 + H_2O$	$2C_6H_6 + 15O_2 \rightarrow 12CO_2 + 6H_2O$
26	$Ca_3(PO_4)_2 + SiO_2 + C \rightarrow CaSiO_3 + CO + P$	$Ca_3(PO_4)_2 + 3SiO_2 + C \rightarrow 3CaSiO_3 + 5CO + 2P$
27	$CH_4 + O_2 \rightarrow CO_2 + H_2O$	$CH_4 + 2O_2 \rightarrow CO_2 + 2H_2O$
28	$FeS_2 + O_2 \rightarrow Fe_2O_3 + SO_2$	$4FeS_2 + 11O_2 \rightarrow 2Fe_2O_3 + 8SO_2$
29	$H_2 + O_2 \rightarrow H_2O$	$2H_2 + O_2 \rightarrow 2H_2O$
30	$H_2 + O_2 \rightarrow H_2O_2$	$H_2 + O_2 \rightarrow H_2O_2$
31	$H_3PO_4 + Ca(OH)_2 \rightarrow Ca_3(PO_4)_2 + H_2O$	$2H_3PO_4 + 3Ca(OH)_2 \rightarrow Ca_3(PO_4)_2 + 6H_2O$
32	$HCl + NaOH \rightarrow NaCl + H_2O$	$HCl + NaOH \rightarrow NaCl + H_2O$
33	$KClO_3 \rightarrow KCl + O_2$	$6K + B_2O_3 \rightarrow 3K_2O + 2B$
34	$KOH + HBr \rightarrow KBr + H_2O$	$KOH + HBr \rightarrow KBr + H_2O$
35	$Li + AlCl_3 \rightarrow LiCl + Al$	$3Li + AlCl_3 \rightarrow 3LiCl + Al$
36	$Li + H_2O \rightarrow LiOH + H_2$	$2Li + 2H_2O \rightarrow 2LiOH + H_2$
37	$Mg + Cl_2 \rightarrow MgCl_2$	$Mg + Cl_2 \rightarrow MgCl_2$
38	$N_2 + H_2 \rightarrow NH_3$	$N_2 + 3H_2 \rightarrow 2NH_3$
39	$N_2 + O_2 \rightarrow N_2O_5$	$2N_2 + 5O_2 \rightarrow 2N_2O_5$
40	$Na + Cl_2 \rightarrow NaCl$	$2Na + Cl_2 \rightarrow 2NaCl$

Part Five

Developing Scientific Research Skills

Chapter Nineteen

Scientific Databases

For the Teacher 373

19.1 Databases in Chemistry 374

19.2 Databases in Biology 378

19.3 Databases in Health 382

19.4 Databases in Earth and Space Science 385

19.5 Databases in Physics 387

Answers to Chapter Activities 389

For the Teacher

The dramatic expansion and dissemination of knowledge is the defining hallmark of our era, a period historians have dubbed the "Information Age." The development of the electronic computer and the Internet has fueled the creation and distribution of information and heightened our need to access, process, and analyze large amounts of data. Electronic databases are the most efficient means of categorizing and retrieving data, and today's students benefit when they learn to use this technology to answer real questions and solve practical problems. Photocopy the database commands section as a reference for your students.

Database Commands

A database is a structured set of data that can be accessed and analyzed in a variety of ways using a computer. Our economy is dependent on electronic databases. Scientific databases fuel the research and development of new products and services, and inventory, employee, product, credit, and client databases help bring products to market. For example, the human genome database is fueling the revolution in biotechnology, and business databases ensure that new biotech products are distributed to interested companies and individuals.

In this chapter, students use real data to answer practical questions and solve real problems. Because there is a diversity of database software and because the design of software changes from version to version, the explanations are given in generic terms. If you or your students have questions regarding the mechanics of a particular program, refer to the help menu associated with that software, entering the names of key words shown in *italics*.

Database Software and Files

All of the database files found in this chapter can be downloaded from the companion Web site (*sciencesourcebook.com*) as Microsoft Excel or text files. *Text files* include minimal formatting and can be imported into virtually any database program. The data printed in the book are excerpted from these files and can be entered manually, should one prefer. Because of its widespread use, Microsoft Excel was chosen to illustrate the principles of database use. Although Excel is primarily a spreadsheet program, it also has standard database features including the ability to *sort, list, group, summarize, select,* and *filter.* To ensure that data *records* stick together, first convert the *records* to a *list.* In *list format,* the top row becomes the *column header* (*category title*), and each row represents a *record.* Students will use database commands to solve the problems posed in this section. Following is a list of the essential database features of Excel and similar programs. Review these commands and features prior to performing the activities in this chapter.

Finding Records To find specific information, perform a *find* (*search*). Type in a portion or all of the term you are looking for, and the cursor will move to the first instance. Repeat the *find* (*search*) to locate other occurrences of the term.

Sorting (Arranging) Data Databases allow users to instantly *sort* (*arrange*) records by *category* (*field*). Table 19.1A shows a database of the longest rivers in the world sorted by length. These rivers can be sorted in either *ascending* (A to Z, 0 to 9) or *descending* (Z to A, 9 to 0) *order* by river name, length, or volume. *Sorting* arranges all items with the same entries adjacent to one another and is a prerequisite to *grouping.*

Grouping and Summarizing Data Once data have been *sorted,* they can be *grouped* and *summarized* (*subtotaled*). For example, the river data in Table 19.1A can be grouped by continent using the *subtotal* command, and then the user can calculate the desired *statistic* (e.g., *sum, count, average, maximum, minimum*). Table 19.1B calculates the combined (*sum*) length, drainage, and discharge of the longest rivers on each continent.

Selecting and Filtering Data In a small database, trends may be apparent, but as the database grows, any trends are obscured by the sheer volume of data. Fortunately, it is possible to select *records* matching specific criteria by employing

a *filter.* A *filter* is a set of *rules* used to extract data from the database. Table 19.1C is a *filtered report* of a database showing rivers that drain watersheds of more than 3 million square kilometers. Filters can be performed sequentially to provide a more specific subset. For example, a user could filter for rivers draining more than 3 million square kilometers *and* greater than 4000 kilometers in length.

19.1 Databases in Chemistry

Forensic science is the application of science to law. Forensic scientists are used as expert witnesses in court cases to establish facts. A physicist might testify concerning ballistics in a murder trial. A chemist might testify regarding the composition of air or water in an environmental lawsuit. A biologist might testify concerning DNA samples in a biotechnology product dispute. Forensic scientists often make their conclusions by comparing current observations with ones compiled in a database. For example, a forensic chemist might identify a pollutant by comparing its NMR (nuclear magnetic resonance) spectrum with the NMR spectra of other chemicals catalogued in an NMR database. In this chapter, we use databases to categorize, sort, compare, and analyze information to answer questions and solve problems.

ACTIVITY 19.1.1 *Choosing the Right Material*

By 1700, only 14 elements (carbon, sulfur, iron, copper, zinc, arsenic, silver, tin, antimony, gold, mercury, lead, bismuth, and phosphorous) and a few compounds were known. The Industrial Revolution, which began in the eighteenth century, established a demand for new resources and gave incentive for chemists to purify, develop, and classify new materials. The phenomenal expansion in commercial products that occurred in the industrial age is a direct result of the development of the chemical and materials sciences.

Materials science focuses on the properties of materials that make them suitable for industrial

Table 19.1 (A) Sorted Database. (B) Grouped Database. (C) Record Selection from Database

A Longest Rivers in the World

River	Length (km)	Drainage Area (km²)	Discharge (m³/sec)	Exit	Continent
Nile	6,690	2,870,000	5,100	Mediterranean Sea	Africa
Amazon	6,387	6,915,000	219,000	Atlantic Ocean	South America
Yangtze	6,380	1,800,000	31,900	East China Sea	Asia
Mississippi — Missouri	6,270	2,980,000	16,200	Gulf of Mexico	North America
Yenisei	5,550	2,580,000	19,600	Kara Sea	Asia
Ob' — Irtysh	5,410	2,990,000	12,800	Gulf of Ob	Asia
Huang He	4,667	745,000	2,110	Bohai Sea	Asia
Congo	4,371	3,680,000	41,800	Atlantic Ocean	Africa
Amur	4,368	1,855,000	11,400	Sea of Okhotsk	Asia
Lena	4,260	2,490,000	17,100	Laptev Sea	Asia
Mackenzie	4,241	1,790,000	10,300	Beaufort Sea	North America
Niger	4,167	2,090,000	9,570	Gulf of Guinea	Africa
Mekong	4,023	810,000	16,000	South China Sea	Asia
Paraná	3,998	3,100,000	25,700	Atlantic Ocean	South America
Murray	3,750	3,490,000	767	Southern Ocean	Australia

B Longest Rivers in the World Grouped by Continent

River	Length (km)	Drainage Area (km²)	Discharge (m³/sec)	Exit	Continent
Nile	6,690	2,870,000	5,100	Mediterranean Sea	Africa
Congo	4,371	3,680,000	41,800	Atlantic Ocean	Africa
Niger	4,167	2,090,000	9,570	Gulf of Guinea	Africa
15,228	*8,640,000*	*56,470*			*Africa Total*
Yangtze	6,380	1,800,000	31,900	East China Sea	Asia
Yenisei	5,550	2,580,000	19,600	Kara Sea	Asia
Ob' — Irtysh	5,410	2,990,000	12,800	Gulf of Ob	Asia
Huang He	4,667	745,000	2,110	Bohai Sea	Asia
Amur	4,368	1,855,000	11,400	Sea of Okhotsk	Asia
Lena	4,260	2,490,000	17,100	Laptev Sea	Asia
Mekong	4,023	810,000	16,000	South China Sea	Asia
34,658	*13,270,000*	*110,910*			*Asia Total*
Murray	3,750	3,490,000	767	Southern Ocean	Australia
3,750	*3,490,000*	*767*			*Australia Total*
Mississippi — Missouri	6,270	2,980,000	16,200	Gulf of Mexico	North America
Mackenzie	4,241	1,790,000	10,300	Beaufort Sea	North America
10,511	*4,770,000*	*26,500*			*North America Total*
Amazon	6,387	6,915,000	219,000	Atlantic Ocean	South America
Paraná	3,998	3,100,000	25,700	Atlantic Ocean	South America
10,385	*10,015,000*	*244,700*			*South America Total*
74,532	*40,185,000*	*439,347*			*Grand Total*

C River	Length (km)	Drainage Area (km²)	Discharge (m³/sec)	Exit	Continent
Amazon	6,387	6,915,000	219,000	Atlantic Ocean	South America
Congo	4,371	3,680,000	41,800	Atlantic Ocean	Africa
Paraná	3,998	3,100,000	25,700	Atlantic Ocean	South America
Murray	3,750	3,490,000	767	Southern Ocean	Australia

applications. Chemists have identified more than 110 elements and more than 23 million compounds, and they are identifying more than 4000 new compounds per day. It is impossible for developers to remember the properties of so many substances, yet they must select the best compounds to produce the best products for today's competitive market. Developers rely on electronic databases to search for materials with desired characteristics. In this activity, you will use a database file of the elements (Table 19.2) to search for those with the specified properties. Download the

Table 19.2 Database of the Elements and Their Properties

Name	At. #	Symbol	Family	MP (K)	BP (K)	Density (g/cm³)	At. Wt.	At. Radius (angstroms)	First IP	Specific Heat Capacity	Thermal Conductivity	Electrical Conductivity	Heat of Fusion	Heat of Vaporization	Electro-negativity	mg/kg Crust	Year
lithium	3	Li	Alkali Metal	454	1619	0.53	6.9	2.05	5.39	3.58	8.5E+01	1.2E+01	3	147	1.0	2.0E+01	1817
sodium	11	Na	Alkali Metal	371	1155	0.97	23.0	2.23	5.14	1.23	1.4E+02	2.0E+01	3	98	0.9	2.8E+03	1807
potassium	19	K	Alkali Metal	337	1039	0.86	39.1	2.77	4.34	0.76	1.0E+02	1.6E+01	2	77	0.8	2.1E+04	1807
rubidium	37	Rb	Alkali Metal	313	967	1.532	85.5	2.98	4.18	0.36	5.8E+01	4.8E+01	2	69	0.8	9.0E+01	1861
cesium	55	Cs	Alkali Metal	302	952	1.87	132.9	3.34	3.89	0.24	3.6E+01	5.3E+00	2	68	0.8	3.0E+00	1860
francium	87	Fr	Alkali Metal	300			223.0	2.7			1.5E+01		2	64	0.7		1939
beryllium	4	Be	Alkaline Earth	1560	2757	1.85	9.0	1.4	9.32	1.83	2.0E+02	2.5E+01	12	297	1.6	2.8E+00	1798
magnesium	12	Mg	Alkaline Earth	922	1378	1.74	24.3	1.72	7.65	1.02	1.6E+02	2.2E+01	9	128	1.3	2.3E+04	1808
calcium	20	Ca	Alkaline Earth	111 2	1757	1.55	40.1	2.23	6.11	0.65	2.0E+02	3.1E+01	9	155	1.0	4.2E+04	1808
strontium	38	Sr	Alkaline Earth	1042	1654	2.54	87.6	2.45	5.70	0.30	3.5E+00	5.0E+00	8	137	1.0	3.7E+02	1790
barium	56	Ba	Alkaline Earth	1002	2122	3.59	137.3	2.76	5.21	0.20	1.8E+01	2.8E+00	8	140	0.9	4.3E+02	1808
radium	88	Ra	Alkaline Earth	973	2010	5	226.0	2.23	5.28	0.09	1.9E+01	1.0E+00	8	137	0.9	9.0E-07	1898
boron	5	B	Boron	2365	3931	2.34	10.8	1.17	5.30	1.03	2.7E+01	5.0E-12	23	508	2.0	1.0E+01	1808
aluminum	13	Al	Boron	934	2720	2.7	27.0	1.62	5.99	0.90	2.4E+02	3.8E+01	11	291	1.6	8.2E+04	1825
gallium	31	Ga	Boron	303	2253	5.91	69.7	1.81	6.00	0.37	4.1E+01	1.8E+00	6	256	1.8	1.9E+01	1875
indium	49	In	Boron	430	2343	7.31	114.8	2	5.79	0.23	8.2E+01	3.4E+00	3	226	1.8	2.5E-01	1863
thallium	81	Tl	Boron	577	1760	11.85	204.4	2.08	6.11	0.13	4.6E+01	5.6E+00	4	162	2.0	8.5E-01	1861
carbon	6	C	Carbon	3825	5100	2.26	12.0	0.91	11.26	0.71		7.0E-02		715	2.6	2.0E+02	ancient
silicon	14	Si	Carbon	1683	2953	2.33	28.1	1.44	8.15	0.70	1.5E+02	4.0E-04	50	359	1.9	2.8E+05	1824
germanium	32	Ge	Carbon	1212	3125	5.32	72.6	1.52	7.90	0.32	6.0E+01	3.0E-06	32	334	2.0	1.5E+00	1886
tin	50	Sn	Carbon	505	2896	7.31	118.7	1.72	7.34	0.23	6.7E+01	8.7E+00	7	290	2.0	2.3E+00	ancient
lead	82	Pb	Carbon	601	2024	11.35	207.2	1.81	7.42	0.13	3.5E+01	4.8E+00	5	178	2.3	1.4E-01	ancient
oxygen	8	O	Chalcogen	55	90	1.429	16.0	0.65	13.62	0.92	2.7E-01		0.2	3	3.4	4.6E+05	1774
sulfur	16	S	Chalcogen	392	718	2.07	32.1	1.09	10.36	0.71	2.7E-01	5.0E-16	2	10	2.6	3.5E+02	ancient
selenium	34	Se	Chalcogen	494	958	4.79	79.0	1.22	9.75	0.32	2.0E+00	8.0E+00	6	26	2.6	5.0E-02	1818
tellurium	52	Te	Chalcogen	723	1282	6.24	127.6	1.42	9.01	0.20	2.4E+00	2.0E-04	17	51	2.1	1.0E-03	1782
polonium	84	Po	Chalcogen	527	1235	9.3	209.0	1.53	8.42		2.0E+01	7.0E-01	13	120	2.0	2.0E-10	1898
fluorine	9	F	Halogen	54	85	1.696	19.0	0.57	17.42	0.82	2.8E-02		0.3	3	4.0	5.9E+02	1886
chlorine	17	Cl	Halogen	172	239	3.214	35.5	0.97	12.97	0.48	8.9E-03		3	10	3.2	1.5E+02	1774
bromine	35	Br	Halogen	266	332	3.12	79.9	1.12	11.81	0.23	1.2E-01	1.0E-16	5	15	3.0	2.4E+00	1826
iodine	53	I	Halogen	387	457	4.93	126.9	1.32	10.45	0.15	4.5E-01	1.0E-11	8	21	2.7	4.5E-01	1811
astatine	85	At	Halogen	575	607		210.0	1.43			1.7E+00		12	30	2.2		1940
hydrogen	1	H	Hydrogen	14	20	0.0899	1.0	0.79	13.60		1.8E-01		0.1	0	2.2	1.4E+03	1766
helium	2	He	Noble gas	1	4	0.1785	4.0	0.49	24.59		1.5E-01		0.02	0		8.0E-03	1895
neon	10	Ne	Noble gas	25	27	0.9	20.2	0.51	21.56	1.03	4.9E-02		0.3	2		5.0E-03	1898
argon	18	Ar	Noble gas	84	87	1.784	39.9	0.88	15.76	0.52	1.8E-02		1	7		3.5E+00	1894
krypton	36	Kr	Noble gas	116	120	3.75	83.8	1.03	14.00	0.25	9.5E-03		2	9		1.0E-04	1898
xenon	54	Xe	Noble gas	161	165	5.9	131.3	1.24	12.13	0.16	5.7E-03		2	13		3.0E-05	1898
radon	86	Rn	Noble gas	202	211	9.73	222.0	1.34	10.75	0.09	3.6E-03		3	16		4.0E-13	1898
nitrogen	7	N	Pnictide	63	77	1.251	14.0	0.75	14.53	1.04	2.6E-02		0.4	3	3.0	1.9E+01	1772
phosphorus	15	P	Pnictide	317	553	1.82	31.0	1.23	10.49	0.77	2.4E-01	1.0E-16	1	12	2.2	1.1E+03	1669
arsenic	33	As	Pnictide	1090	885	5.78	74.9	1.33	9.81	0.33	5.0E+01	3.8E+00	28	32	2.2	1.8E+00	ancient
antimony	51	Sb	Pnictide	904	1913	6.69	121.8	1.53	8.64	0.21	2.4E+01	2.6E+00	20	68	2.1	2.0E-01	ancient
bismuth	83	Bi	Pnictide	545	1852	9.75	209.0	1.63	7.29	0.12	7.9E+00	9.0E-01	11	179	2.0	8.5E-03	ancient
scandium	21	Sc	Transition Metal	1814	3003	2.99	45.0	2.09	6.54	0.57	1.6E+01	1.5E+00	16	305	1.4	2.2E+01	1879
titanium	22	Ti	Transition Metal	1935	3562	4.54	47.9	2	6.82	0.52	2.2E+01	2.6E+00	19	425	1.5	5.7E+03	1791
vanadium	23	V	Transition Metal	2163	3682	6.11	50.9	1.92	6.74	0.49	3.1E+01	4.0E+00	23	447	1.6	1.2E+02	1830
chromium	24	Cr	Transition Metal	2130	2945	7.19	52.0	1.85	6.77	0.45	9.4E+01	7.9E+00	20	340	1.7	1.0E+02	1797
manganese	25	Mn	Transition Metal	1518	2393	7.44	54.9	1.79	7.44	0.48	7.8E+00	5.0E-01	15	220	1.6	9.5E+02	1774
iron	26	Fe	Transition Metal	1808	3146	7.874	55.8	1.72	7.87	0.45	8.0E+01	1.1E+01	14	350	1.8	5.6E+04	ancient
cobalt	27	Co	Transition Metal	1768	3170	8.9	58.9	1.67	7.86	0.42	1.0E+02	1.8E+01	16	373	1.9	2.5E+01	1739
nickel	28	Ni	Transition Metal	1726	3193	8.9	58.7	1.62	7.64	0.44	9.1E+01	1.5E+01	17	378	1.9	8.4E+01	1751
copper	29	Cu	Transition Metal	1357	2855	8.96	63.5	1.57	7.73	0.39	4.0E+02	6.1E+01	13	301	1.9	6.0E+01	ancient
zinc	30	Zn	Transition Metal	693	1184	7.13	65.4	1.53	9.39	0.39	1.2E+02	1.7E+01	7	115	1.7	7.0E+01	ancient
yttrium	39	Y	Transition Metal	1795	3577	4.47	88.9	2.27	6.38	0.30	1.7E+01	1.8E+00	17	393	1.2	3.3E+01	1789
zirconium	40	Zr	Transition Metal	2128	4777	6.51	91.2	2.16	6.34	0.28	2.3E+01	2.3E+00	21	591	1.3	1.7E+02	1789
niobium	41	Nb	Transition Metal	2742	5136	8.57	92.9	2.08	6.88	0.27	5.4E+01	6.6E+00	27	690	1.6	2.0E+01	1801
molybdenum	42	Mo	Transition Metal	2896	4919	10.22	95.9	2.01	7.10	0.25	1.4E+02	1.7E+01	36	590	2.2	1.2E+00	1778
technetium	43	Tc	Transition Metal	2477	4840	11.5	98.0	1.95	7.28	0.24	5.1E+01	1.0E-03	23	502	1.9		1937
ruthenium	44	Ru	Transition Metal	2610	4392	12.37	101.1	1.89	7.37	0.24	1.2E+02	1.5E+01	26	568	2.2	1.0E-03	1844
rhodium	45	Rh	Transition Metal	2236	4000	12.41	102.9	1.83	7.46	0.24	1.5E+02	2.3E+01	22	495	2.3	1.0E-03	1803
palladium	46	Pd	Transition Metal	1825	3213	12	106.4	1.79	8.34	0.24	7.2E+01	1.0E+01	17	393	2.2	1.5E-02	1803
silver	47	Ag	Transition Metal	1235	2437	10.5	107.9	1.75	7.58	0.24	4.3E+02	6.3E+01	11	251	1.9	7.5E-02	ancient
cadmium	48	Cd	Transition Metal	594	1040	8.65	112.4	1.71	8.99	0.23	9.7E+01	1.5E+01	6	100	1.7	1.5E-01	1817
hafnium	72	Hf	Transition Metal	2504	4723	13.31	178.5	2.16	6.65	0.14	2.3E+01	3.4E+00	22	661	1.3	3.0E+00	1923
tantalum	73	Ta	Transition Metal	3293	5786	16.65	180.9	2.09	7.89	0.14	5.8E+01	8.1E+00	36	737	1.5	2.0E+00	1802
tungsten	74	W	Transition Metal	3695	5936	19.3	183.9	2.02	7.98	0.13	1.7E+02	1.8E+01	35	423	2.4	1.3E+00	1783
rhenium	75	Re	Transition Metal	3455	5960	21	186.2	1.97	7.88	0.14	4.8E+01	5.8E+00	33	707	1.9	7.0E-04	1925
osmium	76	Os	Transition Metal	3300	5770	22.6	190.2	1.92	8.70	0.13	8.8E+01	1.2E+01	29	628	2.2	1.5E-03	1804
iridium	77	Ir	Transition Metal	2720	4662	22.6	192.2	1.87	9.10	0.13	1.5E+02	2.1E+01	26	564	2.2	1.0E-03	1804
platinum	78	Pt	Transition Metal	2042	4097	21.45	195.1	1.83	9.00	0.13	7.2E+01	9.4E+00	20	510	2.3	5.0E-03	1735
gold	79	Au	Transition Metal	1338	3081	19.3	197.0	1.79	9.23	0.13	3.2E+02	4.9E+01	12	324	2.5	4.0E-03	ancient
mercury	80	Hg	Transition Metal	234	630	13.55	200.6	1.76	10.44	0.14	8.3E+00	1.0E+00	2	59	2.0	8.5E-02	ancient

elements file (from *sciencesourcebook.com*) or enter the data from Table 19.2 into a new file.

1. *Electronic circuits:* When designing electronic circuits, computer hardware engineers must use materials that have extremely high conductivity so signals travel easily with little loss of energy. *Sort (arrange)* the database *list* on electrical conductivity to determine the three best elements for use in electric circuitry. Where are these three elements found in the periodic table? Perform an Internet search to determine if these elements are indeed used in electrical circuits.

2. *Aircraft design:* Aircraft designers need materials that can withstand extreme temperatures and are lightweight, malleable, and abundant. Determine the element that best fits these criteria. Using a *filter,* select those substances that are metallic (all metals are malleable), have a melting point in excess of 600 K, and have a density less than 3 g/cm^3. Finally, sort these elements by abundance in the Earth's crust to determine which is the most abundant. Which element fills these criteria? Perform an Internet search to determine the element of which most airplanes are made. Is this the same element you selected using your database filter?

3. *Electric switches:* Certain applications require fluid conductors—materials that conduct electricity and yet flow at room temperature. Perform a *record selection (filter)* for elements with a melting point less than 298 K and a boiling point greater than 298 K. This selects for those elements that are liquid at room temperature, 298 K (25°C). Following this *record selection (filter)*, *sort descending* on electrical conductivity. The element at the top of the list will be the best liquid conductor at room temperature. What is this element?

ACTIVITY 19.1.2 *Arranging Elements by Physical Properties*

1. *Abundance:* Coins and jewelry are normally made of rare elements so that they have intrinsic value and are difficult to counterfeit.

By contrast, metals used in construction are abundant and inexpensive, keeping construction costs down. *Sort (arrange)* the elements database (Table 19.2, available online at *sciencesourcebook.com*) by abundance in the Earth's crust and determine if these generalizations hold true. Research the relative abundance of gold, iron, copper, aluminum, silver, and platinum and determine which are better suited for coins or construction on the basis of this single criteria.

2. *Element symbols:* Most element symbols are derived from the first one or two letters of the element name. For example, the symbol for oxygen is O, and the symbol for helium is He. This is not true for all elements, however. For example, the symbol for potassium is K, even though there is no K in the word. Determine if there is a correlation between the date of discovery and the symbol and name convention. *Sort (arrange)* the elements by date of discovery, and compare the element names with the symbol names. Is there greater correlation between the names of elements and their symbols for recently discovered elements or for ones discovered many years ago? Explain your answer.

3. *Ionization potential:* Ionization potential (energy) is the energy required to remove an electron from a neutral atom. Elements with a low ionization energy easily lose electrons and become cations, while those with high ionization energy hold on to their valence electrons much more firmly. Where in the periodic table are the elements located that frequently lose valence electrons to become cations? *Sort* the elemental data from low to high ionization potential (*ascending sort*). Which elements have the lowest ionization energy, and where are they found in the periodic table? Which elements have the highest ionization energy, and where are they found?

ACTIVITY 19.1.3 *Discovering Family Similarities*

Dimitri Mendeleyev, a Russian chemist, created the first version of the periodic table of the

			Ti=50	Zr=90	?[2]=180
			V=51	Nb=94	Ta=182
			Cr=52	Mo=96	W=186
			Mn=55	Rh=104.4	Pt=197.4
			Fe=56	Ru=104.4	Ir=198
			Ni=Co=59	Pd=106.6	Os=199
H=1			Cu=63.4	Ag=108	Hg=200
	Be=9.4	Mg=24	Zn=65.2	Cd=112	
	B=11	Al=27.4	?[6]=68	Ur=116	Au=197?
	C=12	Si=28	?[8]=70	Sn=118	
	N=14	P=31	As=75	Sb=122	Bi=210?
	O=16	S=32	Se=79.4	Te=128?	
	F=19	Cl=35.5	Br=80	J=127	
Li=7	Na=23	K=39	Rb=85.4	Cs=133	Tl=204
		Ca=40	Sr=87.6	Ba=137	Pb=207
		?[10]=45	Ce=92		
		?Er=56	La=94		
		?Yt=60	Di=95		
		?In=75.6	Th=118?		

Figure 19.1 The First Periodic Table, by Dimitri Mendeleyev

elements (Figure 19.1) in 1869. When he ordered the elements according to increasing atomic weight in columns so that rows contained analogous elements, he saw patterns that allowed him to predict the properties of elements yet to be discovered. Mendeleyev's task was formidable because there were relatively few data to work with and no electronic tools to organize the information. Today, however, we have an abundance of information as well as database tools that allow us to instantly group data by common characteristics. Database technology has fueled the Information Revolution by allowing us to store and examine large amounts of data. In this activity, you will use a database program to separate data by groups and summarize your findings.

Figure 19.1 arranges the elements in terms of increasing atomic number. No patterns or trends are seen when the elements are displayed in this fashion. If, however, elements are arranged as seen in the periodic table, those with similar properties are grouped together. Each column represents a family of elements that have a similar electron configuration and similar chemical properties. Although the periodic table makes it easy to see which elements have similar properties (those in the same family or column), comparing these properties is not easy. By contrast, Table 19.2 lists much specific information about the properties of the elements but does not allow comparison of family (group) data, unless first arranged by group.

Sort the elements by group. Then calculate *average* group values for heat of fusion, specific heat, thermal conductivity, and other properties of your choice using the *subtotal* command and *average* option. List your results.

1. Which families are most similar to each other?
2. Which families are most dissimilar to each other?

19.2 Databases in Biology

Francis Bacon, one of the most prominent philosophers of the scientific revolution, stated: "Knowledge is power." Bacon's axiom resonates today as biological researchers use knowledge to solve real-life problems. Researchers share their findings, and other researchers use such knowledge to solve additional problems. The data generated are immense, necessitating the use of databases to store and analyze the information. In this section, students will analyze databases to answer biological questions.

ACTIVITY 19.2.1 *Species Diversity*

Ecologists have identified loss of species diversity as one of the largest ecological problems today. To prevent the extinction of species and loss of species diversity, it is important to track the health and distribution of species and store the information in a database from which researchers can retrieve information. Table 19.3 is a database of common and important North American trees. This database file can be downloaded from *sciencesourcebook.com*. Researchers can add many more categories to this table to include such important details as germination time, pest problems, and life expectancy. The U.S. Department of Agriculture maintains a database that provides a wealth of information for ecologists and other researchers (go to plants.usda.gov, or search "plants USDA database").[1]

1. Which three families have the greatest representation in the database? *Sort* (*arrange*) the database according to family. Then perform a *subtotal*, using the *count* option to determine the number belonging to each family.
2. Which two genera have the greatest representation? *Sort* (*arrange*) the database according to genus. Then perform a *subtotal* function, using the *count* option to determine the number belonging to each genus.
3. Which family is best represented in the western United States? Sort by the following regions: California (CA), Pacific Northwest (NW), Southwest (SW), and Rocky Mountains (RM).
4. Where are oaks (genus *Quercus*) most common? Sort by genus and match with regions.

ACTIVITY 19.2.2 *Properties of Amino Acids*

Proteins are necessary for the structure and function of all forms of life. Some proteins serve as enzymes, facilitating biochemical reactions in the body, while others provide cellular structure or serve specialized roles, including immune response. Amino acids are the building blocks of all proteins. The sequence and frequency of amino acids in a protein influence its structure and function. Table 19.4 records some of the common properties of amino acids. This database file can be downloaded from *sciencesourcebook.com*. Use the database commands to answer the following questions:

1. Which amino acids are coded for by these codons: CCU, UAU, UCG, UUG? Perform a *search* (*find*) for each codon sequence.
2. What is the rarest polar amino acid in vertebrates? *Sort* (*arrange*) in *ascending* polarity, and look for the first polar amino acid in the list.
3. What percentage of proteins are composed of essential amino acids (those that cannot be synthesized by the human body, but must be acquired in food). *Arrange* (*sort*) by essential/nonessential. Perform a *subtotal* of the *average* percentage composition at each change in the "essential" category.
4. Which amino acids compose less than 7 percent of proteins in vertebrates, are neutral, and are polar? Perform three successive *filters* (less than 7 percent, neutral, and polar). Make certain to *show all* records before performing subsequent operations, or you will be working only with the results of the filter.
5. Which amino acid has a molecular weight greater than 150 g/mole, is polar, and is neutral? Perform three successive filters (mass greater than 150, polar, neutral). Make certain to *show all* records before performing subsequent operations.

ACTIVITY 19.2.3 *Human Genome*

The Human Genome Project has discovered approximately 25,000 human genes and 3 billion DNA subunits, and it has published much of this information on the Internet through online databases, such as the human genome database (gene map of the human genome) provided by National Center for Biotechnology Information (NCBI).[2]

Table 19.3 Database of Common North American Trees

Family	Genus	Species	Common Name	NE	SE	CN	NW	CA	SW	RM
Cupressaceae	Chamaecyparis	nootkatensis	Alaska-cedar				1			
Tiliaceae	Tilia	americana	American basswood	1						
Fagaceae	Fagus	grandifolia	American beech	1						
Fagaceae	Castanea	dentata	American chestnut	1	1					
Ulmaceae	Ulmus	americana	American elm	1	1	1				
Aquifoliaceae	Ilex	opaca	American holly		1					
Cupressaceae	Cupressus	arizonica	Arizona cypress						1	
Cupressaceae	Taxodium	distichum	baldcypress		1					
Pinaceae	Abies	balsamea	balsam fir	1						
Salicaceae	Populus	balsamifera	balsam poplar	1						
Fagaceae	Quercus	velutina	black oak	1	1					
Juglandaceae	Juglans	nigra	black walnut	1	1					
Pinaceae	Pinus	aristata	bristlecone pine					1	1	1
Pinaceae	Picea	pungens	Colorado blue spruce				1	1	1	1
Cupressaceae	Juniperus	communis	common juniper				1	1	1	1
Pinaceae	Pseudotsuga	menziesii	Douglas fir				1	1	1	1
Pinaceae	Picea	engelmannii	Engelmann spruce				1		1	1
Cupressaceae	Sequoiadendron	giganteum	giant sequoia					1		
Leguminosae	Gleditsia	triacanthos	honey locust		1					
Cupressaceae	Calocedrus	decurrens	incense-cedar				1	1		
Pinaceae	Pinus	jeffreyi	Jeffrey pine					1		
Pinaceae	Pinus	flexilis	limber pine					1	1	1
Fagaceae	Quercus	virginiana	live oak		1					
Pinaceae	Pinus	taeda	loblolly pine		1					
Pinaceae	Pinus	contorta	lodgepole pine							
Pinaceae	Abies	procera	noble fir				1	1	1	1
Cupressaceae	Thuja	occidentalis	northern white cedar	1						
Hippocastanaceae	Aesculus	glabra	Ohio buckeye	1	1	1				
Betulaceae	Betula	papyrifera	paper birch	1						
Juglandaceae	Carya	illinoensis	pecan	1	1					
Pinaceae	Pinus	edulis	pinyon						1	1
Pinaceae	Pinus	ponderosa	ponderosa pine				1	1	1	1
Salicaceae	Populus	tremuloides	quaking aspen	1				1	1	1
Pinaceae	Pinus	resinosa	red pine	1						
Pinaceae	Picea	rubens	red spruce	1						
Cupressaceae	Sequoia	sempervirens	redwood					1		
Lauraceae	Sassafras	albidum	sassafras	1	1					
Pinaceae	Pinus	echinata	shortleaf pine		1					
Aceraceae	Acer	saccharinum	silver maple	1	1	1				
Pinaceae	Picea	sitchensis	Sitka spruce				1			
Magnoliaceae	Magnolia	grandiflora	southern magnolia		1					
Fagaceae	Quercus	falcata	southern red oak	1	1					
Aceraceae	Acer	saccharum	sugar maple	1						
Hamamelidaceae	Liquidambar	styraciflua	sweet gum		1					
Platanaceae	Platanus	occidentalis	sycamore	1	1	1				
Magnoliaceae	Liriodendron	tulipifera	tulip tree	1	1					
Cornaceae	Nyssa	aquatica	water tupelo		1					
Pinaceae	Tsuga	heterophylla	western hemlock				1			1
Cupressaceae	Thuja	plicata	western red cedar				1			1
Oleaceae	Fraxinus	americana	white ash	1	1	1				
Pinaceae	Abies	concolor	white fir				1	1	1	1
Fagaceae	Quercus	alba	white oak	1	1					
Pinaceae	Picea	glauca	white spruce	1						
Pinaceae	Pinus	albicaulis	whitebark pine				1			1

Note: NE = Northeast, SE = Southeast, CN = Canada, NW = Northwest, CA = California, SW = Southwest, RM = Rocky Mountains.

Table 19.4 Database of Amino Acids

Amino acid		Mass (g/m)	abundance-vertebrates	polarity	pH	codon	essential
Alanine	ala	89	7.4%	nonpolar	neutral	GCU, GCC, GCA, GCG	N
Arginine	arg	174	4.2%	polar	strongly basic	CGU, CGC, CGA, CGG, AGA, AGG	Y
Asparagine	asn	132	5.9%	polar	acidic	AAU, AAC	N
Aspartate	asp	133	4.4%	polar	neutral	GAU, GAC	N
Cysteine	cys	121	3.3%	nonpolar	neutral	UGU, UGC	N
Glutamate	glu	147	5.8%	polar	acidic	CAA, CAG	N
Glutamine	gln	146	3.7%	polar	neutral	GAA, GAG	N
Glycine	gly	75	7.4%	nonpolar	neutral	GGU, GGC, GGA, GGG	N
Histidine	his	155	2.9%	polar	weakly basic	CAU, CAC	Y
Isoleucine	ile	131	3.8%	nonpolar	neutral	AUU, AUC, AUA	Y
Leucine	leu	131	7.6%	nonpolar	neutral	UUA, UUG, CUU, CUC, CUA, CUG	Y
Lysine	lys	146	7.2%	polar	basic	AAA, AAG	Y
Methionine	met	149	1.8%	nonpolar	neutral	AUG	Y
Phenylalanine	phe	165	4.0%	nonpolar	neutral	UUU, UUC	Y
Proline	pro	115	5.0%	nonpolar	neutral	CCU, CCC, CCA, CCG	N
Serine	ser	105	8.1%	polar	neutral	UCU, UCC, UCA, UCG, AGU, AGC	N
Threonine	thr	119	6.2%	polar	neutral	ACU, ACC, ACA, ACG	Y
Tryptophan	trp	204	1.3%	nonpolar	neutral	UGG	Y
Tyrosine	tyr	181	3.3%	polar	neutral	UAU, UAC	N
Valine	val	117	6.8%	nonpolar	neutral	GUU, GUC, GUA, GUG	Y

1. Using information gathered from a general Internet search, summarize the nature of the following genetic disorders: cystic fibrosis, achondroplasia, albinism, and hemochromatosis. Locate the gene that results in each disorder by performing a search using the online human genome database (see *sciencesource book.com*, www.ncbi.nlm.nih.gov, or www.gdb. org, or search "human genome database"). Print out a gene map showing the location of each gene on its chromosome.

2. Many conditions result from the insufficiency or overproduction of hormones. For example, diabetes results from an insufficiency of insulin. Print out a gene map showing the location of a gene responsible for insulin production.

3. Congenital hypothyroidism is a condition that affects infants from birth and results from a partial or complete loss of thyroid function (hypothyroidism). Its symptoms may include fatigue, weakness, and weight gain since thyroxin, the hormone of the thyroid gland, controls metabolism and is lacking in such individuals. Mutations in the PAX8, SLC5A5, TG, TPO, TSHB, and TSHR genes cause congenital hypothyroidism. Print a gene map showing the location on chromosomes of one or more genes that may lead to hypothyroidism.

ACTIVITY 19.2.4 *Protein Structure*

Proteins are essential to the structure and function of all living cells. Some proteins are enzymes or antibodies, and others serve structural, mechanical, or storage roles. Biological and medical researchers are extremely interested in the shapes of proteins because structure determines function. The Protein Data Bank is a repository for the processing and distribution of the three-dimensional structure of proteins (look on *sciencesource book.com* or www.pdb.org, or search "protein data bank").[3] Search the Protein Data Bank for the following proteins using the PDB code listed in capital letters. Each is viewable in three dimensions and can be rotated and enlarged within a Web browser. Print pictures of the three-dimensional structure of each of the following:

1. Insulin 3INS (hormone used in sugar regulation)

2. Hemoglobin 1GZX (oxygen-carrying molecule in the blood)
3. Ferritin 1AEW (iron reservoir in the spleen)
4. Manganese peroxidase 1MNP (an enzyme for breaking down peroxides)
5. NS1-protein 1AIL (a protein from flu virus)

ACTIVITY 19.2.5 *Classification and Taxonomy*

Plants provide us with food, wood, paper, medicines, oxygen, and many other essential or useful products. The U.S. Department of Agriculture (USDA) maintains the online Plants Database (plants.usda.gov) from which users can find the distribution, classification, and use of plants found in North America.

1. Using this online database, obtain a picture and record the classification (kingdom, division, class, order, family, genus, species) and distribution (states in which they grow) of the following record-holding tree species: (a) giant redwood (*Sequoiadendron giganteum*), the largest living thing; (b) bristlecone pine (*Pinus longaeva*), the oldest living thing; and (c) coast redwood (*Sequoia sempervirens*), the tallest living thing. What similarities, if any, exist in the classification and distribution of these species? Include photographs and distribution maps of each.
2. Using the Plants Database, obtain a picture, and record the classification (kingdom, division, class, order, family, genus, species) and distribution (states in which they grow) of your state flower and tree.

19.3 Databases in Health

Americans are preoccupied with losing weight and staying healthy, and a multibillion dollar diet food industry has developed to feed this preoccupation. The South Beach, Atkins, Slim Fast, and 3-Day diets are a few of the hundreds of plans that have been developed to help people reduce weight and stay healthy. Dietitians have developed plans using databases such as that shown in Table 19.5 (download this file from *sciencesourcebook.com*), selecting foods that meet specific nutritional criteria. The activities in this section show how dieti-

tians or consumers may use a database of foods to analyze content and assemble appropriate diets.

Contact a professional before making any major dietary decisions. The activities in this section are merely for the purpose of illustration.

ACTIVITY 19.3.1 *Selecting Foods to Reduce the Risk of Osteoporosis*

Osteoporosis is a metabolic disease in which bones become porous. Approximately 10 million Americans suffer from this debilitating disease with symptoms that include curvature of the spine and bone fractures. Although osteoporosis is often considered to be a disease of the elderly, steps to prevent it can be taken throughout life. Medical researchers have shown that osteoporosis results from an insufficiency of calcium during the growing years as well as later in life.

Nutrition experts agree that the best way to prevent nutrient deficiencies is to eat a balanced diet. However, an individual who is showing symptoms of calcium deficiency may be advised to increase his or her dietary intake. Calcium is best absorbed in foods that contain approximately equivalent amounts of calcium and phosphorous. Vitamin D is known to aid calcium absorption, and excessive dietary protein reduces it. The nutritional database (Table 19.5, which you can download from *sciencesourcebook.com*) provides information about the composition of some common foods. Your goal is to determine foods to recommend to an individual showing symptoms of calcium deficiency. You will need to select foods that (a) are high in calcium, (b) have moderate to low protein content, and (c) have a calcium-to-phosphorous ratio of approximately 1:1.

1. (a) *Select* (*filter*) for those foods with more than 25 mg of calcium per serving size. (b) *Select* (*filter*) for those foods with a protein content less than 10 g/serving (c) and a calcium/phosphorus ratio between 0.7 and 1.3.

ACTIVITY 19.3.2 *Selecting Foods to Reduce the Threat of Cardiovascular Disease*

More than half of American adults die from some form of cardiovascular disease (e.g., heart failure, aneurysms, strokes) in which the heart or

Table 19.5 Nutrition Data

Food	Serving Size	Calcium [mg]	Energy [kcal]	Protein [g]	Carbohydrate [g]	Cholesterol [mg]	Total Fat [g]	Saturate Fat [g]	Polyunsat Fat [g]	Sodium [mg]	Phosphorous [mg]	Ca:P ratio	Niacin [mg]	Thiamin [mg]	Riboflavin [mg]	Vit A [RE]	Vit B6 [mg]	Vit C [mg]	Food type
apple	1 ea	10	80	0.3	21.0	0.0	0.5	0.1	0.1	1	10	1	0.11	0.02	0.02	7	0.07	8	fr
apple pie	1 slice	3	403	3.0	60.0	0.0	18.0	4.2	4.9	474	50	0.06	1.59	0.17	0.13	29	0.09	0	bg
asparagus	1/2 cup	22	22	2.3	4.0	0.0	0.3	0.1	0.1	4	55	0.4	0.95	0.09	0.11	75	0.13	25	v
avocado	1 ea	19	305	4.0	12.0	0.0	30.0	4.5	3.5	21	73	0.26	3.32	0.19	0.21	106	0.48	14	fr
bacon	3 pce	2	109	5.8	0.1	16.0	9.3	3.3	1.1	303	64	0.03	1.39	0.13	0.05	0	0.05	6	m
bagel, plain	1 ea	29	200	7.5	38.2	0.0	1.8	0.3	0.7	245	46	0.63	2.4	0.26	0.2	0	0.03	0	bg
banana	1 ea	7	105	1.2	26.7	0.0	0.5	0.2	0.1	1	22	0.32	0.62	0.05	0.11	9	0.66	10	fr
beef burrito	1 ea	165	390	21.0	40.0	52.0	17.5	6.8	2.3	516	274	0.6	4.36	0.26	0.29	58	0.73	5	mx
broccoli	1 spear	205	53	5.3	10.0	0.0	0.5	0.1	0.2	20	86	2.38	1.36	0.15	0.37	254	0.36	113	v
canned pudding	5 oz	74	205	3.0	30.0	1.0	11.0	9.5	0.1	285	117	0.63	0.6	0.04	0.17	31	0.03	0	d
cantaloupe	1/2 ea	29	94	2.4	22.3	0.0	0.7	0.1	0.2	24	45	0.64	1.53	0.1	0.06	861	0.31	113	fr
cheese crackers	10 ea	11	50	1.0	6.0	6.0	3.0	0.9	0.3	112	17	0.65	0.4	0.05	0.04	5	0.01	0	bg
chicken	1 cup	21	266	40.5	0.0	125.0	10.4	2.9	2.4	120	273	0.08	12.8	0.1	0.25	22	0.65	0	p
choc.chip cookies	4 ea	16	180	2.3	28.0	5.0	8.8	2.9	2.6	140	41	0.39	0.9	0.1	0.23	15	0.02	0	bg
cole slaw	1 cup	54	84	1.5	14.9	10.0	3.1	0.5	1.6	28	38	1.42	0.33	0.08	0.07	98	0.17	39	mx
corn	1 ear	2	83	2.6	19.4	0.0	1.0	0.0	0.5	13	79	0.03	1.24	0.17	0.06	17	0.18	5	v
corn chips	1 oz	35	155	2.0	16.0	0.0	9.0	1.4	3.7	233	52	0.67	0.4	0.04	0.05	11	0.04	1	bg
corn dog	1 ea	34	330	10.0	27.3	37.0	20.0	8.4	1.4	1252	303	0.11	3.27	0.28	0.17	0	0.11	3	mx
cottage cheese	1 cup	126	215	26.2	5.6	31.0	8.9	6.0	0.3	850	277	0.45	0.27	0.04	0.34	101	0.14	0	d
duck	1/2 duck	27	445	51.9	0.0	198.0	24.8	9.2	3.1	143	449	0.06	11.3	0.57	1.04	51	0.55	0	p
egg noodles	1 cup	16	200	6.6	37.3	50.0	2.0	0.5	0.6	3	94	0.17	1.9	0.22	0.13	34	0.01	0	g
eggplant	1 cup	10	45	1.3	10.6	0.0	0.4	0.1	0.1	5	35	0.29	0.96	0.12	0.03	10	0.14	2	v
eggs	1 ea	54	95	6.0	1.4	282.0	7.1	3.0	0.8	176	109	0.5	0.04	0.04	0.18	102	0.06	0	e
enchilada	1 ea	322	235	20.0	24.0	19.0	16.0	7.7	0.6	1332	198	1.63	0	0.18	0.26	352	0.25	0	mx
english muffin	1 ea	96	140	4.5	26.2	0.0	1.1	0.3	0.3	378	67	1.43	2.14	0.26	0.18	0	0.02	0	bg
fish sticks	2 ea	22	140	12.0	8.0	52.0	6.0	1.6	1.6	106	116	0.19	1.2	0.06	0.1	10	0.12	0	f
frankfurter	1 ea	5	145	5.1	1.1	23.0	13.1	4.8	1.2	504	39	0.13	1.18	0.09	0.05	0	0.06	12	m
french fries	10 strips	10	158	2.0	19.8	0.0	8.3	2.5	3.8	108	47	0.21	1.63	0.09	0.01	0	0.12	5	v
graham crackers	2 ea	6	60	1.0	10.8	0.0	1.5	0.4	0.4	86	20	0.3	0.6	0.02	0.03	0	0.01	0	g
Grape-Nuts cereal	1/2 cup	22	202	6.6	26.4	0.0	0.2	0.0	0.2	394	142	0.15	10	0.8	0.8	753	1	0	g
ground beef lean	3 oz	9	230	21.0	0.0	74.0	16.0	6.2	0.6	65	134	0.07	4.4	0.04	0.18	0	0.39	0	m
ground beef regular	3 oz	9	245	20.0	0.0	76.0	17.8	6.9	0.7	70	144	0.06	4.9	0.03	0.16	0	0.39	0	m
ham	1 pce	1	70	2.6	0.4	13.0	6.4	2.3	0.8	271	17	0.06	0.66	0.08	0.04	0	0.04	0	m
honey dew	1 pce	8	45	0.6	11.8	0.0	0.1	0.0	0.0	13	13	0.62	0.77	0.1	0.02	5	0.08	32	fr
ice cream	1 cup	351	269	4.8	31.8	60.0	14.4	8.9	0.5	116	134	2.62	0.14	0.05	0.33	133	0.06	1	d
lima beans	1/2 cup	19	85	5.2	16.0	0.0	0.3	0.1	0.1	45	54	0.35	0.91	0.06	0.05	16	0.1	11	v
liver	3 oz	9	185	23.0	7.0	410.0	7.0	2.5	1.3	90	392	0.02	12.3	0.18	3.52	9120	0.31	23	m
macaroni	1 cup	14	190	6.5	39.1	0.0	0.7	0.1	0.3	1	85	0.16	1.82	0.23	0.13	0	0.01	0	g
melba toast	1 pce	6	20	1.0	4.0	0.0	0.3	0.1	0.1	44	10	0.6	0.1	0.01	0.01	0	0.01	0	bg
milk - 2% low fat	1 cup	297	121	8.1	11.7	22.0	4.8	2.9	0.2	122	232	1.28	0.21	0.1	0.4	140	0.1	2	d
muffins blueberry,	1 ea	15	140	2.7	22.0	45.0	4.9	1.4	1.2	225	90	0.17	1.17	0.11	0.13	40	0.01	0.5	bg
orange juice	1 cup	27	111	1.7	25.8	0.0	0.5	0.1	0.1	2	42	0.64	0.99	0.22	0.07	50	0.11	124	fr
oysters	1 cup	202	160	21.0	8.0	120.0	5.0	1.8	1.8	185	379	0.53	6	0.29	0.43	223	0.13	24	f
peaches	1 ea	4	37	0.6	9.6	0.0	0.1	0.0	0.0	0	10	0.4	0.86	0.01	0.04	47	0.02	6	fr
pears	1 ea	19	98	0.7	25.1	0.0	0.7	0.0	0.2	1	18	1.06	0.17	0.03	0.07	3	0.03	7	fr
peas	1 cup	40	224	14.4	40.4	0.0	1.1	0.3	0.5	9	208	0.19	1.24	0.42	0.11	13	0.16	4	v
pineapple	1 cup	43	140	0.8	34.4	0.0	0.2	0.0	0.1	3	20	2.15	0.64	0.14	0.06	1	0	27	fr
pineapple	1 cup	11	76	0.6	19.2	0.0	0.7	0.0	0.2	2	11	1	0.65	0.14	0.06	4	0.14	24	fr
pinto beans	1 cup	86	265	15.0	49.0	0.0	0.8	0.1	0.5	3	296	0.29	0.7	0.33	0.16	1	0.33	0	v
plums	3 ea	10	55	0.5	14.4	0.0	0.1	0.0	0.0	1	15	0.67	0.45	0.02	0.06	96	0.04	3	fr
pork	3.1 oz	4	275	23.9	0.0	84.0	19.2	7.0	2.2	61	184	0.02	4.35	0.87	0.24	3	0.35	0.3	m
potato chips	14 chips	7	148	1.8	14.7	0.0	10.1	2.6	5.2	133	43	0.16	1.19	0.04	0.01	0	0.14	12	v
potatoes	1 cup	55	162	4.1	36.9	4.0	1.2	0.7	0.1	636	100	0.55	2.35	0.18	0.08	12	0.49	14	v
pretzels	10 ea	1	10	0.3	2.4	0.0	0.1	0.0	0.0	48	3	0.33	0.13	0.01	0.01	0	0.01	0	bg
raisins	1 cup	71	435	4.7	115.0	0.0	0.7	0.2	0.2	17	140	0.51	1.19	0.23	0.13	1	0.36	5	fr
rye wafers	2 ea	7	55	1.0	10.0	0.0	1.0	0.3	0.3	115	44	0.16	0.5	0.06	0.03	0	0.03	0	bg
salmon	3 oz	167	120	17.0	0.0	34.0	5.0	0.9	2.1	443	243	0.69	6.8	0.03	0.15	18	0.38	0	f
sherbet (2% fat)	1 cup	103	270	2.2	59.0	14.1	3.8	2.4	0.2	87	74	1.39	0.13	0.03	0.09	38.5	0.02	4	d
spinach	1 cup	55	12	1.6	2.0	0.0	0.2	0.0	0.1	44	27	2.04	0.41	0.04	0.11	376	0.11	16	v
strawberries	1 cup	28	245	1.4	66.1	0.0	0.3	0.0	0.2	8	33	0.85	1.2	0.04	0.13	6	0.08	106	fr
tomatoes	1 tomato	9	24	1.1	5.3	0.0	0.3	0.0	0.1	10	28	0.32	0.74	0.07	0.06	139	0.09	22	v
trout	3 oz	26	175	21.0	0.3	71.0	9.0	4.1	1.6	122	259	0.1	2.3	0.07	0.07	60	0.41	1	f
tuna	3 oz	7	165	24.0	0.0	55.0	7.0	1.4	3.1	303	199	0.04	10.1	0.04	0.09	20	0.47	0	f
turkey	3 oz	21	145	24.9	0.0	64.0	4.2	1.4	1.2	60	181	0.12	4.63	0.05	0.15	0	0.39	0	p
veal	3 oz	9	185	23.0	0.0	109.0	9.4	4.1	0.6	56	196	0.05	4.6	0.06	0.21	0	0.27	0	m
wheat bread	1 pce	32	65	2.4	11.8	0.0	1.0	0.2	0.3	135	47	0.68	1.13	0.12	0.08	0	0.03	0	bg
white bread	1 pce	32	65	2.1	12.2	0.0	1.0	0.3	0.2	129	27	1.19	0.94	0.12	0.08	0	0.01	0	bg
white rice	1 cup	44	670	12.4	149.0	0.0	0.7	0.2	0.3	9	174	0.25	6.48	0.81	0.06	0	0.3	0	g
yogurt	1 cup	275	138	7.9	10.6	29.0	7.4	4.8	0.2	104	216	1.27	0.17	0.07	0.32	68	0.07	1	d

Source: U.S. Department of Agriculture.

blood vessels, or both, fail to function properly. The underlying cause for many cardiovascular conditions is atherosclerosis (sometimes referred to as hardening of the arteries). In atherosclerosis, fats accumulate on the inner walls of vessels, reducing their flexibility and restricting blood flow. As a result of increased resistance, the heart generates greater pressure to ensure that oxygen and nutrients get to all tissues of the body. Unfortunately this extra stress on the heart can cause it to wear out faster. Excessively high blood pressure may cause vessels to balloon at points of weakness. Such enlargements are known as aneurysms and may burst and lead to substantial internal bleeding. Finally, atherosclerosis may stimulate the formation of blood clots. Such clots cause the death of tissue when they block blood flow. Clots in the brain cause strokes, and those in the coronary artery cause heart attacks.

Fortunately, we know dietary risk factors associated with cardiovascular disease and can reduce the risk by minimizing certain foods in our diets. Many physicians recommend that patients substitute polyunsaturated for saturated fats (increase unsaturated-to-saturated ratio), reduce sodium intake, and minimize cholesterol. Determine foods that should be minimized or eliminated to reduce the risk of cardiovascular disease.

1. (a) Define a *new category* (*insert column*) for the ratio of unsaturated-to-saturated fat. Define the first cell as the ratio of unsaturated fat to saturated fat for that record (divide the unsaturated fat cell by the saturated fat cell), and *copy* this formula *relatively* (to reflect the contents of each record) to all other records in the column (Table 19.6). Perform a *filter* (*record selection*) for foods with a unsaturated to saturated fat ratio less than or equal to 0.3. (b) Perform a *filter* (*record selection*) for foods

Table 19.6 Calculated Category

Food	saturate fat [g]	unsaturated fat [g]	Unsaturated: Saturated
apple	0.1	0.1	=J2/I2
apple pie	4.2	4.9	=J2/I3
asparagus	0.1	0.1	=J2/I4
avocado	4.5	3.5	=J2/I5

with a sodium content greater than 100 mg/serving. (c) Perform a *filter* (*record selection*) for foods with cholesterol greater than 10 mg/serving size. Include a printout of the foods that meet all three criteria. These foods should be minimized or eliminated in diets of those who are at risk of cardiovascular disease. What are these foods? To return to the full list, *show all records* before proceeding with another activity.

ACTIVITY 19.3.3 *Selecting Foods to Treat Vitamin Deficiencies*

Researchers have linked vitamin deficiencies with specific syndromes listed below:

Vitamin	Deficiency Syndromes
Vitamin A	night blindness; brittle skin; damaged respiratory tract
Thiamin (B$_1$)	beriberi (muscle atrophy, paralysis, congestive heart failure)
Riboflavin (B$_2$)	dermatitis, hypersensitivity to light, reddening of the cornea
Niacin	pellagra (dermatitis, diarrhea, mental confusion, irritability)
Vitamin B$_6$	dermatitis, irritation of sweat glands, convulsions
Vitamin C	scurvy (bleeding gums, anemia, painful joints, poor healing)

1. Using a database program and the nutrition database (Table 19.5), determine three foods that a nutritionist might recommend to alleviate or eliminate each of the syndromes listed. This information can be obtained by performing a *descending sort* according to the vitamin in question.

ACTIVITY 19.3.4 *Dieting and Weight Loss*

The caloric content of a food (calories per serving size) is a measure of the stored energy it possesses.

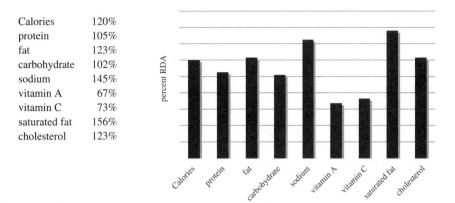

Calories	120%
protein	105%
fat	123%
carbohydrate	102%
sodium	145%
vitamin A	67%
vitamin C	73%
saturated fat	156%
cholesterol	123%

Figure 19.2 Analysis of a Personal Daily Diet

As foods are metabolized, energy is released to perform biological functions. If an individual consumes more calories than necessary, excess energy will be stored as fat. Although a certain amount of fat is essential, excessive quantities may contribute to a variety of physical problems. People who have difficulty maintaining their weight below recommended values should reduce their caloric intake. (*Note:* The following are for illustration purposes only. Consult a professional dietitian to construct the appropriate diet to meet your needs.)

1. Using the database in Table 19.5, sort (*arrange*) foods in *descending order* of caloric content per serving. Which five foods have the greatest caloric value per serving size? Which food group(s) do these foods represent (g-grain, p-poultry, fr-fruit, bg-baked goods, mx-mixed, v-vegetables, m-meat, d-dessert)? Do these results surprise you, or are they what you expect? Explain.

2. Construct a list of foods that have high vitamin content while offering a minimum of calories. Select three vitamins (A, C, riboflavin, niacin, B_6), and perform three successive *filters* (*record selections*) for foods that exceed the following values per serving size: vitamin C (10 mg), vitamin A (120 RE), riboflavin (0.30 mg), niacin (2.4 mg), vitamin B_6 (.30). *Sort* (*arrange*) this list in ascending order in terms of calories per serving size. What five foods in your list have the lowest caloric content? Which food group(s) do these foods

represent? People struggling to reduce their weight should consider including these in their diet.

ACTIVITY 19.3.5 *Analyze Your Diet*
How balanced is your diet? Record the quantities of all foods you eat in a typical day. Enter these values into an Internet-based nutritional analysis service such as the Nutritional Analysis Tool (look on *science sourcebook.com* or nat.crgq.com, or search "nutritional analysis tool").[4] Analyze your diet with respect to the USDA recommended daily allowances (RDA).

1. Generate a graph or table of your diet (Figure 19.2), and write a brief analysis, highlighting areas where your diet deviates significantly from the USDA's recommended daily allowances.

2. What can you do to improve your nutrition?

19.4 Databases in Earth and Space Science

For years, the International Star Registry has advertised that it will name a star after you or a loved one for a nominal fee. Although it claims to have "named" over a million stars, the only place where such names are recognized is in its own book, for the ISR is a private company with no authority to name stars. The International Astronomical Union, a group of professional astronomers that records the precise location of stars, officially names stars on the basis of objective criteria such as location and brightness. The precise coordinates and details of stars are recorded in databases.

It appears as though the International Star Registry and other entrepreneurs have the potential to make much more money since astronomers estimate that there are more than 200 billion stars in the universe (some estimate as many as 3000 million billion!). In the activities that follow, students will use databases to answer questions about objects closer to home: planets, asteroids, and Earth.

ACTIVITY 19.4.1 *Comparing and Contrasting the Properties of the Planets*

Astronomy books group the inner planets (Mercury, Venus, Earth, and Mars) separately from the outer planets (Jupiter, Saturn, Uranus, and Neptune). Are there any characteristics the inner planets share other than their proximity to the Sun? Are there any characteristics the outer planets share other than their great distance from the Sun?

Table 19.7 is a summary of planetary data arranged so one can sort according to a variety of characteristics (the file can be downloaded from *sciencesourcebook.com*). The outer planets are italicized. *Sort* (*arrange*) the planet database on each characteristic, and examine the listing for similarities within the two groups.

1. Identify properties that characterize the inner planets and outer planets.

2. Identify properties that cannot be used to differentiate inner and outer planets.

ACTIVITY 19.4.2 *Analyzing Asteroids*

Asteroids (Figure 19.3A) are rocky or metallic objects that orbit the Sun but are much smaller than planets. Most asteroids orbit the Sun in a belt between the orbits of Mars and Jupiter, but some have eccentric orbits, and occasionally one has an orbit that intersects the orbit of earth. The Barringer meteor crater near Winslow, Arizona (Figure 19.3B), is evidence of such a path. Figure 19.3C lists the largest asteroids, their date of discovery, distance from the sun (in astronomical units (au); 1 au = distance from the Sun to Earth), and orbital period (years). This file can be downloaded from *sciencesourcebook.com*.

1. Is there any relationship between the distance from the Sun and the time it takes to orbit (orbital period)? Explain your answer. To see if such a relationship exists, *sort* the asteroids in *ascending order* of distance from the Sun, and look for trends in orbital period.

2. Is there any relationship between the size of an asteroid and its date of discovery? Explain your answer. *Sort* asteroids in *ascending order* of discovery date and compare with diameter.

ACTIVITY 19.4.3 *Comparing and Contrasting Natural Disasters*

Earth scientists study disasters such as earthquakes, tsunamis, hurricanes (cyclones, typhoons), tornados,

Table 19.7 Planetary Data

Planet	Distance from Sun/million km	Year Length /Earth years	Day Length /Earth Days	Orbital Speed /km/s	Diameter /km	Mass /1022 kg	Density /kg/m3	Surface Gravity/m/s2	Escape Velocity/km/s	Temperature (mean)/C	composition
Uranus	2,871.00	84.01	−0.75	6.8	51,118	8,680	1,290	7.75	21.30	−216	gaseous
Neptune	4,497.10	164.79	0.80	5.4	49,528	10,200	1,640	10.99	23.30	−216	gaseous
Saturn	1,427.00	29.46	0.43	9.6	120,536	56,900	690	9.12	35.50	−180	gaseous
Jupiter	778.30	11.86	0.41	13.1	142,984	190,000	1,330	22.96	59.60	−110	gaseous
Mars	227.90	1.88	1.03	24.1	6,786	64	3,950	3.73	5.00	−60	rocky
Earth	149.60	1.00	1.00	29.8	12,756	598	5,520	9.81	11.20	20	rocky
Mercury	57.90	0.24	58.65	47.9	4,878	33.03	5,430	3.83	4.30	260	rocky
Venus	108.20	0.62	−243.01	35.0	12,102	487	5,250	8.63	10.40	480	rocky

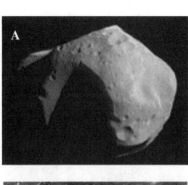

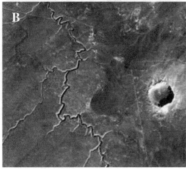

Name	C discovered	diameter (km)	distance (AU)	orbital period (y)
Ceres	1801	918	2.77	4.61
Pallas	1802	522	2.77	4.61
Juno	1804	244	2.67	4.36
Vesta	1807	500	2.36	3.63
Iris	1847	204	2.39	3.68
Hebe	1847	192	2.43	3.78
Hygiea	1849	430	3.14	5.59
Egeria	1850	114	2.58	4.14
Eunomia	1851	272	2.64	4.30
Kalliope	1852	188	2.91	4.97
Psyche	1852	264	2.92	5.00
Amphitrite	1854	240	2.55	4.08
Euphrosyne	1854	248	3.16	5.58
Daphne	1856	182	2.77	4.59
Eugenia	1857	114	2.72	4.49
Doris	1857	226	3.11	5.48
Europa	1858	312	3.10	5.46
Elpis	1860	174	2.71	4.47
Cybele	1861	246	3.43	6.37
Freia	1862	190	3.39	5.49
Sylvia	1866	272	3.49	6.52
Camilla	1868	236	3.49	6.50
Mathilde	1885	61	2.46	4.30
Eros	1898	33	1.46	33.00
Chiron	1977	180	13.72	50.80
Toutatis	1989	4.6	2.51	3.98

Figure 19.3 (A) Asteroid. (B) Barringer Meteor Crater. (C) Database

Sources: (A) Asteroid (253) Mathilde. Photo taken June 27, 1997, by the NEAR Shoemaker spacecraft. Photo courtesy of NASA. (B) Barringer Meteor Crater in Arizona seen from space. Photo taken December 14, 1982, by the Landsat satellite. Photo courtesy of NASA.

volcanoes, floods, and drought. Table 19.8 lists the 30 worst natural disasters of the twentieth century.

1. Of the events listed, which type of disaster caused the greatest loss of life in the twentieth century? To determine this, perform an *ascending sort* on the type of disaster; then perform a *subtotal/sum* after each *group* of disasters to calculate the loss of life from each.
2. Which countries suffered most from natural disasters in the twentieth century? Perform an *ascending sort* on the country and a *subtotal/ sum* on deaths, *grouping* by country, to calculate the loss of life per country.

19.5 Databases in Physics

Physicists use databases to record and access experimental data and analyze the findings of others. In this section, we explore two very different uses of databases in physics. Activity 19.5.1 looks at the classification of subatomic particles, and Activity 19.5.2 looks at the interaction of discoveries in physics and the inventions they lead to.

ACTIVITY 19.5.1 *Classification of Subatomic Particles*

Recent developments in subatomic theory have changed our perception of the nature of matter. Rather than just three fundamental particles (neutrons, electrons, protons), nuclear physicists now believe there are 12 or more, including 6 leptons and 6 quarks (Table 19.9, which you can download from *sciencesourcebook.com*). The electron, which is a type of lepton, is fundamental (composed of no other particles). Protons and neutrons are not fundamental because they are composed of quarks. The field of particle physics is changing

Table 19.8 Disasters of the Twentieth Century

Country	Year	Disaster	Continent	Killed
China	1922	Cyclone	Asia	100,000
Bangladesh	1970	Cyclone	Asia	300,000
Bangladesh	1991	Cyclone	Asia	138,866
India	1900	Drought	Asia	1,250,000
China	1920	Drought	Asia	500,000
Soviet Union	1921	Drought	Europe	1,200,000
China	1928	Drought	Asia	3,000,000
India	1942	Drought	Asia	1,500,000
India	1965	Drought	Asia	500,000
India	1966	Drought	Asia	500,000
India	1967	Drought	Asia	500,000
Ethiopia	1973	Drought	Africa	100,000
Ethiopia	1974	Drought	Africa	200,000
Ethiopia	1984	Drought	Africa	300,000
Sudan	1984	Drought	Africa	150,000
Mozambique	1985	Drought	Africa	100,000
Italy	1908	Earthquake	Europe	75,000
China	1920	Earthquake	Asia	180,000
Japan	1923	Earthquake	Asia	143,000
China	1927	Earthquake	Asia	200,000
China	1932	Earthquake	Asia	70,000
Soviet Union	1948	Earthquake	Europe	110,000
China	1976	Earthquake	Asia	242,000
China	1908	Flood	Asia	100,000
China	1911	Flood	Asia	100,000
China	1931	Flood	Asia	3,700,000
China	1935	Flood	Asia	142,000
China	1938	Flood	Asia	500,000
China	1939	Flood	Asia	500,000
China	1959	Flood	Asia	2,000,000

Table 19.9 Database of Subatomic Particles

Particle Family	Subatomic Particle	Mass (MeV)	Symbol
Leptons	Electron	0.511	e-
Leptons	Muon	105.7	m
Mesons	Pion	140	p
Mesons	K-Meson	494	K
Mesons	h-Meson	547	h
Mesons	r-Meson	769	r
Baryons	Proton	938	p
Baryons	Neutron	940	n
Baryons	L-Baryon	1116	L
Baryons	S-Baryon	1189	S
Baryons	D-Baryon	1232	D
Baryons	X-Baryon	1315	X
Baryons	W-Baryon	1672	W
Leptons	Tau-Le pton	1777	t
Mesons	D-Meson	1869	D
Mesons	y-Meson	3097	y
Mesons	B-Meson	5278	B
Mesons	U-Meson	9460	`
Leptons	Muon Neutrino	0.3	m
Leptons	Electron Neutrino	10	n
Leptons	Tau Neutrino	40	t

rapidly, and new discoveries cause us to reevaluate old classifications. Originally subatomic particles were classified on the basis of their masses. The tiniest particles were known as leptons (*lep-* means "small" in Greek), and the heaviest particles were classified as baryons (*bary-* means "heavy" in Greek). Particles of intermediate size were termed mesons (*mes-* means "middle" in Greek).

1. Is the original classification scheme of subatomic particles still applicable? *Sort* subatomic particles in the table in *ascending order* according to mass. Are baryons always the heaviest particles and leptons the lightest? Is the original classification scheme still relevant? Explain.

ACTIVITY 19.5.2 *Discovering the Interaction of Discoveries and Inventions*

Isaac Newton, one of the greatest physicists of all time, wrote in a letter to a colleague, "If I have been able to see further, it was only because I stood on the shoulders of giants." Indeed, Newton made his discoveries not in a vacuum, but only after analyzing the observations, data, and writings of his predecessors and colleagues. Today's breakthroughs are possible because modern scientists, engineers, and inventors are also "standing on the shoulders of giants." Table 19.10 (which you can download from *sciencesourcebook.com*) lists a few of the giants in the history of physics. Each of these scientists made one or more significant contributions that facilitated the work of others. For example, the invention of the radio by Guglielmo Marconi in 1896 would have been impossible without the discovery and research of Michael Faraday, James Maxwell, Heinrich Hertz, Oliver Lodge, and Nikola Tesla.

1. Create a time line of discoveries in physics by *sorting* the table in *ascending order* by the year the invention was made.
2. Discoveries in science are made only when the appropriate technology is available, and these discoveries can lead to the development of new technologies. Table 19.10 lists some significant inventions and discover-

ies made during the past five centuries. *Sort* the database in an *ascending order* by date of discovery or invention. Identify discoveries or inventions that were necessary to lead to other discoveries or inventions.

Answers to Chapter Activities

19.1.1 (1) Silver, copper, and gold. These elements are located in the same family within the transition elements. Copper is the most commonly used element in household circuits. Silver and gold are used in computer circuitry and other specialty applications. (2) Aluminum fits these criteria and is the most common element in the construction of airplanes. (3) Mercury is frequently used as a fluid conductor.

19.1.2 (1) Copper, silver, gold, and platinum are rare metals and are used in coins and jewelry. Iron and aluminum are common metals and are frequently used in construction. (2) Elements discovered many years ago, such as lead (Pb), gold (Au), and iron (Fe), have symbols that do not match their names. This is because the symbol convention was adopted before the English names were. Plumbum was the original Latin name for lead, and thus the symbol Pb was adopted. Similarly, aurum (Au) was the Latin name for gold and argentum (Ag) for silver. (3) The elements with the highest ionization energies are the noble gases, found in the right-hand column of the periodic table. Elements with the lowest ionization energies are found in the first family, the alkali metals.

19.1.3 (1) The alkali metals (family 1) and alkaline earths (family 2) are more similar to each other than are other families. (2) The alkali metals and the halogens are the most dissimilar.

19.2.1 (1) Pinaceae, Cupressaceae, Fagaceae. (2) Pinus (pine) and Quercus (oak). (3) Pinaceae. (4) Northeast and Southeast.

19.2.2 (1) proline, tyrosine, serine, leucine; (2) histidine; (3) essential: 45.8 percent; (4) tyrosine, glutamine, aspartate, threonine; (5) tyrosine.

19.2.3 Students will access the human genome database, search for the information listed, and find maps showing the locations of the various traits listed.

19.2.4 Each of these is a complex protein and will appear differently depending on the perspective viewed when printing. Emphasize that the structure of a protein determines its function (see section 12.4).

19.2.5 (1) All three of these are conifers in the order Pinales. The bristlecone pine is in Pinaceae, and the two redwoods are in Cupressaceae. All three are native to California. The bristlecone pine is also found on desert mountain ranges in the Great Basin. (2) Students will print the picture, classification, and distribution of each species.

19.3.1 (1) The list may include foods such as strawberries, white bread, yogurt, and milk.

Table 19.10 Discoveries and Inventions in Physics in the Past 500 Years

Year	Scientist	Discovery
1512	Nicholas Copernicus	heliocentic theory
1577	Tycho Brahe	nature of comets
1589	Galileo Galilei	acceleration studies
1590	Zacharias Janssen	compound microscope
1608	Hans Lippershey	refracting telescope
1609	Johannes Kepler	laws of planetary motion
1621	Willebrord Snell	law of refraction
1643	Evangelista Torricelli	mercury barometer
1645	Otto von Guericke	vacuum pump
1656	Christian Huygens	pendulum clock
1665	Isaac Newton	calculus
1668	John Wallis	law of conservation of momentum
1668	Isaac Newton	reflecting telescope
1672	Isaac Newton	theory of light and colors
1678	Christian Huygens	principle of wavefront sources
1684	Isaac Newton	Kepler's Laws proved
1698	Thomas Savery	steam pump
1705	Edmond Halley	periodicity of Halley's comet proposed
1712	Thomas Newcomen	steam engine
1724	Gabriel Fahrenheit	mercury thermometer
1769	James Watt	improved steam engine
1786	John Fitch	steam engine
1798	Henry Cavendish	determines the mass of the Earth
1799	Alessandro Volta	battery
1801	Thomas Young	wave nature of light, interference
1814	George Stephenson	steam locomotive
1814	Joseph Niepce	camera
1820	Louis Ampere	electric currents exert force
1820	Hans Christian Oersted	electricity and magnetism related
1821	Michael Faraday	electric motor
1823	William Sturgeon	electromagnet
1824	Sadi Carnot	heat engines analyzed
1826	Simon Ohm	law of electrical resistance
1831	Michael Faraday	electromagnetic induction
1837	Samuel Morse	telegraph
1843	James Joule	heat is a form of energy
1848	Lord Kelvin	absolute zero
1873	James Maxwell	light is electromagnetism
1888	Heinrich Hertz	radio waves discovered
1888	Nicola Tesla	AC motor & transformer
1896	Antoine Becquerel	radioactivity
1896	Guglielmo Marconi	radio
1897	Joseph Thomson	electron discovered
1899	Ernest Rutheford	alpha and beta particles
1904	Christian Hulsmeyer	radar
1923	Vladimir Zworykin	cathode ray tube
1928	Edwin Land	polarization
1930	Vannever Bush	computer
1932	James Chadwick	neutron
1932	Carl Anderson	positron
1933	Wolfgang Pauli	neutrinos
1942	Enrico Fermi	first controlled nuclear chain reaction
1945	Manhattan Project	atomic bomb
1947	Barden Brattain, Schoclkey	transistor
1954	Chaplin, Fuller, Pearson	solar cell
1958	Jack Kilby, Robert Noyce	integrated circuit
1963	Murray Gell-Mann	quark model
1979	Seymour Cray	super computer
1990	Tim Berners Lee	World Wide Web protocol

	Giant, Redwood	**Bristlecone Pine**	**Coast Redwood**
Kingdom	Plantae	Plantae	Plantae
Division	Coniferophyta	Coniferophyta	Coniferophyta
Class	Pinopsida	Pinopsida	Pinopsida
Order	Pinales	Pinales	Pinales
Family	Cupressaceae	Pinaceae	Cupressaceae
Genus	Sequoiadendron	Pinus	Sequoia
Species	giganteum	longaeva	sempervirens

19.3.2 (1) The list of foods to avoid may include eggs, ice cream, corn dogs, cottage cheese, yogurt, frankfurters, enchiladas, and bacon.

19.3.3 (1) vitamin A (liver, cantaloupe, Grape-Nuts), thiamin B_1 (pork, white rice, Grape-Nuts), riboflavin B_2 (liver, duck, Grape-Nuts), niacin (chicken, liver, duck, Grape-Nuts), vitamin B_6 (Grape-Nuts, beef burrito, banana), vitamin C (orange juice, broccoli, cantaloupe).

19.3.4 (1) white rice, duck, raisins, apple pie, beef burrito, representing a variety of food groups. (2) Answers will vary.

19.3.5 (1) Student answers will vary, but should resemble Figure 19.2 in form. (2) Student answers will vary.

19.4.1 (1) Distance from Sun, year length, orbital speed, diameter, mass, density, escape velocity, temperature, composition. (2) Surface gravity and day length.

19.4.2 (1) There is a direct relationship between the distance from the Sun and the orbital period. The longer the orbit, the more time it will take to orbit. (2) In general, larger asteroids were discovered first because they were easier to see; however, some larger ones were discovered later, probably because they were farther from the Sun, and therefore appeared smaller.

19.4.3 (1) Drought caused the greatest loss of life, followed by flood, earthquake, and cyclone. (2) China and India suffered the most from natural disasters.

19.5.1 (1) No. There are some mesons and leptons that are more massive than baryons.

19.5.2 (1) Students generate a time line. (2) There are many examples; for example, the transistor (1947) was a component of the integrated circuit (1958), which in turn laid the foundation for the first supercomputer (1979).

Chapter Twenty

Spreadsheets, Graphs, and Scientific Data Analysis

For the Teacher 392

20.1 Calculations and Computer Modeling 394

20.2 Relating Graphs with Real-World Experiences 398

20.3 Graphing Stories 400

20.4 Scatter and Line Graphs 402

20.5 Column and Bar Graphs 406

20.6 Pie and Area Graphs 410

20.7 High-Low, Combination, and Log Plots 413

20.8 Statistics 418

Answers to Chapter Activities 420

For the Teacher

The first personal computers were designed for electronics hobbyists and were of little use to the general population. That changed in 1979 with the release of VisiCalc, the world's first electronic spreadsheet for personal computers. Although it resembled a traditional accounting ledger, VisiCalc performed operations automatically, based on formulas entered by the user. Calculations that would normally take hours could now be performed in seconds. Immediately scientists, engineers, and others recognized the potential for personal computers, fueling the personal computer revolution.

The electronic spreadsheet has stimulated dramatic growth in scientific research by freeing scientists from tedious calculations, allowing them to focus their time and efforts generating hypotheses, designing and conducting experiments, and evaluating results. Modern spreadsheet programs can be used to perform calculations, graph data, and organize information. They are an essential tool for students of science, as well as scientific researchers. The information in this section is applicable to all common spreadsheet programs, but the examples and files downloadable from *sciencesourcebook. com* were made using Microsoft Excel. In this chapter, students will learn how to use spreadsheet programs to record, graph, and analyze laboratory data and other scientific information. Such skills are invaluable to students in the Information Age.

All of the exercises in this chapter employ scientific data and can be used to teach science concepts. Although there is discussion regarding spreadsheet mechanics, the emphasis is on using spreadsheets to analyze and interpret scientific data the way scientific researchers do. Mechanics vary by spreadsheet programs and versions of programs. As a result, I have not included specific mechanics in this chapter, but rather encourage students to use the software help menu for program-specific

questions. Search the help menus of your software for the terms and concepts written in *italics* in this chapter.

Spreadsheet Basics

The activities in this chapter use basic mathematics operations. Note that the keys for addition, subtraction, multiplication, division, exponent, and scientific notation are $+$, $-$, $*$, $/$, $\wedge$, and E, respectively (Figure 20.1B). The *order of operation* (sequence in which calculations are performed within a cell) is algebraic (Figure 20.1C).

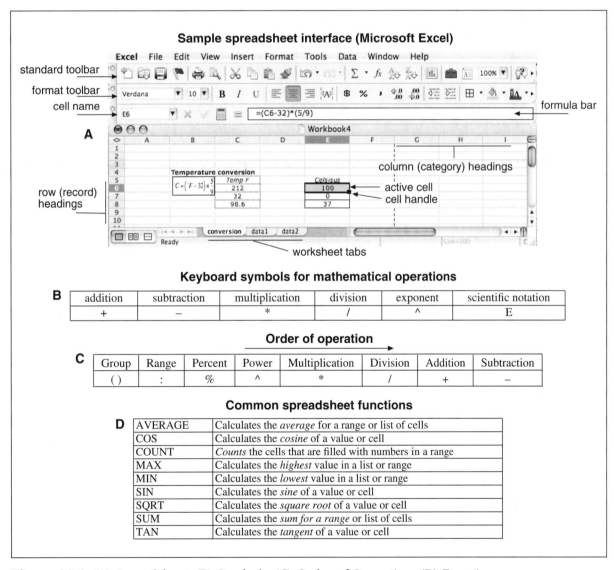

Figure 20.1 (A) Spreadsheet. (B) Symbols. (C) Order of Operation. (D) Functions

Table 20.1 Different Types of Visual Representation

	Table	Graph	Map	Diagram	Chart
Key features	precision of information	quantitative comparison	spatial relationships	nonquantitative relationships	variable
Examples	frequency table reference table spreadsheet time table	area graph bar graph histogram line graph nomograph Pareto graph scatter plot	contour map demographic map distribution map geological map relief map weather map	conceptual diagram decision chart flowchart procedural diagram	pie chart proportional chart ranking chart tree chart Venn diagram

Calculations are preceded by an equals sign (=), and functions operate on data enclosed in parentheses or brackets (the *argument*). For example, =COS(D5) returns the value for the cosine of the contents of cell D5. A range of variables is designated by a colon (:) between the beginning and ending cells. For example, =SUM(B4:B12) gives the sum of all values between B4 and B12. One can also specify a series of values by separating them with commas. For example, =SUM(B6,B9) delivers the sum of these two cells, and =SUM(B6,B7,B10: B12) delivers the sum of the two individual cells, B6 and B7, and the sum of the range from B10 to B12. Figure 20.1D lists the most frequently used *functions* in teaching science.

Spreadsheets allow *formulas* to be copied to adjacent cells. In general, formulas are copied *relatively,* meaning that the copied formula is adjusted relative to its new position. For example, if the formula =B4/B13 is copied down a cell, it will be B5/B14. Similarly, if it is copied up a cell, it will have the value B3/B12. If you want part of the formula to refer to a specific cell so the reference does not change when copied, it is necessary to use an *absolute reference,* indicated by a dollar sign ($). For example, if the formula =B4/$B$13 is copied down a cell, the first value changes relatively, while the second remains the same, =B5/$B$13.

Although all spreadsheet programs have the same fundamental capabilities, they differ in mechanics, and as a result this chapter provides only generic instructions. To plot data, the user must select relevant cells and the desired graph

format (e.g., bar, line, X-Y). Once a graph has been made, the user may redefine the *source data* (location of *data series, x-values, y-values), titles* (*chart title, x-axis title, y-axis title), axes, gridlines, legends,* and *data labels.* In most programs, users can change a feature by selecting it (right- or double-clicking on it) and choosing the options that accompany the contextual menu that appears.

In this chapter, students gain competence developing and interpreting the most common types of tables and graphs used in science (Table 20.1). *Tables* are best when precision is required, and *graphs* are best when the need is to make quantitative comparisons or see trends and relationships. However, if a user wants to show spatial relationships, it is better to use *maps*; to show nonquantitative relationships, *diagrams* are best. *Charts* can be used for a wide range of purposes. Spreadsheet programs generate *tables, graphs,* and *charts.*

20.1 Calculations and Computer Modeling

An electronic spreadsheet, such as Microsoft Excel, presents data in *worksheets* (Figure 20.1A), documents that can store, manipulate, calculate, and analyze data. Data are placed in *cells* formed at the intersection of *columns* and *rows. Cells* can hold *numbers, formulas,* or *labels.* The *address* or *reference* of a cell is the combination of the *column* and *row headings.* For example, the address B5 refers to data found at the intersection of the column B and row 5. Cells may contain *formulas* linked to the contents of other cells. For example, the formula =A5+B5 refers to the sum of the contents of cells A5 and B5. When the value of a cell is changed, all cells with formulas referring to that cell are *updated*. Note that the keys for addition, subtraction, multiplication, division, exponent, and scientific notation are +, −, *, /, ^, and E, respectively.

Figure 20.2 is a spreadsheet that shows a variety of calculations common in science. The shaded boxes on the right side of the spreadsheet reveal the formulas that are embedded in the boxed cells immediately to their left. The temperature conversion equations convert Fahrenheit to Celsius (Figure 20.2A). To convert, one must first subtract 32°F, then multiply by 5/9. The formula in D3 reads =(B3 − 32)*5/9, where B3 represents the Fahrenheit temperature in cell B3 and * indicates multiplication. The formulas in cells D4 and D5 parallel D3, referencing the temperatures in B4 and B5.

The formula for calculating the distance an object travels in free fall is $d = 1/2gt^2$, where g is the acceleration due to gravity and t is the elapsed time (Figure 20.2B). The formula in D9 is =1/2*$B$9*(C9)^2. Since g (the acceleration due to gravity) does not change, the formulas for D10 (=1/2*$B$9*(C10)^2) and D11 (=1/2*$B$9*(C11)^2) both refer to B9 where the value of g is found. A dollar sign ($) in a cell reference makes it an absolute reference for the purpose of copying. If the formula is copied to another cell, $B$9 remains the same, while the other reference (C9) changes to C10 or C11 depending on the row to which it is copied. To calculate the acceleration due to gravity on the Moon or another planet, one merely needs to substitute the applicable value for g in cell B9.

In Figure 20.2C, the force of gravity on an object at the earth's surface is calculated using Newton's Universal Law of Gravitation. The

	A	B	C	D	E	F
1	**Temperature conversion**					
2		Temp F		Celsisus		
3	$^{\circ}C = \left(^{\circ}F - 32\right) \times \dfrac{5}{9}$	212		100 ←	=(B3-32)*(5/9)	
4		32		0 ←	=(B4-32)*(5/9)	
5		98.6		37 ←	=(B5-32)*(5/9)	
6						
7	**Object in freefall**					
8		g(m/s²)	t(s)	d (m)		
9	$d = \dfrac{1}{2}gt^2$	9.8	1	4.9 ←	=1/2*$B$9*(C9)^2	
10			2	19.6 ←	=1/2*$B$9*(C10)^2	
11			3	44.1 ←	=1/2*$B$9*(C11)^2	
12						
13	**Universal Law of Gravitation**					
14				Force (N)		
15	$F = G\dfrac{m_{object}m_{earth}}{r^2}$	G	6.67E-11	9.80E+02 ←	=C15*(C16*C17)/C18^2	
16		m(object)	100			
17		m(earth)	5.97E+24			
18		r	6.38E+06			
19						
20	**Statistics**					
21		Volume (L)	Statistic	Value (L)		
22	$\displaystyle\sum_0^n v$	22.3	Sum	156.9 ←	=SUM(B22:B28)	
23		22.1	Max	23.5 ←	=MAX(B22:B28)	
24		22.4	Min	21.3 ←	=MIN(B22:B28)	
25		21.3	Aver age	22.4 ←	=AVERAGE(B22:B28)	
26		23.1	Std. Dev	0.7 ←	=STDEV(B22:B28)	
27		23.5				
28		22.2				
29						
30	**Escape velocity**					
31		Velocity (m/s)	escapes?			
32	*If...then...*	41000	yes ←	=IF(+B32>=40200,"yes","no")		
33		39000	no ←	=IF(+B33>=40200,"yes","no")		
34		37000	no ←	=IF(+B34>=40200,"yes","no")		
35		42000	yes ←	=IF(+B35>=40200,"yes","no")		

Figure 20.2 Sample Spreadsheet Calculations

equation in D15 reads =C15*(C16*C17)/C18^2/ where cell C15 contains the universal gravitational constant; *G*, C16 contains the mass of the object, C17 contains the mass of the Earth; C18 contains the radius of the Earth; and the ^ character indicates an exponent. By changing the contents of C16, the mass of the object, one can determine the force (weight) of any object. Note that mass of the Earth (C16, in kg) and the radius of the earth (C17, in meters) are so large that they must be represented in scientific format with exponential notation. 5.97E + 24 is the spreadsheet format for 5.97×10^{24} kg, the mass of the Earth, and 6.38E + 06 is the spreadsheet equivalent of 6.38×10^6 m, the radius of the Earth.

Figure 20.3D illustrates some basic statistics. The values in B22–B28 represent experimental values for the volume of 1 mole of gas at standard temperature and pressure, measured in liters. The values in D22 to D26 represent the *sum, maximum, minimum, average,* and *standard deviation* of these volumes. In each case, the statistical function is applied over the *range* of experimental values (B22:B28). Changing values in cells B22 to B28 may result in a change in the average molar volume, as well as the associated statistics. Such statistics are frequently used in laboratory experiments.

The formula in Figure 20.2E determines if a projectile going a given speed (the values listed in B32, B33, B34, or B35) will reach escape velocity and leave the Earth's gravitational field. Escape velocity is 40,200 km/h. The formulas embedded in cells C32 to C35 are logic statements =IF(+B32 > = 40200, "yes," "no"). If the contents of cell B32 (the velocity of the first craft) is greater than or equal to 40,200 km/h, then it will escape the earth's gravitational field and the formula returns the conclusion, **"yes,** it will escape." If, however, the velocity is less than 40,200 km/h, then the formula returns the conclusion, **"no,** it will not escape." The spreadsheets for this activity are available online at *sciencesourcebook.com*.

ACTIVITY 20.1.1 *Using Formulas*

Examine the formulas shown in the boxes on the left of Figure 20.3, and determine the spreadsheet representation of the formulas embedded in the shaded cells. Remember that the keys for addition, subtraction, multiplication, division, exponent, and scientific notation are +, −, *, /, ^, and E, respectively.

ACTIVITY 20.1.2 *Performing Calculations*

Figure 20.4 compares the speed of a variety of things expressed in miles per hour. Download the spreadsheet from *sciencesourcebook.com,* and convert the first entry (D3) to the metric equivalent (kilometers/hour) using the formula 5C3*1.61 (there are 1.61 km per mile); then *copy* this formula (in a *relative* manner) down the column. The new contents of D4 should read 5C4*1.61. In most spreadsheet programs, a formula can be copied by dragging the *cell handle* (Figure 20.1A) in the lower right corner of the source cell over the destination cells.

Compare the speed of the fastest human relative to each item in the list by dividing the speed of the human (35.4 km/h) by the speed of the object. For example, the formula in E3 should read 35.4/D3. Copy this formula in a relative manner throughout the column.

1. How many times faster is the fastest human than the average snail?
2. What fraction of the speed of sound can the fastest person run?

ACTIVITY 20.1.3 *Making a Conversion Tool*

Virtually all scientists use the metric system when performing measurements and calculations. Unfortunately, many Americans cannot relate to meters and liters because they have grown up using customary units such as feet and quarts.

In this activity, you will make a conversion spreadsheet that will convert metric units to customary units. Construct a spreadsheet in which you can enter a volume in liters and receive a volume measured in gallons, pecks, pints (liquid), and quarts (liquid). Refer to Table 20.2 for conversion factors. Construct a second conversion chart in which you enter a distance in meters and receive measurements in feet, miles, and yards.

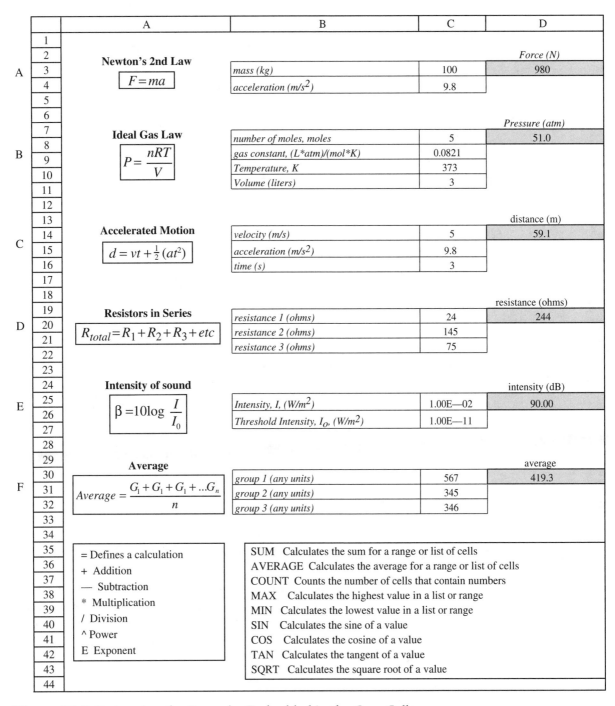

Figure 20.3 Determine the Formulas Embedded in the Gray Cells

ACTIVITY 20.1.4 *Computer Modeling of Greenhouse Gas Emissions*

One of the most powerful uses of a "number-cruncher" (spreadsheet) is to answer the question "What if . . . ?" The spreadsheet allows the user to produce models and predict outcomes. Ecologists use spreadsheets to make predictions concerning the influence of various chemicals on global warming. Figure 20.5 lists the global warming potentials (GWP) of the most common greenhouse gases. The GWP is a measure of the estimated global warming contribution due to

	A	B	C	D	E
1	**Comparison of Speeds**				
2			speed (mi/h)	speed (km/h)	speed relative to fastest human
3	Human Growth Rate		6E-09		
4	Average Snail		0.01		
5	Average Walking Pace		3		
6	First Gasoline Automobile		9		
7	Fastest Human		22	35.4	1.00
8	1908 Model T Ford		40		
9	Cheetahs' Top Speed		65		
10	Fastest Horsefly		90		
11	Fastest Roller Coaster		100		
12	Fastest Falcon Species		105		
13	Fastest Skier		154		
14	High Speed Train		186		
15	Dodge Viper's Top Speed		212		
16	Fastest Wind		318		
17	Speed of Sound		750		
18	Mach 3		2250		
19	Fastest Fighter Jet		4500		
20	Speed of Light		670000000		

Figure 20.4 Comparison of Speeds

Table 20.2 Conversion Factors

Customary	Metric	Factor
liters	gallons	0.2642
liters	pecks	0.1135
liters	pints	2.1134
liters	quarts	1.0567
meters	feet	3.2808
meters	miles	0.0006214
meters	yards	1.0936

Greenhouse Gas:	GWP	kilograms	kg CO$_2$ equivalent
Carbon dioxide (CO$_2$)	1		
Methane (CH$_4$)	21		
Nitrous Oxide (N$_2$O)	310		
CFC-11 Freon	3400		
CFC-12	7100		
sulfur hexaflouride (SF$_6$)	23,900		
Equivalent mass of carbon dioxide released			

Figure 20.5 Global Warming Potentials of Greenhouse Gases
Sources: U.S. Environmental Protection Agency. (1999). Inventory of U.S. Greenhouse Gas Emissions and Sinks: 1990–1997. *EPA 236-R-003.*

emission of 1 kg of the gas compared to the emission of 1 kg of carbon dioxide. Note that the other gases listed have GWPs substantially greater than carbon dioxide. Suppose Company X releases 34 kg of Freon, 15 kg of nitrous oxide, and 1 kg of sulfur hexafluoride, while Company Y releases

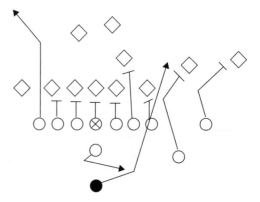

Figure 20.6 Football Offensive Play Diagram

450 kg of carbon dioxide and 120 kg of CFC-12. Which company would contribute more to global warming? Answer this question by completing the spreadsheet shown in Figure 20.5 with the appropriate formulas.

20.2 Relating Graphs to Real-World Experiences

Football coaches develop plays based on the strength and talents of their players and opponents. A playbook includes many diagrams like the one illustrated in Figure 20.6. Each circle represents a player, each diamond an opponent, and each line a planned movement. Team members must memorize many such diagrams so they can quickly assemble the correct formation when the quarterback calls for a play. In a similar manner, choreographers develop diagrams to show dancers how to move, and marching band directors develop maps to show how half-time shows will be performed. Although football players, dancers, or drum majors may comprehend such diagrams, they do not fully understand them until they have put them into action. In a similar manner,

it is difficult to fully understand a scientific graph until you have done the activity it represents. In this section, students will learn motion graphs by doing the motions they represent.

ACTIVITY 20.2.1 *Walking Through Motion Graphs*

The instructor will select graphs for you to demonstrate by walking (Figure 20.7). Examine the graph carefully, noting the axes and defining

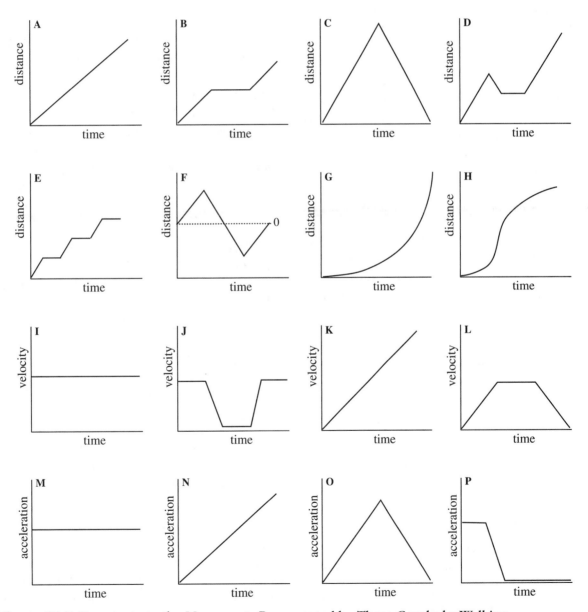

Figure 20.7 Demonstrate the Movements Represented by These Graphs by Walking

your zero point before beginning. Classmates should evaluate your movement to see if it correctly reflects the graph. If available, use a motion detector and associated probeware to compare your movement with the graph (see Chapter Twenty-Two).

20.3 Graphing Stories

In 1958 C. David Keeling of the Scripps Institution of Oceanography started recording the atmospheric carbon dioxide levels at the Mauna Loa Observatory in Hawaii.[1] His work was later adopted by the National Oceanic and Atmospheric Administration (NOAA), which continuously plots carbon dioxide data year-around. The graph of these data (Figure 20.8) tells one of the most important stories in science. The spreadsheet of these data is available online (see *sciencesourcebook.com*, or search "Mauna Loa carbon dioxide graph").

Hawaii is in the middle of the Pacific Ocean, far from other population centers. It is therefore a good location for monitoring global atmospheric change. Note that there are predictable seasonal variations (the small teeth on the graph) and a definite trend of increasing carbon dioxide concentration. In the 40 years between 1966 and 2006, the average yearly atmospheric carbon dioxide concentration increased from approximately 320 ppm to 380 ppm, an increase of nearly 20 percent! Carbon dioxide is known to capture infrared radiation and retain heat. The picture in Figure 20.8 tells an interesting and worrisome story. Since carbon dioxide traps infrared radiation, if carbon dioxide concentration continues to increase, then global temperatures can be expected to rise. The rapid increase in carbon dioxide and the resulting rapid change in climate may cause great problems for agriculture and natural ecosystems. Figure 20.8 tells the story of the main cause of global warming: the increase in atmospheric carbon dioxide concentrations that results from the burning of fossil fuels (coal, natural gas, and petroleum) and the removal of vegetation that consumes carbon dioxide (deforestation, desertification).

Graph reading and interpretation are an important aspect of literacy. You cannot understand the financial, weather, or sports sections of the newspaper without being able to interpret statistics and graphs, much less scientific and environmental stories like that told by Figure 20.8. In Activity 20.3.1, you will learn how to recognize stories in graphs and create stories from graphs.

ACTIVITY 20.3.1 *Matching Stories with Graphs*

Examine the four graphs in each set that refers to the following questions in Figure 20.9. Identify the graph that best represents each of the following stories:

1. A commuter bus stops at a series of major intersections.
2. A swinging pendulum experiences substantial friction.
3. A driver cautiously accelerates from a stop sign and enters a freeway.
4. A rocket engine fires continuously on a spacecraft in orbit around the Earth.

ACTIVITY 20.3.2 *Creating Stories from Graphs*

Figures 20.10A to 20.10D are distance versus time graphs for runners in a marathon. Write a plausible story for each runner that can explain the corresponding graph. Figures 20.10E to 20.10H plot the water level in a small child's swimming pool as

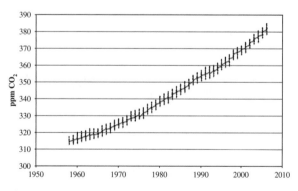

Figure 20.8 Atmospheric Carbon Dioxide Concentrations at the Mauna Loa Observatory
Source: National Oceanic and Atmospheric Administration. (2007). *Atmospheric carbon dioxide at the Mauna Loa Observatory.* Earth System Research Laboratory, Global Monitoring Division. Retrieved May 1, 2007, from http://www.esrl.noaa.gov/gmd/ccgg/trends.

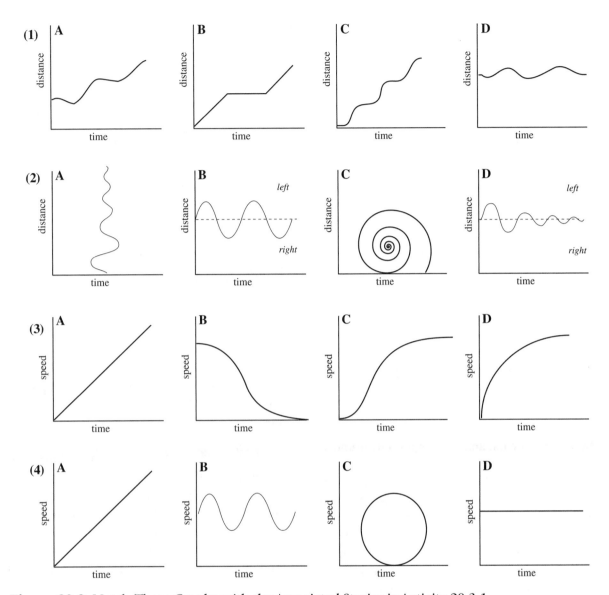

Figure 20.9 Match These Graphs with the Associated Stories in Activity 20.3.1

a function of time on each of three days. Write a story to explain each.

ACTIVITY 20.3.3 *Creating Graphs from Stories*

Draw graphs of each of the following stories. Analyze the story, select the appropriate *x*-axis (independent variable) and *y*-axis (dependent variable) labels, and plot a rough graph.

1. Dribbling a basketball
2. Traveling up the lift hill and down the first drop of a roller-coaster
3. Money placed in the bank at a constant rate of interest

4. A thermostatically controlled air conditioner is turned on in a warm room
5. The movement of bridesmaids in a wedding march
6. The height of grass of a well-maintained lawn during growing season
7. The radioactive decay of the unstable isotope uranium-238
8. A trumpet player practicing scales from middle C to high C and back twice
9. The speed of an orbiting spacecraft
10. The population growth of mice introduced to a very small island, where the population is ultimately limited by the food supply

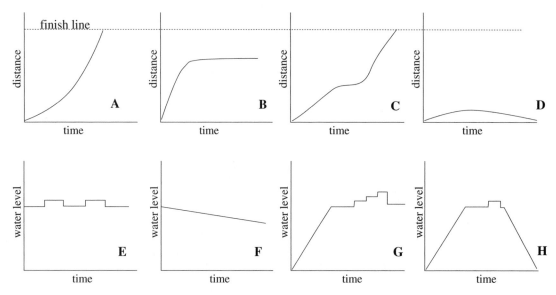

Figure 20.10 Create Stories from These Graphs

20.4 Scatter and Line Graphs

Spreadsheet programs offer scientists a variety of ways to graph data, and it is important to understand the nature of the data before selecting a type of graph. The data to be graphed should be entered in corresponding rows or columns, as illustrated in Figure 20.11A. Select the data to be plotted, and then use the graphing or charting tool to create the appropriate graph. Label the axes on your chart. *Note:* The instructions in this section are general because the mechanics vary from program to program. Refer to the spreadsheet help menu for details not mentioned in this section. (Associated spreadsheet files and links may be found at *sciencesourcebook.com.*) Initially you may find it easiest simply to change the values in the existing spreadsheets and observe changes in the associated graphs.

ACTIVITY 20.4.1: *Displaying Data as a Scatter (x-y) Plot*

Perhaps the most common format for plotting experimental data is the *scatter plot* (*x-y plot*) that can show a relationship between two variables (Figure 20.11B). The independent variable is placed on the *x*-axis and the dependent variable on the *y*-axis. The independent variable must represent a continuum, such as temperature, time, or light intensity, rather than discrete points or factors such as blood type, habitat, or wing design. For example, there is a continuum between any two times (e.g., one can divide the time between 5.0 and 5.2 seconds ad infinitum), but not between blood types (you have A, B, AB, or O, but nothing in between). Figure 20.11B is a scatter (x-y) plot of atmospheric ozone concentration in the Los Angeles basin as a function of time for a smoggy day in September 2006. Although the measurements were made at 1 hr intervals, they could have been made at any time in between because time is a continuous variable. When the data points are plotted, the relationship between time and ozone concentration is clear. The atmospheric ozone concentration varies throughout the day, regardless of location. It is highest in the early afternoon and lowest at night.

1. *Air pollution trends:* Figure 20.11B demonstrates changes in ozone concentration in a 24 hr period in the mountains and valleys of Los Angeles for a given day in September. Compare these data with those from the same day at the beach by plotting the data from the "beach" column. Does ozone pollution at

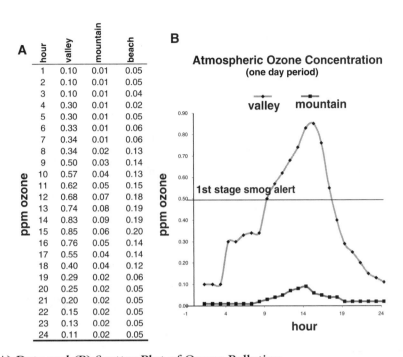

hour	valley	mountain	beach
1	0.10	0.01	0.05
2	0.10	0.01	0.05
3	0.10	0.01	0.04
4	0.30	0.01	0.02
5	0.30	0.01	0.05
6	0.33	0.01	0.06
7	0.34	0.01	0.06
8	0.34	0.02	0.13
9	0.50	0.03	0.14
10	0.57	0.04	0.13
11	0.62	0.05	0.15
12	0.68	0.07	0.18
13	0.74	0.08	0.19
14	0.83	0.09	0.19
15	0.85	0.06	0.20
16	0.76	0.05	0.14
17	0.55	0.04	0.14
18	0.40	0.04	0.12
19	0.29	0.02	0.06
20	0.25	0.02	0.05
21	0.20	0.02	0.05
22	0.15	0.02	0.05
23	0.13	0.02	0.05
24	0.11	0.02	0.05

Figure 20.11 (A) Data and (B) Scatter Plot of Ozone Pollution

Source: Environmental Protection Agency (2006). *Air quality maps—Los Angeles basin.* Retrieved May 2, 2007, from http://airnow.gov.

the beach show the same daily fluctuations? Where is ozone pollution the worst?

2. *Air pollution trends in your region.* Access the Environmental Protection Agency Web site (epa.gov) or your local air quality management district Web site, and obtain the values for ozone or other air pollutants for a given day in the closest large city. Record the time in one column and the pollution concentration in the adjacent column. It is not necessary to have data at even time intervals since time is a continuous variable. Plot data such that time is on the *x*-axis (independent variable) and pollution concentration is on the *y*-axis. Adjust the *y*-axis *scale* so daily variations can be clearly seen. Plot data for three days on three separate plots, and summarize the trends.

3. *Body size and brain size:* Scientific researchers are always searching for correlations between variables in an attempt to better understand the world around us. Such studies have led to many important discoveries, such as the link between smoking and lung cancer and the link between alcohol consumption and fetal alcohol syndrome. Figure 20.12A reports data for average body weight and brain size for a variety of animals. Plot these data such that body weight is on the *x*-axis and brain weight is on the *y*-axis. Does there appear to be a relationship between body weight and brain size? Add a linear *trend line* (best-fit line) to the chart. Are humans above or below the trend line? Explain your answer.

4. *Classifying stars:* Astronomers classify stars according to their temperature and absolute brightness. A plot of absolute brightness versus temperature is known as a Hertzsprung-Russell diagram and is used to identify stars as main sequence stars, white dwarfs, giants, and super giants. Figure 20.12B shows the temperature and absolute brightness measures for stars easily seen from earth. Make a Hertzsprung-Russell diagram by creating an x-y (scatter plot) plot in which temperature is on the *x*-axis and absolute brightness is on the

Brain wt vs. body wt.

species	body wt. (kg)	brain wt. (g)
Mountain beaver	.35	8.1
Gray wolf	36.33	119.5
Guinea pig	1.04	5.5
Asian elephant	2547	4603
Potar monkey	10	115
Giraffe	529	680
Gorilla	207	406
Human	62	1320
African elephant	6654	5712
Rhesus monkey	6.8	179
Mouse	0.023	0.4
Rabbit	2.5	12.1
Jaguar	100	157
Chimpanzee	52.16	440
Rat	0.28	1.9
Mole	0.122	3

Brightest Stars

Star	Temp	M(V)
Delta Canis Majoris	6100	−8
Deneb	9340	−7.2
Rigel	12,140	−7.2
Alnitak	33,600	−5.9
Betelgeuse	3200	−5.7
Theta Scorpii	7400	−5.6
Adhara	23,000	−5.2
Antares	3340	−5.2
Beta Centauri	25,500	−5.1
Beta Crucis	28,000	−4.7
Mirfak	7700	−4.6
Polaris	6100	−4.6
Bellatrix	23,000	−4.3
Shaula	25,500	−3.4
Spica	25,500	−3.4
Alpha Crucis B	20,500	−3.3
Achemar	20,500	−2.4
Avior	4900	−2.1
Elnath	12,400	−1.6
Aldebaran	4130	−0.8
Regulus	13,260	−0.8
Capella	5150	−0.6
Gacrux	3750	−0.5
Arcturus	4590	−0.4
Alhena	9900	0
Dubhe	4900	0.2
Vega	9900	0.5
Sirius A	9620	1.4
Fomalhaut	9060	2
Altair	8060	2.2
Procyon A	6580	2.6
Alpha Centari A	5840	4.3
Sun	5840	4.8

Sunspots per year

year	#	year	#
1964	10	1980	155
1965	15	1981	140
1966	47	1982	116
1967	94	1983	67
1968	106	1984	46
1969	106	1985	18
1970	105	1986	13
1971	67	1987	29
1972	69	1988	100
1973	38	1989	158
1974	35	1990	143
1975	16	1991	146
1976	13	1992	94
1977	28	1993	55
1978	93	1994	30
1979	155	1995	18

Figure 20.12 Data on (A) Body and Brain Weight, (B) Star Intensity, and (C) Sunspot Activity

Source: Gurman, J. (2001). Huge sunspot group—Active region 9393. Solar and Heliospheric Observatory. Retrieved May 2, 2007, from http://sohowww.nascom.nasa.gov. Data and image courtesy of NASA.

y-axis. Draw a line through the dots that form a trend diagonally across the chart. These stars are part of the main sequence. Is the Sun a main sequence star?

5. *Sunspots:* A sunspot is a relatively cool region of the photosphere (Sun's surface) that is characterized by intense magnetic activity. Figure 20.12C records some the major sunspots by year from 1970 to 1999. Plot the number of sunspots as a function of time on an x-y (scatter plot). Describe the pattern you see.

ACTIVITY 20.4.2 *Displaying Data with Line Graphs*

A *line graph* is similar to an x-y plot, except that the independent variable is discrete and evenly spaced. For example, Figure 20.13 shows the relationship of atomic radius to atomic number. The atomic radius is one of the most important properties of an atom and influences a number of other properties, such as boiling point, melting point, and reactivity. Atomic radius is a continuous variable, but atomic number is a discrete, evenly spaced variable. Atomic number represents the quantity of protons in the nucleus of an atom and therefore can be represented only by whole numbers. There can be two or three protons in a nucleus but not 2.2 or 2.356.

Chemistry

1. *Is boiling point a periodic property?* The periodic table of the elements derives its name from the fact that many properties are *periodic,* or repeating. Members of a family (column) share similar characteristics, so when a property is plotted as a function of atomic number, the repeating patterns are noticeable. Notice that atomic radius is periodic (Figure 20.13B), with

A

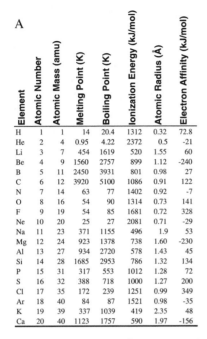

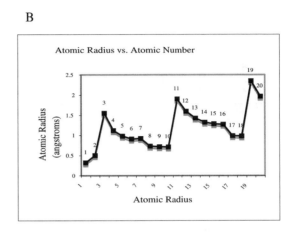

B

Element	Atomic Number	Atomic Mass (amu)	Melting Point (K)	Boiling Point (K)	Ionization Energy (kJ/mol)	Atomic Radius (Å)	Electron Affinity (kJ/mol)
H	1	1	14	20.4	1312	0.32	72.8
He	2	4	0.95	4.22	2372	0.5	-21
Li	3	7	454	1619	520	1.55	60
Be	4	9	1560	2757	899	1.12	-240
B	5	11	2450	3931	801	0.98	27
C	6	12	3920	5100	1086	0.91	122
N	7	14	63	77	1402	0.92	-7
O	8	16	54	90	1314	0.73	141
F	9	19	54	85	1681	0.72	328
Ne	10	20	25	27	2081	0.71	-29
Na	11	23	371	1155	496	1.9	53
Mg	12	24	923	1378	738	1.60	-230
Al	13	27	934	2720	578	1.43	45
Si	14	28	1685	2953	786	1.32	134
P	15	31	317	553	1012	1.28	72
S	16	32	388	718	1000	1.27	200
Cl	17	35	172	239	1251	0.99	349
Ar	18	40	84	87	1521	0.98	-35
K	19	39	337	1039	419	2.35	48
Ca	20	40	1123	1757	590	1.97	-156

Figure 20.13 (A) Data on Elements 1–20. (B) Atomic Radius Versus Atomic Number

relatively high radii in the first family (elements 3, 11, and 19) and small radii in the noble gases (elements 2, 8, 18). Create a line graph of boiling point versus atomic number for the first 20 elements using the data provided in Figure 20.13A. Is boiling point a periodic property? Which families have the highest and lowest boiling points?

2. *Is melting point a periodic property?* Create a line graph of melting point versus atomic number for the first 20 elements using the data provided in Figure 20.13A. Is melting point a periodic property? Which families have the highest and lowest melting points?

3. *Is atomic mass a periodic property?* Create a line graph of atomic mass versus atomic number for the first 20 elements using the data provided in Figure 20.13A. Is atomic weight a periodic property?

4. *Is first ionization energy a periodic property?* First ionization energy is the energy required to remove the first electron from an atom and is a measure of how reactive an element is. Elements with extremely high ionization energies will not ionize to form ionic bonds.

Create a line graph of first ionization energy for the first 20 elements using the data provided in Figure 20.13A. Is first ionization energy periodic? Which families have the highest and lowest ionization energies?

5. *Is electron affinity a periodic property?* Create a line graph of electron affinity for the first 20 elements using the data provided in Figure 20.13A. Is electron affinity a periodic property? Which families have the highest and lowest electron affinities?

Biology

6. *How did life expectancy change during the twentieth century?* Life expectancy is defined as the average number of years that a person can be expected to live. Figure 20.14A shows the average life expectancy for Americans born in the years specified. Create a line graph of life expectancy as a function of birth year, and summarize your findings. List the factors that you believe have influenced the trends you see.

7. *What are the trends in the causes of death?* The twentieth century was marked by dramatic improvements in medicine, as reflected in the

A	year born	life expectancy (y)	deaths from tuberculosis	deaths from cancer	deaths from cardiovascular problems
	1900	49	194	64	345
	1910	52	154	76	372
	1920	56	113	83	365
	1930	59	71	97	414
	1940	63	46	120	486
	1950	68	23	140	511
	1960	70	6	149	522
	1970	71	3	163	496
	1980	74	1	184	436
	1990	75	1	203	368
	2000	77	0	201	340

B	mammals	birds	amphibians	reptiles	fish	plants
1980	36	61	25	8	47	59
1985	48	72	26	8	64	118
1990	61	83	32	11	86	240
1995	66	91	33	12	105	525
2000	72	93	36	18	114	736

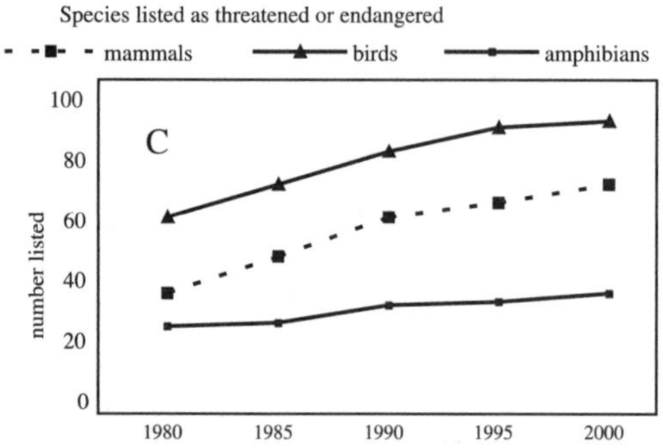

Figure 20.14 (A) Life Expectancy. (B) Endangered Species. (C) Endangered Species Growth
Sources: (A) U.S. Census Bureau. (2007). *Vital statistics.* Retrieved May 1, 2007, from http://www.census.gov. (C) U.S. Fish and Wildlife Service. (2007). *Rare and endangered species.* Retrieved May 2, 2007, from http://www.fws.gov/endangered.

increase in life expectancy (Figure 20.14A). Are people still dying of the same diseases? Create a line graph of death rate (deaths per 100,000 population) for tuberculosis, cancer, and cardiovascular disease such as heart attacks. Explain the trends you see.

8. *Rare and endangered species:* In an effort to preserve biodiversity, the U.S. Wildlife service lists species that are threatened or endangered with extinction. Figure 20.14B shows the number of species that have received this designation between 1980 and 2000. Figure 20.14C plots the trends for mammals, birds, and amphibians. Plot the values for reptiles, fish, and plants on a similar graph and summarize your findings.

20.5 Column and Bar Graphs

Spreadsheet programs allow users to plot data in columns. This is particularly useful when the dependent variable is neither continuous nor evenly spaced, or when the researcher wants to highlight specific divisions of data. Column and bar graphs include the following forms: *columns, stacked columns, Pareto, bar,* and *clustered bar,* each has advantages for displaying certain types of data. The following activities demonstrate the usefulness of column and bar graphs in science.

ACTIVITY 20.5.1 *Column Chart: Comparing Between Different Items*

A *column graph* allows comparisons between different items. Categories are organized horizontally and values vertically. A stacked column chart allows comparison between items in a group, as well as between groups (Figure 20.15A). Figure 20.15B shows the population profiles of the United States and Afghanistan in 2000. The vertical axis represents the percentage of the population in a particular age bracket. Note that Afghanistan had a much younger population than the United States, with a very small older population. Such differences result from the high birthrates and low life expectancies characteristic of many developing nations.

1. *Biology: Population profiles:* Plot the population age profile for Germany using data from Figure 20.15A. Does this profile more closely

Age Profiles (2004)
source: US Census Bureau

Wolf Repopulation
in Yellowstone NP

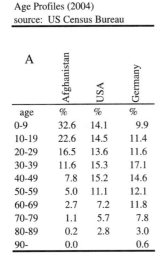

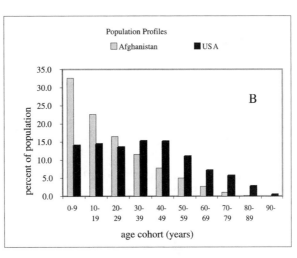

A	Afghanistan	USA	Germany
age	%	%	%
0-9	32.6	14.1	9.9
10-19	22.6	14.5	11.4
20-29	16.5	13.6	11.6
30-39	11.6	15.3	17.1
40-49	7.8	15.2	14.6
50-59	5.0	11.1	12.1
60-69	2.7	7.2	11.8
70-79	1.1	5.7	7.8
80-89	0.2	2.8	3.0
90-	0.0		0.6

C year	Yellowstone	Northern Range
1995	21	21
1996	37	30
1997	69	32
1998	83	42
1999	72	35
2000	117	65
2001	131	70
2002	148	78
2003	174	98

Figure 20.15 (A) Age Profile Data. (B) Graph of Age Profile Data. (C) Wolf Repopulation Data
Source: Smith, D., Stahler, D., & Guernsey, D. (2004). *Yellowstone wolf project: Annual report, 2003.* Yellowstone National Park, WY: National Park Service.

resemble that of the United States or Afghanistan? Explain your answer. Obtain population profile data of three countries of your choice from the U.S. Census Bureau Web site or other reputable source (see *sciencesourcebook.com* or www.census.gov). Create column graphs, and determine if their population profiles more closely resemble those of developed or developing nations.

2. *Ecology: Wolf repopulation in Yellowstone National Park:* In the nineteenth century, ranchers, farmers, and hunters made a concerted effort to eradicate wolves from the western United States. Wolves are a predatory animal that travel in packs and were seen as a nuisance for ranchers and farmers because they prey on livestock and other animals. Removing wolves upset the food web and allowed the excessive growth of elk and deer populations, which subsequently overgrazed rangelands and woodlands. In 1995 the National Park Service reintroduced wolves into Yellowstone National Park in order to reestablish the natural balance. The wolves were originally introduced in the northern range of the park but have now spread to other regions. Produce a column graph of the wolf population of the northern range compared to the park as a whole

using the data in Figure 20.15C. Describe the growth and distribution of the wolf population between 1995 and 2003.

ACTIVITY 20.5.2 *Stacked Column Charts: Comparing Within and Between Groups*

A stacked column chart allows comparison between items in a group, as well as between groups. Figure 20.16B is a stacked column plot of the snowfall by month at Mammoth Mountain, California, one of America's premier ski resorts. Comparisons of snowfall in the same month in subsequent years can be made by examining a single column. Alternatively, one can compare the average snowfall from month to month by comparing the heights of columns.

1. *Environmental science: Rechargeable batteries:* Batteries have become an essential commodity in developed societies, powering a wide array of portable electronic devices. People use rechargeable batteries because they seem more environmentally friendly than disposable ones. Unfortunately, one of the most popular rechargeable varieties, the nickel-cadmium, contains a toxic heavy metal, cadmium, that has been found in aquifers, probably as a result of leaching from batteries dumped in

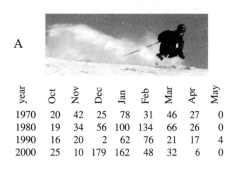

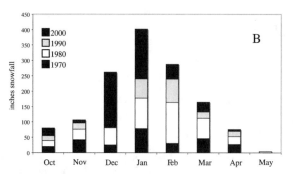

year	Oct	Nov	Dec	Jan	Feb	Mar	Apr	May
1970	20	42	25	78	31	46	27	0
1980	19	34	56	100	134	66	26	0
1990	16	20	2	62	76	21	17	4
2000	25	10	179	162	48	32	6	0

Figure 20.16 Stacked Column Graph at Mammoth Mountain, California
Source: California Department of Water Resources. (2007). *Snow course data.* Retrieved May 1, 2007, from http://cdec.water.ca.gov.

Table 20.3 Rechargeable Batteries: Percentage Market Share

	1992	1993	1994	1995	1996	1997
Nickel cadmium	100%	89%	83%	73%	58%	45%
Nickel metal hydride	0%	11%	17%	25%	32%	41%
Lithium ion	0%	0%	0%	2%	11%	14%

landfills. Recognizing the need to produce more environmentally friendly rechargeable batteries, chemists developed the nickel-metal-hydride and eventually the lithium battery. Table 20.3 shows the transition in rechargeable battery sales from 1992 to 1997. Plot these data in stacked columns, so that each column shows the percentage market share of each battery type each year.

ACTIVITY 20.5.3 *Pareto Charts: Ranking Data Graphically*

A *Pareto chart* is a specialized form of a column chart in which the categories are arranged so that the tallest bar is on the left, descending to the shortest bar on the right. Generally the space between subsequent columns is removed. By arranging the bars in order of height, attention is given to the more important categories. Figure 20.17A illustrates the elemental composition of the human body in descending percentage from hydrogen to sulfur, clearly showing that the body is made up mostly of hydrogen, oxygen, and carbon.

1. *Earth science: Seawater composition:* Seawater is uniformly saline, meaning that the relative concentration of ions is similar throughout the world. Minerals and ions enter the ocean from rivers, thermal vents, volcanoes, and the leaching of rocks on the ocean floor. Water evaporates from the surface of the ocean, leaving behind minerals and ions that make ocean water "salty." Create a Pareto chart of the main ions found in seawater using the data in Figure 20.17B.

2. *Ecology: Threatened and endangered species.* In 1973, the United States passed the Endangered Species Act, regulating a wide range of activities that might affect species threatened with extinction. An organism is classified as endangered if it is in immediate danger of extinction and threatened if it is likely to become endangered in the foreseeable future. The law protects threatened and endangered species and requires the protection of habitat necessary for their survival and recovery. Using data from Figure 20.17C, create a Pareto graph showing the states with the rarest and most endangered species. Offer an explanation for the large numbers of endangered species in the top two states.

ACTIVITY 20.5.4 *Bar Charts: Graphing Qualitative Independent Variables*

A *bar chart* is similar to a column chart, but the axes are reversed. Bar charts are best suited for qualitative independent variables. Figure 20.18 shows the mineral composition of the Earth and

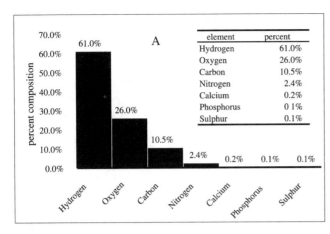

Figure 20.17 Elemental Composition of (A) Humans and (B) Seawater. (C) Endangered Species per State

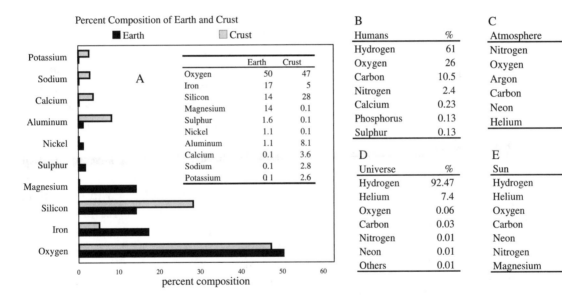

Figure 20.18 Compositions of (A) Earth, (B) Humans, (C) Atmosphere, (D) Universe, (E) Sun

Earth's crust. The independent variable is mineral type, which is a qualitative, discrete variable.

1. *What is the universe made of?* Create a bar graph showing the elemental composition of the universe.
2. *What is the atmosphere made of?* Create a bar graph showing the elemental composition of the atmosphere.
3. *What is the ocean made of?* Create a bar graph showing the elemental composition of the oceans.

4. *What are humans made of?* Create a bar graph showing the elemental composition of the human body. Is the composition of the human body more similar to the Sun, the atmosphere, or the oceans?

ACTIVITY 20.5.5 *Clustered Bar Charts: Comparing Composition of Various Items*

A *clustered bar chart* allows rapid comparison of the composition of different items. For example, Figure 20.19 shows the comparative composition of vegetable oils. A quick glance reveals

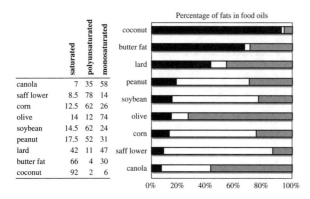

Figure 20.19 Clustered Bar Chart of Oil Composition in Foods

Table 20.4 Blood Types as Percentage of Population

	O	A	B	AB
Koreans	28	32	30	10
Egyptians	32	36	24	8
Kenyan	60	19	20	1
English	46	42	9	3
Navajo	73	27	0	0

that coconut oil has a very high percentage of saturated fats, and safflower oil has a very low percentage. Nutritionists advise diets low in saturated fats since these fats have been shown to stimulate blood cholesterol and contribute to cardiovascular diseases. The clustered bar chart allows consumers to make a quick comparison among different oils.

1. *Physiology: Is blood type distribution the same for all ethnicities?* Human blood is classified as A, B, AB, or O, depending on whether it contains the A antigen, B antigen, both the A and B antigens, or neither. Blood transfusions may be necessary to sustain life following accidents or surgery, but the wrong mixture of blood types may be fatal. For this reason, blood specialists must classify all donor blood according to type. Construct a clustered bar chart from the data in Table 20.4, and summarize any significant differences in the distribution of blood types between these groups.

20.6 Pie and Area Graphs

Pie charts (Figure 20.20B) illustrate the relative magnitude of a category by the portion of a circle it occupies. *Area graphs* (Figure 20.22B) illustrate the magnitude of change over time. Pie and area charts use the size of the plot, rather than its position, to emphasize key features.

ACTIVITY 20.6.1 *Pie Charts: Comparing Relative Magnitude Within a Data Series*
Pie charts show only one data series and are useful when emphasizing a significant element. For example, Figure 20.20B shows the leading causes of death in the United States.

1. *What are the causes of death in developing and developed countries?* Figures 20.20C and 20.20D list the leading causes of death in developed and developing countries according to data collected by the World Health Organization. (Note that the classifications differ from those reported for the United States by the U.S. Center for Disease Control in Figure 20.20A.) Construct a pie chart of the 10 leading causes of death in developing countries, and compare it with the 10 leading causes of death in developed countries. Describe the differences, and offer an explanation for these differences.

2. *Which biomes are most productive?* Figure 20.21A lists the approximate percentages of the Earth's surface that are covered by various biomes and the percentages of the total productivity (amount of biomass produced) accounted for by each biome. Develop pie charts showing the percentage coverage and the percentage productivity such as those shown in Figures 20.21B and 20.21C. Which biomes have the highest and lowest productivity per unit area? Why is deforestation of the tropical rain forests a global concern?

3. *Sources of energy:* The United States and many other developed nations are dependent on foreign sources of energy, particularly oil, to fuel their economies. What percentage of America's

A	Causes of Death in the US 2005	
1	heart disease	654,092
2	cancer	550,270
3	stroke	150,147
4	chronic respiratory diseases	123,884
5	accidents	108,694
6	influenza & pneumonia	61,472
7	diabetes	72,815
8	Alzheimers disease	65,829
9	all other causes	500,000

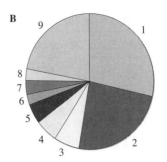

Leading Causes of Death, 2001

C	Developed nations		D	Developing nations	
	Heart disease	3,512,000		HIV-AIDS	2,678,000
	Stroke	3,346,000		Lower respiratory infections	2,643,000
	Respiratory disease (COPD)[a]	1,829,000		Ischemic heart disease	2,484,000
	Lower respiratory infections	1,180,000		Diarrhea	1,793,000
	Lung cancer	938,000		Cerebrovascular disease	1,381,000
	Car accident	669,000		Childhood diseases	1,217,000
	Stomach cancer	657,000		Malaria	1,103,000
	High blood pressure	635,000		Tuberculosis	1,021,000
	Tuberculosis	571,000		Respiratory disease (COPD)[a]	748,000

[a] chronic obstructive pulmonary disease

Figure 20.20 Causes of Death in (A) the United States, (B) Pie chart of A, (C) Developed Nations, and (D) Developing Nations
Sources: (A) National Center for Health Statistics. (2007). *Deaths—Leading causes.* Centers for Disease Control. Retrieved May 2, 2007, from http://www.cdc.gov. (C, D) World Health Organization. (2007). *Mortality database.* Retrieved May 2, 2007, from http://www.who.int.

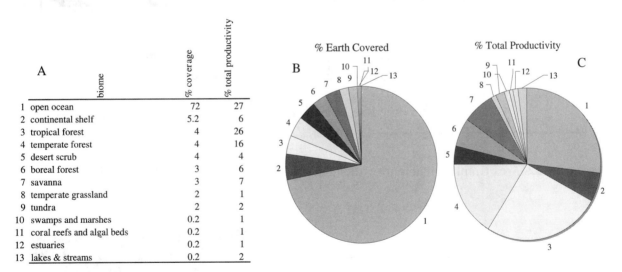

A	biome	% coverage	% total productivity
1	open ocean	72	27
2	continental shelf	5.2	6
3	tropical forest	4	26
4	temperate forest	4	16
5	desert scrub	4	4
6	boreal forest	3	6
7	savanna	3	7
8	temperate grassland	2	1
9	tundra	2	2
10	swamps and marshes	0.2	1
11	coral reefs and algal beds	0.2	1
12	estuaries	0.2	1
13	lakes & streams	0.2	2

Figure 20.21 (A) Size of Each Biome. (B) Percentage of Earth Covered by Biome. (C) Percentage Total Productivity

energy comes from the burning of fossil fuels (oil, coal, natural gas)? Create a pie chart of American energy consumption from the data in Table 20.5. Shade the renewable resources

in a different color from the nonrenewable resources. What percentage of our energy comes from renewable sources (hydroelectric, geothermal, wind, biomass, and solar)?

Table 20.5 U.S. Energy

Source	Percentage
Oil	38.8
Natural Gas	23.2
Coal	22.9
Nuclear	7.6
Hydroelectric	3.8
Biomass	3.2
Geothermal	0.3
Solar	0.1
Wind	0.04

ACTIVITY 20.6.2 *Area Graphs: Illustrating the Magnitude of Change over Time*

Area charts emphasize the magnitude of change over time. By displaying the sum of plotted values, an *area chart* shows the relationship of parts to the whole. Figure 20.22A shows a table of the number of trees infected on each slope. Figure 20.22B documents the spread of an infestation of bark beetles on four sides of a mountain over a period of 10 months. The graph shows that the spread has been most severe on the south and east slopes.

1. *Seed germination:* Area graphs are an excellent tool for plotting experimental data such as those shown in Figure 20.23A. Fifty seeds each of a wild, hybrid, and mutant plant were observed for 2 weeks after planting. Graph the cumulative seed germination rate using an area graph.
2. *Commercial satellite launches:* The Information Revolution has created a large demand for communications satellites to relay information from one part of the Earth to another. Private

Trees infected on each slope

	month	north	east	south	west
A	1	2	4	1	1
	2	4	3	3	4
	3	6	6	7	13
	4	7	8	15	12
	5	6	10	27	13
	6	8	15	32	13
	7	3	21	43	13
	8	7	24	56	13
	9	8	25	67	15
	10	7	36	74	16

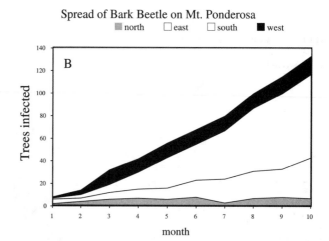

Figure 20.22 Area Graph Documenting the Magnitude of a Beetle Infestation over Time

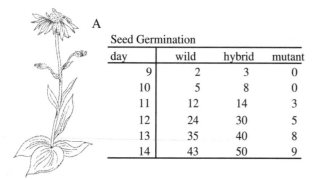

Seed Germination

day	wild	hybrid	mutant
9	2	3	0
10	5	8	0
11	12	14	3
12	24	30	5
13	35	40	8
14	43	50	9

Commercial Satellite Launches

	USA	Russia	Europe	Multi-Nat
2001	3	3	8	2
2002	5	8	20	1
2003	5	5	4	3

Figure 20.23 Data for (A) Seed Germination and (B) Commercial Satellite Launches

Source: National Aeronautics and Space Administration. (various dates). *NASA image exchange.* Public domain rocket photographs courtesy of NASA. Retrieved May 1, 2007, from http://nix.larc.nasa.gov.

companies recognize the potential to make money in this expanding market. Create an area graph of the data in Figure 20.23B to show the growth of the commercial satellite business in the early years between 2001 and 2003.

20.7 High-Low, Combination, and Log Plots

In many instances it is necessary to plot more than one type of data on the same chart. *High-low (stock) graphs* give scientists the ability to plot three values (high/low and average) on the same chart, while *combination plots* provide the capability of plotting two totally different variables on the same graph by using two different y-axes. In other instances, scientists use *logarithmic (log) plots* either to study exponential functions or ones in which there is a large range of values.

ACTIVITY 20.7.1 *High-Low Graphs (Stock): Plotting Means and Ranges of Data*
Researchers often want to plot a range of data, rather than individual points. For this, the high-low graph is often appropriate (see Figure 20.24A). Stock market analysts are familiar with this type of graph because companies report the high, low, and closing values for stocks each day, month, or year. Scientists often report data in a similar manner. Figure 20.24B shows the average high, low, and daily temperature for New York City. The top of each line represents the average monthly high, the bottom represents the average monthly low, and the dot represents the monthly average.

1. *How does a continental climate differ from a maritime climate?* Denver (39° N, 105° W) and San Francisco (37° N, 122° W) are situated at approximately the same latitude, but San Francisco is near the ocean, and Denver is land-locked. San Francisco is in a maritime environment, sitting on a peninsula with the Pacific Ocean on one side and San Francisco Bay on the other. Denver is in a continental environment, close to the center of the

continent and far from large bodies of water (Figure 20.24C). Climatologists say that San Francisco has an equable climate, meaning that there is little daily, seasonal, or yearly variation in temperature. By contrast, they characterize Denver's climate as continental, with substantial changes in seasonal temperature. Create high-low graphs of the temperature profiles for both of these cities. Do your graphs support the climatologists' characterization? Explain your answer. *Note:* Make certain both graphs use the same scale.

ACTIVITY 20.7.2 *Combination Graphs: Graphing Two Types of Data on One Chart*
It is often helpful to plot two different types of data on the same graph. For example, a climograph (Figure 20.24F) is a single graph that charts both the average temperature and precipitation for a given locale throughout the course of the year, using separate axes for each variable. Figure 20.24D shows the average monthly temperature and rainfall in Chicago. As shown in Figure 20.24F, the line graph represents temperature, and the bar chart represents precipitation. The horizontal axis represents the months of the year. The climograph not only shows average temperatures for each month, but also illustrates seasonal variations in temperature over the course of the year. And the climograph reveals monthly precipitation and seasonal variations in precipitation. Combination graphs like the climograph must have the same independent variable (*x*-axis) but can have different dependent variables (*y*-axes). Note that the axis on the left is precipitation, measured in millimeters of rainfall, and the axis on the right is temperature, measured in degrees Celsius.

1. *Analyzing climates with climographs.* Compare the climographs for Iquitos, Peru, and Barrow, Alaska (Figure 20.25). The graphs look very different with respect to temperature and rainfall, indicating that these are very different climates. The temperature graph for Iquitos is linear and flat, indicating little or no variation in temperature during the course of the year. By contrast, the temperature

A

New York, NY

year	Jan	Feb	Mar	Apr	May	Jun	Jul	Aug	Sep	Oct	Nov	Dec
Average High	3	4	10	16	22	26	29	28	24	18	12	5
Average Low	-3	-2	1	6	12	17	20	19	15	9	5	0
Average	0	0	5	11	17	22	24	24	20	14	8	2

Denver, CO

year	Jan	Feb	Mar	Apr	May	Jun	Jul	Aug	Sep	Oct	Nov	Dec
Average High	5.2	7.7	11.5	17.2	22.3	28.2	32	30.7	25.7	19.6	11.2	6.1
Average Low	-11.5	-8.6	-5.2	-0.5	4.8	9.7	13.2	12.1	7.1	0.7	-5.7	-10.5
Average	-3.1	-0.4	3.1	8.3	13.6	19	22.6	21.4	16.4	10.1	2.7	-2.1

San Francisco, CA

year	Jan	Feb	Mar	Apr	May	Jun	Jul	Aug	Sep	Oct	Nov	Dec
Average High	13.5	15.5	16	16.7	17	17.8	18.1	18.6	20.3	20.3	17	13.5
Average Low	7.6	9.2	9.4	9.8	10.2	11.4	11.9	12.5	13.2	12.8	10.8	8.3
Average	10.6	12.4	12.7	13.3	13.6	14.6	15	15.6	16.8	16.6	14	10.9

Source: worldclimate.com

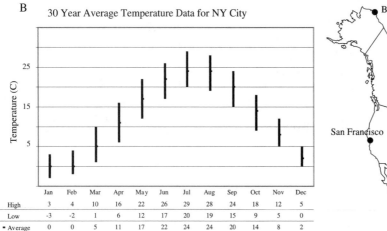

B   30 Year Average Temperature Data for NY City

	Jan	Feb	Mar	Apr	May	Jun	Jul	Aug	Sep	Oct	Nov	Dec
High	3	4	10	16	22	26	29	28	24	18	12	5
Low	-3	-2	1	6	12	17	20	19	15	9	5	0
▪ Average	0	0	5	11	17	22	24	24	20	14	8	2

C

D   Average monthly temperature and rainfall
Chicago, IL

	J	F	M	A	M	J
¡C	-4	-2.5	2.6	8.9	14.9	20.3
mm	46.7	44.6	68.2	80	88	93

	J	A	S	O	N	D
¡C	23.4	22.8	18.9	12.6	5	-1.4
mm	89.2	86.2	81.4	64.3	61.9	54.5

E   Average monthly temperature and rainfall
Dallas, TX

	J	F	M	A	M	J
¡C	6.3	8.8	13.7	18.6	22.6	27.2
mm	49.2	59.9	80	79.7	146.6	83.7

	J	A	S	O	N	D
¡C	29.6	29.3	25.2	19.5	13.4	8.2
mm	55.4	53	65	97.1	59.3	58.4

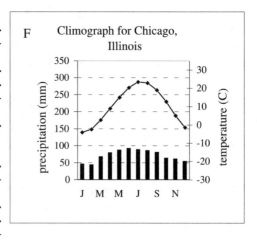

F   Climograph for Chicago, Illinois

Figure 20.24 (A, B, D, E) High-Low Graphs, (C) Locations of Different Climate Areas, and (F) Combination Graphs of Climate Data

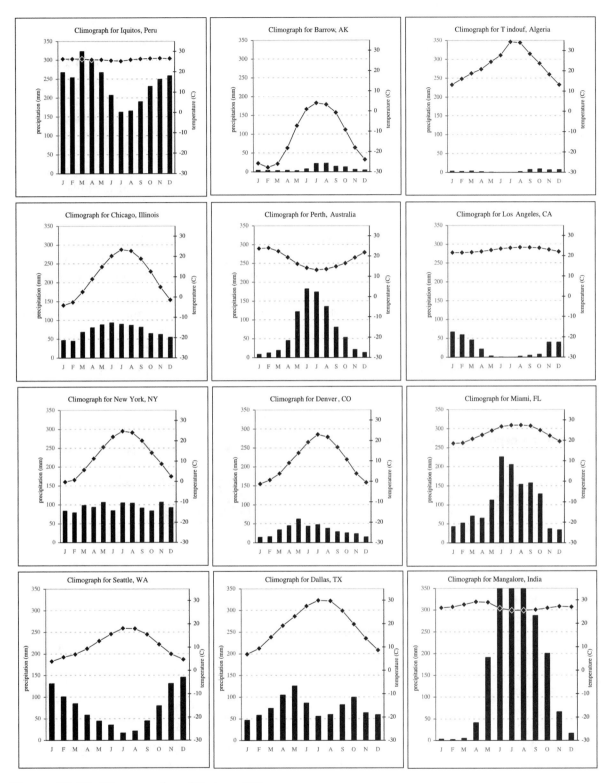

Figure 20.25 Climographs of Various Cities

graph for Barrow appears like a sine wave, with a maximum in June, July, and August and a minimum in December, January, and February. From this we can conclude that Barrow is in the Northern Hemisphere (a city in the Southern Hemisphere would have maximum temperatures during December, January, and February). Although the summer months are much warmer than the winter months in Barrow, they are still very cool, indicating that this city must be located very far north. Indeed, Barrow is on the northern coast of Alaska (Figure 20.24C). The climate in Barrow is cold and dry. It is so cold, however, that water rarely evaporates from the soil, leaving the soil wet and often frozen, a characteristic of arctic tundra. By contrast, the climate in Iquitos is warm and wet, indicating it supports a large amount of vegetation; indeed it is found in the tropical rain forests of Peru. Analyze the climographs in Figure 20.25 to answer the following questions.

a. Which city has the most equable (constant) climate? Explain.

b. Which city has what most people would consider the most comfortable climate?

c. Chicago and New York have approximately the same climographs, except that Chicago's winter is colder. Why might this be?

d. Which of these cities is located in a hot desert?

e. Which city is in the Southern Hemisphere?

f. Which of these cities is located in tropical rain forest?

g. Which two of these cities have a Mediterranean climate, characterized by mild winters and warm, dry summers?

h. Which city would experience monsoon-type rains (heavy summer rains)?

i. Which city has the coldest, driest summers?

j. Which of the following cities has the most annual rainfall: Chicago, New York, Dallas, or Miami?

k. Which of the following has more summer rainfall: Denver, Los Angeles, or Seattle?

l. Which city has a climate most similar to Chicago?

m. Which of the following cities would be best suited for outdoor ice skating rinks: Chicago, New York, Dallas, or Miami?

n. Which has more winter rainfall: Mangalore, India, or Seattle, Washington?

o. Which city has two wet seasons?

2. *Biome/climograph posters:* Perform an Internet image search to find photographs of the biome in which each city listed in Figure 20.25 is located. Make posters for the bulletin board that include photos of the natural vegetation of the biome, correlated with climographs and written descriptions (Figure 20.26).

3. *Create a climograph for a city close to you.* Collect average rainfall and temperature data for a city near you using an online almanac, NOAA (National Oceanic and Atmospheric Administration) Web site, or similar resource (*sciencesourcebook.com,* worldclimate.com or www.noaa.gov, or search "world climate").

Coniferous Forests

Coniferous forests are made up mainly of cone-bearing or coniferous trees, such as spruces, hemlocks, pines and firs. The leaves of these trees are either small and needle-like or scale-like and most stay green all year around (evergreen).

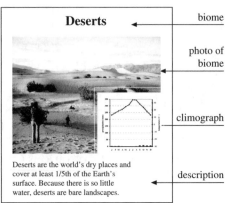

Deserts

biome

photo of biome

climograph

Deserts are the world's dry places and cover at least 1/5th of the Earth's surface. Because there is so little water, deserts are bare landscapes.

description

Figure 20.26 Biome and Climograph Posters

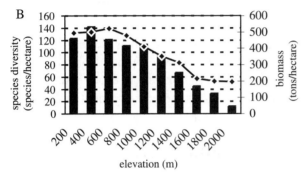

A

Elevation (m)	species (n/ha)	biomass (tons/ha)
200	123	495
400	142	501
600	121	523
800	111	480
1000	113	412
1200	95	352
1400	67	312
1600	45	216
1800	33	200
2000	12	195

B

Figure 20.27 (A) Table and (B) Graph of Species Diversity and Biomass Versus Elevation

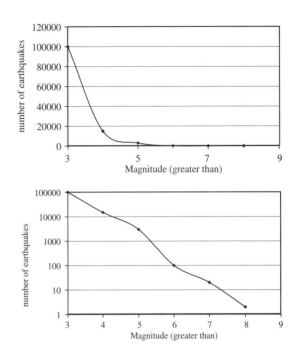

Figure 20.28 Distribution of Earthquakes by Magnitude on (A) Linear and (B) Semilog Scales
Source: U.S. Geological Survey. (2007). *Earthquake hazards program.* Retrieved May 2, 2007, from http://earthquake.usgs.gov.

Plot monthly precipitation using columns and monthly temperature using a line graph. Alternatively, you can use the data for Dallas, Texas, shown in Figure 20.24E. Describe the climate you have plotted.

4. *How do species diversity and biomass change with elevation?* Figure 20.27A contains hypothetical data one might find in the mountains of the western United States. Species diversity is measured as the average number of animal and plant species found within a 1 hectare (10,000 square meter) plot of land. *Average biomass* refers to the average mass of all of the organisms in the same plot. Generate a combination graph that plots species diversity on the left axis, and biomass on the right axis. Your graph should look like Figure 20.27B.

ACTIVITY 20.7.3 *Semilogarithmic Plots: Plotting Wide Range Data*

Some data are difficult to plot because of an extremely wide data range. Figure 20.28 shows

such data for the distribution of earthquakes by magnitude. Note that in an average year, there are more than 100,000 earthquakes worldwide between magnitude 3 and 4, and only 2 greater than magnitude 8. If the data are plotted on a simple linear scale (Figure 20.28A), the number of larger earthquakes is virtually invisible because the number of small earthquakes dwarfs it. Although massive earthquakes are much more important, they do not appear due to the scale of the graph. However, data plotted on a *semilogarithmic* graph (Figure 20.28B) clearly show the number of earthquakes of any magnitude. The graph is referred to as a semilogarithmic (semilog) plot because the *y*-axis is logarithmic, while the *x*-axis is linear. A *logarithmic scale* is constructed so that the data are plotted in powers of 10 to yield a maximum range while maintaining resolution at the low end of the scale. Semilogarithmic plots are also useful when demonstrating exponential relationships.

Figure 20.29 shows the growth of a colony of bacteria as a function of time, where *t* represents

A

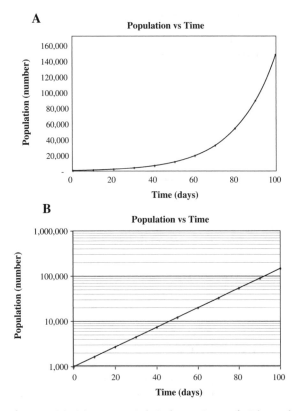

Table 20.6 Strontium-90

Time (y)	Sr = 90 (g)
0	100
25	50
50	25
75	12.5
100	6.25
125	3.125
150	1.5625
175	0.78125

Figure 20.29 Bacterial Colony Growth Plotted on (A) Linear and (B) Semilogarithmic Scales

the time interval and P_t represents the size of the population at any given time, *t*. When the data are plotted on a standard linear scale, a curve is drawn as shown in Figure 20.29A. This is a classic exponential growth curve. If the data are plotted on a semilogarithmic graph (Figure 20.29B), they plot as a straight line. Straight lines on semilog plots indicate an exponential relationship. In this case the relationship is: $P_t = P_0 e^{rt}$ where *r* is the growth rate, defined as $\frac{\ln(P_n/P_0)}{t}$.

1. *Do radioactive elements decay in an exponential manner?* Data in Table 20.6 show the mass of strontium-90, a radioactive isotope with a half-life of 28 years. Strontium-90 is one of the isotopes that may accompany a nuclear accident. It is potentially hazardous not only because it is radioactive, but also because it mimics calcium and accumulates in bone. Graph the data in Table 20.6, first with a linear

scale and then as a semilog graph. If the line becomes straight when plotted on a semilog graph, the relationship is exponential. Does strontium-90 experience exponential decay?

20.8 Statistics

In 1989, two researchers announced that they had achieved nuclear fusion with a simple apparatus at room temperature. Fusion, the process in which two atomic nuclei combine to form a larger nucleus, has been touted as the answer to the world's energy problems, but it has been achieved only in high-temperature, high-energy environments. The announcement of "cold fusion" was of interest to scientists and energy planners worldwide. But no one was ever able to replicate the researchers' purported findings. Although the researchers may have been earnest in their report, they did not have any independent confirmation of their work. A sample size of one is not sufficient to prove anything in science, and the researchers should not have presented their findings to the media without sufficient verification from repeated experimentation.

Scientific research relies on independent confirmation and *statistics,* the branch of mathematics that deals with the analysis and interpretation of numerical data. The school science laboratory is an excellent place to employ statistics because many students and lab groups may collect data on the same experiment. Rather than relying on one data point from one group, it is better to take the mean of all groups. An average (or mean) is perhaps the most common statistical measure, but there are others that can also assist scientists in their interpretation of data. Spreadsheet programs provide tools to perform many statistical tests, but we focus on those most commonly used in science: basic descriptive measures (*percentage, per capita, mean, median, mode, maximum, minimum*) and *curve fitting*.

ACTIVITY 20.8.1 *Descriptive Statistics: Making Sense of the Data*

In 1952 a sulfur-laden smog covered London, England, leading to the deaths of approximately 4000 people. In 1963 an air pollution inversion occurred in New York City, leading to 168 deaths. Shocking tragedies such as these led to the passage of the Air Quality Control Act in the United States and similar measures in other parts of the world. Since the passage of this landmark act in 1967, agencies have been commissioned to measure pollution and set standards.

Figure 20.30 shows the number of unhealthful air days per year in some of the major cities in the United States in 1999. To determine the percentage of days that are considered to have unhealthful air, divide the number of unhealthy days by 365 days per year and convert to percentage. Once the formula has been entered in the top cell, it can be copied to the remaining cells. When you have completed this calculation, determine the *average* (=AVERAGE(*first cell: last cell*)) and *median* (=MEDIAN(*first cell: last cell*)) number of unhealthful days for the cities listed. Finally, determine the city with the largest number of unhealthful days (=MAX(*first cell: last cell*)) and the city with the least (=MIN(*first cell: last cell*)).

ACTIVITY 20.8.2 *Trend Lines: Discovering Relationships in the Data*

A *trend line* is a best-fit line through a series of data points. It can be a *linear, exponential, power, logarithmic,* or *polynomial* function. Trend lines help researchers visualize relationships. The best trend line is the one that best fits the data.

1. *Motion:* Table 20.7A lists time and distance data for an accelerating automobile. Graph these data, and determine the best trend line. Try all types to see which fits the data best.
2. *Pendulums:* In 1656, Christian Huygens, a Dutch scientist, invented the first pendulum clock. What formulas govern the movement of pendulums? Plot the experimental data from Table 20.7B, and determine the best trend line. Is the relationship linear, exponential, power, logarithmic, or polynomial? What is the basic equation of the pendulum?

Table 20.7 Plot These Data and Determine the Best Trend Line

(A) Car Motion Data		(B) Pendulum Data	
Time (s)	Distance (m)	Length (m)	Period (s)
1	4.9	1	2.01
2	20	2	2.84
3	50	3	3.48
4	57	4	4.01
5	135	5	4.49
6	176	6	4.92
7	280	7	5.31
8	290	8	5.68
9	420	9	6.02
10	515	10	6.35

Atlanta GA	Bakersfield CA	Baltimore MD	Boston MA	Buffalo NY	Charlotte NC	Chicago IL	Cleveland OH	Dallas TX	Detroit MI	Fresno CA	Houston TX	Indianapolis IN	Knoxville TN	Los Angeles CA	Memphis TN	Nashville, TN	New Orleans LA	New York City NY	Philadelphia PA	Phoenix AZ	Riverside CA	Sacramento CA	San Antonio TX	San Diego CA	St. Louis MO	Washington DC
61	88	40	5	8	34	12	18	23	15	81	50	21	59	27	36	33	18	24	32	12	93	38	9	16	29	39

Figure 20.30 Number of Unhealthful Air Days per Year in Major American Cities, 1999
Source: Environmental Protection Agency. (2000). *National air quality and emissions trends report, 1999.* Research Triangle Park, NC: Air Quality Trends Analysis Group.

Answers to Chapter Activities

20.1.1 (A) Newton's 2nd law =C3*C4, (B) ideal gas law =(C8*C9*C10)/C11, (C) accelerated motion =(C14*C16)+1/2*(C15*C16^2),(D) resistors in series =C19+C20+C21, (E) intensity of sound =10*LOG10(C25/C26), (F) experimental data =AVERAGE(C30:C32) or =AVERAGE(C30,C31,C32) or =SUM(C30:C32)/3.

20.1.2 (1) The speed of the fastest human is nearly 2200 times that of a snail. (2) The speed of the fastest human is approximately 3 percent the speed of sound. See Figure 20.31.

20.1.3 The spreadsheet should contain formulas that are the product of the value in liters times the appropriate volume conversion factor from Figure 20.2, or the value in meters times the appropriate length conversion factor.

20.1.4 Students should complete the spreadsheet formulas and determine that Company X contributes more to global warming.

20.2.1 This should be done outdoors, in the hallway, or wherever else there is a sufficiently clear area to walk. (A) Constant velocity (same as I). (B) Constant velocity for first third; then pause for the second third before proceeding at the initial rate. (C) Walking forward a given distance and then walking back to the starting point at the same speed. (D) Walking forward at constant speed, then taking a few steps back at the same rate before pausing, then proceeding forward at the initial rate. (E) Forward, pause; forward, pause; forward pause; as in the gait of bridesmaids at a wedding. (F) Forward at a constant speed, then reversing at the same speed for twice as long before returning to the original speed. (G) Constant acceleration (same as K and M). (H) Forward at a gradually increasing rate, then slowing down at a gradually decreasing rate.

(I) Constant velocity (same as A). Students will need to walk at a constant rate before crossing the zero point. (J) Constant velocity, then deceleration to zero followed by acceleration until the original velocity is resumed. Students must start walking before the zero point to achieve the initial velocity. (K) Constant acceleration (same as G and M). (L) Constant acceleration followed by constant velocity and then constant deceleration. (M) Constant acceleration (same as K and G). (N) Constantly increasing acceleration. (O). Constantly increasing acceleration followed by constantly decreasing acceleration. (P). Constant acceleration followed by decreasing acceleration and then no acceleration.

20.3.1 (1) C, (2) D, (3) C, (4) A.

20.3.2 The following are sample stories that match the data. Student answers may vary. (A) This was a strong runner. He finished in the least amount of time and had sufficient energy to accelerate during the last portion of the race. (B) This runner was a "jack-rabbit." He started out extremely fast but ran out of energy and gave up two-thirds of the way through the race. (C) This runner started at a moderate pace but had to take a break. He got his "second wind" and went on to finish the race, running fast at the end. (D) This runner started off extremely slowly, gave up, and turned around. (E) A child jumps in the pool, leaves the pool, returns, and then leaves again. (F) The pool has sprung a leak. (G) The pool is filled with water from a hose, after which one child enters, followed by a second and a third. They all leave the pool at the same time. (H) The pool is filled by a hose, after which a child jumps in the pool, gets out, and drains the pool.

	A	B	C	D	E
1	**Comparison of Speeds**				
2			speed (mi/h)	speed (km/h)	speed relative to fastest human
3	Human Growth Rate		6E-09	9.66E-09	3.66E+09
4	Average Snail		0.01	0.0161	2198.76
5	Average Walking Pace		3	4.83	7.33
6	First Gasoline Automobile		9	14.49	2.44
7	Fastest Human		22	35.42	1.00
8	1908 Model T Ford		40	64.4	0.55
9	Cheetahs' Top Speed		65	104.65	0.34
10	Fastest Horsefly		90	144.9	0.24
11	Fastest Roller Coaster		100	161	0.22
12	Fastest Falcon Species		105	169.05	0.21
13	Fastest Skier		154	247.94	0.14
14	High Speed Train		186	299.46	0.12
15	Dodge Viper's Top Speed		212	341.32	0.10
16	Fastest Wind		318	511.98	0.07
17	Speed of Sound		750	1207.5	0.03
18	Mach 3		2250	3622.5	0.01
19	Fastest Fighter Jet		4500	7245	0.00
20	Speed of Light		670000000	1078700000	0.00

Figure 20.31 Calculated Spreadsheet: Comparison of Speeds

20.3.3 The independent variable should be plotted on the *x*-axis and the dependent variable on the *y*-axis. Student graphs may vary in appearance but should have the following axes (*x*-independent, *y*-dependent): (1) independent variable: time; dependent variable: height above floor; (2) independent variable: time; dependent variable: height; (3) independent variable: time; dependent variable: amount of money; (4) independent variable: time; dependent variable: temperature; (5) independent variable: time; dependent variable: distance; (6) independent variable: time;

dependent variable: height of grass; (7) independent variable: time; dependent variable: amount of uranium-238; (8) independent variable: time; dependent variable: frequency; (9) independent variable: time; dependent variable: speed; (10) independent variable: time; dependent variable: population.

20.4.1 (1) Students should produce a graph such as Figure 20.32 showing that ozone is highest during the afternoon and lowest at night, regardless of location. Ozone pollution is greatest in the valleys and least in the mountains. (2) Students will produce graphs similar to 20.11B and comment on fluctuations in air quality. Ozone is an element of photochemical smog, and as such is highest at midday. (3) Students should produce a graph similar to Figure 20.33A. Brain size is somewhat proportional to body size, but humans have a disproportionately large brain relative to their body size and are above the trend line. (4) Students should produce a graph similar to Figure 20.33B. The Sun is a main sequence star. (5) Sunspot frequency varies over an approximately 11-year cycle (see Figure 20.34).

20.4.2 (1) Boiling point is a periodic or repeating property, as shown in Figure 20.35A. Members of the carbon family (group 6; elements 6, 14) have the highest boiling points, while the noble gases (group 8; elements 2, 10,

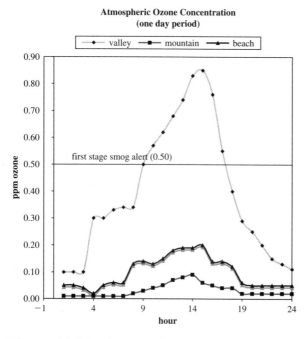

Figure 20.32 Plotting of Data for Atmospheric Ozone

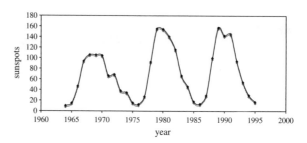

Figure 20.34 Sunspot Cycle

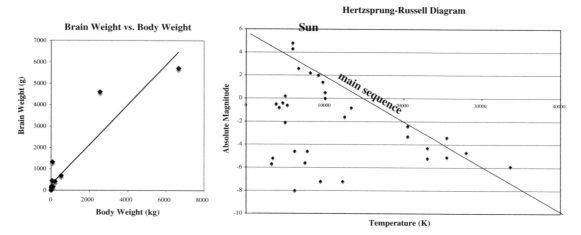

Figure 20.33 (A) Brain Weight Versus Body Weight. (B) Hertzprung-Russell Diagram

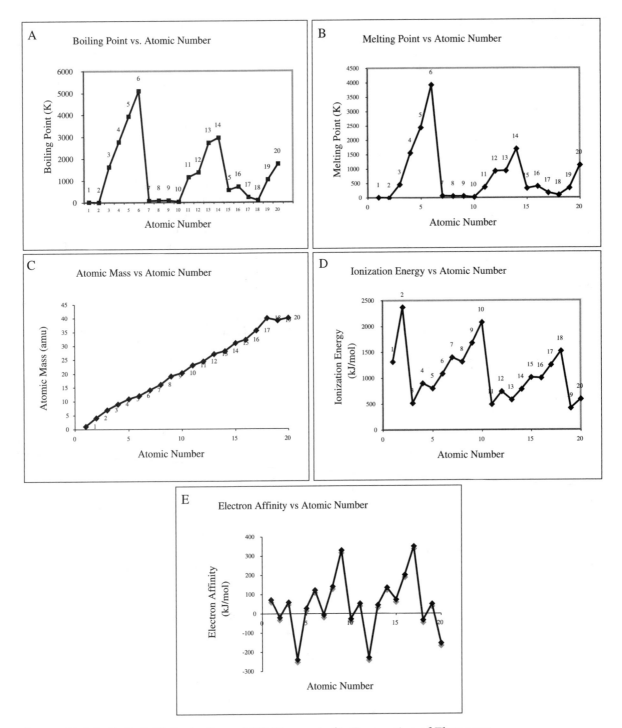

Figure 20.35 (A, B, D, E) Periodic and (C) Nonperiodic Properties of Elements

18) have the lowest boiling points. (2) Melting point is a periodic property (Figure 20.35B). Members of the carbon family (group 6; elements 6, 14) have the highest melting points, and the noble gases (group 8; elements 2, 10, 18) have the lowest. (3) Atomic mass is not a periodic property. The mass increases as the atomic number increases, with no repeating (periodic) patterns (Figure 20.35C). (4) First ionization energy is a periodic property (Figure 20.35D). The Noble gases (group 8; elements 2, 10, 18) have the highest ionization energies, and the alkali metals (group 1; elements 3, 11, 19) have the lowest. (5) Electron affinity

is a periodic property (Figure 20.35E). Members of the halogens (group 7; elements 9, 17) have the highest electron affinities. Members of the calcium family (group 2; elements 4, 12) have the lowest electron affinities. (6) Life expectancy (Figure 20.36A) increased continuously from 1900 to 2000 due largely to better medicine, housing, and other technological factors. (7) Tuberculosis was a major killer in 1900 but was almost extinct by 2000 due to improvements in antibiotics and public health (Figure 20.36B). As people lived longer, they were more prone to suffer symptoms associated with aging, such as cardiovascular disease. Advances in medicine, nutrition, and surgery reduced the rate of cardiovascular disease in the second half of the twentieth century, and the population continued to live even longer so that they were now more likely to develop cancer due to lengthy exposure to radiation, carcinogenic chemicals, and other environmental and biological factors. (8) Students will add the other three groups to the spreadsheet.

20.5.1 (1) The population profile of Germany closely resembles that of the United States. Like other developed nations, Germany has a low birth rate and high life expectancy. By contrast, developing nations generally have younger profiles due to a higher birth rate and lower life expectancy. Students will graph a population profile of Germany. (2) Students should produce a graph showing that the wolf population experienced relatively constant growth and spread to other parts of the park.

20.5.2 (1) See the stacked column of market share for rechargeable batteries, Figure 20.37A.

20.5.3 (1) Students provide a Pareto graph (similar to Figure 20.17A) of seawater. (2) Students provide a Pareto graph showing the greatest number of threatened and endangered species in California and Hawaii. California is a large and geographically diverse state with a large number of species. One would expect more endangered species in California simply because it has such a large number of species. Habitat destruction is the leading cause of extinction. Both California and Florida are experiencing rapid population growth. The development of farms and cities destroys natural habitats and may lead to extinction.

20.5.4 (1–4) Students develop bar graphs such as Figure 20.18A. The elemental composition of the human body shows more similarity to the oceans.

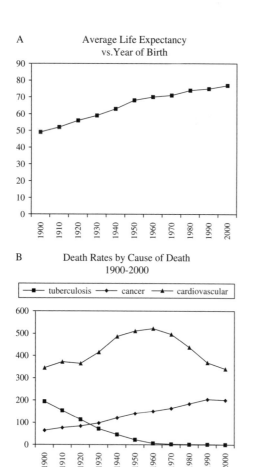

Figure 20.36 (A) Life Expectancy and (B) Causes of Death

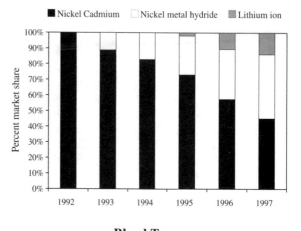

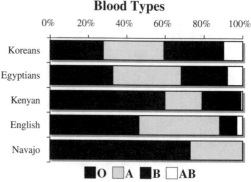

Figure 20.37 Stacked Charts of (A) Battery Market Share and (B) Blood Type Distribution

20.5.5 (1) See Figure 20.37B. Types B and AB are absent in the Navajo population. Koreans have the broadest distribution of blood types. Kenyans have the lowest percentage of type A blood.

20.6.1 (1) Students will develop pie charts resembling Figure 20.20B. Communicable diseases (AIDS, tuberculosis, and measles) are much more common causes of death in developing countries, while diseases associated with aging (heart disease, stroke, and cancer) are more common causes of death in developed countries. Health standards are higher in developed countries, reducing communicable diseases and allowing people to live to the age where diseases associated with aging become a greater issue. (2) Students will develop pie charts for area coverage and productivity (Figure 20.21B). Tropical rain forests, while occupying 4 percent of the Earth's surface, account for 27 percent of the world's productivity. Destruction of the world's tropical forests leads to a dramatic reduction in biomass production and an increase in carbon dioxide, a primary greenhouse gas that contributes to global climate change. (3) Students develop a pie chart of energy consumption by energy source. About 85 percent comes from fossil fuels, and about 8 percent from renewable sources.

20.6.2 (1) See Figure 20.38. (2) Students generate an area graph for satellite launches.

20.7.1 (1) Students develop temperature plots for Denver and San Francisco and find that Denver has a continental climate with great seasonal temperature variations, while San Francisco has an equable, maritime climate.

20.7.2 (1) (a) Iquitos, Peru. The average temperature in Iquitos is very constant, as illustrated by the straight temperature graph. The rainfall does vary from season to season, but is relatively heavy each month. (b) Los Angeles, California. The average temperature varies little from month to month, averaging about 18°C. Room temperature is 22°C (72°F). (c) Chicago is inland, while New York is on the coast. Water has a very high

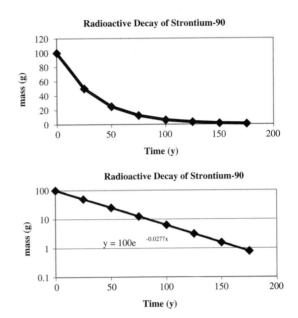

Figure 20.39 Radioactive Decay of Strontium-90: (A) Linear Scale and (B) Semilog Plot

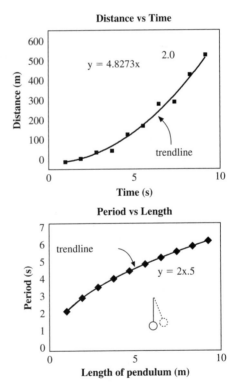

Figure 20.40 Trend Lines and Best-Fit Equations for (A) Acceleration and (B) Pendulum

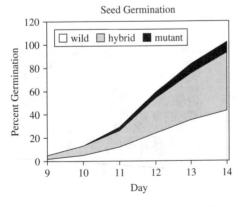

Figure 20.38 Area Graph of Germination

specific heat (it is difficult to change the temperature of water), and therefore it is difficult to change the temperature of oceans and the environments that border them. (d) Tindouf, Algeria. The precipitation shows only trace amounts of rain in a few months of the year. (e) Perth, Australia. Note that the temperature curve is inverted from the others, with the warmest months in the period from May through September. (f) Iquitos, Peru. It has a warm (averaging 26°C) and wet (2880 mm rain annually) climate. (g) Los Angeles, California, and Perth, Australia. Note that Perth is in the Southern Hemisphere, and therefore the winter months are opposite those in the Northern Hemisphere. (h) Mangalore, India. (i) Barrow, Alaska. (j) Miami (1285 mm). (k) Denver. (l) New York. The climographs are very similar, although Chicago has colder winters. (m) Chicago. It has the coldest winters. (n) Seattle. (o) Dallas. There are two spikes on the precipitation graph. (2) Students will make biome posters as shown in Figure 20.26. (3) Students will generate a climograph for their city in the format shown in Figure 20.24F. (4) Students should replicate Figure 20.27B, a combination graph that plots species diversity and biomass as a function of elevation.

20.7.3 (1) Figure 20.39A plots radioactive decay on a linear scale and Figure 20.39B on a logarithmic scale (semi-log plot). Strontium-90 experiences exponential decay, as indicated by the straight line when plotted on a logarithmic scale.

20.8.1 (1) The following statistics are for the cities listed. Average unhealthful days/year: 34 (9 percent). Median number of unhealthful days/year: 29 (8 percent). Maximum number of unhealthful days/year: 93 (25 percent) in Riverside, California. Minimum number of unhealthful days/year: 5 (1 percent) Boston, Massachusetts.

20.8.2 (1) Figure 20.40A is a plot of distance versus time for an accelerating automobile. The best-fit line is a squared function (power), $y = 4.8 \ x^2$. (2) The relationship of period to length in a pendulum is shown in Figure 20.40B. The best-fit line is a square root function (power) with an equation $y = 2x^{.5}$. The full equation for the period of a pendulum is $T = 2\pi (L/g)^{0.5}$, where L is the length of the pendulum, and g is the acceleration due to gravity (9.8 m/s^2).

Chapter Twenty-One

Mapping and Visualizing Scientific Data

For the Teacher 426

21.1 Map Construction 427

21.2 Topographic Maps 428

21.3 Mapping Data Electronically 434

21.4 Weather Maps 438

21.5 Environmental Maps 444

21.6 Astronomy Maps 446

21.7 Interpreting Aerial and Satellite Photographs 452

Answers to Chapter Activities 454

For the Teacher

Mapmaking is one of the oldest and most basic forms of written communication and is essential to modern science. Scientists map everything from the structure of the atom to the structure of the universe. The Human Genome Project has sequenced the human genome, and researchers are mapping the 100,000 or more genes on chromosomes (Figure 21.1).[1] At the other end of the spectrum, the Sloan Digital Sky Survey is creating a three-dimensional map of about a million galaxies and quasars.[2]

As our knowledge continues to grow, so has the need to represent it in graphic form. Map development and map reading are basic skills that all students should acquire. Geological, hydrological, topographic, botanical, distribution, gene, soil, astronomical, climatic, and weather maps are but a few of the many types of maps that are essential to science. In this chapter, students are provided with opportunities to design and interpret maps from a wide variety of scientific disciplines.

Many of the activities require Internet resources that can be accessed from *sciencesource book.com* or by an Internet search. Some resources allow students to collect and map data in conjunction with other students and researchers. In such cases, the data are managed on a Web site so all participants can analyze them. For example, students participating in the Journey North project contribute information on the sightings of orioles

Figure 21.1 Sample Gene Map: Position of Human Leukocyte Antigen on Chromosome 6

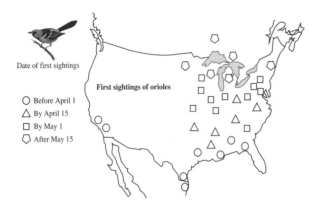

Figure 21.2 Map of the First Spring Sightings of Orioles

on their migration north with the onset of spring.[3] Figure 21.2 is an example of a map generated using such data and shows not only the migration of the orioles but also the advance of spring north toward Canada. Other projects engage students in an array of data collection activities, such as weather data, cosmic ray detection, and magnetic field intensity. The activities in this chapter are designed to help students master scientific mapping and interpretation skills.

21.1 Map Construction

Thomas Edison received 1093 U.S. patents for his inventions, including the electric light bulb, motion picture, and phonograph.[4] Although he is remembered for these inventions, his greatest contribution to science and technology was the development of the independent research laboratory. Edison had extensive laboratories in New Jersey and hired the best chemists, physicists, machinists, and inventors he could find. Edison was successful in the laboratory because he worked collaboratively with others who shared his vision. Edison was excellent at communicating his ideas to those on his research

teams, and as a result, they were able to combine their talents and efforts to solve many real-world problems.

If you walk into modern research laboratories you will likely find blackboards, whiteboards, computer screens, and paper, filled with diagrams and pictures representing the topics being researched. Researchers use these media to communicate difficult concepts to one another. If a picture is worth a thousand words, then a good diagram or map is worth ten thousand! Diagrams and maps represent relationships and allow researchers to communicate more easily with one another. The following mapmaking activities in this chapter are designed to help students follow and deliver clear instructions.

ACTIVITY 21.1.1 *Creating a Map from Written Directions*

Create a map from the following written directions. Use a fine-tip pencil and the appropriate symbols from Figure 21.3.

1. Draw a school symbol in the center of a blank sheet of paper to represent "Granite High School" and a compass in the upper right corner.
2. Exit through the south gate of Granite High School.
3. Turn west on the primary highway on which the school is located, and travel 1 km to the county border.
4. Continue traveling west 2 km until you see a church on your right.
5. Travel northwest for 2 km on the light-duty road that intersects the highway just west of the church.
6. At 2 km you cross railroad tracks that are perpendicular to the road.
7. Turn northeast on the dirt road that parallels the train tracks.

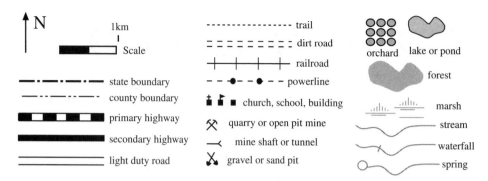

Figure 21.3 Traditional Map Symbols

8. Travel 2 km northeast on the dirt road until you cross a stream.
9. Get out of the car, and follow the meandering stream in a westward direction for approximately 3 km until it enters a forest.
10. Look for the entrance to a mine on the north side of the creek immediately after entering the forest. This is your destination.

ACTIVITY 21.1.2 *Creating a Map from Spoken Directions*

Create a map from the following spoken instructions. Your instructor will read these aloud. Use a fine-tip pencil and the appropriate symbols from Figure 21.3.

1. Draw a school symbol in the center of a blank sheet of paper to represent "Sequoia High School" and a compass in the upper right corner.
2. Exit through the south gate of Sequoia High School.
3. Travel due east for 0.5 km on the secondary highway on which the school is located.
4. Turn due south on the trail that is on the east border of the orchard.
5. After 0.5 km, the orchard ends, and you cross under power lines.
6. Continue south for another 0.5 km until you come to a dirt road.
7. Travel east on the dirt road for 1.0 km, at which point you will reach a marsh.
8. The road turns southeast. Follow it for 1.0 km, at which point you will reach a stream that crosses under the road and flows into the marsh.

9. Follow the stream west for approximately 3 km until you reach a lake.
10. Walk around the south shore of the lake for 1 km to the other side, where you reach a cluster of cabins.
11. In the middle of the cabins, you will find a trail. Travel south 1 km, passing through the woods.
12. When the trail emerges from the woods, it turns east.
13. Hike east on the trail for 1.5 km until you reach the gravel pit on the north side of the trail.
14. Just past the gravel pit, the trail splits. Follow the branch that leads southeast 0.5 km to the cabin. This is your destination.

ACTIVITY 21.1.3 *Writing Clear Directions*

Write clear, explicit directions for how to get from your school to your home or from the entrance of your school to your science classroom. Present your instructions to a lab partner, who can draw an accurate map based on your instructions. The better your instructions are, the more accurate your partner will be able to draw. Compare the map to your home with driving directions retrieved from an Internet mapping program, such as those found at *sciencesourcebook.com* or maps.google.com, or search street "maps."

21.2 Topographic Maps

Topographic maps are two-dimensional representations of the three-dimensional surface of the Earth. Cartographers (mapmakers) represent this

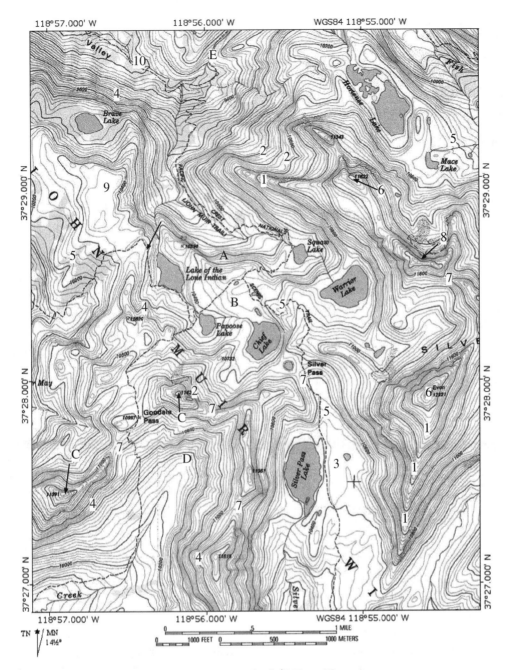

Figure 21.4 Contour Map with a Contour Interval of 40 Feet Elevation
Source: U.S. Geological Survey. (2003). Public domain USGS topographic maps, printed from National Geographic TOPO! software.

three-dimensional surface on paper using contour lines—lines that represent locations of equal elevation. Place your pen on any line on the contour map in Figure 21.4, and follow it as far as you can. All points on the line you have drawn are at same elevation.

ACTIVITY 21.2.1 *Reading a Topographic Map*

Hikers frequently "contour" around a mountain or hill when hiking cross-country (without a trail). They choose to contour so they don't have to gain or lose elevation. If you could plot their path on a map, it would represent a contour line like those shown in Figure 21.4. The distance between contour lines is consistent on an individual map but may vary from map to map. On Figure 21.4, the elevation between contour lines is 40 feet, and therefore the distance between two dark lines is 200 feet (there are five divisions between dark lines). The closer the lines are together, the steeper the slope (A), and the farther the lines are apart, the less steep the slope (B). Extremely close lines indicate cliffs.

Examine Figure 21.4, and note the locations of peaks (C). The contours around the peaks are in concentric rings, indicating that you can traverse completely around a peak without changing elevation. The innermost ring indicates the summit. If the inner ring is very small, the peak is pointed, but if it is large, the peak is flat. Contour lines form U or V shapes when representing ridges (D) or canyons (E). If surrounded by lower elevation contours, the feature is a ridge, and if surrounded by higher elevation contours, the feature is canyon. Match each of the numbered features on the map in Figure 21.4 with one of the following landforms:

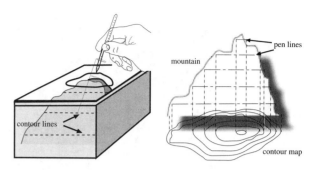

Figure 21.5 (A) Drawing a Contour Map. (B) The Resulting Map

canyon	gentle slope	pass
cliff	flat region (basin)	ridge
plateau	pointed summit	valley
steep slope		

ACTIVITY 21.2.2 *Drawing a Contour Map*

In this activity, you will construct a three-dimensional model of a mountain and draw a two-dimensional contour (topographic) map to represent its shape. The model can be made of clay, modeling clay, papier-mâché, salt dough, or other similar material. Your "mountain" should be attached to a piece of cardboard and should fit inside a shoebox or similar container.

Obtain a set of books or boards that have the same thickness. Set the first book or board close to the "mountain." Place a pen flat on this surface, keep it at right angles to the mountain, and draw a ring around the mountain. Place a second book

or board on top of the first, and draw another line. Repeat until you have reached the top. Each ring represents an elevation difference equal to the thickness of the books or boards. Place the "mountain" in a shoebox or similar container, and stretch and tape clear plastic food wrap over the opening (Figure 21.5A). Look straight down on the model mountain. Using an overhead pen or similar marker, draw lines on the plastic wrap to match the lines you drew on the mountain. When you have traced all of the lines you will have a two-dimensional topographic map of your artificial landform. Figure 21.5B illustrates how the contour map correlates with the lines drawn on the "mountain."

ACTIVITY 21.2.3 *Identifying Ecological and Geological Transects*

Figure 21.6 is a topographic map of hilly terrain in the foothills of the Sierra Nevada mountains of California. The five lines on the map represent transects: equal-length lines along which biologists, geologists, or ecologists collect environmental and biological data when studying a region. The five transects in Figure 21.6 are each 1 mi in length. Scientists make records of what they observe at even intervals along the transect. After collecting such data, they construct an elevation profile so they can correlate plant and animal distribution with slope, exposure, and elevation. Figure 21.7 shows five profiles. For each of the transects, find the matching profile. Assume you are walking from left to right across the map. The

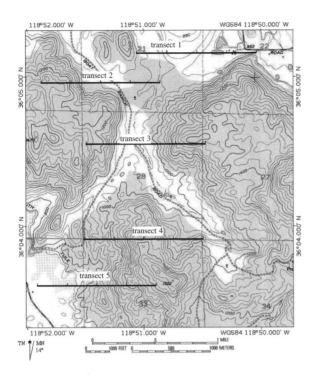

Figure 21.6 Topographic Map with Transects
Source: U.S. Geological Survey. (2003). Public domain USGS topographic maps, printed from National Geographic TOPO! software.

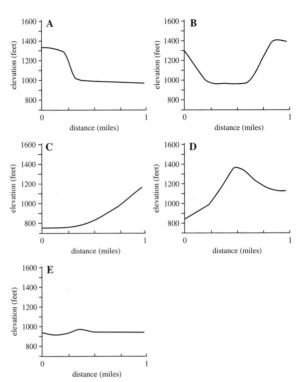

Figure 21.7 Elevation Profiles of Transects in Figure 21.6

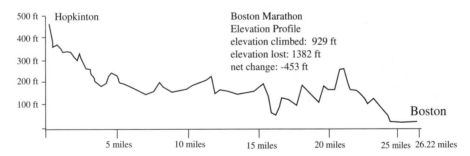

Figure 21.8 Elevation Profile for the Boston Marathon
Source: Boston Athletic Association. (2007). The Boston Marathon course map. Retrieved May 8, 2007, from http://www.bostonmarathon.org.

closer together the contour lines are, the steeper the slope is. The farther apart the lines are, the flatter the terrain is.

ACTIVITY 21.2.4 *Interpreting Elevation Profiles*

The Boston Marathon is the world's oldest annual marathon and one of the most prestigious foot races in the world. Runners study the course in detail so they can plan their running strategy. Of particular interest is the elevation profile (Figure 21.8), a graph that plots elevation as a function of distance. Runners note that although there is a net loss in elevation as they run from rural Hopkinton to the center of Boston, they encounter a number of uphill sections, particularly between miles 16 and 21, when they climb the infamous Heartbreak Hill. Elevation profiles are made by plotting elevation

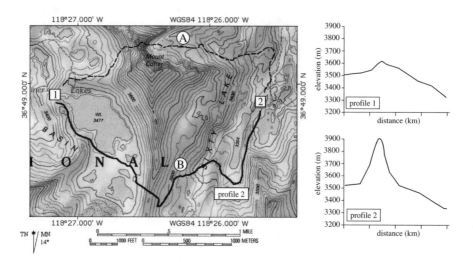

Figure 21.9 Topographic Map with Routes and Matching Elevation Profiles
Source: U.S. Geological Survey. (2003). Public domain USGS topographic maps, printed from National Geographic TOPO! software.

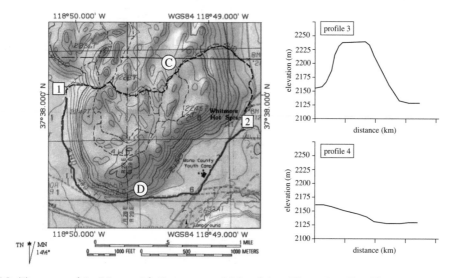

Figure 21.10 Topographic Map with Routes and Matching Elevation Profiles
Source: U.S. Geological Survey. (2003). Public domain USGS topographic maps, printed from National Geographic TOPO! software.

(determined by the closest contour line) as a function of linear distance along the path.

In this activity you will find five maps of varied terrain in California's Sierra Nevada Mountains (Figures 21.9 to 21.12). On each map there are two alternative routes from point 1 to point 2. One is a trail, marked with a dashed line, and the other a cross-country route, marked with a solid line. Examine the map, and match the routes with the profiles.

For each pair of routes, specify which option follows an easier (less elevation change) course.

ACTIVITY 21.2.5 *Constructing Profiles from Topographic Maps*

In 1871, the preservationist John Muir published his first work, "Yosemite Glaciers," in the *New York Tribune*. In this influential article, Muir hypothesized that the great valleys of Yosemite were carved by

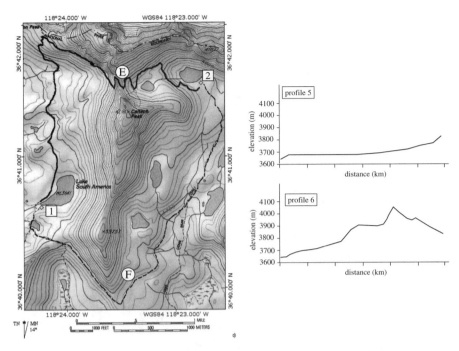

Figure 21.11 Topographic Map with Routes and Matching Elevation Profiles
Source: U.S. Geological Survey. (2003). Public domain USGS topographic maps, printed from National Geographic TOPO! software.

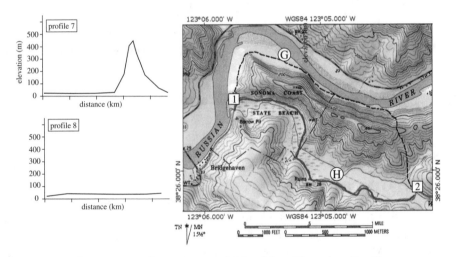

Figure 21.12 Topographic Map with Routes and Matching Elevation Profiles
Source: U.S. Geological Survey. (2003). Public domain USGS topographic maps, printed from National Geographic TOPO! software.

ancient glaciers that had long since receded to the upper peaks of the mountains.

Since the introduction of this idea, geologists and glaciologists have been fascinated with the work of glaciers in Yosemite and elsewhere in the world. Glaciologists still study the features in Yosemite in an effort to gain a better understanding of the work of ancient glaciers.

Figure 21.13 shows four transects in an area north of Yosemite Valley. Using the contour map provided, draw a simple profile illustrating how elevation changes as a function of distance from the first letter to the second. The *x*-axis should be distance, and the *y*-axis elevation. Which of the transects most closely resembles a glacial, U-shaped valley?

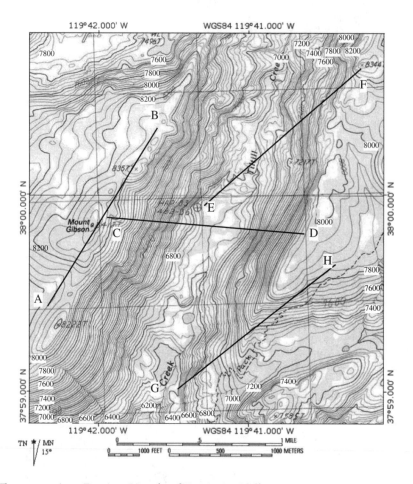

Figure 21.13 Transects in a Region North of Yosemite Valley
Source: U.S. Geological Survey. (2003). Public domain USGS topographic maps, printed from National Geographic TOPO! software.

21.3 Mapping Data Electronically

Monarch butterflies are beautiful insects and an important part of the food web. They may fly 3500 km from Canada to Mexico, where they spend the winter. At the end of March, they migrate northward to the U.S. Gulf states, where they lay their eggs and die. The next generation continues the migration back toward Canada, where the cycle begins again. Monarchs return to the oyamel (fir) forests in the mountains of Mexico where they spend the winter. Unfortunately, these forests are threatened from overlogging, and ecologists are concerned that if these habitats are destroyed, the annual monarch butterfly migration could stop. Environmentalists are working to save the oyamel forests and pro-

tect the monarch butterfly and other species that depend on it.

Each year thousands of school children and others record the date that monarch butterflies appear in their neighborhoods and submit this information to a central database. Researchers enter the longitude and latitude of these sightings into geographic information system (GIS) software and plot them on a map to show migration patterns (Figure 21.14).

Such information was used to show the vital role of the Mexican fir forests to the survival of the monarch. Although GIS software is the best way to map geographic data, such data can also be graphed manually or with spreadsheet software such as Microsoft Excel. Longitude and latitude are plotted on an XY scatter plot, with longitude serving as

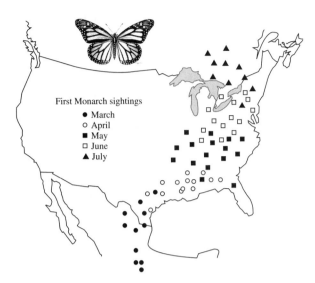

Figure 21.14 Mapping a Monarch Butterfly Migration

the X (horizontal) coordinate and latitude as the Y (vertical) coordinate. Such data are acquired using a handheld global positioning system (GPS) device or by locating the site on a topographic map.

A scanned map should be placed in the background of the XY scatter plot and the scales adjusted so the minimum and maximum X and Y values correspond to the longitude and latitude limits of the map. In the activities that follow, you will plot these data using Excel, GIS, or other plotting software. If this software is not available to you, the data can be plotted manually on a map. U.S. Geological Survey topographic maps of all portions of the United States are freely available on the Internet. (See *sciencesourcebook.com* or topozone. com, or search for "USGS topographic maps.")

ACTIVITY 21.3.1 *Mapping Animal Populations*

In 1804, Meriwether Lewis, of the Lewis and Clark Expedition, made the first scientific observations of "barking squirrels," an animal now known as the prairie dog. As the plains were settled and cultivated, the habitat of the prairie dog shrank, and now some species are listed as threatened or endangered.

For a species to obtain threatened or endangered status and the special protection it ensures, data must be collected on its historic and current ranges. This is best done by maintaining historic data in a database and plotting the information with GIS or spreadsheet software. Figure 12.15A includes the GPS coordinates (longitude followed by latitude) of Colorado's tallest peaks, as well as the coordinates of populations of the white-tailed prairie dog, the black-tailed prairie dog, and another rodent, the marmot. Plot the peaks and populations on Figure 12.15B or on the spreadsheet available on *sciencesourcebook.com*.

1. Describe the distribution of both the black- and white-tailed prairie dogs in Colorado. Do they have distinct or overlapping ranges?
2. How does the distribution of the marmot compare with the distribution of the prairie dogs.

ACTIVITY 21.3.2 *Mapping Patterns of Earthquake Activity*

Earthquakes can cause tremendous loss of human life as buildings collapse and tsunamis flood beachside towns. It is estimated that 830,000 people died in the Shasi earthquake in China in 1556, and more recently 255,000 people lost their lives in the Tangshan, China, earthquake of 1976. In 2004, an earthquake in the Indian Ocean off the coast of Sumatra, Indonesia, caused a tsunami that spread destruction throughout the coastal regions of southern Asia, claiming more than 200,000 lives. Although seismologists (scientists who study earthquakes) are unable to accurately predict the time and location of earthquakes, they have been able to state the likelihood of earthquakes by examining historical records. These data are provided to insurance companies so they can set earthquake insurance rates and to city planners so they can set building codes that address the threat.

Figure 21.16A records the location of large (magnitude 7.3 or greater) earthquakes in the United States during the past 200 years. If these data are plotted, one can determine the location of greatest earthquake hazard. Using the spreadsheet downloaded from *sciencesourcebook.com*, develop an XY scatter plot of the data, using longitude as the *x*-value and latitude as the *y*-value. The spreadsheet already has a map in the background to facilitate plotting. Alternatively, you can plot

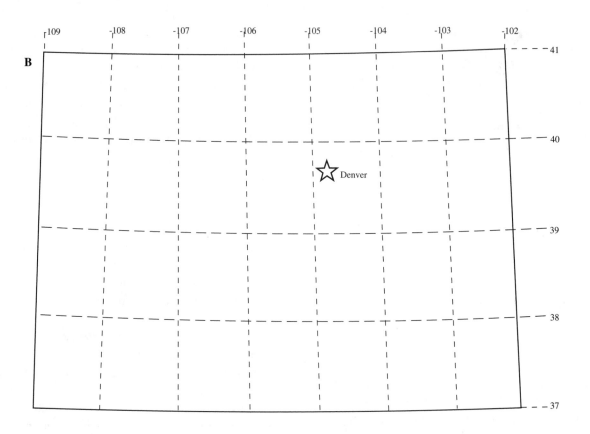

Higest Peaks					Marmot				Black-tailed PD		
Elbert, Mount	-106.44	39.11	14433		pop.	long	lat		pop.	long	lat
Massive, Mount	-106.47	39.18	14421		1	-106.1	39.2		1	-103.11	40.9
Harvard, Mount	-106.32	38.92	14420		2	-105.56	37.95		2	-103.31	40.3
La Plata Peak	-106.47	39.02	14361		3	-105.6	39.5		3	-103.4	40.7
Blanca Peak	-105.48	37.57	14345		4	-105.64	39.58		4	-103.1	39.5
Uncompahgre Pk	-107.46	38.07	14309		5	-106.1	38.5		5	-102.5	40.4
Crestone Peaks	-105.56	37.95	14294		6	-106.18	39.2		6	-103.8	38
Crestone Peak	-105.58	37.96	14294		7	-106.47	39.18		7	-102.8	37.8
Lincoln, Mount	-106.11	39.35	14286		8	-106.47	39.02		8	-103	39
Front Range	-105.81	39.63	14274		9	-106.86	39		9	-103.4	38.3
Grays Peak	-105.81	39.63	14274		10	-107.99	37.83		10	-102.6	38.5
Antero, Mount	-106.24	38.67	14269								
Torreys Peak	-105.82	39.64	14267								
Castle Peak	-106.86	39	14265		White-tailed PD						
Quandary Peak	-106.1	39.39	14265		pop.	long	lat				
Evans, Mount	-105.64	39.58	14264		1	-108.6	40				
Longs Peak	-105.61	40.25	14255		2	-108.9	40.9				
Wilson, Mount	-107.99	37.83	14246		3	-107.6	40.3				
Cameron, Mount	-106.11	39.34	14238		4	-107.2	40.7				
Shavano, Mount	-106.23	38.61	14229		5	-107.4	40.4				

Figure 21.15 (A) GPS Coordinates and (B) Colorado Map for Plotting Populations

B

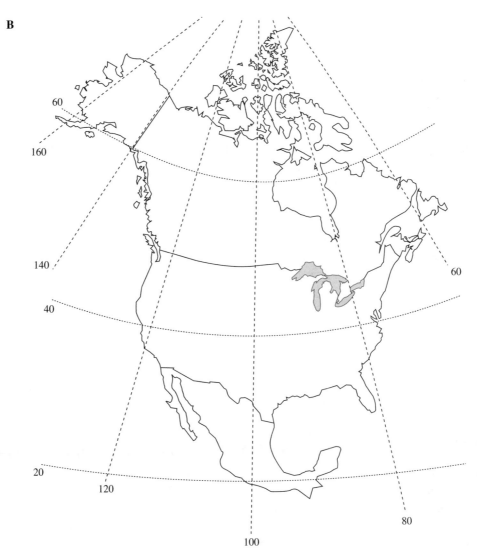

A US earthquakes of magnitude 7.3 or greater (1800-2000)

yr	long	lat	mag	yr	long	lat	mag	yr	long	lat	mag
1964	-147.7	61.0	9.2	1906	-122.5	37.7	7.8	1904	-148.1	64.7	7.3
1957	-175.6	51.3	9.1	1929	-169.7	50.9	7.8	1905	-178.6	50.7	7.3
1965	-178.6	51.3	8.7	1988	-143.0	57.0	7.8	1906	-153.9	56.9	7.3
1938	-158.4	55.5	8.2	1811	-90.4	35.6	7.7	1912	-155.0	57.5	7.3
1812	-89.6	36.5	8.0	1900	-153.5	57.1	7.7	1922	-125.5	41.0	7.3
1899	-140.0	60.0	8.0	1958	-136.5	58.3	7.7	1929	-177.9	51.6	7.3
1986	-174.8	51.3	8.0	1872	-118.1	36.7	7.6	1937	-147.1	64.6	7.3
1857	-120.3	35.7	7.9	1972	-135.7	56.8	7.6	1938	-157.6	55.5	7.3
1868	-155.5	19.0	7.9	1979	-141.6	60.6	7.6	1946	-163.2	53.3	7.3
1899	-142.0	60.0	7.9	1948	-160.9	54.7	7.5	1952	-119.0	35.0	7.3
1917	-159.1	54.8	7.9	1899	-140.0	60.0	7.4	1957	-166.3	52.2	7.3
1987	-142.8	58.7	7.9	1909	-169.0	52.5	7.4	1958	-156.6	66.0	7.3
1996	-177.6	51.6	7.9	1916	-170.0	53.3	7.4	1959	-111.2	44.7	7.3
2002	-147.4	63.5	7.9	1943	-150.8	61.9	7.4	1992	-116.4	34.2	7.3
1812	-89.6	36.3	7.8	1872	-120.3	47.9	7.3	1996	-176.9	51.5	7.3
1892	-115.6	32.6	7.8	1886	-80.0	32.9	7.3				

Figure 21.16 (A) GPS Coordinates of Earthquakes to Plot on the (B) Map

the points manually on a large wall map or on Figure 21.16B.

1. Is earthquake activity evenly distributed throughout the United States or concentrated in certain regions? Describe the distribution of seismic activity.
2. Some cities require that new housing construction include shear walls (the attachment of plywood sheets to building frames) to prevent excessive damage in earthquakes. Examine your plot, and predict which of the following cities would likely have such a code: San Francisco, Miami, Minneapolis, Los Angeles, Anchorage, Baltimore, Dallas, and Denver. Explain your answer.

ACTIVITY 21.3.3 *Mapping Shark Populations*

Hawaii is one of the most popular tourist destinations in the world, yet many visitors are fearful of swimming in the ocean because Hawaii is home to 40 species of sharks. Most species of sharks nevertheless are harmless, and shark-related injuries are relatively rare. Figure 21.17A shows hypothetical sightings of three of the most common sharks in Hawaiian waters as recorded by a group of researchers. Using the spreadsheet from *sciencesourebook.com* or GIS software (search "GIS"), develop an XY scatter plot of the data for sightings of hammerhead and pygmy sharks, using longitude as the x-value and latitude as the y-value. Alternatively, plot the data manually on the map provided (Figure 21.17B).

1. Describe the distribution of whitetip reef sharks found in this study.
2. Are pygmy sharks more likely to be seen in the open ocean or in reefs surrounding the islands? How about hammerhead sharks?

ACTIVITY 21.3.4 *Mapping Your Movement with a GPS Device*

For centuries, people have tried to develop a dependable way to determine their location with respect to camps, cities, and other destinations. Ancient sailors followed coastlines and later traveled in open seas,

studying the stars to determine locations and directions. Techniques improved significantly with the development of the compass, sextant, and chronometer, but the most significant improvements took place with the advent of satellite technology.

Today's global positioning system (GPS) was developed by the U.S. military and is used to determine the precise latitude, longitude, and elevation of any object on the Earth's surface equipped with a GPS device. The GPS device receives radio messages from different satellites, determines the distance to each by studying the time delay of the signal, and triangulates the position by noting the relative distances to each of the satellites.

Using a handheld GPS device provided by your teacher, record the GPS coordinates for three locations such as your classroom, home, local park, or other notable place.

1. Enter the coordinates provided by your GPS device into an online mapping site (available at *sciencesourcebook.com*, maps.google.com, earth.google.com, or www.topozone.com), and generate a topographic map, street map, and aerial photograph of each location. In most cases, street and topographic mapping sites allow latitude and longitude input. On each map or photograph, circle the location at which you recorded the coordinates. Note that most mapping programs accept the latitude before the longitude.
2. Describe how GPS devices can be used in geology, ecology, marine biology, oceanography, seismology, or other science.

21.4 Weather Maps

ACTIVITY 21.4.1 *Interpreting Weather Maps*

Meteorologists report their findings and predictions on weather maps using international symbols such as those shown in Figure 21.18. A circle is placed at the location of the weather station. An empty circle indicates clear skies, and a filled circle indicates complete cloud cover. A quarter-filled circle indicates 25 percent cloud cover, a

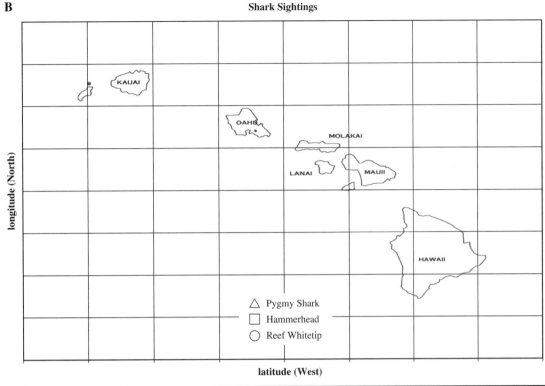

B   **Shark Sightings**

longitude (North)

latitude (West)

	Reef Whitetip		Pygmy Shark		Hammerhead	
	Longitude	Latitude	Longitude	Latitude	Longitude	Latitude
A	-160.2	22	-160.5	19.4	-158	21.6
	-156	20.9	-153.5	20.1	-157.5	22.1
	-155.3	21.3	-155	22.4	-157.2	21.7
	-156.2	21.4	-160.3	20.1	-157.4	21.5
	-155.4	21.3	-159.2	19.7	-157.9	21.8
	-155.9	21.4	-157	20.1	-155.1	19.7
	-159.1	22.1	-160.1	19.8	-154.2	19.9
	-159.3	22.1	-159.7	20.1	-159	22.3
	-155.8	21.4	-160	21.1	-156	21.2
	-155.6	21.4	-153.8	22.4	-154	20.4

Figure 21.17 (A) Data of Shark Sightings and (B) Map of Hawaiian Islands Region

half-filled circle indicates 50 percent cloud cover, and a three-quarters-filled circle indicates 75 percent cloud coverage. A number next to the circle indicates the temperature in degrees Fahrenheit. If the winds are calm, no lines are attached to the circle. Precipitation is indicated by a symbol to the left of the circle. A dot (.) indicates rain, an asterisk (*) snow, bars (=) fog, a comma (,) drizzle, and a bolt, thunderstorms. To indicate the presence of a wind, a line ("barb") is attached to the circle from the direction of the wind. For example, a northern wind would be shown by a line at the top of the circle, and an eastern wind would be indicated by a line on the right side. The strength of the wind is indicated by flags or bars emanating from this line. A long flag is added for each 10 knots (1 knot = 1.15 mph or 1.85 km/hr) of wind speed, and a short flag is added for an additional 5 knots. Thus, two long flags and one short flag indicate a wind speed of 25 knots.

Thus, the weather symbol shown in the key of Figure 21.18 indicates that it is raining at the weather station, and the temperature is 45°F, with 50 percent cloud cover and a wind of 25 knots

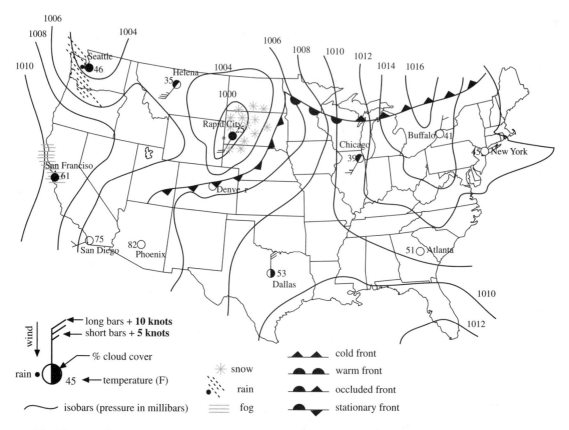

Figure 21.18 Weather Map and Symbols

from the north. Some weather maps record pressure, dew point, and precipitation next to the symbol. Often only the last three digits of pressure are recorded, so 014 = 1014 millibars, and 995 = 995 millibars. The dew point is the temperature at which dew or condensation forms and is recorded in degrees Fahrenheit. This weather map includes isobars, lines of equal pressure. You may note that the 1004 millibar line is adjacent to Seattle, Washington, indicating that the current air pressure in Seattle is approximately 1004 millibars.

1. Referring to Figure 21.18, record the conditions in Dallas, Rapid City, and Atlanta in Table 21.1.
2. Identify the city that is experiencing the following conditions: (a) 10 knot winds from the northeast; (b) the onset of a cold front; (c) onshore breeze of 10 knots; (d) offshore wind of 15 knots; (e) partially cloudy skies and a northeast wind of 35 knots; (f) close to the center of a high-pressure zone; (g) in the center of a low-pressure zone; (h) fog.

ACTIVITY 21.4.2 *Predicting Weather*

Meteorology is the science of the Earth's atmosphere, particularly its patterns of climate and weather. Meteorologists study weather patterns so they can predict future patterns and trends. Predictions are important not only for individuals who are planning picnics and outings, but for farmers, water district managers, firefighters, and others who need to make informed decisions based on the likelihood of future weather. Using an Internet weather service (look on *sciencesourcebook.com* or www.nws.noaa.gov, or search "weather maps"), print satellite photographs (visible and radar) and weather maps (including pressure, fronts, temperature, rain) of North America for the past four days.

Locate zones of high- (H) and low-pressure (L). On a blank map (Figure 21.19) indicate the centers for all four days, using H_1 to indicate the center of a high-pressure zone on day 1, H_2 the high-pressure center on day 2, and so on.

Draw arrows to show the movement of each high- and low-pressure zone during the past four

Table 21.1 Data Table for Reading a Weather Map

	Seattle, WA	Dallas, TX	Rapid City, SD	Atlanta, GA
Temperature (˚F)	46			
Cloud cover	100%			
Weather	rain			
Wind speed (knots)	calm			
Direction of wind	no wind			
Atmospheric pressure (mb)	1004 mb			

Figure 21.19 Outline Map of North America for Plotting Weather Conditions

days, and predict where you expect these zones to be tomorrow. Log on to the same Web site tomorrow and check your predictions. Repeat this for cold fronts (lines with triangles) and warm fronts (lines with half circles).

1. Do high- and low-pressure systems appear randomly arranged from day to day, or do they appear to flow in lines across the map? Explain your answer.
2. How did your predictions of high- and low-pressure zones compare with what occurred?
3. How did your predictions of the positions of the weather fronts compare with what occurred?

4. In the Northern Hemisphere, winds flow counterclockwise around low-pressure centers, creating cyclones. Using wind barbs, predict the direction of air movement around the centers of low pressure on your map.
5. Low-pressure zones are often associated with cloud formation and rain. Indicate the locations on your map most likely to be covered by clouds; then compare this with satellite photos (showing clouds) and radar maps (showing rain). Summarize your findings.

ACTIVITY 21.4.3 *Tracking Hurricanes*

A tropical cyclone is a large circular storm with wind speeds in excess of 73 mph (117 km/hour). Such storms are known as typhoons in the Pacific, cyclones in the Indian Ocean, and hurricanes in the Atlantic. They start over open oceans in tropical regions and move heat energy away from the equators toward the poles. Hurricanes cause significant damage if they make landfall in populated regions, as happened when a hurricane hit Galveston, Texas, in 1900. Winds of 120 mph generated a 20 ft storm surge that swept over the entire island, destroying 3500 homes and killing as many as 8000 people, making it the worst disaster in American history. In August 1992, a stronger hurricane, Andrew, hit Florida with sustained winds of 145 mph and gusts in excess of 175 mph! More than 60,000 homes were destroyed, yet only 53 lives were lost. Although Andrew was stronger, satellite data allowed meteorologists to plot the progress of the storm and warn residents of the impending danger.

The National Oceanic and Atmospheric Administration (NOAA) maintains the National Hurricane Center (www.nhc.noaa.gov), an organization committed to plotting the movement of hurricanes and warning people of approaching storms. Storms, however, can change course, and meteorologists must note these changes and update their predictions.

In this activity, you will assume the role of a forecaster, issuing warnings to residents based on GPS coordinates (latitude and longitude). Table 21.2 shows the GPS coordinates for one of the most destructive hurricanes in American history. Plot these data on the hurricane-tracking map provided by NOAA and the National Weather Service (Figure 21.20). After every three measurements, predict which state the hurricane will hit. After it has made landfall, continue to plot its course.

Table 21.2 Hurricane Tracking Data

Latitude	Longitude	mph	Predicted Landfall
13.2	−20	30	
13.2	−23.7	35	
12.8	−27.3	35	
12.5	−31	45	
12.5	−34.8	50	
12.6	−38.2	65	
12.8	−41.8	70	
12.9	−44.9	80	
13.2	−7.8	100	
13.8	−50.5	115	
14.2	−53.3	145	
14.8	−56.1	155	
15.4	−58.4	140	
16.1	−60.4	140	
16.6	−62.5	145	
17.2	−64.1	150	
18.2	−65.5	125	
19.7	−66.8	115	
21.6	−68	105	
23.5	−69.3	105	
25.2	−71	110	
27.2	−73.4	115	
29	−76.1	125	
31.7	−78.8	140	
35.9	−81.7	65	
42.2	−80.2	40	
49	−69	45	
52	−62	45	

1. How accurate were your predictions? Did you need to change them as time progressed?
2. These data were from Hurricane Hugo, a destructive 1989 hurricane. Where in the United States did the hurricane make landfall? Through which states did the storm travel?
3. In 2005, Hurricane Katrina flooded New Orleans and much of the Gulf Coast. Track this hurricane on the NOAA map (Figure 21.20) using the coordinates provided in Table 21.3.

Table 21.3 Tracking Data for Hurricane Katrina, 2005

	Latitude	Longitude	mph
1	23.1	−75.1	30
2	23.4	−75.7	30
3	23.8	−76.2	30
4	24.5	−76.5	35
5	25.4	−76.9	40
6	26.0	−77.7	45
7	26.1	−78.4	50
8	26.2	−79.0	55
9	26.2	−79.6	60
10	25.9	−80.3	70
11	25.4	−81.3	65
12	25.1	−82.0	75
13	24.9	−82.6	85
14	24.6	−83.3	90
15	24.4	−84.0	95
16	24.4	−84.7	100
17	24.5	−85.3	100
18	24.8	−85.9	100
19	25.2	−86.7	125
20	25.7	−87.7	145
21	26.3	−88.6	150
22	27.2	−89.2	140
23	28.2	−89.6	125
24	29.5	−89.6	110
25	31.1	−89.6	80
26	32.6	−89.1	50
27	34.1	−88.6	40
28	35.6	−88.0	30
29	37.0	−87.0	30
30	38.6	−85.3	30

Source: National Oceanic and Atmospheric Administration. (2007). *Historical hurricane tracks—Hurricane Katrina.* Retrieved May 8, 2007, from http://maps.csc.noaa.gov.

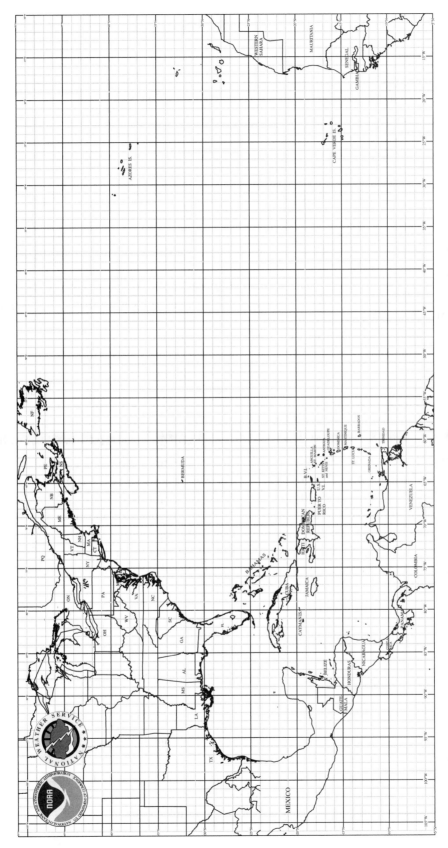

Figure 21.20 Atlantic Basin Hurricane Tracking Chart, National Hurricane Center, Miami, Florida

Source: National Oceanic and Atmospheric Administration. (2007). *Atlantic Basin hurricane tracking chart.* Retrieved May 8, 2007, from http://www.nhc.noaa.gov.

4. Use the historical hurricane tracking tool from NOAA (hurricane.csc.noaa.gov), look on *sciencesourcebook.com,* or search "national hurricane center, hurricane tracks," to plot the tracks of the following famous Atlantic hurricanes: Camille, Carla, Floyd, and Andrew. Are there any similarities in the tracks of these hurricanes? Explain your answer.

21.5 Environmental Maps

When the U.S. Environmental Protection Agency (EPA) was established in 1970, it was commissioned by Congress to protect America's air, water, and land resources. The EPA and other organizations develop careful maps so they can accurately and efficiently communicate environmental concerns. In this section students will develop environmental maps using data from the EPA and other organizations.

ACTIVITY 21.5.1 *Tracking Radioactive Fallout*

In 1953, the U.S. Atomic Energy Commission predicted that nuclear generators would eventually make electricity "too cheap to meter." In the years that followed, the nuclear power industry grew dramatically, but the promise of extremely cheap electricity was never realized, due in part to expensive safety measures necessary to contain such reactions and the radioactive waste generated. The

Figure 21.21 Map for Plotting the Spread of the Radioactive Cloud from Chernobyl, 1986

need for such safety requirements was underscored by an explosion at a nuclear reactor in Chernobyl, Ukraine, on April 26, 1986. Radioactive materials were spewed high in the atmosphere, and winds carried the radioactive cloud west into Europe and east across Asia, straining relations with nations that experienced radioactive fallout.

The tragic explosion provided meteorologists a rare opportunity to study wind movement. Table 21.4 lists the dates on which the radioactive cloud was first detected in parts of Europe. On the map provided in Figure 21.21, chart the flow of the radioactive cloud across Europe by placing the number

Table 21.4 Tracing Radioactive Fallout from Chernobyl, 1986

Day	Date	City
1	April 26	Chernobyl, Ukraine
2	April 27	Gdansk, Poland
3	April 28	Stockholm, Sweden; Helsinki, Finland; Oslo, Norway
4	April 29	Trondheim, Norway; Copenhagen, Denmark; Prague, Czechoslovakia
5	April 30	Munich, Germany; Vienna, Austria; Geneva, Switzerland
6	May 1	Rome, Italy; Budapest, Hungary; Zagreb, Yugoslavia; Paris, France
7	May 2	Reykjavik, Iceland; Bucharest, Romania; Brussels, Belgium; London, England
8	May 3	Glasgow, Scotland; Athens, Greece; Ankara, Turkey
9	May 4	Beirut, Lebanon

of the day on the appropriate cities. Use an online atlas or European map to locate places with which you are unfamiliar (look on *sciencesourcebook.com*, or search "Europe map").

1. Describe the path of the radioactive cloud.
2. What other events can meteorologists use to track large movements of air?

ACTIVITY 21.5.2 *Tracking Air Pollution*
One of the many tasks of the EPA is to measure air pollution and report findings to the public. Each day the EPA, in cooperation with other federal and local agencies, measures five major air pollutants

regulated by the Clean Air Act (ground-level ozone, particulate matter, carbon monoxide, sulfur dioxide, and nitrogen dioxide) and reports the current and predicted air quality index (AQI) to the public using the Internet. AQI values less than 100 are considered acceptable; those over 100 are not (Figure 21.22).

When AQI numbers are high (bad air quality), schools may be required to cancel physical education and sports activities, and industries may be required to reduce polluting activities.

What is the air quality in your region? Log on to the EPA air quality Web site (airnow.gov), look on *sciencesourcebook.com*, or search "EPA air quality

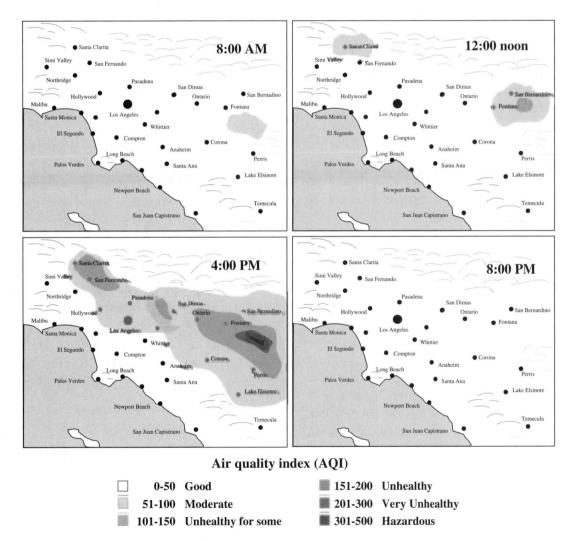

Air quality index (AQI)

☐	0-50 Good		▨	151-200 Unhealthy
▨	51-100 Moderate		▨	201-300 Very Unhealthy
▨	101-150 Unhealthy for some		▨	301-500 Hazardous

Figure 21.22 Sample Air Quality Index Map for a Summer Day in Los Angeles
Source: U.S. Environmental Protection Agency. (2004). Adapted from a Los Angeles ozone animated map. Retrieved May 8, 2007, from http://www.airnow.gov.

maps" and determine the current air quality for the area closest to you.

1. Report the current composite air quality index (AQI), as well as the values for ozone and particulate matter.
2. Examine map archives for air quality (e.g., ground-level ozone, particulates) during the past year for your same region. Identify the month during which the air pollution appears to be worst.
3. Compare daily animated maps for this month to see if there are any daily trends in air ozone levels. For example, do ozone levels vary during the day, and if so, at what times are they highest and lowest.
4. Open the animated map archive for the Los Angeles basin in California, an area known for air pollution. Examine the animation thumbnails (small pictures), and select a month during which ozone pollution seems to be a problem (e.g., September). Run the animations, and record the approximate time of day that ozone pollution appears to be the worst (see Figure 21.22). Is this true for other days during this month? What man-made and natural factors may explain this trend?

ACTIVITY 21.5.3 *Environmental Hazards in Your Community*

The mission of the U.S. Environmental Protection Agency (EPA) is to protect human health and the environment. The EPA enforces the regulations of environmental laws enacted by Congress. All companies or organizations that produce, ship, or store hazardous chemicals must register with the EPA, and in turn the EPA shares this information with the public. Citizens can learn about the potential hazards in their neighborhoods by looking at maps produced by the EPA (EnviroMapper at epa. gov), or look on *sciencesourcebook.com* or search "EnviroMapper, EPA maps."

Figure 21.23 is a map of a hypothetical community showing the location of hazardous waste producers, air pollutant emitters, and Superfund sites. Hazardous waste sites include any entity that

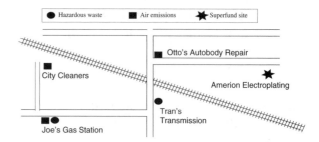

Figure 21.23 Sample Map of EPA Regulated Sites

generates, transports, treats, stores, or disposes of hazardous waste. For example, automobile service centers must register with the EPA as hazardous waste sites if they change engine oil or radiator fluid. Many electric power plants, steel mills, factories, and other heavy industries release pollutants into the air and must therefore register as "air emissions" sites. These sites may be forced to curtail activity if air pollution values rise too high. Superfund sites require federal intervention to clean up.

Use the EPA or similar Internet resource to generate environmental maps showing the hazardous waste producers, air pollutant emitters, and superfund sites in your community and in a local industrial area.

1. Are there EPA registered sites in either of the two sites you selected?
2. Identify the EPA registered sites on your maps, and determine the toxic substances they use, produce, or release.
3. Is there any correlation between the registered sites and geographic features such as rivers, lakes, streets, or railroads? Explain your answer.

21.6 Astronomy Maps

Early explorers relied on their knowledge of the night sky to determine latitude and longitude. Latitude can be determined by measuring the altitude (angle above the horizon) of Polaris, the North Star (Figure 21.24). If, for example, Polaris is 45 degrees above the horizon, you can conclude

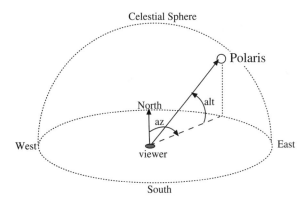

Figure 21.24 Determining the Latitude from Polaris

that you are on the 45th parallel (45 degrees north latitude), and if it is at 50 degrees, you must be on the 50th parallel.

Explorers Robert Perry and Matthew Henson knew in 1909 they had reached the geographic North Pole (90th parallel) when the North Star was directly overhead (90 degrees above the horizon). Although latitude was easy for early explorers to determine, longitude was more difficult and required knowledge of the appearance of the night sky at different times of the year. The planisphere, an intricate dynamic star chart, was a device that provided such information. By matching the appearance of the night sky with a time- and latitude-dependent window in the planisphere, navigators could determine their longitude. Today the planisphere is used primarily by amateur astronomers to locate and reference stars. In this activity, you will construct a planisphere and use it to identify stars and constellations in the night sky.

ACTIVITY 21.6.1 *Mapping the Stars*

Figure 21.25(A–C) is a star chart showing the brightest stars in the sky (listed in italics) and the major constellations visible from the Northern Hemisphere. The size of a dot on the star chart is proportional to its brightness. Early astronomers imagined shapes of animals and heroes among the stars and gave these constellations (apparent groupings of stars) names that we still use. Today these constellations are typically illustrated by lines

connecting the major stars that only vaguely represent the shapes the ancients envisioned. For example, Draco (near the center of the chart in Figure 21.25) vaguely resembles a dragon, from which its name is derived.

Constellations help us locate stars and other celestial bodies. For example, each November, the Earth passes through the tail of an ancient comet, causing the Leonid meteor shower. These "shooting stars" appear to radiate from the region of the constellation known as Leo, hence the name. Figure 21.26 shows the same stars as Figure 21.25 but does not include the constellations or names.

1. Draw and label each of the following constellations on Figure 21.26 by referring to Figure 21.25: Cygnus (the Northern Cross), Ursa Major (the Great Bear, or Big Dipper), Ursa Minor (the Little Bear, or Little Dipper), Draco, Corona Borealis (the Northern Crown), Bootes, Pegasus, and Hercules.

2. Find and label these notable bright stars: Altair, Vega, Deneb, Sirius, Arcturus, and Betelgeuse. In many cities these may be the only identifiable stars due to light pollution.

3. Each August, stargazers see many "shooting stars" from the Perseid Meteor shower (emanating from the sky around Perseus). Indicate on Figure 21.26 the location from which these meteors appear to originate.

4. Galaxies orbit around their center of mass, termed the galactic center. It is believed that the galactic center of our galaxy, the Milky Way, is in the direction of Sagittarius. On Figure 21.26, label this region as the galactic center.

ACTIVITY 21.6.2 *Identifying Constellations*

A planisphere is used to identify stars, constellations, star clusters, and galaxies. In this activity, you will build your own planisphere using Figures 21.25 and 21.27. Glue a paper photocopy of Figure 21.25 to a piece of stiff cardboard. Photocopy Figure 21.27 on transparency film, and cut off everything outside the perimeter of the circle. Attach this circle to the cardboard using a

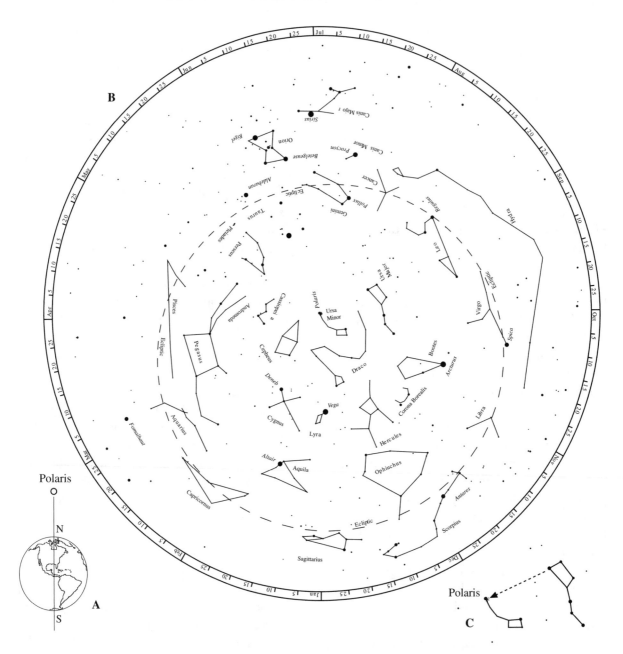

Figure 21.25 (A) Polaris, the Pole Star. (B) Locating Polaris. (C) Base of Planisphere

pin, brad, or similar fastener so that the top circle rotates directly over the circle on the bottom. Rotate the upper sheet so current time on its dial matches the current date on the bottom sheet. For example, if it is 7:00 P.M. on March 1, align the 7 P.M marker with the March 1 marker. The objects shown in the window will be visible from the Northern Hemisphere if it is night and there is no cloud cover or light pollution.

Match 12:00 midnight on the upper circle with January 1 on the bottom circle and note which stars are visible. Repeat at 12:00 midnight for the first of each month, and notice that the view changes throughout the year. The stars visible at midnight on January 1 are considerably different from those on July 1, hence astronomers refer to a "winter sky" and a "summer sky." Realize, however, that the sky changes throughout the night as well.

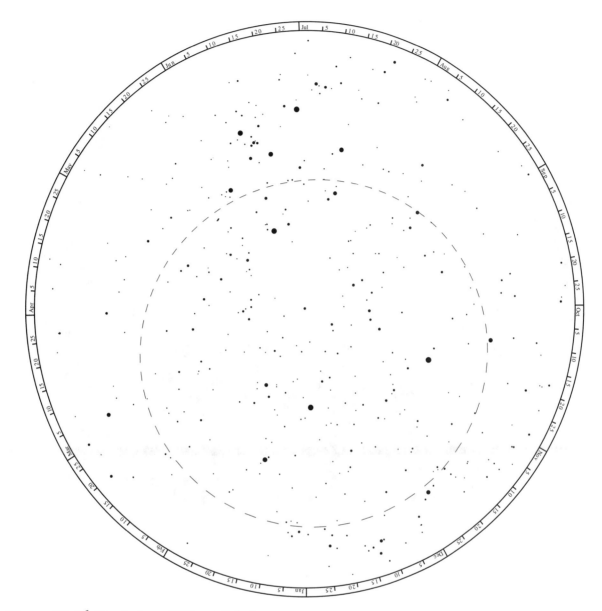

Figure 21.26 Planisphere Without Labels

Set the planisphere for 5:00 P.M. on January 1, and then rotate slowly toward 6:00 A.M. and note that stars appear to swirl around Polaris, the North Star. In 24 hours, the stars appear to have rotated back to the position from which they began. This apparent rotation is due to the rotation of the Earth on its axis. Since Polaris is aligned with the Earth's axis (Figure 21.25A), all other stars appear to rotate around it. Figure 21.28A is a 4 hr exposure showing the apparent movement of the stars. The North Star is behind the peak, at the center of the con-

centric arcs formed by the apparent movement of the stars.

To identify stars in the sky, hold the planisphere above your head with the arrow pointing north. Light pollution, clouds, and smog will reduce your ability to see, so it is suggested that you use this at least 2 hr after sunset in a rural location when there is no moonlight (New Moon). To view the planisphere, use red light (red cellophane over a flashlight works well) so your pupils do not constrict when looking at the chart.

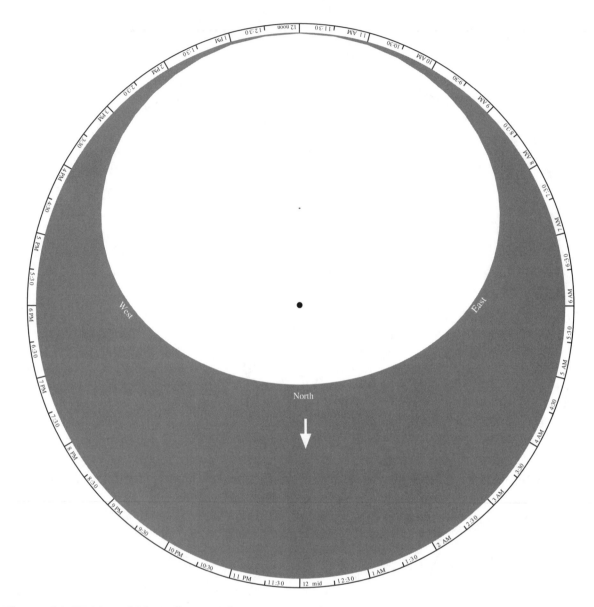

Figure 21.27 Top of Planisphere with Viewing Window

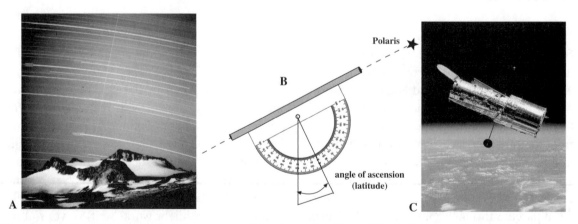

Figure 21.28 (A) Four-Hour Exposure of the Stars. (B) Home-Made Sextant. (C) Hubble Telescope

Source: National Aeronautics and Space Administration. (2007). Hubble Telescope. Retrieved May 20, 2007, from http://www.nasa.gov.

Note that the planisphere used in this activity is designed for 40 degrees north latitude, the approximate latitude of Denver or Philadelphia, but is adequate for most other major American and Canadian cities as well. You may also wish to use astronomy software that will generate the night sky for any day of the year, such as Starry Night software from starrynight.com, or look on *sciencesourcebook.com* or search "astronomy software."

1. Looking toward the northern horizon, identify Ursa Major (the Big Dipper), the most easily recognizable constellation on the northern horizon due to its bright stars and distinctive dipper-like shape. The two stars at the end of the dipper "cup" can be used to point to Polaris, the pole star or North Star (Figure 21.25C), a much dimmer star at the end of the handle in the Ursa Minor (the Little Dipper).

2. A sextant is a device used to determine the angle of elevation of a star, planet, or other object, and has been used for centuries by navigators to determine their position at sea. Make a simple sextant using a protractor, straw, string, tape, and rock as shown in Figure 21.28B. Tape the straw to the protractor and hang a rock or other object from a line connected to the protractor to create a plumb line (vertical line). Sight at a star, planet, or other object through the straw. The angle of elevation is measured as the angle between the plumb line and the ninety-degree (right angle) mark as shown in the Figure.

3. Use Polaris as a reference to identify as many of the following constellations as are visible: Cygnus (the Northern Cross), Ursa Major (the Great Bear, or Big Dipper), Ursa Minor (the Little Bear, or Little Dipper), Draco, Corona Borealis (the Northern Crown), Bootes, Pegasus, and Hercules. List the constellations you have identified.

ACTIVITY 21.6.3 *Identifying and Tracking Satellites*

In October 1957, the Soviets launched *Sputnik*, the first artificial satellite to orbit the Earth. In the years since, thousands of satellites have been thrust into orbit to provide weather forecasts, relay phone messages, perform experiments, monitor foreign armies, document environmental problems, and study the universe. Many of these satellites can be seen with the unaided eye, appearing as tiny bright dots, moving against the backdrop of the dark night sky. The straight line in Figure 21.28A is the trace left by a satellite. The tracks of satellites are predictable and are made public through various agencies. Certain satellites, such as the Hubble Space Telescope (Figure 21.28C) and the International Space Station (ISS), are particularly brilliant because of their large size and reflective panels.

The goal of this activity is to identify satellites in the night sky using their current azimuth and altitude as reported on the Internet. Brightness is measured by magnitude. Vega, one of the best-known stars, is said to have a brightness of zero. Things brighter than Vega have negative values, and those that are dimmer have positive values. The Sun is the brightest object in the sky, having a brightness of −26.7. The full Moon has a brightness of −12.7, and the International Space Station can have a brightness of −2 if conditions are just right.

Review satellite forecasts, and select a convenient time when a satellite of interest is particularly bright as seen from your location. Satellite orbits are highly predictable, and their flight schedules can be found on the Internet (see *sciencesourcebook. com* or www.heavens-above.com, or search "satellite tracking").

Record the date, magnitude, time, altitude, and azimuth for viewing three notable satellites from your location (Table 21.5). *Altitude* is the angle of the satellite with reference to the horizon (Figure 21.24), and *azimuth* is the angle from true north. An object on the horizon has an altitude of 0°, and one directly overhead has an altitude of 90°. An azimuth of W indicates that the satellite is visible in the west, and an azimuth of WNW indicates that the satellite is visible between west and northwest. Some agencies may report the azimuth in degrees, with 0° or 360° = north, 90° = east, 180° = south, and 270° = west.

Using a compass, map, or GPS device, orient with respect to true north, and look in the appropriate region of the sky for your chosen satellite at the designated time. It should appear as a tiny white dot moving across the background of stars.

Table 21.5 Satellite Tracking and Viewing Data

Satellite	Date	Magnitude	Starts			Maximum Altitude			Ends		
			Time	Alt.	Az.	Time	Alt.	Az.	Time	Alt.	Az.
ISS	3/25/05	0.0	19:29:56	10	WNW	19:32:43	46	SW	19:33:23	39	S

Note: Alt. = Altitude; Az. = Azimuth.

Red lights or flashing lights are from airplanes, not satellites. The International Space Station is the largest and brightest satellite and can often be seen even in regions with substantial light pollution.

1. Which satellites were you able to observe?
2. Examine the prediction tables, and determine the time of day that satellites appear brightest. Explain why this is so.

21.7 Interpreting Aerial and Satellite Photographs

From the earliest days of the space program, scientists have recognized the potential of satellites for collecting data on our planet. One of the earliest American satellites, the *Explorer VII*, launched in 1959, was equipped with an infrared sensor to study heat patterns on the surface of the Earth. Today scientific instruments onboard orbiting satellites provide researchers with data to study the Earth's environment and potential problems such as ozone depletion, deforestation, climate change, earthquakes, volcanoes, hurricanes, and ocean temperature variations. For example, the Topex/Poseidon satellite program has helped oceanographers understand and predict El Niño patterns, temperature changes in the Pacific Ocean that dramatically influence weather worldwide. In this section, students will examine aerial and satellite data to better understand Earth.

ACTIVITY 21.7.1 *Interpreting Aerial/Satellite Photos of Earth*

A variety of sites on the Internet (such as *sciencesource book.com*, maps.google.com, earth.google.com, or terraserver.com, or search "satellite photos") offer satellite and aerial photographs of the Earth's surface. Many street mapping services also offer hybrid views in which street names are superimposed on images. You can locate positions by address or GPS coordinates (latitude and longitude). For example, the GPS coordinates 46.20213, −122.20177 locate a satellite view of Mount Saint Helens, a composite volcano in the Cascades of Washington that erupted in 1980. The first number in a GPS coordinate pair generally represents latitude, and the second represents longitude, measured in degrees. A positive latitude indicates a position north of the equator, and a negative longitude indicates a position west of the prime meridian that separates the Eastern and Western Hemispheres. If you enter the coordinates 36.01524, −114.73856 and zoom in, you will see Hoover Dam, a structure that stores water and provides hydroelectric power for much of the American Southwest. Table 21.6 shows the GPS coordinates of a number of sites of scientific interest.

1. Using the online aerial and satellite photo resources, match the coordinates in Table 21.6 with the places listed below. Put the number of each location in the box immediately to the left of the latitude. Make certain you are using a satellite, aerial, or hybrid view. Zoom in to higher magnification to see each feature clearly. If you are using a resource such as Google Earth, you can tilt the images to get a three-dimensional perspective.
2. Print satellite or aerial photographs of each feature.
3. Locate and print land-based photographs of each location using an image search engine (such as *sciencesourcebook.com* or images.google.com).

Table 21.6 Match the GPS Coordinates with Points of Scientific Interest

Latitude	Longitude	Location
31.43563	−109.90147	
35.02666	−111.02193	
35.99714	−113.75961	
33.35634	−116.86565	
35.42517	−116.88874	
37.74710	−119.53775	
46.86077	−121.77235	
38.13501	−122.88135	
40.15506	−76.72356	
43.08451	−79.06886	
28.60965	−80.59909	
41.83296	−88.25235	
29.55402	−95.09417	
40.74846	−73.98658	
35.07370	−118.26500	

1. *Barringer Meteor Crater*, near Winslow, Arizona, is one of the best-preserved meteor craters on Earth.

2. *Empire State Building* in New York City has been named by the American Society of Civil Engineers as one of the Seven Wonders of the Modern World.

3. *Fermi National Accelerator Laboratory* is a center for the study of the fundamental nature of matter and energy. Its massive circular accelerator has been the site of many discoveries in high-energy physics.

4. *Goldstone Deep Space Antenna* is one of three telescopes in an international array that supports interplanetary spacecraft missions and performs radio and radar astronomy of the solar system and universe.

5. *Grand Canyon*, one of the Seven Wonders of the World, is a mile-deep canyon formed by the Colorado River, which has worn through a plateau in northern Arizona.

6. *Half Dome* is a massive granite rock that dominates Yosemite Valley, California. Geologists have proposed that an extinct glacier cut off the front of the dome along a major fissure, revealing its massive sheer granite face.

7. *Kennedy Space Center*, at Cape Canaveral, Florida, is NASA's space vehicle launch complex.

All manned U.S. missions have launched from this location.

8. *Lavender Copper Mine*, near Bisbee, Arizona, is a classic example of open pit mining.

9. *Mount Rainier*, Washington, is a composite volcano whose glaciers serve as the headwaters for five rivers.

10. *Niagara Falls* is the most voluminous waterfall in North America and is the site of massive power-generating stations that provide power to Canada and much of the northeastern United States.

11. *Palomar Observatory* houses the Hale reflecting telescope, an invaluable tool in astronomy that was the largest telescope in the world for more than 40 years.

12. *San Andreas Fault* is a right-lateral strike-slip fault in western California. It is clearly visible in aerial photographs of the Carizzo Plain.

13. *Tehachapi Windmill Farm*, California, is one of the largest wind-powered electricity generation plants in the world.

14. *The Saturn V Rocket* was the largest rocket ever built and was used to carry American astronauts to the Moon.

15. *Three Mile Island* is a nuclear power generating station that experienced a partial core meltdown in 1979, making it the site of the worst nuclear accident in U.S. history.

ACTIVITY 21.7.2 *Interpreting Satellite Images of Other Planets*

In 1996, the National Aeronautic and Space Administration (NASA) launched the *Mars Global Surveyor*. For five years it photographed and surveyed the Martian environment. Much of the imagery is available online (look on sciencesroucebook.com or mars.google.com, or search "Google Mars").

1. Search the Martian surface for the following features: (a) volcanoes, (b) impact craters, (c) faults and cracks, (d) alluvial fans, (e) plains, (f) canyons apparently cut by water, (g) polar ice caps, (h) dunes, and (i) ridges. It may be easier to see features using the false-color elevation view rather than the visible or infrared views. Print photographs of each.

2. Search for the features in question 1 on Earth using Google Earth or other resources used in the previous activity. Print and compare photographs of features on Mars with those on Earth. Describe similarities and differences.

Answers to Chapter Activities

21.1.1–21.1.2 See Figure 21.29.
21.1.3 Responses will vary.

21.2.1 1—ridge, 2—canyon, 3—flat region (basin), 4—steep slope, 5—gentle slope, 6—pointed summit, 7—pass, 8—cliff, 9—plateau, 10—valley.
21.2.2 Students will draw a simple topographic map similar to Figure 21.5B.
21.2.3 (A) transect—2, (B) transect—3, (C) transect—5, (D) transect—4, (E) transect—1.
21.2.4 (A) profile—2 (B) profile—1 (easier), (C) profile—3, (D) profile—4 (easier), (E) profile—6, (F) profile—5 (easier), (G) profile—7, (H) profile—8 (easier).
21.2.5 See the profiles in Figure 21.30. Transect C-D has a U-shaped profile characteristic of a glacial carved valley.

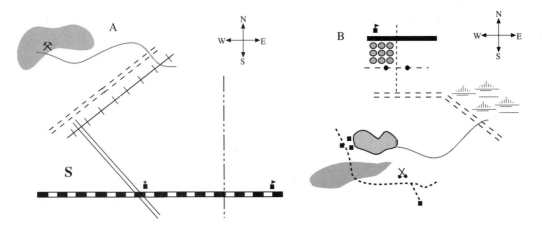

Figure 21.29 Sample Maps for (A) Activity 21.1.1 and (B) Activity 21.1.2

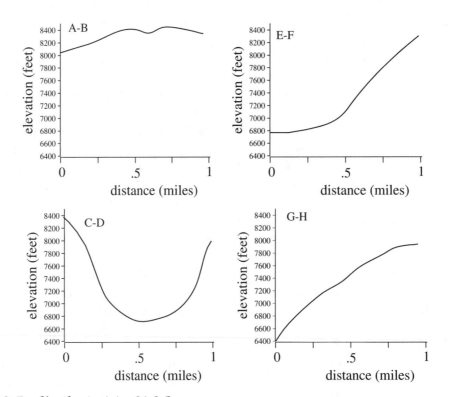

Figure 21.30 Profiles for Activity 21.2.5

21.3.1 (1) The white-tailed prairie dogs are located in the northwest portion of the state, and the black-tailed prairie dogs are located in the plains along the eastern boundary. (2) Marmots are found high in the mountains near the tallest peaks. Figure 21.31A is a spreadsheet plot of their distribution.

21.3.2 Students plot a map such as Figure 21.31B using the spreadsheet from the Web site or plot a similar map on paper. Earthquake activity is distributed along the western coast of the United States and Canada. San Francisco, Anchorage, and Los Angeles are in earthquake zones and require shear wall and other earthquake safety features.

21.3.3 Whitetip reef sharks were commonly found in coastal waters, particularly near Maui and Kauai. Pigmy sharks were more likely to be found in the open ocean, and hammerheads in reefs around islands. Figure 21.32 is an XY scatter plot from the spreadsheet file showing where the sharks were seen.

21.3.4 (1) Students will plot locations with GPS coordinates (precise latitude and longitude) using an online mapping program such as Google Earth. (2) Field scientists use global positioning systems to locate field sites. For example, a marine biologist might record the GPS coordinates of a submerged reef. Given the coordinates, he or she can return periodically to study coral bleaching or other aspects of the coral reef ecosystem.

21.4.1 (1) Table 21.7 shows the answers for Table 21.1. (2) (a) Buffalo, N.Y.; (b) Denver, Colo.; (c) San Diego, Calif.; (d) Chicago, Ill.; (e) Helena, Mont.; (f) Buffalo, N.Y.; (g) Rapid City, S.D.; (h) San Francisco, Calif.

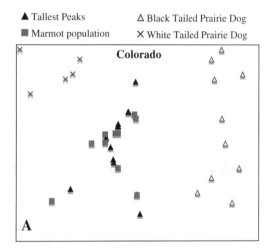

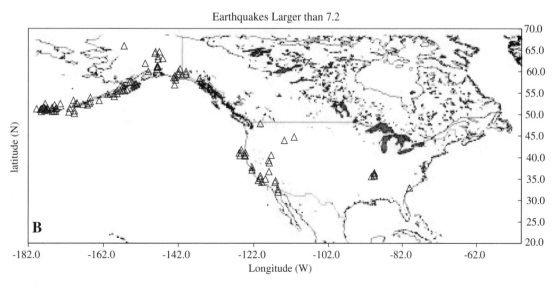

Figure 21.31 (A) Spreadsheet-Generated Map of Prairie Dog Populations and (B) Spreadsheet-Generated Map of Earthquakes

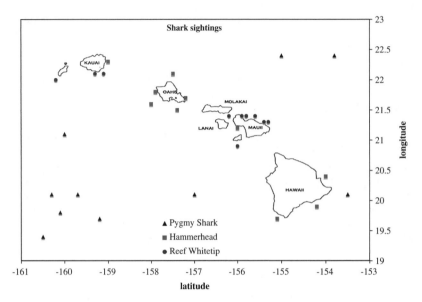

Figure 21.32 Scatter Plot of Shark-Sighting Data

Table 21.7 Data for Activity 2.4.1

	Seattle, WA	Dallas, TX	Rapid City, SD	Atlanta, GA
Temperature (°F)	46	53	25	51
Cloud cover	100%	50%	100%	0%
Weather	rain	no rain	snow	clear
Wind speed (knots)	calm	30 knots	20 knots	none
Direction of wind	no wind	north	southwest	none
Atmospheric pressure (mb)	1004 mb	1009	1000	1010

21.4.2 (1–3) Students should note that high- and low-pressure zones often move, and past patterns can be used to predict future weather. For example, the past four days' data can be used to predict the location where one might expect to find high- and low-pressure systems tomorrow. Many factors affect weather, making accurate predictions a complex task. (4–5) Student responses will vary.

21.4.3 (1) Student answers will vary. (2) Hurricane Hugo made landfall in South Carolina and traveled through South Carolina, North Carolina, Virginia, and West Virginia before dying down in Ohio. (3) See maps. csc.noaa.gov/hurricanes. (4) Atlantic hurricanes generally start in the subtropical waters of the eastern Atlantic and move west toward the Caribbean or the Southeastern United States. They lose intensity when they hit land and tend to turn to the right, often going back into the Atlantic.

21.5.1 (1) The radioactive cloud moved west across northern Europe and Scandinavia, then south over central and southern Europe. (2) Meteorologists learn much about wind patterns by tracking debris from volcanoes and large fires.

21.5.2 (1) Answers will vary. (2) Answers will vary. (3) Ozone peaks in the afternoon since it is a component of photochemical smog, formed as a result of the interaction of light and other pollutants. Ozone concentrations drop late in the day and remain low through midmorning. (4) See question 3.

21.5.3 (1) Answers will vary. (2) Answers will vary. (3) Heavy industries rely on large-scale transportation to receive and deliver products. As a result, they are often clustered near railways, major highways, and shipping lanes. These areas characteristically have worse pollution problems than surrounding regions.

21.6.1 (1–4) Refer to Figure 21.25 for star and constellation positions.

21.6.2 (1) Students locate Polaris. (2) Students calculate their latitude from the altitude (angle above the horizon) of Polaris. (3) Answers will vary.

21.6.3 (1) The International Space Station and the Hubble Space Telescope are the easiest to see. (2) Satellites appear brightest just after dusk or just before dawn. At these times, they are outside the Earth's shadow and reflecting light from the Sun. Since it is relatively dark at these times, they appear bright and easy to see. During the middle of the night, satellites are not easily seen because they are generally in the shadow of the Earth.

21.7.1 See Table 21.8.

21.7.2.(1) Students may find many examples of each feature. Some of the most notable features are Olympus Mons (the tallest volcano in the Solar System, 18° N, 133° W), Valles Marineris (the largest canyon/crevice in the Solar System), and Hellas Planitia (the largest impact basin on Mars, with a diameter of 2300 km). (2) Students should note great similarities between the surface of Earth and Mars. Mars, however, does not have rain, and hence little erosion, although ancient evidence of erosion is abundant. Impact craters and other geological features are more noticeable on Mars than on Earth due to the lack of rain and erosion.

Table 21.8 GPS Coordinates Matched with Points of Scientific Interest

	Latitude	Longitude
8	31.43563	−109.90147
1	35.02666	−111.02193
5	35.99714	−113.75961
11	33.35634	−116.86565
4	35.42517	−116.88874
6	37.74710	−119.53775
9	46.86077	−121.77235
12	38.13501	−122.88135
15	40.15506	−76.72356
10	43.08451	−79.06886
7	28.60965	−80.59909
3	41.83296	−88.25235
14	29.55402	−95.09417
2	40.74846	−73.98658
13	35.07370	−118.26500

Chapter Twenty-Two

Science Inquiry and Research

For the Teacher 458

22.1 Inquiry 459

22.2 Sensors and Probeware 461

22.3 Problem-Based Learning 465

22.4 Forums and Debates 466

22.5 Rotating Laboratories 468

22.6 Citing Research 470

Answers to Chapter Activities 471

For the Teacher

Science is the systematic study of the structure and behavior of the physical and natural world through observation and experiment. Science is investigative, and an emphasis on inquiry must be modeled in the classroom, just as it is practiced in the research laboratory. This chapter provides strategies and activities to engage students in scientific research in which they define *and* answer their own questions.

The National Science Education Standards were developed by the National Research Council to "promote a scientifically literate citizenry." The standards frequently encourage the use of inquiry in the science classroom, defining it as "a multifaceted activity that involves making observations; posing questions; examining books and other sources of information to see what is already known; planning investigations; reviewing what is already known in the light of experimental evidence; using tools to gather, analyze, and interpret data; proposing answers, explanations, and predictions; and communicating the results. Inquiry requires identification of assumptions, use of critical and logical thinking, and consideration of alternative explanations."[1] These skills are addressed in a wide variety of activities in this book, as referenced below:

- Making observations (Activities in section 5.2)
- Posing questions (Activities in section 23.1)
- Examining resources and reviewing what is known (Activities in sections 3.1, 22.5)
- Planning investigations (Activities in sections 5.5, 5.6, and 5.7)
- Using tools to gather, analyze, and interpret data (Activities in sections 19.1 to 19.5 and 22.2)
- Proposing answers, explanations, and predictions (Activities in sections 6.2 and 6.3)
- Communicating results (Activities 3.2, 3.4, and 3.5)

A special case of inquiry learning is *problem-based learning (PBL)*. Students are assigned to teams and provided an ill-defined problem. Teams must organize themselves, define objectives, assign responsibilities, conduct research, analyze results, and present conclusions. The problems are purposely ill defined, causing team members to work collaboratively to define specific issues, problems, and objectives. Such tasks mimic the problem-solving skills that professionals engage in, whether repairing automobiles or treating cancer patients. Problem-based learning employs open-ended questions that are not limited to a single correct answer. The questions elicit diverse ideas and opinions and require students to work as a group. Problem-based learning naturally integrates various fields of study as students search beyond the traditional curricular boundaries to develop solutions. The activities in this chapter provide students opportunities to develop scientific reasoning and skills through problem-based learning and other inquiry-based activities.

Researchers have found that inquiry is a very effective learning technique.[2] A helpful way to visualize inquiry learning is with the 5-E model proposed by Richard Bybee.[3] The 5-E model (Table 22.1) is a *constructivist approach,* which provides students the opportunity to use logic and prior knowledge to build understanding.[4]

The 5-E model seeks to engage students in the lesson before exploration or explanation. This contrasts with traditional instruction in which teachers present principles that students verify in the laboratory. Although inquiry is a powerful approach, it is time-consuming and should be integrated with other instructional strategies. More recently, a 7-E model has been proposed: Elicit, Engage, Explore, Explain, Elaborate, Evaluate, and Extend.[5]

22.1 Inquiry

Alfred Nobel, the Swedish chemist and industrialist who invented dynamite, dedicated his fortune to the establishment of yearly prizes for those making the most significant contributions to physics, chemistry, literature, peace, physiology, and economics. Today the Nobel Prize is widely recognized as the supreme commendation in these fields of study. Table 22.2 lists a few of the Nobel Prize winners and what their discoveries led to. The Nobel Prize is awarded only to those who have asked *and* answered important questions. Each winner is an expert in inquiry.

Scientific inquiry is a process in which one asks testable questions and sets out to discover the answers. There is no single method of inquiry, but classroom science inquiry is characterized by the five elements listed in Table 22.3. These elements are not necessarily linear and may occur at any time during an inquiry.

Table 22.1 The 5-E Learning Cycle and Instructional Model

Engage: Provide activities that access prior knowledge, capture student interest, and stimulate student thinking. Possible activities include counterintuitive demonstrations, intriguing movie clips, current events, and hypothetical questions.

Explore: Provide students the opportunity to plan, collect, and organize data. Possible activities include designing and performing an investigation, solving a problem, and reading to collect further information.

Explain: Students analyze data they have collected and formulate explanations. Possible activities include comparing, classifying, and analyzing data; building explanations; and supporting ideas with evidence.

Elaborate: Students expand their understanding by applying it to real-world situations. Possible activities include giving examples of how the principles apply to other phenomena and making decisions based on new understandings.

Evaluate: Students evaluate their understanding. Possible activities include determining the limits to findings and evaluating the authenticity and accuracy of information and conclusions.

Table 22.2 A Few Notable Nobel Prize Laureates

Year	Researcher	Discovery	Applications
1909	Guglilmo Marconi (Italy) Ferdinand Braun (Germany)	Communication via radio waves	Radio, TV, wireless Internet, satellite communication, cell phones
1918	Fritz Haber (Germany)	Production of ammonia	Synthetic fertilizers that increased worldwide agricultural production 50 percent
1962	Francis Crick (USA) James Watson (USA) Maurice Wilkins (USA)	Structure of the DNA molecule	Biotechnology, genetic analysis, understanding of genetics and inheritance
1965	William Shockley (USA) Walter H. Brattain (USA) John Bardeen (USA)	Electronic transistor	Computers, cell phones, cameras, calculators, global positioning systems, and other electronic devices
1995	Sherwood Rowland (USA) Mario Molina (USA) Paul Crutzen (Netherlands)	Ozone depletion by chlorofluoro-carbons (CFCs)	Led to the banning of CFC production and development of an international effort to protect Earth's ozone layer

Source: Nobel Foundation. (2007). *Nobel laureates.* Retrieved May 15, 2007, from http://nobelprize.org.

Table 22.3 Characteristics of Classroom Inquiry

Ask testable questions.	Ask scientifically oriented questions that can be investigated with available resources.
Give priority to evidence in responding to questions.	Examine evidence from a variety of sources when responding to a question.
Formulate explanations from evidence.	Develop explanations based on observations, measurements, and the work of others.
Connect explanations to scientific knowledge.	Connect work and findings to the research and findings of others.
Communicate explanations.	Share findings with others through dialogue, conferences, publications, and/or the Internet.

Source: System-Wide Change for All Learners and Educators. (2007). *What makes things float? An immersion unit investigating density and buoyancy.* NSF Award No. 0227016.

ACTIVITY 22.1.1 *Inquiry: What Factors Determine Termite Movement?*

Termites are insects that live in colonies, feed on wood, and can be highly destructive to wooden structures and trees. Entomologists (those who study insects) are quite interested in termite behavior because of their economic impact.

Your teacher will provide you with termites obtained from a scientific supply company. Draw a full-page figure eight on a blank white sheet of paper with a Papermate or Scripto ballpoint pen (Figure 22.1). (*Note:* The brand of pen used is important.) Place a termite on the pen mark, and record its movement. Develop and test one or more questions related to termite movement

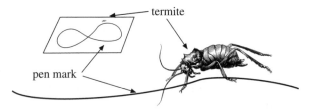

Figure 22.1 Inquiry Activity: Termites and Ink

and pen marks. Communicate your findings to the class.

ACTIVITY 22.1.2 *Inquiry: What Makes Things Float or Sink?*

Place a can of diet soda and a can of regular soda in a container of water, and note that the diet

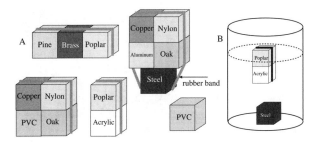

Figure 22.2 (A) Assemble Different Combinations of Blocks (A) to See If They Float or Sink (B)

soda floats while the regular soda sinks. Why? Try to answer this question in the following inquiry investigation.

Your teacher will provide you with a set of density blocks obtained from a scientific supply company (see *sciencesourcebook.com,* carolina.com, or search "density blocks"). All of the blocks are the same size and thus have the same volume, but some sink and some float in water. Determine the volume of the blocks by cubing the length of a side. Express the volume in cubic centimeters. Many supply companies provide blocks with a volume of 1 cubic inch (1 in.^{3} = 16.4 cm^3). Test all blocks in a container of water, and record those that float and those that sink. What makes some blocks float and others sink? What will happen if you combine blocks? Connect blocks with rubber bands and record whether they sink or float (Figure 22.2).

Record the mass of each combination and the number of blocks, and note whether it sinks or floats. Plot the mass of each combination on the *y*-axis, and the volume on the *x*-axis. Indicate "floaters" with an open circle and "sinkers" with a closed circle. Try to get combinations that neither float nor sink but stay suspended in the middle of the water column. Examine the evidence you have collected and answer the question, "What determines if an object will sink or float?"

22.2 Sensors and Probeware

A sensor (probe) is a device that continuously detects and responds to stimuli such as temperature, light, or motion. For example, an automobile is equipped with an acceleration sensor to detect rapid deceleration as occurs in serious accidents. Under normal acceleration and deceleration, no signal is sent to the airbag, but during rapid deceleration, a command is sent to deploy the airbag with the intent of protecting passengers from injury. Sensors are used to monitor and control a wide array of industrial, medical, and consumer products, a few of which are listed below.

- *Accelerometers:* Accelerometers in cars detect rapid deceleration and trigger airbag deployment in accidents. Accelerometers in laptop computers detect when the device is dropped, sending a command to park the hard drive to prevent loss of data.
- *Temperature sensors:* Buildings are equipped with thermostats that trigger air conditioners or heaters to keep temperatures in an acceptable range. Many fire alarm systems employ temperature sensors to detect fire.
- *Light sensors:* Streetlights are often equipped with light sensors that shut off electricity during daylight hours. Video cameras continuously monitor lighting conditions and control the aperture to ensure proper lighting while recording.
- *Motion sensors:* Doppler shift security systems detect motion and trigger burglar alarms. Professional baseball stadiums use motion sensors to record pitching speeds.
- *Oxygen sensors:* Cars are equipped with oxygen sensors to ensure complete combustion and reduce auto emissions. Cardiologists use oxygen sensors to monitor blood oxygen levels during surgery.
- *Electromagnetic sensors:* Traffic engineers install electromagnetic sensors to detect the presence of automobiles and trigger traffic lights to optimize traffic flow. Metal detectors rely on changes in the electromagnetic field to locate hidden metal objects in structures or the ground.
- *Pressure sensors:* Airplanes are equipped with pressure sensors to detect air speed, elevation, and rate of climb. Industrial robots use pressure sensors to detect when they have made contact with the object they are assembling or repairing.

Sensors and probeware have revolutionized scientific research. Prior to the development of electronic sensors and computers, researchers had to continuously monitor experiments and record data. Manual data recording is a tedious, error-prone task, and researchers are unable to examine events that take place very quickly or over very long periods of time by traditional manual methods.

ACTIVITY 22.2.1 *Commercial and Industrial Uses of Sensors*

Table 22.4 lists sensors that are commonly used in the classroom or laboratory. Each of these sensors has commercial applications as well. Identify a possible commercial application for each of the sensors listed in Table 22.4.

ACTIVITY 22.2.2 *Probeware Experiments*

Probeware automates data collection and allows researchers to collect data continuously, even when the researcher is not present (Figure 22.3). Table 22.4 lists the sensors that are commonly used in secondary school and college classrooms. These sensors (probes) are available from various scientific supply companies (such as pasco.com, vernier.com, or search "probeware") and can be purchased on the Internet.

- *Develop a question.* Write a research question that can be answered using the probeware you have available. For example, "What is the effect of light intensity on photosynthesis in *Elodea*?" Tables 22.5 to 22.8 list investigations that can be performed with the appropriate sensors.

Table 22.4 Common Sensors

accelerometer	heart rate	pressure
barometer	humidity	radiation
carbon dioxide	light	sound frequency
colorimeter	magnetic field	sound level
conductivity	mass (scale)	temperature
dissolved oxygen	motion	turbidity
electrocardio-graph	oxygen gas	voltage/current/
	pH	resistance
force		

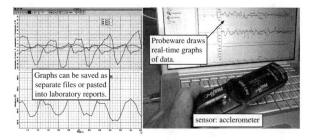

Figure 22.3 Probeware Facilitates Continuous Data Collection and Graphing

Table 22.5 Physics Investigations Performed Using Specified Sensors

Acceleration due to gravity (motion)
Angle of incline and normal forces (force)
Centripetal force (force)
Centripetal motion (accelerometer)
Coefficient of friction (motion)
Color and the absorption of light (temperature)
Conservation of momentum (force)
Friction and thermal energy (temperature)
Heat versus temperature (temperature)
Hooke's law (force)
Impulse (force and motion)
Inverse square law (light, magnetic field, or radiation)
Motion in three dimensions (accelerometer)
Newton's second law (force and motion sensor)
Ohm's law (multimeter: voltage, current, resistance)
Parallel and series circuits (multimeter: voltage, current, resistance)
Pendulums—periodic motion (force)
Position versus time (motion sensor)
Relationship of weight and mass (force)

- *Design an experiment.* Design an experiment that uses sensors to collect data. If you are having difficulty designing an experiment, you may wish to search the Internet for probeware-based experiments that are related to your research question. Make certain to define your control and experimental treatments, as well as your independent and dependent variables (see section 5.5 in Chapter Five).

Table 22.6 Chemistry Investigations Performed Using Specified Sensors

Acid-base reactions (pH)
Acid-base titration (pH)
Boyle's law (pressure)
Chemical reactions (colorimeter or temperature)
Combustion (oxygen or carbon dioxide or electronic balance)
Conductivity of solutions (conductivity sensor)
Endothermic reactions (temperature)
Evaporative cooling (temperature)
Exothermic reactions (temperature)
Freezing and melting points (temperature)
Heat of fusion (temperature)
Heats of fusion and vaporization (temperature)
Ideal gas law (pressure, temperature)
Ion concentration (conductivity)
Vaporization (electronic balance)

Table 22.7 Biology Investigations Performed Using Specified Sensors

Caloric value of food (temperature)
Exercise and heart rate (heart rate)
Exercise and heart activity (electrocardiograph)
Exercise and muscle fatigue (force)
Exercise and respiration (carbon dioxide)
Germination and respiration (carbon dioxide)
Microbial activity (pH, carbon dioxide, or temperature)
Photosynthesis in aquatic plants (dissolved oxygen)
Photosynthesis in terrestrial plants (atmospheric oxygen)
Relationship of sound frequency and pitch (sound frequency)
Respiration (carbon dioxide)
Skin temperature response time (temperature)
Surface body temperatures (temperature)
Temperature and metabolism (temperature)
Transpiration (humidity or pressure)

- *Conduct an experiment.* Connect your sensors to your computer or handheld interface, and collect the desired data. The software associated with your sensors will collect and plot data as shown in Figure 22.3.

Table 22.8 Earth Science Investigations Performed with Specified Sensors

Acid rain, soil, and water pH (pH)
Air pressure and weather (barometer)
Classroom air quality changes (carbon dioxide and/ or oxygen)
Convection and conduction (temperature)
Convection currents (temperature)
Daily patterns in light intensity (light sensor)
Geographic temperature variation (temperature)
Noise pollution (sound level sensor)
Radiation (radiation or light)
Rainfall and water quality (turbidity sensor)
Seasonal variations in light intensity (light sensor)
Soil salinity (conductivity)
Specific heat of land versus water (temperature)
Temperature and relative humidity (temperature and humidity)

- *Write a report.* Interpret the data in the light of the question you asked.

ACTIVITY 22.2.3 *Creating Real-World Events to Match Graphs*

Although technology solves many problems, it can create others. For example, although calculators allow people to perform complex tasks, many become so dependent on them that they never master basic arithmetic skills. Probeware could have this same effect since data are automatically collected and plotted, allowing students to perform difficult experiments while never mastering skills of data collection and interpretation. This activity is designed to ensure that you develop an understanding of the graphs produced by the computer.

Figure 22.4 shows a series of graphs. Recreate these graphs using probeware and activities of your design. For example, Figure 22.4S shows a steadily declining mass. A constant downward slope like this may be achieved by placing a burning candle or a hot cup of water on the electronic balance. As the candle burns, mass is lost to the atmosphere. As water evaporates from the cup, a similar graph is produced. In replicating the graphs, focus on general trends, and don't worry about matching the graphs precisely.

Activities using the **temperature** sensor

Activities using the **force** sensor

Activities using the **light** sensor

Activities using the **accelerometer**

Activities using the **mass** sensor (balance)

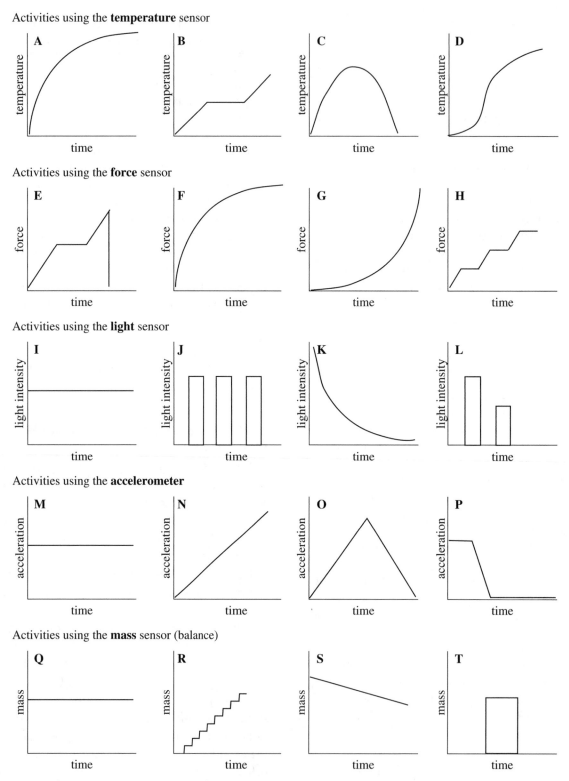

Figure 22.4 Perform Activities Using Probeware to Recreate These Graphs

22.3 Problem-Based Learning

Although much legislation deals with issues related to science and technology, few legislators have a strong background in science. Legislators often rely on commissions, think tanks, special interest groups, lobbyists, and others who have greater understanding of the issues. The Brookings Institute, Rand Corporation, Hoover Institution, World Resources Institute, and Heritage Foundation are a few of the many think tanks that generate reports that legislators use to guide their decision-making process.

In the activities that follow, you will be a member of a think tank and generate a report to share with "legislators." Follow the steps in the problem-based learning (PBL) model as you prepare your report, policy, or action plan.

1. *Knowns:* What does your study group already know? List all relevant information pertaining to the subject.
2. *Ideas:* What ideas or hypotheses do you have based on information you already possess? List your current ideas prior to research.
3. *Unknowns:* What do you need to know? What are your learning needs? Prepare a list of questions that should be answered before you proceed.
4. *Plan:* Who will collect the information? Assign responsibilities for data collection.
5. *Problem:* What is your problem? Define your problem in a one- to two-sentence statement.
6. *Analysis:* What do the data say? Analyze and discuss your data as they pertain to the problem.
7. *Report:* Prepare a report in which you state your findings, inferences, predictions, and recommendations. Support arguments, conclusions, and recommendations with evidence, and state any assumptions that have been made.

ACTIVITY 22.3.1 *Preparing Reports, Policies, and Action Plans*

Select one of the following issues, and prepare a report following the PBL steps listed above.

- *Preparing for disaster:* Your city council has just appointed you to an earthquake (or tornado, hurricane, flood, volcano, fire, meteor strike, or other natural disaster) preparedness committee. Your committee is charged with assessing the risks, creating a disaster preparedness plan, and informing the community.
- *Saving endangered species:* The mountain gorilla is a rare and endangered species living in the mountains of Rwanda, Uganda, and the Democratic Republic of Congo. Develop a plan for saving the mountain gorilla from extinction. Alternatively, your committee may develop a plan for saving the Asian elephant, giant panda, black rhinoceros, chimpanzee, tiger, or other endangered species.
- *Predicting the impact of tropical deforestation:* Tropical rain forests comprise less than 2 percent of the Earth's surface area but account for more than 50 percent of all plant and animal species. Satellite photos from NASA show extensive deforestation in the Amazonian basin, equatorial Africa, and southeastern Asia. The United Nations has contracted your company to write a report predicting the biological, hydrological, climactic, economic, and social impacts of tropical rain forest deforestation.
- *Evaluating environmental legislation and treaties:* The Montreal Protocol on Substances That Deplete the Ozone Layer is an international treaty designed to protect the Earth's ozone layer from destruction by man-made chemicals. Nearly all nations have signed the treaty, making it the most widely adopted treaty to date. The United Nations has hired your team to evaluate the economic, scientific, environmental, and social impacts of the treaty. Alternatively, your team may select to evaluate the Kyoto Protocol to the United Nations Framework Convention on Climate Change, the United States Endangered Species Act, the Safe Drinking Water Act, or the National Environmental Policy Act.
- *Developing an energy policy:* Many experts agree that we have passed the period of peak oil production and that worldwide demand for oil will exceed production in the years to come.

The U.S. Department of Energy has hired your company to serve as a consultant for drafting a new energy policy. Your company must evaluate the seriousness of the issue and develop a plan that will incorporate a wide variety of innovative technologies to keep energy supply at pace with growing energy demand.

- *Serving as an expert witness in court:* Lawyers often call on the technical expertise of scientists when preparing their cases for the courtroom. A prominent legal team has hired your company to evaluate the claims of clients who say that groundwater pollution from a local landfill has entered the water supply, resulting in increased illness in the community.

- *Judging medical malpractice:* As a member of an arbitration team, you are often called to settle disputes. Both parties agree to abide by your decisions, but expect a fair and impartial ruling based on solid evidence. Your current case deals with an athlete who claims that his physician did not adequately repair his anterior cruciate ligament, and as a result he can no longer play professional football.

- *Protecting the coasts:* More than 60 percent of the population of the United States lives within 50 mi of the coast (Pacific Ocean, Atlantic Ocean, Arctic Ocean, or the Great Lakes). This percentage is expected to increase as America ages and retirees move to coastal communities. Coastal development has resulted in degraded coastal water quality, a reduction in the quantity and diversity of coastal wildlife, increased coastal and shoreline erosion, decreased open space for public use, and other ecological problems. Develop a report for the U.S. Interior Department and state coastal commissions. Your report should address concerns and trends, and propose workable solutions to protect coastal resources during a period of population growth.

22.4 Forums and Debates

Scientific research flourishes when there is open dialogue among researchers. The principal forums for such dialogue are professional meetings, journals, and online discussions. There are numerous organizations devoted to scientific research, ranging from very broad-based interest groups such as the American Association for the Advancement of Science to highly specialized groups such as the Society of Neuroscience, Society of Wetland Scientists, and Soil Science Society of America. Nearly all of these organizations hold periodic meetings at which members present their latest research and findings. In addition, these organizations sponsor journals in which research is published and disseminated. These journals require *peer review,* meaning that experts in the field have reviewed and approved the article for publication. The following are some of the best-known journals:

Science—American Association for the Advancement of Science
Physics Today—Institute of Physics
Journal of the American Chemical Society—American Chemical Society
Journal of the American Medical Association—American Medical Association
Geology—Geological Society of America
Proceedings of the National Academy of Sciences—National Academy of Sciences

Scientists share their findings with the public through general interest journals such as *Nature, Scientific American,* and *Science News.* Although these journals and organizations are essential to science, they do not provide a forum for young or novice researchers. Fortunately, there are venues, such as *Journal of Student Research Abstracts* (an annual journal for young investigators and their teachers) and science fairs (see Chapter Twenty-Three) where young researchers can present their findings. In addition, young researchers can publish their findings on the Web so that other students and scientists can see their work.

ACTIVITY 22.4.1 *Developing Electronic Forums, Blogs, and Web Sites*

A threaded electronic discussion group or forum affords students the opportunity to post their ideas or research so others can read and comment. Figure 22.5 shows the framework of a typical discussion group.

The instructor establishes the basic framework of the forum, and students reply within these threads. In this example, the instructor established the major thread (major topic): environmental issues. Students then started minor threads (minor topics) of deforestation, ozone hole, global warming, and desertification. Students interested in writing about deforestation would select this thread and read all of the related messages before posting their own reply.

Using a threaded discussion group, students can post the findings of their research and request comments and suggestions. Alternatively, teachers can post questions or activities, and students can reply online, and read or critique the contributions of their peers. Newsgroups can be used for a variety of purposes. Prompts for the individual discussions should invite comment. For example, in Figure 22.5, a prompt at the top level of the deforestation discussion could be, "Explain the reasons for rapid deforestation in the past 50 years" or "What are the effects of deforestation in the Amazon rain forest?"

Create an electronic discussion group using a free online service, or respond to the online prompts of a discussion group created by your instructor. Alternatively, you may want to publish a Blog (web log) showing the progress of a science project you are working on, develop a Web site in which you publish your experimental or library science research, or publish a movie of your work to an amateur movie database (look on *science sourcebook.com*, groups.google.com, or movies. google.com, or search "newsgroups").

ACTIVITY 22.4.2 *Science, Technology, and Public Policy Debates*

Debate is a formal method of presenting arguments with the purpose of persuading others of the merits of a particular position on an issue. Legislators debate issues so they can make informed decisions. Candidates debate issues so citizens can decide how to cast their votes. Debates follow structure protocols, and participants must follow specific rules. Traditionally one side presents its case, followed by the opposing side. Each side is then provided time for a rebuttal to refute the arguments or claims of its opponent, and then there is time for a closing argument from both sides.

In this activity, you will debate various issues on their scientific, technological, and social merit. Unless otherwise specified by your teacher, use the format that follows (Figure 22.6):

Debate Format

Prior to the debate. Each debater submits his or her notes to the teacher, citing references as appropriate (see section 22.6).

Introduction (2 minutes per debater). Each debater delivers a prepared speech, focusing on one or more issues relevant to the debate statement. All members of the team in favor of the statement speak first, followed by all members of the team opposing the statement.

Preparation for rebuttal (3 minutes). Debaters are given the opportunity to prepare a rebuttal.

Rebuttal (1.5 minutes per debater). Each debater is given the opportunity to refute or contradict the statements of opponents.

Questions. The audience is given opportunity to ask questions of the debaters.

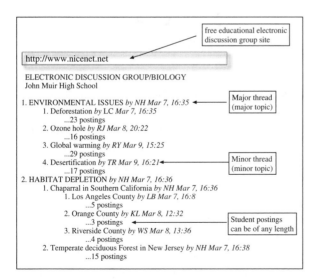

Figure 22.5 Sample Electronic Discussion Group

Science & Technology Debate Schedule
time - 20 minutes
one student per topic
topics/students can be added as necessary

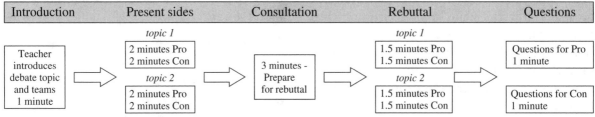

| Introduction | Present sides | Consultation | Rebuttal | Questions |

topic 1

Teacher introduces debate topic and teams 1 minute

2 minutes Pro
2 minutes Con

topic 2

2 minutes Pro
2 minutes Con

3 minutes - Prepare for rebuttal

topic 1

1.5 minutes Pro
1.5 minutes Con

topic 2

1.5 minutes Pro
1.5 minutes Con

Questions for Pro
1 minute

Questions for Con
1 minute

Figure 22.6 Sample Science and Technology Debate Format

Sample Debate Statements

Teams speak in favor of or in opposition to the statement.

- A superconducting supercollider should be built with federal tax dollars.
- NASA should pursue a manned mission to Mars.
- Aquaculture is an environmentally friendly way to increase the food supply.
- Global warming is a direct result of human activity.
- The ozone hole is a direct result of human activity.
- State and local governments should release earthquake predictions.
- Transgenic fish should be released in the oceans to increase food production.
- Federal air quality standards should be stricter.
- Fuel cell technology will eliminate the U.S. need for imported oil.
- The federal government should establish renewable-fuel standards.
- Nuclear power should be expanded.
- Recent severe weather patterns are a result of global warming.
- Tradable pollution credits safeguard the environment.
- Government funding of the space program helps the national economy.
- Ethanol-fuel production should be subsidized by the government.

- Transgenic monoculture crops should be banned.
- Conservation is a luxury only wealthy nations can afford.
- Local sanitary landfill standards are too lax.
- The local community should build a trash-to-electricity generator.
- Increases in skin cancer are a result of a diminished ozone layer.
- The federal government should subsidize the search for new oil reserves.
- The federal government should establish a fishing quota program.

22.5 Rotating Laboratories

Many schools are unable to offer their students adequate laboratory experiences due to limited resources. It is often unfeasible to offer activities that use microscopes, computers, probeware, oscilloscopes, and other expensive laboratory equipment. To provide meaningful hands-on experiences with limited equipment, teachers should consider rotating students through laboratory activities rather than engaging them simultaneously in the same activity. Using the rotational approach, students are divided into lab groups and assigned to a sequence of activities. Since only a fraction of the class is engaged in a given activity on any day, teachers need only acquire a fraction of the equipment than if all of the students performed the same activity simultaneously.

Figure 22.7 shows a schedule for a class of 36 students in which 3 students are assigned to each of 12 laboratory groups. On day 1, groups 1, 5, and 9 do activity 1; groups 2, 6, and 10 do activity 2; groups 3, 7, and 11 do activity 3; and groups 4, 8, and 12 do activity 4. On day 2, all of the teams move to a new activity (Figure 22.7B). In this example, the teacher must acquire only one-fourth as much equipment as would be needed if all of the students performed the activity simultaneously (Figure 22.7C).

Figure 22.7A shows a hypothetical schedule for a team of three students. Each student serves as captain, teacher, and scout at least once in every rotation. For example, student 1 serves as the captain of the enzyme and genetics activities, as the teacher of the respiration activity, and as the scout during the photosynthesis lab. The captain of an activity has the responsibility of organizing the investigation, collecting the written contributions of all team members, and editing and submitting the final laboratory report. The scout participates in the current investigation with his or her team, but also looks for opportunities to observe the activity that his or her group will be doing next. As time permits, the scout consults with the teacher of the upcoming activity to learn the procedure

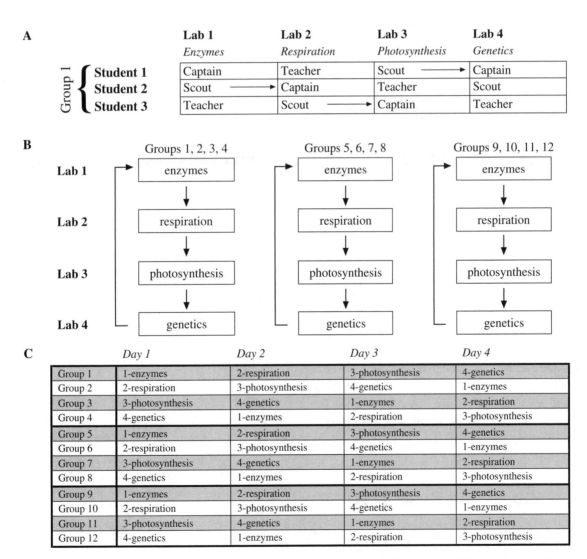

Figure 22.7 Rotating Laboratory: (A) Team Assignments. (B) Lab Sequence. (C) Lab Schedule

and how it may be improved. It is the teacher's responsibility to provide the scout of the next team with information that will allow it to move more efficiently through the activity. In the example (Figure 22.7), the scout of group 1 consults with the teacher of group 2 so that he or she can be an effective captain of that activity on the next day of the rotation. Similarly, the scout of group 2 consults with the teacher of group 3, so he or she can be prepared to serve as captain of this activity on the next day of the rotation.

In a traditional (nonrotating) scheme, the instructor prepares the entire class for the laboratory on the day prior to the activity. Such preparation is generally not feasible in the rotating scheme because of the variety of simultaneous activities. You may wish to provide an extra day at the beginning of the rotation since groups will not have had the opportunity to watch their peers. Extra time allows each group to perfect its first activity so it can get better results and more adequately prepare subsequent groups. Since each group builds on the experiences of those who precede them, the performance of the last group to do a given activity should be better than that of the first group. For example, group 1 should do best on the genetics activity (Figure 22.7B) because the members will have learned from group 3, which learned from group 2, which learned from group 1.

The rotational laboratory approach affords students the opportunity to work with equipment and perform experiments and activities that would otherwise be unavailable to them. It also fosters a cooperative environment in which students learn from each other and ultimately develop better techniques and obtain better results than they do in a one-day, one-activity approach. The rotational laboratory approach more closely models the world of scientific investigation in which research teams share their findings with their colleagues.

22.6 Citing Research

Scientists do not work in a vacuum. They rely heavily on the ideas and findings of others. It is essential that scientists, as well as other researchers and writers, appropriately cite the work of others. Presenting the writing of another as one's own work is known as *plagiarism* and is considered a serious form of academic dishonesty. Plagiarism is sometimes intentional, but often it is unintentional as writers forget to adequately cite the ideas and writings of others. Writers should place borrowed text in quotations, and provide footnotes or endnotes that reference the source of the quoted work. Similarly, it is important to cite the ideas of others. Science teachers can check for potential plagiarism in many ways, the easiest of which is through a commercial service such as Turnitin (www.turnitin.com), which checks student work against millions of Web sites and other student papers.

To avoid accidental plagiarism, students should keep notes copied from the Internet in a different file from the paper they write and place all copied material in quotes, citing their references. They should also cite ideas that come from other sources.

ACTIVITY 22.6.1 *Detecting Plagiarism*
Plagiarism is very easy to detect with a commercial resource such as Turnitin. It can also be detected using Internet search engines. Search for identical text on two or more pages, and see if proper citations have been used. To do this, copy a sentence from a science article on one Web site (e.g., Wikipedia), and place it within quotes in the Find window of a search engine. The quotes force the search engine to look for the string of words in the order you have placed them. Compare the text against others on the Internet to see if text has been adequately cited or plagiarized.

ACTIVITY 22.6.2 *Building a Bibliography*
Various organizations have established guidelines for writing style and the citation of references. The standards established by the American Psychological Association (APA),[6] Modern Language Association (MLA),[7] and the Council of Science Editors (CSE)[8] are widely used, but differ one from another. I recommend science students use the CSE standards and have provided

examples in Figure 22.8. Find five or more references on a science topic of relevance, including at least one book, one journal article, and one Web site. Cite your references according to the Council of Science Editors guidelines.

Answers to Chapter Activities

22.1.1 Students will find that termites will follow a fresh trail left by any Papermate or Scripto ballpoint pen. They may generate and test a variety of questions such as: Do termites exhibit any pattern in their movement? What do termites do if they miss a turn in the

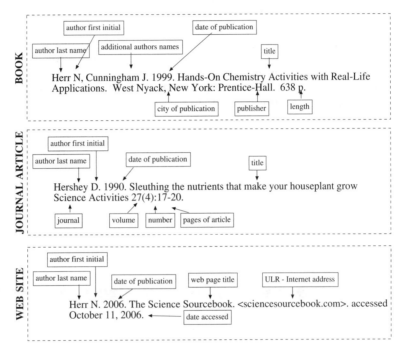

Figure 22.8 Council of Science Editors Bibliographical Citation Guidelines

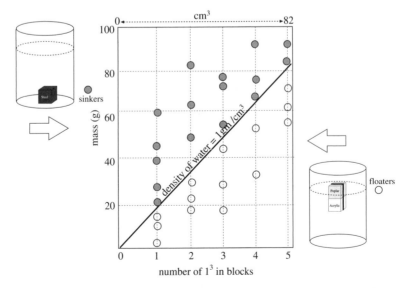

Figure 22.9 Students Discover the Mass-to-Volume Ratio Determines If an Object Will Float

line? What will happen if termites travel in opposite directions on the pen line and meet? Do workers and soldiers follow the trail equally well? Do they follow all colors of ink equally well? Are they following the ink trail or the indentation left in the paper by the pen? Will they follow pencil marks? Are they able to follow pen trails on newsprint, photocopy, and notebook paper equally well? Do they follow all manufacturers' pens equally well? Look for and encourage the characteristics of classroom inquiry (Table 22.3) as students engage in this activity.

22.1.2 Put all student data on the board or projector. Students can then plot these data on graph paper or with a spreadsheet program (see Chapter Twenty and Figure 22.9). Students may note that an imaginary line separates the floaters from the sinkers and that the slope of this line is 1 g/cm³. You may then ask them

to measure the mass of a given volume of water using a beaker or graduated cylinder. When they plot this point on the chart, they will note that it falls on the line. Thus, they have discovered that things with a density greater than water sink and those with a density less than water float. Note that I have not mentioned the term *density* except with reference to the blocks. Rather than introducing students to the concept of density and having them verify it through measurement, the activity allows them to discover the concept and use it to answer questions and make predictions. Students have constructed their own understanding of density using prior knowledge and experience.

22.2.1 Student answers will vary, but should have the form shown in the introductory portion of section 22.2.

22.2.2–22.6 Answers will vary.

Chapter Twenty-Three

Science Projects and Fairs

For the Teacher 473

23.1 Writing Research Questions 474

23.2 Developing a Research Proposal 486

23.3 Conducting Research 487

23.4 Sharing Your Findings 488

Answers to Chapter Activities 490

For the Teacher

Science projects and fairs offer students a rare opportunity to engage in scientific research. Unlike traditional classroom experiments and demonstrations, science projects challenge students to develop their own questions, design their own experiments, conduct their own research, and present their own findings. Students present their work with posters (Figure 23.1A) and presentations to peers, parents, and other members of the community (Figure 23.1B). Most science fairs provide recognition and awards for those who excel.

The first national science fair took place in 1942, when Science Service and the Westinghouse Corporation offered the first Science Talent Search.[1] Since then, numerous school, district, county, and state science fairs have been developed to encourage students in scientific research. The best-known international event is the Intel International Science and Engineering Fair,[2] which sponsors precollege research and provides millions of dollars in college scholarships.

Science fairs spur adolescents toward academic excellence, much the way sporting events drive them toward athletic excellence. This effect is chronicled in the Universal Pictures movie *October Sky*, in which four boys from an impoverished coal-mining town in Appalachia earn top honors at the national science fair for their design and development of homemade rockets. This story, based on a historical novel by Homer Hickham (*Rocket Boys*), may inspire students to think big as they plan their projects.[3]

The benefits of science projects and fairs may last a lifetime, as they have for me, when my eighth-grade work in the development of a pinhole camera sparked an interest in science that has never died. Unfortunately science projects and fairs can also engender a dislike toward research and science. Most students are ill prepared to engage in scientific research, and most parents are unprepared to assist them. Unable to organize ideas, design experiments, or acquire needed materials, many become overwhelmed and frustrated. It is therefore critical that science projects and fairs be structured to provide clear paths for

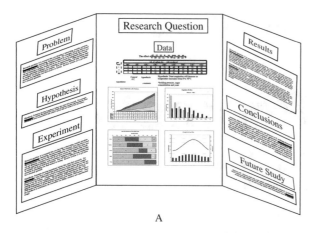

Figure 23.1 (A) Science Project Poster and (B) A Local Science Fair Poster Session

student success. If students are frustrated with their projects, they may become disinterested in science and research.

For many years, American and Canadian colleges and universities have graduated an insufficient supply of scientists and engineers to meet the demands of our technologically driven societies.[4] Low enrollment in college science programs is due in part to a culture of science-phobia that is prevalent in many schools. Aware that science projects may contribute to this phobia, teachers should prepare their students well to ensure they have a positive experience and opportunity for success.

This chapter provides information that will help students write research questions, proposals, and reports. I suggest that you review these materials and adapt them for your student population. If you teach in a school whose students come from well-educated families, you will likely experience greater success with the science fair. If you teach in

a school whose students come from less-educated families, the science fair will be much more challenging, but potentially more valuable, if done well.

Perhaps the greatest challenge students face when conducting their own research is learning to write suitable research questions. The research question must be answerable, of interest to the student, and possible given the resources available to the student. Review section 23.1 on writing research questions, and adapt it to the needs of your students. Students should become proficient in writing research questions before they settle on one for their science project.

"People don't plan to fail, they just fail to plan!" This truism is particularly apt as it relates to science projects. There is a tendency to want to answer the question before thinking deeply about how it can be answered. For this reason, it is important to require students to develop a research proposal before they begin their science projects. Section 23.2 provides directions for writing a research proposal, and these should be adapted to the needs of your students. Finally, section 23.3 sets out guidelines for conducting research and section 23.4 for writing reports and sharing results.

23.1 Writing Research Questions

Most of us ask "research" questions on a regular basis, whether we realize it or not. Sometimes we ask *observational* questions, such as, "What is my gas mileage?" and other times we ask *cause-and-effect questions*, such as "Will my car get better gas mileage at 60 or 65 miles per hour?" Both types of questions are important but must be phrased well if they are to guide scientific investigation. The following activities provide an opportunity to practice writing observational and cause-and-effect questions.

ACTIVITY 23.1.1 *Writing Observational Research Questions*

Most research starts with observations. The researcher documents patterns and trends that may provide the foundation for later causal research studies. Observational studies can be *quantitative* (measured with numbers) or *qualitative* (based on description), but they are not experimental. The researcher records measurements and descriptions but does not alter independent variables to see their effect. Review the following observational questions and identify which are *quantitative* (require the recording of specific numbers) and which are *qualitative* (based on quality or character):

1. Are AM or FM radio signals stronger in tunnels?
2. Do soap bubbles last longer on warm or cold days?
3. What percentage of my class is right-eye-dominant?
4. Is the density of aphids greater on the top or bottom of rose leaves?
5. What is the current pH of my home tap water?
6. What is the average height of 2-week-old radish seedlings?
7. What is the maximum acceleration of the world's fastest roller coaster?
8. Are earthquakes more common near the coasts or inland?
9. Which cloud types are associated with rainstorms?
10. What is the average base height of cumulus clouds?
11. Write two quantitative and two qualitative observational questions. These questions should be related to the subject you are currently studying in class.

ACTIVITY 23.1.2 *Writing Experimental Research Questions*

An experiment is a scientific procedure designed to test a *hypothesis* or make a discovery. The researcher compares the results of an *experimental sample* against those from a *control sample* that is treated the same except for the factor under investigation. Experimental research questions must include an *independent variable, dependent variable,* and *subject* (see sections 5.5 and 5.6).

The *independent variable* is the variable that the researcher selects or manipulates to determine if it produces changes in the *dependent variable*. The researcher looks for evidence that changes in the independent variable are correlated with changes in the dependent variable. Establishing a relationship between the independent and dependent variable may suggest or confirm cause and effect. The independent variable is independent of the dependent variable. It may be changed or controlled by the experimenter, but it is not affected by changes in the dependent variable. By contrast, the dependent variable is (potentially) dependent on the independent variable. If there is a relationship between the independent and dependent variables, then changes in the independent variable will result in changes in the dependent variable. The researcher should hold all other factors constant to make certain that changes in the independent variable are responsible for changes in the dependent variable.

Researchers must specify the subject of the study to clarify the extent to which the findings can be generalized. For example, a researcher may demonstrate that the optimal elevation for the giant redwood (*Sequoiadendron giganteum*), the largest living species, is 1400 to 2000 m in California's Sierra Nevada Mountains. No one can say, however, that this is the optimal elevation for the growth of the closely related coastal redwood (*Sequoia sempervirens*), the tallest living species that grows near sea level in California's Coast Range. The researcher must state the subject and conditions to which his or her findings apply.

The *conditions* are the parameters under which the study is conducted and may include any of a variety of key factors such as temperature, light intensity, and pH. There are many ways to write an experimental question, but the following formulas work well because they include *independent variable, dependent variable, subject,* and *conditions:*

"What is the effect of (*independent variable*) on (*dependent variable*) in (*subject*) at (*conditions*)?"
"What is the relationship of (*independent variable*) to (*dependent variable*) in (*subject*) at (*conditions*)?"

Tables 23.1 to 23.4 list common independent variables, dependent variables, and subjects for research. Some subjects illustrate properties

A

**Components of
Experimental Design**

Title: The title should summarize the research study and should include the name of the independent variable, the dependent variable(s), and the subject.

Hypothesis: The hypothesis is a prediction concerning the relationship of the independent and dependent variables.

Independent variable: The independent variable is manipulated, measured, or selected by the researcher to see if there is a change in the dependent variable. In a cause-and-effect relationship, the independent variable is the cause while the dependent variable is the effect or outcome.

Dependent variable: The responding variable; a factor or condition that might change as a result of a change in the manipulated independent variable.

Constants: All factors that remain the same for both the experimental and control treatments. The list of constants is extremely long and will vary with each experimental design. Constants may include environmental factors (e.g. temperature, pH, humidity, pressure, light intensity), as well as subject factors (e.g. composition, age, species). Everything should be kept constant between treatments except the independent variable.

Control treatment: The standard against which the experimental treatment is compared. Usually the independent variable is in the "default," or normal state.

Experimental treatment: The test group in which the independent variable is varied to see if there is a change in the dependent variable.

Repetition: All experiments should be repeated to determine average values and trends.

B   **Experimental Design & Data Tables**

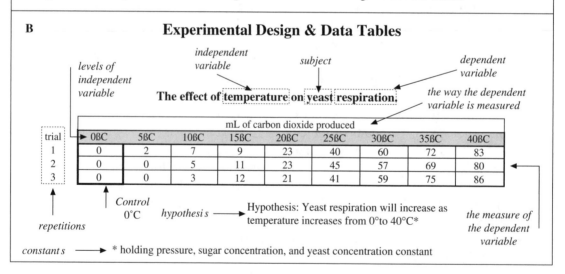

Figure 23.2 (A) Components of Experimental Design. (B) Data Table with These Components

particularly well and are identified as such in the tables. Figure 23.2A lists the components of experimental design, and Figure 23.2B shows how these components are reflected in data tables. Make certain to include these components in your research and report.

1. Identify the independent variable, dependent variable, subject, and conditions in each of the sample life science questions that follow:
   (a) What is the effect of running at different speeds on the heart rate of healthy 17-year-old boys at National High School?

(b) How does the photosynthetic rate of pondweed (*Elodea canadensis*) vary with light intensity at 30°C?

(c) At what temperature does baker's yeast (*Saccharomyces cerevisiae*) respire the most when placed in 0.1 molar sucrose solution?

(d) At which concentration of polyacrylamide gel do blood proteins separate the best when performing gel electrophoresis?

(e) Which antibiotic is most effective in killing *Staphylococcus* growth in agar plates kept at 37°C?

2. Identify the independent variable, dependent variable, subject, and conditions in each of the sample physical science questions that follow:

(a) How is the diffusion rate of air freshener affected by temperature at standard atmospheric pressure?

(b) What effect does temperature have on the rate of sugar (sucrose) crystal formation in saturated sugar solutions?

(c) What is the relationship of the number of turns of 20-gauge copper wire to magnetic field strength in a simple electromagnet?

(d) Which metal serves as the best electrode for producing hydrogen in an electrolysis device at standard temperature and pressure?

(e) What effect does the volume of nitrogen gas have on temperature if pressure is kept constant?

3. Causal research questions in the life sciences:
(a) Write five causal life science research questions using the variables and subjects listed in Tables 23.1 and 23.2 or ones that you think of on your own. (b) Construct appropriate blank data tables as shown in Figure 23.2B. (c) Describe the significance and implications of your questions.

4. Causal research questions in human physiology: (a) Write five causal physiology research questions using the variables and subjects listed in Table 23.3 or ones that you think of on your own. (b) Construct appropriate blank data tables as shown in Figure 23.2B. (c) Describe the significance and implications of your questions.

5. Causal research questions in the physical and earth sciences: (a) Write five causal physical or earth science research questions using the variables and subjects listed in Table 23.4 or ones that you think of on your own. (b) Construct appropriate blank data tables as shown in Figure 23.2B. (c) Describe the significance and implications of your questions.

Table 23.1 Research with Plants, Protozoa, Bacteria, and Fungi

Possible Independent Variables
Air movement (wind speeds, wind direction)
Atmospheric carbon dioxide (low to high concentrations)
Atmospheric humidity (low to high humidity)
Atmospheric pollution (fresh air to polluted air)
Chemical concentration (low to high concentration)
Chemicals (none versus household chemicals)
Competition (no competition, interspecific, intraspecific)
Environment (laboratory, yard, field)
Hormone concentration (low to high)
Hormone (auxins, gibberellins, cytokinins)
Insects (presence, absence, density of insects)
Light angle (overhead, oblique, angle)
Light color (red, orange, yellow, green, blue, violet)
Light intensity (absence or presence; high to low intensity)
Light quality (incandescent, fluorescent, natural)
Nutrient application (foliar, systemic)

(Continued)

Table 23.1 (*Continued*)

Nutrients (N, P, K concentrations)
Nutrients (natural, synthetic, manufacturer)
Pesticide application (foliar, water, injection)
Pesticide concentration (low to high)
Pesticide type (insecticides, snail killers, fungicides)
Planting density (one to many per pot)
Salinity (fresh versus saline, low to high, sodium chloride versus other salts)
Soil biomatter (debris from conifers, broad leaf trees, or grasses)
Soil classification (alfisols, andisols, aridisols, entisols)
Soil pH (alkaline, neutral, acidic)
Soil profile (humus, top soil, elluviation, subsoil, regolith, bedrock)
Soil source (field, stream bank, mountain side, sediment)
Soil type (sand, clay, silt, loam)
Temperature (high to low, boiling, freezing)
Temperature treatments (duration, regimen)
Water application (foliar, basin, subsurface)
Water pH (acidic, basic, neutral, pH 0–14)
Water pollution (household chemicals, acid, base)
Water source (tap, distilled, bottled, stream, lake, ocean)

Possible Dependent Variables
Breadth (breadth of branches, breadth of roots)
Cell (cell size, stage of mitosis, cell turgor)
Chlorophyll (content, distribution, ratio of a to b)
Color (leaf color, stem color, fruit color)
Energy (calories, distribution within plant parts)
Fruit (quantity, appearance, size, texture, quality)
Fruit quality (nutrients, shape, size, quantity)
Germination (percent, time to germination, survival)
Growth response (nutation, etiolation, geotropism, phototropism)
Growth rings (number, width, spacing)
Guttation (rate, content, distribution)
Height (height of plant, length of shoots, length of roots)
Life stages (time to flower, time to produce fruits, time of fruit drop)
Longevity (lifetime of plant, mortality rate)
Mass (wet mass, dry mass, estimated mass)
Metabolism (rate of photosynthesis, rate of respiration)
Mortality (antibiotic sensitivity, herbicide sensitivity, mortality rate)
Movement (phototropism, geotropism, nastic movement)
Pests (molds, rusts, mildews, insects, snails, rodents, birds)
Plant structures (trichomes, pubescence, appearance under microscope)
Protein (tissue concentration, distribution, presence)
Reproduction rate (number of offspring, generation time)
Seeds (quantity, appearance, size, viability)
Shape (shapes of leaves, plant shape, root shape)
Starch (concentration, distribution)
Surface area (leaf size, exposed surfaces)
Translocation (speed of dye movement, location of dye movement)
Transpiration (water loss over time, water loss in leaves)

Table 23.1 (*Continued*)

Transport (osmosis, diffusion, active transport)
Width (thickness of stems, thickness of roots)

Possible Subjects[a]

Alfalfa (*Medicago sativa*): competition with grasses, germination

Annual ryegrass (*Lolium species*): guttation, response to fertilizer or herbicide

Bacteria (*Acinetobacter calcoaceticus*): genetic transformation, recombinant DNA, antibiotic sensitivity, exponential growth, disinfectant sensitivity

Beans (*Phaseolus vulgaris*): translocation, phototropism, geotropism, calories in seeds, germination, growth and development

Bread mold (*Rhizopus nigrans*): spore production, preservative sensitivity

Celery (*Apium graveolens*): translocation, transpiration, xylem anatomy

Corn (*Zea mays*): growth density, salinity sensitivity, genetics

Duckweed (*Wolffia globosa*): reproduction, chemical sensitivity

Fast plants (*Brassica rapa*): genetics, growth and development, variation, physiology, flowering

Lettuce (*Latuca sativa*): photoperiodism, germination

Mold (*Penicillium notatum*): antibiotics, enzymes

Onion (*Allium cepa*): mitosis, root growth

Peas (*Pisium sativum*): mutation, growth and development, seed respiration, germination

Potatoes (*Solanum tuberosum*): diffusion, osmosis, starch production, enzymes

Radish (*Raphanus sativus*): etiolation, factors effecting germination

Sensitive plant (*Mimosa pudica*): nyctinasty, "sleep movement," motion response

Sunflower (*Helianthus annus*): heliotropism, growth rate, growth and development

Tall fescue (*Festuca species*): guttation, fertilizer response, herbicide response

Tomato (*Solanum lycopersicum*): growth and development, flower and fruit formation

Venus fly trap (*Dionaea muscipula*): carnivorous behavior, nitrogen deprivation

Water weed (*Elodea canadensis*): photosynthesis, cytoplasmic streaming, chloroplast movement

Yeast (*Saccharomyces cerevisiae*): respiration, reproduction, enzyme kinetics

Yeast (*Sordaria*): genetics

[a]Following each organism are subjects that can easily be studied with that organism.

Table 23.2 Research with Animals

Possible Independent Variables

Air movement (wind speeds, wind direction)

Chemical concentration (low to high concentration)

Chemicals (none versus household chemicals)

Dissolved gases (oxygen, carbon dioxide)

Environment (simple, complex, large, small, maze, pen)

Foods (types, enhancers, freshness)

Light color (red, orange, yellow, green, blue, violet)

Light intensity (absence or presence. high to low intensity)

Light quality (incandescent, fluorescent, natural)

Nutrients (natural versus synthetic; commercial brand A versus brand B)

Salinity (fresh versus saline, low to high, sodium chloride versus other salts)

Sound (volume, pitch, rhythm, music)

Temperature treatments (cold to hot, pattern of exposure)

(Continued)

Table 23.2 *(Continued)*

Water pH (acidic, basic, neutral, pH 0–14)
Water source (tap, distilled, bottled, stream, lake, ocean)

Possible Dependent Variables
Barotaxis (avoidance, directionality)
Chemotaxis (avoidance, directionality)
Food preference (avoidance, target)
Genetics (inheritable traits, dominance)
Gravitaxis (degree of movement, direction of movement)
Growth and development (fertilization, embryology, maturation)
Habitat selection (avoidance, selection, persistence)
Heart rate (rate, consistency, recovery)
Length (height, length of limbs)
Life stages (time to maturity, time to reproduction)
Longevity (lifetime, survivorship)
Mass (wet mass, dry mass, estimated mass)
Memory and reasoning (trainability, conditioned response, insight)
Metabolism (rate of respiration, eating schedule, diet)
Metamorphosis (timing of phases, length of phases)
Muscle strength (force, duration, speed)
Perception (time, perspective, relationship, position)
pH sensitivity (movement, survival)
Phototaxis (degree of movement, direction of movement)
Population dynamics (growth rate, growth cycles, growth curve, carrying capacity, predation)
Regeneration (degree of regeneration, time for regeneration)
Reproduction rate (offspring rate, generation time)
Respiration (breathing rate, tidal volume)
Response to environment (response to touch, light, chemicals)
Social behavior (division of labor, nesting and foraging behaviors, hierarchy)
Temperature (core temperature, surface temperature)
Thermotaxis (avoidance, temperature sensitivity, directionality)
Thigmotaxis (avoidance, directionality)
Weight (overall weight, distribution)

Possible Subjects[a]
Ants (various spp.): sociobiology, caste structure, colonial behavior, reproduction and development
Brine shrimp (*Artemia*): habitat selection, effect of salinity on growth, phototaxis, geotaxis, hatching
Crickets (*Gryllus texensis*): respiration, behavior, growth and development, metamorphosis, population dynamics, temperature response
Daphnia (*Daphnia*): heart rate, circulation, response to alcohol and caffeine
Earth worms (*Isoptera* spp.): thermotaxis, phototaxis, temperature sensitivity
Euglena (*Euglena*): gravitaxis, phototaxis
Frog (*Xenopus*): egg fertilization, embryology
Fruit flies (*Drosophila melongaster*): genetics, light and color, temperature sensitivity
Gold fish (*Carassius auratus*): circulation, breathing rate, response to dissolved oxygen
Halobacterium (*Halobacterium salinarium*): DNA, survival in extremes, exponential growth rate
Hydra (*Hydra littoralis*): budding, regeneration, vegetative reproduction
Laboratory rat (*Rattus norvegicus*): memory, behavior, exercise

Table 23.2 *(Continued)*

Lady beetle (*Hippodamia convergens*): predation, biological pest control, lifecycle

Land snails (*Solatopupa*): response to gravity, touch, light, and chemicals; environmental preferences; movement

Mealworm (*Tenebrio molito*): metamorphosis, taxis, kinesis, binary choices

Paramecium (*Paramecium caudatum*): phototaxis, cilia propulsion

Planaria (*Seriata*): regeneration; light, temperature, and pH sensitivity

Silkworm (*Bombyx mori*): development, metamorphosis, food preference, eating

Termites (*Isoptera* spp.): chemotaxis, nesting and foraging behavior, division of labor

[a]Following each organism are subjects that can easily be studied with that organism.

Table 23.3 Research with Humans

Possible Independent Variables

Activity (sleeping, studying, sports)

Air movement (wind speeds, wind direction)

Concentration (focus, distraction)

Exercise (duration, intensity, regimen)

Foods (types, enhancers)

Instruction (kinesthetic, visual, auditory)

Instruction (traditional, multimedia, hands-on)

Learning environment (classroom, home, field)

Light color (red, orange, yellow, green, blue, violet)

Light intensity (absence or presence, high to low intensity)

Light quality (incandescent, fluorescent, natural)

Nutrients (natural versus synthetic)

Odor (regimen, intensity, type)

Sound (silence, music, noise, talking)

Stimulus (sound, light, touch)

Temperature treatments (cold to hot, pattern of exposure)

Possible Dependent Variables

Blood pressure (systolic, diastolic, changes in blood pressure)

Conductivity (skin conductivity, perspiration, electrocardiogram patterns)

Eyes (pupil constriction, dilation, rate of dilation, movement, blinking, stereoscopic vision)

Fatigue (reduction in grip strength, grip frequency)

Focus (depth of focus, eye dominance)

Heart rate (rate, recovery rate)

Memory (sequence, number, shape, concept, frequency, attenuation)

Muscle strength (force, duration, speed)

Perception (time, perspective, relationship, position)

Reaction rate (eye movement, hand movement, verbal response)

Reflex (knee jerk, eye blink, time of reflex, strength of reflex)

Respiration (tidal volume, breathing rate)

Smell (odor, discrimination, accommodation, recognition)

Sound (volume, pitch, discrimination, attenuation, accommodation)

Spatial (sense of up, down, relationship of objects, position)

Stride (pace, length, rate)

Taste (flavor, discrimination, accommodation, recognition, attenuation)

(Continued)

Table 23.3 (*Continued*)

Temperature (core temperature, surface temperature)
Temperature sensation (heat, cold, discrimination, accommodation)
Touch (pressure, location discrimination, attenuation, recognition)
Vision (resolution, recognition, color, distinction, appearance, accommodation)

Possible Subjects
Age (infant, child, youth, adult, elderly)
Education (high school, middle school, college)
Gender (male, female)
Occupation (student, career, unemployed)
Physique (height, weight)
Population (students in class, workers on job, teachers at school)

Table 23.4   Research in Physical and Earth Science

Possible Independent and Dependent Variables
Absolute humidity (grams water vapor/liter of air)
Acceleration (meters /second^2)
Acidity (pH)
Altitude (meters)
Angle (degrees, percent slope)
Appearance (color, size, shape, texture)
Area (square meters, acres, hectares)
Buoyancy (newtons)
Color (wavelength, identifiable color)
Concentration (molarity, molality, normality, pH)
Conductivity (siemens, mho)
Convection (direction of heat flow, watts/square meter)
Crystal shape (isometric, tetragonal, hexagonal, orthorhombic)
Density (grams/cubic centimeter, kilograms/liter)
Dew point (degrees Celsius, degrees Fahrenheit, Kelvin)
Dissolved oxygen (ppm, milligrams of gas per liter of water)
Distance (meters, kilometers)
Efficiency (percent)
Electrical capacitance (farads)
Electrical current (milliamps, amps AC, amps DC)
Electrical potential (millivolts, volts)
Electrical resistance (milliohms, ohms)
Energy (calories, joules, kilojoules, kilowatt-hours)
Flow rate (milliliters/minute)
Focal length (millimeters, meters)
Force (newtons)
Frequency (hertz)
Friction (newtons)
Gas concentration (ppm, molar)
Hardness (mohs rating)
Heat (calories, calories, joules)

Table 23.4 (*Continued*)

Heat capacity (calories/degree Celsius, joules/Kelvin)

Heat flux (watts/square meter)

Heat transfer (watts)

Inductance (henries)

Ion concentration (molar)

Light quality (incandescent, fluorescent, sunlight)

Luminous flux (lumens)

Luminous intensity (candela)

Magnetic field strength (newtons/amp·meter)

Magnetic flux (webers)

Mass (grams, kilograms)

Moment of inertia (kilogram·meters^2)

Power (watts, kilowatts)

Pressure (pascals, psi, mm Hg, torr, bar, millibar)

Purity (percent)

Quantity (count, moles)

Radiation (becquerel/seconds, curies/second, millirems)

Relative humidity (percent)

Solubility (molar)

Sound intensity (decibel)

Specific heat (calories/gram degree Celsius)

Surface area (square meters)

Surface area/volume ratio (meters^{-1})

Surface tension (millinewtons/meter)

Temperature (Kelvin, degrees Celsius, degrees Fahrenheit)

Time (seconds, minutes, hours, days, weeks, years)

Turbidity (newton-second per coulomb-meter)

Velocity (meters/second, kilometers/hour)

Viscosity (poise)

Volume (cubic centimeter, liter, milliliter, cubic meter)

Wavelength (nanometers, millimeters, meters)

Wind speed (meters/second)

Work (joules)

Yield (grams)

Possible Subjects

Acids and bases (acid rain, acidic soils, soil chemistry, acids in industry, properties of acids and bases, antacids, buffers, pH, neutralization, corrosion)

Aerodynamics (flight, lift, drag, weight, thrust, airplane design, terminal velocity)

Alloys (alloy formation, brass, bronze, steel, sterling silver, pewter, solder)

Applied optics (converging lenses, diverging lenses, Fresnel lenses, telescopes, microscopes, glasses)

Atmosphere (air quality, pollutants, wind speed, wind patterns, humidity)

Buoyancy (density, floating, sinking, displacement, ship design, submarines, hot air balloons)

Chemical bonding (ionic, covalent, hydrogen, metallic, chemical reactions)

Chemical changes (yield, purity, products, reactants)

Chemical energetics (endothermic reactions, exothermic reactions, home and industrial applications of endothermic and exothermic reactions)

Chemical movement (diffusion, osmosis, kinetic theory, temperature effects)

Chemical reaction rates (catalysis, enzymes, denaturing enzymes, chemical equilibrium, chemical kinetics, product comparison for glues, epoxies, and other household chemical reactions)

(Continued)

Table 23.4 (*Continued*)

Chemical reactions (addition reactions, single replacement, double replacement, catalysis, chain reactions, combustion, oxidation-reduction, electrolysis, electroplating, oxidizers, reducers, combination, electrochemical, dehydration, synthesis)

Colligative properties (boiling point elevation, freezing point depression, osmotic pressure, antifreeze, deicers)

Combustion (flame tests, wood, fuel, fires, oxidation, fire management)

Convection (cold air drainage, downdrafts, updrafts, heat transfer, ocean currents, seasonal overturn in lakes, thermoclines, thermals, gliding)

Corrosion (oxidation reduction, rusting, tarnish, oxides, materials engineering)

Crystallization (composition, patterns, growth factors, crystals, stalactites, stalagmites, cave formations, mineral formations, industrial uses of crystals)

Density (buoyancy, centrifugation, density gradient, thermocline, halocline, ocean currents, earth crustal densities)

Earth dynamics (earthquakes, volcanoes, faults, seismology, earthquake detection and measurement, plate tectonics)

Electric circuit components (resistors, capacitors, transistors, inductors, electrodes, conductors, insulators)

Electric circuits (current, conductivity, Ohm's law, series circuits, parallel circuits, circuit design, electronics)

Electric conductivity (insulators, conductors, superconductors, semiconductors, electric hazards)

Electric currents (alternating current, direct current, generators, motors, electric power generation, resistivity, temperature effects)

Electric devices (generators, alternators, solenoids, relays, transmitters, receivers, motors, transformers, microphones, speakers)

Electric energy (conservation, thermoelectricity, Seebeck effect, Peltier effect, thermocouples)

Electric power (generator, battery, Daniell cell, Galvanic pile, fuel cells, solar cells, transformers, energy conversion, alternative sources of energy)

Electrical inductance (mutual inductance, transformers, alternating current)

Electricity (electric charge, electric field, electric potential, electric energy, electric power, electrical engineering)

Electrochemistry (electrolysis, electroplating, electrochemical cells, batteries, electrolytes)

Electronics (circuit design, simple electronic devices, photoelectric effect, thermoelectric effect, piezoelectric effect, hysteresis)

Electrostatics (electroscope, electrostatic repulsion, electrostatic attraction, transfer, Coulomb's law, induction, distribution, static electricity, home and industrial applications of static electricity)

Energy (potential energy, kinetic energy, entropy, enthalpy, alternative energy sources, conservation, consumption, work, efficiency)

Engineering (structural design, materials strength, materials properties, circuit design)

Expansion (thermal expansion, contraction, thermostats, properties of matter)

Fluids (surface tension, heat capacity, solubility, conductivity, adhesion, cohesion)

Forces (Newton's laws, gravity, normal, friction, torque, weightlessness, propulsion)

Fuels (methane, propane, butane, coal, biodiesel, methanol, alternative fuels, biofuels, internal combustion engine)

Gasses (Boyle's law, Charles's law, ideal gas law, Hero's engine, steam engine, propulsion, steam generators)

Geology (landforms, soil profiles, erosion patterns, weathering, landform formation)

Inverse square law (radiation, light, magnetism, gravity, sound, static electricity)

Leverage (first-class, second-class, third-class, torque; equilibrium; mechanics; simple tools)

Light (fluorescent, incandescent, halogen, chemiluminesence, phosphorescence, photoelectric effect, lasers, sunlight, wavelength, frequency, prisms, dispersion, recombination, spectrum, infrared, primary colors, complementary colors, spectra, complementary colors, color printing, color projection shadows, eclipses, phases of moon)

Machines (lever, inclined plane, block and tackle, wheel, efficiency, mechanical advantage, multiplying force, multiplying speed)

Table 23.4 (*Continued*)

Magnetization (polarity, magnetic fields, magnetic force, retentivity, inverse square law, magnetic shielding, permeability, flux density, geomagnetism, Curie temperature, induction, demagnetization, electric motors, electric generators, electromagnets, compass, bar, permanent, magnetic recording)

Mapping (topographic, surveying, triangulation, global positioning system)

Measurement (accuracy, precision, indirect measurement, direct measurement, scaling, instrumentation)

Metals (iron, copper, silver, aluminum, activity series, metallurgy, ores, mining, extraction, purification, uses of metals)

Minerals (classification, types, properties, distribution, formation, crystals, home and industrial applications)

Mixtures (homogeneous mixtures, heterogeneous mixtures, suspensions, surfactants, gels, foams, bubbles, films, surface tension, soaps, household product comparisons, aerosols, chromatography, colloidal suspensions, colloids, dispersions, emulsification, emulsions)

Momentum (linear, collisions, impulse, conservation, angular, precession)

Motion (inertia, action-reaction, acceleration, Newton's laws, angular velocity, rotational inertia, angular acceleration, centripetal, trajectories, collisions, momentum, inertia, center of mass)

Optics (cameras, projectors, illusions, pinhole camera, polarization, reflection, transmission, Moiré patterns, oil films, interference, diffraction, refraction, chromatic aberration, scattering, interference, fiber optics, Snell's law, total internal reflection, critical angle, magnification, optical density, mirrors)

Periodic motion (Foucault pendulum, torsion pendulum, simple harmonic motion, uniform circular motion, springs, Hooke's law, oscillations, timekeeping, satellites, sound vibration)

Phases of matter (solids, liquids, gases, plasma, phase changes, melting, freezing, boiling, sublimation, condensation, weather, magma)

Polymers (recycling plastics, properties of plastics, polymer formation, thermoplastics, thermoset plastics, plastic product comparisons)

Pressure (Pascal's law, fluid pressure, barometric, weather forecasting, vapor pressure, siphons, Bernoulli's principle, streamlines, air drag, osmotic pressure, vapor pressure, pressure-volume relationships)

Propulsion (steam propulsion, jet propulsion, internal combustion, movement, engine design, engine efficiency)

Radio waves (radar, radio wave polarity, crystal radio design and construction, antennae theory, transmission conditions, interference)

Radioactivity (Geiger counters, cosmic ray detection, alpha radiation, beta radiation, ultraviolet radiation, isotopes, half-life, critical mass, industrial applications of radioactivity)

Rocks (igneous, metamorphic, sedimentary, classification, identification, formation, properties, distribution, hardness, weathering, rock cycle, geochemistry, home and industrial uses of rock products)

Separation (distillation, sedimentation, electrophoresis, precipitation, paper chromatography, thin layer chromatography)

Soils (classification, types, properties, distribution, formation, soil profiles, horizons, erosion, soil conservation, groundwater pollution)

Solutions (solubility, gas solubility, heat of solution, solutes, polar solvents, nonpolar solvents, solution chemistry, product comparisons of household solutions)

Sound (frequency, amplitude, harmonics, speed, resonance, transmission, vibration, Doppler effect, echoes, reflection, superposition, diffraction, interference, laws of strings, sonar, musical instruments)

Thermodynamics (laws of thermodynamics, heat, heat capacity, specific heat, thermal expansion, conduction, convection, Brownian motion, heat effects on viscosity, reaction rate, heat conductivity, heat of crystallization, heat of dilution, heat of fusion, heat of neutralization, heat of reaction, heat of solution, heat of vaporization, heat transfer)

Water (properties of water, acid rain, water quality, clarity, turbidity, water pollution, water conservation, erosion, stream formation, weather)

Waves (fluid waves, sound waves, light waves, seismic waves, wavelength, amplitude, frequency, period, transverse, longitudinal, superposition, attenuation, amplitude, interaction of waves, interference, standing waves, propagation, reflection, refraction, diffraction, interference, wave patterns, wave behaviors)

Weather (cloud types, wind, storms, humidity, temperature, weather prediction, meteorology)

23.2 Developing a Research Proposal

Researchers should develop a plan for what they want to accomplish and how they intend to do so. Such a plan is known as a *research proposal.* Professional scientists submit research proposals to major funding agencies to receive the funds necessary to do their research. The National Institutes of Health (NIH) and National Science Foundation (NSF) are two of the many agencies that review proposals and award grants to scientists who have presented interesting, useful questions, and clear plans for how they intend to answer them. Student researchers should develop proposals before they engage in research as well.

A research proposal addresses each of the following points:

- *Topic:* Specify the domain, field, and topic of the research. For example, if you are researching the factors that influence electrolysis, the *domain* is chemistry, the *field* is electrochemistry, and the *topic* is electrolysis.
- *Research question:* Develop an interesting, testable question. Some questions are interesting but not testable. For example, you may have heard that cockroaches can survive the radiation emitted by a nuclear bomb, but since you cannot detonate a nuclear bomb and do not have access to equipment that would provide equivalent radiation, this question is not testable. Other questions may be testable but do not hold your interest. You will have a difficult time conducting research if you find it useless or boring. Review section 23.1 for ideas for a research question.
- *Hypothesis:* A hypothesis is a proposed explanation or prediction and serves as the starting point for an investigation. Good hypotheses are based on careful observation and good reasoning. For example, you may have noted that termites follow trails made by blue and black Papermate pens but do not follow trails made by other pens or pencils. You might hypothesize that there is a special chemical in Papermate inks that attracts termites, and hypothesize that termites will follow tracks

made by green and red Papermate pens as well. A hypothesis should be based on observation, developed with logic, and able to be tested.

- *Independent variable:* The researcher manipulates, measures, or selects the independent variable to see if there is a change in the dependent variable. In a cause-and-effect relationship, the independent variable is the cause, and the dependent variable is the effect or outcome. For example, in a study of the effect of temperature on the rate of diffusion of air freshener, temperature is the independent variable that the experimenter changes to see its effect on the dependent variable, the rate of diffusion.
- *Dependent variable:* The dependent variable is the responding variable—a factor or condition that might change as a result of a change in a manipulated, independent variable. For example, in a study of the effect of the color of light on plant growth, plant growth is the dependent variable.
- *Control:* A control is the standard against which the experimental treatment is compared. Usually the independent variable is in the *default,* or normal, state. For example, if you were interested in the effect of fertilizer on plant growth, you would compare growth against a control, natural state in which no fertilizer is applied.
- *Constant:* Constants are the factors that remain the same for both the experimental and control treatments. The list of possible constants is extremely long and varies with experimental design. Constants may include environmental factors (e.g. temperature, pH, humidity, pressure, light intensity), as well as subject factors (e.g., composition, age, species). Everything should be kept constant between the experimental and control groups, except the treatments or independent variable.
- *Measuring the variables and constants:* Science requires measurement. Sometimes measurements can be made directly, but other times they must be made indirectly. A researcher who wants to measure seed production can do so directly by counting the number of seeds produced. By contrast, the researcher who wants to determine the rate of photosynthesis must do so indirectly

by measuring the rate of carbon dioxide consumption, the rate of sugar production, or the rate of oxygen release. Specify whether your measurements will be direct or indirect, and describe the way you will make the measurements. Many science experiments rely on appearance rather than an easily measurable quantity such as length or time. In such instances, provide as accurate descriptions as possible.

- *Materials:* List the materials and resources you will need to conduct the experiment, and describe how you will acquire them.
- *Experimental procedure:* List the steps necessary to complete the experiment and answer your questions.
- *References:* Include a list of books, journal articles, Web sites, scientists, and other resources you have used to gain background knowledge on this topic. Cite your references as described in section 22.6.
- *Approval:* Get approval from your teacher to ensure that your question is appropriate and your investigation feasible. Get approval from your parents to make certain that you will have their support and access to resources necessary to complete the research project.

23.3 Conducting Research

Discoveries don't just happen. Isaac Newton didn't discover the laws of gravity just because an apple fell on his head, and Archimedes didn't discover buoyancy just by taking a bath. Newton, the father of classical mechanics and one of the greatest scientists of all times said, "If I have ever made any valuable discoveries, it has been owing more to patient attention, than to any other talent."[5] Similarly, Thomas Edison, one of the most prolific and influential inventors of all time, commented, "Genius is one per cent inspiration, ninety-nine per cent perspiration."[6]

Popular literature describes "Eureka!" moments or "Aha!" discoveries when scientists experience great breakthroughs, but such apparently sudden discoveries don't occur in a vacuum. Louis Pasteur, the Father of Microbiology, aptly said, "In the fields of observation chance favors only those minds which are prepared."[7] Pasteur's vast array of accomplishments, including the development of the germ theory of disease, the process of pasteurization for preserving foods, and the development of the first vaccine for rabies, didn't happen by chance. Pasteur, like all other scientists, had a "prepared mind" and therefore was able to see the significance of the "chance events" that occurred in his laboratory and the world around him. Discoveries don't just happen; they are the result of significant preparation, observation, dialogue, and reasoning.

Scientific research requires a commitment of resources and time. One must acquire the tools necessary to do research and carefully record observations and the results of experiments. The activities in this section focus on these fundamental processes.

ACTIVITY 23.3.1 *Developing a Budget and Acquiring Equipment*

Review the materials list from your proposal, and develop a budget for your project. Think of how you can acquire the materials with as little cost and time as possible. Indicate the source and cost of each item as illustrated in Figure 23.3. Submit your budget to your instructor for review. Use inexpensive household alternatives whenever possible. For example, plastic cups can substitute for glass beakers in a variety of applications, but be certain to check with your instructor to ensure that such substitutions are safe and viable. Section 22.6 lists common and inexpensive sources for chemicals, but again it is necessary to check with your instructor about the safety and viability of such products in the context of your investigation.

item	source	notes	cost
balance	E-Bay	online auction	$25
styrofoam cups	Snack-Shack	ask manager	free
bean seeds	market	find in soup section	$2
colored cellophane	garage	wrapping leftovers	free
meter stick	hardware store	promotional	free
fan	house	ask parents	free
watering can	garage	old bottle	free
digital camera	home	borrow from uncle	free

Figure 23.3 Sample Budget from a Science Project

		water	notes	height of sample (mm)					average
				1	2	3	4	5	
Monday	1-Oct	x		0	0	0	0	0	0
Tuesday	2-Oct		overcast	0	0	0	0	0	0
Wednesday	3-Oct	x		0	0	0	0	0	0
Thursday	4-Oct			0	0	0	0	0	0
Friday	5-Oct	x	foggy	0	0	0	0	0	0
Saturday	6-Oct			0	0	0	0	0	0
Sunday	7-Oct	x		0	0	0	0	0	0
Monday	8-Oct		germination	1	0	0	1	1	0.6
Tuesday	9-Oct	x		3	0	2	2	4	2.2
Wednesday	10-Oct		2 & 3 yellow	5	1	3	3	6	3.6
Thursday	11-Oct	x		7	2	4	4	8	5
Friday	12-Oct		all now green	8	4	4	4	9	5.8
Saturday	13-Oct	x		9	6	6	5	10	7.2
Sunday	14-Oct		ungus on #4	11	9	9	7	13	9.8
Monday	15-Oct								
Tuesday	16-Oct								
Wednesday	17-Oct								
Thursday	18-Oct								
Friday	19-Oct								

Treatment - green light ← specify treatment

include units → height of sample (mm)

record observations — record measurements

note date of all observations

Figure 23.4 Sample Research Log

ACTIVITY 23.3.2 *Keeping a Research Log or Science Notebook*

Don't rely on your memory when collecting data and making observations. Scientists make written records of *all* observations and data because they do not know which will be of most value in making discoveries or answering questions. Create a research log in which you record all relevant information. Record the time and date of each observation in a clear format, such as that illustrated in Figure 23.4. Include your research log as an appendix to your final report.

23.4 Sharing Your Findings

The renowned scientist Isaac Newton said, "If I have seen further it is by standing on the shoulders of giants"[8] Newton could not have made his discoveries in astronomy, motion, forces, and calculus if it were not for the information he had learned from earlier researchers. Scientists share their findings with others in many ways.

They may talk on the phone, work in each other's laboratories, publish their findings in journals, maintain logs on the Internet, or share with colleagues at professional meetings. The following are some of the major professional science organizations and the journals they offer as forums for scientific research:

- American Association for the Advancement of Science: *Science*
- American Astronomical Society: *Astronomical Journal*
- American Chemical Society: *Journal of the American Chemical Society*
- American Geological Institute: *Geotimes*
- American Physical Society: *Journal of the American Physical Society*
- Biophysical Society: *Biophysical Journal*

School science fairs provide an opportunity for students to share their research with peers, parents, teachers, and other interested members of the community. Just as many organizations honor scientists for outstanding research, so science fair judges award special honors to students whose research is exceptional. Table 23.5 shows standard science fair judging criteria. Review these criteria and the criteria of your local science fair before planning your poster and presentation.

ACTIVITY 23.4.1 *Writing a Research Report*

Research reports should have these sections:

1. *Title page:* Include a descriptive title of your project, your name, e-mail address, school, grade, class, and science teacher.

2. *Introduction:* The introduction includes your hypothesis and a rationale for why you chose this topic and think it is interesting or important. Refer to section 23.2 on formulating a research proposal before writing this section. Be certain to include:
   - *Topic:* List the domain, field, and topic of your research.
   - *Literature review:* Describe what others have found. Cite references.
   - *Research question:* Describe the question and why you are interested.

Table 23.5 Criteria for Judging Science Fair Projects

Research Design (20%)
Problem: Is the research problem stated completely and concisely?
Background research: Is the library research thorough, and are citations complete?
Research question: Is the research question meaningful and clearly stated?
Hypothesis: Is the hypothesis appropriate and clearly stated?
Independent variable: Is the independent variable appropriate to the question?
Dependent variable(s): Are dependent variables appropriate to the question?
Control: Is an appropriate control selected?
Constant: Are all conditions held constant except the independent variable?
Procedure: Is the procedure appropriate for the question?

Ingenuity and Creativity (20%)
Innovation: Are the research question and design innovative?
Resource: Does the researcher make good use of materials and resources?
Relevance: Does the researcher show why this research is important?
Challenge: Is this research challenging?

Experiment (20%)
Technique: Is the researcher's technique skillful and consistent?
Sample size: Is the sample size sufficient to draw reasonable conclusions?
Repetition: Have enough repetitions been conducted to draw conclusions?
Units: Are appropriate units applied to all measurements?
Logs: Were data recorded accurately while the experiment was in progress?

Analysis (20%)
Data: Do graphs and charts adequately display the data?
Hypothesis: Was the hypothesis appropriately accepted or rejected?
Interpretation: Are there data to support the conclusions?
Conclusions: Are the conclusions reasonable given the data collected?
Related research: Does the researcher show how this is related to other studies?
Limitations: Does the researcher express the limitations of the study?

Presentation (20%)
Board: Does the display board contain all required components?
Relevance: Does the researcher show the relevance of this study?
Clarity: Is the research presented professionally?
Interview: Does the interview demonstrate the researcher's understanding?

- *Hypothesis:* Explain what you predicted would happen.
3. *Experiment and procedure:* Describe in detail the method used to organize your observations and collect your data. Your procedure should be detailed enough that another researcher could repeat your experiment. Be certain to include the following information (see section 23.2 for detailed explanations):
   - independent variable
   - dependent variable(s)
   - control
   - constants
   - method of measurement
   - materials and methods
   - procedures
   - photographs
   - diagrams
4. *Discussion:* Explain the process by which you reached your conclusions:
   - interpretation of data
   - analysis of hypothesis
   - how conclusions were reached
   - design errors
   - experimental errors
   - suggestions for improvement
   - suggestions for further research

5. *Conclusion:* Answer your research question, and evaluate your hypothesis in the light of the data. Refine or reformulate your hypothesis, reasoning from the evidence gathered in your research.
6. *Acknowledgments:* Give credit to all who assisted you in the research—family members, teachers, students, businesses, institutions, and others—and specify the role each played.
7. *References:* Cite all of your references following the format outlined in section 22.6.

ACTIVITY 23.4.2 *Developing a Research Poster*

Construct a poster of your research as shown in Figure 23.1. Your poster should include a discussion of the problem, research question, hypothesis, experiment, data, results, conclusion, and ideas for future study, and should be accompanied by your research log (Figure 23.4). Present your poster at a science fair.

Answers to Chapter Activities

23.1.1 (1) qualitative, (2) qualitative, (3) quantitative, (4) qualitative, (5) quantitative, (6) quantitative, (7) quantitative, (8) qualitative, (9) qualitative, (10) quantitative, (11) student responses will vary.

23.1.2

1.

	Independent Variable	Dependent Variable	Subject	Conditions
(a)	running rate	heart rate	17-year-old boys	National High School
(b)	light intensity	photosynthesis	pondweed	30°C
(c)	temperature	respiration	baker's yeast	0.1 M sucrose
(d)	concentration	separation	blood proteins	electrophoresis
(e)	antibiotic	death of bacteria	*Staphylococcus*	agar at 37°C

2.

	Independent Variable	Dependent Variable	Subject	Conditions
(a)	temperature	diffusion rate	air freshener	1 atm
(b)	temperature	rate of crystallization	sucrose	saturated solutions
(c)	turns	magnetic field	20 gauge Cu wire	electromagnet
(d)	metal	H production	electrode	1 atm, 0°C
(e)	volume	temperature	nitrogen gas	constant P

23.1.3–23.1.5 Student answers will vary.

Part Six

Resources for Teaching Science

Chapter Twenty-Four

Science Curriculum and Instruction

24.1 The Nature of Science 493

24.2 Theories and Perspectives in Science Education 496

24.3 Developments in Science Curriculum and Instruction 498

24.4 The Science Curriculum 502

24.5 Advanced Placement and International Baccalaureate Curricula 504

24.6 Teaching Science Inquiry 506

24.7 Teaching Science to English Language Learners 508

24.8 Teaching Science with Humor 511

24.9 Professional Development in Science Education 513

24.10 Science Field Trips and Guest Speakers 515

24.1 The Nature of Science

Teachers and students should know the nature, capabilities, and limitations of science.[1] A summary is provided in the position statement on the following page by the National Science Teachers' Association (NSTA).[2]

Reflections by Scientists on the Nature of Science

Each of us has reasons for choosing our professions, and it is helpful to share these with young people so they can better understand the career planning and decision-making process. This section provides quotes about the nature of science and the reasons that famous scientists selected their career:

- *George Washington Carver*, African American botanist and inventor (1863–1943). Carver invented numerous uses for the peanut and other plants.

  I love to think of nature as an unlimited broadcasting station, through which God speaks to us every hour, if we will only tune in.

- *Marie Curie*, Polish physicist and chemist (1867–1934). Marie Curie, one of the most

The Nature of Science: A Position Statement of NSTA

Preamble: All those involved with science teaching and learning should have a common, accurate view of the nature of science. Science is characterized by the systematic gathering of information through various forms of direct and indirect observations and the testing of this information by methods including, but not limited to, experimentation. The principal product of science is knowledge in the form of naturalistic concepts and the laws and theories related to those concepts.

Declaration: The National Science Teachers Association endorses the proposition that science, along with its methods, explanations and generalizations, must be the sole focus of instruction in science classes to the exclusion of all non-scientific or pseudoscientific methods, explanations, generalizations and products. The following premises are important to understanding the nature of science.

- Scientific knowledge is simultaneously reliable and tentative. Having confidence in scientific knowledge is reasonable while realizing that such knowledge may be abandoned or modified in light of new evidence or reconceptualization of prior evidence and knowledge.

- Although no single universal step-by-step scientific method captures the complexity of doing science, a number of shared values and perspectives characterize a scientific approach to understanding nature. Among these are a demand for naturalistic explanations supported by empirical evidence that are, at least in principle, testable against the natural world. Other shared elements include observations, rational argument, inference, skepticism, peer review and replicability of work.

- Creativity is a vital, yet personal, ingredient in the production of scientific knowledge.

- Science, by definition, is limited to naturalistic methods and explanations and, as such, is precluded from using supernatural elements in the production of scientific knowledge.

- A primary goal of science is the formation of theories and laws, which are terms with very specific meanings.

  (1) Laws are generalizations or universal relationships related to the way that some aspect of the natural world behaves under certain conditions.

  (2) Theories are inferred explanations of some aspect of the natural world. Theories do not become laws even with additional evidence; they explain laws. However, not all scientific laws have accompanying explanatory theories.

  (3) Well-established laws and theories must

     - be internally consistent and compatible with the best available evidence;

     - be successfully tested against a wide range of applicable phenomena and evidence;

     - possess appropriately broad and demonstrable effectiveness in further research.

- Contributions to science can be made and have been made by people the world over.

- The scientific questions asked, the observations made, and the conclusions in science are to some extent influenced by the existing state of scientific knowledge, the social and cultural context of the researcher and the observer's experiences and expectations.

- The history of science reveals both evolutionary and revolutionary changes. With new evidence and interpretation, old ideas are replaced or supplemented by newer ones.

- While science and technology do impact each other, basic scientific research is not directly concerned with practical outcomes, but rather with gaining an understanding of the natural world for its own sake.

famous of all women scientists, was a pioneer in the field of radioactivity.

All my life through, the new sights of Nature made me rejoice like a child. . . . It was like a new world opened to me, . . . which I was at last permitted to know in all liberty.

- *Thomas Alva Edison,* American inventor (1847–1931). Edison established the first industrial research laboratory. He was one of the most prolific inventors of all time, inventing a sound recording device (phonograph), motion pictures, and the first practical incandescent light bulb. He received patents for 1090 inventions.

I never did anything worth doing by accident, nor did any of my inventions come by accident; they came by work.

Genius is one per cent inspiration and ninety-nine per cent perspiration.

I have not failed. I've just found 10,000 ways that won't work.

To invent, you need a good imagination and a pile of junk.

- *Albert Einstein,* German American theoretical physicist (1879–1955). Einstein formulated the special and general theories of relativity and made significant contributions to quantum theory and statistical mechanics.

The most incomprehensible thing about our universe is that it can be comprehended.

The important thing is not to stop questioning. Curiosity has its own reason for existing.

Imagination is more important than knowledge.

- *Enrico Fermi,* Italian-American physicist (1901–1954). Fermi developed quantum theory and the first nuclear reactor.

There are two possible outcomes: If the result confirms the hypothesis, then you've made a measurement. If the result is contrary to the hypothesis, then you've made a discovery.

- *Galileo Galilei,* Italian astronomer (1564–1642). Galileo was the father of modern astronomy and physics.

I do not feel obliged to believe that the same God who has endowed us with sense, reason, and intellect has intended us to forgo their use.

- *Robert Goddard,* American physicist, chemist, and engineer (1882–1945). Goddard was the pioneer of controlled, liquid-fueled rocketry.

It is difficult to say what is impossible, for the dream of yesterday is the hope of today and the reality of tomorrow.

- *Edwin Hubble,* American astronomer (1889–1953). Hubble discovered cosmological red-shift and laid the foundation for physical cosmology. He was the first to discover galaxies beyond the Milky Way.

Equipped with his five senses, man explores the universe around him and calls the adventure Science.

- *James Prescott Joule,* English physicist (1818–1889). Joule discovered the first law of thermodynamics (conservation of energy) and the relationship of heat to mechanical work.

It is evident that an acquaintance with natural laws means no less than an acquaintance with the mind of God therein expressed.

- *Johannes Kepler,* German astronomer and mathematician (1571–1630). Kepler discovered the three laws of planetary motion.

The diversity of the phenomena of nature is so great, and the treasures hidden in the heavens so rich, precisely in order that the human mind shall never be lacking in fresh nourishment.

- *Isaac Newton,* English physicist, astronomer, theologian (1643–1727). Newton discovered the universal law of gravitation and laws of motion. He laid the foundations for classical mechanics and the development of calculus.

I do not know what I may appear to the world, but to myself I seem to have been only a boy playing on the sea-shore, and diverting myself in now and then finding a smoother pebble or a prettier shell than ordinary, whilst the great ocean of truth lay all undiscovered before me.

If I have ever made any valuable discoveries, it has been owing more to patient attention, than to any other talent.

- *Louis Pasteur,* French biologist and chemist (1822–1895). Pasteur developed the process of pasteurization, helped establish the germ theory of disease, was a cofounder of bacteriology, and developed new vaccines.

Science belongs to no one country.

In the field of observation, chance favors only the prepared mind.

- *Nikola Tesla,* Serb-American inventor, physicist, and engineer (1856–1943). Tesla invented polyphase power distribution systems and the AC motor, laying the foundation for the second industrial revolution.

I do not think there is any thrill that can go through the human heart like that felt by the inventor as he sees some creation of the brain unfolding to success.

- *Wernher Von Braun,* German-American physicist and engineer (1912–1977). Von Braun was the father of the American space program and chief architect of the *Saturn V* rocket that took men to the Moon.

Research is what I'm doing when I don't know what I'm doing.

24.2 Theories and Perspectives in Science Education

Numerous theories and perspectives concerning the teaching and learning of science are addressed in this book. Here we look at a few of the more prominent ones. The numbers in parentheses refer to activity numbers in this book.

Active Learning: Learn by Doing

Active learning is a set of strategies that posits the responsibility for learning with the student.[3] Discovery learning,[4] problem-based learning (22.3), experiential learning, and inquiry-based instruction

(22.1) are examples of active learning. Discussion, debate (22.4), student questioning (5.1, 22.1, 23.1), think-pair-share (25.7), quick-writes (25.7), polling, role playing, cooperative learning (22.3, 22.5), group projects (13.1–8, 22.5), and student presentations (22.4) are a few of the many activities that are learner driven. It should be noted, however, that even lecture can be an active learning event if students process and filter information as it is provided. Cornell notes (3.1) and diagramming (16.2) are a couple of activities that can make lectures active learning events.

Teaching to Multiple Learning Modalities

We can learn through any of our five senses, but the three most valuable are vision, hearing, and touch. Theorists and practitioners claim that learners have a preference for one learning style over another. *Visual learners* learn best by watching, *auditory learners* learn best by verbal instruction, and *kinesthetic learners* learn best by manipulation. Because of the demands of the profession, teachers often resort to the instructional style that requires the least time and preparation: lecture and discussion. Although these may be valuable approaches to teaching and learning, they fail to take advantage of other learning modalities and disenfranchise students whose primary modality is visual or kinesthetic. This book emphasizes the use of all three modalities in teaching and learning.

Teaching to Multiple Intelligences

Intelligence is a property of the mind that includes many related abilities, such as the capacities to reason, plan, solve problems, comprehend language and ideas, learn new concepts, and think abstractly. Historically, psychometricians have measured intelligence with a single score (intelligence quotient, IQ) on a standardized test, finding that such scores are predictive of later intellectual achievement. Howard Gardner and others assert that there are multiple intelligences, and that no single score can accurately reflect a person's intelligence.[5]

More important, the *theory of multiple intelligences* implies that people learn better through certain modalities than others and that science teachers should design curriculum to address as many modalities as possible. Gardner identifies seven intelligences (the numbers in parentheses indicate sections in this book that address each intelligence):

- *Logical/mathematical intelligence* is used when thinking conceptually (6.1–6.4, 7.1–7.7, 10.1–10.5, 13.9, 16.1–26.6, 18.1–18.3), computing (14.1–14.3, 15.1–15.7, 17.1–17.7, 20.1, 20.8), looking for patterns (1.1–1.4, 16.4, 16.6, 17.5–17.7), and classifying (8.1–8.6, 19.1–19.5).
- *Linguistic/language intelligence* is used when learning by listening (21.1), verbalizing (1.1–1.4, 3.1–3.4, 11.2–11.4, 22.6), reading (2.1–2.4), translating (14.1–14.3), and discussing (8.6, 22.4).
- *Naturalist intelligence* is used to question (5.1, 22.1, 23.1), observe (5.2–5.3, 22.2), investigate (23.2), and experiment (5.1–5.10, 23.3–23.4).
- *Visual/spatial intelligence* is used when learning with models (12.1–12.5), photographs (16.4, 16.6), videos (16.5), diagrams (8.1–8.6, 16.1–16.3, 20.2–20.7), maps (21.1–21.7), and charts (20.2–20.7).
- *Bodily kinesthetic intelligence* is used to process knowledge through bodily sensations (12.2), movements (12.2), and manipulation (22.2).
- *Interpersonal intelligence* is used when learning through cooperative learning experiences (22.3, 22.5), group games (13.1–13.8), group lab work (22.5), and dialogue (8.6, 23.4).
- *Intrapersonal intelligence* is used when learning through self-dialogue (7.1–7.3, 11.1), studying (11.2–11.4), and self-assessment (7.4–7.7).
- *Musical intelligence* is used when learning through rhythm, melody, and nonverbal sounds in the environment (24.8).

Metacognition: Teaching Students to Think About Their Thinking

John Flavell argues that learning is maximized when students learn to think about their thinking

and consciously employ strategies to maximize their reasoning and problem solving capabilities.[6] Metacognitive thinkers know when and how they learn best and employ strategies to overcome barriers to learning. As students learn to regulate and monitor their thought processes and understanding, they learn to adapt to new learning challenges. Expert problem solvers first seek to develop an understanding of problems by thinking in terms of core concepts and major principles (6.1–6.4, 7.1–7.7, 11.1–11.4). By contrast, novice problem solvers have not learned this metacognitive strategy and are more likely to approach problems simply by trying to find the right formulas into which they can insert the right numbers. A major goal of education is to prepare students to be flexible for new problems and settings. The ability to transfer concepts from school to the work or home environment is a hallmark of a metacognitive thinker (6.4).

Developing Higher-Order Reasoning

Perhaps the most widely used classification of human thought is Bloom's taxonomy.[7] Benjamin Bloom and his team of researchers wrote extensively on the subject, particularly on the six basic levels of cognitive outcomes they identified: knowledge, comprehension, application, analysis, synthesis, and evaluation. Bloom's taxonomy (6.1) is hierarchical, with knowledge, comprehension, and application as fundamental levels and analysis, synthesis, and evaluation as advanced (6.1–6.4). When educators refer to "higher-level reasoning," they are generally referring to analysis, synthesis, and evaluation. One of the major themes of this book is to develop higher-order thinking skills through the teaching of science.

Constructivism: Helping Students Build Their Understanding of Science

Constructivism is a major learning theory, and is particularly applicable to the teaching and learning of science.[8] Piaget suggested that through accommodation and assimilation, individuals construct new knowledge from their experiences.[9] Constructivism views learning as a process in which students actively construct or build new ideas and concepts based on prior knowledge and new information. The constructivist teacher is a facilitator who encourages students to discover principles and construct knowledge within a given framework or structure.

Throughout this book, I emphasize the importance of helping students connect with prior knowledge and experiences as new information is presented so they can dispense with their misconceptions (7.4–7.7) and build a correct understanding. Seymour Papert, a student of Piaget, asserted that learning occurs particularly well when people are engaged in constructing a product.[10] Papert's approach, known as *constructionism,* is facilitated by model building (12.5), robotics, video editing (16.5), and similar construction projects.

Pedagogical Content Knowledge in Science

An expert scientist is not necessarily an effective teacher. An expert science teacher, however, knows the difficulties students face and the misconceptions they develop and knows how to tap prior knowledge while presenting new ideas so students can build new, correct understandings. Schulman refers to such expertise as *pedagogical content knowledge* (PCK) and says that excellent teachers have both expert content knowledge and expert PCK.[11] In *How People Learn,* Bransford, Brown, and Cocking state, "Expert teachers have a firm understanding of their respective disciplines, knowledge of the conceptual barriers that students face in learning about the discipline, and knowledge of effective strategies for working with students. Teachers' knowledge of their disciplines provides a cognitive roadmap to guide their assignments to students, to gauge student progress, and to support the questions students ask."[12] Expert teachers are aware of common misconceptions and help students resolve them. This book is dedicated to improving science teacher pedagogical content knowledge.

24.3 Developments in Science Curriculum and Instruction

Science is a dynamic endeavor, and each day brings new discoveries and raises new questions. It should come as no surprise, therefore, that the secondary school science curriculum is constantly evolving. Unlike many other countries, the United States does not have a federal system of education. As the Supreme Court stated in *Everson* v. *Board of Education of Ewing Township,* "The Constitution says nothing of education. It lays no obligation on the states to provide schools and does not undertake to regulate state systems of education if they see fit to maintain them."[13] Although the exclusion clause of the U.S. Constitution places education in the hands of the states, the federal government does affect policy by providing or withholding funds to states, districts, and schools that do or do not conform to federal policies.

The development of American science education is varied and diverse, as each state, district, and school has had a voice in the way science is taught. Despite this decentralized approach, there are many national trends in American science education, and many initiatives and reforms have had national and international consequence. We look next at a few of them.

1893: Harvard Committee of Ten—Precollegiate Science Curriculum

In 1892, the National Education Association organized the Harvard Committee of Ten to recommend uniform college entrance requirements.[14] The committee recommended science prerequisites for college applicants. In addition, it recommended that high school science classes have a significant laboratory component and that biology precede chemistry and physics. High schools conformed to the committee's recommendation, giving birth to the traditional laboratory-based science curriculum, with biology preceding the physical sciences. By 1920, general science, biology, chemistry, and physics were established as sequential year-long courses in most American high schools, and today most still offer science in this "layer-cake" sequence.[15]

1950: National Science Foundation—Federal Funding for Science Education

Prior to World War II, academic research in science and engineering was not considered to be a federal responsibility, and almost all support came from industry and private contributions. In 1950, President Truman signed Public Law 507, creating the National Science Foundation (NSF) as an independent government agency supporting fundamental research and education in science and engineering. Through the years, NSF has provided substantial funding for training science educators and developing science curriculum.

1955: Advanced Placement Program—College-Level Science Courses

In 1955, the College Board established the Advanced Placement Program (AP) to provide students the opportunity to do college-level work while still in high school. The College Board defines curriculum and offers yearly tests in more than 30 curricular fields. Students around the world take the standardized examinations, which include multiple-choice and free-response components. Most colleges offer applicants credit or advanced standing for suitable test scores. The Advanced Placement Program has experienced steady growth since its inception and is a model of sustained educational reform.

Research indicates that that the Advanced Placement Program increases academic expectations,[16] standards, professional development,[17] and student involvement at participating high schools.[18] The College Board offers Advanced Placement Programs in the sciences in biology, chemistry, physics, and environmental science. In 2006, AP courses were offered in more than 16,000 schools to more than 1.3 million students, many of whom were enrolled in one or more of the science offerings.[19] Most high schools and colleges calculate weighted grade point averages in which Advanced Placement classes are graded on a five-point rather than a four-point scale.[20] It is very difficult to get into many selective institutions without Advanced Placement credits and the extra grade points they provide, and this has fueled interest in the program.[21]

1958: National Defense Education Act—Developing Science Curricula

In October 1957 the Soviet Union launched *Sputnik 1*, the first artificial satellite to orbit the Earth. The fear that the United States had become technologically inferior to its cold war foe awakened a nationwide interest in science and technology education. The 1958 National Defense Education Act (NDEA) provided federal aid for secondary science instruction and funded college students to pursue degrees in science and engineering. In addition, the NDEA and NSF funded numerous science curriculum development projects, including BSCS (Biological Sciences Curriculum Study), Chem Study (Chemical Education Materials Study), PSSC Physics (Physical Science Study Committee), and ESCP (Earth Science Curriculum Project). These curricula became widely used throughout the United States, creating nationwide (not national or federal) science curricula and ushering in what some have called the Golden Age of Science Education.

1969: National Assessment of Educational Progress— America's Report Card

The National Assessment of Educational Progress (NAEP) was developed by the National Center for Education Statistics to be "the Nation's Report Card." It remains the only nationally representative, ongoing assessment of what America's students know.[22] The NAEP assesses student knowledge in science and seven other areas. The 1996 assessment revealed that less than one-third of students were performing at or above the proficiency level in mathematics and science. Poor performance on the NAEP has been an impetus for many educational reforms.

1983: Nation at Risk Report—The Call for Standards-Based Reform

In 1983 the National Commission on Excellence in Education published an alarming report, *A Nation at Risk,* stating that "if an unfriendly foreign power had attempted to impose on America the mediocre educational performance that exists today, we might well have viewed it as an act of war. As it stands, we have allowed this to happen to ourselves. We have even squandered the gains in student achievement made in the wake of the Sputnik challenge. Moreover, we have dismantled essential support systems which helped make those gains possible. We have, in effect, been committing an act of unthinking, unilateral educational disarmament."[23] *A Nation at Risk* emphasized the need for educational standards and standards-based assessments, both of which were instituted in succeeding reforms. In addition, it recommended that American high schools require three years of science for graduation and that the federal government support curriculum improvement and research on teaching, learning, and the management of schools.[24]

1990: Project 2061: Science for All Americans—Science Literacy and STS

In 1990 the American Association for the Advancement of Science, the world's largest scientific society, issued a call for a long-term science education reform in its landmark report, *Project 2061: Science for All Americans.*[25] The report focused on the need for science literacy and said that a "scientifically literate person is one who understands key concepts and principles of science, [and] uses scientific knowledge and reasoning for individual and social purposes." *Project 2061* emphasized the need to organize science around conceptual, transdisciplinary themes that would allow learners to link science concepts with mathematics, history, economics, language, literature,

political science, and the arts. *Project 2061* encouraged an emphasis on conceptual themes to provide understanding across traditional curricular boundaries. In addition, it published *Benchmarks for Scientific Literacy* with specific goals and objectives for science curriculum.[26] *Project 2061* has been widely cited in subsequent curricular reforms.

1990: Scope, Sequence, and Coordination— Integrated Science

The National Science Teachers Association's (NSTA) *Scope, Sequence, and Coordination Report* (SS&C) recommended that all secondary students study every science every year for six years, in courses integrating physics, chemistry, biology, and earth and space science.[27] Its recommendation was based in part on an international model and called for an integrated approach to science that was radically different from the traditional layer-cake curriculum in which each science was taught in separate year-long courses.

In the years following the SS&C report, numerous schools instituted integrated science curricula with the expectation that students would learn concepts across curricular lines in a coordinated program, starting with descriptive and phenomenological aspects of science and moving through empirical and quantitative treatments to the abstract and theoretical concepts. Unfortunately very few curricular resources were developed to support integrated science, and few teachers were prepared to teach across curricular lines. The introduction of state standards with yearly assessments based on the traditional layer-cake sequence contributed to the demise of integrated science in many parts of the country.

1995: Trends in International Mathematics and Science Study—Evaluating Science Education in an International Context

Every four years since 1995, the National Center for Education Statistics has conducted an assessment to see how American students perform in an international context. The Trends in International Mathematics and Science Study (TIMMS) documents a gradual decline in performance and interest in mathematics and science as American students get older, paralleling a drop in standardized science scores.[28] Among the 20 countries assessed in advanced mathematics and physics in 1999, none scored significantly lower than the United States in mathematics, and only one scored significantly lower in physics. The TIMMS is the largest and most comprehensive study ever undertaken of mathematics and science education. The study focuses on children who are in fourth, eighth, and twelfth grades. The 1999 TIMMS charged that American science courses were unfocused and shallow ("a mile wide and an inch deep"), providing arguments for later reforms.

1996: National Science Education Standards Project—National Standards

The National Research Council developed the National Science Education Standards to provide the qualitative criteria and framework for judging the content, instruction, and assessment of science education in schools across the nation.[29] The standards define the understanding that all students should develop and present criteria for judging science education content at specific grade levels. These standards are national in the sense that they are offered by a national organization, but they are not federal since education is the prerogative of the states. The standards offer many recommendations, including greater emphasis on pedagogical content knowledge, student understanding, inquiry, and integration.

1998: California Science Content Standards—What Students Should Know

In 1998, the California State Board of Education adopted science content standards for sixth (earth science), seventh (life science), and eighth (physical science) grades, as well as for high school

biology, chemistry, earth science, and physics.[30] The standards define specific concepts students should master and provide the benchmark for district and state assessments. Other states followed California's example by defining the science facts and concepts students should know after each grade or subject.

2001: No Child Left Behind—Holding Schools Accountable for Learning

In 2001, the U.S. Congress passed the No Child Left Behind Act (NCLB), emphasizing "increased accountability for states, school districts, and schools; greater choice for parents and students, particularly those attending low-performing schools; more flexibility for states and local educational agencies (LEAs) in the use of federal education dollars; and a stronger emphasis on reading."[31] NCLB is based on the belief that what gets measured gets done. States are required to test student and school performance according to their established state standards if they are to receive full federal funding.

Today anyone can look online to examine the test scores of specific schools and districts. States and districts must provide data on student achievement by subgroup, inform parents and the community of the scores of each school, and disseminate report cards on school and district performance. NCLB fueled a variety of state and local initiatives in standards-based reform and performance-based education.

2005: Rising Above the Gathering Storm—The Need for Scientists

In response to soaring trade deficits and the export of numerous high-tech jobs to rapidly developing nations, the National Academy of Sciences, National Academy of Engineering, and Institute of Medicine commissioned *Rising Above the Gathering Storm: Energizing and Employing America for a Brighter Economic Future,* a report that noted:

Without basic scientific literacy, adults cannot participate effectively in a world increasingly shaped by science and technology. Without a flourishing scientific and engineering community, young people are not motivated to dream of what can be, and they will have no motivation to become the next generation of scientists and engineers who can address persistent national problems, including national and homeland security. . . For the first time in generations, the nation's children could face poorer prospects than their parents and grandparents did. We owe our current prosperity, security, and good health to the investments of past generations, and we are obliged to renew those commitments in education, research, and innovation policies to ensure that the American people continue to benefit from the remarkable opportunities provided by the rapid development of the global economy and its not inconsiderable underpinning in science and technology. . . Because other nations have, and probably will continue to have, the competitive advantage of a low wage structure, the United States must compete by optimizing its knowledge-based resources, particularly in science and technology, and by sustaining the most fertile environment for new and revitalized industries and the well-paying jobs they bring. We have already seen that capital, factories, and laboratories readily move wherever they are thought to have the greatest promise of return to investors.[32]

Similar writings by the Education Testing Service (*America's Perfect Storm*)[33] and Thomas Friedman (*The World Is Flat*)[34] show that America must give greater emphasis to developing and retaining scientists, engineers, and science and technology educators.

24.4 The Science Curriculum

Most countries have a national system of education and, hence, national curricula. In the United States, education is a responsibility of the state, and curricular decisions are made at the state, county,

district, and school levels. The only nationwide science curricula in the United States are the College Board's Advanced Placement (AP) Program[35] and the International Baccalaureate (see section 24.5). Both sponsoring organizations publish course outlines, test materials, and laboratory activities, and as a result, there is a high degree of standardization nationwide.[36] The Advanced Placement and International Baccalaureate programs are also offered at many international schools and are the most prominent models of internationally recognized science curricula.

Although there is no national system of education in the United States, recommendations by national organizations, such as the American Association for the Advancement of Science, National Science Teachers Association, and National Research Council, have a profound influence on state and local curricular decisions. For example, after the National Commission on Excellence in Education's landmark *Nation at Risk* report in 1983,[37] schools and districts gave greater emphasis to science, and by the end of the decade, the number of graduating seniors who had taken science had increased as follows: biology, from 75 to 92 percent; chemistry, from 31 to 50 percent; and physics, from 14 to 22 percent. Although this represented a significant increase in the amount of science instruction American students received, it was still significantly less than in many countries, particularly with respect to the physical sciences. For example in the early 1990s, it was found that Chinese secondary students spent 140 percent as much instructional time in biology, 200 percent as much time in chemistry, and 280 percent as much time in physics.[38]

Figure 24.1 shows standard curricular sequences for American and Chinese high school students. Note that in grades 8, 10, 11, and 12, Chinese students receive 9 hours of science instruction, comprising 3 hours each of biology, chemistry, and physics. This same study observed that "the Chinese science curriculum is uniform, narrow, and deep, while the American curriculum is varied, broad, and flat. The Chinese curriculum is vertical and spiral in nature—the same science concepts and skills appear again and again in the curricular materials at different levels

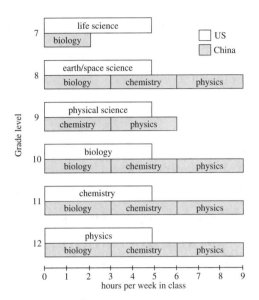

Figure 24.1 Comparisons of Chinese and American Curriculum

of schooling, with greater knowledge and deeper understandings at the higher levels."[39] Comparisons with other developed nations have been similar, and the U.S. science and math curriculum has been described as "a mile wide and an inch deep" when compared to that of other developed nations.[40]

Although AP and International Baccalaureate science curricula and assessments are accepted across the United States, no others are, and there is great variation from one school to the next among middle school, general program, college preparatory, and elective science courses. The sections that follow describe and list the titles of some of the more common science courses taught in American schools.

Middle and Junior High School Science

Middle schools generally serve grades 6 to 8, while junior high schools serve grades 7 to 9. The courses offered are a function of the grades served:

- *General Science:* introduction to the life and physical sciences
- *Earth Science:* introduction to geology, hydrology, meteorology, and astronomy
- *Life Science:* introduction to biology, and to human anatomy and physiology

- *Physical Science:* introduction to chemistry and physics
- *Integrated Science 1 and 2:* all sciences are taught around unifying themes

High School Science

General Program General program courses may or may not have a laboratory component. They satisfy graduation requirements but are generally not accepted as prerequisites for admission to four-year colleges and universities.

- *Physical Science:* introduction to physics and chemistry
- *Life Science:* introduction to biology

Integrated Science Many integrated science courses were developed in response to the National Science Teachers Association's Scope Sequence and Coordination Project, with the goal of offering every student, every science, every year. Integrated science courses are often taught thematically according to major unifying principles such as energy, matter, equilibrium, and change.

- *Integrated Science 1,2,3,4:* science based around common themes

College Preparatory and Honors College preparatory sciences are laboratory-based courses that meet the entrance requirements at most colleges and universities.[41] Honors or academically enriched classes are advanced versions of college preparatory courses and may or may not receive an extra point when colleges are tabulating grade point averages for candidates for admission:

- *Biology, Honors Biology:* Traditional high school biology with lab
- *Chemistry, Honors Chemistry:* Traditional high school chemistry with lab
- *Physics, Honors Physics:* Traditional high school physics with lab

Elective Sciences Many high schools offer elective sciences that allow students to pursue specialized interests. These may be offered as general program, college preparatory, or honors courses. Those that are offered at the college preparatory or honors level offer a laboratory component and generally satisfy college science admissions requirements:

- *Botany:* the study of plant biology
- *Anatomy and Physiology:* the study of human structure and function
- *Marine Biology:* the study of marine organisms and ecosystems
- *Geology:* the study of the physical structure, substance, and history of the Earth
- *Astronomy:* the study of all celestial objects and the physical universe
- *Earth and Space Science:* the study of geology and astronomy
- *Conceptual Physics:* a nonmathematical introduction to physics

Advanced Placement   These courses are offered to high school juniors and seniors, and occasionally to sophomores and freshmen. These are laboratory sciences that meet the science prerequisites for admission to colleges and universities. Students may earn credit and advanced standing by performing high enough on a standardized exam. Many colleges award an extra grade point for A and B grades in AP courses that candidates for admission have taken:

- AP Biology
- AP Chemistry
- AP Physics B: Classical and modern physics (not calculus based)
- AP Physics C: Mechanics (calculus based)
- AP Physics C: Electromagnetism (calculus based)
- AP Environmental Science

International Baccalaureate   These courses are offered to high school juniors and seniors at participating schools. These are laboratory sciences that meet the science prerequisites for admission to colleges and universities. Students may earn

credit and advanced standing for sufficient scores on standardized assessments. Many colleges award an extra grade point for A and B grades in IB courses to their candidates for admission:

- IB Physics
- IB Chemistry
- IB Biology
- IB Environmental Systems

24.5 Advanced Placement and International Baccalaureate Curricula

Most colleges and universities have an AP policy granting incoming students credit, placement, or both on the basis of their AP Exam grades, and many grant up to a full year of college credit (sophomore standing) to students who earn a sufficient number of qualifying AP grades. In this section we briefly describe the curricula. More information can be found online at *sciencesource book.com* and www.collegeboard.com, or search "advanced placement."

Advanced Placement Biology

The AP Biology curriculum includes the following:

- *Molecules and cells:* chemistry of life, cells, cellular energetics
- *Heredity and evolution:* heredity, molecular genetics, evolutionary biology
- *Organisms and populations:* diversity of organisms, structure, and function of plants and animals, ecology[42]

Recommended AP Biology laboratory activities are published by the College Board.[43] The following activities are commonly used in AP Biology classes:

- Diffusion and osmosis
- Enzyme catalysis
- Mitosis and meiosis
- Plant pigments and photosynthesis

- Cellular respiration
- Molecular biology
- Genetics of organisms
- Population genetics and evolution
- Transpiration
- Physiology of the circulatory system
- Animal behavior
- Dissolved oxygen and aquatic primary productivity

Advanced Placement Chemistry

The AP Chemistry curriculum includes the following:

- *Structure of matter:* atomic theory and structure, chemical bonding, nuclear chemistry, nuclear equations, half-lives, radioactivity, chemical applications
- *States of matter:* gases, liquids, solids, solutions
- *Reactions:* reaction types, stoichiometry, equilibrium, kinetics, thermodynamics
- Descriptive chemistry
- Laboratory
- *Problem solving:* The AP Chemistry exam requires much problem solving, including problems dealing with percentage composition, empirical and molecular formulas from experimental data, molar masses from gas density, freezing-point measurements, boiling-point measurements, gas laws, Dalton's law, Graham's law, stoichiometric relations, titration calculations, mole fractions, molar and molal solutions, Faraday's laws of electrolysis, equilibrium constants and their applications, standard electrode potentials and their use, Nernst equation, thermodynamic and thermochemical calculations, and kinetics calculations.[44]

Advanced Placement Physics B

The AP Physics B curriculum covers topics in classical and modern physics. It requires use of algebra and trigonometry but not calculus:

- *Newtonian mechanics:* kinematics, Newton's laws of motion, work, energy, power, systems of particles, linear momentum, circular motion, rotation, oscillations, gravitation
- *Electricity and magnetism:* electrostatics, conductors, capacitors, dielectrics, electric circuits, magnetic fields, electromagnetism
- *Fluid mechanics and thermal physics:* fluid mechanics, temperature, heat, kinetic theory, thermodynamics
- *Waves and optics:* wave motion, sound, physical optics, geometric optics
- *Atomic and nuclear physics:* atomic physics, quantum effects, nuclear physics[45]

Advanced Placement Physics C

The Physics C curriculum has two components: classical mechanics, and electricity and magnetism. A student can take one or both exams. Physics C classes require use of calculus in problem solving, derivations, and formulating principles. The curriculum is narrower than the curriculum of Physics B but requires greater analytical and mathematical sophistication.

- *Newtonian mechanics:* kinematics, Newton's laws of motion, work, energy, power, systems of particles, linear momentum, circular motion, rotation, oscillations, gravitation
- *Electricity and magnetism:* electrostatics, conductors, capacitors, dielectrics, electric circuits, magnetic fields, electromagnetism

Advanced Placement Environmental Science

The AP Environmental Science curriculum includes the following:

- *Earth systems and resources:* Earth science concepts, atmosphere, global water resources and use, soil and soil dynamics
- *The living world:* ecosystem structure, energy flow, ecosystem diversity, natural ecosystem change, natural biogeochemical cycles
- *Population:* population biology concepts, human population

- *Land and water use:* agriculture, forestry, rangelands, other land use, mining, fishing, global economics
- *Energy resources and consumption:* energy concepts, energy consumption, fossil fuel resources and use, nuclear energy, hydroelectric power, energy conservation, renewable energy
- *Pollution:* pollution types, impacts on the environment and human health, economic impacts
- *Global change:* stratospheric ozone, global warming, loss of biodiversity[46]

International Baccalaureate

A growing number of schools offer the International Baccalaureate (IB), an international curriculum and assessment program administered by the International Baccalaureate Organization (IBO), headquartered in Geneva, Switzerland (see *science sourcebook.com* or www.ibo.org, or search "international baccalaureate"). The IB program is taught in more than 120 countries and is particularly popular at international schools such as those that serve the families of embassy workers and other expatriate professionals. Like the AP program, the IB offers yearly assessments in physics, chemistry, biology, and environmental systems. Many American colleges offer credit for a performance of 5 or better on a scale of 1 to 7, although each college sets its own standards. The IB is a comprehensive curriculum designed to prepare students for liberal arts education at the tertiary level. The mission of the IBO is "to develop inquiring, knowledgeable and caring young people who help to create a better and more peaceful world through intercultural understanding and respect."[47]

24.6 Teaching Science Inquiry

Teaching and learning science through inquiry is one of the themes of this book.[48] Inquiry is advocated in the National Science Education Standards,[49] the Benchmarks for Science Literacy,[50] and the National Science Teachers Association.

Think-Aloud

Students learn how to reason by observing the reasoning of others. *Think-aloud* is a strategy in which the teacher makes thinking and reasoning processes explicit by describing the thought processes involved. During think-alouds, teachers help students see the invisible processes of the mind by explaining what and how they are thinking. Teachers should describe how and when they are using the five essential features of inquiry (22.1), aspects of the scientific methods (5.4–5.10), and all of the other strategies introduced in preceding chapters.

Teachers often want to prepare overhead transparencies or computer presentations showing how problems are solved. I strongly recommend against this as it makes the presentation "canned" and gives students a window only on the teacher's reading ability rather than his or her true thought process. I suggest starting with a blank transparency or whiteboard when solving a problem and with only outline diagrams when describing anatomical or other structural features. Explain your logic as you solve problems and fill in details so students can learn from your thought processes.

Scientific Inquiry: A Position Statement of the National Science Teachers Association

The National Science Education Standards (NSES) defines scientific inquiry as "the diverse ways in which scientists study the natural world and propose explanations based on the evidence derived from their work. Scientific inquiry also refers to the activities through which students develop knowledge and understanding of scientific ideas, as well as an understanding of how scientists study the natural world."[51] The Science as Inquiry Standard in NSES includes the abilities necessary to do scientific inquiry and understanding about scientific inquiry.

Scientific inquiry reflects how scientists come to understand the natural world, and it is at the heart of how students learn. From a very early age, children interact with their environment, ask questions, and seek ways to answer those questions.

Understanding science content is significantly enhanced when ideas are anchored to inquiry experiences.

Scientific inquiry is a powerful way of understanding science content. Students learn how to ask questions and use evidence to answer them. In the process of learning the strategies of scientific inquiry, students conduct an investigation and collect evidence from a variety of sources, develop an explanation from the data, and communicate and defend their conclusions.

The National Science Teachers Association (NSTA) recommends that all K–16 teachers embrace scientific inquiry and is committed to helping educators make it the centerpiece of the science classroom. The use of scientific inquiry will help ensure that students develop a deep understanding of science and scientific inquiry.

Regarding the use of scientific inquiry as a teaching approach, NSTA recommends that science teachers:

- Plan an inquiry-based science program for their students by developing both short- and long-term goals that incorporate appropriate content knowledge.
- Implement approaches to teaching science that cause students to question and explore and to use those experiences to raise and answer questions about the natural world. The learning cycle approach is one of many effective strategies for bringing explorations and questioning into the classroom.
- Guide and facilitate learning using inquiry by selecting teaching strategies that nurture and assess students' developing understandings and abilities.
- Design and manage learning environments that provide students with the time, space, and resources needed for learning science through inquiry.
- Receive adequate administrative support for the pursuit of science as inquiry in the classroom. Support can take the form of professional development on how to teach scientific inquiry, content, and the nature of science; the allocation of time to do scientific inquiry

effectively; and the availability of necessary materials and equipment.
- Experience science as inquiry as part of their teacher preparation program. Preparation should include learning how to develop questioning strategies, writing lesson plans that promote abilities and understanding of scientific inquiry, and analyzing instructional materials to determine whether they promote scientific inquiry.

Regarding students' abilities to do scientific inquiry, NSTA recommends that teachers help students:

- Learn how to identify and ask appropriate questions that can be answered through scientific investigations.
- Design and conduct investigations to collect the evidence needed to answer a variety of questions.
- Use appropriate equipment and tools to interpret and analyze data.
- Learn how to draw conclusions and think critically and logically to create explanations based on their evidence.
- Communicate and defend their results to their peers and others.

Regarding students' understanding about scientific inquiry, NSTA recommends that teachers help students understand:

- That science involves asking questions about the world and then developing scientific investigations to answer their questions.
- That there is no fixed sequence of steps that all scientific investigations follow. Different kinds of questions suggest different kinds of scientific investigations.
- That scientific inquiry is central to the learning of science and reflects how science is done.
- The importance of gathering empirical data using appropriate tools and instruments.
- That the evidence they collect can change their perceptions about the world and increase their scientific knowledge.

- The importance of being skeptical when they assess their own work and the work of others.
- That the scientific community seeks explanations that are empirically based and logically consistent.

24.7 Teaching Science to English Language Learners

In 2003, 42 percent of American public school students were of racial or ethnic minorities, up 22 percent from 30 years before.[52] Most of this increase in diversity was due to immigration from Latin America and Asia, and with this increase in ethnic diversity came a corresponding increase in linguistic diversity. For example, in 2002, nearly 42 percent of students in Los Angeles Unified School District, the second largest district in the country, were classified as English language learners.

The Institute of Education Sciences of the U.S. Department of Education defines *English language learners (ELL)* as

individuals who (1) were not born in the United States or whose native language is a language other than English; or (2) come from environments where a language other than English is dominant; or (3) are American Indians and Alaskan Natives and who come from environments where a language other than English has had a significant impact on their level of English proficiency; and who, by reason thereof, have sufficient difficulty speaking, reading, writing, or understanding the English language, to deny such individuals the opportunity to learn successfully in classrooms where the language of instruction is English or to participate fully in our society.[53]

Today's science teachers must be prepared to teach students whose first language is not English. In this section we reference ELL strategies and activities that are found throughout this book.

The science classroom is often a frustrating place for English language learners. Science has a complex vocabulary that is difficult even for native English speakers to learn. Difficulty learning English should not be confused with an inability to think scientifically. Many of the strategies that are useful for English language learners are effective for differentiating instruction for other students as well. Use a variety of methods to see which work best with your teaching style and students.

Listening

• *Speak slowly and distinctly, and write down key terms.* Anyone who has learned a foreign language in class, then traveled to a country where the language is spoken, has noticed that it is difficult to understand natives because they seem to "talk too fast." What seems normal speed to a native speaker is extremely fast to a language learner or a student with a hearing impairment. The addition of the complex terms and concepts of science can make learning even more difficult. Write down key terms so students can see them and connect them to the spoken word.

• *Closed captioning.* Most science videos are equipped with closed captioning. Turn on the closed captioning so students can see what narrators and actors are saying (Activity 16.5.4). This helps English language learners correlate written and spoken English and helps them see spelling and sentence construction. Closed captioning is also invaluable for the hearing impaired.

Visualization

• *Emphasize visual literacy.* It is often said that math and music are universal languages—ones that can be read regardless of one's primary language. Although these claims are debatable, it is clear that an English-speaking student can read and understand an equation in a Swahili textbook and a Greek musician can play a score drafted by a Japanese composer. Regardless of linguistic background, people around the world can interpret mathematical equations and musical scores. In addition, they can also interpret pictures and, with minimal linguistic skills, interpret charts and graphs. Visual literacy, or the ability to evaluate, apply, or create conceptual visual representation, is relatively independent of language and is therefore invaluable to learning science and English simultaneously. Vector diagrams (16.1), scientific diagrams (16.2), pictorial riddles (16.3), photographic analysis (16.4), movie analysis (16.5), and map development and analysis (21.1–21.7) are a few of the many activities that can be used to build visual literacy.

• *Graphic organizers.* Graphic organizers are a means of introducing and assessing concepts in a manner that encourages meaningful learning. They are diagrams or maps that show the relationship between new and existing concepts, thereby facilitating integration of new and familiar ideas. They require minimal language and are helpful tools when teaching science to English language learners. Conceptual grids (9.1), Venn diagrams (9.2), flowcharts (9.3), mind maps (9.4), and concept maps (9.5) are some of the more common graphic organizers.

• *Use charts, graphs and figures.* Scatter and line graphs (20.4), column and bar charts (20.5), pie and area graphs (20.5), and high-low, combination and log plots (20.7) can communicate concepts with minimal use of spoken or written language. The layout of such visual aids should be clear and uncluttered.

• *Manual video control.* Science videos often introduce a variety of new terms and concepts, most of which even native speakers have difficulty remembering. Pause the video to discuss key concepts. Use the bookmark and video clip features to return to precise sequences for review (Activity 16.5.4). Use the step-frame, slow motion, and replay features to focus student attention on key concepts.

Interpersonal Strategies

• *Group projects and cooperative learning.* Many of the activities in this book employ group work and cooperative learning. Such activities provide opportunities for students to exchange, write, and present ideas. Projects use a variety of skills that work together to increase understanding and retention.

• *Partner English learners with strong English speakers.* The best way to learn something is to teach it. Partnering English learners with strong English speakers benefits both students. It may be particularly beneficial to pair English learners with bilingual students who can translate laboratory and activity procedures. Develop a seating chart so English language learners are sitting near the front of class and adjacent to bilingual students who can assist them.

• *Think/pair/share.* Students learn to speak English by speaking English, but it is often counterproductive to ask English language learners to read passages or give descriptions to the entire class. Students are often embarrassed by their minimal science knowledge and English skills, and public exposure may make them more uncomfortable and reserved. By contrast, English language learners are often eager to share their ideas in their new language with their peers. The think/pair/share strategy gives all students the opportunity to practice English by explaining science concepts.[54] Provide students with time to write a response to a thought-provoking question, then additional time to discuss it with their neighbor before sharing their conclusion with the class. The think/pair/share technique increases student participation and involvement and is a particularly effective way of encouraging English language learners to express science concepts in English.

• *Encourage participation.* Many English learners come from countries in which student participation is not encouraged. They may be reluctant to speak, not only because of their lack of proficiency in English, but also because they are uncomfortable in an environment where they are asked to share their ideas. A positive and supportive environment has a significant influence on student comfort level, participation, and success. Requiring English language learners to speak in front of class may be counterproductive and cause great anxiety. Encourage them to express themselves, but don't force them onto the stage prematurely.

Structure

• *Consistent routines:* English learners are freer to concentrate on new concepts if they are familiar with classroom routines.

• *Road map to science:* English language learners benefit greatly from a "road map" that shows where they are in the science curriculum. Use organizational structures when teaching earth and space science (8.2), biology (8.3), chemistry (8.4), or physics (8.5) to English language learners.

• *Outlines:* Provide students with a copy of your lecture or discussion outline. This will help ELL students know where you are and where you are going with your lesson.

• *Relate to prior knowledge:* Make use of student background knowledge of science concepts. Discover what your students already know about a given topic, and build on this knowledge.

Laboratory

• *Hand-on activities:* Kinesthetic learning events provide an excellent learning environment for English language learners. The books I coauthored with James Cunningham, *Hands-On Chemistry Activities with Real-Life Applications,* and *Hands-On Physics Activities with Real-Life Applications,* provide numerous hands-on activities of benefit for English language learners.

Demonstrations

• *Clear, procedural steps:* The science laboratory can be a confusing and potentially dangerous setting for English language learners. Present procedures clearly using flowcharts, pictures, and outlines.

• *Model laboratory activities:* Demonstrate activities in front of the class to ensure that English language learners can see the procedures before engaging in an activity.

• *Pictorial guide:* Provide a visual reference to glassware and other materials used in experiments and activities. Review safety symbols, and post them in the room and in the lab handout.

Reading and Writing

• *Journaling:* Students become better writers by writing. Require English language learners to keep science journals (Activity 3.2.1) in which they write lecture notes, new terms, and responses to prompts.

• *Science reading comprehension activities:* Cloze (2.1) and jigsaw (2.2) are two techniques for developing and assessing reading comprehension and can be used when making formative assessments of language and science learning.

Instruction

• *Wait time:* Teachers are often uncomfortable with silence and either call on the first student to raise a hand or answer questions themselves, thereby short-circuiting the thought processes of most students, particularly English language learners who are trying to translate terms while formulating an explanation. Let students know that you expect all to be mentally engaged, and for this reason you provide wait time sufficient for the majority to develop an answer before calling on any individual.

• *Analogies:* Use analogies to relate new concepts to previously learned concepts (10.2–10.5).

Vocabulary

• *Language-based science games:* Reinforce vocabulary with Science Bingo (13.3) and concepts with Science Pictionary (13.4). These games require minimal spoken language and provide an excellent review of science vocabulary.

• *Picture glossary:* One of the best ways to learn the vocabulary of a new language is with pictorial flash cards. A picture of the concept is on one side, and the term (in the language to be learned) is on the reverse. The student learns to correlate concepts directly with words, eliminating the need for translation.

• *Common lexicon:* People construct understanding by integrating new ideas with preexisting knowledge. Ask students what they already know; then develop a common classroom vocabulary that can be used to develop new understandings.

• *Root words:* A knowledge of Greek and Latin prefixes, suffixes, and roots can greatly enhance student understanding of scientific terms and facilitate a better understanding of English and other European languages. Approximately 50 percent of all words in English have Latin roots, many of which are shared with Spanish, French, Portuguese, and Italian. Learning scientific root words therefore helps one understand the vocabulary of a variety of languages, particularly English (1.1–1.4).

• *Cognates:* Many science terms are used internationally. Identify such terms (2.3, 2.4), and ask your students to notify you whenever they recognize a new term that is pronounced or written similarly in their first language. This helps build your knowledge of cognates (words that are similar in two or more languages) so you can help future learners master science vocabulary.

• *Mathematics translation:* English language learners find word problems much more challenging than symbolic math problems. The English language is exceedingly complex, with numerous nuances that must be learned. Students need to be able to translate common words to math symbols (14.1), natural language to algebraic expressions (14.2), and algebraic expressions to natural language (14.3). The activities in this book help students develop such skills.

• *Word wall:* Post new vocabulary terms on the wall in an organized, grouped manner. For example, you may wish to post new biology terms in columns according to the level of organization (e.g., cell, tissue, organ) (8.3).

24.8 Teaching Science with Humor

A good sense of humor can help create a positive learning environment and reduce the tension that makes many students dislike school. Humor should be clean, respectful, and related to the curriculum. Each teacher needs to develop his or her own style of humor, but it helps to have some ideas to work with. This section provides a few samples of science humor that may add a little levity to your classroom.

Puns

A pun is a figure of speech that consists of a deliberate confusion of similar words or phrases. Here are a few examples:

- Absolute zero is cool!
- The speed of time is 1 second per second.

- The unit on optics requires some light reading.
- Free radicals have revolutionized chemistry.
- If you chop an avocado into 6.02×10^{23} pieces, you get guacamole.
- The chemical company became insolvent after spilling benzene in the river.
- The microbiologist was crushed by the cover slip.
- During nucleotides, biochemicals wash up onto the beach.
- A person who is ambidextrose can eat L-glucose or D-glucose.
- Biology grows on you.
- Seismologists are fault finders.
- Geologists have their faults
- Geologists are gneiss, don't take things for granite, and have a good apatite.
- Excellent vulcanology students graduate magma cum laude.
- Geologists never lose their luster.
- Geologists don't wrinkle; they show lineation.
- When a bridge collapses in California, it is the San Andreas Fault!
- Do molecular biologists wear designer genes?
- Geology rocks!
- 10^{12} microphones = 1 megaphone.
- 10^6 bicycles = 2 megacycles.
- 454 graham crackers = 1 pound cake.
- 10 millipedes = 1 centipede.
- 10 monologs = 5 dialogues.
- 2 monograms = 1 diagram.
- 8 nickels = 2 paradigms.
- Visual puns: Some puns can be displayed diagrammatically such as the "chemicals" in Figure 24.2.

Imponderable Questions

The term *imponderable* was popularized by David Feldman, author of a series of books that examine, investigate, and explain puzzling phenomena.[55] Many imponderables are humorous and can be used as warm-up activities, or simply to add levity to the classroom. Here are a few "imponderable" questions:

- Why does the Department of Interior oversee the outdoors?

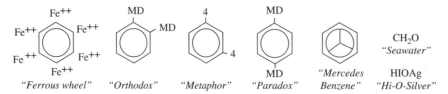

Figure 24.2 Visual Puns in Chemistry

- Why do scientists call it "research" when looking for something new?
- Why does the number of cells multiply when cells divide?
- Have you ever imagined a world with no hypothetical situations?
- How does Teflon stick to a pan?
- If it's zero degrees outside today and it's supposed to be twice as cold tomorrow, how cold is it going to be?
- What's the speed of dark?
- Why is it called "after dark" when it really is "after light"?
- If something doesn't matter, does it have no mass?
- If sound does not travel in a vacuum, why is a vacuum so noisy?
- When do fish sleep?
- How do they keep soda in soft drink machines from freezing in winter?
- Why don't lizards get sunburned?
- Why do bottled water containers have expiration dates?
- Do identical twins have identical fingerprints?
- How do birds know where to peck for worms?

Science Songs

Students who have great difficulty memorizing science facts may be able to memorize lengthy song lyrics with little difficulty. The rhythm, rhyme, and melody of songs make it easy to remember the lyrics. Certain performers, like J.P. Taylor and the Academics, have capitalized on this fact and have written songs to help students memorize science facts and concepts. *The Academics* have written songs such as "The Rock Cycle" (on the formation of igneous, sedimentary,

and metamorphic rocks), "The Rain Forest Song" (on the ecology and value of the rain forest), and "Get Your Molecules Movin" (on conduction, convection, and radiation). "The Elements Song," written and sung by Tom Lehrer in 1959, has been used for years to introduce students to the periodic table. These and other science songs can be acquired from iTunes and other Internet music stores. To capitalize on musical intelligence (24.2), have your students write and sing songs on science topics such as the solar system, mitosis, or chemical reactions.

Science Celebrations

Some science teachers have found celebrations to be good tools for engaging students and setting the tone of the class. Classes can celebrate the birthdays of scientists, famous days in science, and other notable days. Two of the most commonly celebrated days are Mole Day and Pi Day.

- *Mole Day* is celebrated in chemistry classes on October 23 between 6:02 A.M. and 6:02 P.M., making the date 6:02 10/23 (American style of writing dates). The time and date reflect Avogadro's number (6.02×10^{23}), which represents the number of atoms or molecules in a mole, the SI unit for measuring quantity. Classes can celebrate in a variety of ways, many of which are listed on Mole Day Web sites.
- *Pi Day* is celebrated in mathematics and physics classes in recognition of the irrational number pi (π), the ratio of the circumference to the diameter of a circle. The value of π is approximately 3.14159, so classes celebrate on March 14 (3/14 U.S. date format) at 1:59 P.M. Classes can celebrate in a variety of ways, many of which are listed on Internet Pi Day Web sites.

- *Scientists' birthdays.* Classes may celebrate scientists' birthdays to reflect their contributions to science and society. The following is a month-by-month starter list. The birthdays of many scientists can be found using an online encyclopedia such as Wikipedia (www.wikipedia.org):
  - January 4, 1643: Isaac Newton—mechanics, gravity, calculus
  - February 8, 1834: Dimitri Mendeleyev—periodic table
  - March 14, 1879: Albert Einstein—relativity, mass energy equivalence
  - April 21, 1838: John Muir—ecology, conservation, preservation
  - May 27, 1907: Rachel Carson—environmental movement
  - June 13, 1831: James Clerk Maxwell—electromagnetism
  - July 10, 1856: Nikola Tesla—alternating current
  - August 30, 1871: Ernest Rutherford—nuclear physics
  - September 22, 1791: Michael Faraday—electrochemistry
  - October 5, 1882: Robert Goddard—rocket propulsion
  - November 7, 1867: Marie Curie—radioactivity
  - December 27, 1822: Louis Pasteur—microbiology

Science Comics

A variety of cartoonists make humorous comics pertaining to topics in science. Perhaps the most famous is Gary Larson, whose syndicated "Far Side" cartoons often have a scientific theme. Larson's single-framed cartoons are humorous because of their anthropomorphic portrayal of plants, animals, protozoans, fungi, and bacteria.

Science Spoofs

A spoof is a humorous story, parody, or satire. One of the most famous science spoofs is the work of Nathan Zohner, a student at Eagle Rock Junior High School in Idaho Falls, Idaho. Zohner's science fair project, entitled "How Gullible Are We?" examined the response of his fellow students to a "petition" to ban dihydrogen monoxide (DHMO). Zohner wrote a "petition" stating the dangers of DHMO in such a way that most readers thought it was a dangerous product of an industrial lab rather than what it really is, water (H_2O). Soon Zohner's petition was posted on the Internet and e-mailed around the world. Zohner's petition begins: "Dihydrogen monoxide is colorless, odorless, tasteless, and kills uncounted thousands of people every year. Most of these deaths are caused by accidental inhalation of DHMO, but the dangers of dihydrogen monoxide do not end there. Prolonged exposure to its solid form causes severe tissue damage. Symptoms of DHMO ingestion can include excessive sweating and urination, and possibly a bloated feeling, nausea, vomiting and body electrolyte imbalance. For those who have become dependent, DHMO withdrawal means certain death."[56] Each of these statements is true but phrased so those reading the petition do not recognize that it is about water (DHMO = H_2O). You may wish to find the original petition on the Internet and use it for a lesson in gullibility (see *sciencesourcebook.com,* or search "ban DHMO").

24.9 Professional Development in Science Education

Professional Organizations and Journals

A *profession* is an occupation that requires extensive study and training and mastery of a specialized body of knowledge. Professions are governed and represented by professional associations, have an ethical code, and have a process of licensing or certification. Teaching is a profession. Table 24.1 lists professional organizations and journals for science teachers. Science teachers can keep current of recent developments by attending local and national conferences and reading professional journals.

Table 24.1 Science Organizations and Their Journals

Organization	Journals
American Association of Physics Teachers www.aapt.org	*American Physics Teacher:* Research, applied physics, curriculum, pedagogy, lab equipment, book reviews *American Journal of Physics:* Physics, culture, education
Association for the Advancement of Computing in Education www.aace.org	*Journal of Computers in Mathematics and Science Teaching:* Information technology in the teaching of mathematics and science
American Chemical Society www.acs.org	*Journal of Chemical Education:* Resources to improve college and high school chemistry education
American Physiological Society www.the-aps.org	*Advances in Physiology Education:* Teaching and learning of physiology
National Association of Biology Teachers www.nabt.org	*American Biology Teacher:* Pedagogy, demonstrations, experiments, and resources in biology education
National Association of Geoscience Teachers www.nagt.org	*Journal of Geoscience Education:* Pedagogy, assessment, and philosophy of teaching and learning about the geosciences
National Earth Science Teachers Association www.nestanet.org	*Earth Scientist:* Teaching of geology, astronomy, physical geography, and environmental sciences
National Association for Research in Science Teaching www.narst.org	*Journal of Research in Science Teaching:* Issues of science teaching and learning, science education policy
National Science Teachers Association www.nsta.org	*Science and Children:* Elementary school science *Science Scope:* Middle school science *Science Teacher:* Middle and high school science *Journal of College Science Teaching:* College science
School Science and Mathematics Association www.ssma.org	*School Science and Mathematics:* Issues, concerns, and lessons within and between science and mathematics

Professional Development

Many school districts and organizations offer professional development workshops for science teachers. Such workshops are designed to expand the pedagogical content knowledge of participating faculty. One way that this is accomplished is by giving teachers the opportunity to participate in lessons as adult learners. Teachers and facilitators start a workshop lesson in "teacher mode," discussing the purpose and pedagogy of the training. They then enter "student mode," where they practice the lesson as adult learners, performing the same activities required of secondary school students,

but responding to questions and prompts with the full knowledge of adult professionals. After the "student session" is completed, the training moves again to the "teacher mode" where all reflect on the lesson and offer suggestions for improvement.[57]

Lesson Study

A related approach to professional development is known as Lesson Study, a process in which teachers work together to plan, observe, analyze, and refine actual classroom lessons.[58] Lesson Study is used widely in Japan, and many credit it for improvements in Japanese mathematics and science instruction. In lesson study, teachers work together to (1) establish long-term goals of instruction, (2) consider goals of a particular subject, unit, or lesson, (3) plan classroom research lessons that operationalize long term and specific subject-matter goals, and (4) study how students respond to these lessons.

National Board Certification

The National Board for Professional Teaching Standards (NBTPS) was created in 1987 after the Carnegie Forum on Education and the Economy's Task Force on Teaching as a Profession released *A Nation Prepared: Teachers for the 21st Century*.[59] The NBTPS is an independent, nonprofit, nongovernmental organization designed to advance the quality of teaching by developing professional standards for accomplished teaching. It has created a voluntary system to certify teachers who meet these standards. More information about national board certification can be found on the Internet at *sciencesourcebook.com* or www.nbtps.org, or search "national board certification nbtps."

24.10 Science Field Trips and Guest Speakers

Students benefit from a variety of teachers, both formal and informal. Variety provides new perspectives and ideas and opens minds to new goals and careers. Teachers can provide such variety by taking students on field trips, where they learn from displays, docents, and real-world examples, and by inviting guest speakers who provide expertise from research and industry.

Science Field Trips

Although science studies the real world, many students study it only vicariously through books, lectures, and videos. To gain a deeper appreciation for science, students should be exposed to the real thing. We may talk about constellations and galaxies, but if students have never seen the Milky Way,

it is difficult for them to relate to lectures on the stars. We can talk about biomes and ecosystems, but if they have never been out of the city, such talk may seem irrelevant.

Field trips are an excellent way to connect students with true subject matter—the real world. Students should always be provided with a printed field trip guide to help them understand what they are seeing and to make them accountable for learning. Teachers should provide activities for students to do while on the trip, such as gathering data, collecting samples, making observations, answering questions, taking photographs, recording coordinates, or writing reports.

Table 24.2 lists possible field trip destinations. Look online for the field trip sites closest to your school (look on *sciencesourcebook.com* or search by destination).

Guest Speakers

The best source of guest speakers for your science classroom may be the parents of your students. If possible, determine the occupations of your students' parents through a questionnaire, the parent teacher association, or back-to-school night. Tables 4.2 to 4.5 list hundreds of occupations related to science. Parents who work in any of these fields may be able to provide presentations on their professions to your class. Such presentations build bridges between industry and education, and they may open the eyes of students to career possibilities and help them see how to prepare academically. In addition, you may wish to inquire at the speakers' bureaus of local industries and agencies, a few of which are listed below.

- *Government agencies:* fish and game, waste management, air resources
- *Colleges:* professors, public lecture series, educational outreach, recruitment
- *Professional societies:* American Chemical Society, American Physical Society
- *Health societies:* Cancer Society, Diabetes Association, Heart Association
- *Special interest groups:* Audubon Society, Nature Conservancy, Sierra Club

Table 24.2 Science Field Trip Ideas

Museums	state parks	universities	dairies
aeronautics museums	tide pools	weather stations	dams
automotive museums	wetlands		engineering firms
invention museums	wilderness areas	**Interpretive Centers**	electric substations
natural history museums	wildlife preserves	animal parks	factories
science museums		arboretums	farms
technology museums	**Research**	aviaries	greenhouses
transportation museums	agricultural research	botanical gardens	harbors
	stations	fish hatcheries	hospitals
Wild Lands	federal research stations	marine aquariums	hydroelectric plants
beaches	launch sites	nature centers	landfills
county parks	marine research stations	planetariums	mining operations
deserts	mountain research	zoos	nuclear power plants
forests	stations		ranches
marine preserves	NASA centers	**Industry**	refineries
mountains	observatories	aqueducts	solar farms
national parks	research laboratories	airports	Superfund sites
ocean cruises	research vessels	biotechnology firms	water treatment plants
rangelands	tracking stations	coal power plants	wind farms

WebQuests

WebQuests are inquiry oriented Internet-based activities.[60] Students solve problems and answer questions using data from the Web. For example, an environmental science WebQuest may ask students to assess the air quality in their city.

The WebQuest home page might provide links to archived ozone and particulate maps, current pollution indexes, the National Weather Service, local newspapers, and municipal webcams. WebQuests can be located by searching for the subject of interest and the term "WebQuest."

Chapter Twenty-Five

Planning and Managing Science Instruction

25.1 Establishing Science Learning Objectives 517

25.2 Developing a Science Lesson Plan 517

25.3 Developing a Science Semester Plan 519

25.4 Getting to Know Your Students 519

25.5 Managing the Classroom Effectively 522

25.6 Assessing Student Performance 525

25.7 Evaluating Teaching Performance 528

This chapter provides a variety of professional resources to aid new and experienced science teachers in planning and managing science instruction. Although similar information can be found in many teacher education books, the ideas and information here are designed with science teachers in mind. I encourage you to browse these resources and adopt and adapt those you find useful.

25.1 Establishing Science Learning Objectives

Science teachers should write *learning objectives* that communicate and describe intended learning outcomes.[1] Objectives should be stated in terms of what the student will be able to do when the lesson is completed. Objectives should include verbs, such as those listed in Table 25.1, to define specific,

observable, and measurable student behavior.[2] A learning objective contains (1) a statement of what students will be able to do when a lesson is completed, (2) the conditions under which the students will be able to perform the task, and (3) the criteria for evaluating student performance. While *goals* describe global learning outcomes, *learning objectives* are statements of specific performances that contribute to the attainment of goals. Learning objectives should help guide curriculum development, instructional strategies, selection of instructional materials, and development of assessments.

25.2 Developing a Science Lesson Plan

Dwight Eisenhower, Supreme Commander of Allied Forces in Europe and thirty-fourth president

Table 25.1 Verbs for Use in Writing Learning Objectives

Knowledge	Comprehension	Application	Analysis	Synthesis	Evaluation
cite	associate	administer	analyze	adapt	appraise
collect	classify	apply	arrange	assemble	argue
copy	convert	calculate	breakdown	collaborate	assess
define	describe	change	categorize	combine	conclude
describe	differentiate	chart	classify	compile	convince
duplicate	discuss	choose	compare	compose	criticize
enumerate	distinguish	collect	connect	concoct	decide
identify	estimate	compute	contrast	construct	deduce
label	explain	construct	correlate	contrive	defend
list	express	demonstrate	detect	create	determine
match	extend	determine	diagram	design	discriminate
memorize	group	develop	differentiate	develop	infer
name	identify	discover	discriminate	devise	interpret
order	indicate	employ	dissect	formulate	judge
quote	order	establish	distinguish	generalize	justify
recall	paraphrase	examine	divide	generate	persuade
recognize	predict	exhibit	examine	hypothesize	prioritize
record	report	illustrate	experiment	imagine	rate
recount	restate	interview	group	incorporate	rank
relate	retell	manipulate	identify	integrate	recommend
repeat	review	modify	illustrate	invent	relate
reproduce	select	operate	inspect	modify	revise
show	summarize	practice	interpret	organize	score
specify	translate	predicts	investigate	originate	support
state	understand	prepare	order	plan	value
tabulate		produce	organize	predict	validate
tell		relate	outline	produce	
when		report	probe	propose	
what		schedule	question	reconstruct	
where		show	relate	reorganize	
who		sketch	select	revise	
		solve	separate	speculate	
		transfer	survey	systematize	
		use	test		

of the United States, said, "In preparing for battle I have always found that plans are useless, but planning is indispensable." Eisenhower knew that it was essential to plan yet remain flexible. Planning helps teachers be more flexible as they become acquainted with various options. Lesson planning is a critical part of every teacher's work, but it is important to be flexible to accommodate the real and immediate needs of students. Just as there is no single scientific method, so there is no single way of planning lessons.[3] In general, however, lessons should include *objectives, standards, anticipatory sets, teaching, guided practice* (input, modeling, check of understanding), *closure,* and *independent practice.*[4] Table 25.2 lists factors to consider when planning a lesson.

Table 25.2 Elements of a Lesson Plan

Goals and Objectives (before class)
Goals and learning objectives
Concepts and content standards

Preparation (before class)
Equipment and supplies
Prior knowledge students must have

Lesson introduction (in class)
Anticipatory set[a]
Purpose or objective of lesson
Relationship to previous lessons and standards

Lesson (in class)

Spoken and Written	**Graphics**	**Activities**
lecture notes	diagrams	demonstrations
discussion	video clips	experiments
handouts	digital photos	projects
worksheets	bulletin board	field trip
text references	transparencies	guest speakers

Guided Practice (in class)
Worksheets
Activities

Closure (in class)[b]
Summary
Assessment of learning

Independent Practice: Homework (at home)
Readings
Questions and problems

[a]The purpose of an anticipatory set is to focus the attention of all learners on the lesson. Counterintuitive demonstrations, stories, news items, anecdotes, and dispatch activities are among the many things that can be used as an anticipatory set to "make sure everyone is on the train before it leaves the station."
[b]Closure involves the completion of a daily or unit lesson. It summarizes the lesson, relates the lesson to the objectives, and assesses understanding. Closure is facilitated by the teacher but should be an act of the learner.

25.3 Developing a Science Semester Plan

It is essential that every science teacher develop a long-term plan. Such plans help pace instruction to ensure sufficient time for key concepts, activities, and assessments. It is helpful to develop a semester plan using a grid such as shown in Table 25.3. Each column represents a week or other unit of time, and each row represents an element in the teaching plan. This format makes it very easy to see the semester at a glance.

25.4 Getting to Know Your Students

The classroom should be an environment characterized by *respect*—respect for the mission of the school, respect for the teacher, respect for the staff and administration, respect for school and personal property, respect for the taxpayers or parents who are paying the bills, and respect for one another. To establish an environment of respect, teachers should practice the Golden Rule: "Do unto others as you would have them do unto you."

Table 25.3 Sample Semester Plan: First Four Weeks of Physics

	Week 1 Sept. 1–5	Week 2 Sept. 8–12	Week 3 Sept. 15–19	Week 4 Sept. 22–26
Topics	• 1D kinematics • speed • reference frames	• coordinate systems • velocity • acceleration • falling bodies	• 2D kinematics • vectors • vector addition • vector multiplication	• methods for adding vectors • relative velocity • projectile motion
Standards	Physics: 1a–f	Physics: 1b, c, l; 2c	Physics: 1j	Physics: 1i, 1j
Lecture	1.1.1–1.2.5	1.2.6–1.3.6	2.1.1–2.2.3	2.2.3–2.4.7
Readings	Chapter 1 Sections 1–7	Chapter 1 Sections 8–11	Chapter 2 Sections 1– 5	Chapter 2 Sections 6–10
Homework	Chapter 1 #1, 3, 4, 7, 10, 11	Chapter 1 #15–17, 19–23	Chapter 2 #3, 9, 10, 11, 12	Chapter 2 #13–20, 24–34, 39

Labs		• lab handout:
		  Reaction Time
		• bottle rocket
		  design specs
			• lab book 2.1:
			  Kinematics
				• lab book 2.4:
				  Projectiles
				• bottle rocket
				  contest

Electronic	Video of last year's rocket contest (10 min clip)	*National Geographic* Special on Goddard (10 min clip)	vector addition software	education.nasa.gov
Demos	Demo: compressed air rocket	Acceleration (Cunningham & Herr 2.3)	Accelerometer (Cunningham & Herr 3.1)	
Special		Guest speaker: Dr. Tom Johnson, JPL rocket engineer		Remind students of JPL open house this Saturday
Tests		Ch. 1 quiz		Ch. 1–2 unit test
Points	Homework: 30	Quiz: 25 Homework: 30 Lab: 50	Homework: 30 Lab: 50	Test: 100 Homework: 30 Project: 50

Teachers who demonstrate respect for students, the school, the administration, and their colleagues are more likely to have respectful classroom environments. Teachers demonstrate respect for their students when they express a genuine interest in them as individuals.

The following strategies provide opportunities for the teacher to do this by learning the names, backgrounds, ideas, interests, and aspirations of their students. Showing interest in your students demonstrates your respect for them and helps build rapport, making the classroom a more pleasant place for all.

Learning Student Names: Tips and Techniques

It is a formidable task to learn the names of 150 to 200 students, but it is easier if you can associate them with a photograph, activity, event, interest, or hobby. The more you know about your students, the easier it is to remember their names.

The following techniques help you learn student names, and those in subsequent sections help you understand who they are. Use multiple techniques in different contexts to promote long-term memory of student names:

- *Yearbook photos.* Match last year's yearbook photographs with the names of the students on your roster. Learn as many student names as possible prior to the first day of class, and surprise your students by greeting them by name when you meet them.
- *Photographic seating chart.* Use seating chart software to position individual student photographs in a flexible grid that can be rearranged as needed. Alternatively, you may take a photograph of your classroom with students in their assigned seats. Leave a photographic seating chart in your desk or on your computer, where it may be accessed by a substitute teacher.
- *Class photograph.* Take a digital photograph of your class, print it out, and pass it around, asking students to write their names under their photos.
- *Name cards.* Ask your students to write their names on a folded sheet of card stock in large enough letters that everyone can read them. Students should place their name cards on their desks or above their lab stations.
- *Paper distribution.* Match student names with faces as you hand back student work. Save those you don't know for last, and use the process of elimination to match student names with faces.
- *Calling on students by name.* Call on students by name, and refer to their ideas and contributions by the name of student who provided them.
- *Student introductions.* Instruct your students to ask a series of questions of their neighbors and then introduce them to the class using what they have learned.
- *Greeting students at the door.* Greet your students by name at the door as they enter. This helps you memorize their names and helps establish rapport and accountability.
- *Write personalized responses.* Address students by name when writing comments on their papers.

Learning Who Your Students Are: Questionnaires

Questionnaires are a valuable tool to learn about the students in your classes. They should be voluntary, approved by an administrator, and collected early in the first week of class. Study each questionnaire, associating personal information with student pictures from your photographic seating chart.

Following are sample questions. Select ones you think will provide the most useful information, and blend them with questions of your own. The category titles are for your reference only and should not be included on your final questionnaire.

Goals
- What are your career goals?
- What are your educational goals after high school?
- What college would you like to attend?
- What do you see yourself doing in the next 5 to 10 years?
- How do you plan to get to where you want to be 5 to 10 years from now?

Family and Home Environment
- How many brothers and sisters do you have?
- Do you take the bus to school?
- Do you bring your own lunch to school?
- What language do you speak at home?
- Whom do you know, other than a teacher, who has gone to college?

Personal Information
- Who are your friends in this class?
- What are you are most proud of?
- What do you enjoy doing in your free time?
- What extracurricular activities are you involved in?
- What are your hobbies?

Attitudes Toward School
- What is your favorite thing about school?
- What is your least favorite thing about school?
- What was your favorite class last year? Why?
- Why did you enroll in this class?
- What school clubs and other organizations do you belong to?
- What school sports are you involved with?

Educational Background

- What was your most recent mathematics course?
- List your class schedule.
- List the science courses you have taken.

Writing Ability (Writing Prompts)

- If I could go anywhere, I would . . .
- I learn the most when the teacher . . .
- I learn the most when I . . .
- After high school, I will probably . . .
- My ideal job would be . . .
- Three adjectives others might use to describe me are . . .
- My definition of [biology, chemistry, physics, earth science] is . . . .

Establishing a Positive Classroom Environment: Icebreakers

An icebreaker is an activity that helps students get to know one another and become comfortable in the classroom setting. There are numerous ice-breakers, but the following are particularly helpful in getting to know students.

Commonalities Provide students with a 3" by 5" note card, and instruct them to write their name on the front. They should then flip the card and write things that they share in common with others in the class as follows: (a) true of all, (b) true of most, (c) true of about half, (d) true of a few, (e) true of only themselves. The teacher selects cards at random and reads a statement. All students for whom the statement is true should stand and remain standing until a statement is read that does not describe them.

People Bingo Give each student a "people bingo" card with questions such as those shown in Figure 25.1. Give students 5 minutes to collect the initials of others in the class for which each statement is true. Each person can sign a card only once. The winners are the first five to get a Bingo (five initials in a column, row, or diagonal).

If questions are selected well, they can serve as segues to science lessons. For example, the broccoli question raises a number of interesting questions

Has seen the sunrise	Plays an instrument	Born out of state	Likes broccoli	Driven in a biofuel vehicle
Plays chess	Has seen a volcano	Traveled abroad	Has seen an eclipse	Has broken a bone
Has felt an earthquake	Takes the bus to school	Is bilingual	Has climbed a mountain	likes sudoku puzzles
Needs quiet to study	favorite season is autumn	Has an aquarium	Likes math	Carpools to school
Is left handed	Plays on a team sport	Favorite color is green	Studies with music	Has been to the ocean

Figure 25.1 Sample Card for "People Bingo"

concerning chemistry, genetics, and perception. Why do some people like broccoli, while others hate it? Scientists now believe that certain tastes are not acquired but genetic. Teachers can illustrate this by distributing phenylthiocarbamide (PTC) paper, easily available from scientific supply companies. Some students find PTC extremely distasteful, while others don't taste a thing. Geneticists have identified the TAS2R38 gene as responsible for the ability to taste bitter chemicals similar to PTC.[5]

25.5 Managing the Classroom Effectively

Classroom management is a term teachers use to describe techniques and strategies employed to ensure that classroom lectures, discussions, activities, and experiments are conducted efficiently and effectively. Classroom management involves planning and implementation of lessons, as well as strategies to engage and manage students. Student misbehavior is a threat to any classroom, and teachers need to develop a workable approach to discipline that is consistent with school policy and appropriate for their students.

Classroom management is best established when there is an environment of *respect* and *rapport*.

"Tyranny" results when teachers emphasize respect but do nothing to develop rapport with their students. "Anarchy" results when teachers emphasize rapport but do nothing to develop a respectful environment. Here are some tips to establish respect and rapport in the classroom.

Communicate and Enforce Policies

- *School policies:* Make certain that you support and enforce school and district policies. Undermining the authority of the administration gives students license to undermine your authority.
- *Behavior standards:* Develop and communicate a clear and simple set of behavior standards. Long lists invite confusion and loopholes. Do not establish policies that you are unwilling or unable to enforce.

Build a Respectful Environment

- *Respect:* Students learn respect from teachers who demonstrate respect for students, colleagues, administrators, parents, education, and the school. Teachers should avoid threats, bribery, sarcasm, and similar control mechanisms. Such shortsighted techniques may produce immediate compliance but foment long-term anger and disrespect.
- *Honesty:* Admit when you don't know something, and use it is an opportunity to illustrate your desire to learn. Apologize if you have said or done something rude or hurtful. Set the standard of honesty that you want your students to follow.
- *Be firm, fair, and consistent:* Enforce policies firmly, fairly, and consistently. Partiality breeds contempt. Students should never be able to identify a teacher's pet.

Establish Rapport

- *Know your students:* Illustrate your interest in students by engaging them in classroom discussion and talking with them outside class. It is valuable to attend school plays, sporting events, social gatherings, and other extracurricular activities to learn about your students and demonstrate that you are interested in them as individuals. It is helpful to conduct a student survey at the beginning of the semester to gather information and learn about your students.
- *Concern for students:* Demonstrate that you teach students, *not* material. Model the type of concern you want your students to show to one another.
- *Humor:* Maintain a good sense of humor. Laugh with your students but never at them. Humor can defuse many problems, but sarcasm and offensive statements will harm your relationship with your class.

Establish Goals and Expectations

- *Syllabus:* A syllabus describes the course content, calendar, grading standards, and behavior standards. Students and parents should sign a form indicating that they have read and understand the syllabus.
- *High expectations:* Maintain high expectations for yourself as a teacher and lifelong learner. You cannot expect students to have high expectations as learners if they perceive that you have low goals as a teacher. Maintain high but appropriate expectations for your students.[6] Work toward developing an atmosphere of personal accountability.
- *Enthusiasm for learning:* Demonstrate an enthusiasm for the subject you teach and for learning in general.
- *Assignment sheets:* Students should have access to their assignments and grades at any time. Such information can be provided through the Internet or through assignment sheets such as shown in Figure 25.2. The student completes the form and calculates his or her cumulative total and percent as illustrated.
- *Objectives and standards:* Display your objectives and content standards at the beginning of each session, referring to them as the lesson progresses. Show how the content relates to prior lessons.

Plan and Deliver

- *Overplan:* Plan more activities than you think you will have time for, but prioritize them so you cover the most important ones first. Idle time is the source of many behavior problems.

#	due date	Description	points possible	my score	assignment %	total possible	my total	cumulative %
1	5-Sep	hw - chapter 1; 2-6	5	5	100%	5	5	100%
2	7-Sep	hw - ch 1; 10-14	5	3	60%	10	8	80%
3	9-Sep	quiz - ch 1	10	8	80%	20	16	80%
4	12-Sep	lab 1 - photosynthesis	20	18	90%	40	34	85%
5	14-Sep	hw - ch 2; 1-10	10	8	80%	50	42	84%
6	16-Sep	journal - climate change	10	6	60%	60	48	80%
7	19-Sep	hw 2; 11-14	5	4	80%	65	52	80%
8	20-Sep	quiz - ch 2	10	8	80%	75	60	80%
9	22-Sep	lab 2 - respiration	20	15	75%	95	75	79%
10	23-Sep	unit 1 test	50	45	90%	145	120	83%

Figure 25.2 Sample Student Assignment Sheet

- *Use time efficiently:* Students are in school to learn. Respect their time. Don't shortchange them by poor time management.
- *Make content relevant:* Students are more likely to buy into your educational goals if they see how the subject matter relates to everyday life.
- *Avoid busywork:* Assignments should be designed to further understanding, not occupy student time. Don't waste valuable student time by meaningless busywork.
- *Use your voice wisely:* Modulate your voice to provide emphasis and interest. Do not raise your voice to be heard over students. If you do, students may raise their voices to be heard over you! Consider using a wireless microphone so you can be heard without raising or straining your voice.
- *Engage students:* Students who are engaged learn. The best way to engage students is through interesting, relevant, and significant activities. One way to keep students on their toes is to call on them randomly. Put student names on craft sticks (popsicle sticks) or cards and pull the cards from a jar at random.

Monitor Student Behavior

- *Proximity:* Move around the classroom to maintain proximity to all students. Students are more likely to stay on task when the teacher is close by.
- *Maintain eye contact:* Eye contact communicates concern, awareness, and accountability. Greet your students by name as they enter the class. This affirms your interest in them and helps

Figure 25.3 Sample Extra-Credit Note

them know they will be accountable for their behavior.

- *Catch students doing something right:* Reward good behavior. Figure 25.3 illustrates an extra-credit note that can be issued to students who are "caught doing something right." Extra-credit points boost student morale and can help improve the classroom climate. Students keep their extra-credit points until the end of a grading period, when they sign them and turn them in to the teacher.

Maintain an Optimal Learning Environment

- *Ventilation and temperature:* Make certain room temperatures are appropriate and ventilation is adequate. Warm, stuffy air may contribute to sleepiness, particularly after lunch. Hot, unpleasant environments contribute to irritation, conflict, and lethargy. Studies have shown that students perform significantly better on academic tasks at 22.5°C (72.5°F) than at 26°C (79°F).
- *Decoration:* Blank walls are boring. Decorate your walls with posters and other materials that stimulate interest and showcase student work.

- *Organization:* Don't expect your students to be organized if you are not. Clean, organized classrooms and laboratories are safer and more pleasant than messy, disorganized rooms.
- *Instruction for substitutes:* Keep a guide for substitutes in your classroom desk: a photographic seating chart, list of classroom rules and procedures, daily and weekly schedule, semester plan, lesson plans, procedures for collecting and disseminating papers, and extra worksheets and curricular materials that can be used at any time. Include your e-mail address and telephone number so substitutes can call for clarification.
- *Praise students appropriately:* Offer genuine praise. Intermittent praise is the most powerful way to reinforce positive behavior. If you praise students all the time or simply for doing what is expected, they may not strive to do more. Tell them when they have excelled and how they can improve. Be specific.
- *Provide wait time:* Teachers often allow only a few seconds of silence after asking questions. In such situations, many students don't bother formulating answers because it is easier to wait for one of the "regulars" to do so. Wait time encourages greater student involvement and more thoughtful and developed responses.
- *Use silent clues for getting attention:* Do not proceed with instruction when there is class noise, and don't raise your voice to get student attention. Silent methods, such as dimming the light or having students raise their hands and close their mouths whenever you raise your hand, are generally far more effective and less energy intensive.

Discipline Fairly and Consistently
- *Minimize interruptions:* Deal with disruptions with as little interruption as possible. Many problems can be taken care of after class or during guided practice. Don't allow student misbehavior to steal time away from other students.
- *Have clear expectations:* Establish clear, written behavior standards and explicit consequences. Be consistent in your enforcement of standards.

- *Don't argue with students:* Arguments are emotional encounters, provide an opportunity for offending students to justify their actions, and may undermine your authority, particularly when occurring in front of other students.
- *Start fresh everyday:* Don't hold grudges. It hurts you, your reputation, and your relationship to all your students.
- *Never give schoolwork as punishment:* Giving homework as a punishment suggests that learning is a punishment.
- *Assertive discipline:* Lee and Marlene Canter advocate a take-control approach to management in which teachers establish clear rules and directions and identify the limits of acceptable behavior. More information on assertive discipline can be obtained by reading their books or by searching online (search "assertive discipline").[7]
- *Positive classroom discipline:* Fred Jones is the author of *Positive Classroom Discipline,* a nonadversarial approach to managing student disruption, emphasizing high behavior standards and personal responsibility.[8] More information on positive discipline can be obtained from books or online (search positive discipline).[9]

25.6 Assessing Student Performance

Assessment is the process of documenting the knowledge, skills, and attitudes of students. Assessment can be formative, summative, subjective, objective, criterion-referenced, or norm-referenced.

Formative Assessment

Madeline Hunter, an influential American educator and author of numerous works on curriculum and instruction, wrote, "To say that you have taught when students haven't learned is to say you have sold when no one has bought. But how can you know that students have learned without spending hours correcting tests and papers? . . . Check students' understanding *while you are teaching* (not at 10 o'clock at night when you're correcting papers) so you don't move on with unlearned material that can accumulate like a snowball and eventually engulf the student in confusion and despair."[10] Hunter was speaking of the need for *formative assessment*—feedback from learning activities that is used by the instructor to adapt teaching to meet the immediate needs of learners. The following are techniques for formative assessment:[11]

- *Audience response systems:* Audience response systems (personal response systems) can be used to collect and analyze student responses to multiple-choice and true-false questions. Such devices provide immediate feedback to specific prompts, but do not allow full text entry as is needed for free-response questions (Figure 25.4).
- *Electronic groups:* If your classroom has access to the Internet, use an electronic chatroom or newsgroup to elicit student responses to your questions (see *sciencesourcebook.com*).
- *Think/pair/share:* Provide students with time to write a response to a thought-provoking question, then additional time to discuss it with their neighbor before sharing their conclusion with the class.
- *Interview:* Interview students about their thinking as they solve problems. This metacognitive strategy works well during guided practice or in the laboratory when using rotating labs (section 22.5).
- *Whiteboards:* Prepare student whiteboards by cutting white shower board (inexpensive, laminated, waterproof board sold at home

improvement centers for lining showers) into small rectangles. Many home improvement stores will cut it for you. Provide students with dry erase markers and ask them to write, draw, or diagram answers to questions you pose. When asked, all students should hold up their boards simultaneously, providing you with a quick assessment of what students understand.
- *Voting:* Provide several possible answers to a question. Then ask students to vote for the answer by raising their hands.
- *Quick-writes:* Throughout your lesson, ask students to demonstrate their understanding by answering prompts in their science notebooks.[12] You can scan student responses as you move through the class. If few are writing, then it is likely that few understand.

Summative Assessment

Summative assessments are provided at the end of a unit to determine how much students have learned. They provide information for determining grades and giving students feedback on their performance. Summative assessments may come in the form of papers, homework problems, lab reports (Activity 3.4.1), projects (sections 22.3 and 23.1–23.4), quizzes, and tests, and can include objective or subjective tasks. *Objective* tasks have clear right and wrong answers, examples of which include mathematical solutions, multiple choice, true-false, and fill-in-the-blank questions. *Subjective* tasks are more open-ended, do not have obvious right and wrong answers, and must be evaluated

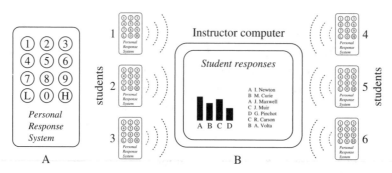

Figure 25.4 (A) Personal Response Device and (B) Instructor Computer That Receives All Student Input

Table 25.4 Teaching Evaluation Form

	5 (Outstanding)	4 (Strong)	3 (Satisfactory)	2 (Marginal)	1 (Unsatisfactory)
A. Making Science Comprehensible to Students Knows subject matter Demonstrates subject-specific pedagogical skills Teaches state-adopted academic content standards					
B. Assessing Student Learning Monitors student learning Paces instruction appropriately Reteaches content when necessary Uses multiple means of assessment Communicates progress to students and family Encourages student self-assessment					
C. Engaging and Supporting Students in Learning Uses a variety of teaching techniques Encourages application of knowledge Integrates computer technology into instruction Delivers clear, organized lessons Communicates instructional objectives Ensures participation of all students Establishes challenging academic expectations Fosters higher order thinking and problem solving Adapts instruction and materials for diverse needs Teaches English learners effectively					
D. Planning Instruction Learns about students to maximize learning opportunities Prepares complete and sequential lesson plans Prepares appropriate, standards-based objectives Incorporates reading/literacy instruction					
E. Creating Effective Learning Environment Maximizes instructional time Maintains effective classroom control Uses facilities and equipment effectively Manages classroom routine effectively Is consistent in enforcing policies Communicates effectively in oral/written English Creates a positive climate for learning					
F. Developing as a Professional Educator Maintains good rapport with faculty and staff Maintains good rapport with students Demonstrates cultural sensitivity Meets commitments and deadlines Meets professional, legal, and ethical obligations Analyzes and evaluates own teaching					

by professionals who truly understand the material. *Criterion-referenced assessments* are based on content expectations, and *norm-referenced assessments* compare students to others who have taken the same test. Students pass criterion-referenced tests by obtaining a score in excess of a predetermined cut score; they pass norm-referenced tests by performing better than a given percentage of others who took the same test.

25.7 Evaluating Teaching Performance

Teachers should be reflective practitioners. They should evaluate their lessons and take steps to improve them.

Perhaps the easiest way to evaluate your teaching is by examining video clips of classroom lessons. Set up a video camera on a tripod in the back of the room, and make a recording of a class session. Make certain to secure approval from your administration before videotaping students. Watch the video and evaluate using the criteria in Table 25.4. It is helpful to view the video with the sound off, and then listen to it with the picture off. Is there enough visual information to understand the lesson in the absence of sound? Is there enough auditory information to understand the lesson in the absence of video? Table 25.4 is adapted from the student teaching evaluation for secondary school teachers at California State University, Northridge, and may also be used to evaluate teachers you mentor.

Chapter Twenty-Six

The Science Laboratory

26.1 Equipping the Science Laboratory 529

26.2 Writing Successful Grant Proposals 533

26.3 Common and Inexpensive Sources of Chemicals 534

26.4 Preparing Solutions 538

26.5 Laboratory Safety 540

26.6 Safety Equipment Checklist 540

26.7 Chemical Hazards and Storage 542

26.8 Disposal of Chemicals 546

26.9 Accidents 547

26.1 Equipping the Science Laboratory

Science activities and experiments require a variety of equipment and materials. Although most science departments have budgets, the funds are generally insufficient to fully equip middle or high school science laboratories. Nevertheless, there are ways that science teachers can equip or augment their laboratories.

Cash Purchases

Science Budget Most schools have line-item budgets for their science departments. The amount of the budget varies from school to school but is generally relatively small on a per-student basis. Department members should submit their requests to their chair in writing, and the department chair should maintain a spreadsheet of proposed expenditures (Figure 26.1). Most schools work on annual budgets, and unspent money from the science department is returned to the general fund. A department that does not use all of its funds is usually allotted less in the following year under the assumption that it does not need what was previously budgeted. The department chair should keep a close watch on the budget and make specific requests at the time the administration is drafting the next year's budget.

Petty Cash Teachers often need to purchase items at a grocery, hardware, or online store to complement a laboratory exercise. Many schools reimburse teachers for such purchases through a petty cash system. Teachers should photocopy and submit all receipts for reimbursement.

	A	B	C	D	E	F
1	**Science Department "wish-list"**		Cost	$4,406.70		
2	**Spreadsheet**		Tax	$363.55		
3			Total	**$4,770.25**		
4						
5		**Vendor**	**Catalog #**	**Price**	**Qty**	**Extension**
6	1 ml dropper bulbs (pack of 24)	Fisher	s34793	$10.90	3	$32.70
7	30 centimeter rules (pack of 12)	Fisher	s40637	$9.60	10	$96.00
8	30 meter tape measure	Carolina	CB2213	$45.90	10	$459.00
9	acid pump	Carolina	CB2253	$22.90	15	$343.50
10	acid reagent bottle holder	Carolina	CB2312	$40.00	3	$120.00
11	assorted corks sizes 3-16	Boreal	b12-123	$19.00	3	$57.00
12	beaker brush	Boreal	b13-3452	$10.30	4	$41.20
13	beaker tongs with fiberglass jaws	Boreal	b25-2245	$36.50	8	$292.00
14	brush	Fisher	s30409	$6.90	12	$82.80
15	butane burner	Fisher	s41872	$36.30	15	$544.50
16	capillary tubes (100)	Fisher	s17029	$6.10	10	$61.00

Figure 26.1 Science Department Wish List Spreadsheet

Year-End Funds   Most schools operate on a yearly budget, with the new budget year beginning in July or shortly after the closing of the academic session. Science chairs should maintain spreadsheets (Figure 26.1) of their "wish lists" and present them to their administrators in the event that there are surplus funds in science department or discretionary budgets. It is common for administrators to make purchases to empty discretionary accounts at the end of the fiscal year, and science departments can benefit by submitting requests at this time.

Grants   A variety of public and private agencies offer grants for improving science education. Teachers are advised to search the Internet and talk with their district science specialists to identify realistic opportunities. In addition, many schools and districts maintain a grants Web site to summarize current opportunities for secondary education. It is critical to follow the guidelines specified in the request for proposal (RFP) provided by the funding agency. Section 26.2 lists tips for writing successful proposals.

Online Auctions and Sales   Many items can be obtained at bargain prices by purchasing them from private parties who are marketing them through online auctions. Unfortunately, these firms rarely offer any warranty, so the buyer should beware. Although risks are higher than with traditional scientific supply companies, the monetary savings can be substantial. Many schools have policies to reimburse teachers for online equipment purchases.

In-Kind Contributions

Parents and Community Members   Parents are often eager to provide resources for the science classes at their children's schools. You can connect with the parents of your students through school newsletters, the school Web site, your class Web site, the parent-teacher association, back-to-school night, open house, and flyers sent home with your students. We suggest that you prepare a letter (Figure 26.2) expressing your needs, accompanied by a tax-deductible donation form. The form should meet the guidelines of your school, district, and state and should have the approval of your administrative staff.

Students   Teachers often spend much time collecting resources that could be more easily collected by students. Students who contribute by providing resources tend to have a greater sense of ownership and commitment to class, so engaging them in the process not only saves the teacher time but also

Ways to Support the Science Program

1 Be a guest speaker in one of our science classes!

Professionals Needed!	*Science experts needed!*

Share information about your career in

- biology
- chemistry
- physics
- geology
- research
- biotechnology
- meteorology
- astronomy
- engineering
- health
- medicine
- related fields

Talk about your area of science expertise

- vision (optometrists and opticians)
- body systems (physicians)
- teeth and digestion (dentists)
- flight (pilots, aerospace engineers)
- earthquakes (geologists, civil engineers)
- and other science topics!

2 Give your discards to benefit our science program!

- *auto stereo technicians*—old speakers, wires, magnets …
- *bankers and businesspeople*—computers, peripherals, monitors, file cabinets, software …
- *butchers*—samples for dissection: heart, liver, wings …
- *carpenters*—wood, screws, nails, building material …
- *chemists*—old or imperfect glassware, old equipment, storage bottles …
- *custodians*—paper towels, boxes, photocopy paper, towels, cleaners, containers …
- *electricians*—thin gauge wire, lamps, electrician tape, wire nuts, old tools …
- *engineers*—computers, calculators, test equipment, oscilloscopes …
- *fast food workers*—cups, containers, straws, ice, towels …
- *florists*—flowers for dissection, plant specimens …
- *geologists*—rock samples, topographic maps, old GPS devices, old UV lamps …
- *hardware store*—assorted fasteners, wood, supplies …
- *home supply*—wood and metal scraps, broken bags of fertilizer, damaged tools …
- *horticulturists*—pots, bedding trays, heat lights, drip lines, fertilizer, potting soil …
- *machinists*—metal samples, metal filings, used tools …
- *pet store workers*—crickets, pondweed, mealworms, aquariums …
- *photographers*—digital cameras, film canisters, developing chemicals …
- *physicians*—models, charts, diagrams …
- *radiologists*—X-rays, CAT scans, PET scans, etc. (remove names) …
- *many others*—Think about what you no longer need that we could use … .

3 Support our science program with your gifts!

You can make a tax-deductible cash donation to the science materials budget and receive a receipt for tax purposes.

Figure 26.2 Letter Requesting Support for the Science Program

(Continued)

Receipt for Tax Deductible Donation

This confirms that _____ donated $_____ cash

OR supplies and equipment valued at $_____ to the science education program at

_____ School.

Donated item	Cash value	Donated item	Cash value
_____	_____	_____	_____
_____	_____	_____	_____
_____	_____	_____	_____
_____	_____	_____	_____

Received by _____ (school administrator) on _____ (date)

gets students more involved in their education. Following is a list of the kinds of free resources that students can gather from the Internet, their homes, or the field. *Caution:* Students should never be instructed to collect anything that is hazardous, and parents should be notified of your requests:

- *Earth science:* soil samples, rocks, minerals, petrified wood, crystals, weather maps, weather reports, current maps, water samples, containers, tide reports, earthquake reports, hurricane maps, topographic maps, digital images
- *Biology:* pond water, water quality samples, mold, flowers, leaves, fruits, seeds, teeth, owl pellets, yeast, containers, cleaning supplies, casts of animal tracks, digital photos of ecosystems
- *Chemistry:* household chemicals (see section 26.3), plastic bottles, paper towels, cleaning supplies, goggles, containers, stirrers, Styrofoam cups, food coloring, candles
- *Physics:* old electronic equipment, computers, meter sticks, lenses, magnets, candles, hardware, marbles, balls, carts, timers, tape, string, rope, wood, fasteners

Parent-Teacher Association Parent-teacher associations (PTA) often raise money to support special activities and events. Many science teachers have found that their PTA is eager to support academic activities once they know what those activities are. Make your needs known to the PTA and attend meetings. Remember, it is a parent-*teacher* association.

Major Firms Engineering firms, hospitals, universities, and other large institutions periodically donate used computers, furniture, glassware, and electronic equipment. Contact the asset management office at an institution near you and learn how it dispenses with old equipment. Much of the time it is donated to local schools, but only when faculty make a specific request. Many tax-supported agencies (such as public universities) are required to offer other tax-supported agencies (such as public schools) first choice when dispensing with old equipment.

Businesses Businesses often discard equipment that may nevertheless be useful in the science lab. For example, car stereo installation companies throw away old speakers that could be used to study sound or taken apart for strong magnets, and office supply companies throw away paper and supplies from damaged packages. Business owners are generally eager to donate such materials to local schools and are often willing to provide new materials as well. Businesses may receive credit for tax-deductible donations to school science laboratories (Figure 26.2). Many colleges and businesses offer local schools equipment they no longer use, and science classrooms can receive computer networks and other significant resources through such donations. In addition, federal organizations such as NASA are required to offer schools excess or old laboratory equipment. Figure 26.2 lists things that businesses can provide.

Making Your Own Equipment Much scientific equipment can be constructed from things in your garage. Expensive solutions can be made inexpensively through dilutions such as shown in section 26.4.

Book and Video Libraries Many public libraries allow teachers to check out more books and movies than other patrons and keep them for longer periods of time. Most libraries have numerous science-related movies (such as *Scientific American Frontiers, Nova, Discover Channel,* and *Bill Nye*) that can be checked out or downloaded to your computer. Libraries frequently discard older books and magazines that they no longer have room to store. Ask your librarian to save science-related books and magazines such as *Astronomy, Discover, National Geographic, Popular Science, Science, Science Daily, Science News, Science Now, Scientific American, Sky and Telescope, Smithsonian,* and *The Scientist.*

26.2 Writing Successful Grant Proposals

A variety of public and private agencies offer grants for improving science education. Teachers are advised to search the Internet and talk with their district science specialists to identify realistic opportunities. In addition, many schools and districts maintain a grants Web Site to summarize current opportunities for secondary education. It is critical to follow the guidelines specified in the request for proposal (RFP) provided by the funding agency. Following are tips for writing successful proposals:

• *Cover letter (1 page maximum):* The cover letter should be written on school stationery and signed by a school administrator. Describe the purpose in terms that are consistent with the organization's RFP. Explain how your project will accomplish its goals and improve science education for the students at your school. Provide contact information, including telephone, e-mail addresses, and relevant Web sites.

• *Abstract (1–3 paragraphs, 300 words maximum):* The abstract is the first portion of the proposal and should be no more than 300 words. Describe the project, including the needs that are addressed, the equipment that is to be acquired, and the methods for implementation. Describe the project goals and expected outcomes, and explain how these will be met. Summarize the costs, and provide the expected date of completion.

• *Background:* Funding agencies provide resources to those they believe will best fulfill the goals and objectives of the RFP. Provide evidence that you have done thorough research on the topic, include relevant literature, and reference external benchmarks and standards. For example, if you are requesting funds to equip your laboratory with probeware, cite research articles showing how probeware improves student research or cite standards calling for accurate data measurement.

• *Statement of need:* Explain the significance of this project to your students, the learning community, or education in general. Outline current resources that address the issues, identify gaps in these resources, and explain how your project will fill these gaps.

• *Project description:* Explain your project in detail. Describe how you will conduct the research or implement the project you have proposed. Agencies usually will not fund equipment-based proposals unless there is assurance that such equipment will be put to good use in *action research* (research conducted by classroom teachers concurrent with their teaching) to develop a new program or offer students new opportunities.[1] If your proposal includes a research component, describe the methodology. Express the potential long-term impact and influence of the project.

• *Goals and evaluation criteria:* What specific goals are you trying to achieve? What measurable criteria will you reach in meeting those goals?

How will you know whether you are achieving your goals? What records and information will you keep so you can measure your progress? How will you disseminate the information gained from this grant? Explain how you will evaluate the success and merit of the project and, if appropriate, how you will disseminate your findings.

• *Budget:* Prepare a line-item budget for all costs of your project, using bids and estimates if available.

• *Calendar:* Develop a calendar for the project, indicating when key phases will be completed.

• *Résumés:* Explain how you are prepared to manage this grant. Include the résumés of all project leaders.

26.3 Common and Inexpensive Sources of Chemicals

Many chemicals may be purchased from the grocery store, drugstore, pet store, or hardware store at lower prices than from scientific supply companies. Students gain a greater appreciation for the applicability of chemistry to everyday life if they are able to use household products to conduct their experiments and investigations. Although the products listed in Table 26.1 are less expensive than comparable products from a scientific supply company, they may contain additives.

Table 26.1 Common and Inexpensive Sources of Chemicals

Chemical	Formula	Source/Description
Acetic acid	CH_3COOH	**Vinegars** vary between 4% and 5.5% acetic acid; more concentrated acetic acid (28%) may be purchased at photography supply stores.
Acetone	CH_3COCH_3	**Nail polish remover** is generally acetone; **fiberglass cleaner** is also generally made of acetone and is available at boating supply stores.
Aluminum	Al	**Aluminum foil; aluminum turnings** are available as scrap from machine shops.
Potassium aluminum sulfate	$KAl(SO_4)_2 \cdot 12H_2O$	**Alum** is available at most drugstores. It is used as an astringent to shrink mucous membranes.
Ammonia	$NH_3(aq); NH_4OH$	**Household ammonia** (ammonium hydroxide) is an aqueous solution of ammonia. *Note:* This often has additives.
Ammonium nitrate	NH_4NO_3	**Nitrate of ammonia** fertilizer is available at most garden supply stores.
Amylose	$(C_6H_9O_5)_n$	**Cornstarch** is available at most grocery store and is used extensively in cooking.
Anthocyanin		Anthocyanin solution can be prepared by cutting, boiling, and filtering **red cabbage.**
Ascorbic acid	$C_6H_8O_6$	**Vitamin C tablets** sold at the grocery store are primarily ascorbic acid.
Bromthymol blue	$C_{27}H_{28}Br_2O_5S$	**Aquarium pH test** kits often employ bromthymol blue because it changes color in the 6.0–7.6 range.
Butane	C_4H_{10}	The lighter **fluid** in handheld fire starters or **cigarette lighters** is usually liquid butane.

Chemical	Formula	Source/Description
Calcium carbonate	$CaCO_3$	**Chalk, limestone,** and **marble chips** are good sources of solid calcium carbonate; some **antacids** are largely calcium carbonate.
Calcium chloride	$CaCl_2$	Much of the **road salt (de-icer)** used to de-ice roads in cold climates is calcium chloride.
Calcium hydroxide	$Ca(OH)_2$	Some **antacids** are primarily calcium hydroxide; **slaked lime** is calcium hydroxide and is used in **lime-softening water treatment** and in plastering.
Calcium hypochlorite	$Ca(ClO)_2$	**Bleaching powder** and some **swimming pool disinfectants** contain calcium hypochlorite. Available from cleaning or swimming pool supply companies.
Calcium oxide	CaO	In the past **quicklime** was a material plasterers used in making plaster. It can still can be acquired from some hardware stores.
Carbon	C	**Charcoal** used in cooking, **activated charcoal** used in fish tank filters, and **graphite** used in pencil leads are good sources of carbon.
Carbon dioxide	CO_2	**Dry ice** is available from party stores, refrigeration supply companies, and ice cream companies.
Carbonic acid	H_2CO_3	**Soda water** is simply carbonated water, a dilute solution of carbonic acid.
Copper	Cu	**Electrical wire, copper pipe,** and **copper sheeting** are available at hardware stores; **American pennies** (minted 1944–1946, 1962–1982) are 95% copper and 5% zinc.
Copper sulfate pentahydrate	$CuSO_4 \cdot 5H_2O$	**Basicop** or **Bluestone algaecide** used to kill algae and other aquatic pests contains copper sulfate.
Ethylene glycol	CH_2OHCH_2OH	Some engine **antifreezes** are primarily ethylene glycol.
Glucose	$C_6H_{12}O_6$	**Dextrose** (glucose) is available in many drugstores; some specialty throat lozenges are dextrose.
Glycerol	$C_3H_8O_3$	**Glycerin** is an emollient used to soften skin by delaying the evaporation of water. It is available at most drugstores.
Gold	Au	Gold **jewelry** is generally not pure gold. Gold is generally alloyed with other metals to increase strength.
Helium	He	**Helium** can be obtained from party stores or wherever else helium balloons are available.
Hydrochloric acid	HCl	**Muriatic acid** (the common name for HCl) is used in swimming pool maintenance. It is also sold as **masonry cleaner** and is available at hardware stores. Percentage concentrations vary.

(Continued)

Table 26.1 *(Continued)*

Chemical	Formula	Source/Description
Hydrogen peroxide	H_2O_2	**Hydrogen peroxide antiseptic** (3%) is available from the drugstore. **Clairoxide hair bleach** by Clairol is much more concentrated and is available from beauty supply stores.
Iodine	I_2	**Tincture of iodine,** a topical antiseptic used for treating wounds, is a solution of iodine dissolved in ethyl alcohol. It is available at most drugstores.
Iron	Fe	**Steel wool, iron nails, iron bolts, nuts,** and **screws** are good sources of iron. You can get iron filings by dragging a strong magnet through sand.
Ferric oxide	Fe_2O_3	**Ceramic rust** is used to add a red color to pottery and can be purchased at ceramic stores.
Kerosene	C_nH_{2n+1} (n = 12–16)	**Lamp oil** or **kerosene** is sold in the paint departments of most hardware stores.
Lead	Pb	**Lead shot** and **lead sinkers** are used by fishermen and are available at sporting goods stores.
Magnesium hydroxide	$Mg(OH)_2$	**Milk of magnesia** is an antacid used to settle sour (acidic) stomachs. Some **antacid tablets** also contain magnesium hydroxide.
Magnesium silicate	$Mg_3Si_4O_{10}(OH)_2$	**Talcum powder** comes from **talc,** the softest of all minerals, and is used as a **dusting powder** for babies. It is available in the body care section of the drugstore.
Magnesium sulfate	$MgSO_4{\cdot}7H_2O$	**Epsom salt** is sold at most drugstores and is used as a laxative or as an anti-inflammatory soak.
Methanol	CH_3OH	**Methanol** is sold as a solvent in paint supply stores under the names **"wood alcohol"** or **"methyl alcohol."**
Methylene blue	$C_{16}H_{18}ClN_3S$	**Methylene blue (Methidote antiseptic)** is used to treat small, injured fish and is available at pet stores.
Mineral oil	complex mixture of hydrocarbons	**Mineral oil** is sold in drugstores as an emollient. Some **baby oils** are essentially mineral oil and fragrance.
Nickel	Ni	**Pre-1985 Canadian nickels** are made of nickel. *Note:* American "nickels" are composed of 25% nickel and 75% copper.
Oxygen	O_2	Portable **welding oxygen** tanks are available at welding shops and some hardware stores.
Paraffin	CnH_{2n+2} (n > 19)	**Candle wax** is made of paraffin. Some grocery stores sell paraffin as a sealant for home canning.
Phosphoric acid	H_3PO_4	Some pH reducers (available at pet stores) used in fish tanks are simply dilute solutions of phosphoric acid.
Potassium bitartrate	$KHC_4H_4O_6$	**Cream of tartar** is available at the grocery store and is used to stabilize delicate foods like meringue toppings and other baked egg-white products.

Chemical	Formula	Source/Description
Potassium carbonate	K_2CO_3	Some agricultural supply companies sell **potash** to farmers who need to increase the potassium content in their soils.
Potassium bromide	KBr	Potassium bromide may be purchased from photography stores where it is used in photographic development.
Potassium chloride	KCl	**Lite Salt** is used as a salt substitute by people who must limit their sodium intake and is available at most grocery stores.
Potassium iron (II) hexacyanoferrate(iii)	$KFe[Fe(CN)_6]$	Mrs. Stewart's **Bluing** is used to whiten clothes and may be found in the detergents section of the grocery store.
Potassium nitrate	KNO_3	**Saltpeter** or **quick salt** is used to cure homemade sausages and corned beef and may be available at some butcher shops.
Potassium permanganate	$KMnO_4$	**Clearwater** is a solution of approximately 50% potassium permanganate and is used to remove odors and cloudiness from water to be used in aquariums.
Propane	C_3H_8	**Gas barbecue fuel** is generally made of propane and is available at many gasoline stations or picnic supply stores.
2-propanol	$CH_3CHOHCH_3$	**Rubbing alcohol** (isopropyl alcohol) is a concentrated solution (generally 70%) of 2-propanol and may be found in most drugstores.
Silicon dioxide	SiO_2	**Quartz sand** is relatively pure silicon dioxide and is available at most building supply stores.
Silver	Ag	**Older nonclad American dimes, quarters, half dollars,** and **silver dollars.** are 90% silver and 10% copper.
Sodium acetate	$NaC_2H_3O_2$	**Re-Heater** and other **hand warmers** are available at sporting goods stores.
Sodium bicarbonate	$NaHCO_3$	**Baking soda** is pure sodium bicarbonate and may be found in the baking section of the grocery story.
Sodium carbonate	Na_2CO_3	**Washing soda** is used to treat wool fibers and is available at spinning, weaving, and art supply stores.
Sodium chloride	NaCl	The **table salt** used in cooking is sodium chloride. **Iodized salt** contains a trace of sodium iodide.
Sodium hydroxide	NaOH	Known also as **caustic soda** and **lye,** sodium hydroxide is used in many commercial drain cleaners.
Sodium hypochlorite	NaClO	**Household bleach** is generally a 5% solution of sodium hypochlorite.
Sodium phosphate	Na_3PO_4	**Trisodium phosphate,** commonly known as **TSP,** is available at hardware stores and is used to clean walls prior to painting.
Sodium tetraborate decahydrate	$Na_2B_4O_7 \cdot 10H_2O$	**Borax,** such as **Twenty Mule Team Borax Laundry Booster,** is sodium tetraborate decahydrate.
Sodium thiosulfate	$Na_2S_2O_3$	**Photographer's hypo** is used in photograph development and is available at photography supply stores.

(Continued)

Table 26.1 *(Continued)*

Chemical	Formula	Source/Description
Sucrose	$C_{12}H_{22}O_{11}$	**Table sugar** is available at grocery stores.
Sulfur	S	Sulfur is sold at some garden stores to treat certain plant diseases.
Sulfuric acid	H_2SO_4	**Battery acid,** also known as **oil of vitriol,** is sulfuric acid and may be obtained at some auto supply stores.
Tungsten	W	The **filament in incandescent light bulbs** is made of tungsten.
Zinc	Zn	**Recent American pennies** (1982–present) are 97.5% zinc with a 2.5% copper coating.

Most additives do not affect performance, but you should examine ingredients to note the percentage concentration and adjust quantities as necessary. You should perform all experiments yourself and assess safety concerns prior to classroom implementation.

26.4 Preparing Solutions

Preparing Stock Solutions

Many laboratory activities require specific molar concentrations of aqueous stock solutions of soluble inorganic and organic compounds. *Molarity* is defined as the number of *moles of solute per liter of solution*. Before making a stock solution, calculate the formula weight (generally written on the side of the container), and measure the appropriate mass of solute. For example, to make a 1 mol solution of NaCl, measure out 58.5 g of NaCl (NaCl has a formula weight of 58.5 g/mol) and place in a volumetric flask. Add water slowly while stirring until a solution volume of 1 L is reached. To make a 2 mol solution of NaCl, it is necessary to dissolve 117 g of NaCl (117 g represents two moles of NaCl) and add water until the 1 L mark is reached. Many activities are qualitative and do not require precise concentrations. In such situations, it is appropriate to use less precise containers, such as graduated cylinders, to prepare stock solutions.

If the formula weight is not printed on the container, it may be calculated by adding the masses of the component atoms (see the periodic table in Figure 27.1). For example, $NaHCO_3$ is 84 g/mol = 1 sodium (23 g/mol) + 1 hydrogen (1 g/mol) + 1 carbon (12 g/mol) + 3 oxygens (16 g/mol) = 23 + 1 + 12 + 3(16) = 84 g/mol.

Performing Dilutions

A dilute solution can be made by adding solvent to a more concentrated solution. The number of moles of solute before dilution equals the number of moles following dilution. Knowing this, the dilution formula can be derived:

$$M_1 V_1 = M_2 V_2$$

where M_1 is the initial molarity, V_1 is the initial volume, M_2 is the final molarity, and V_2 is the final volume. If the concentration (C) of a solution is expressed in grams solute/liter solution, the dilution equation becomes

$$C_1 V_1 = C_2 V_2$$

This equation is derived from the principle that the initial number of grams of solute must equal the final number (conservation of mass).

Sample Dilution Problem (Molarity) Prepare a 100 mL solution of 0.1 M NaOH from a stock solution of 1.0 M NaOH,

Table 26.2 Preparing Acid and Base Stock Solutions

To Make These Solutions . . .	Dissolve This in 1 L of Solution.	To Make These Solutions . . .	Dissolve This in 1 L of Solution.
acetic acid $HC_2H_3O_2$	glacial acetic acid (17.5M)	aqueous ammonia NH_4OH	concentrated ammonia (15M)
5.0 M	286 mL	5.0 M	333 mL
2.0 M	114 mL	2.0 M	132 mL
1.0 M	57 mL	1.0 M	67 mL
0.10M	5.7 mL	0.10M	6.7 mL
hydrochloric acid HCl	concentrated HCl (12 M)	sodium hydroxide NaOH	sodium hydroxide (pellets or powder)
6.0 M	500 mL	6.0 M	240 g
2.0 M	167 mL	2.0 M	80 g
1.0 M	83 mL	1.0 M	40 g
0.1 M	8.3 mL	0.1 M	4.0 g
sulfuric acid H_2SO_4	concentrated H_2SO_4 (18 M)	nitric acid HNO_3	conc. nitric acid (16 M)
2.0 M	111 mL	2.0 M	125 mL
1.0 M	55 mL	1.0 M	63 mL
0.1 M	5.5 mL	0.1 M	6.3 mL

$M_1 = 1.0$ M NaOH (initial molarity)

$V_1 = ?$ (initial volume)

$M_2 = 0.1$ M NaOH (final molarity)

$V_2 = 100$ mL (final volume)

$$V_1 = M_2V_2/M_1 = (0.1 \text{ M NaOH})(100 \text{ mL})/$$
$$(1.0 \text{ M NaOH}) = 10 \text{ mL}$$

Therefore, dilute 10 mL of 1.0 M NaOH solution by adding solvent to a final volume of 100 mL.

Sample Dilution Problem (Grams/Liter)

A solution contains 20 g of sodium chloride per liter of solution. Dilute so the resulting solution contains only 4 g of sodium chloride per liter of solution.

$C_1 = (20 \text{ g NaCl})/L$ $V_1 = 1$ L
$C_2 = (4 \text{ g NaCl})/L$ $V_2 = ?$

$$V_2 = C_1V_1/C_2 =$$
$$(20 \text{ g NaCl/L})(1 \text{ L})/(4 \text{ g NaCl/L}) = 5 \text{ L}.$$

Thus, dilute 1 L of the original solution to a final volume of 5 L.

Preparing Acid and Base Solutions

Perform dilutions in only a fume hood or other well-ventilated area. Acids irritate skin and acid vapors damage the eyes and respiratory system. Always wear goggles and a lab coat when working with acids and bases. Table 26.2 illustrates how to make dilutions from concentrated reagents.

- When diluting, always add acid to water. *Never add water to acid* due to the danger of splattering.
- Neutralize acid spills with baking soda ($NaHCO_3$, sodium hydrogen carbonate) before wiping up with water.
- Always add the acid or base slowly, and stir with a glass rod.
- Only teachers or other professionals should dilute concentrated acids and bases.

26.5 Laboratory Safety

Teachers, administrators, school board members, and school district science specialists are responsible for maintaining a safe school environment. Any or all of these parties may be held liable for injury if they have been negligent in their duties to protect student health and safety. All teachers must abide by their school, district, county, and state safety policies!

Science teachers should provide safety instruction, supervise all activities in the classroom and laboratory, and ensure that safety equipment and facilities are well maintained. They should pass a district or school-approved safety and first-aid course.

It is wise for teachers to talk with their personal and school insurance representatives to make sure that they carry the appropriate liability insurance. Although schools and districts generally carry insurance policies, you should not assume that these policies provide adequate protection for teachers in all situations. In the event of a lawsuit pertaining to student injury, the courts may analyze the actions of the school, district, and individual to determine the degree of responsibility that can be attributed to each. Teachers must be diligent to promote a safe laboratory environment and model all safety procedures. The following is a list of things that should be done to promote a safe laboratory experience.

Teachers Should:
- Post state, district, and school-approved safety guidelines and procedures.
- Post emergency contact numbers (see section 26.8).
- Post emergency (procedures for fires earthquakes, and other disasters).
- Abide by state, district, and school policies.
- Avoid activities that are unsafe given the equipment and facilities.
- Monitor all student activity in the laboratory.
- Pass a district- or state-approved safety and first-aid course.
- Perform routine laboratory safety checks.
- Ensure that safety and first-aid equipment is available and maintained.
- Provide students with prelaboratory activities that highlight safety concerns.
- Remind students of general and specific hazards.

To Be Admitted to the Laboratory, Students Should First
- Pass a laboratory safety test.
- Return a signed school or district-approved safety agreement (Figure 26.3).
- Complete all prelaboratory activities as required by the teacher.

26.6 Safety Equipment Checklist

The following safety equipment should be available in the science laboratory.

For Spills and Disposal
- Acetic acid solution, for neutralizing spilled bases
- Sodium bicarbonate (saturated solution), for neutralizing spilled acids
- Sand or absorbent, to dam around spills and smother fires
- Earthenware crocks, for disposal of solid chemicals (don't mix chemicals)
- Glass containers, for disposal of liquid chemicals (don't mix chemicals)
- Mercury cleanup kit (it is best to not use mercury thermometers)

First Aid
adhesive bandages	first-aid manual
adhesive tape	flashlight and
alcohol wipes	extra batteries
antibiotic cream	mouthpiece for
	administering CPR
	plastic gloves

The student agrees to:

PREPARE FOR LABORATORY WORK

- Study laboratory procedures prior to class.
- Keep lab bench organized and free of clutter.
- Know the location and operation of all safety equipment.

CONDUCT

- Act in a responsible manner at all times.
- Follow written and oral instructions.
- Do not perform unauthorized experiments.
- Do not eat or drink in the lab.
- Notify the teacher of any unsafe conditions.
- Monitor experiment at all times.

DRESS FOR LABORATORY WORK

- Tie back long hair.
- Do not wear loose sleeves or dangling jewelry.
- Wear shoes with tops.
- Wear lab coats or aprons during laboratory sessions.
- Wear safety goggles during laboratory sessions.
- Wear gloves when using hazardous chemicals.

AVOID CONTACT WITH CHEMICALS

- Never taste or "sniff" chemicals.
- Never draw materials in a pipette with your mouth.
- When heating substances, point containers away from people.
- Never carry dangerous chemicals or hot equipment near others.

AVOID HAZARDS

- Keep combustibles away from open flames.
- Use caution when handling hot glassware.
- When diluting, add acid slowly to water; never water to acid.
- Use lubricant when inserting tubing in stoppers.
- Twist slowly at base when inserting tubing through stoppers.
- Turn off burners when not in use.
- Keep caps on reagent bottles. Never switch caps.
- Place heated glassware on insulating pads to cool.
- Allow glassware to cool before handling after heating.
- Shield sharp objects when transporting.
- Do not connect power to circuits until approved by instructor.

Figure 26.3 Laboratory Safety Agreement

(Continued)

CLEAN UP

- Consult teacher for proper disposal of chemicals.
- Wash hands thoroughly following experiments.
- Leave laboratory bench clean and neat.

IN CASE OF ACCIDENT

- Report all accidents and spills immediately.
- Place broken glass in designated containers. Do not use hands.
- Wash chemicals immediately with plenty of soap and water.
- If chemicals enter eyes, wash for a minimum of 15 minutes.

I, _____ (student's name), have read and agree to follow all of the safety rules set forth in this agreement. I realize that I must obey these rules to ensure my own safety, and that of my fellow students and instructors. I will cooperate to the fullest extent with my instructor and fellow students to maintain a safe lab environment. I will also closely follow the oral and written instructions provided by the instructor. I am aware that any violation of this safety contract or misbehavior on my part may result in removal from the laboratory and appropriate disciplinary action.

_____ Student Signature _____ Date

Your signature on this agreement indicates that you have read this Student Safety Contract, are aware of the measures taken to insure the safety of your son/daughter in the science laboratory, and will instruct your son/daughter to uphold his/her agreement to follow these rules and procedures in the laboratory.

_____ Parent/Guardian Signature _____ Date

Note: For illustration purposes only. Use your school, district, or state approved agreement.

---

antiseptic solution	safety pins
cotton	sharp scissors
antiseptic wipes	soap
blanket (stored nearby)	sterile gauze
instant cold	tweezers
packs	list of emergency
elastic bandage	phone numbers

Protective Equipment

face shields	lab coats or aprons
fume hood	protective gloves
goggles	safety shield
insulated gloves	

Emergency Equipment

eye wash	fire extinguisher
emergency shower	telephone
fire blanket	accident report log

26.7 Chemical Hazards and Storage

Material Safety Data Sheets (MSDS)

Chemical manufacturers provide material safety data sheets (MSDS) with the chemicals they sell (see Figure 26.4), or you can find them online (look on *sciencesourcebook.com* or search "msds"). These sheets include pertinent safety and health information compiled by OSHA (Occupational Safety and Health Administration), the EPA (Environmental Protection Agency), and the National Library of Medicine. Keep this information in an appropriate location, and be mindful of the possible dangers of chemicals in the laboratory.

Material Safety Data Sheet (MSDS)
Sample

BENZOIC ACID
XYZ SCIENTIFIC   EMERGENCY NUMBER: (555) 555-555
CHEMICAL DIVISION   Company Phone   Company Address

SUBSTANCE IDENTIFICATION

SUBSTANCE: **BENZOIC ACID**   CHEMICAL FAMILY: Carboxylic acid, aromatic

TRADE NAMES/SYNONYMS: benzenecarboxylic acid; carboxybenzene

MOLECULAR FORMULA: $C_6H_5CO_2H$ MOLECULAR WEIGHT: 122.12

CERCLA RATINGS (SCALE 0-3): health=3 fire=1 reactivity=0 persistence=2
NFPA RATINGS (SCALE 0-4): health=2 fire=1 reactivity=u

COMPONENTS AND CONTAMINANTS

PHYSICAL DATA

DESCRIPTION: White powder or crystals with an odor of benzoin or benzaldehyde.

BOILING POINT: 480 F (249 C)   MELTING POINT: 252 F (122 C)

SPECIFIC GRAVITY: 1.2659 @ 15 C   VAPOR PRESSURE: 1 mmHg @ 205 F

pH: 2.8 (saturated solution)   SOLUBILITY IN WATER: 2.9% @ 20 C VAPOR DENSITY: 4.2

SOLVENT SOLUBILITY: Soluble in alcohol, ether, benzene, chloroform, acetone, carbon disulfide, oil of turpentine, carbon tetrachloride, fixed and volatile oils; slightly soluble in petroleum ether, hexane.

FIRE AND EXPLOSION DATA

TOXICITY

HEALTH EFFECTS AND FIRST AID

INHALATION: FIRST AID- Remove from exposure area to fresh air immediately. If breathing has stopped, perform artificial respiration. Keep person warm and at rest. Treat symptomatically and supportively. Get medical attention immediately.

SKIN CONTACT: FIRST AID- Remove contaminated clothing and shoes immediately. Wash affected area with soap or mild detergent and large amounts of water until no evidence of chemical remains (approximately 15-20 minutes). Get medical attention immediately.

EYE CONTACT: FIRST AID- Wash eyes immediately with large amounts of water or normal saline, occasionally lifting upper and lower lids, until no evidence of chemical remains (approximately 15-20 minutes). Get medical attention immediately.

INGESTION: FIRST AID- Treat symptomatically and supportively. Get medical attention immediately. If vomiting occurs, keep head lower than hips to prevent aspiration.

REACTIVITY

STORAGE AND DISPOSAL
Store away from incompatible substances.

CONDITIONS TO AVOID
May burn but does not ignite readily. Avoid contact with strong oxidizers, excessive heat, sparks, or open flame.

SPILL AND LEAK PROCEDURES

Figure 26.4 Sample Material Safety Data Sheet

NFPA Hazard Codes

The National Fire Protection Association has developed a standard label to display chemical hazard ratings (Figure 26.5). The NFPA label is required by many institutions, industries, and municipalities and is found on most new chemical reagent containers. The left diamond is blue and indicates toxicity (health hazard), the top diamond is red and indicates flammability, the right diamond is yellow and indicates reactivity. The bottom diamond is white and is reserved for special warnings such as radioactivity or reactivity with water.

Fire and Fire Extinguisher Codes

Fire extinguishers are classified by the fires they extinguish. For example, an ABC extinguisher can

Label	Description of hazard	Examples
FLAMMABLE 3	**Flammable** – Any solid, liquid, vapor, or gas that can be ignited readily. Burns so strongly as to create a serious hazard. The Department of Transportation defines a flammable liquid as a liquid with a flash point of less than 141°F (60.5°C).	acetone acetic acid, glacial benzene cyclohexane ethanol methanol isopropyl alcohol
CORROSIVE 8	**Corrosive** – A liquid or solid that causes visible destruction of, or irreversible alterations in, living tissue by chemical action at the site of contact; or a liquid that causes a severe corrosion rate on steel or aluminum.	ammonia, aqueous nitric acid phosphoric acid glacial acetic acid hydrochloric acid sodium hydroxide sulfuric acid
NON-FLAMMABLE GAS 2	**Pressurized gas** – A pressurized dissolved gas, or a gas liquefied by compression or refrigeration. Refrigerated gases may cause frostbite on contact.	argon carbon dioxide chlorine nitrogen sulfur dioxide
OXIDIZER 5.1	**Oxidizer** – A chemical that initiates or promotes combustion in other materials, causing fire either by itself or through the release of oxygen or other gases. Oxidizers must be stored away from all flammable materials.	chlorates nitrates nitrites bromates peroxides permanganates
Diborane [4/3/W] *Ignites spontaneously in moist air.*	**Hazards** *US National Fire Protection Association Label* Blue (left): health hazard Red (top): fire hazard Yellow (right): reactivity hazard White (bottom): special hazard	0=minimal hazard 1=slight hazard 2=moderate hazard 3=serious hazard 4=severe hazard
(biohazard symbol)	**Biohazard** – Biohazardous materials are those of biological origin that are capable of causing disease or infection.	microbes cell cultures blood recombinant DNA human tissue cultures
(radioactive symbol)	**Radioactive** – Radioactive materials emit potentially damaging high-energy rays or particles.	alpha emitters gamma emitters smoke detectors camping lantern mantles photographic antistatic brushes
(electrical shock symbol)	**Risk of Electrical Shock**–All electrical appliances pose the risk of electric shock, especially if there is damaged wiring or contact with water.	electrical panels power generators electrical equipment

Figure 26.5 Common Hazard Labels

be used on class A, B, and C fires. The National Fire Protection Association (NFPA) classifies fires as follows:

- *Class A fires* involve ordinary combustibles such as wood, paper, and cloth and can be extinguished by water.
- *Class B fires* involve flammable and combustible liquids, greases, and similar materials. They are best extinguished by smothering with noncombustible gases such as carbon dioxide or halon.
- *Class C fires* involve electrical equipment and should be extinguished with a material that is electrically nonconducting to avoid shock hazard.
- *Class D fires* involve combustible metals like magnesium and must be extinguished by a heat-absorbing material that does not react with the burning metal.

Chemical Storage Categories

Explosions, fires, toxic fumes, and other hazards can arise if incompatible chemicals are accidentally mixed. For a list of reactive chemicals, see *Bretherick's Handbook of Reactive Chemical Hazards.*[2] To minimize the possibility of such hazards, the fronts of all chemical storage shelves should be equipped with horizontal bars so chemicals will not fall in the event of an earthquake. Chemicals should also be stored with other compatible chemicals and separated by appropriate distances from incompatible chemicals. The following storage classification system was suggested by the California State Department of Education:[3]

- *Metals:* All metals except mercury can be stored together. Metals should be stored separate from all oxidizers, halogens, organic compounds, and moisture.
- *Oxidizers (except ammonium nitrate):* Oxidizers include such chemicals as nitrates, nitrites, permanganates, chromates, dichromates, chlorates, perchlorates, and peroxides. They should

be separated from metals, acids, organic materials, and ammonium nitrate. They should be separated from flammable liquids by a 1 hour firewall or a distance of 8 meters.

- *Ammonium nitrate:* Ammonium nitrate should be stored in isolation from all other chemicals.
- *Bases:* All strong bases, such as sodium hydroxide or potassium hydroxide, should be stored in a dedicated corrosive chemicals cabinet that is coated with corrosion-resistant material.
- *Acids:* All inorganic acids (except nitric acid) and all regulated organic acids should be stored in a cabinet constructed of corrosion-resistant material. Acids may be stored with bases, but fumes from acids and bases may produce an annoying coating of salt crystals on the outside of reagent containers. Nitric acid should be stored separately from acetic acid. Fuming nitric acid should never be used in the school laboratory.
- *Flammables:* Flammables should be stored in a dedicated flammable materials cabinet, 8 meters away from all oxidizers. The cabinet should be coated with flame retardant paint and should be labeled with the notice: FLAMMABLE LIQUID STORAGE. KEEP FIRE AWAY!
- *Poisons:* Highly toxic substances such as cyanides should **never** be used in a school laboratory. Poisons approved by state and district education boards should be stored in a locked cabinet away from the acids cabinet.
- *Compressed gases:* Compressed gas cylinders should be strapped to the wall. Oxidizing gases such as oxygen should be stored far away from flammable liquids, gases, and metals. Flammable gases should be separated from oxidizers and oxidizing gases by a 1 hour firewall or a distance of 8 meters.
- *Low-hazard chemicals:* Many weak bases, oxides, sulfides, indicators, amino acids, sugars, stains, and carbonates are classified as low-hazard chemicals. These chemicals may be stored on open shelves with bars to prevent accidental spillage.

Storage Codes

Some manufacturers provide color-coded labels to categorize chemicals for storage purposes (Table 26.3). Chemicals with a common storage color may be stored together, except when indicated otherwise. Chemicals with different storage color labels should be stored in different areas.

Hazard Symbols

Hazard symbols are designed to warn about hazardous materials or locations. Figure 26.5 lists some of the more common hazard labels.

Table 26.3 Chemical Storage Codes

Storage code **Red**	**Flammable.** Store in area designated for flammable reagents.
Storage code **Yellow**	**Reactive and oxidizing.** May react violently with air, water, or other substances. Store away from flammable and combustible materials.
Storage code **Blue**	**Health hazard.** These chemicals are toxic if inhaled, ingested, or absorbed through the skin. They should be stored in a locked cabinet.
Storage code **White**	**Corrosive.** These chemicals may harm skin, eyes, and mucous membranes. They should be stored away from red-, yellow-, and blue-coded reagents.
Storage code **Gray**	**Moderate or minimal hazard.** According to current data, these chemicals do not pose more than a moderate hazard in any category.

26.8 Disposal of Chemicals

Regulations

It is important that your school is in compliance with all federal, state, local, and district regulations pertaining to the handling, storage, and disposal of chemical wastes. Consult your local environmental health and safety specialist regarding the policies and regulations in your school, community, and state.

Drain Disposal

The National Research Council's Committee on Hazardous Substances in the Laboratory has published detailed information regarding the handling of chemical waste.[4] The committee approves compounds of the following low-toxic-hazard cations and anions for disposal down the drain with excess water in quantities up to 100 g at a time (Table 26.4). Any strongly acidic or basic substances should be neutralized before disposal. *Always consult local policies and regulations before disposing of chemical wastes in your laboratory drain.*

Trash Disposal

In most areas, nonhazardous solids can be disposed of in the trash (Table 26.5). Liquid wastes are generally not allowed in sanitary landfills and should not be placed in the trash. The following types of solid laboratory waste are generally considered nonhazardous or of low toxicity and may be placed in the trash, depending on quantities involved. *Always consult local policies before disposing of chemical wastes in the trash.*

Table 26.4 Low-Toxicity Ions

Low-Toxicity Cations				Low-Toxicity Anions			
Al^{3+}	H^+	Na^+	$Ti^{3+,4+}$	BO_3^{3-}	Cl^-	OH^-	PO_4^{3-}
Ca^{2+}	K^+	NH_4^+	Zn^{2+}	$B_4O_7^{2-}$	HSO_3^-	I^-	SO_4^{2-}
Cu^{2+}	Li^+	Sn^{2+}	Zr^{2+}	Br^-	OCN^-	NO_3^-	SCN^-
$Fe^{2+,3+}$	Mg^{2+}	Sr^{2+}		CO_3^{2-}			

Table 26.5 Nonhazardous Solids That Can Be Disposed of in the Trash

Inorganic Chemicals	Organic Chemicals
borates of Na, K, Mg, Ca	naturally occurring a-amino acids and salts
carbonates of Na, K, Mg, Ca, Sr, NH$_4$	citric acid and its Na, K, Mg, Ca, and NH$_4$ salts
chlorides of Na, K, Mg	lactic acid and its Na, K, Mg, Ca, and NH$_4$ salts
fluorides of Ca	sugars and starches
oxides of B, Mg, Ca, Sr, Al, Si, Ti, Mn, Fe, Co, Cu, Zn	
phosphates of Na, K, Mg, Ca, Sr, NH$_4$	**Laboratory Materials Not Contaminated with Hazardous Materials**
sulfates of Na, K, Mg, Ca, Sr, NH$_4$	chromatographic paper and absorbents, filter paper, filter aids, glassware, and rubber and plastic protective clothing

26.9 Accidents

Accidents happen regardless of preparation and protocol. Teachers should have emergency contact numbers readily available (Figure 26.6) and should accurately document the circumstances of all accidents (Figure 26.7).

Emergency	*911*	*Campus Police*	
School Nurse		*School Office*	
School Safety Officer		*District Science Specialist*	
Animal Control		*Toxic Substances Control*	
County Health Department		*State Department of Education*	
OSHA	*osha.gov*	*EPA*	*epa.gov*

Figure 26.6 Emergency Contacts with Local Numbers

Accident Report		
Room	Date	Time
Person(s) involved in incident		
Description of incident		
Immediate action in responding to incident		
Action taken (or required) to prevent such incidents in the future		
Witnesses to the incident	Reported by: Signature:	

Figure 26.7 Sample Accident Report Form

Chapter Twenty-Seven

Science Reference Information

27.1 Writing Style Guidelines 549

27.2 Units, Constants, and Conversions 551

27.3 Chemical Properties 554

27.4 Graph Paper, Protractors, and Rulers 559

27.1 Writing Style Guidelines

SI Units

Le Systéme International des Unités (SI) is an internationally recognized system of measurement adopted in 1960 by the General Conference of Weights and Measures. Scientists are encouraged to express all measurements in SI units so colleagues around the world can interpret them readily.

Fundamental SI Units

A fundamental unit is one that cannot be expressed in simpler terms. It is defined by a physical standard of measurement. The seven fundamental quantities and their SI units are as follows:

Quantity	Unit	Symbol
length	meter	m
mass	kilogram	kg
time	second	s
temperature	kelvin	K
amount	mole	mol
charge	coulomb	C
luminous intensity	candela	cd

Derived SI Units

A derived unit is one that can be expressed in terms of fundamental units. Volume, for example, is expressed as length cubed, and velocity is expressed as length (distance) per time. Table 27.1 lists the seven fundamental SI units and a variety of derived SI units in terms of these fundamental units.

Capitalization

Unit Names When written in full, all units begin with a lowercase letter:

> *Correct:* kelvin, farad, newton, joule, hertz, degree
>
> *Incorrect:* Kelvin, Farad, Newton, Joule, Hertz, Degree

Unit Symbols The first letter in a unit symbol is uppercase when the unit name is derived from a person's name. The following is a list of units that are named after famous scientists. Note that the unit name is not capitalized, but the unit symbol is.

ampere	A	André Ampère: discovered basic principles of electrodynamics.
coulomb	C	Charles Coulomb: discovered the law of force between charged bodies.
farad	F	Michael Faraday: pioneered research in electricity and magnetism.
henry	H	Joseph Henry: discovered electromagnetic induction and self-induction.
hertz	Hz	Heinrich Hertz: discovered radio waves.
joule	J	James Joule: pioneered research in thermodynamics.
kelvin	K	William Thomson (Lord Kelvin): developed the absolute temperature scale.
newton	N	Isaac Newton: pioneered work in forces, calculus, optics, and gravitation.
ohm	Ω	Georg Ohm: discovered the relationship between current, voltage, and resistance.
Pascal	Pa	Blaise Pascal: discovered basic principles of hydrostatics.
tesla	T	Nikola Tesla: developed the AC motor and high-voltage transformers.
volt	V	Allesandro Volta: invented the first battery.
watt	W	James Watt: developed the steam engine as a practical power source.
weber	Wb	Wilhelm Weber: performed early research in electricity and magnetism.

The following units are not named after people, and therefore their symbols are not capitalized: meter, m; kilogram, kg; second, s; mole, mol; candle, cd; lux, lx; degree,°.

Prefixes   The symbols for all prefixes representing factors less than 1 million are never capitalized (a, f, p, n, μ, m, c, d, da, h, k). The symbols representing factors greater than or equal to 1 million are always capitalized (M, G, T, P, E).

Periods

Periods are never used after a symbol, except at the end of a sentence.

Decimals

For numbers less than 1, a zero is written before the decimal point.

Correct:	0.03256	0.5234
Incorrect:	.03256	.5234

Compound Units

A centered dot is used to indicate that a unit is the product of two or more units.

Correct:	N·m	kg·m/s^2
Incorrect:	Nm	kgm/s^2

Differentiating Quantity Symbols and Unit Symbols

By convention, quantity symbols are italicized, but unit symbols are not. Quantity symbols represent a physical quantity such as time, mass, and length, while unit symbols represent specific measures of those quantities, such as seconds, kilograms, and meters.

Quantity Symbols (Italicized)	Unit Symbols (Not Italicized)
time, *t*	seconds, s
mass, *m*	kilograms, kg
length, *l*	meter, m
heat, *Q*	joule, J

27.2 Units, Constants, and Conversions

Table 27.1 Physical Quantities and Their SI Units

	Symbol	SI Measurement Units	Symbol	Unit Dimensions
distance	d	meter	m	m
Mass	m	kilogram	kg	kg
time	t	second	s	s
electric charge[a]	Q	coulomb	C	C
temperature	T	Kelvin	K	K
amount of substance	n	mole	mol	mol
luminous intensity	I	candela	cd	cd
acceleration	a	meter per second squared	m/s^2	m/s^2
area	A	square meter	m^2	m^2
capacitance	C	farad	F	$C^2 \cdot s^2/kg \cdot m^2$
concentration	$[C]$	molar	M	mol/dm^3
density	D	kilogram per cubic meter	kg/m^3	kg/m^3
electric current	I	ampere	A	C/s
electric field intensity	E	newton per coulomb	N/C	$kg \cdot m/C \cdot s^2$
electric resistance	R	ohm	Ω	$kg \cdot m^2/C^2 \cdot s$
emf	ϕ	volt	V	$kg \cdot m^2/C \cdot s^2$
energy	E	joule	J	$kg \cdot m^2/s^2$
force	F	newton	N	$kg \cdot m/s^2$
frequency	f	hertz	Hz	s^{-1}
heat	Q	joule	J	$kg \cdot m^2/s^2$
illumination	E	lux (lumen per square meter)	lx	cd/m^2
inductance	L	henry	H	$kg \cdot m^2/C^2$
magnetic flux	π	weber	Wb	$kg \cdot m^2/C \cdot s$
potential difference	V	volt	V	$kg \cdot m^2/C \cdot s^2$
power	P	watt	W	$kg \cdot m^2/s^3$
pressure	p	pascal (newton per square meter)	Pa	$kg/m \cdot s^2$
velocity	v	meter per second	m/s	m/s
volume	V	cubic meter	m^3	m^3
work	W	joule	J	$kg \cdot m^2/s^2$

[a]The official SI quantity is electrical current, and the base unit is the ampere. Electrical current is the amount of electrical charge (measured in coulombs) per unit of time.

Table 27.2 Metric System Prefixes

Factor	Decimal Representation	Prefix	Symbol
10^{18}	1,000,000,000,000,000,000	exa	E
10^{15}	1,000,000,000,000,000	peta	P
10^{12}	1,000,000,000,000	tera	T
10^9	1,000,000,000	giga	G
10^6	1,000,000	mega	M
10^3	1,000	kilo	k
10^2	100	hecto	h
10^1	10	deka	da
10^0	1		
10^{-1}	0.1	deci	d
1^{-2}	0.01	centi	c
1^{-3}	0.001	milli	m
1^{-6}	0.000 001	micro	μ
1^{-9}	0.000 000 001	nano	n
1^{-12}	0.000 000 000 001	pico	p
1^{-15}	0.000 000 000 000 001	femto	f
1^{-18}	0.000 000 000 000 000 001	atto	a

Table 27.3 Physical Constants

Planck constant	h	$6.6260755 \cdot 10^{-34}$ J·s
Boltzmann constant	k_B	$1.380658 \cdot 10^{-23}$ J/K
Elementary charge	e	$1.60217733 \cdot 10^{-19}$ C
Avogadro's number	N_A	$6.0221367 \cdot 10^{23}$ particles/mol
Speed of light	c	$2.99792458 \cdot 10^8$ m/s
Electron rest mass	m_e	$9.1093897 \cdot 10^{-31}$ kg
Proton rest mass	m_p	$1.6726231 \cdot 10^{-27}$ kg
Neutron rest mass	m_n	$1.6749286 \cdot 10^{-27}$ kg
Atomic mass unit	amu	$1.66054 \cdot 10^{-27}$ kg
Gas constant	R	8.31451 m²·kg/s²·K·mol
Molar volume	V_{mol}	22.41383 m³/kmol
Faraday constant	F	$9.64846 \cdot 10^4$ C/mol
Gravitational constant	G	$6.673 \cdot 10^{-11}$ m³/kg·s²
Acceleration due to gravity	g	9.80665 m/s²

27.4 SI and Customary Units and Conversions

Quantity	SI Unit	Symbol	Customary Unit	Symbol	Conversion
Length	meter	m	foot	ft	$1\ m = 3280\ ft$
Area	square meter	m^2	square foot	ft^2	$1\ m^2 = 10.76\ ft^2$
Volume	cubic meter	m^3	cubic foot	ft^3	$1\ m^3 = 35.32\ ft^3$
Speed	meter per second	m/s	foot per second	ft/s	$1\ m/s = 3.280\ ft/s$
Acceleration	meter per second per second	m/s^2	feet per second per second	ft/s^2	$1\ m/s^2 = 3.280\ ft/s^2$
Force	newton	N	pound	lb	$1\ N = 0.2248\ lb$
Work (energy)	joule	J	foot-pound	ft·lb	$1\ J = 0.7376\ ft·lb$
Power	watt	W	foot-pound per second	ft·lb/s	$1\ W = 0.7376\ ft·lb/s$
Pressure	pascal	Pa	pound per square inch	lb/in^2	$1\ Pa = 1.450 \times 10^{-4}\ lb/in^2$
Density	kilogram per cubic meter	kg/m^3	pound per cubic foot	lb/ft^3	$1\ kg/m^3 = 6.243 \times 10^{-2}\ lb/ft^3$

27.5 SI and Customary Units and Conversions

Quantity	Customary Unit	Metric Unit	Customary/Metric	Metric/Customary
Length	inch (in.)	millimeter (mm)	1 in. = 25.4 mm	1 mm = 0.0394 in
	foot (ft)	meter (m)	1 ft = 0.305 m	1 m = 3.28 ft
	yard (yd)	meter (m)	1 yd = 0.914 m	1 m = 1.09 yd
	mile (mi)	kilometer (km)	1 mi = 1.61 km	1 km = 0.621 mi
Area	square inch (in^2)	square centimeter (cm^2)	$1\ in^2 = 6.45\ cm^2$	$1\ cm^2 = 0.155\ in^2$
	square foot (ft^2)	square meter (m^2)	$1\ ft^2 = 0.0929\ m^2$	$1\ m^2 = 10.8\ ft^2$
	square yard (yd^2)	square meter (m^2)	$1\ yd^2 = 0.836\ m^2$	$1\ m^2 = 1.20\ yd^2$
	acre (acre)	hectare (ha)	1 acre = 0.405 ha	1 ha = 2.47 acre
Volume	cubic inch (in^3)	cubic centimeter (cm^3)	$1\ in^3 = 16.39\ cm^3$	$1\ cm^3 = 0.0610\ in^3$
	cubic foot (ft^3)	cubic meter (m^3)	$1\ ft^3 = 0.0283\ m^3$	$1\ m^3 = 35.3\ ft^3$
	cubic yard (yd^3)	cubic meter (m^3)	$1\ yd^3 = 0.765\ m^3$	$1\ m^3 = 1.31\ yd^3$
	quart (qt)	liter (L)	1 qt = 0.946 L	1 L = 1.06 qt
Mass	ounce (oz)	gram (g)	1 oz = 28.4 g	1 g = 0.0352 oz
	pound (lb)	kilogram (kg)	1 lb = 0.454 kg	1 kg = 2.20 lb
	ton (ton)	metric ton (t)	1 ton = 0.907 t	1 t = 1.10 ton
Weight	pound (lb)	newton (N)	1 lb = 4.45 N	1 N = 0.225 lb

27.3 Chemical Properties

PERIODIC TABLE OF THE ELEMENTS

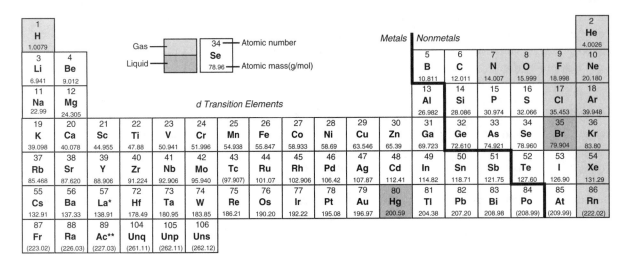

Figure 27.1 Periodic Table of the Elements

Table 27.4 Atomic Symbols, Numbers, and Masses

Actinium	**Ac**	**89**	**227.03**	**Actinium**	**Ac**	**89**	**227.03**
Aluminum	Al	13	26.98	Cesium	Cs	55	132.91
Americium	Am	95	243.06	Chlorine	Cl	17	35.45
Antimony	Sb	51	121.76	Chromium	Cr	24	52.00
Argon	Ar	18	39.95	Cobalt	Co	27	58.93
Arsenic	As	33	74.92	Copper	Cu	29	63.55
Astatine	At	85	209.99	Curium	Cm	96	247.07
Barium	Ba	56	137.33	Dysprosium	Dy	66	162.50
Berkelium	Bk	97	247.07	Einsteinium	Es	99	252.08
Beryllium	Be	4	9.01	Erbium	Er	68	167.26
Bismuth	Bi	83	208.98	Europium	Eu	63	151.97
Boron	B	5	10.81	Fermium	Fm	100	257.10
Bromine	Br	35	79.90	Fluorine	F	9	19.00
Cadmium	Cd	48	112.41	Francium	Fr	87	223.02
Calcium	Ca	20	40.08	Gadolinium	Gd	64	157.25
Californium	Cf	98	251.08	Gallium	Ga	31	69.72
Carbon	C	6	12.01	Germanium	Ge	32	72.61
Cerium	Ce	58	140.12	Gold	Au	79	196.97

Actinium	Ac	89	227.03	Actinium	Ac	89	227.03
Hafnium	Hf	72	178.49	Praseodymium	Pr	59	140.91
Hahnium	Ha	105	262.11	Promethium	Pm	61	144.91
Helium	He	2	4.00	Protactinium	Pa	91	231.04
Hessium	Hs	108	265.13	Radium	Ra	88	226.03
Holmium	Ho	67	164.93	Radon	Rn	86	222.02
Hydrogen	H	1	1.01	Rhenium	Re	75	186.21
Indium	In	49	114.82	Rhodium	Rh	45	102.91
Iodine	I	53	126.90	Rubidium	Rb	37	85.47
Iridium	Ir	77	192.22	Ruthenium	Ru	44	101.07
Iron	Fe	26	55.85	Rutherfordium	Rf	104	261.11
Krypton	Kr	36	83.80	Samarium	Sm	62	150.36
Lanthanum	La	57	138.91	Scandium	Sc	21	44.96
Lawrencium	Lr	103	262.11	Seaborgium	Sg	106	263.12
Lead	Pb	82	207.20	Selenium	Se	34	78.96
Lithium	Li	3	6.94	Silicon	Si	14	28.09
Lutetium	Lu	71	174.97	Silver	Ag	47	107.87
Magnesium	Mg	12	24.31	Sodium	Na	11	22.99
Manganese	Mn	25	54.94	Strontium	Sr	38	87.62
Mendelevium	Md	101	258.10	Sulfur	S	16	32.07
Mercury	Hg	80	200.59	Tantalum	Ta	73	180.95
Mietnerium	Mt	109	266.14	Technetium	Tc	43	97.91
Molybdenum	Mo	42	95.94	Tellurium	Te	52	127.60
Neodymium	Nd	60	144.24	Terbium	Tb	65	158.93
Neon	Ne	10	20.18	Thallium	Tl	81	204.38
Neptunium	Np	93	237.05	Thorium	Th	90	232.04
Nickel	Ni	28	58.69	Thulium	Tm	69	168.93
Nielsbohrium	Ns	107	262.12	Tin	Sn	50	118.71
Niobium	Nb	41	92.91	Titanium	Ti	22	47.88
Nitrogen	N	7	14.01	Tungsten	W	74	183.84
Nobelium	No	102	259.10	Unnunnilium	Unn	110	268.00
Osmium	Os	76	190.23	Unnununium	Unu	111	269.00
Oxygen	O	8	16.00	Uranium	U	92	238.03
Palladium	Pd	46	106.42	Vanadium	V	23	50.94
Phosphorus	P	15	30.97	Xenon	Xe	54	131.29
Platinum	Pt	78	195.08	Ytterbium	Yb	70	173.04
Plutonium	Pu	94	244.06	Yttrium	Y	39	88.91
Polonium	Po	84	208.98	Zinc	Zn	30	65.39
Potassium	K	19	39.10	Zirconium	Zr	40	91.22

Table 27.5 Properties of Common Elements

Element	Symbol	Atomic Mass	Common Oxidation States	Phase 25˚C	Color	Density g/cm³
Aluminum	Al	27.0	+3	s	Silver	2.70
Antimony	Sb	121.8	−3,+3,+5	s	Silver	6.69
Arsenic	As	74.9	−3,+3,+5	s	Gray	5.73
Barium	Ba	137.3	+2	s	Silver	3.51
Bismuth	Bi	209.0	+3, +5	s	Silver	9.75
Bromine	Br	79.9	−1,+1,+3,+5,+7	l	Red/brown	3.12
Calcium	Ca	40.1	+2	s	Silver	1.55
Carbon (graphite)	C	12.0	+2,+4,−4	s	Blk/clear	2.26
Chlorine	Cl	35.5	−1,+1,+3,+5,+7	g	Grn/yellow	0.0032
Chromium	Cr	52.0	+2,+3,+6	s	Silver	7.19
Cobalt	Co	59.0	+2,+3	s	Silver	8.90
Copper	Cu	63.5	+1,+2	s	Red	8.96
Fluorine	F	19.0	−1	g	Yellow	0.0017
Gold	Au	197.0	+1,+3	s	Yellow	19.3
Hydrogen	H	1.0	−1,+1	g	None	0.00009
Iodine	I	126.9	−1,+1,+3,+5,+7	s	Blue/black	4.93
Iron	Fe	55.8	+2,+3	s	Silver	7.87
Lead	Pb	207.2	+2,+4	s	Silver	11.4
Magnesium	Mg	24.3	+2	s	Silver	1.74
Manganese	Mn	54.9	+2,+3,+4,+6,+7	s	Silver	7.3
Mercury	Hg	200.6	+1,+2	l	Silver	13.5
Nickel	Ni	58.7	+2,+3	s	Silver	8.90
Nitrogen	N	14.0	−1,+3,+5	g	None	0.0012
Oxygen	O	16.0	−2,−1	g	None	0.0014
Phosphorous	P	31.0	+3,+5	s	Yellow/red	1.82
Platinum	Pt	195.1	+2,+4	s	Silver	21.4
Potassium	K	39.1	+1	s	Silver	0.86
Silicon	Si	28.1	+2,+4	s	Gray	2.33
Silver	Ag	107.9	+1	s	Silver	10.5
Sodium	Na	23.0	+1	s	Silver	0.97
Strontium	Sr	87.6	+2	s	Silver	2.54
Sulfur	S	32.1	−2,+4,+6	s	Yellow	2.07
Tin	Sn	118.7	+2,+4	s	Silver	7.31
Titanium	Ti	47.9	+2,+3,+4	s	Silver	4.54
Tungsten	W	183.8	+6	s	Gray	19.3
Zinc	Zn	65.4	+2	s	Silver	7.13

Table 27.6 Common Ions

Common Cations		Common Anions	
aluminum	Al^{3+}	acetate	$(C_2H_3O)_2^-$
ammonium	NH_4^+	bromide	Br^-
barium	Ba^{2+}	carbonate	CO_3^{2-}
calcium	Ca^{2+}	chlorate	ClO_3^{2-}
chromium(III)	Cr^{3+}	chloride	Cl^-
cobalt(II)	Co^{2+}	chlorite	ClO_2^-
copper(I)	Cu^+	chromate	CrO_4^{2-}
copper(II)	Cu^{2+}	cyanide	CN^-
hydronium	H_3O^+	dichromate	$Cr_2O_7^{2-}$
iron(II)	Fe^{2+}	fluoride	F^-
iron(III)	Fe^{3+}	hexacyanoferrate(II)	$Fe(CN)_6^{4-}$
lead(II)	Pb^{2+}	hexacyanoferrate(III)	$Fe(CN)_6^{3-}$
magnesium	Mg^{2+}	hydride	H^-
mercury(I)	Hg_2^{2+}	hydrogen carbonate	HCO_3^-
mercury(II)	Hg^{2+}	hydrogen sulfate	HSO_4^-
nickel(II)	Ni^{2+}	hydroxide	OH^-
potassium	K^+	hypochlorite	ClO^-
silver	Ag^+	iodide	I^-
sodium	Na^+	nitrate	NO_3^-
tin(II)	Sn^{2+}	nitrite	NO_2^-
tin(IV)	Sn^{4+}	oxide	O^{2-}
zinc	Zn^{2+}	perchlorate	ClO_4^-
		permanganate	MnO_4^-
		peroxide	O_2^{2-}
		phosphate	PO_4^{3-}
		sulfate	SO_4^{2-}
		sulfide	S^{2-}
		sulfite	SO_3^{2-}

Table 27.7 Standard Reduction Potentials

Half-Reaction	E° (V)	Half-Reaction	E° (V)
$Li^+(aq) + e^- \rightarrow Li(s)$	-3.05	$Cu^{2+}(aq) + e^- \rightarrow Cu^+(aq)$	$+0.16$
$K^+(aq) + e^- \rightarrow K(s)$	-2.92	$Cu^{2+}(aq) + 2e^- \rightarrow Cu(s)$	$+0.34$
$Ba^{2+}(aq) + 2e^- \rightarrow Ba(s)$	-2.90	$O_2(g) + 2H_2O + 4e^- \rightarrow 4OH^-(aq)$	$+0.40$
$Ca^{2+}(aq) + 2e^- \rightarrow Ca(s)$	-2.76	$I_2(s) + 2e^- \rightarrow 2I^-(aq)$	$+0.54$
$Na^+(aq) + e^- \rightarrow Na(s)$	-2.71	$O_2(g) + 2H^+(aq) + 2e^- \rightarrow H_2O_2(aq)$	$+0.68$
$Mg^{2+}(aq) + 2e^- \rightarrow Mg(s)$	-2.37	$Fe^{3+}(aq) + e^- \rightarrow Fe^{2+}(aq)$	$+0.77$
$Al^{3+}(aq) + 3e^- \rightarrow Al(s)$	-1.66	$Hg_2^{2+}(aq) + 2e^- \rightarrow 2Hg(l)$	$+0.80$
$2H_2O + 2e^- \rightarrow H_2(g) + 2OH^-(aq)$	-0.83	$Ag^+(aq) + e^- \rightarrow Ag(s)$	$+0.80$
$Zn^{2+}(aq) + 2e^- \rightarrow Zn(s)$	-0.76	$Hg^{2+}(aq) + 2e^- \rightarrow Hg(l)$	$+0.85$
$Cr^{3+}(aq) + 3e^- \rightarrow Cr(s)$	-0.73	$NO_3^-(aq) + 4H^+(aq) + 3e^- \rightarrow NO(g) + 2H_2O$	$+0.96$
$Fe^{2+}(aq) + 2e^- \rightarrow Fe(s)$	-0.44	$Br_2(l) + 2e^- \rightarrow 2Br^-(aq)$	$+1.09$
$Cd^{2+}(aq) + 2e^- \rightarrow Cd(s)$	-0.40	$O_2(g) + 4H^+(aq) + 4e^- \rightarrow 2H_2O$	$+1.23$
$Co^{2+}(aq) + 2e^- \rightarrow Co(s)$	-0.28	$Cl_2(g) + 2e^- \rightarrow 2Cl^-(aq)$	$+1.36$
$Ni^{2+}(aq) + 2e^- \rightarrow Ni(s)$	-0.23	$MnO_4^-(aq) + 8H^+(aq) + 5e^- \rightarrow Mn^{2+}(aq) + 4H_2O(l)$	$+1.51$
$Sn^{2+}(aq) + 2e^- \rightarrow Sn(s)$	-0.14	$Au^{3+} + 3e^- \rightarrow Au$	$+1.50$
$Pb^{2+}(aq) + 2e^- \rightarrow Pb(s)$	-0.13	$H_2O_2(aq) + 2H^+(aq) + 2e^- \rightarrow 2H_2O$	$+1.78$
$2H^+(aq) + 2e^- \rightarrow H_2(g)$	**0.00**	$F_2(g) + 2e^- \rightarrow 2F^-(aq)$	$+2.87$

Note: Standard reduction potentials at 25˚C. For all half-reactions, the concentration is 1 *M* for dissolved species and the pressure is 1 atm for gases.

Table 27.8 Units of Pressure

Unit	Definition	Pascal Equivalents	When It Is Used
Pascal (Pa)	N/m^2	1	Standard SI Unit. Used when mass is measured in kg and area in meters.
kiloPascal (kPa)	$1000 \ N/m^2$	1000	Practical metric unit of measuring gaseous, fluid or mechanical pressure (Pa is generally too small).
bar	$10,000 \ N/m^2$	100,000	Practical metric unit of measuring atmospheric pressure. One bar is approximately 1 atmosphere.
millibar (mb)	$100 \ N/m^2$	100	Weather reports. *Note:* Some weather maps drop the first two digits (e.g., 1013.3 mb may be reported as 13.3).
barye (dyne/cm²)	$0.1 \ N/m^2$	0.1	Standard CGS unit. Used when measurements are made in centimeters and grams.
torr	1/760 of standard atmospheric pressure	133.3	Used when pressure is measured with a mercury manometer or barometer.
mm Hg	Pressure required to support a column of Hg 1 mm in height	133.3	Blood pressure measurements. Standard blood pressure is 120/80 (systolic/diastolic).
cm H_2O	Pressure required to support a column of water 1 cm in height	98.1	Used when pressure is measured using simple water barometer or manometer.
atmosphere (atm)	Atmospheric pressure at sea level	101,325	Used when a comparison to standard atmospheric pressure is desired.
PSI	lb/in.²	6894	Common measurement in mechanical and structural engineering. Tire pressures are rated in PSI.

Table 27.9 Vapor Pressure of Water

Temperature °C	Pressure kPa	Temperature °C	Pressure kPa	Temperature °C	Pressure kPa
0	0.6	20	2.3	30	4.2
3	0.8	21	2.5	32	4.8
5	0.9	22	2.6	35	5.6
8	1.1	23	2.8	40	7.4
10	1.2	24	3.0	50	12.3
12	1.4	25	3.2	60	19.9
14	1.6	26	3.4	70	31.2
16	1.8	27	3.6	80	47.3
18	2.1	28	3.8	90	70.1
19	2.2	29	4.0	100	101.3

Note: 1 mm H_2O = 0.00981 kPa; 1 cm H_2O = 0.0981 kPa.

27.4 Graph Paper, Protractors, and Rulers

You may provide your students with graph paper by copying the following pages. If you copy them on transparency film, you can use them as measurement tools. For example, you can lay the transparent rulers over an object to measure its length, or place the centimeter graph paper over an irregular object to measure its area. You can also use them on the overhead projector to plot data and measure objects. Students will find it much easier to learn how to plot data if they can watch the instructor plot the same data on the same type of graph paper. You can make inexpensive rulers by copying the image onto transparency film and then cutting them apart with scissors. This section provides linear graph paper, semilog paper, log-log graph paper, polar graph paper, and rulers.

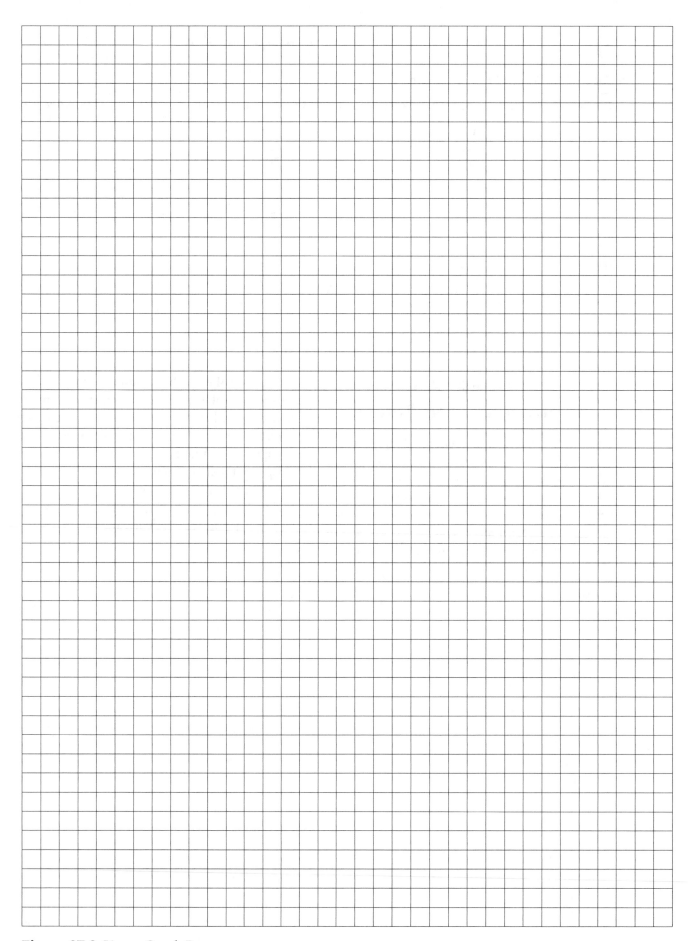

Figure 27.2 Linear Graph Paper

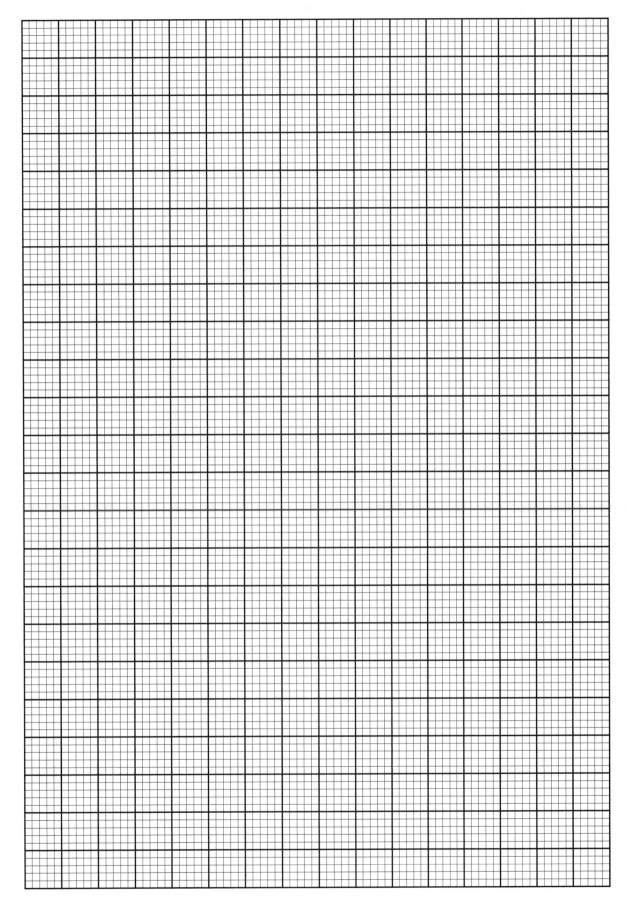

Figure 27.3 Centimeter Graph Paper

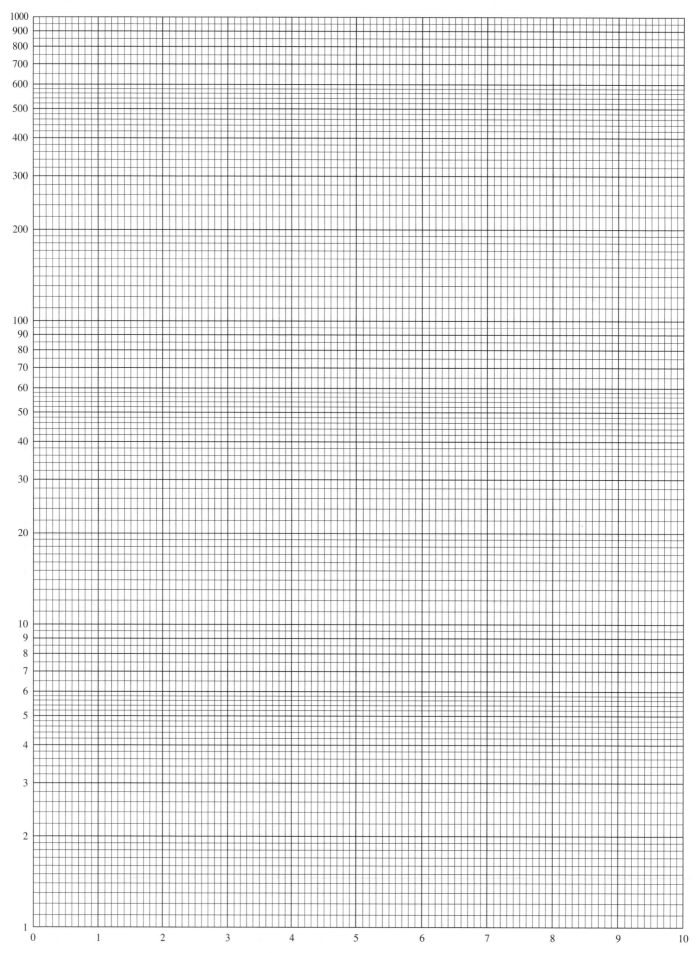

Figure 27.4 Semilogarithmic Graph Paper

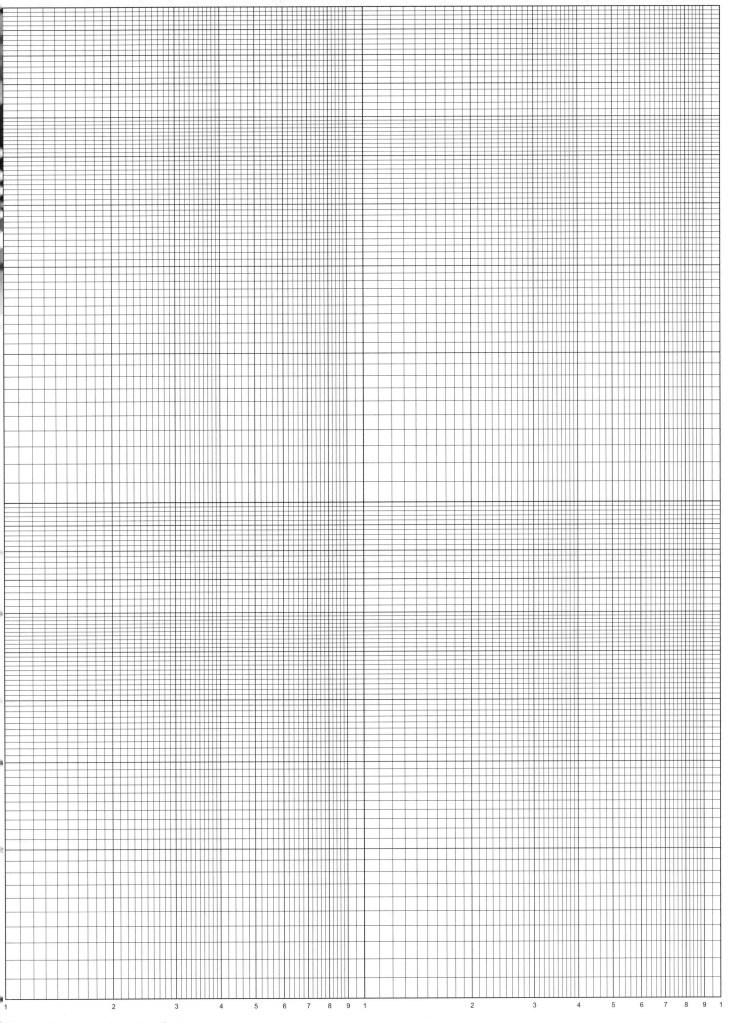

Figure 27.5 Log-Log Graph Paper

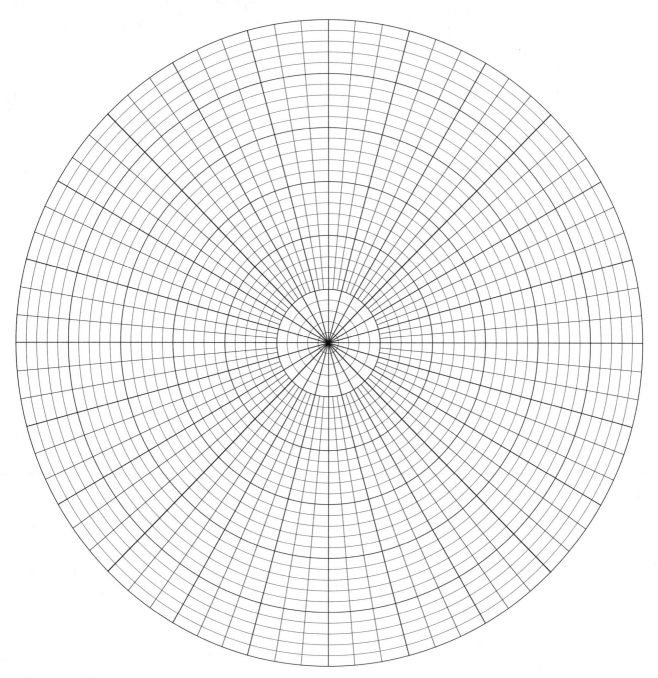

Figure 27.6 Log-Log Graph Paper

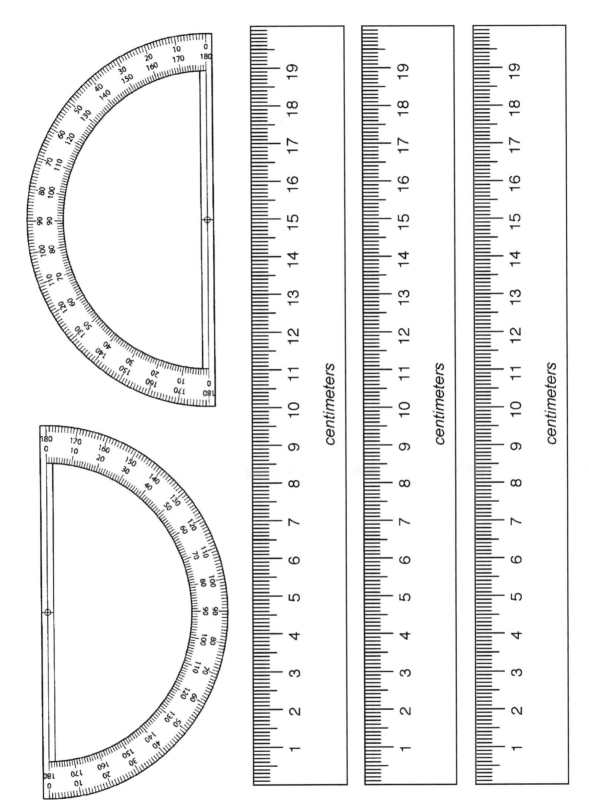

Figure 27.7 Rulers and Protractors

Notes

Chapter Two

1. Rutherford, F. (1990). *Project 2061: Science for all Americans.* American Association for the Advancement of Science. New York: Oxford University Press.
2. National Research Council. (1996). *National science education standards.* Washington, DC: National Academy Press.
3. OECD Programme for International Student Assessment. (1999). *Measuring student knowledge and skills: A new framework for assessment.* Paris: OECD.

Chapter Three

1. Storms, E. (2000). Excess power production from platinum cathodes using the Pons-Fleischmann effect. In *Proceedings of the 8th International Conference on Cold Fusion, 2000.* Bologna, Italy: Italian Physical Society.
2. Killion, J. (1999). Journaling. *Journal of Staff Development, 20*(3). Retrieved February 21, 2008, from http://www.nsdc.org/library/publications/jsd/killion203.cfm.

Chapter Four

1. U.S. Bureau of Labor Statistics. (2006). *Occupational outlook handbook, 2006–07 edition.* Washington, DC: Bureau of Labor Statistics, U.S. Department of Labor.
2. Edison, T. A. (1889, November). The dangers of electric lighting. *North American Review,* 625–635.

Chapter Five

1. Merriam-Webster. (2003). Merriam-Webster's *collegiate dictionary* (11th ed.). Springfield, MA: Author.
2. Bridgman, P. (1980). *Reflections of a physicist.* New York: Arno Press.
3. Cunningham, J., & Herr, N. (1994). *Hands-on physics activities with real-life applications.* San Francisco: Jossey-Bass. Herr, N., & Cunningham, J. (1999). *Hands-on chemistry activities with real-life applications.* San Francisco: Jossey-Bass.
4. Faraday, M. (1963). *Chemical history of a candle.* New York: Viking Press.
5. Osheroff, D. (1997, May 19). *Puttering around in the basement on the road to Stockholm.* Keynote address to the California State Science Fair, Sacramento.

Chapter Six

1. Flavell, J. H. (1979). Metacognition and cognitive monitoring: A new area of cognitive-developmental inquiry. *American Psychologist, 34,* 906–911.
2. Bloom, B. S. (Ed.). (1956). *Taxonomy of educational objectives: The classification of educational goals.* New York: McKay.
3. Anderson, L. W., & Krathwohl, D. R. (Eds.). (2001). *A taxonomy for learning, teaching, and assessing: A revision of Bloom's taxonomy of educational objectives.* New York: Longman.
4. Cunningham, J., & Herr, N. (1994). *Hands-on physics activities with real-life applications.* San Francisco: Jossey-Bass. Herr, N., & Cunningham, J. (1999). *Hands-on chemistry activities with real-life applications.* San Francisco: Jossey-Bass.

Chapter Seven

1. Mokdad, A., Marks, J., Stroup, D., & Gerberding, J. (2004). Actual cause of death in the United States. *Journal of the American Medical Association, 291,* 1238–1245.
2. Greenfield, A. (1998). *Analysis of national data on the prevalence of alcohol involvement in crime.* Washington, DC: U.S. Department of Justice, Office of Justice Programs, Bureau of Justice Statistics.
3. Grant, B. (2000). Estimates of U.S. children exposed to alcohol abuse and dependence in the family. *American Journal of Public Health, 90,* 112.
4. Smith, G., Branas, C., & Miller, T. (1999). Fatal non-traffic injuries involving alcohol: A meta-analysis. *Annals of Emergency Medicine, 33,* 659–668.
5. Alan Guttmacher Institute. (2004). *Teen sex and pregnancy.* Accessed March 18, 2004, www.guttmacher.org/.
6. National Highway Traffic Safety Administration. (2005). *Traffic safety facts 2004: Alcohol.* Washington, DC: U.S. Department of Transportation.
7. National Highway Traffic Safety Administration. (2005).
8. Naimi, T., Brewer, B., Mokdad, A., Serdula, M., Denny, C., & Marks, J. (2003). Binge drinking among U.S. adults. *Journal of the American Medical Association, 289,* 70–75.

Chapter Eight

1. Ausubel, D. P. (1960). The use of advance organizers in the learning and retention of meaningful verbal material. *Journal of Educational Psychology, 51,* 267–272. Ausubel, D. (1978). In defense of advance organizers: A reply to the critics. *Review of Educational Research, 48,* 251–257.
2. Boeke, K. (1957). *Cosmic view: The universe in 40 jumps.* New York: John Day.
3. Eames, C., & Eames, R. (1977). *Powers of ten.* Santa Monica, CA: Eames Office.

Chapter Nine

1. Buzan, T. (1995). *The mindmap book* (2nd ed.). London: BBC Books.
2. Lawson, M. J. (1994). Concept mapping. In T. Husén & T. N. Postlethwaite (Eds.), *The international encyclopedia of education* (2nd ed., vol. 2, pp. 1026–1031). Oxford: Elsevier Science.
3. Novak, J. D. (1991). Clarify with concept maps: A tool for students and teachers alike. *Science Teacher, 58*(7), 45–49. Ausubel, D. P. (1960). The use of advance organizers in the learning and retention of meaningful verbal material. *Journal of Educational Psychology, 51,* 267–272.

4. Burke, J. (2007). *Connections.* New York: Simon & Schuster. Burke, J. (2001). *Connections 1, 2, 3.* [DVD]. New York: BBC and Time Life.

Chapter Ten

1. Tobin, K. (Ed.) (1993). *The practice of constructivism in science education.* Washington, DC: AAAS Press. Fosnot, C. (Ed.). *Constructivism: Theory, perspectives, and practice.* New York: Plenum. Driver, R., Asoko, H., Leach, J., Mortimer, E., & Scott, P. (1994). Constructing scientific knowledge in the classroom. *Educational Researcher, 23*(7), 5–12.
2. Glynn, S. M., Duit, R., & Thiele, R. B. (1995). Teaching science with analogies: A strategy for constructing knowledge. In S. M. Glynn & R. Duit (Eds.), *Learning science in the schools: Research reforming practice* (pp. 247–273). Mahwah, NJ: Erlbaum.

Chapter Eleven

1. Bjork, R. A. (1975). Short-term storage: The ordered output of a central processor. In F. Restle et al. (Eds.), *Cognitive theory* (Vol. 1). Mahwah, NJ: Erlbaum. Baddeley, A. (1982). *Human memory: A user's guide.* New York: Macmillan, 1982.
2. Craik, F.I.M., & Tulving, T. (1985). Depth of processing and the retention of words in episodic memory. *Journal of Experimental Psychology: General, 104,* 268–294.
3. Craik, F.I.M. (1981). Encoding and retrieval effects in human memory: A partial review. In A. D. Baddeley & J. Long (Eds.), *Attention and performance, IX.* Mahwah, NJ: Erlbaum, 1981.
4. Cunningham, J., & Herr, N. (1994). *Hands-on physics activities with real-life applications.* San Francisco: Jossey-Bass. Herr, N., & Cunningham, J. (1999). *Hands-on chemistry activities with real-life applications.* San Francisco: Jossey-Bass.
5. Bjork, R. A. (1979). *Retrieval practice.* Invited paper, Conference on Developmental and Experimental Approaches to Human Memory, Ann Arbor, MI.

Chapter Twelve

1. Gardner, H. (1993). *Frames of mind: The theory of multiple intelligences.* New York: Basic Books.

Chapter Thirteen

1. Owens, K. D. (1997). Playing to learn: Science games in the classroom. *Science Scope, 20*(5), 31–33. Hounshell, P. B., & Trollinger, I. R. (1977). *Games for the science classroom. An annotated bibliography.* Washington, DC: National Science Teachers Association.
2. Bonwell, C. C., & Eison, J. A. (1991). Creating excitement in the classroom. *ERIC Digest.* (ERIC Document Reproduction Service No. ED340272)
3. Winn, W. D., & Holliday, W. G. (1981, April). *Learning from diagrams: Theoretical and instructional considerations.* Paper presented at the Annual Convention of the Association for Educational Communications and Technology, Philadelphia.
4. Hooke, R. (1665). *Micrographia: or, Some physiological descriptions of minute bodies made by magnifying glasses.* London: J. Martyn and J. Allestry.

Chapter Fifteen

1. Haldane, J.B.S. (1928). On being the right size: An essay discussing the proportions in the animal world.
2. Bailey, B., & Briars, G. (1996). Estimating the surface area of the human body. *Statistics in Medicine, 15,* 1325–1332.

Chapter Sixteen

1. Nielsen Media Research. (2005). Nielsen reports Americans watch TV at record levels. *Nielsen Media Research.* Retrieved April 2007 from http://www.nielsenmedia.com/newsreleases/2005.
2. Anderson, R., Crespo C., Bartlett S., Cheskin, L., & Pratt, M. (1998). Relationship of physical activity and television watching with body weight and level of fatness among children. *Journal of the American Medical Association, 279,* 938–942.
3. Hancox, R., Milne B., & Poulton, R. (2005). Association of television viewing during childhood with poor educational achievement. *Archives of Pediatrics and Adolescent Medicine, 159,* 607–619.

Chapter Seventeen

1. Wilford, J. (1999, September 24). Mars orbiting craft presumed destroyed by navigation error. *New York Times,* p. A:1.
2. Kohn, L., Corrigan, J., & Donaldson, M. (eds.). (2000). *To err is human: Building a safer health system.* Committee on Quality of Health Care in America. Washington, DC: National Academy Press.
3. Eleventh General Conference on Weights and Measures. (1960). *The International System of Units (SI).* Paris: Organisation Intergouvernementale de la Convention du Mètre.

Chapter Nineteen

1. U.S. Department of Agriculture. (2007). *Plants database.* Retrieved June 11, 2007, from http://plants.usda.gov.
2. National Institutes of Health. (2007). *Human genome database.* National Center for Biotechnology Information, National Institutes of Health. Retrieved June 11, 2007, from www.ncbi.nlm.nih.gov.
3. Brookhaven National Laboratory. (2007). *Protein data bank.* Retrieved June 11, 2007, from http://www.rcsb.org.
4. Fiber Gel Technologies. (2007). *Nutritional analysis tools and system, using data from the United States Department of Agriculture.* Retrieved June 11, 2007, from http://nat.crgq.com.

Chapter Twenty

1. Keeling, C., Bacastow, R., Bainbridge, A., Ekdahl, C., Guenther, R., & Waterman, L. (1976). Atmospheric carbon dioxide variations at Mauna Loa Observatory, Hawaii. *Tellus, 28,* 538–551.

Chapter Twenty-One

1. National Institutes of Health. (2007). *Human genome project.* National Human Genome Research Institute. http://www.genome.gov.
2. Astrophysical Research Consortium. (2007). *Sloan digital sky survey.* Retrieved May 8, 2007, from http://www.sdss.org.

3. Annenberg Media. (2007). *Journey north.* Retrieved May 8, 2007, from http://www.learner.org/jnorth.

4. U.S. Department of Commerce. (2007). United States Patent and Trademark Office. Retrieved May 8, 2007, from http://www.uspto.gov.

Chapter Twenty-Two

1. National Academy of Sciences. (1996). *National science education standards.* Washington, DC: National Academy Press.

2. Bransford, J., Brown, A., & Cocking, R. (Eds.). (2000). *How people learn.* Washington, DC: National Academy Press.

3. Bybee, R. W. (1997). *Achieving scientific literacy.* Portsmouth, NH: Heinemann.

4. Wheatley, G. (1991). Constructivist perspectives on science and mathematics learning. *Science Education, 75*(1), 9–21.

5. Eisencraft, A. (2003). Expanding the 5-E model. *Science Teacher, 70*(6), 56–59.

6. American Psychological Association. (2005). *Concise rules of APA Style.* Washington, DC: Author.

7. Gibaldi, J. (2003). *MLA handbook for writers of research papers* (6th ed.). New York: Modern Language Association.

8. Council of Science Editors. (2006). *Scientific style and format.* Reston, VA: Council of Science Educators.

Chapter Twenty-Three

1. Science Service. (2007). *Science talent search.* Retrieved May 17, 2007, from http://www.sciserv.org.

2. Science Service. (2007). *Intel International Science and Engineering Fair.* Retrieved May 17, 2007, from http://www.sciserv.org/isef.

3. Hickham, R. (2000). *Rocket boys.* New York: Delta.

4. Bishop, J., & Carter, S. (1991). The worsening shortage of college-graduate workers. *Educational Evaluation and Policy Analysis, 13*(3), 221–246. Jackson, S. (2003). *Envisioning a 21st century science and engineering workforce for the United States: Tasks for university, industry, and government.* Washington, DC: National Academy Press.

5. Newton, I. (1675). Letter to Robert Hooke, with reference to his dependency on Galileo's and Kepler's work in physics and astronomy, February 5, 1675. From Cook, J. (2007). *The book of positive quotations* (p. 604). Minneapolis: Fairview Press.

6. Edison, T. (1903). Remark by Edison. *Harper's Monthly.* New York, Sept. 1932.

7. Pasteur, L. (1854, December 7). Inaugural lecture as professor and dean of the faculty of science, University of Lille, Douai, France, quoted in Peterson, H. (ed.). (1954). *A treasury of the world's great speeches* (p. 473). New York: Simon & Schuster.

8. Bartlet, J. (1919). *Familiar quotations.* Boston: Little, Brown and Company.

Chapter Twenty-Four

1. McComas, W., Clough, M., & Almazroa, H. (1998). The role and character of the nature of science. In W. F. McComas (Ed.), *The nature of science in science education: Rationales and strategies* (pp. 3–39). Norwell, MA: Kluwer Academic.

2. National Science Teachers Association. (2000). *The nature of science: A position statement of NSTA.* Washington, DC: Author.

3. Bonwell, C., & Eison, J. (1991). *Active learning: Creating excitement in the classroom.* AEHE-ERIC Higher Education Report, No. 1. San Francisco: Jossey-Bass.

4. Bruner, J. S. (1961). The act of discovery. *Harvard Educational Review, 31*(1), 21–32.

5. Gardner, H. (1993). *Frames of mind: The theory of multiple intelligences.* New York: Basic Books.

6. Flavell, J. H. (1979). Metacognition and cognitive monitoring: A new area of cognitive-developmental inquiry. *American Psychologist, 34,* 906–911.

7. Bloom, B. S. (Ed.). (1956). *Taxonomy of educational objectives: The classification of educational goals.* New York: McKay.

8. Bodner, G. (1986). Constructivism: A theory of knowledge. *Journal of Chemical Education, 63*(10), 873–877.

9. Piaget, J. (1950). *The psychology of intelligence.* New York: Routledge.

10. Papert, S. (1993). *Mindstorms: Children, computers, and powerful ideas.* New York: Basic Books.

11. Schulman, L. S. (1986). Those who understand: Knowledge growth in teaching. *Educational Researcher, 15*(2), 4–14.

12. Bransford, D., Brown, E., & Cocking, R. (Eds.) (1999). *How people learn: Brain, mind, experience, and school.* Committee on Developments in the Science of Learning, National Research Council. Washington, DC: National Academy Press.

13. Menez, J., & Vile, J. (2004). *Summaries of leading cases on the Constitution* (243–244). Lanham, MD: Rowan and Littlefield.

14. Sheppard, K., & Robbins, D. (2002). Lessons from the Committee of Ten. *Physics Teacher, 40*(7), 426–431.

15. Vázquez, J. (2006). High school biology today: What the Committee of Ten did not anticipate. *CBE Life Science Education, 5*(1), 29–33.

16. Herr, N. (1990). Advanced science instruction in American high schools: A comparative analysis of the perceived influence of Advanced Placement and honors programs on the quality of science education. *Dissertation Abstracts International, 51,* 07A.

17. Herr, N. (1991). The influence of program format on the professional development of science teachers: A within-subjects analysis of the perceptions of teachers who have taught AP and honors science to comparable student populations. *Science Education, 75*(6), 619–621.

18. Herr, N. (1992). A comparative analysis of the perceived influence of Advanced Placement and honors programs upon science instruction. *Journal of Research in Science Education, 29*(5), 521–532.

19. College Board. (2007). *Advanced Placement Program.* Retrieved May 22, 2007, from http://apcentral.collegeboard.com.

20. Herr, N. (1991). Perspectives and policies regarding Advanced Placement and honors coursework. *College and University, 62*(2), 47–54.

21. Herr, N. (1992, May). Administrative policies regarding Advanced Placement and honors coursework. *National Association of Secondary School Principals Bulletin,* 80–87.

22. National Center for Education Statistics. (2007). *The Nation's Report Card.* retrieved May 22, 2007, from http://nces.ed.gov/nationsreportcard.

23. U.S. National Commission on Excellence in Education. (1983). *A nation at risk: The imperative for educational reform: A report to the nation and the secretary of education.* Washington, DC: Author.

24. Wong, K., Guthrie, J., & Harris, D. (eds.). (2003). *A nation at risk:* A twenty-year re-appraisal: A Symposium of the *Peabody Journal of Education.*

25. Rutherford, F. (1990). *Project 2061: Science for all Americans.* American Association for the Advancement of Science. New York: Oxford University Press.

26. AAAS. (1993). *Benchmarks of science literacy.* American Association for the Advancement of Science. New York: Oxford University Press.

27. National Science Teachers Association. (1990). *A national curriculum and development policy for high school science education.* Reston, VA: Author.

28. National Center for Education Statistics. (2007). *Trends in International Mathematics and Science Study.* Retrieved May 22, 2007, from http://nces.ed.gov/timss.

29. National Research Council. (1996). *National science education standards.* Washington, DC: National Academy Press.

30. California State Board of Education. (1998). *California Science Content Standards.* Sacramento: Author.

31. No Child Left Behind Act of 2001. (2002). P.L. 107–110.

32. Committee on Prospering in the 21st Century. (2005). *Rising above the gathering storm: Energizing and employing America for a brighter economic future.* National Academy of Sciences, National Academy of Engineering, Institute of Medicine. Washington, DC: National Academies Press.

33. Educational Testing Service. (2007). *America's perfect storm: Three forces changing our nation's future.* Princeton, NJ: ETS.

34. Friedman, T. L. (2005) *The world is flat: A brief history of the twenty-first century.* New York: Farrar, Straus and Giroux.

35. Herr, N. (1993). National curricula for advanced science classes in American high schools? The influence of the College Board's Advanced Placement Program on Science Curricula. *International Journal of Science Education, 15*(3), 297–306.

36. Herr. (1992).

37. National Commission on Excellence in Education. (1983).

38. U.S. Department of Education. (1992). *Education standards in the Asia-Pacific region.* Washington, DC: U.S. Department of Education.

39. Su, Z., Goldstein, S., & Su, J. (1995). Science education goals and curriculum designs in American and Chinese high schools. *International Review of Education, 41*(5), 371–388.

40. U.S. National Research Center for the Third International Mathematics and Science Study. (1996). *A splintered vision: An investigation of U.S. science and mathematics education.* Ann Arbor: Michigan State University.

41. Herr, N. (1993). The relationship between Advanced Placement and honors science courses. *School Science and Mathematics, 93*(4), 183–187.

42. College Board. (2005). *AP Biology course description.* New York: College Board.

43. College Board. (2001). *AP Biology lab manual for students.* New York: College Board.

44. College Board. (2006). *AP Chemistry course description for May 2007, 2008.* New York: College Board.

45. College Board. (2005). *AP Physics course description for May 2006, 2007.* New York: College Board.

46. College Board. (2005). *AP Environmental Science course description for May 2006, 2007.* New York: College Board.

47. International Baccalaureate Program. (2007). *International Baccalaureate.* Retrieved May 30, 2007, from http://www.ibo.org.

48. National Research Council. (2000). *Inquiry and the national science education standards: A guide for teaching and learning.* Washington, DC: National Academy Press.

49. National Research Council. (1996).

50. American Association for the Advancement of Science. (1993). *Benchmarks for science literacy.* New York: Oxford University Press.

51. National Science Teachers Association. (2004). *Scientific inquiry: A position statement of NSTA.* Washington, DC: Author.

52. Wirt, J., Rooney, P., Husar, B., Choy, S., Provasnik, S., & Hampden-Thompson, G. (2005). *The condition of education 2005*. Washington, DC: National Center for Education Statistics.

53. National Center for Education Statistics. (2005). *Characteristics of the 100 largest public elementary and secondary school districts in the U.S., 2001–2002*. Washington, DC: U.S. Department of Education.

54. Lymna, F. (1981). The responsive classroom discussion. In A. Anderson (Ed.), *Mainstreaming digest*. College Park, MD: University of Maryland College of Education.

55. Feldman, D. (1996). *How do astronauts scratch an itch? An imponderable book*. New York: Berkley Books.

56. Associated Press. (1997, November 2). Sophomore's project makes people think. *St. Louis Post-Dispatch*, E4.

57. Loucks-Horsley, S., Love, N., Stiles, K., Mundry, S., & Hewson, P. (2003). *Designing professional development for teachers of science and mathematics*. Thousand Oaks, CA: Corwin Press.

58. Lewis, C. (2000). *Lesson study: The core of Japanese professional development*. Invited address to the Special Interest Group on Research in Mathematics Education, American Educational Research Association National Meeting, New Orleans, LA.

59. Carnegie Forum on Education and the Economy's Task Force on Teaching as a Profession. (1987). *A nation prepared: Teachers for the 21st century*. Report of the Task Force on Teaching as a Profession. Hyattsville, MD: Carnegie Forum on Education and the Economy.

60. Dodge, B. (1995). WebQuests: A technique for Internet-based learning. *Distance Educator, 1*(2), 10–13.

Chapter Twenty-Five

1. Metfessel, N., Michael, W., & Kirsner, D. (1969). Instrumentation of Bloom's and Krathwohl's taxonomies for the writing of educational objectives. *Psychology in the Schools, 4*(3), 227–231.

2. Bloom, B. M. (Ed.). (1956). *Taxonomy of educational objectives: The classification of educational goals*. New York: McKay.

3. Wolfe, P. (1987, February). What the "seven-step lesson plan" isn't. *Educational Leadership*, 70–71.

4. Hunter, M. (1982). *Mastery teaching*. El Segundo, CA: TIP Publications.

5. Bowerman, S. (2007). Hate broccoli? Spinach? Blame your genes. Extra taste buds create an aversion, for some, to bitter vegetables and other foods. *Los Angeles Times* (February 9, 2007).

6. Bruns, J. H. (1992). *They can but they don't: Helping students overcome work inhibition*. New York: Viking Penguin.

7. Canter, L., & Canter, M. (1992). *Assertive discipline: Positive behavior management for today's classroom*. Santa Monica, CA: Canter and Associates. Canter, L., & Canter, M. (1993). *Succeeding with difficult students: New strategies for reaching your most challenging students*. Santa Monica, CA: Canter and Associates.

8. Jones, F. (1987). *Positive classroom discipline*. New York: McGraw-Hill.

9. Nelson, J., Lott, L., & Glenn, H. (2000). *Positive discipline in the classroom*. New York: Three Rivers Press.

10. Hunter, M. (1989). *Newsletters*. U.S. Department of Education. Retrieved June 4, 2007, from http://www.ed.gov/news/newsletters/achiever/2002/08122002.html.

11. Cowie, B., & Bell, B. (1999). A model of formative assessment in science education. *Assessment in Education, 6*, 101–116.

12. Klentschy, M. P., & Molina-De La Torre, E. (2004). Student's science notebooks and the inquiry process. *Crossing borders in literacy and science instruction: Perspectives on theory and practice*. Arlington, VA: International Reading Association/National Science Teachers Association.

Chapter Twenty-Six

1. Anders, D. J. (1966). Action research. In S. Kemmis & R. McTaggart (Eds.), *The action research reader* (3rd ed., pp. 317–321). Victoria: Deakin University.

2. Bretherick, L. 1990. *Bretherick's handbook of reactive chemical hazards* (4th ed.). London: Butterworths.

3. California State Department of Education. (1987). *Science safety handbook for California high schools.* Sacramento: California State Department of Education.

4. National Academy Press. (1983). *Prudent practices for disposal of chemicals from laboratories.* Washington, DC: National Academy Press.

Index

A

abbreviations, 11.2.2, 11.2.3, 11.2.4, 11.3, 11.3.1
absolute reference, 20.0
abstract, 3.4.5
acceleration, 3.5, 7.4.1, 14.3, 16.5.1, 17.3, 17.7, 17.17, 27.2
accidents, 26.9
acidic solutions, 18.0, 26.4
acronyms, 11.0, 11.2.2, 11.2.3, 11.2.4, 11.3, 11.3.1
acrostics, 11.0, 11.4, 11.4.1, 11.4.2, 11.4.3, 11.4.4
action potential, 10.4.1
activated complex, 10.3, 10.4
active learning, 24.2
adhesion, 12.4.2
advance organizers, 2.0, 8.0, 8.1, 8.1.1
Advanced Placement, 3.3, 8.4, 8.4.1, 24.3, 24.4, 24.5
Advanced Placement, Biology, 24.5
Advanced Placement, Chemistry, 24.5
Advanced Placement, Environmental Science, 24.5
Advanced Placement, Physics, 24.5
advertisements, evaluating, 7.2.1, 7.2.2, 7.2.3
aerial photography, 21.7
aerodynamic forces, 16.1
air pollution, 20.4, 21.5.2
air pressure, 5.1.2
air quality index (AQI), 21.5.2
aircraft, design of, 19.1.1
alcohol, medical, and social costs, 7.2.2, 7.6
algebra, 6.3.3
algebraic expressions, 6.3.3, 14.2, 14.2.1, 14.2.3, 14.3
alternating current (AC), 9.1.4
American Association for the Advancement of Science (AAAS), 2.0
American Association of Physics Teachers (AAPT), 24.9
American Chemical Society (ACS), 24.9
American Physiological Society (APS), 24.9

American Psychological Association (APA) format, 3.4
amino acids, 19.2.2
ammeter, 10.1.1
amount of substance, 3.5, 17.3, 17.17, 27.2
analogies, 10.0, 10.1.1, 10.1.2, 10.1.3, 10.1.4, 10.1.5, 24.7
analogue concept, 10.0, 10.1.1, 10.1.2, 10.1.3, 10.1.4, 10.1.5
analysis (learning objectives), 5.4.1, 6.1, 25.1
analytical chemistry, 8.4.1
anatomy, 12.5.6
angular acceleration, 10.2, 10.2.1
angular velocity, 10.2
animation, 16.7
anions, 18.3
antennae, 15.6.4, 15.7.1
antibodies, 15.6.4
anticipatory sets, 25.2
application (learning objectives), 6.1, 25.1
Archimedes principle, 5.3.2
area, 3.5, 17.3, 17.17, 27.2
area graph, 20.0, 20.6
argument, 20.0
arthropods, 9.1.1
assessment, student performance, 25.6
assessment, teacher, 25.7
Association for the Advancement of Computing in Education (AACE), 24.9
asteroids, 19.4.2
astronomical unit (AU), 15.6.3
atherosclerosis, 19.3.2
atmosphere, 8.6
atom, 5.9.2
atomic mass, 6.2.2, 20.4.2, 27.3
atomic number, 19.1.3
atomic radii, 6.1.3, 6.3.2
atomic spectra, 10.3.1
atomic symbols, 27.3
atoms, 8.3, 8.3.1, 8.3.2, 8.3.3
ATP, 10.0
auctions, 26.1
audience response system, 25.6

auditory learning, 11.0, 16.0, 24.2
azimuth, 21.6.3

B

back-to-school night, 26.1
Bacon, Francis, 7.0, 19.2
bacteria, 9.2.1
Banting, Frederick, 5.8.2
bar graph, 20.0, 20.5
baryons, 19.5.1
basic solutions, 18.0, 26.4
batteries, 10.1.1
Bell, Jocelyn, 5.8.2
Benchmarks for Scientific Literacy, 24.3
beriberi, 5.8.1
Bingo, 13.3, 25.4
binomial nomenclature, 10.4.1
biochemistry, 8.4.1, 9.2.2, 10.4
Biological Sciences Curriculum Study (BSCS), 24.3
biology vocabulary, 1.1
biomes, 8.3, 8.3.1, 8.3.2, 8.3.3, 20.6.1
biomolecules, 9.1.1
biosphere, 8.3, 8.3.1, 8.3.2, 8.3.3, 8.6
black box experiments, 5.4.2, 5.9.1, 5.9.2
blood, 12.0, 20.5.5
blood types, 20.5.5
Bloom, Benjamin, 6.0
Bloom's taxonomy, 6.0
bodily kinesthetic intelligence, 24.2
body, composition of, 20.5.4
boiling point, 20.4.2
bonding, 9.2.2, 10.3
bones, 12.2.2, 12.5.4
brainstorming, 5.4, 5.4.1
bridge building, 12.5.1
bridges (hashiwokakero), 13.9.3
budgeting, 23.3.1
buoyancy, 5.3.2
buoyant force, 5.3.2

C

cancer, 16.4.3
candle, observations, of, 5.2.1, 5.2.2
Canter, Lee, 25.5

capacitance, 3.5, 10.1.1, 17.3, 17.5.1, 17.17, 27.2
carbon, 12.4
carbon dioxide, 20.3
cardiovascular disease, 19.3.2
Carothers, Wallace, 5.8.2
Carver, George Washington, 24.1
cash, petty, 26.1
Cassini, Giovanni, 16.4
categorical variables, 5.0
cations, 18.3
causal research questions, 23.1
celebrations, science, 24.8
celestial equator, 15.7.1
cell cycle, 6.2.3
cells, 8.3, 8.3.1, 8.3.2, 8.3.3, 10.1.3, 12.5.5, 16.3.1
Celsius, 17.2.1
Centers for Disease Control (CDC), 20.6.1
CGS system, 17.0, 17.4
chain reaction, 10.3
Chem Study, 24.3
chemical reactions (*see* reactions)
chemical weathering, 18.0
chemicals, 26.3
chemistry vocabulary, 1.2
Chernobyl, 21.5.1
chlorofluorocarbons (CFCs), 8.6.1
Christmas Lectures, Faraday's, 5.2
chromatography, 14.3
chromosome, 10.1.3
chunking, 11.0, 11.2, 11.2.1, 11.2.5
cilia, 16.5.1
circle, 15.7, 15.7.1
circulation, 10.4.1, 12.0
citations, 3.4, 22.6
classification, 1.1.3, 16.3.2, 19.2.5
climate, 20.7.1
climate change, 20.1.4, 20.3
climographs, 20.7.2
closed captioning, 16.5.4, 24.7
closure, 25.2
clouds, 9.2.4
cloze, 2.1
clustered bar graph, 20.5, 20.5.5
code breaker (Mastermind), 13.9, 13.9.1
codons, 19.2.2
cognates, 2.3, 2.4, 24.7
cognitive science, 11.0
cohesion, 12.4.2
cold fusion, 3.0
College Bowl, 13.5.1
Columbus, Christopher, 5.8.1
column graph, 20.5, 20.5.1
combination graph, 20.7
combustion, 16.5.2

combustion reaction, 18.3
comets, 8.6.1, 9.1.3, 16.3.1
comics, science, 24.8
communicable diseases, 6.3.3
communicating findings, 3.2, 3.4, 3.5
communities, 8.3, 8.3.1, 8.3.2, 8.3.3
composition reactions, 9.2.2
compounds, 19.1
comprehension (learning objectives), 6.1, 25.1
computed tomography (CT), 16.0, 16.4.3, 16.4.4
computer modeling, 20.1
concentration, 3.5, 17.3, 17.17, 27.2
concept maps, 2.0, 9.5, 9.5.1, 9.5.2, 9.5.3, 9.5.4
conceptual diagram, 20.0
conceptual grid, 9.1, 9.1.1, 9.1.2, 9.1.3, 9.1.4
conceptual physics, 24.4
conductor, 10.1.1
Conference of Weights and Measures, 3.5
conic sections, 15.7, 15.7.1
consensus building, 5.4.1
conservation of angular momentum, 18.0
conservation of energy, 18.0
conservation of mass, 18.0, 18.3
conservation of momentum, 16.3.3, 18.0
constants, 5.0, 5.5, 5.5.1, 5.6.1, 5.8.1, 27.2, 27.3
constellations, 11.4.3, 21.6.1, 21.6.2
constructivism, 24.2
contour maps, 20.0, 21.2
contributions, 26.1
controls, 5.0, 5.5, 5.5.1, 5.6.1, 5.8.1, 6.3.3, 23.1
convection, 10.5
conversion factors, 27.2, 27.4, 27.5
conversions, 17.4, 17.5, 17.7, 20.2
cooperative learning, 24.7
Coriolis effect, 7.7.1
Cornell notes, 2.0, 3.1
Coulomb's law, 6.3.2, 10.0, 10.2
Coulomb's law of electrostatics, 14.3
counterintuitive event, 5.4.2
creativity, 6.0
Crick, Francis, 5.8.2
critical thinking, 6.0, 7.1, 7.2, 7.3
crystal formation, 16.5.1, 16.5.2
cubes, 15.4.1
Curie, Marie, 24.1
current, 10.1.1
current events, 3.2
curriculum, 8.3, 8.4, 8.5, 8.6, 24.3
curriculum, biology, 8.3

curriculum, chemistry, 8.4, 8.6
curriculum, physics, 8.5
cytoplasmic streaming, 16.5.1

D

data analysis, 20.0
data comparison table, 7.0
data interpretation, 19.1, 19.2, 19.3, 19.4, 19.5, 22.2
data series, 20.0
database categories, 19.3.2
database commands, 19.0
database filters, 19.3
database formulas, 20.0
database record selection, 19.3.2
database reports, 19.0
database software, 19.0
database sort, 19.3.4
database subtotal, 19.4.3
databases, 19.1, 19.2, 19.3, 19.4, 19.5
death, causes of, 6.3.3, 20.4.2, 20.6.1
debates and forums, 22.4
deBono, Edward, 6.4.1
decision chart, 20.0
decision-making matrix, 7.3, 7.3.1, 7.3.2
decomposition reactions, 9.2.2
deduction, 6.3.1, 6.3.2, 6.3.3, 13.1, 13.2, 13.3, 13.4, 13.5, 13.6, 13.7, 13.8, 13.9, 18.3.1
deductive reasoning, 6.0, 6.3, 6.3.1
defense of position, 5.4.1
deforestation, 8.6.1
demographic map, 20.0
density, 3.5, 5.3.2, 14.2.3, 14.3, 17.3, 17.7, 17.17, 27.2
dependent variable, 5.0, 5.5, 5.5.1, 5.6.1, 5.8.1, 15.6.3, 20.3.3, 23.1, 23.2
derived units, 3.5, 17.2, 17.3, 17.5, 17.17, 27.2
descriptive statistics, 20.8.1
development, 16.3.1
diabetes, 19.2.3
diagrams, 13.7.2, 16.2.2, 21.1
dichotomous key, 13.8, 13.8.1
dicots, 7.1, 9.1.1
dieting and weight loss, 19.3, 19.3.3
diffusion, 4.3, 10.3
digit span, 11.2
dihydrogen monoxide (DHMO), 24.8
dilutions, 26.4
dimensional analysis, 17.1, 17.2, 17.3, 17.4, 17.5, 17.6, 17.7
dimensions (*see* units)
direct current (DC), 9.1.4
direct measurement, 15.2.1
directions, writing, 21.3
discipline, 25.5

discovery learning, 24.2
discrepant events, 5.1, 5.1.1, 5.1.2, 5.1.3, 5.4.2, 11.0
diseases, communicable, 6.3.3
disposal, chemical, 26.8
distance, 3.5, 17.3, 17.17, 27.2
distribution map, 20.0
DNA, 5.8.2, 7.6.1, 10.0, 10.1.3, 10.4
donations, 26.1
Doppler effect, 10.2
double replacement reaction, 18.3

E

Earth Science Curriculum Project (ESCP), 24.3
Earth science vocabulary, 1.4
Earth systems interactions, 8.6, 8.6.1
Earth, circumference, 15.3
Earth's crust, 20.5.4
earthquakes, 6.2.4, 6.3.3, 16.3.1, 21.3.2
ecological transects, 21.2.3
ecology, 2.4
ecosystems, 8.3, 8.3.1, 8.3.2, 8.3.3
Edison, Thomas, 5.8.1, 5.10.1, 21.1, 24.1
educational objectives, 6.1.5
egg drop, 12.5.2
Eijkman, Christiaan, 5.8.1
Einstein, Albert, 15.6, 24.1
elaboration, 6.0
electric charge, 3.5, 17.3, 17.17, 27.2
electric circuits, 10.1.1
electric current, 3.5, 17.3, 17.17, 27.2
electric field, 15.6
electric field intensity, 3.5, 17.3, 17.17, 27.2
electric resistance, 3.5, 17.3, 17.17, 27.2
electric switches, 19.1.1
electrical ground, 10.1.1
electricity, 8.5, 10.1.1
electrocardiogram, 16.3.1
electrolysis, 18.0
electromagnetic waves, 10.2
electromagnetism, 5.8.2, 9.1.4, 9.2.3
electron, 5.8.2, 5.9.2
electron affinity, 20.4.2
electron configuration, 6.1.3
electron energy diagram, 10.1.2
electron orbitals, 11.4.2
electron transport chain, 10.4.1
electronegativity, 9.1.2
electronic circuits, 19.1.1
electronic presentations, 16.5.5
electrons, 10.1.2
electrophoresis, 10.4
electrostatic attraction, 6.3.2, 17.6.1
element abundance, 19.1.2

element formation, 18.0
element names, 1.2
element symbols, 19.1.2
elements, 19.1, 27.3
elevation profiles, 21.2.4, 21.2.5
ellipse, 15.7, 15.7.1
emf, 3.5, 17.3, 17.17, 27.2
Endangered Species Act, 20.5.3
endoplasmic reticulum, 10.1.3
energy, 3.5, 7.3.1, 7.4.1, 14.3, 17.3, 17.5.1, 17.17, 20.6.1, 27.2
energy, alternative, 7.3.1
energy, kinetic, 7.4.1
energy, sources of, 20.6.1
engineering, 12.1, 12.1.1, 12.1.2, 12.5.1, 12.5.2, 12.5.7
English learners, strategies for, 2.0, 2.3, 2.4, 3.0, 24.7
enthalpy, 14.2.3
entropy, 10.3, 14.2.3
environmental issues, 7.3.2
environmental maps, 21.5
Environmental Protection Agency (EPA), 21.5, 26.7
enzyme, 10.4, 12.4.1
epicenter, 6.3.3
epidemiology, 6.3.3
equation balancing, 18.1, 18.2, 18.3
equations, 17.5.1
equilibrium constant, 14.3
equipment, science, 26.1
Eratosthenes, 15.3
essay writing, 3.3, 3.3.1, 3.3.2, 3.4.2, 3.4.3
evaluating claims, 7.2.1, 7.2.2, 7.2.3
evaluating hypotheses, 5.10
evaluation (learning objectives), 5.4.1, 5.10, 6.1, 7.0, 7.1.2, 7.2, 25.1
evaluation, teacher, 25.7
evidence, 7.0
Excel, Microsoft, 19, 20
expanding universe, 10.5.1
experiential learning, 24.2
experimental design, 5.5, 5.8.1
experimental procedures, 5.7
experimental research questions, 23.1
expert learners, 6.0
exponential notation, 8.2.1, 8.2.2
extrapolation, 13.7.2, 16.6
eye, 10.4.1

F

factor label method (*see* dimensional analysis)
Fahrenheit, 17.2.1
families, chemical, 9.1.2, 9.1.3, 9.2.2
Faraday, 5.2, 19.5.2
fats, 19.3.2

faults, 9.2.4, 16.3.1
Feldman, David, 24.8
Fermi, Enrico, 24.1
fertilization, 16.5.1
field trips, 24.10
filter, 19.0
fire, 8.6
fire extinguishers, 26.7
first law of thermodynamics, 18.0
fission, 9.1.2, 10.3, 18.0
Flavel, John, 24.2
Fleming, Alexander, 5.1
flexibility, 6.0
flowcharts, 9.3, 20.0
flowers, 12.3, 12.3.1
fluency, 6.0
fluid mechanics and thermal physics, 8.5
focal length, 16.2.1
Food and Drug Administration (FDA), 17.1
force, 3.5, 9.1.4, 14.2.3, 17.3, 17.6.1, 17.7, 17.17, 27.2
force vectors, 16.1.1
form and function, 12.1
formative assessment, 25.6
forums and debates, 22.4
fossil fuels, 8.6.1
frame of reference, 7.7.1
free fall, 15.6.4
freezing, 12.4.2
French/English cognates, 2.4
frequency, 3.5, 17.3, 17.17, 27.2
frequency table, 20.0
friction, 14.2.3, 16.1
fruits, 12.2.3
functions, 20.8.2
fundamental particles, 8.3, 8.3.1, 8.3.2, 8.3.3
fundamental units, 3.5, 17.2, 17.3, 17.5, 17.17, 27.2
funds, year-end, 26.1
Funk, Casimir, 5.8.1
fusion, 9.1.2, 10.3, 18.0

G

galaxies, 5.8.2, 10.5.1
Galileo Galilei, 6.1.1, 24.1
games, 13.0, 13.1, 13.2, 13.3, 13.4, 13.5, 13.6, 13.7, 13.8
Gardner, Howard, 24.2
gas exchange, 12.0
gas laws, 10.5, 14.1, 14.3
gene maps, 19.2.3
generalization, 13.7.2
generation effect, 11.0
genetic disorders, 19.2.3
genome (*see* Human Genome Project)

genotype, 6.1.2
genre, science, 3.4
geological eras, 11.4.3
geological map, 20.0
geological transects, 21.2.3
geometrical principles, 15.1, 15.2, 15.3, 15.4, 15.5, 15.6, 15.7
German/English cognates, 2.4
germination, 16.5.2, 20.6.2
germs, 5.8.1
getting to know your students, 25.4
Gibbs free energy, 14.2.3
global positioning system (GPS), 15.1, 21.3, 21.7
global warming, 20.1.4, 20.3
glossary, 1.1.2, 1.2.2, 1.3.4, 1.4.2
Goddard, Robert, 24.1
Golgi apparatus, 10.1.3
granite, 10.1.4, 16.3.3
grants, 26.1, 26.2
graph paper, 27.4
graphic information system (GIS), 21.3
graphic organizers, 24.7
graphing, 5.5, 5.5.1, 6.2.1
graphing stories, 20.3
graphs, 20.0
grasslands, 9.2.1
gravity, 7.7.1, 9.1.4, 9.2.3, 10.0, 15.4, 15.6, 15.6.4, 17.6.1
Great Red Spot, 16.4.
greenhouse effect, 7.7.1, 20.1.4, 20.3
greenhouse gases, 20.1.4, 20.3
group projects, 24.7
growth rate, 20.7.3
guest speakers, 24.10
guide questions, 2.0
guided practice, 25.2

H

half-reactions, 18.0
hands-on science, 24.7
hardness, 11.4.3
Harvard Committee of Ten, 24.3
hashiwokakero (bridges), 13.9.3
hazard symbols, 26.7
hazardous waste, 21.5.3
hazards, chemical, 26.7
health hazards, 26.7
heartbeat, 16.5.1
heat, 3.5, 7.5.1, 14.3, 15.4.1, 15.5.3, 17.3, 17.17, 27.2
heat loss, 15.5.3
heat transfer, 15.5.3, 9.1.4
hemoglobin, 12.0
Henry, William, 5.3.2
Henry's law, 5.3.2
Hertzprung-Russell diagram, 20.4.1

heuristics, 17.7
higher-order reasoning, 6.0, 6.1, 24.2
high-low graphs, 20.7
Hippocrates, 5.8.1
histogram, 20.0
history and science, 5.8
HIV/AIDS, 6.3.3
hoaxes, 16.4.6
homeostasis, 10.4
honors science, 24.4
How People Learn, 24.2
Hubble Space Telescope, 21.6.3
Hubble, Edwin, 5.8.2, 24.1
Human Genome Project, 19.2.3, 21.0
humor, science, 24.8
Hunter, Madeline, 25.6
hurricane tracking, 21.4.3
hurricanes, 9.1.3, 21.4.3
Huygens, Christian, 20.8.2
hydrogen bonding, 12.4.2
hydrosphere, 8.6
hyperbola, 15.7, 15.7.1
hypothesis, 4.3.1, 5.4, 5.4.2, 5.8.1, 5.10.1, 23.1, 23.2
hypothyroidism, 19.2.3

I

icebreakers, 25.4
igneous, 9.1.3, 9.2.4, 10.1.4, 10.5
illumination, 3.5, 15.6, 15.6.1, 15.6.3, 16.2.2, 17.3, 17.17, 27.2
immune system, 10.4.1, 15.6.4
immunotherapy, 15.6.4
imponderable questions, 24.8
impulse, 12.5.2, 14.3, 17.5.1
independent variable, 5.0, 5.5, 5.5.1, 5.6, 5.6.1, 5.8.1, 15.6.3, 20.3.3, 23.1, 23.2
indirect evidence, 5.9, 5.9.1, 5.9.2
indirect measurement, 15.2.1, 15.2.2, 15.2.3
inductance, 3.5, 17.3, 17.17, 27.2
inductive reasoning, 6.0, 6.2.1, 6.2.2, 6.2.3, 6.2.4
inertia, 9.2.3
inference, 5.3, 5.3.1, 5.3.2, 6.2.3, 6.3.1, 13.1, 13.2, 13.3, 13.4, 13.5, 13.6, 13.7, 13.8, 13.9, 16.4.2, 16.4.3
Information Age, 19.0, 20.0, 20.6.2
inorganic chemistry, 8.4.1
inquiry, 22.0, 22.1, 24.6
insight, 6.4.1
instructions, 5.7.1, 5.7.2, 21.2
insulin, 5.8.2, 19.2.4
integrated science, 24.3, 24.4
intelligence, 12.5, 24.2
intelligence quotient (IQ), 24.2
International Baccalaureate (IB), 24.4, 24.5

International Space Station, 15.7.1, 21.6.3
International Union of Pure and Applied Chemists (IUPAC), 17.3
Internet, 16.7
interpersonal intelligence, 24.2
interpersonal strategies, 24.7
interpreting graphs, 5.5.1
interpretive centers, 24.10
interviews, 25.6
intrapersonal intelligence, 24.2
inventions, 9.5.3, 19.5.2
inverse square law, 15.6
ionic compounds, 18.2.2
ionization energy, 6.1.3, 20.4.2
ionization potential, 9.1.2, 19.1.2
ions, 18.1, 18.1.1, 27.3
isotopes, 5.8.2, 20.7.3
Italian/English cognates, 2.4

J

jigsaw, 2.1
Jones, Fred, 25.5
Joule, James, 21.4.2
journaling, 3.2, 3.2.1, 3.4.5, 24.7
journals, 3.2, 3.4.5
journals, professional, 27.9
journals, science, 23.4
Journey North, 21.0

K

kakuro (cross sums), 13.9
Kelvin, 17.2.1
Kepler, Johannes, 21.4.2
kinesthetic learning, 11.0, 16.0, 24.2
kinetic energy, 14.3, 16.3.3
knowledge (learning objectives), 6.1, 25.1
Krebs cycle, 11.4.1
KWL, 2.0, 8.0

L

lab reports, 3.4.1
laboratory, science, 22.5, 26.1–26.9
languages, common, 2.4.1
languages, uncommon, 2.4.2
lateral thinking, 6.0, 6.4, 6.4.1
latitude, 21.6.2
law of lenses, 14.2.3
Le Four Solaire at Font-Romeur, 15.7.1
Le Systéme International des Unités (*see* SI)
learning, 6.0
learning modalities, 24.2
learning objectives, 25.1
learning plan, 6.0
learning strategies, 6.0
length, 17.3.1, 17.7

leptons, 19.5.1
lesson plans, 25.2
Lesson Study, 24.9
levels of organization, 8.3, 8.3.1,
    8.3.2, 8.3.3
levers, 9.2.3
lexicon, 24.7
library research, 3.4.4
life expectancy, 20.4.2
light intensity, 15.6, 15.6.1, 15.6.3
Lind, James, 5.8.1
line graph, 20.0, 20.4
line method, 17.6, 17.6.1
lingua franca, 1.0
linguistic/language intelligence, 24.2
liquid pressure, 5.4.2
listening strategies, 24.7
lithosphere, 8.6
log plot, 20.7
logarithmic paper, 27.4
logic, 7.0, 7.1, 7.2, 7.3, 7.4, 7.5, 7.6, 7.7
logic games, 13.9, 13.9.1, 13.9.2, 13.9.3,
    13.9.4, 13.9.5
logical/mathematical intelligence, 24.2
longitudinal studies, 3.2
lost on the moon, 5.4.1
luminous intensity, 3.5, 17.3, 17.17, 27.2

M

macromolecules, 8.3, 8.3.1, 8.3.2, 8.3.3
magnetic flux, 3.5, 17.3, 17.17, 27.2
magnetic resonance imaging
    (MRI), 16.4.4
magnetism, 8.5, 15.6, 15.6.2, 16.3.1
magnetometer, 15.6.2
maintenance rehearsal, 11.0
management, classroom, 25.5
map, construction of, 21.1, 21.2
mapping, 6.2.4, 21.3, 21.5
Marconi, 19.5.2
Mars, 21.7.2
Mars Climate Orbiter, 17.1
Mars Global Surveyor, 5.7, 21.7.2
Mars Pathfinder, 17.7
mass, 3.5, 17.3, 17.3.1, 17.7, 17.17, 27.2
Mastermind (code breaker), 13.9, 13.9.1
material safety data sheets
    (MSDS), 26.7
math phobia, 14.0
mathematics translation, 14.1, 14.2,
    14.3, 24.7
Maxwell, James Clerk, 15.6
measurement, 8.2.1, 8.2.2, 15.0, 15.1.1
measurement scales, 15.1.1
medical images, 16.4.3
medication, 17.1.1, 17.6.1, 17.7
melting point, 6.1.3

membranes, 10.1.3, 10.4
memory, long term, 11.0
memory, sensory, 11.0
memory, short term, 11.0, 11.2
Mendel, Gregor, 6.1.2
Mendeleev, Dmitri, 6.2.2, 19.1.3
mesons, 19.5.1
metacognition, 6.0, 9.1, 9.2, 9.3, 9.4,
    9.5, 24.2
metals, 9.1.2
metamorphic rocks, 9.1.3, 9.2.4
metamorphosis, 16.3.3
meteors, 19.4.2
metric system, 11.4.2, 27.2
micrographs, 16.0, 16.4.3
micromolecules, 8.3, 8.3.1, 8.3.2, 8.3.3
microscopy, 13.7, 16.6
migration, 21.0, 21.3
mind maps, 2.0, 9.4, 9.4.1, 9.4.2, 9.4.3
mineral composition, 20.5.4
Minkowski, Hermann, 15.0
misconceptions, 3.2, 7.0, 7.4, 7.5, 7.6,
    7.7, 16.4.5
misconceptions, biology, 7.6, 7.6.1
misconceptions, chemistry, 7.5, 7.5.1
misconceptions, earth and space science,
    7.7, 7.7.1
misconceptions, physics, 7.4, 7.4.1
misnomers, 7.6.1
mitochondria, 10.0, 10.1.3
mitosis, 11.4.1
MKS system, 17.0, 17.4
model building, 12.5
models, 12.5.5, 12.5.6, 12.5.7
modern physics, 8.5
Mole Day, 24.8
molecular assemblies, 8.3, 8.3.1,
    8.3.2, 8.3.3
molecules, 11.4.2, 12.4, 12.4.1
momentum, 9.2.3, 14.3
monarch butterflies, 21.3
monocots, 7.1, 9.1.1
Moon, 11.4.3, 15.2.2, 15.7.1, 16.2.2,
    16.4.1, 16.4.5, 16.5.2
motion, 20.8.2
movies (*see* video)
multimedia, 16.5.5
multiple intelligences, 24.2
multiple modalities, 11.0
muscles, 11.4.1, 12.0, 12.2.1
musical intelligence, 24.2
mysterious bottle activity, 5.4.2

N

names, learning students', 25.4
Nation at Risk report, 24.3
National Academy of Science, 2.0

National Assessment of Educational
    Progress (NAEP), 24.3
National Association for Research in
    Science Teaching (NARST), 24.9
National Association of Biology
    Teachers (NABT), 24.9
National Association of Geoscience
    Teachers (NAGT), 24.9
National Board Certification, 24.9
National Center for Biotechnology
    Information (NCBI), 19.2.3
National Defense Education Act, 24.3
National Earth Science Teachers
    Association, 24.9
National Oceanic and Atmospheric
    Administration (NOAA), 20.3, 21.4.3
National Science Education Standards
    (NSES), 22.0
National Science Education Standards
    Project, 24.3
National Science Foundation
    (NSF), 24.3
National Science Teachers Association
    (NSTA), 24.1, 24.6, 24.9
natural disasters, 19.4.3
naturalist intelligence, 24.2
nature of science, 24.1
nerves, 11.4.1
newsgroups, 25.6
Newton, Isaac, 5.8, 15.0, 21.4.2
Newton's law of gravitation, 10.0,
    10.2, 14.3
Newton's law of interaction, 16.5.1
Newtonian mechanics, 8.5
NFPA hazard codes, 26.7
Niépce, Nicéphore, 16.4
nitrogen fixation, 18.0
No Child Left Behind Act, 24.3
Nobel prize, 5.2, 5.8.1
nomograph, 20.0
note taking, 2.0, 3.1
notebooks (*see* science notebooks)
novice learners, 6.0
nuclear chemistry, 8.4.1
nuclear magnetic resonance imaging,
    (NMR), 19.1
nuclear winter, 9.5.1
nucleus, 5.9.2
nutrients, 11.4.1
nutrition, 17.1.1
nutritional analysis, 19.3.5
nylon, 5.8.2

O

objectives, 25.2
observation, 3.2, 5.2, 5.3.1, 5.3.2,
    5.6.1, 5.8.1

Occupational Safety and Health
   Administration (OSHA), 26.7
ocean composition, 20.5.4
octane rating, 18.3
octet, 18.1, 18.1.2,
oncology, 16.4.3
open essay, 3.4.2
open house, 26.1
optical density, 10.2.1
optics, 16.2.1
orbit, 15.7.1
orbitals, 18.1.2
order of magnitude, 8.2, 8.2.2
organelles, 10.1.3
organic chemicals, 7.5.1, 8.4.1
organic chemistry, 9.2.2
organizational hierarchy, 8.3, 8.4, 8.5, 8.6
organizations (*see* professional
   organizations)
organ systems, 8.3, 8.3.1, 8.3.2, 8.3.3
organs, 8.3, 8.3.1, 8.3.2, 8.3.3
originality, 6.0
Ørsted, Hans Christian, 5.8.2, 15.6
Osheroff, Douglas, 5.2
osmosis, 16.3.1
osteoporosis, 19.3.1
oxidation, 11.4.2, 18.0
oxidation states, 18.1, 18.1.1, 18.1.2, 27.3
oxidizers, 26.7
oxygen, 12.0, 15.4, 18.0, 18.3

P

Papert, Seymour, 24.2
parabola, 15.7, 15.7.1
Pareto graph, 20.0, 20.5.3, 20.5
partner learners, 24.7
Pasteur, Louis, 5.8.1, 21.4.2
pathogens, 6.3.3
Pauli exclusion principle, 10.1.2
pedagogical content knowledge,
   24.2, 24.9
peer review, 3.0
peer teaching, 2.2.1
pendulum, 6.2.1, 14.3, 20.8.2
perception, 5.1.3
performance, teacher, 25.7
periodic properties, 6.1.3, 6.3.2, 20.4.2
periodic table, 1.2, 6.2.2, 9.1.2, 19.1.3,
   20.4.2, 27.3
phagocytosis, 16.5.1
phase change, 12.4.2
phases of matter, 10.3.1
phenotype, 6.1.2
phonemes, 11.2.5
photography, 16.4, 16.5, 16.5.2, 21.7
photography, aerial, 21.7
photon energy, 14.3

photons, 14.2.3
photosynthesis, 7.6.1, 9.2.1, 16.2.2,
   16.5.2, 17.7, 18.0
physical chemistry, 8.4.1, 9.2.2
physical laws, 17.5
Physical Science Study Committee
   (PSSC), 24.3
physics databases, 19.5
physics vocabulary, 1.3
Pictionary, 13.4
pictorial guide, 24.7
pictorial riddles, 16.3, 16.3.1
picture glossary, 24.7
pie chart, 20.0, 20.6
planets, 9.1.3, 10.5, 11.4.3, 15.6.3,
   16.4, 19.4.1
planisphere, 21.6.2
plankton, 15.4
planning investigations, 5.5, 5.6, 5.7
plant distribution, 19.2.5
plants database, 19.2.5
plate tectonics, 6.2.4
polar graph paper, 27.4
Polaris (North Star), 16.2.2, 16.5.2, 21.6
polio vaccine, 5.8.2
pollination, 12.3, 12.3.1
pollution, 7.3.2, 18.0
polyatomic ions, 18.2, 18.2.1
population growth rate, 14.3
population profiles, 20.5.1
populations, 8.3, 8.3.1, 8.3.2, 8.3.3
positron emission tomography (PET)
   scans, 16.0, 16.4.3, 16.4.4
potential difference, 3.5, 17.3, 17.17, 27.2
potential energy, 14.3
power, 3.5, 14.3, 17.5.1, 17.3, 17.7, 27.2
PowerPoint, 16.5.5
powers of ten, 8.2
preconceptions, 7.0
predator-prey interactions, 20.5.1
predators, 8.6.1, 20.5.1
predictions, 6.2, 6.3
prefixes, 1.1, 1.2, 1.3, 1.4
premises, 6.3, 6.3.1, 6.3.2, 6.3.3
pressure, 3.5, 5.1.2, 5.4.2, 7.5.1, 14.2.3,
   17.5.1, 17.3, 17.7, 17.17, 21.4.2,
   27.2, 27.3
primacy effect, 3.3, 11.1
primary rehearsal, 11.0
primary structure, 12.4.1
prior knowledge, 3.2
probeware, 22.2
problem-based learning (PBL),
   22.3, 24.2
procedural diagram, 20.0
procedures, 5.7, 5.7.1, 5.7.2
productivity, 20.6.1

products, 18.2
profession, 24.9
professional development, 24.9
professional organizations, 24.9, 24.10
profiles, elevation, 21.2.4, 21.2.5
Programme for International Student
   Assessment, 2.0
Project 2061, 24.3
proportional chart, 20.0
proposals (*see* grants)
protein data bank, 19.2.4
proteins, 11.4.1, 12.4.1, 19.2.2, 19.2.4
protozoans, 9.2.1
protractors, 27.4
pseudoscientists, 15.6.4
PSSC Physics, 24.3
pulsars, 5.8.2, 10.5.1
puns, science, 24.8
p-waves, 6.3.3

Q

qualitative studies, 23.1
qualitative variables, 20.5.4
quality control, 16.3.2
quantitative studies, 23.1
quantum number, 10.1.2
quarks, 19.5.1
quasars, 10.2.1
quaternary structure, 12.4.4
questionnaires, student, 25.4
questions, 6.1.5, 7.0, 13.1, 13.2, 13.3,
   13.4, 13.5, 13.6, 13.7, 13.8, 13.9
quick-writes, 25.6
quotes, 24.1

R

radio telescopes, 15.6.4
radioactive decay, 20.7.3
radioactivity, 21.5.1
rain shadow, 16.3.3
raisin buoyancy, 5.3.2
ranking chart, 20.0
rapport, establishing, 25.5
rare and endangered species, 20.4.2, 20.5.3
ratios, 15.1.1, 15.2, 15.2.2, 15.2.3, 15.2.4,
   15.3, 15.3.1, 15.4
ray diagrams, 16.2.1
reactants, 18.2
reactions, 5.1.1, 9.2.2, 10.3.1, 18.0
reading comprehension, 2.1, 2.2
reading, strategic, 2.0
reasoning, 6.0, 6.1, 6.2, 6.3, 24.2
reasoning, higher-order, 24.2
recency effect, 3.3, 11.1
rechargeable batteries, 20.5.2
records, finding and sorting, 19.0
red shift, 10.2

redox reactions, 18.0
reduction, 11.4.2
reduction potentials, 27.3
redwood, 19.2.5
reference table, 20.0
references, 3.4, 3.4.5
reflection, 10.2
relativity, 14.3
relevance of science, 4.0, 4.2, 4.3, 4.4
relief map, 20.0
replacement reactions, 9.2.2
research, laboratory, 5.10.1
research, library, 3.3.4
research, log, 23.3.2
research, poster, 23.4.2
research, proposal, 23.2
research, questions, 5.0, 5.2, 5.3, 5.8.1,
    23.1, 23.2
research, report, 23.4.1
research, subjects, 23.1
resistance, 10.1.1
resistors, 11.4.2
resonance, 6.3.1
respect, establishing, 25.5
respiration, 18.0
results, 3.4.5
retention factor, 14.3
retinal fatigue, 5.1.3
retrieval practice, 11.0
retrograde motion, 10.5
reversible reactions, 5.1.1
review sessions, 13.0
Rising Above the Gathering Storm, 24.3
RNA, 9.1.1, 10.1.3, 10.4
road map to science, 24.7
robotics, 12.5.7
rockets, 12.5.3, 16.5.1
rocks, 9.1.3, 9.2.4, 10.5, 10.5.1
Roentgen, Wilhelm, 16.4.4
root words, 1.1, 1.2, 1.3, 1.4
rotating labs, 22.5
Royal Society, 5.2
rulers, 27.4
running, 20.3.2, 21.2.4
Rutherford, Ernest, 5.9.2

S

safety agreement, 26.5
safety, equipment checklist, 26.6
safety, lab, 26.5, 26.6
Salk, Jonas, 5.8.2
satellite photography, 21.7
satellites, 20.6.2, 21.6.3, 21.7.2
scaling, 15.5, 15.5.1
scatter plot, 20.0, 20.4, 20.4.1
School Science and Mathematics
    Association (SSMA), 24.9

Schulman, Lee, 24.2
Science Baseball, 13.6
Science Bowl, 13.5
science content standards, 24.3
science curriculum, 24.3, 24.4, 24.5
science fairs, 23.1, 23.2, 23.3, 23.4, 23.5
Science for All Americans, 24.3
science humor, 24.8
science inquiry, 24.6
Science Jeopardy, 13.1
science journaling (*see* journaling)
science literacy, 2.0
science notebooks, 3.2, 3.2.1, 23.3.2
science projects, 23.1, 23.2, 23.3,
    23.4, 23.5
science research, 23.1, 23.2, 23.3, 23.4, 23.5
Science Talent Search, 23.0
science writing style, 3.5
Science, Technology, Society (STS), 4.0,
    4.1, 4.2, 4.3, 4.4, 19.5.2
scientific journal, 3.4.5
scientific literacy, 22.0
scientific method, 5.8, 5.8.1
scientific notation, 8.2.1
scientific writing, 3.5
*Scope, Sequence, and Coordination
    Report* (SS&C), 24.3
scurvy, 5.8.1
seawater, 20.5.3
secondary structure, 12.4.2
sedimentary rocks, 9.1.3, 9.2.4, 10.5
seed dispersal, 12.2.3
seeds, 12.2.3
seismic patterns, 6.2.4
seismology, 21.3.2
semantic depth, 11.0
semantic maps, 2.0, 9.4
semester plan, 25.3
semilog plots, 20.7.3, 27.4
semilogarithmic paper, 27.4
sensor, 22.2
shadows, 16.4.5
sharks, 21.3.3
SI (International System), 3.5, 5.7,
    17.0, 17.2, 17.4, 27.1
SI units (*see* SI)
significance of science, 4.0, 4.1
siphon, 5.4.2
size, animals, 15.5, 15.5.1, 15.5.2
skeletal system, 12.2.2, 12.5.4
Sloan Digital Sky Survey, 21.0
smog, 20.4, 21.5.2
snow crystals, 16.3.3
solar system, 19.4.1
solubility, 15.5.3
solutions, preparing, 26.4
solvent, 12.4.2

songs, science, 24.8
sonography, 16.4.4
sound, 15.7.1
sound intensity, 14.3, 15.6, 15.6.2
sound waves, 10.2.1
space science vocabulary, 1.4
space shuttle, 16.3.2, 16.4.1, 17.7
space-time, 10.5.1
Spanish/English cognates, 2.4
species diversity, 19.2.1
specific heat, 12.4.2
spectrum, 11.4.2
speed, 17.7
spheres, 15.4.1
spoofs, science, 24.8
spreadsheet calculations, 20.1
spreadsheets, 20.0, 20.1, 20.2, 20.3, 20.4,
    20.5, 20.6, 20.7, 20.8
Sputnik, 21.6.3
SQ3R, 2.0, 8.0
stacked column graph, 20.5.2
standard units, 3.5
standing waves, 6.3.1
star maps, 21.6
stars, 9.2.4, 16.2.2, 16.3.1, 21.6
statistics, 20.8
stoichiometry, 18.1, 18.2, 18.3
storage codes, 26.7
storage, chemical, 26.7
strategic reading, 2.0
strong nuclear force, 9.1.4, 9.2.3
structure and function, 12.1.1, 12.1.2,
    12.2, 12.3, 12.3.1, 12.3.2, 12.4
subatomic particles, 8.3, 8.3.1, 8.3.2,
    8.3.3, 19.5.1
sudoku puzzle, 7.1.2, 13.9
suffixes, 1.1, 1.2, 1.3, 1.4
summative assessment, 25.6
Sun, 16.2.2, 17.7, 20.4.1
sunspots, 20.4.1
surface-area-to-volume ratio, 14.3, 15.4,
    15.4.1, 15.5, 15.5.1, 15.5.2, 15.5.3
surface tension, 12.4.2
s-waves, 6.3.3
syllabus, 25.5
synthesis (learning objectives), 6.1, 25.1

T

taboo, 13.2
tangrams, 5.10.1
target concept, 10.0, 10.1.1, 10.1.2,
    10.1.3, 10.1.4, 10.1.5
taxonomic key, 13.8.2
taxonomy, 1.1.3, 9.3.1, 11.4.1, 13.8.2,
    19.2.5
teamwork, 5.10.1, 13.1, 13.2, 13.3, 13.4,
    13.5, 13.6, 13.7, 13.8, 13.9

television, 16.5.4
temperature, 3.5, 7.5.1, 17.3, 17.17, 27.2
terminology, 11.2, 11.2.3, 11.2.4,
    11.2.5, 12.0
tertiary structure, 12.4.3
Tesla, Nikola, 21.4.2
textbooks, 2.0
think-aloud strategy, 24.6
think-pair-share, 24.7, 25.6
Thompson, J. J., 5.8.2, 5.9.2
time, 3.5, 17.3, 17.17, 27.2
time-lapse photography, 16.5, 16.5.2
time line, 19.5.2
time table, 20.0
tissues, 8.3, 8.3.1, 8.3.2, 8.3.3, 9.2.1
titration, 16.5.1
tobacco, 7.2.1, 7.6
tomography, 7.6.1
topographical maps, 21.2
tornadoes, 9.1.3, 9.2.4
transcription, 10.4
transects, 21.2.3
transfer appropriateness, 11.0
transferability, 6.0
transference, 13.7.2
translation, 10.4
translation (math), 14.0, 14.1, 14.1.1,
    14.1.2
tree chart, 20.0
trend lines, 20.4, 20.8.1
Trends in International Mathematics
    and Science Study (TIMSS), 24.3
tsunami, 7.7.1
Twenty-One Questions, 13.8

U

unit analysis (*see* dimensional analysis)
units, 17.1, 17.2, 17.3, 17.4, 17.5, 17.6,
    17.7; *see also* SI
units, customary, 27.4, 27.5
units, derived, 27.1

units, fundamental, 27.1
units, SI, 27.2, 27.4
universe, composition of, 20.5.4
USGS, 21.3

V

vaccination, 6.3.3
valence electrons, 18.1
vapor pressure, 27.3
vaporization, heat of, 12.4.3
variables, 5.0, 5.5, 5.5.1, 5.6, 5.6.1, 5.8.1,
    15.6.3, 20.3.3, 20.5.4, 23.1, 23.2
vectors, 16.1, 16.1.1
velocity, 3.5, 17.3, 17.17, 27.2
velocity vectors, 16.1.1
Venn diagrams, 9.2, 9.2.1, 9.2.2, 9.2.3,
    9.2.4, 20.0
vertebrae, 12.2.2
video, 16.5, 16.5.4, 24.7, 26.1
video, editing, 16.5, 16.5.4
video, remote, 16.5.4
Viking 1, 17.7
viruses, 7.6.1
vision, 5.1.3
visual learners, 24.2
visual learning, 11.0, 13.4, 13.4.1, 13.7,
    13.7.1, 13.7.2, 16.0, 24.2
visual literacy, 24.7
visual/spatial intelligence, 12.5, 24.2
visual/verbal integration, 11.0
vitamin D, 19.3.1
vitamin deficiency, 19.3.3
vitamins, 5.8.1
vocabulary, 1.1, 1.2, 1.3, 1.4, 13.1,
    13.2, 13.3, 13.4, 13.5, 13.6, 13.7,
    13.8, 24.7
vocabulary, biology, 1.1
vocabulary, chemistry, 1.2
vocabulary, earth science, 1.4
vocabulary, physics, 1.3
vocabulary, space science, 1.4

volcanoes, 6.2.4, 8.6, 10.1, 10.5
voltage, 10.1.1
volume, 3.5, 14.3, 17.3, 17.7, 17.17, 27.2
Voyager 1, 2, 15.6.3, 15.7, 16.4

W

wait time, 24.7
walking through graphs, 20.2.1
water, 12.4.2
Watson, James, 5.8.2
wave model, 10.2.1
wavelength, 6.3.1
waves, 6.3.1, 9.1.4, 10.2, 10.2.1, 16.3.1
waves and optics, 8.5
waves, electromagnetic, 10.2
waves, radio, 16.3.1
waves, sound, 10.2.1
waves, water, 10.2
weak nuclear force, 9.1.4, 9.2.3
weather forecasting, 21.4.2, 21.4.3
weather map, 20.0, 21.4, 21.4.2
WebQuests, 24.10
Web sites, 26.1
weight, 7.4.1, 17.7
weightlessness, 15.7.1
wild lands, 24.10
wolf repopulation, 20.5.1
word equation, 18.3
word problems, 11.4.2, 14.0, 14.1,
    14.2, 14.3
word wall, 8.3, 24.7
work, 3.5, 14.2.3, 17.3, 17.17, 27.2
writing style, scientific, 27.1

X

X-rays, 13.7.2, 16.0, 16.4.3, 16.4.4
x-y plot, 20.4.1

Z

z-scheme, 16.2.2